ON LINE

DRAMA
for Students

DRAMA
for Students

Presenting Analysis, Context and Criticism on Commonly Studied Dramas

Volume 7

David Galens, Editor

GALE GROUP

Detroit
San Francisco
London
Boston
Woodbridge, CT

National Advisory Board

Dr. Lynn F. Carhart: Supervisor at Monmouth Regional High School, in Tinton Falls, New Jersey. Received the 1999 New Jersey English Educator of the Year Award.

Jim Heiman: Liaison officer, Kansas Council of Teachers of English, Kansas City, Missouri.

Heidi Huckabee: English Instructor at Eastern New Mexico University and at Mason Middle School, both in Roswell, New Mexico. Named Middle School Teacher of the Year and received the Roswell Laureate Teaching Award for Excellence.

Sally Joranko: Instructor of composition and literature and director of the writing center at John Carroll University in Cleveland, Ohio. Contributor to a recent publication, *Short Stories in the Classroom.*

Rose F. Schmitt: Teacher at Florida Air Academy, in Melbourne, Florida. 1997-98 President of the Florida Council of Teachers of English.

Deborah Kelly Woelflein: Vice Principal at Merrimack High School in Merrimack, New Hampshire. Named 1996 New Hampshire Teacher of the Year.

Drama for Students

Staff

Editorial: David M. Galens, *Editor*. Tim Akers, Andrea Henry, Mark Milne, and Kathleen Wilson, *Contributing Editors*. James Draper, *Managing Editor*. David Galens and Lynn Koch, *"For Students'' Line Coordinators*. Jeffery Chapman, *Programmer/Analyst*.

Research: Victoria B. Cariappa, *Research Manager*. Andrew Guy Malonis, Barbara McNeil, Gary J. Oudersluys, Maureen Richards, and Cheryl L. Warnock, *Research Specialists*. Patricia Tsune Ballard, Wendy K. Festerling, Tamara C. Nott, Tracie A. Richardson, Corrine A. Stocker, and, Robert Whaley, *Research Associates*. Phyllis J. Blackman, Tim Lehnerer, and Patricia L. Love, *Research Assistants*.

Permissions: Maria Franklin, *Permissions Manager*. Kimberly F. Smilay, *Permissions Specialist*. Kelly A. Quin, *Permissions Associate*. Sandra K. Gore, *Permissions Assistant*.

Graphic Services: Randy Bassett, *Image Database Supervisor*. Robert Duncan and Michael Logusz, *Imaging Specialists*. Pamela A. Reed, *Imaging Coordinator*. Gary Leach, *Macintosh Artist*.

Product Design: Cynthia Baldwin, *Product Design Manager*. Cover Design: Michelle DiMercurio, *Art Director*. Page Design: Pamela A. E. Galbreath, *Senior Art Director*.

0124540 9

Table of Contents

The Study of Drama

We study drama in order to learn what meaning others have made of life, to comprehend what it takes to produce a work of art, and to glean some understanding of ourselves. Drama produces in a separate, aesthetic world, a moment of being for the audience to experience, while maintaining the detachment of a reflective observer.

Drama is a representational art, a visible and audible narrative presenting virtual, fictional characters within a virtual, fictional universe. Dramatic realizations may pretend to approximate reality or else stubbornly defy, distort, and deform reality into an artistic statement. From this separate universe that is obviously not ''real life'' we expect a valid reflection upon reality, yet drama never is mistaken for reality—the methods of theater are integral to its form and meaning. Theater is art, and art's appeal lies in its ability both to approximate life and to depart from it. By presenting its distorted version of life to our consciousness, art gives us a new perspective and appreciation of reality. Although, to some extent, all aesthetic experiences perform this service, theater does it most effectively by creating a separate, cohesive universe that freely acknowledges its status as an art form.

And what is the purpose of the aesthetic universe of drama? The potential answers to such a question are nearly as many and varied as there are plays written, performed, and enjoyed. Dramatic texts can be problems posed, answers asserted, or moments portrayed. Dramas (tragedies as well as comedies) may serve strictly ''to ease the anguish of a torturing hour'' (as stated in William Shakespeare's *A Midsummer Night's Dream*)—to divert and entertain—or aspire to move the viewer to action with social issues. Whether to entertain or to instruct, affirm or influence, pacify or shock, dramatic art wraps us in the spell of its imaginary world for the length of the work and then dispenses us back to the real world, entertained, purged, as Aristotle said, of pity and fear, and edified—or at least weary enough to sleep peacefully.

It is commonly thought that theater, being an art of performance, must be experienced—that is, seen—in order to be appreciated fully. However, to view a production of a dramatic text is to be limited to a single interpretation of that text—all other interpretations are for the moment closed off, inaccessible. In the process of producing a play, the director, stage designer, and performers interpret and transform the script into a work of art that always departs in some measure from the author's original conception. Novelist and critic Umberto Eco, in his *The Role of the Reader: Explorations in the Semiotics of Texts,* explained, ''In short, we can say that every performance offers us a complete and satisfying version of the work, but at the same time makes it incomplete for us, because it cannot simultaneously give all the other artistic solutions which the work may admit.''

Thus Laurence Olivier's coldly formal and neurotic film presentation of Shakespeare's *Hamlet* (in which he played the title character as well as directed) shows marked differences from subsequent adaptations. While Olivier's Hamlet is clearly entangled in a Freudian relationship with his mother, Gertrude, he would be incapable of shushing her with the impassioned kiss that Mel Gibson's mercurial Hamlet (in director Franco Zeffirelli's 1990 film) does. Although each of the performances rings true to Shakespeare's text, each is also a mutually exclusive work of art. Also important to consider are the time periods in which each of these films were produced: Olivier made his film in 1948, a time in which overt references to sexuality (especially incest) were frowned upon. Gibson and Zeffirelli made their film in a culture more relaxed and comfortable with these issues. Just as actors and directors can influence the presentation of drama, so too can the time period of the production affect what the audience will see.

A play script is an open text from which an infinity of specific realizations may be derived. Dramatic scripts that are more open to interpretive creativity (such as those of Ntozake Shange and Tomson Highway) actually require the creative improvisation of the production troupe in order to complete the text. Even the most prescriptive scripts (those of Neil Simon, Lillian Hellman, and Robert Bolt, for example), can never fully control the actualization of live performance, and circumstantial events, including the attitude and receptivity of the audience, make every performance a unique event. Thus, while it is important to view a production of a dramatic piece, if one wants to understand a drama fully it is equally important to read the original dramatic text.

The reader of a dramatic text or script is not limited by either the specific interpretation of a given production or by the unstoppable action of a moving spectacle. The reader of a dramatic text may discover the nuances of the play's language, structure, and events at their own pace. Yet studied alone, the author's blueprint for artistic production does not tell the whole story of a play's life and significance. One also needs to assess the play's critical reviews to discover how it resonated to cultural themes at the time of its debut and how the shifting tides of cultural interest have revised its interpretation and impact on audiences. And to do this, one needs to know a little about the culture of the times which produced the play as well as the author who penned it.

Drama for Students supplies this material in a useful compendium for the student of dramatic theater. Covering a range of dramatic works that span from the fifth century B.C. to the 1990s, this book focuses on significant theatrical works whose themes and form transcend the uncertainty of dramatic fads. These are plays that have proven to be both memorable and teachable. *Drama for Students* seeks to enhance appreciation of these dramatic texts by providing scholarly materials written with the secondary and college/university student in mind. It provides for each play a concise summary of the plot and characters as well as a detailed explanation of its themes and techniques. In addition, background material on the historical context of the play, its critical reception, and the author's life help the student to understand the work's position in the chronicle of dramatic history. For each play entry a new work of scholarly criticism is also included, as well as segments of other significant critical works for handy reference. A thorough bibliography provides a starting point for further research.

These inaugural two volumes offer comprehensive educational resources for students of drama. *Drama for Students* is a vital book for dramatic interpretation and a valuable addition to any reference library.

Source: Eco, Umberto, *The Role of the Reader: Explorations in the Semiotics of Texts,* Indiana University Press, 1979.

Carole L. Hamilton
Author and Instructor of English
Cary Academy
Cary, North Carolina

Introduction

Purpose of **Drama for Students**

The purpose of *Drama for Students* (*DfS*) is to provide readers with a guide to understanding, enjoying, and studying dramas by giving them easy access to information about the work. Part of Gale's "For Students" literature line, *DfS* is specifically designed to meet the curricular needs of high school and undergraduate college students and their teachers, as well as the interests of general readers and researchers considering specific plays. While each volume contains entries on "classic" dramas frequently studied in classrooms, there are also entries containing hard-to-find information on contemporary plays, including works by multicultural, international, and women playwrights.

The information covered in each entry includes an introduction to the play and the work's author; a plot summary, to help readers unravel and understand the events in a drama; descriptions of important characters, including explanation of a given character's role in the drama as well as discussion about that character's relationship to other characters in the play; analysis of important themes in the drama; and an explanation of important literary techniques and movements as they are demonstrated in the play.

In addition to this material, which helps the readers analyze the play itself, students are also provided with important information on the literary and historical background informing each work.

This includes a historical context essay, a box comparing the time or place the drama was written to modern Western culture, a critical overview essay, and excerpts from critical essays on the play. A unique feature of *DfS* is a specially commissioned overview essay on each drama by an academic expert, targeted toward the student reader.

To further aid the student in studying and enjoying each play, information on media adaptations is provided, as well as reading suggestions for works of fiction and nonfiction on similar themes and topics. Classroom aids include ideas for research papers and lists of critical sources that provide additional material on each drama.

Selection Criteria

The titles for each volume of *DfS* were selected by surveying numerous sources on teaching literature and analyzing course curricula for various school districts. Some of the sources surveyed included: literature anthologies; *Reading Lists for College-Bound Students: The Books Most Recommended by America's Top Colleges;* textbooks on teaching dramas; a College Board survey of plays commonly studied in high schools; a National Council of Teachers of English (NCTE) survey of plays commonly studied in high schools; St. James Press's *International Dictionary of Theatre;* and Arthur Applebee's 1993 study *Literature in the Secondary School: Studies of Curriculum and Instruction in the United States.*

Input was also solicited from our expert advisory board (both experienced educators specializing in English), as well as educators from various areas. From these discussions, it was determined that each volume should have a mix of "classic" dramas (those works commonly taught in literature classes) and contemporary dramas for which information is often hard to find. Because of the interest in expanding the canon of literature, an emphasis was also placed on including works by international, multicultural, and women playwrights. Our advisory board members—current high school teachers—helped pare down the list for each volume. If a work was not selected for the present volume, it was often noted as a possibility for a future volume. As always, the editor welcomes suggestions for titles to be included in future volumes.

How Each Entry Is Organized

Each entry, or chapter, in *DfS* focuses on one play. Each entry heading lists the full name of the play, the author's name, and the date of the play's first production or publication. The following elements are contained in each entry:

- **Introduction:** a brief overview of the drama which provides information about its first appearance, its literary standing, any controversies surrounding the work, and major conflicts or themes within the work.

- **Author Biography:** this section includes basic facts about the author's life, and focuses on events and times in the author's life that inspired the drama in question.

- **Plot Summary:** a description of the major events in the play, with interpretation of how these events help articulate the play's themes. Subheads demarcate the plays' various acts or scenes.

- **Characters:** an alphabetical listing of major characters in the play. Each character name is followed by a brief to an extensive description of the character's role in the plays, as well as discussion of the character's actions, relationships, and possible motivation.

  Characters are listed alphabetically by last name. If a character is unnamed—for instance, the Stage Manager in *Our Town*—the character is listed as "The Stage Manager" and alphabetized as "Stage Manager." If a character's first name is the only one given, the name will appear alphabetically by the name.

Variant names are also included for each character. Thus, the nickname "Babe" would head the listing for a character in *Crimes of the Heart,* but below that listing would be her less-mentioned married name "Rebecca Botrelle."

- **Themes:** a thorough overview of how the major topics, themes, and issues are addressed within the play. Each theme discussed appears in a separate subhead, and is easily accessed through the boldface entries in the Subject/Theme Index.

- **Style:** this section addresses important style elements of the drama, such as setting, point of view, and narration; important literary devices used, such as imagery, foreshadowing, symbolism; and, if applicable, genres to which the work might have belonged, such as Gothicism or Romanticism. Literary terms are explained within the entry, but can also be found in the Glossary.

- **Historical and Cultural Context:** This section outlines the social, political, and cultural climate *in which the author lived and the play was created.* This section may include descriptions of related historical events, pertinent aspects of daily life in the culture, and the artistic and literary sensibilities of the time in which the work was written. If the play is a historical work, information regarding the time in which the play is set is also included. Each section is broken down with helpful subheads.

- **Critical Overview:** this section provides background on the critical reputation of the play, including bannings or any other public controversies surrounding the work. For older plays, this section includes a history of how the drama was first received and how perceptions of it may have changed over the years; for more recent plays, direct quotes from early reviews may also be included.

- **For Further Study:** an alphabetical list of other critical sources which may prove useful for the student. Includes full bibliographical information and a brief annotation.

- **Sources:** an alphabetical list of critical material quoted in the entry, with full bibliographical information.

- **Criticism:** an essay commissioned by *DfS* which specifically deals with the play and is written specifically for the student audience, as well as excerpts from previously published criticism on the work.

In addition, each entry contains the following highlighted sections, set separate from the main text:

- **Media Adaptations:** a list of important film and television adaptations of the play, including source information. The list may also include such variations on the work as audio recordings, musical adaptations, and other stage interpretations.

- **Compare and Contrast Box:** an ''at-a-glance'' comparison of the cultural and historical differences between the author's time and culture and late twentieth-century Western culture. This box includes pertinent parallels between the major scientific, political, and cultural movements of the time or place the drama was written, the time or place the play was set (if a historical work), and modern Western culture. Works written after the mid-1970s may not have this box.

- **What Do I Read Next?:** a list of works that might complement the featured play or serve as a contrast to it. This includes works by the same author and others, works of fiction and nonfiction, and works from various genres, cultures, and eras.

- **Study Questions:** a list of potential study questions or research topics dealing with the play. This section includes questions related to other disciplines the student may be studying, such as American history, world history, science, math, government, business, geography, economics, psychology, etc.

Other Features

DfS includes ''The Study of Drama,'' a foreword by Carole Hamilton, an educator and author who specializes in dramatic works. This essay examines the basis for drama in societies and what drives people to study such work. Hamilton also discusses how *Drama for Students* can help teachers show students how to enrich their own reading/viewing experiences.

A Cumulative Author/Title Index lists the authors and titles covered in each volume of the *DfS* series.

A Cumulative Nationality/Ethnicity Index breaks down the authors and titles covered in each volume of the *DfS* series by nationality and ethnicity.

A Subject/Theme Index, specific to each volume, provides easy reference for users who may be studying a particular subject or theme rather than a single work. Significant subjects from events to

broad themes are included, and the entries pointing to the specific theme discussions in each entry are indicated in **boldface.**

Each entry has several illustrations, including photos of the author, stills from stage productions, and stills from film adaptations.

Citing Drama for Students

When writing papers, students who quote directly from any volume of *Drama for Students* may use the following general forms. These examples are based on MLA style; teachers may request that students adhere to a different style, so the following examples may be adapted as needed.

When citing text from *DfS* that is not attributed to a particular author (i.e., the Themes, Style, Historical Context sections, etc.), the following format should be used in the bibliography section:

''Our Town,'' *Drama for Students.* Ed. David Galens and Lynn Spampinato. Vol. 1. Farmington Hills: Gale, 1997. 8–9.

When quoting the specially commissioned essay from *DfS* (usually the first piece under the ''Criticism'' subhead), the following format should be used:

Fiero, John. Essay on ''Twilight: Los Angeles, 1992.'' *Drama for Students.* Ed. David Galens and Lynn Spampinato. Vol. 1. Farmington Hills: Gale, 1997. 8–9.

When quoting a journal or newspaper essay that is reprinted in a volume of *DfS,* the following form may be used:

Rich, Frank. ''Theatre: A Mamet Play, 'Glengarry Glen Ross'.'' *New York Theatre Critics' Review* Vol. 45, No. 4 (March 5, 1984), 5–7; excerpted and reprinted in *Drama for Students,* Vol. 1, ed. David Galens and Lynn Spampinato (Farmington Hills: Gale, 1997), pp. 61–64.

When quoting material reprinted from a book that appears in a volume of *DfS,* the following form may be used:

Kerr, Walter. ''The Miracle Worker,'' in *The Theatre in Spite of Itself* (Simon & Schuster, 1963, 255–57; excerpted and reprinted in *Drama for Students,* Vol. 1, ed. Dave Galens and Lynn Spampinato (Farmington Hills: Gale, 1997), pp. 59–61.

We Welcome Your Suggestions

The editor of *Drama for Students* welcomes your comments and ideas. Readers who wish to suggest dramas to appear in future volumes, or who have other suggestions, are cordially invited to contact the editor. You may contact the editor via

E-mail at: **david.galens@gale.com.** Or write to the editor at:

David Galens, *Drama for Students*
The Gale Group
27500 Drake Rd.
Farmington Hills, MI 48331-3535

Literary Chronology

c. 1495: *Everyman* is first published.

1586: John Ford is born in Islington, Devonshire, England.

1633: *'Tis a Pity She's a Whore* is first published.

c. 1639: John Ford dies.

1860: J. M. Barrie is born on May 9, in Kirriemuir, Scotland.

1890: Karel Capek is born in January, in Male Svatonovice, Bohemia (now Czechoslovakia).

1904: *Peter Pan* is first performed in London, England, on December 27, at the Duke of York Theatre.

1906: Samuel Beckett is born Samuel Barclay Beckett at Cooldrinagh (his family's home) in Foxrock, County Dublin, Ireland, on Good Friday, April 13.

1911: Tennessee Williams is born Thomas Lanier Williams on March 26, in Columbus, Mississippi.

1912: Joseph Stein is born on May 30, in New York City.

1921: *R.U.R.* is first produced in Prague, Czechoslovakia, at the National Theater, January 25.

1923: Brendan Behan is born on February 9, in Dublin, Ireland.

1930: Harold Pinter is born October 30, in Hackney, London, England.

1937: Arthur Kopit is born in New York City on May 10.

1937: J. M. Barrie dies on June 19, in London, England.

1938: Karel Capek dies of pneumonia, December 25, in Prague, Czechoslovakia.

1939: Alan Ayckbourn is born on April 12, in the London, England, suburb of Hampstead.

1939: Shelagh Delaney is born November 25, in Salford, Lancashire, England.

1943: Sam Shepard is born Samuel Shepard Rogers in Fort Sheridan, Illinois, on November 5.

1944: Tim Rice is born November 10, in Amersham, Buckinghamshire, England.

1945: August Wilson is born Frederick August Kittel in Pittsburgh, Pennsylvania.

1946: Larry Shue is born on July 23, in New Orleans, Louisiana.

1947: David Hare is born on June 5, in St. Leonard's-on-Sea , Sussex, England.

1948: Andrew Lloyd Webber is born March 22, in London, England.

1958: *A Taste of Honey* opens at the Theatre Royal, Stratford East in London, England, on May 27; the play moves to Wyndham's Theatre in London's West End on February 10, 1959; on October 4, 1960, the play opens on Broadway at New York City's Lyceum Theatre.

1958: *The Hostage* opens on October 14, at the Theater Royal in Stratford, London, England.

1960: *Oh Dad, Poor Dad* is first produced in a playwriting contest at Harvard University; the play's success prompts a move to the commercial Agassiz Theatre in Cambridge, Massachusetts; the play eventually moves to the Off-Broadway Phoenix Theatre in New York City on February 26, 1962, running for 454 performances.

1960: *The Caretaker* by Harold Pinter is first produced on April 27, at the Arts Theatre in London, England.

1961: *Night of the Iguana* is first performed on December 28, on Broadway in the Royale Theatre.

1964: Brendan Behan dies on March 20, from complications resulting from alcohol abuse, diabetes, and jaundice.

1964: *Fiddler on the Roof* debuts on September 22, at Broadway's Imperial Theatre.

1971: *Jesus Christ Superstar* is first produced.

1983: Tennessee Williams chokes to death on February 24, in his suite at Hotel Elysee, New York, New York; he is buried in St. Louis, Missouri.

1983: *Fool for Love* is first produced at the Magic Theatre in San Francisco, California, in February; the play moves to the Off-Broadway Circle Repertory Theatre in May.

1983: *The Foreigner* is first produced at the Milwaukee Repertory Theatre in January; the play is later produced Off-Broadway in November, 1984, at the Astor Place Theatre in New York City.

1984: *A Chorus of Disapproval* premieres at the Stephen Joseph Theater in the Round in Scarborough, England, in May; following a sell-out season in Scarborough, the play opens at the National Theater in London, England, in August, 1985.

1985: Larry Shue dies in a commuter plane crash near Weyer's Cave, Virginia, on September 23.

1987: *The Piano Lesson* is first produced in New Haven, Connecticut, at the Yale Repertory Theatre; the play later moves to Broadway.

1989: Samuel Beckett dies in France on December 22.

1998: David Hare's *The Blue Room* debuts in London, England; the play later debuts on Broadway in December of the same year.

Acknowledgments

The editors wish to thank the copyright holders of the excerpted criticism included in this volume and the permissions managers of many book and magazine publishing companies for assisting us in securing reproduction rights. We are also grateful to the staffs of the Detroit Public Library, the Library of Congress, the University of Detroit Mercy Library, Wayne State University Purdy/Kresge Library Complex, and the University of Michigan Libraries for making their resources available to us. Following is a list of the copyright holders who have granted us permission to reproduce material in this volume of *DFS.* Every effort has been made to trace copyright, but if omissions have been made, please let us know.

COPYRIGHTED EXCERPTS IN *DFS,* VOLUME 7, WERE REPRODUCED FROM THE FOLLOWING PERIODICALS:

America, v. 174, May 4, 1996. © 1996. All rights reserved. Reproduced with permission of America Press, Inc.,106 West 56th Street, New York, NY 10019.—*Catholic Library World,* v. 123, August, 1971. Copyright 1971 by The Missionary Society of St. Paul the Apostle in the State of New York. Reproduced by permission of Paulist Press.—*College English,* v. 22, October, 1960 for "Time and the Timeless in Everyman and Dr. Faustus" by David Kuala. Copyright © 1960 by the National Council of Teachers of English. Reproduced by permission of the publisher.—*Common-weal,* v. LII, May 12, 1950; v. LXXV, January 26, 1962. Copyright 1950, 1962 Commonweal Publishing Co., Inc. Both reproduced by permission of Commonweal Foundation.—*The Explicator,* v. 37, Summer, 1979. Copyright © 1986 by Helen Dwight Reid Educational Foundation. Reproduced with permission of the Helen Dwight Reid Educational Foundation, published by Heldref Publications, 1319 18th Street, NW, Washington, DC 20036-1802.—*The Georgia Review,* v. XXXVII, Fall, 1983. Copyright, © 1983, by the University of Georgia. Reproduced by permission.—*The Hudson Review,* v. XIII, Winter, 1960-61 for "Theatre Chronicle" by John Simon. Copyright © 1960-61 by The Hudson Review, Inc. Reproduced by permission of the author./v. XLIII, Autumn, 1990. Copyright © 1990 by The Hudson Review, Inc. Reproduced by permission.—*Maclean's,* v. 100, August 31, 1987. © 1987 by Maclean's Magazine. Reproduced by permission.—*Modern Drama,* v. 9, December, 1966. © 1966 University of Toronto, Graduate Centre for Study of Drama. Reproduced by permission.—*The Nation,* New York, v. 199, October 12, 1964; v. 252, January 7-14, 1991. Copyright 1964, 1991 *The Nation magazine* The Nation Company, Inc. Both reproduced by permission.—*The New Republic,* v. 122, May 8, 1950; v. 143, October 3, 1960; v. 145, October 23, 1961; v. 146, January 22, 1962; v. 201, September 11, 1989; v. 206, May 11, 1992; v. 209, November 1, 1993. Copyright 1950, 1960, 1961, 1962, 1989, 1992,

1993 The New Republic, Inc. All reproduced by permission of *The New Republic.*—*Newsweek,* v. 132, October 5, 1998. © 1998 Newsweek, Inc. All rights reserved. Reproduced by permission—*New York,* Magazine, v. 17, June 13, 1983; v. 17, November 12, 1984; v. 26, November 29, 1993; v. 31, January 4, 1999. Copyright © 1983, 1984, 1993, 1999 PRIMEDIA Magazine Corporation. All rights reserved. All reproduced with the permission of *New York* Magazine.—*The New Yorker,* v. LIX, June 6, 1983; v. 60, November 19, 1984. © 1983, 1984 by The New Yorker Magazine, Inc. All rights reserved. All reproduced by permission./ v. XXXVI, October 15, 1960 for ''Lancashire Lass'' by John McCarter. © 1960 by The New Yorker Magazine, Inc.—*The New York Times Book Review,* October 13, 1971, October 24, 1971; December 30, 1998. Copyright © 1998 by The New York Times Company. All reproduced by permission.—*The Saturday Review,* v. 43, January 30, 1960. © 1960 Saturday Review Magazine, © 1979 General Media International, Inc. Reproduced by permission of *The Saturday Review.*—*Time,* New York, v. 133, January 30, 1989. Copyright © 1989 Time Warner Inc. All rights reserved. Reproduced by permission from *Time.*—*Tulane Drama Review,* v. 11, Spring, 1967. Copyright © 1967, Tulane Drama Review. Reproduced by permission of MIT Press, Cambridge, Massachusetts.

COPYRIGHTED EXCERPTS IN *DFS*, VOLUME 7, WERE REPRODUCED FROM THE FOLLOWING BOOKS:

Brustein, Robert S. From ''The New American Playwrights: Arthur Kopit'' in *Modern Occasions.* Edited by Philip Rahv. Farrar, Straus, and Giroux, 1966. Copyright © 1966 by Farrar, Straus, and Giroux, Inc. All rights reserved. Reproduced by permission of the author.—Kerr, Walter. From *The Theater in Spite of Itself.* Simon and Schuster, 1963. Copyright © 1963 by Walter Kerr, renewed 1991. All rights reserved. Reproduced by permission of the Literary Estate of Walter Kerr.

PHOTOGRAPHS AND ILLUSTRATIONS APPEARING IN *DFS*, VOLUME 7, WERE RECEIVED FROM THE FOLLOWING SOURCES:

Anderson, Carl, as Judas Iscariot in *Jesus Christ Superstar* by Andrew Lloyd Webber and Tim Rice, July 13, 1971, photograph. AP/Wide World Photos. Reproduced by permission.—Ayckbourn, Alan, photograph. AP/Wide World Photos. Reproduced by permission.—Barrie, Sir James M., photograph.

AP/Wide World Photos. Reproduced by permission.—Beckett, Samuel, photograph. Archive Photos, Inc. Reproduced by permission.—Behan, Brendan, photograph. AP/Wide World Photos. Reproduced by permission.—Capek, Karel, photograph. The Library of Congress.—Delaney, Shelagh, photograph. AP/Wide World Photos. Reproduced by permission.—Elliman, Yvonne, as Mary Magdalene in *Jesus Christ Superstar* by Andrew Lloyd Webber and Tim Rice, July 13, 1971, photograph. AP/Wide World Photos. Reproduced by permission.—From a movie still of *A Taste of Honey* by Shelagh Delaney, Directed by Tony Richardson, with Dora Bryan as Helen and Rita Tushingham as Jo, British Lion, 1961, photograph. BRITISH LION. Courtesy of The Kobal Collection. Reproduced by permission.—From a movie still of *A Taste of Honey* by Shelagh Delaney, Directed by Tony Richardson, with Rita Tushingham as Jo and Murray Melvin as Geoffrey, British Lion, 1961, photograph. BRITISH LION. Courtesy of The Kobal Collection. Reproduced by permission.—From a movie still of *A Taste of Honey* by Shelagh Delaney, Directed by Tony Richardson, with Dora Bryan as Helen, British Lion, 1961, photograph. BRITISH LION. Courtesy of The Kobal Collection. Reproduced by permission.—From a movie still of *Chorus of Disapproval* by Alan Ayckbourn, Directed by Michael Winner, with Patsy Kensit as , Jeremy Irons as Guy Jones, and Prunella Scales as Hannah Ap Llewellyn, 1988, photograph. HOBO/CURZON/PALISADES. Courtesy of The Kobal Collection. Reproduced by permission.—From a movie still of *Fool for Love* by Sam Shepard, Directed by Robert Altman, with Kim Basinger as May, Canno Films, 1985, photograph. CANNON FILMS. Courtesy of The Kobal Collection. Reproduced by permission.—From a movie still of *Fool for Love* by Sam Shepard, Directed by Robert Altman, with Sam Shepard as Eddie, the cowboy, Canno Films, 1985, photograph by Robert Altman. CANNON FILMS. Courtesy of The Kobal Collection. Reproduced by permission.—From a movie still of *Oh Dad, Poor Dad, Mamma's Hung You in the Closet and I'm Feelin' So Sad* by Arthur Kopit, Directed by Richard Quine, with Rosalind Russell as Madame Rosepettle and Jonathan Winters, 1965, Paramount, Russell watches appalled as Winter's stuffs his face at the table, photograph. Paramount. Courtesy of The Kobal Collection. Reproduced by permission.—From a movie still of *Oh Dad, Poor Dad, Mamma's Hung You in the Closet and I'm Feelin' So Sad* by Arthur Kopit, Directed by Richard Quine, with Rosalind Russell as Madame Rosepettle and

Jonathan Winters, 1965, Paramount, Russell watches wide eyed as Winter smiles in his sleep, photograph. Paramount. Courtesy of The Kobal Collection. Reproduced by permission.—From a movie still of *Peter Pan* by J. M. Barrie, with Peter Pan, Tinker Bell, Wendy, Michael and John with his teddy bear, flying past Big Ben, 1953, Walt Disney, photograph. Walt Disney. Courtesy of The Kobal Collection. Reproduced by permission.—From a movie still of *The Night of the Iguana* by Tennessee Williams, Directed by John Huston, with Ava Gardner as Maxine Faulk and Richard Burton as The Rev. T. Lawrence Shannon, M-G-M, 1964, photograph. M-G-M. Courtesy of The Kobal Collection. Reproduced by permission.—From a movie still of *The Night of the Iguana* by Tennessee Williams, Directed by John Huston, with Richard Burton as The Rev. T. Lawrence Shannon and Sue Lyon as Charlotte Goodall, M-G-M, 1964, photograph. M-G-M. Courtesy of The Kobal Collection. Reproduced by permission.—From a theatre production of *Everyman* by Anonymous, with Paul Hamilton, Joseph Mydell, Edward Woodall and Johnny Lodi, RSC/The Other Place, November 14, 1996, photograph. © Donald Cooper/Photostage. Reproduced by permission.—From a theatre production of *Everyman* by Anonymous, with Paul Hamilton, Joseph Mydell, Edward Woodall and Johnny Lodi, RSC/The Other Place, November 14, 1996, photograph. © Donald Cooper/Photostage. Reproduced by permission.—From a theatre production of *Fiddler on the Roof* by Joseph Stein, with (l-r) Austin Pendleton as Zero Mostel, and his family played by Mr. Mostel, Mavis Karnoliva, Joanna Merlin, Julia Migenes, Tanya Everet, Marilyn Rogers and Linda Ross, 1965, photograph. AP/Wide World Photos. Reproduced by permission.—From a theatre production of *Fiddler on the Roof* by Joseph Stein, with Peg Murray and Paul Lipson as Golds and Tevye, Harold Prince Musical at the Broadway Theatre, March, 1971, photograph. AP/Wide World Photos. Reproduced by permission.—From a theatre production of *Jesus Christ Superstar* by by Andrew Lloyd Webber and Tim Rice, with Jeff Fenholt as Jesus, photograph. AP/Wide World Photos. Reproduced by permission.—From a theatre production of *Krapp's Last Tape* by Samuel Beckett, with Edward Petherbridge as Krapp, RSC/Arts Theatre, October 1, 1999, photograph. © Donald Cooper/Photostage. Reproduced by permission.—From a theatre production of *Krapp's Last Tape* by Samuel Beckett, with Max Wall as Krapp, Greenwich Theatre, London, 1975, photograph. © Donald Cooper/Photostage. Repro-

duced by permission.—From a theatre production of *Peter Pan* by J. M. Barrie with Mary Martin as Peter Pan and Cyril Ritchard as Captain Hook, February 25, 1955, photograph. AP/Wide World Photos. Reproduced by permission.—From a theatre production of *R.U.R.* by Karel Capek, Directed by Mark Wolgar with Gemma Barnetson as Lady Helen Glory and Amanda Mannion as Robot Radius at The Courtyard Theatre, November, 1998, Robot Radius stands waiting for instruction from Lady Helen Glory, photograph by Amanda j. Ifrah. © 1998 by Amanda j. Ifrah. Reproduced by permission.—From a theatre production of *The Blue Room* by David Hare, adaptation of Arthur Schnitzler's ''La Ronde,'' Directed by Sam Mendes with (l-r) Iain Glen and Nicole Kidman, New York, December 13, 1998, photograph by Adam Nadel. AP/Wide World Photos/Adam Nadel. Reproduced by permission.—From a theatre production of *The Hostage* by Brendan Behan, RSC/Barbican Theatre, London, September, 1994, photograph. © Donald Cooper/Photostage. Reproduced by permission.—From a theatre production of *The Hostage* by Brendan Behan, with (l-r) Dermot Crowley as Pat, Damien Lyne as Leslie Williams and John Woodvine as Monsewer, RSC/Barbican Theatre, London, September, 1994, photograph. © Donald Cooper/Photostage. Reproduced by permission.—Hare, David, photograph by Daniel Locus. © Daniel Locus. Reproduced by permission of the photographer.—Kopit, Arthur, photograph. AP/Wide World Photos. Reproduced by permission.—Neeley, Ted, as Jesus, on Mount Calvary, in the 1973 film, *Jesus Christ Superstar,* a Norman Jewison Film, photograph. Archive Photos, Inc. Reproduced by permission.—Pinter, Harold, 1961, photograph. The Library of Congress.—Pleasance, Donald, and Harold Pinter rehearse *The Caretaker* written by Harold Pinter, ca. 1965, photograph. CORBIS/Hulton-Deutsch Collection. Reproduced by permission.—Shepard, Sam, May 23, 1996, photograph by Andy King. AP/Wide World Photo/Andy King. Reproduced by permission.—Stein, Joseph, photograph. © Joseph Stein. Reproduced by permission.—The December, 1990, Playbill for August Wilson's *The Piano Lesson,* Directed by Lloyd Richards, with Charles S. Dutton as Boy Willie, at the Walter Kerr Theater, NY, photograph. PLAYBILL (r) is a registered trademark of Playbill Incorporated, N.Y.C. All rights reserved. Reproduced by permission.—The January, 1985, Showbill for Larry Shue's *The Foreigner,* Directed by Jerry Zaks, with Larry Shue as ''Froggy'' LeSueur, at the Astor Place Theater, NY, photograph. SHOWBILL (r) is

Contributors

Clare Cross: Doctoral candidate, University of Michigan, Ann Arbor. Entry on *The Caretaker.*

John Fiero: Professor Emeritus of Drama and Playwriting, University of Southwestern Louisiana. Entry on *Oh Dad, Poor Dad.*

Lane A. Glenn: Author, educator, director, and actor, Lansing, Michigan. Entry on *The Blue Room.*

Carole Hamilton: Freelance writer and instructor at Cary Academy, Cary, North Carolina. Entry on *Jesus Christ Superstar.*

Helena Ifeka: Doctoral candidate, Columbia University, and freelance author. Entries on *A Chorus of Disapproval, The Hostage,* and *The Piano Lesson.*

Sheri Metzger: Freelance writer and Ph.D., Albuquerque, NM. Entries on *Everyman, R.U.R.,* and *A Taste of Honey.*

Daniel Moran: Educator and author, Monmouth Junction, NY. Entry on *Krapp's Last Tape.*

Terry Nienhuis: Associate Professor of English, Western Carolina University. Entry on *The Foreigner.*

Annette Petrusso: Freelance author and screenwriter, Austin, TX. Entries on *Fiddler on the Roof, Fool for Love, Night of the Iguana,* and *Peter Pan.*

Arnold Schmidt: Professor of English, California State University, Stanislaus. Entry on *'Tis a Pity She's a Whore.*

The Blue Room

DAVID HARE

1998

When David Hare's *The Blue Room* opened on Broadway in December, 1998, it became part of a record-setting year for the prolific playwright. In a twelve-month period, the British author managed to send *four* of his latest plays across the Atlantic to New York's stages. The others included *The Judas Kiss, Amy's View,* and Hare's one-man autobiographical staged memoir, *Via Dolorosa.*

The Blue Room is based on *Reigen,* a series of vignettes written by Dr. Arthur Schnitzler in 1896. *Reigen,* German for "round dance," was set in Schnitzler's own *fin de siecle* Vienna and depicted a number of characters in a continuous chain of sexual liaisons, suggesting that the meaningless physical relationships they shared, as well as venereal diseases they picked up along the way, were passed along in a mechanical, dehumanizing chain. When the work was actually performed in Vienna in 1921, it was closed by police for its scandalous sexual content. Actors in a Berlin production the same year were taken to court on obscenity charges. The film version, *La Ronde,* created by Max Ophuls in 1950, lifted some sense of the taboo surrounding the story and replaced it with a wistful nostalgia and only minor titillation.

In the introduction to his adaptation of the play, Hare claims he first learned about Schnitzler's clever story as a boy, when his father promised him he could one day watch "his favorite film of all time." More recently, it was director Sam Mendes

who asked Hare to adapt Schnitzler's work for a modernized stage version. For Hare, who has written many times about deception and dissatisfaction in relationships, the story was a natural draw. "[Schnitzler's] essential subject is the gulf between what we imagine, what we remember, and what we actually experience," the playwright suggests.

In Hare's retelling, the story remains the same, ten characters fall in and out of bed with each other, never quite finding fulfillment but the setting and some of the ideas have changed. No longer Vienna, the backdrop for *The Blue Room* is described ambiguously as "one of the great cities of the world, in the present day." Although it is not a major issue in the play, AIDS has replaced less harmful venereal diseases as a communicable worry in the minds of some of Hare's characters, and the shock audiences may have experienced upon witnessing a staged sexual roundelay nearly a century ago has turned into curious titillation for New Yorkers interested in seeing a famous film star in the buff (a reference to star Nicole Kidman's nude scene). As critic Charles Isherwood noted in *Variety,* "At the last turn of the century, when the original was written, it was considered too dangerous to be published and later inspired police action; on the cusp of the next, the new text has become virtually insignificant, lost in the swirl of celebrity hype that has surrounded the production." Seemingly the more things change, the more they stay the same: audiences still flocked to both productions.

AUTHOR BIOGRAPHY

British playwright David Hare was born on June 5, 1947, in St. Leonard's-on-Sea in Sussex along the southeastern coast of England. Though he doesn't like "psychologizing," or over-emphasizing the importance of his early years to his current artistic output, in an interview with Mel Gussow published in the *New York Times Magazine,* Hare admitted his birth was "on the wave of postwar optimism. Everyone came home from the war and had children. Bang on the day I was born, the Marshall Plan was announced, and Europe became Europe." Accordingly, like many of his contemporaries, this Postwar period in British history has figured prominently in Hare's plays.

Hare began his career in the "Fringe Theatre" movement of London in the late-1960s and early-

1970s. He was a literary manager at the Royal Court Theatre in 1969, where he earned about $15 a week plowing through dozens of hopeful manuscripts in search of produceable material. It was a time of artistic experimentation, revolutionary writing, and anti-establishment politics. Some of his earliest plays include *England's Ireland* (1972), a collaborative documentary play about political controversy and bloodshed caused by the English presence in Northern Ireland; *Fanshen* (1975), an adaptation of William Hinton's novel about the Chinese Revolution; and *Plenty* (1978), an original work about the failure of Great Britain to live up to its post-World War II promise.

Hare has long since graduated from the Fringe movement to popular acclaim and public subsidy at the Royal National Theatre in London, where most of his plays have originated during the past twenty years. Throughout the 1980s and early-1990s, he was particularly known for criticizing the Conservative government of Prime Minister Margaret Thatcher in his plays. *The Secret Rapture* (1988) concerns three women struggling to thrive in the greed and excess of 1980s Thatcherite England. In an amazing feat of journalistic research and creative fiction writing in the early-1990s, Hare tackled the Church of England, Britain's legal system, and English politics in a trilogy of plays about British social institutions. *Racing Demon* (1990) earned Hare an Olivier Award for best play in London's West End as well as an Antoinette "Tony" Perry Award for best play on Broadway. *Murmuring Judges* (1991) and *The Absence of War* (1993) completed the series, which was presented in its nearly nine hour entirety at the National Theatre.

Since England's liberal Labour Party recaptured the goverment in the mid-1990s, some of the political fervency has left Hare's writing, and he has been drawn toward other forms of drama. His popularity, however, is as stong as ever, particularly in America. *Skylight* (1995) and *Amy's View* (1996) are intimate portrayals of individual relationships between a woman and her lover and a girl and her mother, respectively. *The Judas Kiss* (1998) is a biographical story about playwright Oscar Wilde (*The Importance of Being Earnest*), and *Via Dolorosa* (1998) is a one-man, staged autobiography that Hare himself performed in London and New York. When *The Blue Room,* an adaptation of Arthur Schnitzler's *Reigen,* appeared in New York in the fall of 1998, it joined *The Judas Kiss, Amy's View,* and *Via Dolorosa* as one of four new Hare plays to appear on Broadway within a single year.

PLOT SUMMARY

Scene One: The Girl and The Cab Driver

The first scene of *The Blue Room* is an encounter between The Girl and The Cab Driver. The Girl is a prostitute, young, amateurish, and new to the work. She is waiting in a park, dressed in a short, black leather skirt, trying to catch the eye of a potential customer when The Cab Driver walks past her, twice. Taking the initiative, The Girl invites The Cab Driver home with her. The savvy driver knows her game and tells her he doesn't have any money. She persists, telling him she doesn't care about money, and they end up walking down to the nearby river in order to have sex off the main pathway in the park.

The lights darken, and a projected slide reads ''THREE MINUTES,'' the time it takes for The Cab Driver to finish and pull his pants back up. When the lights return, the driver brushes himself off, pulls The Girl up off the ground, and heads off to go back to work. In spite of her earlier claim, The Girl asks The Cab Driver for some money. He refuses and leaves, while she promises, ''I'll be here tomorrow.''

Scene Two: The Cab Driver and The Au Pair

With the sound of an Elvis Presley ballad echoing at a dance in the outside ballroom, The Cab Driver and The Au Pair duck into a darkened storage closet. The Au Pair, whose name is Marie, is foreign, and her job is caring for a family and their children. She has just met The Cab Driver, who now introduces himself as Fred. He has brought her into the storage room, he says, to escape the dance. His real motive is to seduce the young lady.

Before The Au Pair will agree to have sex with The Cab Driver, she tells him he must reassure her that ''it means something.'' Parroting her request, Fred tells Marie, ''It means something. I promise.'' The lights go out and the slide projection reads ''NINE MINUTES.'' As a dim light slowly reveals the two of them atop some crushed cardboard boxes, The Au Pair asks her Cab Driver what he feels. Fred stammers that he doesn't know. ''Feel's a big word,'' he complains. But the experience seems to have had a greater effect on him than his encounter with The Girl in the park. He admits he feels confused and is in no hurry to leave this girl. Instead, he asks her to stay a bit while he goes to get

David Hare

them both a beer. He heads off on his mission while The Au Pair sits alone and the lights go out.

Scene Three: The Au Pair and The Student

The third scene takes place in the fancy modern kitchen of the lavish home where The Au Pair works. She is seated at a table in the middle of the room writing a letter to The Cab Driver, who she recently met at the dance, when The Student comes downstairs from his studies for a glass of water. He asks about a phone call he has been expecting, then takes his water back up to his room. A moment later, the phone rings. Apparently it is The Student again, asking for another drink. The Au Pair hangs up the phone, and just as she finishes pouring a fresh glass The Student reappears. It is obvious he has manufactured the need for more water as an excuse to see her again.

This time down The Student wastes no time. He begins flirting with The Au Pair, complementing her shirt and shoes, before kissing her and unbuttoning her clothes. For modesty's sake, or perhaps to preserve her job, The Au Pair asks The Student to at least close the blinds before they continue, which he does. As he pushes her up onto the table, she warns him they may be interrupted by the door, or by the phone call he is expecting from his friend, but The Student pretends not care. The lights blacken momentarily and a slide projection reads ''FORTY-FIVE SECONDS,'' before the doorbell begins ringing. The mood is broken. The Student panics. He asks The Au Pair to check the door while he quickly dresses himself. When she returns his manner is changed. He is once again the son of the family in charge and announces he is leaving for the cafe. Instead of kind words or tenderness, he leaves The Au Pair with a directive to tell his friend where he has gone, should he finally call.

Scene Four: The Student and The Married Woman

The ''friend'' The Student was anticipating in the previous scene was apparently The Married Woman, Emma, who appears in Scene Four. Up in his bedroom, The Student, whose name is now revealed as Anton, has been preparing for her visit. He has assembled a collection of hors d'oeuvres wrapped in an aluminum container and a bottle of cognac. Offstage, the doorbell rings, and The Married Woman is greeted by The Au Pair. When Emma makes it upstairs, she is obviously a public figure the wife of a prominent politician who is trying to keep her tryst with The Student a secret. She has worn a scarf and dark glasses and complains to her soon-to-be lover that she must not be discovered, because the press have no values or respect and would make her life miserable.

To make matters worse, or at least more dangerous, The Married Woman is a friend of The Student's parents. The two briefly discuss her marital woes (she is unhappy in her husband's world of deception and lies), and The Student actually admits he is in love with her. Then they fall into bed together. The lights are only out briefly, long enough for a slide projection to read ''0 MINUTES,'' before the room is bright again and The Student sits on the edge of the bed, frustrated and nervously impotent. While he tries to find excuses for his condition and berates himself, she tells jokes and tries to make light of the situation. Finally, The Married Woman solves the problem. She tells The Student to simply lie very still on the bed. She stands over him and the lights fade to black. The slide projection now reads ''THIRTY-TWO MINUTES'' and, in the darkness, she murmurs in a satisfied voice, ''Oh my beautiful boy.''

Quickly, however, The Married Woman realizes she must get back home to her husband. While they both dress they agree they will see each other the next day, in public, at a political rally for her husband, and two days later they will meet again in private. Left alone, The Student sits down, eats a few hors d'oeuvres, and brags to himself, ''I'm fucking a married woman.''

Scene Five: The Married Woman and The Politician

Back at home, the source of The Married Woman's unhappiness is revealed. Emma and her husband, Charlie, The Politician, share a single bedroom but sleep in different beds. It is an arrangement The Politician dubs mature, convenient, and wise, since it ensures their marriage will not be based on sex alone, but on friendship and mutual respect for each other's lives as individuals. The lesson is a hollow one for The Married Woman, who really longs for the passion they shared when they met eight years earlier in Venice.

As the couple talk just before bedtime, The Married Woman asks her husband about his life before her. He admits (though they have had the conversation before) that he was foolish, sleeping with many, many women, at least one of whom was even married. Now, though, he has seen the error of his ways. He claims he is in love with Emma, and she is all he needs. The lights go out, and a slide projection reads ''FIFTEEN MINUTES.'' When they are finished, The Married Woman tells her husband she longs for the feeling of Venice again. The Politician, ever politic, tells her that is the wonderful thing about marriage; that one day there may be time for Venice again.

Scene Six: The Politician and The Model

Romance and Venice aside, the next time The Politician appears he is sitting on a sofa in a hotel room, contentedly smoking a cigar and watching a seventeen-year-old girl he has just picked up on the street dance to a rock video and eat chocolate ice cream. The Model, Kelly, is no innocent abroad. She admits she has been with men before, though she is insulted when The Politician guesses she has entertained as many as fifty previous lovers. She snorts cocaine and pops pills throughout the scene, and complains about a previous lover who looked a lot like The Politician.

In a seemingly uncharacteristic move, The Politician takes a handful of pills himself. The begin to have sex and the lights fade to black. The projected slide reads ''TWO HOURS TWENTY-EIGHT MINUTES.'' In the haze following their drug-influenced sexual encounter, The Model and The Politician talk about their next moves and the possible effects of cheating on a marriage. The Politician is enraged at The Model's suggestion that, since he cheats on his wife, she must be cheating on him, too. He is hypocritical and ironically blind to something his young partner finds very obvious. Finally, The Politician tries to convince The Model to let him find her an apartment of her own, where he can pay her expenses and keep her available for future trysts. Foolishly, he asks her, ''Isn't that what women want?''

Scene Seven: The Model and The Playwright

Like The Politician before him, The Playwright apparently found The Model on the street or in a club somewhere and immediately brought her home, under the premise that he will sing a song for her. She initially protests that she will only stay for the song, but once The Playwright sings for her (the composition is ''The Blue Room''), she is smitten, and stays long enough to be seduced. For his part, The Playwright enjoys that The Model doesn't recognize him as a celebrity artist, and he uses his deftness with words to confuse and impress her into bed with him. He promises to take her to India, ''to the Rajasthan,'' where they will see the sights and enjoy passionate lovemaking. As in the previous scenes, the lights fade and a slide projection reads ''FORTY-NINE MINUTES.''

Afterward, still playing the romantic gentleman, The Playwright promises her tickets to a sold-out performance of his latest work (which is meaningless to her), and vows to see her again. They leave for a late evening dinner.

Scene Eight: The Playwright and The Actress

The Playwright meets his match in his next assignation. He accompanies The Actress to a country hotel, to get away from the city and the theatre where they both spend their lives. The Actress, a few years older than he and quite a bit more composed, seems able to play the writer like a fiddle. She teases him about his point of pride, his vocabulary, telling the stunned man, ''You do talk more bollocks per square meter than any man I've ever met.'' She even goes so far as to insult his plays. Then, just when The Playwright thinks things are going his way, The Actress tells him she has booked him another room in the hotel and the time has come for goodnight. Nevertheless, they do end up in bed together. The lights go to black and a slide projection reads ''TWENTY-FIVE MINUTES.'' Humorously, the lights come back up to reveal the two in each other's arms, then darkness falls again and the slide reads ''TWELVE MINUTES.''

In the post-coital bliss that follows, The Actress admits to The Playwright, ''You write brilliant plays,'' and that, even though everyone else in their theatre hates him because he seems conceited, she defends him by saying he has a lot to be conceited about. A backhanded compliment, but he misses the insinuation. Lying in bed together a little while longer, they debate about the sounds of nature outside (Is the chirping they hear created by crickets or frogs?) and The Actress continues her taunts, alternately poking fun at The Playwright and telling him she is in love with him; The Playwright cannot tell if she is serious or only acting.

Scene Nine: The Actress and The Aristocrat

In this scene, Hare's play starts to look in on itself. The Actress is seen on an imaginary stage, taking a bow after a performance of a play by Schnitzler, the author of *Reigen,* the work that was the original material for *The Blue Room.* Apparently, The Actress is starring in the very play Hare's audience is watching, while at the same time really living the fictional events in her fictional world.

Back in her dressing room after the performance, The Actress is visited by The Aristocrat, a wealthy admirer who has been courting her and has just seen her perform onstage for the first time. Like many of the earlier encounters, theirs begins with some verbal jousting. The Actress insinuates The Aristocrat is here while cheating on another mistress, and the Aristocrat pleads innocence and noble intentions. He even suggests they should delay their sexual gratification until they can get to a proper room with a bed, where the right mood can be established.

Very quickly, however, mood becomes unimportant. The Actress and The Aristocrat couple on the dressing room's chaise lounge as the lights fade to black. The slide projection this time reads ''ONE HOUR ONE MINUTE.'' Afterward, The Aristocrat is fully clothed, and picking at leftover Chinese food when he muses on one of the play's central themes. ''Do you think any of us is ever just one person?'' he asks his paramour. ''Don't you think we all change, all the time? With one person we're one person, and with another we're another.'' Even though they both agree their affair is destined to end in misery, The Aristocrat agrees to return to the theatre the next day.

Scene Ten: The Aristocrat and The Girl

A year has passed since the first scene of the play, and the story has come full circle. In a dingy room above a sex shop in the red light district of the city, The Aristocrat has just spent a drunken night with The Girl from scene one. When he awakens, fully clothed in a chair across the room from the sleeping prostitute, he imagines (hopes, actually) that he passed out, inebriated, before they had sex. He gets up, pays her for her time, and kisses her on the eyelids, imagining, romantically, that his kiss is the only physical thing that passed between them. His delusion is shattered, however, when The Girl tells him that they actually did have sex the night before, and he can return anytime he likes, ''Just ask for Irene.''

Through the room's curtained window the day starts to appear. Music plays as The Girl gets up to bid her one-night beau goodbye. ''Goodnight,'' The Aristocrat tells her. ''Good morning,'' she reminds him.

CHARACTERS

The Actress

The unnamed Actress is in her forties, brash, alluring, and one of the most consistently strong personalities in the play. While the other characters all seem to encounter someone capable of disarming their defenses, this remarkable woman never seems to lose, possibly because, of everyone, she seems best able to recognize and accept the imperfections inherent in people and relationships. During her rendezvous with The Playwright, she insults his work and his propensity for fancy wordplay. She pretends Catholic piety, then pulls him into bed with her for multiple rounds of sex. One moment naughty, the next nice, even the cultured and sophisticated Playwright is unable to guess her true intentions. Later, with the well-heeled Aristocrat, she is more sincere, because she seems to like him more, but she is no less wise. She acknowledges that he has other women in his life, sees directly through his false diffidence and, in spite of knowing their relationship is doomed to fail, encourages him to stay the course. ''We're alive!'' she cries to him, and experiencing life is the only way of learning.

Anton

See The Student

The Aristocrat

Malcolm, The Aristocrat, is in his early thirties. His wealth derives from his family's farming estate, and his personality seems to be a combination of the best and worst the aristocracy has to offer. He is intelligent, though not very articulate; earnest, but deceptive, even to himself; sophisticated, but base and animalistic as any of the other men in the play. ''My life is a search . . . for a love which stays real,'' he tells The Actress when he meets her in her dressing room. And it may be that he has good intentions on his search, but he is easily led astray. He suggests to The Actress that they put off their lovemaking until the next day, when they can find a proper room with a bed. However, she very easily seduces him into their first sexual encounter right there in her dressing room. The Aristocrat has glimpses of true insight, and in fact voices one of the most important ideas of the play, that everyone plays different parts with different people, and we're all constantly changing. Despite his aspirations toward virtue, truth, and propriety, however, The Aristocrat has a darker side he is unable to control. In the final scene of the play he awakens from a night of drunken lovemaking with a prostitute and cannot remember where he is or how he got there. To his credit, he still hopes for the best, that nothing happened between himself and The Girl. When he is told otherwise, however, his wistful, philosophic side returns. ''On we go,'' he laments.

The Au Pair

Marie, The Au Pair, is foreign, and cares for a family and their children. Her origins (or, indeed, the origins of the family she cares for) are not described. She begins her encounter with Fred, The Cab Driver, by refusing his advances, even though she compromised herself by following him into a darkened storage closet. To help justify her actions to herself, she permits Fred to have sex with her after forcing him to tell her that it will mean something. She pretends to be fooled in order to allow herself a few minutes of guilty pleasure. After the act it is she who tries to leave first, though she is convinced to stay awhile with Fred, drinking beer and listening to the dance outside their tiny room.

Back at home, The Au Pair seems no more in control of her environment than at the dance. Whether to preserve her job, or because she lacks dignity, Marie allows herself to be treated with scorn and derision by The Student, at the same time that she permits him to have sex with her.

The Cab Driver

The Cab Driver (who later introduces himself as Fred) is shrewd, self-centered, and businesslike. Although it is he who sends out the first signals of sexual interest to the prostitute in the park (he walks past The Girl twice, with no particular destination in mind), he waits for her to make the first contact. He deflects any conversation about his personal life or a relationship beyond a brief sexual encounter, warning The Girl she would only get jealous because "I'm irresistible. Women can't resist me." He only agrees to sex when he is told he will not have to pay for it, then he finishes the act quickly and rushes back to work.

His next encounter, however, is different. He is kinder and gentler (if not altogether sincere) with the Au Pair. Their act of sex takes longer, and they both seem to have enjoyed it. When they are finished, he does not want to rush away but instead asks her to stay with him awhile. He remains awkward with emotions but more interested in her as a person.

Charlie

See The Politician

Emma

See The Married Woman

MEDIA ADAPTATIONS

- David Hare's *The Blue Room* is based on a series of sketches called *Reigen,* written by Arthur Schnitzler in 1896. Director Max Ophuls created a film version of *Reigen* called *La Ronde,* which premiered in 1950 and has since become a favorite of foreign film buffs. The film stars Simone Signoret and Anton Walbrook as the revolving series of intertwined lovers.

Fred

See Cab Driver

The Girl

The Girl, who calls herself Irene, is a teenage prostitute, amateurish and new to her work. She dresses the part, with a short, black leather skirt and heels, and her method of operation seems to be smoking cigarettes on a park bench, waiting to catch the attention of a potential customer. Given the chance, she is bold and aggressive. In order to build her clientele, or perhaps because she is still new, she doesn't force payment for her services. The Cab Driver is momentarily surprised when The Girl tells him she doesn't care if he pays her for sex. Then, after the act, she asks for remuneration anyway and is rejected but not discouraged. "I'll be here tomorrow," she says, purposefully.

She then disappears until the end of the play. A year has passed, and Irene has been plying her trade in a small room above a sex shop in the city. She spent the previous evening with The Aristocrat and admits to him that Fred (The Cab Driver from Scene One) wants to marry her, but she has so far resisted. Her experience during the last year doesn't seem to have hardened her. She is sympathetic toward the plight of The Aristocrat, who clearly regrets the night they spent together.

Irene

See The Girl

Kelly

See The Model

Malcolm

See The Aristocrat

Marie

See The Au Pair

The Married Woman

Emma is The Married Woman. She is in her thirties and has been married to Charlie, a prominent politician, for over eight years. They met in Venice, where they experienced several weeks of wild, romantic, passionate love. Now, however, their marriage and Charlie's career have forever changed the course of the fire that once warmed their relationship. They now sleep in separate beds in the same room, coming together only for occasional sexual encounters. Charlie is constantly working, and Emma pines for the love they once had.

In order to recapture some sense of the drama and excitement she once found with Charlie, The Married Woman begins an affair with a younger man, The Student, who is the son of some friends of the family. With him, The Married Woman is no longer pliant and submissive, she gets *her* way, and she finds it thrilling.

The Model

Like all of the other characters in the play, The Model (Kelly) is both more and less than she appears. As a model, someone admired for her beauty, she might be expected to radiate loveliness. Actually, she complains, "If you're a model you have to look awful. That's the job." A mere seventeen-years-old, The Model has traveled abroad with her mother and three sisters. She is apparently not yet successful enough in her career to afford a life of luxury, or even a place of her own, but she manages to find men more than willing to provide these things for her. The Model seems addicted to cocaine and prone to the abuse of a variety of other substances. She seems to be an even match for The Politician in their sexual encounter, trumping him in a conversation about marriage by telling him that his wife no doubt cheats on him as well. Though she

seems unwilling to commit to any kind of a relationship, she apparently accepts The Politician's offer of an apartment and living expenses in exchange for being his mistress. This does not, however, deter her from other amorous affairs. She follows The Playwright home, not even realizing he is a famous, wealthy, eccentric hyper-intellectual. They have absolutely nothing in common, but she enjoys the song he sings her and the sex they share, and she seems genuinely flattered by his kind, if insincere, compliments.

Robert Phethean

See The Playwright

The Playwright

Robert Phethean is a famous playwright in his early thirties. Judging by his writing studio he is both financially successful and quite eccentric. A large desk is piled with books, scripts, and CDS, and there is a piano in the shadows at the back of the room. He lights his workspace only with candles, a happy discovery, he claims, during a power outage, that now casts a "magical" light on everything. The Playwright may or may not be the voice of David Hare himself, an idea the actual writer of *The Blue Room* no doubt intended to leave ambiguously open to interpretation.

The Playwright complains about scholars who try to pigeonhole him into categories such as "postromantic" and scoffs at the idea that journalists, too, are actually "writers." He plays a song for The Model that he calls his own, but artfully dodges the question of the composition's true authorship. He is skilled with words and seems to enjoy using his wide-ranging vocabulary to impress, to mock, and to play with his female conquests. Because of his eccentric ways, it is difficult to gauge The Playwright's sincerity when he tells The Model he is enamored of her and wants to take her around the world (or at least see her again sometime.)

For all his cleverness and verbal dexterity, however, The Playwright meets his match in The Actress. At a secluded country hotel where they have escaped for an intimate weekend, he allows the older woman to mock and shame him, seemingly because he is so powerfully attracted to her. She insults his writing, his way with words, and his arrogance, yet he keeps coming back for more. In the end, he finds himself as confused by The Actress as The Model was by him.

The Politician

Charlie is a prominent politician who is almost always working. He carries three cellular telephones with him everywhere he goes and has to schedule his time with his wife and family. Before marrying Emma, The Politician conducted a string of youthful affairs, at least one of which was with a married woman. Now, however, in the middle part of his life, he claims to love only The Married Woman, and calls his family his stability, his salvation. They met in Venice and experienced a few weeks of romantic, passionate love before wedding and settling into a more mundane existence that The Politician pronounces safer, since the bed is no longer the only thing holding them together. As if to prove his point, the couple each has their own single bed in the bedroom, and they share a bed only for occasional sex.

At the same time, however, The Politician is taking drugs and starting an affair with The Model, a seventeen-year-old cocaine addict. After two hours of intoxicated love-making, Charlie offers to set The Model up with an apartment of her own, where he can provide financial stability for her, and she can be available to him for sexual rendezvous whenever he wants. "A life of your own," he calls it, "Isn't that what women want?"

The Student

The Student, Anton, is the son of wealthy parents. He is studying law like his father, and has discovered aristocratic, imperial ways at an early age. At times he is foolish, young and naive, and at others impassioned, idealistic, and oddly sophisticated. During his first scene, with The Au Pair, his behavior is detestable. He makes unnecessary and demeaning demands on the family's foreign servant and seems to assume that satisfying him sexually should simply be part of her job. Later, with The Married Woman, he has met his match. With Emma, a friend of his parents, he tries to be mature and seductive but only half-succeeds. She obviously is not interested in him for his worldliness but simply for sex. When he is unable to provide it because of his nervousness with an older, dominant woman, she takes charge and draws excitement from him.

He is helpless, in love with her, and at the same time juvenile and proud of his accomplishment for seducing a married woman.

THEMES

Sex

The most obvious motif in *The Blue Room* is sex, in all its many guises. In the play, sex is shared between a prostitute and a john, a student and an older, married woman, a politician and his wife, an artist and a model, an actress and a writer, and so on and on. In every instance, however, the build-up prior to the sexual act is more energetic and exciting than the act itself which, accordingly, is never shown on the stage. The characters all long for satisfying experiences, and some seem to be seeking meaningful relationships, but their constant changing of partners in a sexual roundelay thwarts their chances of ever finding meaning and substance with other human beings.

At their best, the characters in *The Blue Room* can seem innocent and well-intentioned. Even The Girl, a neophyte prostitute, tells The Cab Driver "The kiss is the best bit," not the act of sex itself; and early on she doesn't even demand payment for her services. Fred, The Cab Driver, for all his callousness in the first scene with The Girl, seems genuinely enamored with the Au Pair at a dance later. Even though he is incapable of discussing his feelings in any meaningful way, he makes an attempt at tenderness and at least stays for a little while after sex.

No matter how rude, incorrigible, or formidable a character in this play's world might seem at first, he or she is likely to meet his or her match just around the corner in the next scene, suggesting that our attitudes toward sex make conquerors, and fools, of us all. Sex, the play seems to suggest, is a merry-go-round of our own making. Human nature is drawn toward lechery, whether we like it or not. It is this realization that causes the frustrated Aristocrat to wail, "How do we change? How do we change who we are?" when he wakes up in a dingy room above a sex shop after a drunken night with a prostitute. Dawn comes, he and The Girl bid fare-

TOPICS FOR FURTHER STUDY

- Schnitzler's original work, *Reigen,* upon which *The Blue Room* is based, suggested that one of the unfortunate things passed along in the "round dance" of loose sexual relations is venereal diseases. Although it is not a prominent feature of Hare's play, AIDS is the modern counterpart to this worry, and a couple of characters do express concerns about proper "hygiene." Research the most recent statistics and medical findings about the AIDS virus. How many people are now affected by this disease? What have governments and physicians been doing to combat the spread of AIDS?

- Watch *La Ronde,* the 1950 film version of Schnitzler's work directed by Max Ophuls, and compare it with David Hare's adaptation, *The Blue Room.* How are the stories and characters similar? How do they differ? What is the effect of Ophuls's faithful recreation of turn-of-the-century Vienna as the setting for his film, versus Hare's ambiguous suggestion that the play simply occur, "in one of the great cities of the world, in the present day"? Finally, how have attitudes toward the characters' sexual looseness changed over the years?

- One of the characters in *The Blue Room* is a playwright, like Hare himself. Examine the scenes involving The Playwright. What is his opinion of the artist's place in society? How does he feel about his audiences? What is his relationship like with the media? With others in the theatre? How much of The Playwright's personality might be shared by the author of *The Blue Room?*

- At the turn of the century, Schnitzler's Vienna was considered a center of European science and culture. Prior to the First World War, two million people occupied the crown jewel of the Austrian Empire. Vienna was the source for the modernist art movement, the origin of Sigmund Freud's psychoanalytical theories, and the capital of European music, home to such famous composers as Joseph Haydn, Wolfgang Amadeus Mozart, and Ludwig van Beethoven. Research *fin de siecle* Vienna. How did the city manage to become so influential in art, music, and thought? When and why did its fortunes change?

well, but the play suggests that by evening the dance will continue on.

Masks

One of the devices people rely on in a lifetime of sexual escapades and failed relationships, the play suggests, is *masks* that hide, and change, their true identities. With his Au Pair, The Student is confident, imperious even. He is the master of the house, and she the servant. Up in his room with the older Married Woman, however, he is insecure, impotent, and romantically naive. Which face is the real Student? For her part, The Married Woman is nervous about possible discovery but as confident with her young paramour as he was the Au Pair. It is

she who controls the situation. Back at home, though, she is cowed by her husband, The Politician, who she really loves but no longer inspires.

Like the sex that passes from partner to partner in scene after scene, the masks the characters wear are constantly changing. The Cab Driver is a crude, anonymous john willing to have sex on a riverbank one day, and a tender, if unpolished, wooer at ballroom dance the next. The Playwright is by turn preening, boastful, and condescending with The Model, and clumsy, reserved, and altogether mastered by The Actress. It is a dilemma summed up by The Aristocrat, in what may be the play's most self-descriptive line. "Do you think any of us is ever just one person?" he asks The Actress after they have had sex in her dressing room. "Don't you think we all change, all the time? With one person we're one person, and with another we're another." True to form, this wealthy, sophisticated gentleman later finds himself rumpled in a chair in a prostitute's bedroom, missing memories of the previous night's debauchery. No one in the play, or perhaps in life, remains what they seem for long.

STYLE

Plot Structure

Quite cleverly, the structure of *The Blue Room* is part of its story. Originally titled *Reigen,* German for "round dance," the play presents a series of characters who meet, have sex, then part ways and move on to a new partner. Ultimately the play ends where it begins, with a sexual transaction between a man and a prostitute.

The larger template of the play is familiar to modern theatergoers. Rather than a single story, told in linear fashion with a handful of characters and only one or two settings, *The Blue Room* presents a series of ten separate, but interrelated, scenes involving many characters who meet in a variety of locations. The unique contribution this play makes to this type of plot structure is that it is not the story but the *characters* that carry over from one scene into the next.

The Cab Driver who meets the prostitute in the opening scene is found in a storage closet with an Au Pair in the next scene. Back at home, The Au Pair dallies with The Student, before The Student meets The Married Woman in his bedroom upstairs. She goes home to her husband, The Politician, who then picks up The Model and takes her to a hotel room. And so on. Taken one at a time, each assignation is unremarkable, common even. Together, though, they present a picture of human beings controlled by physical impulses and seemingly powerless to change their miserable destinies.

Slide Projections

The German playwright and director Bertolt Brecht advocated the use of slide projections as a replacement for scenery, or to interrupt the flow of action, in productions of his "Epic" dramas. For Brecht, slide projections were a means of "alienating" his audiences. Instead of allowing audiences to become comfortable and lulled by familiar, realistic scenery and linear, climactic storytelling, Brecht employed signs and projections that told audiences what the setting for a particular scene was, which often took the place of characters in the play by relaying important plot information.

Since Brecht used this experimental device in the 1930s and 1940s, it has caught on in mainstream theatrical production and is now a common element of modern plays. *The Blue Room* uses slide projections to show the passage of time during scenes, comment on the action of the characters, and provide a touch of humor to the play. Each time two characters come together for sex, the lights fade to black and a slide projection displays the amount of time it took for them to complete the act. The Cab Driver, for example, doesn't particularly favor The Girl. She is a prostitute and he has no emotional attachment to her, so when they have sex down by the river, their projection reads, "THREE MINUTES." Immediately afterward, he is up and gone. Later, with the Au Pair, The Cab Driver extends his time to "NINE MINUTES," with the suggestion that he cares a little more about their tryst.

Sometimes the effect of the slide's judgment on a character can be humiliating, as when The Student panics after "FORTY-FIVE SECONDS" with the Au Pair, or fizzles in "0 MINUTES" with the Married Woman. The Married Woman and her husband, The Politician, achieve a standard, mundane "FIFTEEN MINUTES," while The Politician, under the influence of drugs, logs "TWO HOURS TWENTY-EIGHT MINUTES" with the model.

In each instance, the slide projection represents the literal passage of time, as well as a change of mood in the scene, sometimes for the better, sometimes for the worse. The Playwright is a dapper gentleman to The Model after their respectable "FORTY-NINE MINUTES." Once The Actress spends "TWENTY-FIVE MINUTES" followed by an additional "TWELVE MINUTES" with The Playwright, she stops insulting him and tells him, "You write brilliant plays." Later, though, the effect of "ONE HOUR ONE MINUTE" on The Actress and The Aristocrat is melancholy and the loss of romance.

HISTORICAL CONTEXT

Although David Hare began his playwriting career in England during the turbulent 1960s and 1970s, he grew to popular prominence during the "Thatcher Decade" of the 1980s, an era that has influenced his work to the present day. During the 1980s, Hare was an outspoken critic of the "Iron Lady," as Great Britain's Prime Minister from 1979-1990, Margaret Thatcher, was known. As the leader of the reigning Conservative Party (or "Tories") in Great Britain, Thatcher stood for everything Hare and the liberal Labour Party were against. During her terms in office, she sold and privatized many government-operated businesses such as British Airways and British Telecom. She also fought to damage the influence and control of labor unions in Great Britain, and her administration drastically reduced the welfare benefits offered to Britons, particularly in the areas of education and health.

Thatcher's methods produced boom years for many. Overall wages and standards of living rose during the 1980s, and the decade is often remembered as a period of rampant greed and consumerism, much like the same years in America during Ronald Reagan's presidency. Still, many more people were pushed aside, and the gap between the "haves" and "have-nots" grew wider. During the Thatcher Decade, Hare's plays, such as *Pravda* (1985) and *The Secret Rapture* (1988), were scathing indictments of British society under a Conservative government.

In 1990, Thatcher was turned out of office, thanks largely to a temporary increase in inflation and friction between her administration and governments on continental Europe that were seeking to unify their currency and reduce trade barriers. The Iron Lady was replaced by John Major, another Conservative Party representative. For seven more years, Major and the Conservative Party attempted to curb inflation, stabilize the pound (British currency), and improve relations with the European community and their increasingly hostile colony to the west, Ireland. At one point during his term of office, Major received only a fourteen percent approval rating from the people of Great Britain, the lowest of any Prime Minister in the country's history. During the Major years, Hare continued his attacks on Conservative government with a trilogy of plays aimed at social institutions: *Racing Demon* (1990),

about the Church of England; *Murmuring Judges* (1991), concerning Britain's legal system; and *The Absence of War* (1993), a commentary on politics in England.

Hare's arch-nemeses, the Conservatives, were finally driven from office in 1997, when the long-suffering Labour Party produced Tony Blair as the new Prime Minister of Britain. With Labour back in office, many of the political worries Hare had been critiquing in his plays for so many years were, temporarily at least, held at bay. While Hare was writing *The Blue Room,* Blair was restructuring the health care system in Britain to better serve low- and middle-income families. Blair also created closer ties to the European Union (though by 1999, Great Britain had still not chosen to participate in the new unified European currency system, based on the "Euro"), and, in 1998-99, he helped revive the stalled peace talks over British rule in Northern Ireland.

Throughout the Thatcher Decade, the John Major years, and Tony Blair's "New Labour" administration, a major change also occurred in one of England's most famous institutions: the royal family. English royalty, at one time the ruling kings and queens of one of the largest commonwealth empires the world has ever known, steadily lost their power and prestige during the final years of the twentieth century. While the actual king or queen of Britain has been merely a figurehead for many years, with the real power to create and enforce laws given to the Prime Minister and Parliament, history and tradition combined to at least make the royal family an object of reverence for the people of England. However, the divorce of Diana, the immensely popular Princess of Wales, from her husband, Charles in 1996, followed by the princess's death in an automobile accident in Paris in 1997, caused the people of Great Britain to question the morals and the function of their royal family. By 1999, many politicians and social critics wondered aloud how long it would be before Britain, home to crowned heads from King Alfred the Great to Queen Elizabeth, turned its back on royalty.

CRITICAL OVERVIEW

David Hare's *The Blue Room* has been "freely adapted" from Dr. Arthur Schnitzler's *La Ronde,* which in turn was based on a series of two-character sketches Schnitzler wrote in 1896 entitled *Reigen.* At the time, Schnitzler's scenes were deemed near pornographic. The author claimed he never intended his sketches to be performed publicly but simply to be shared among friends. When the vignettes were finally pulled together on the stage for the first time in Vienna in 1921, police closed the performance. The same year, in Berlin, actors performing the work were hauled into court and subjected to a trial on obscenity charges. In a social turnabout years later, director Max Ophuls's 1950 film version of *La Ronde,* became a cult classic, an appealing blend of nostalgia, enchantment, and titillation.

Sex still sells, and when word went out in 1998 that the well-known screen siren Nicole Kidman was starring in *The Blue Room,* and that she would be naked, or nearly so, in almost every scene, the New York run of the play opened with $4 million in advance ticket sales. Scalped tickets sold for hundreds of dollars a seat, and much of the criticism leveled at the work in the popular press surrounded the production's *hype* (and Kidman's semi-clothed body) rather than the play's literary worth.

For all its promise of sexual stimulation, though, review after review pointed out that one of the actual aims of the play seemed to be to illustrate how tawdry and unsatisfying sex often is. Charles Isherwood wrote in *Variety,* "For all the steamy sexual traffic onstage, watching the play is a chilly, empty experience." In *LI Business News,* Richard Scholem noted "The point of Hare's adaptation seems to be the vapidness and emptiness of often mechanical sex. That the anticipation and pursuit of sex, the precoital shadow boxing that takes place before consummation generates more excitement, hope and interest than the act itself, which is most often an empty disappointment, sometimes a comical fiasco." In the *New York Times* Ben Brantley suggested Hare's main point was that "sex would always have been better somewhere else, at some other time, with another person; erotic satisfaction is a chimera, the elusive quarry of an eternal and fruitless hunt."

In *The Blue Room,* the hunt is indeed everything, and most critics agreed the parade of characters who participate in the daisy chain of sexual affairs was one of the most appealing features of the play. As a playwright, Hare is particularly known for his intimate, multi-dimensional, sympathetic female characters. Many of his plays center around women with strong, forceful personalities (*The Secret Rapture, Plenty,* and *Skylight* are just three examples). Accordingly, a common note sounded by reviewers about the various characters in *The Blue Room* was that, in every instance, the female parts were much more varied and interesting than the male ones.

"The Cab Driver, Student, Politician, Playwright and Aristocrat . . . are rather boorish, macho types," Scholem observed, "not nearly as juicy, complex or even mysterious as the female parts." Brantley wrote, "Mr. Glen [Iain Glen, who played all the male roles] has the harder row to hoe of the two stars, since the men of *The Blue Room* tend to be blind and fatuous, swaggering macho jokes with little redeeming self-consciousness."

While London critics raved about the sensuality and excitement of the play (one critic for the *Daily Telegraph* famously dubbed Nicole Kidman "pure theatrical Viagra"), American reviewers were generally less impressed with the work. "A shrug, and an occasional worldly chuckle, is pretty much all that *The Blue Room* elicits," lamented Brantley, "The entire evening is not unlike Ms. Kidman's much-discussed body: smooth, pale and slender." Also in the *New York Times,* Frank Rich complained, "The director, Sam Mendes, and adapter, David Hare, lent *The Blue Room* their cachet, but not their best efforts." *The Blue Room* "is a lightweight piece by a heavyweight playwright," proclaimed Scholem.

Perhaps seeking an excuse for why such a successful playwright might have floundered on this project, Rod Dreher suggested in the *National Review* that "this dreary, vapid, airless evening of theater is such a depressingly accurate reflection of our time." To Dreher, audiences deserved what they got as a result of the society they had created. He continued:

> I screw, therefore I am. Sex is certainly an ignoble basis for metaphysics, but who can deny that it's the one most people these days seem to swear by? When a society becomes unmoored from traditional religious belief or moral idealism, and in the absence of social stigma as an external reinforcement of inwardly held virtue, it is no surprise that the sex instinct will assert its rule as if by divine right. And a society in which the cheap thrills of celebrity and quickie sex are sovereign is a society willing to pay anything for the chance to see a famous actress's rear end in shallow, pseudo-

Iain Glen and Nicole Kidman enact two of the many personas presented in Hare's play

highbrow erotica which can't even boast of a positive review in the *Times*.

CRITICISM

Lane A. Glenn,

Lane A. Glenn is a Ph.D. specializing in theatre history and literature. In this essay, he discusses the

different cultural climates of fin de siecle *Vienna, when Arthur Schnitzler's* Reigen *was first produced, and the Europe and America of the late-twentieth century, when playwright David Hare updated Schnitzler's work as* The Blue Room.

Dr. Arthur Schnitzler began writing *Reigen*, a "round dance" of sexual escapades among a variety of characters in turn-of-the-century Vienna, during the winter of 1896-97. He initially considered his collection of "dialogues," as he called them, too scandalous to ever be staged, and preferred to

WHAT DO I READ NEXT?

- David Hare is the author or adapter of more than twenty stage plays and a number of screenplays. Some of his best known and most popular plays include *Plenty* (1978), *The Secret Rapture* (1988), and his trilogy of plays about social institutions in Great Britain, *Racing Demon* (for which he earned both an Olivier Award and a Tony Award following its production in 1990), *Murmuring Judges* (1991), and *The Absence of War* (1992).

- Besides writing plays, David Hare is also an accomplished screenwriter, director, and essayist. *Writing Left-Handed* is a collection of his essays that have appeared in newspapers, playbills, and anthologies over the years. The book includes the playwright's insights into his craft, as well as his perspectives on theatre history in Great Britain, and his opinions about a variety of contemporary political issues.

- Various versions of Arthur Schnitzler's original series of dialogues that were the inspiration for *The Blue Room* exist in English translations. Among them are Schnitzler's *Hands Around: A Cycle of Ten Dialogues* (1995) and *The Round Dance* (1983). In both, a series of people conduct sexual affairs that are intertwined, like the characters in Hare's play.

- Schnitzler was also a novelist of some renown.

- *The Road into the Open* (1992) depicts Imperial Vienna at the turn of the century. Before the First World War, the city is a center of European culture, a backdrop against which Schnitzler presents themes ranging from anti-Semitism to the struggles of artists, as well as his more familiar treatment of the complications of love and sex among various men and women.

- John Gray's 1992 best-selling self-help book *Men are from Mars, Women are from Venus* is billed as "a practical guide for improving communication and getting what you want in your relationships." Gray is a relationship counselor who examines some of the differences between men and women and suggests that, in order to develop happier relationships, couples must recognize and accept those differences.

- English Restoration comedies are famous for characters who are constantly chasing each other into and out of sexual relationships. William Wycherley's *The Country Wife* (1673) and William Congreve's *The Way of the World* (1700) both present husbands, wives, and lovers who go to elaborate lengths to deceive each other while carrying on clandestine affairs.

---

simply have them printed, at his own expense, and distributed to friends for their enjoyment. Reportedly, when his fiancee asked to see a copy, he even refused her, saying *Reigen* was not appropriate reading for a young lady.

It wasn't until 1920 that Schnitzler allowed a publicly staged performance of *Reigen,* and even then it opened out of town, in Berlin. The German production met with demonstrations, riots, and the arrest of the cast on charges of obscenity (they were later acquitted). The next year, in 1921, the Viennese premiere of the play was closed by police,

who considered the performance a form of public pornography.

What a difference a century can make. A hundred years after Dr. Schnitzler shocked his society (some of the more sensitive members, anyway) with *Reigen,* the first production of English playwright David Hare's 1998 adaptation of the work, *The Blue Room,* was greeted by a very different kind of disturbance: ticket riots. Publicity for Hare's modernized daisy chain of casual sexual encounters proudly trumpeted the appearance of a scantily clad, and occasionally nude, popular film star, Australian

"IT DOESN'T MATTER WHETHER *THE BLUE ROOM* TAKES PLACE IN VIENNA, VENICE, OR VENTURA, CALIFORNIA, ITS CHARACTERS POSSESS RECOGNIZABLE TRAITS OF PEOPLE THE WORLD OVER, AND THEY STRUGGLE WITH SOME OF THE SAME PROBLEMS INDIVIDUALS IN ADVANCED SOCIETIES HAVE ALWAYS FOUND THEMSELVES STRUGGLING WITH—CLASS CONFLICTS, LOVELESS RELATIONSHIPS, SEXUAL INHIBITION AND ITS COUNTERPART, AGGRESSIVE LICENTIOUSNESS"**

actress Nicole Kidman, and instead of shouting moral outrage, theatregoers clamored in line for tickets. The limited run of the show on Broadway in New York City opened with an amazing $4 million in advance sales, and scalped seats were reportedly going for several hundred dollars a cushion. Same play, same prurience, but a *very* different audience.

The production record of *Reigen* in its various forms throughout the century illustrates the cultural relativity of all literature. What is shocking and abhorrent to one group of people in one particular place at one specific time sometimes becomes quaint, or even comical, to a different society years later. Important, burning issues, particularly those with contemporary political themes, fade into the distant, collective memory of a culture, while new hot topics take their place. It is as true of Shakespeare, Mark Twain, and Harriet Beecher Stowe as it is of Arthur Schnitzler and David Hare: The words remain the same, but they are heard a different way.

In the Introduction to *Hands Around: A Cycle of Ten Dialogues,* a limited-circulation, English language translation of Arthur Schnitzler's *Reigen,* printed for members of the Schnitzler Society in 1929, the anonymous translators of the text observe:

Humanity seems gayest when dancing on the brink of a volcano. The culture of a period preceding a social cataclysm is marked by a spirit of light wit and sophisticated elegance which finds expression in a literature of a distinct type. This literature is lighthearted, audacious and self-conscious. It can treat with the most charming insouciance subjects which in another age would have been awkward or even vulgar. But with the riper experience of a period approaching its end the writers feel untrammeled in the choice of them by pride or prejudice knowing that they will never transgress the line of good taste.

This observation is an attempt to position *Reigen* in its proper place in history. In Schnitzler's Vienna, the twilight years of the nineteenth century (often referred to by the French term *fin de siecle*) were a time of aristocratic sophistication, intellectual and artistic achievement, and social gaiety. In the words of Charles Osborne, another of Schnitzler's English translators, the era "produced significant new movements in the arts in several countries, notably England, France, and Austria. Nowhere, however, did the arts thrive more richly in those years than in Austria, and specifically in its capital city, Vienna, which is where many of the most exciting developments had their beginnings."

Those developments the accomplishments of *fin de siecle* Vienna were created by the hands and minds of an amazing collection of painters, composers, philosophers, playwrights, and scientists, all gathered together in one place and time. Among the notables were the poet and playwright Hugo von Hofmannsthal, the painter Oskar Kokoschka, composer Johann Strauss, and one of the most influential thinkers of the twentieth century, the psychologist Sigmund Freud, whose *Interpretation of Dreams* was published in 1900, laying the foundation for modern psychoanalysis.

When they say humanity is gayest while "dancing on the brink of a volcano," the translators of *Hands Around* are suggesting that, without realizing it, the Viennese of Schnitzler's day and Schnitzler's play were experiencing a last hurrah before proud, cultured, aristocratic Vienna would be consumed and forever changed by the First and Second World Wars. In other words, the creation of this play had to wait until the time was just right, and a little longer would have been too late.

In his description of *The Round Dance,* in *Hauptmann, Wedekind and Schnitzler,* scholar Peter Skrine suggested, "The idea [of the play] was a good one: one wonders why no one had thought of it before. Perhaps someone had, but it was of course unthinkable on the modern stage until in the Vienna of the early-1900s a sufficiently large group of open-minded theatre-goers . . . were able to provide a potential audience in sympathy with what Schnitzler was doing and the encouragement he needed to bring out into the open what he had on his mind.''

Thanks to decades worth of intense exploration into anthropology, biology, sociology, and psychology by scientists in the nineteenth century, Schnitzler was also better armed than any of his predecessor playwrights had been to write such an insightful play. Charles Darwin, Karl Marx, and Auguste Comte contributed to *Reigen,* indirectly at least as much as the atmosphere of aristocratic Vienna. ''Schnitzler was drawing the logical literary consequences from the biological and sociological discoveries of the late-nineteenth century,'' Skrine noted. ''Sex is the basic manifestation of life, and he therefore presents it as the common denominator of a wide cross-section of humanity drawn from the widely differing social strata of Viennese society.''

A century later, that social strata has changed somewhat. Schnitzler's characters remain largely intact in Hare's *Blue Room.* The ''Sweet Young Lady'' of Schnitzler's play, who sips a little too much wine with the Husband character, becomes a cocaine sniffing, pill-popping waifish Model in Hare's updating, but otherwise the people onstage are remarkably similar. Those in the audience, however, have undergone a major transformation.

Schnitzler's audiences claimed to be surprised by the acts of debauchery in *Reigen.* Perhaps to provide a mask of honor for an otherwise dishonorable production, some critics suggested that there was a moral lesson to be learned from the play: Besides the emptiness and emotional despair that are passed along by casual sex, venereal diseases may also find their way from partner to partner. In the 1990s, audiences in Europe and America have seen it all, on the stage and on the screen, and are unlikely to be truly shocked by any mere display of the naked human form. Titillated yes, but shocked, no. They have lived through a decade of proliferating pornography, thanks to the widespread use of the Internet, and witnessed the impeachment of U.S. President Bill Clinton over a variety of sexual affairs, ending with the now infamous White House intern Monica Lewinsky. Their steamy encounters were described in graphic detail by an infamous Special Prosecutor, whose written report, including accounts of oral sex in the president's office, was made public and printed in serial form in newspapers and magazines across the country. As Rod

Dreher dryly noted in a review of *The Blue Room* in the *National Review,* ''It's easy to imagine what a shock these vignettes must have delivered to Schnitzler's cultured audiences in 1920s Vienna, but at this late date in the sexual revolution, especially after the year-long Lewinskian Thermidor, it's all very old hat. Been there, done that, saw it on C-SPAN.''

Modern audiences might be expected, however, to be more frightened by the specter of AIDS, a devastating sexually transmitted disease that killed nearly 7 million people between the time of its discovery in 1981 and the time *The Blue Room* was staged in 1998. Intriguingly, however, Hare does not turn AIDS into a major, or even minor, topic of discussion in the new adaptation. At one point in the sexual roundelay, the Au Pair tells her new beau, the Cab Driver, she wants to wait to have sex ''because of the risk. . . . It's not safe nowadays.'' But when he tells her the act will mean something significant to him, her resolve melts and they fall down together on a bed of cardboard boxes. Occasional glimpses of tentative regrets are all that surface in the play.

Perhaps this seeming lack of social consciousness can be forgiven, in light of Hare's previous track record of socially important works. Describing the playwright's previous work, Robert Viagas wrote in *Back Stage,* ''Hare's plays examine various facets of the troubled late-20th century British soul.'' This is undeniably true of plays like *Plenty, The Secret Rapture,* and Hare's remarkable trilogy of dramas examining British social institutions, *Racing Demon, Murmuring Judges,* and *The Absence of War.* With *The Blue Room,* however, Britain's most popular playwright-polemicist was telling a more *universal* story, and seemed to be less concerned with large social issues, than with intimate, personal crises that are experienced the same the world over, in any time period.

Unlike Schnitzler's original work, which deliberately attempts to evoke the spirit of *fin de siecle* Vienna, *The Blue Room*'s preface suggests only that ''The play is set in one of the great cities of the world, in the present day,'' and, indeed, there is little about the work that ties it to a particular geographic location. Schnitzler's audiences may indeed have seen something uniquely Austrian, or German, about the characters in *Reigen.* In fact, Skrine asserted that without the proper treatment of the language and a delicately nuanced approach to the unique Viennese personality, the play would become something very different than its author intended. ''*The Round Dance* is a play which needs plenty of tact,'' said Skrine. ''If the subtle inflections of Viennese speech and the details of Viennese manners are not captured, the true qualities of the text are apt to evaporate, and we are left with an episodic and rather smutty entertainment in which Schnitzler's delightfully varied and pointed dialogue might just as well be replaced by coarse innuendo and heavy breathing.''

Half a century later, when he filmed *Reigen* as *La Ronde* in 1950, Max Ophuls must have felt the same way. His production, which has become a favorite of cinema buffs everywhere, labors to recreate the same Viennese turn-of-the-century elegance and wistfulness found in Schnitzler's play. Five more decades later though, a full century after Dr. Schnitzler circulated copies of his ''dialogues'' he had printed at his own expense among a select group of friends, Hare's new adaptation has proven that it really is a small world after all. In the last hours of the twentieth century, geographic boundaries and cultural differences are melting away in a flurry of electronic global communications and a powerful world economy. It doesn't matter whether *The Blue Room* takes place in Vienna, Venice, or Ventura, California, its characters possess recognizable traits of people the world over, and they struggle with some of the same problems individuals in advanced societies have always found themselves struggling with—class conflicts, loveless relationships, sexual inhibition, and its counterpart, aggressive licentiousness.

In the 1990s, however, those themes, in this story, haven't achieved the same resonance they once found with audiences less programmed for voyeuristic thrills. As Charles Isherwood noted in his review of *The Blue Room* for *Variety,* ''One notes an irony: At the last turn of the century, when the original was written, it was considered too dangerous to be published and later inspired police action; on the cusp of the next, the new text has become virtually insignificant, lost in the swirl of celebrity hype that has surrounded the production. Play? What play? Draw your own conclusion about the decline of culture.''

Source: Lane A. Glenn, for *Drama for Students,* Gale, 2000.

John Simon

Simon reviews the Broadway debut of Hare's adaptation of Arthur Schnitzler's Reigen, *finding that the new work, while offering dazzling performances, does not live up to its source material.*

Perhaps the one world-theater figure left undervalued many years after his death is Arthur Schnitzler. Esteemed by the cognoscenti, his work performed intermittently (though often in bastardized versions), and dimly known to many theatergoers, he has yet to achieve the honors due a genius in both drama and fiction. Unfortunately, the updating of his comedy *Reigen* by David Hare (rhymes with Guare) as *The Blue Room* will not add many laurels to the great Austrian's reputation.

Reigen (''Round Dance''), known mostly from Max Ophuls's movie version, *La Ronde*—a flamboyant but facile Ophulsification—is a play that astutely views the sexual act as also a sexual leveler and psychological placebo, but only fleetingly satisfying in any capacity. It is both a dance of sex (A screws B, B screws C, and so on until J screws A) and a dance of death—the death of love, as various partners from diverse social strata declare feelings for one another that are transparently transient.

What Schnitzler achieves, and Hare pretty much loses, is a careful demonstration of how sex takes on varying significance depending on the status of the participants, and of how emotions change from before intercourse to after. Yet Hare and his clever director, Sam Mendes, have conceived this modernization as a bravura display piece for one actor and one actress, each playing five parts. That way, however, the sense of a cross section of humankind caught in the act fades, and the focus becomes the versatility of the two performers. Similarly, the startling minimalist décor by Mark Thompson and neon-edged abstract lighting by Hugh Vanstone further detract from Schnitzler's detailed and minutely documented societal and existential exploration.

Still, if all you want is two highly attractive performers—she an Australian-American movie star, he a British-stage leading man—exhibiting their skills and bodies in a sufficiently sophisticated but slick vehicle, more Hare than Schnitzler, *The Blue Room* fills the bill.

I doubt whether there exists a young actress anywhere today who better combines physical allure with histrionic gifts than Nicole Kidman. Here she manages five idiosyncratic and duly varied performances that will not be outshone by an almost continuous dishabille and brief nudity (mostly from the back) that would be enough to eclipse many a lesser talent. For Miss Kidman's is a great and very nearly flawless beauty, extending from hair to toes and skipping nothing, unless, unlike me, you feel that a tall, willowy, essentially girlish figure is inferior to womanly copiousness. But be forewarned: You will see much more of Miss Kidman's face, legs, and feet, superb as they are, than of her torso.

I dwell on body so much because that is what the hype has been all about, dishonest in hype's usual way. You get more nudity on the masculine side, from Iain Glen, an equally fine performer and not inconsiderable looker. But what with capitalization on Miss Kidman's star aura, and underestimation of female and homosexual audiences, Glen's even greater self-baring has gotten less publicity.

The hundred uninterrupted minutes go by without boring you, but do not expect major erotic, any more than artistic, stimulation. No doubt intentionally, the essence of eroticism—the passionately sensual interplay of two performers—has been downplayed, if not exactly curbed. Moreover, what was incomparably daring a century ago (1897, and then in 1900, only privately printed) is mere marginal titillation today. And Hare, to his credit, was not simply after sexual jokiness, although he may still have overemphasized it.

Source: John Simon, review of *The Blue Room* in *New York,* Vol. 31, no. 50, January 4, 1999, p. 69.

Frank Rich

Rich offers a mixed review of The Blue Room, *praising the two lead actors, Nicole Kidman and Iain Glen, but finding the attendant hype surrounding movie star Kidman's presence in the play to overshadow the actual work.*

If the theater is a temple, it's no surprise that the most popular faith on Broadway this holiday season is ''The Blue Room,'' to which pilgrims flock from miles around to worship Nicole Kidman's tush.

But given the competing prurience on tap this year, anyone who sees ''*The Blue Room*'' must be baffled. It's no Starr report. You pay your money—even $35 balcony seats are scalped for hundreds—and all you get is 100 minutes of arch acting—class skits in which Ms. Kidman's backside (and only her backside) is visible undraped for about five seconds. The dim lighting hasn't been turned up a watt since the similar faux-nude tableau in ''Hair'' 30 years ago. Let the sunshine in—please!

The shortfall between the show's lurid reputation and its PG-13 content—as well as that between its status as a highfalutin cultural event and its slim theatrical rewards—once more proves that our wan-

ing century's most powerful invention, publicity, can alter even empirical reality once harnessed to sex to sell a product. The notoriously rapacious promotional machine of Ms. Kidman and her husband, Tom Cruise, has pulled off the feat of making cynical, allegedly sophisticated New Yorkers look like rubes who shell out big bucks for a carny show that's all smoke and mirrors once they're inside the tent.

What brought the product, Ms. Kidman, to Broadway? She isn't a has been, like the usual TV refugees who turned up as novelty acts in ''Grease.'' Nor is she in the category of Christian Slater, currently doing penance in another play, ''Side Man,'' to re-establish his employability after a highly public detox. And she doesn't need her paltry Broadway paycheck. (The entire box-office gross for the 12-week run of ''*The Blue Room*'' equals roughly a fifth of what Mr. Cruise alone makes per picture.)

Officially, yes, Ms. Kidman simply yearned to return to her stage roots in a classic. (''*The Blue Room*'' is an updating of Arthur Schnitzler, albeit in Cliff Notes form.) The actual motive, though, is a stalled screen career. Ms. Kidman's recent movies (''The Peacemaker,'' ''Practical Magic'') didn't set the world on fire, so it's time to manufacture buzz—and where cheaper or easier to do it than on star-and-sex-deprived Broadway, where the biggest celebrities are ''Lion King'' puppets, vanity productions can be assembled for a fraction of Hollywood's cost, and only 1,000 seats a night need be sold to earn the accolade ''smash hit''?

The ''*Blue Room*'' agenda was dictated to a compliant *Newsweek,* which set the tone for the monkey-see media to follow. Ms. Kidman, we were told, is no longer ''Mrs. Tom Cruise, a nepotistic status assigned to her by a twitchy, bitchy Hollywood,'' but a budding superstar heading for ''what may be a career unlike any other.'' Eager to hop on the ''*Blue Room*'' gravy train for its own commercial purposes, Newsweek oversold the sexual come-on, taking a lead from the British critic, apparently on sabbatical from a monastery, who had fatuously labeled Ms. Kidman's performance ''pure theatrical Viagra'' at its debut in London. The magazine's cover announced that ''Nicole Kidman bares all,'' and its article led with the empty promise that the star would be seen on stage ''in various percentages of undress (including a climactic 100 percent).'' The play's artistic bona fides were similarly hyped, the director, Sam Mendes, and adaptor, David Hare, lent ''*The Blue Room*'' their cachet but not their best efforts.

Ms. Kidman is a good actress. If she had found a stage vehicle as challenging as her best movie, ''To Die For,'' she might have had an acting rather than a publicity triumph. Instead she became one of the few stars of recent seasons to be denied a unanimous standing ovation on her Broadway opening night.

The morning after, New York critics blew the whistle on the whole stunt, noting its acute shortfall as both sex show and cultural event. Too little, too late. Ticket buyers had already been suckered into spending some $4 million in advance to subsidize Ms. Kidman's image makeover, and what New Yorker wants to admit he's been had? A ticket to ''*The Blue Room*,'' the terminally tedious club no one can get into, still confirms status, even if anyone in search of pure theatrical Viagra might have had a better shot with the Rockettes.

Source: Frank Rich, ''Nicole Kidman's Behind'' in the *New York Times,* December 30, 1998, p. A17.

Jack Kroll

Kroll focuses on the performance of Nicole Kidman in his review of The Blue Room, *finding the actress to be the greatest attraction to seeing the play.*

The most passionately anticipated movie in years is Stanley Kubrick's ''Eyes Wide Shut,'' starring Tom Cruise and his wife, Nicole Kidman. Now that desire is being partially slaked by the appearance of Kidman onstage in London in David Hare's erotically charged new play *The Blue Room*. While Kubrick edits the closely guarded film in his London lair, Kidman is hitting the boards like a fireball, scorching the normally nonflammable critics. The *Daily Telegraph* swore that Kidman was ''pure sexual Viagra.'' The *Guardian* said, ''She is not just a star, she delivers the goods.'' As for Kidman, she's acting in the 250-seat Donmar Warehouse because ''you cannot look just to movies to be fulfilled.''

''*The Blue Room*'' is Hare's modernized version of Arthur Schnitzler's ''La Ronde,'' in which five men and five women form an inadvertent sexual daisy chain that crosses lines of social class and money. In Hare's version, two actors, Kidman and Iain Glen, play all 10 contemporary copulators. Both give virtuoso performances, switching identities, costumes, accents and positions with speed, elegance, pathos and hilarity. These attributes apply equally to Sam Mendes's staging and to Hare's play, which looks with cool empathy at the illusions and deceptions of the modern mating dance.

As a stage image, Kidman is the essence of escense: luminescent, opalescent, incandescent. As an actress, she evokes with wit and style a teenage hooker, a French au pair, an upscale wife, a coked-up model, an imperious stage diva. Matching her is Glen as a lecherous cabdriver, a callow student, a self-adoring playwright, a philandering politician, a jaded aristocrat. Flinging their clothes off and on with finger-straining abandon, they couple in stage blackouts, to the frazzling accompaniment of an electric buzzer, followed by a sign signaling the length of their liaisons. (Winner: the politician at 2 hours 28 minutes. Flunkout: the student at 0.)

It took guts for movie-star Kidman, 31, to step into the naked reality of the stage in such a risky project. Living in London with Cruise for 18 months while working on Kubrick's project, Kidman felt the call of the theater, where she hadn't worked since she was 19 in her native Australia. The skydiving, mountain-climbing Kidman was undaunted by the relentless sexuality of ''The Blue Room.'' The most erotic scene in the play is one in which the playwright tenderly dresses the model after they've made love. ''That was my idea,'' says Kidman. ''I thought it was sexier for him than ripping her clothes off.''

Kidman has a special insight into the character of the young model. She's frank about her own emotional history and her youthful dalliance with drugs. ''When I was 17, I had a relationship with a 37-year-old man,'' she says. ''Another man was 13 years older than me. He was lovely and kind. He gave me such a strong belief in men, which is a lovely thing to have.'' Kidman studied ballet as a youngster, and later joined a theater group in Sydney. Inevitably the movies grabbed the girl with the red-gold hair and moonglow skin. Her best American role so far was the murderously ambitious TV weather girl in 1995's ''To Die For.'' (Her next film, ''Practical Magic,'' opens mid-October.) Cruise and Kidman—whose previous films together, ''Days of Thunder'' and ''Far and Away,'' were not successful—are as anxious as anyone to see what Kubrick has wrought with them in ''Eyes Wide Shut.''

The director has buttoned the lips of everyone connected with the film (now set to open next summer). But Kidman's awed affection for Kubrick (''He's truly inspired'') threatens to pop one button.

The movie, a thriller about jealousy and sexual obsession, involves scenes of highly charged eroticism with Kidman and Cruise reportedly as husband-and-wife psychiatrists. ''Stanley was extremely respectful of us, of our marriage,'' says Kidman. ''He set those scenes up from the beginning so that he dealt with us separately. He told us, 'I don't want you to direct each other or give each other notes.' He thought that when a threesome works on such sensitive scenes, two can gang up on the third without meaning to.''

''*The Blue Room*'' will run through October, but Kidman won't escape from sex. Her next film is ''In the Cut,'' from novelist Susanna Moore's (what else?) erotic thriller, which Kidman bought for filmmaker Jane Campion, who directed her in ''Portrait of a Lady.'' ''Jane will push me to the limit, she'll ask me to do things I've never done before,'' says Kidman. She doesn't sound like someone who has threatened to give up acting. ''It's the awful scrutiny of your private life that gets you down.'' She and Cruise are currently suing an English magazine that wrote they were getting divorced. Their two children go to English schools, but Kidman says ideally she'd like to raise the kids in Australia. As for her husband, she calls him ''wonderfully American.'' It sounds as if no one country, no one medium, is going to contain her energy and daring.

Source: Jack Kroll, ''Scorched-Earth Strategy'' in *Newsweek,* Vol. 132, May 10, 1998, p. 89.

SOURCES

Anonymous, trans. *Hands Around: A Cycle of Ten Dialogues,* Privately printed for Members of the Schnitzler Society, 1929, pp. ix-xiii.

Brantley, Ben. Review of *The Blue Room,* in the *New York Times,* December 14, 1998.

Dreher, Rod. Review of *The Blue Room,* in the *National Review,* January 25, 1999.

Gussow, Mel. ''David Hare: Playwright as Provocateur,'' in *New York Times Magazine,* September 29, 1985, pp. 42-76.

Hare, David. *The Blue Room,* Grove Press, 1998.

Isherwood, Charles. Review of *The Blue Room,* in *Variety,* December 14, 1998, p. 141.

Osborne, Charles, trans. *The Round Dance and Other Plays,* Carcanet New Press, 1982, pp. vii-x.

Rich, Frank. Review of *The Blue Room,* in the *New York Times,* December 30, 1998.

Scholem, Richard. Review of *The Blue Room,* in *LI Business News,* January 15, 1999, p. 26A.

Skrine, Peter. *Hauptmann, Wedekind and Schnitzler,* St. Martin's Press, 1989, 129-133.

Viagas, Robert. Review of *The Blue Room,* in *Back Stage,* December 18, 1998, p. 3.

FURTHER READING

Liptzin, Solomon and Sol Liptzin. *Arthur Schnitzler (Studies in Austrian Literature, Culture, and Thought),* Ariadne Publishers, 1995.
    At once a history, biography, and literary critique, the Liptzins' study examines Schnitzler's place in Austrian and world literature and illuminates some of the most important themes in the author's work.

Page, Malcolm, compiler. *File on Hare,* Methuen, 1986.
    A collection of excerpted criticism of Hare's plays, taken largely from theatre reviews in London and New York newspapers and magazines. Also includes a chronology of Hare's work.

Schorske, Carl E. *Fin-De-Siecle Vienna: Politics and Culture,* Random House, 1981.
    In seven separate studies, Schorske provides a social and political history of turn-of-the-century Vienna that examines early modernism in art, music, and thought.

Zeifman, Hersh, editor. *David Hare: A Casebook,* Garland Publishing, 1994.
    A collection of essays about Hare's most important plays, accompanied by a chronology of his work and a bibliography of Hare interviews and criticism.

The Caretaker

HAROLD PINTER

1960

The Caretaker was the first of Pinter's plays to bring him artistic and commercial success as well as national recognition. Opening on April 27, 1960, at the Arts Theatre in London, *The Caretaker* was an immediate hit with audiences as well as critics, receiving mostly favorable reviews. In addition, *The Caretaker* received the *Evening Standard* Award for best play of 1960. In the many years since its first production, the play has continued to be the recipient of critical praise. It has been adapted for television as well as film and has seen numerous revivals all over the world, including at least one production with an all-female cast.

The real-world origins of the play lie in Pinter's acquaintance with two brothers who lived together, one of whom brought an old tramp to the house for a brief stay. At the time, Pinter himself had very little money and so identified somewhat with the tramp, with whom he occasionally spoke. Artistically, *The Caretaker* is clearly influenced in both style and subject matter by Samuel Beckett's 1955 classic *Waiting for Godot,* in which two tramps wait endlessly for someone they know only as Godot to come and give meaning and purpose to their lives.

Through the story of the two brothers and the tramp, *The Caretaker* deals with the distance between reality and fantasy, family relationships, and the struggle for power. It also touches on the subjects of mental illness and the plight of the indigent. Pinter uses elements of both comedy and tragedy to

create a play that elicits complex reactions in the audience. The complexity of the play, Pinter's masterful use of dialogue, and the depth and perception shown in Pinter's themes all contribute to *The Caretaker*'s consideration as a modern masterpiece.

AUTHOR BIOGRAPHY

On October 30, 1930, Harold Pinter was born to Jewish parents in Hackney, a working-class neighborhood in London. It was a difficult time for Jews in England. Hitler's rise to power had begun, and the fascism he championed had its British sympathizers. In 1939, Britain entered World War II; during the Blitz, Hitler's intense bombing of London, Pinter, like many young people, was evacuated to the countryside, which was considered safer. Later, Pinter returned to London and experienced the terror of the Blitz firsthand. After the war, difficulties for British Jews continued. Jews were attacked in the streets, and Pinter later recalled his own involvement in a number of altercations.

Pinter attended the Hackney Down Grammar School and, in 1948, received a grant to study at the Royal Academy of the Dramatic Arts but soon dropped out. Shortly afterwards, he started reading the works of Samuel Beckett (*Waiting for Godot*), who became a great influence on Pinter's work. In 1950, two of Pinter's own plays were published. That same year, he began working professionally as an actor, both in London and on tour. During this time he met the actress Vivien Merchant. The two were married in 1956, and their son Daniel was born in 1958. Pinter and Merchant were divorced in 1980, at which time Pinter married Lady Antonia Fraser.

In 1956, John Osborne's play *Look Back in Anger* ushered in a new period of British drama; the period was characterized by playwrights who came to be known as the ''angry young men.'' Pinter's writing came to be identified with this group. In 1957, *The Room* became the first of Pinter's plays to be produced. That year he also wrote *The Dumb Waiter* and *The Birthday Party,* which was initially condemned by critics but has since come to be considered one of the most important plays of the twentieth century. In spite of the earlier critical failure of *The Birthday Party,* Pinter began to achieve a modest success, writing radio and television plays. In 1959, he wrote *The Caretaker,* which was produced in 1960; the play became Pinter's first criti-

Harold Pinter

cally successful play. It was also the first of Pinter's plays to be filmed. The playwright soon began adapting the work of other dramatists for film while continuing to write his own plays. His major works include *The Homecoming* (1965), *Old Times* (1971), and the screenplay for *The French Lieutenant's Woman.* Later plays, such as *One for the Road* (1984) and *Mountain Language* (1988), reflect Pinter's growing interest in leftist politics. Many critics consider the newer more critical plays inferior to Pinter's earlier work, but even if such criticism has merit, his earlier work alone has been enough to establish Pinter as one of the great playwrights of the twentieth century.

PLOT SUMMARY

Act I

Act I opens in a room full of assorted objects, clearly best described as junk. These include an iron bed, paint buckets, numerous boxes, a toaster, a statue of Buddha, a kitchen sink, and a gas stove. A bucket for catching drips hangs from the ceiling. Mick, a man in his twenties, sits alone on the bed, slowly looking around the room, focusing on each object in turn. When the bang of a door is heard, followed by the sound of muffled voices, Mick leaves the room.

Aston, in his thirties, and Davies, an old tramp, enter the room. Aston tells Davies to sit and offers him a cigarette. Davies reveals that he has just been fired from his restaurant job for refusing to do work he considers beneath him. Aston begins working on fixing the toaster while Davies complains about ''Poles, Greeks, Blacks, the lot of them,'' then mentions that he left the bag with his possessions in the restaurant. Davies questions Aston about the house, about how many rooms there are, about Aston's position. Aston replies that he is ''in charge'' of the house and that he is working on building a shed. Davies asks Aston about spare shoes, but when Aston finds some for him, Davies complains that they don't fit.

Aston gives Davies money and offers to let him stay in the room until he gets ''sorted out.'' Davies says that he plans to go to Sidcup, ''if only the weather would break,'' to get his papers, which he says ''prove who I am.'' Davies finally goes to bed while Aston continues to work on the toaster. The lights fade out, indicating night, then come up again, showing that morning has arrived. Aston tells Davies he was making noises in his sleep, and Davies insists that it could not have been him, that it was probably ''them Blacks.'' Aston says he is going to leave for a while, then surprises Davies by saying that he can stay alone in the room.

When Aston leaves, Davies immediately begins looking through the objects in the room. Mick comes in and is unnoticed by Davies until Mick seizes Davies's arm, forcing him down on the floor. Mick then lets go of Davies, sits down, and asks the old man, ''What's the game?''

Act II

Act II opens a few seconds later. Mick starts questioning Davies in a hostile fashion, repeating many of the same questions over and over again. This confuses and frightens the tramp. Davies tells Mick that he was brought to the room by ''the man who lives here,'' but Mick informs Davies that he is in fact the owner of the house and that unless Davies wants to rent the room, Mick can take him to the police. Aston then enters with a bag, which he says belongs to Davies, but Mick grabs the bag and keeps it from the tramp. Mick finally lets Davies have the

bag, then leaves the room. Aston tells Davies that Mick is his brother and that he himself is supposed to be decorating the house and plans to build a shed where he can do woodworking.

Aston asks Davies if he would like to stay on as caretaker, but Davies seems reluctant. The lights fade to blackout, then come up again dimly. Davies enters the room, but is unable to get the light on and stumbles about in the darkness. Suddenly Mick, already in the room, begins vacuuming, frightening Davies with the noise. Mick then takes the vacuum plug out of the socket and replaces the light bulb. Davies and Mick talk, and Mick tells Davies that he is impressed by him and that the two just ''got off on the wrong foot.''

Mick offers Davies a sandwich and, as the two eat together, Mick tells Davies that Aston's trouble is that he doesn't like work. Mick then offers Davies a job as caretaker, and Davies again seems reluctant to accept the position. Finally, however, he agrees. When Mick asks for references, however, Davies claims that his papers are all in Sidcup but that he will go there soon. The lights fade, then come back up, indicating another morning. Aston wakes Davies up, reminding Davies that he had planned to go to Sidcup that day. Davies says he wants to go out for tea. Aston tells him of a cafe nearby, then begins a long monologue, as the lights in the room fade so that only Aston can be seen clearly. Aston tells of how he used to talk to people in that cafe but that he talked too much. He began having hallucinations and was taken to a hospital, where a doctor proposed electroshock therapy.

Aston says that he was a minor at the time, so he knew the doctors could not perform electroshock without his mother's permission. Aston wrote his mother, asking her not to agree to the treatment, but she gave the doctors permission anyway. Aston tried to escape but was caught, and though he physically fought the doctors, he was forced to receive treatment. Ever since, his thoughts have been slow, and he tries to avoid talking to people. He speaks of wanting to find the man who ''did that to me,'' but first, he tells Davies, he wants to build the shed in the garden.

Act III

Act III begins two weeks later. Mick and Davies are together in the room, and Davies is complaining about Aston, who, he says, will not give him a knife for his bread and refuses to keep the Blacks next door from coming into the house and using the lavatory. Davies says that he and Mick could "get this place going," and Mick offers a series of decorating ideas, using the words and images common in house and garden magazines—which seem like ludicrous fantasies for the house he owns.

Mick says that the house would be a palace, and that he and his brother would live in it. Davies asks what would happen to him. Mick ignores his question, and Davies continues to complain about Aston—he will not give Davies a clock, and he wakes Davies up in the night. Mick then leaves, and Aston enters. He has another pair of shoes for Davies, but Davies complains that these shoes also don't fit. Davies then tells Aston that a man has offered him a job. He needs to go to Sidcup but the weather is bad. The lights go out, and a dim light through the window reveals that Davies and Aston are both in bed. Aston switches on the light and wakes Davies, complaining that the tramp is making noises in his sleep. Davies begins insulting Aston, saying that he is not surprised that Aston was put in a mental institution. Davies complains about Aston's treatment of him, and tells Aston that he could be taken back to the hospital and given electroshock treatments again. Aston tells Davies that he needs to find another place to live. Davies tells Aston that Mick will "sort you out," that Davies has been offered a job. Davies then leaves.

The lights go out, then back up. It is early evening. Mick and Davies enter the room, Davies complaining about Aston to Mick, who first listens somewhat sympathetically, then tells Davies he can stay if he is as good an interior decorator as he says he is. When Davies denies being a professional decorator, Mick accuses him of falsely presenting himself. Davies says that Aston must have told Mick that Davies is a decoration. When Davies tells Mick that Aston is "nutty," he goes too far, and Mick begins insulting Davies, calling him a barbarian. Mick then picks up the Buddha and hurls it against the stove, breaking it. Aston comes in. Mick leaves, and Davies begins desperately pleading with Aston, attempting to work out a compromise so that he can stay in the room. Aston says that Davies must leave. Davies continues to beg Aston to let him stay, but Aston turns to the window, ignoring Davies. Finally, the two stand, silent for a moment, Aston still facing the window. The curtain falls.

CHARACTERS

Aston

Aston, in his early thirties, is Mick's brother. He seems quite generous, as is indicated by his rescuing Davies from a potential brawl and later bringing the tramp into his own house. Once he brings Davies home, Aston continues to try to care for him, giving him tobacco, attempting to find shoes for him, and even replacing Davies's bag when it is stolen. Unlike Mick, Aston is gentle and calm, enduring Davies's continual complaints about all that he is offered.

At the end of the second act, Aston reveals what may be at the root of his exceedingly calm nature; sometime before he reached adulthood, he was committed for a time to a mental institution, where he received involuntary electroshock therapy. When in the hospital, Aston says, he counted on his mother to deny permission for the treatments. When she did not, he attempted to escape and, when that failed, physically fought those who attempted to treat him, although his efforts were ultimately futile.

At the time of the play, Aston lives in his brother's house, planning to build a shed that the audience realizes will never materialize. Aston initially accepts a great deal of abuse from Davies, who uses his confession of psychiatric treatment against him. Aston is finally pushed to his limit, however, and tells the old man he must leave. As the play ends, Aston literally turns his back to Davies, as the tramp begs to be allowed to stay.

Mac Davies

Davies is an old man who temporarily moves into the room when Aston rescues him from a brawl. Although Davies was just fired from his menial job, wears old clothes, has no money, and is obviously a tramp, he insists on maintaining what he considers his proper station and refuses to do work he considers beneath him. He also considers himself, as a white Englishman, superior to the Blacks, Greeks, and Poles he rails against. Although Davies does thank Aston for his kindnesses, he complains constantly. Nothing Aston does is good enough for him—the shoes don't fit, the clothes aren't warm enough, and the room itself is too drafty. Davies is also deceitful, even lying about his own name when it suits him. He speaks often of going to Sidcup for the papers he needs in order to find work, but the weather is never good enough. The audience realiz-

MEDIA ADAPTATIONS

- *The Caretaker* was adapted as a film in 1964. This British production stars Alan Bates as Mick, Donald Pleasance as Davies, and Robert Shaw as Aston. The producer was Michael Birkett. The film also appeared under the title *The Guest*.

- A made-for-television version was filmed and shown on the BBC in 1966. This version was directed by Clive Donner and starred Ian MacShane as Mick, John Rees as Aston, and Roy Dotrice as Davies.

es that Davies has no intention of taking the trip, of taking care of himself instead of taking advantage of others.

Davies only thinks of himself. When Aston reveals his history of mental illness, Davies is incapable of any sort of sympathy and taunts Aston with his past. He tries to play the brothers against one another, attempting to ingratiate himself with Mick by criticizing Aston. Finally, Aston tires of Davies's criticism, complaints, and personal attacks, and tells the tramp to leave. Davies desperately begs Aston to reconsider, and the old man finally becomes a pitiable figure, having nowhere to go and no one to whom he can turn. This complicates audience reaction to Davies. He has been depicted as a cunning, deceitful, and ungrateful tramp, but finally becomes also a pathetic and poverty-stricken old man.

Mick

Mick, Aston's brother, is in his late twenties. He is the owner of the building that contains the room in which the play's action occurs. Mick identifies himself as a successful businessman, although whether he is truly successful and what he actually does for a living are not clear. Since Mick allows Aston to live in his house, it seems that in the wake of Aston's electroshock treatments, Mick has become a sort of caretaker for his brother.

Mick is a much more suspicious person than Aston, who is quick to take Davies into the house. Although Mick has to have heard the voices of Aston and Davies together as they came toward the room at the play's beginning, when he finds Davies alone after Aston leaves, Mick physically attacks the old man. Mick follows the physical attack with a verbal attack as he fires quick questions, the same questions over and over, at the frightened tramp. Later, when talking with Davies, Mick alternates between politeness and brutality. Knowing that Davies has no pertinent experience, Mick offers the old man a job as a caretaker, but he later grows angry and accuses Davies of trying to pass himself off as a skilled interior decorator.

Mick also alternates between criticizing and defending his brother. Mick's frequent changes in attitude make it difficult to ascertain his motivations, and his inconsistency seems to indicate that, at least part of the time, he is lying. His one moment of emotional truth comes when he smashes Aston's statue of Buddha against the gas stove.

THEMES

Truth, Lies, and Fantasy

In *The Caretaker* none of the characters can be trusted to speak the truth. All are, to some extent, deceptive, twisting reality in order to manipulate one another and to delude themselves. The character who is the most deceptive is probably Davies. From the beginning, it is clear that he is a liar, first attempting to win Aston's respect by pretending to a past that rings false. ''I've had dinner with the best,'' he says. He also calls everything he says into question when he admits to having used a false name; the audience cannot even be sure that his true name is Davies. Davies's talk of the future is also filled with lies and fantasy and serves two purposes—to manipulate Aston and Mick and to bolster his own self esteem. He speaks of getting even with the man whom he says attacked him: ''One night I'll get him. When I find myself in that direction.''

Davies also tells Aston and Mick that he will go to Sidcup to get his papers. He talks throughout the play of his supposed plans to go to Sidcup, plans he will act on if he acquires shoes, if the weather gets better, plans that the audience soon realizes will never materialize. By his insistence that he is not merely a tramp, that he has a grand past and will support himself in the future, Davies manipulates Aston into continuing to let him stay in the room.

Mick and Aston are not obvious liars like Davies, but the truth of what they say is also questionable. When Mick, after hurling the Buddha against the stove, says, "I got plenty of other things I can worry about . . . I've got my own business to build up," it is unclear whether he is speaking the truth or trying to persuade himself and Davies of his own importance. When he discusses his grandiose plans for turning the house into a vision from a home and garden magazine, he is either playing with Davies or deluding himself with plans for a future that will never arrive.

Aston's honesty is also questionable. Pinter himself has said that a common mistake among audiences watching *The Caretaker* is to assume that Aston is telling the truth about his experiences in the mental hospital. But even if Aston is truthful about that experience, he deludes himself with his talk of building a shed. Like Davies's trip to Sidcup and Mick's decorating plans, Aston's shed is a fantasy that will never materialize.

All of the characters in the play not only deceive one another but also delude themselves. Instead of revealing the truth, communication in the play obscures reality. In the world of *The Caretaker* truth itself becomes an illusion.

Family

Ideally, the family is a source of strength and support for its members, but in *The Caretaker,* family members are disconnected and even hostile. The brothers Mick and Aston say little of their parents; in fact, the audience does not even know if their mother and father are alive. The little they do say, however, reveals relationships that are strained at best. At one point, Mick speaks to Davies of his "uncle's brother," who may simply be another uncle, but who is more likely Mick and Aston's father.

If this is, in fact, the case, Mick is so disconnected from his father that he cannot use the familial term "father" to identify him. "I called him Sid," he tells Davies, and in fact, Mick himself seems unsure of what his relationship with this man is: "I've often thought that maybe . . . my uncle was his brother and he was my uncle." Although Mick's speech is obviously intended to have a comic effect, it does indicate that there is no real relationship between Mick and the man who may be his father.

TOPICS FOR FURTHER STUDY

- *The Caretaker* has often been compared to Samuel Beckett's play *Waiting for Godot.* Compare Beckett's play to Pinter's. How do the tramps Vladimir and Estragon compare to Davies? What are the thematic similarities and differences between the two plays?

- Research the historical treatment of the mentally ill, considering especially societal attitudes, and compare past times with the present. Discuss Aston's treatment and Davies's reaction in terms of the history of the treatment of mental illness.

- None of the women mentioned in *The Caretaker* appear onstage, and the audience only knows of them through what other characters say. What attitudes toward women are reflected in the characters' dialogue? What is the effect of having none of the women onstage?

- Compare the characters and situations of Pinter's *The Birthday Party* to those in *The Caretaker.* How are the two plays alike? How are they different?

- Discuss *The Caretaker* as a comedy. What are the comic elements of the play? What is the effect of Pinter's use of comedy on the plays' ending?

Aston's mention of his mother is brief but revealing. While in the mental hospital, he says, he believed he was safe from electroshock therapy because he was a minor and his mother would have to give permission for such treatment. Although he wrote and asked her not to give permission, she signed the papers anyway, allowing the doctors to give Aston electroshock treatment. Aston's one memory of his mother is of his trust and her betrayal of that trust.

Aston and Mick's relationship is also one of distance, but that distance is relieved with some evidence of familial feelings. Mick has taken some responsibility for Aston—he allows Aston to live in his house, and Mick tells Davies that he and his brother take turns cleaning. And when Davies describes Aston as nutty, Mick takes offense, or pretends to take offense. But the brothers are also disconnected. They rarely speak to one another, rarely, in fact, stay in the same room together. In addition, just after Mick expresses anger at Davies's comment about Aston, he himself picks up Aston's Buddha and destroys it. This action reveals some hostility toward his brother.

The meaning of Mick's action is complicated, however, when Aston enters immediately afterwards, and, for the first time, the two brothers face one another, ''smiling faintly.'' The meaning of the smile, however, is ultimately ambiguous. It may indicate a sort of reconciliation or connection, possibly a united front against Davies. Yet it could also indicate that a surface kindness, an appearance of connection, masks the hostility and estrangement of the brothers. It could even be intended to highlight the ambiguous nature of the brothers' relationship. However, even if the relationship is somewhat ambiguous, what does seem clear is that in *The Caretaker* the family is not an idealized haven from the world but a collection of various relationships, sometimes distant, sometimes hostile, always complicated.

Power

Much of the action in *The Caretaker* follows from the characters' pursuit of power over one another. This is evident from the beginning, when Davies, rescued by Aston from a possible brawl, first attempts to raise Aston's estimation of him by suggesting a past grander than his present, claiming social superiority over those with whom he has been working, and finding fault with virtually everything that anyone does for him. Davies presents himself as one who deserves much more than life has given him and so suggests that he has no reason to feel himself inferior to Aston.

Aston acts kindly toward Davies, but his motives are not entirely clear. For instance, by leaving the tramp in the room alone at the end of the first act, knowing that Mick could come in at any time, Aston leaves the old man vulnerable to Mick's anger—and thus may be asserting a sort of familial power. When Mick does find Davies alone, he first attacks Davies, establishing physical power over him, then threatens to take Davies to the police, reminding the tramp that he has little control over his future. Mick further establishes his power over Davies by his

relentless questioning of the tramp, which leaves Davies confused and frightened.

The remainder of the play sees continual struggles for power. Mick keeps Davies's bag from him, frightens him with the vacuum cleaner, and angrily accuses Davies of falsely presenting himself as an interior decorator. Davies attempts to gain power by trying to get Mick to side with him against Aston. Davies also attempts to assert his own power over Aston by continually reminding Aston that he has been in a mental hospital and telling Aston that he could easily have to back there. Davies's attempts to gain power, however, finally backfire. Mick defends his brother, again establishing a sort of conjoined familial power, and Aston tells the tramp he must leave. In the final scene, it is Davies who is powerless in spite of his efforts. It is he who is alone and has no place to go.

STYLE

Setting

The Caretaker is set in a single room, a dismal space full of assorted junk and with one window half covered by a sack. Among the objects in the room are paint buckets, a lawn-mower, suitcases, a rolled-up carpet, a pile of old newspapers, and a statue of the Buddha atop a gas stove that does not work. A bucket, used to catch water from the leaking roof, hangs from the ceiling. The room has so much junk in it that it seems more a storage area than a place to live. The room stores not only useless junk but, metaphorically, useless people such as Aston, who can no longer have a real life in the outside world, and briefly Davies, who, in a sense, is just another useless thing that Aston has picked up and brought back to the room.

With its collection of junk, its leaky ceiling, and its window with a sack instead of curtains, the room is the antithesis of the kind pictured in home and garden magazines, which are parodied in a speech by Mick in Act III. In that speech, Mick describes for Davies his supposed plans for the room: ''This room you could have as the kitchen . . . I'd have teal-blue, copper and parchment linoleum squares . . . venetian blinds on the window, cork floor, cork tiles.'' This exaggerated description has a comic effect but also serves to highlight the distance between the reality of the room and the assorted fantasies of Mick, Aston, and Davies. And no matter what dreams are spoken of in the play, the room is a constant reminder of harsh reality.

Comedy

In past centuries, a comedy has been a play with a so-called ''happy ending,'' in which the main character's problems are resolved, the ''good'' are rewarded, and the ''bad'' are punished. Modern drama, however, has seen the development of a hybrid of tragedy and comedy, sometimes called tragicomedy, in which there are comic elements with dark undercurrents. *The Caretaker* is such a play.

In *The Caretaker,* Pinter uses numerous comic devices. The character Davies himself is a sort of stock figure from vaudeville, the tramp/clown, which was also used as a persona by actor Charley Chaplin. Similar to the tramp/clown in a vaudeville sketch, Davies provides a great deal of physical, slapstick humor. For instance, Davies removes his trousers to go to bed, and when Mick arrives he takes them, teasing the old man by flicking the trousers in his face, further emphasizing the connection to Vaudeville, in which a man is often stripped of his dignity when his pants fall down. Mick also takes Davies's backpack, which gets tossed around the room as Davies tries to retrieve it. And later, when Davies flees Mick's electrolux (vacuum), this scene of panic also connects him to the classic tramp/clown.

In addition to the physical comedy in the play, there is also a great deal of verbal comedy. In Davies's dialogue, the difference between reality and Davies's words often has a comic effect. ''I've had dinner with the best,'' he tells Aston. ''I've eaten my dinner off the best of plates.'' This highly doubtful statement from the tramp has a humorous effect, as does Davies's story of his experience at the monastery near Luton. In this story, Davies tells a monk, ''I heard you got a stock of shoes here,'' but the monk replies, ''Piss off. . . . If you don't piss off . . . I'll kick you all the way to the gate.'' This story has a comic effect because the monk's supposed response to Davies is so unexpected and because of the contrast between the monk's words, ''Piss off,'' and his traditionally reserved and pious position.

Mick's interrogation of Davies, his quick questions and his claim that Davies represented himself as a professional interior decorator, are also humorous, again because of contrast—this time between the tramp Davies and the professional qualifications Mick describes.

Although there are many comic elements in *The Caretaker,* there is also a dark side to Pinter's play. The ending, in which Davies becomes a frightened old man with no place to go, creates a sense of pity for the tramp's condition. In the final scene, Davies is too pathetic to be funny; in fact, he almost becomes a tragic figure, and the tragedy of his situation is made more profound by the comedy that preceded it.

Symbolism

In literature, a symbol stands for something other than itself. Probably the most important symbol in *The Caretaker* is the Buddha that sits atop the gas stove. This Buddha is an object that Aston has picked up and brought back to the already cluttered room. In this sense, the Buddha resembles Davies, who can also be seen as something useless that Aston has picked up. The Buddha, therefore, could be a symbol of Davies.

It should be noted here, however, that there is not always a clear one-to-one correlation between a symbol and what it represents. A complex symbol can have a number of possible meanings, all of which can be joined together to create a greater whole. Mick's smashing of the Buddha in the third act, therefore, could have several interpretations. Whether the Buddha symbolizes Davies, is a representation of Aston's inner peace, or is just another item that Aston has brought back, Mick may destroy it because it represents his brother, whom he may even hate. The Buddha, however, as another piece of junk in a house that belongs to Mick, could also symbolize the life he leads. In that case, Mick may destroy the Buddha because of his frustration with his life as a whole. The Buddha could represent all of these things, or it could represent something else. Sometimes the success of a symbol lies in its ambiguity.

HISTORICAL CONTEXT

The years following victory in World War II were a time of hardship in Britain. A 1947 fuel crisis left many without heat, and food shortages resulted in the continuation of wartime rationing well into the late-1940s. These years also saw a serious housing shortage. During the war, when construction of housing had ceased, two hundred thousand houses were completely destroyed and half a million more required extensive repair. Some Britons saw hope

COMPARE
&
CONTRAST

- **1960:** Many government programs for the assistance of the poor have been developed, but the efficacy of such programs begins to be called into question.

  Today: Although government programs continue to help millions, many begin to doubt that the government is truly capable of offering real solutions to the problem of poverty. Focus on the assistance of the private sector grows, and there is a new emphasis on volunteerism.

- **1960:** The domestic economy is recovering from its Postwar malaise, and the so-called "consumer culture" grows. Television becomes popular, and people are exposed to more advertising than ever before.

  Today: Emphasis on consumer acquisition continues as corporate power grows and advertising becomes even more pervasive (and persuasive).

- **1960:** New medications begin to revolutionize treatment of the mentally ill, but psychologists and psychiatrists often blame severe illnesses such as schizophrenia and manic-depression on psychological factors.

  Today: Scientific study has revealed a biological basis for major psychiatric illness, but the mentally ill and their families still face discrimination, as the social stigma of mental illness continues.

- **1960:** Immigrants and members of minority groups face difficult times, much prejudicial treatment, and little legal protection.

  Today: Members of minority groups are protected by law, and racism is generally socially unacceptable. The rise of the militant right and hate groups, however, present new threats to immigrants and people of color.

---

for the future in socialism, and the late-1940s saw the development of the Welfare State, which placed responsibility for the relief of the poor on the government. In 1946, the National Insurance Act and the National Health Service Act were passed, providing insurance and medical care to the poor. The National Assistance Act was developed to provide a safety net for the poor. Many believed that new government policies would end poverty altogether.

Such optimistic assessments, however, were soon proven false. In addition, those who saw socialism as a solution to Britain's problems were disillusioned by the Soviet Union's 1956 invasion of Hungary, which showed that a socialist system could be as violent and corrupt as any other political system.

These years also saw a decline in Britain's status among nations. Previous generations had said that the sun would never set on the British empire,

but now that empire was crumbling, with former colonies such as India gaining freedom from British rule. In 1956, the Suez crisis, in which Britain was condemned by the United Nations for its attempt to gain control of the Suez Canal in Egypt, resulted in international humiliation for the former empire. British troops were forced to withdraw, and the Prime Minister resigned over the incident.

In spite of political difficulties, however, the late-1950s saw some domestic economic recovery, and Britain saw the rise of a consumer culture focusing on the acquisition of material goods. Ownership of what were formerly luxury items, such as refrigerators, washing machines, and automobiles, rose significantly between 1953 and 1960. In addition, the development of television led to a new perceived need. Magazines enticed consumers to buy with photographs and descriptions of beautifully decorated homes. Not surprisingly, British citizens were exposed to more advertising than ever before. It is, in fact, the language of house and garden magazines and of advertisements that Mick uses when he describes for Davies his vision for the future of *The Caretaker*'s squalid setting.

In the 1950s, treatment of the mentally ill was undergoing change, as the introduction of new psychiatric medications made it possible for patients to leave institutions and live in their communities. Nonetheless, many patients remained institutionalized and, although more humane than those of past eras, mental hospitals of the time were sometimes little better than warehouses for those whose illnesses had no real cure. In addition, in spite of advances in medications, little was known about the biological causes of severe mental illness, and such illnesses were still generally believed to have psychological bases. Psychiatrists often blamed the family unit for illnesses such as schizophrenia and manic-depressive disorder, and particular blame was laid at the feet of the mother and the ways in which she brought up her children.

As early as the sixteenth century, physicians had attempted to cure schizophrenia by inducing convulsions with camphor. In the 1930s, modern electroconvulsive therapy (ECT) was developed in Rome. In the 1950s, ECT was commonly used to treat depression and schizophrenia. At that time, however, treatments were often given without muscle relaxants, which prevent broken bones during seizures, or general anesthesia. In addition, the mentally ill had not yet benefited from the patients' rights movement of the 1960s, and so the involuntary ECT that Aston was subjected to was much more common than it is today.

CRITICAL OVERVIEW

The first production of *The Caretaker* at the Arts Theatre in London on April 27, 1960, met with an enthusiastic audience response. In his book *The Life and Work of Harold Pinter,* biographer Michael Billington quoted the *Daily Herald*'s description of the play's reception: "Tumultuous chaos. Twelve curtain calls. And then, when the lights went up, the whole audience rose to applaud the author who sat beaming in the circle." Early reactions from the critics were positive as well. Billington noted that the *News Chronicle*'s critic wrote, "This is the best play in London." Michael Scott, in his book *Harold Pinter: The Birthday Party, The Caretaker, The*

Homecoming, quoted critic Charles Marowitz: "*The Caretaker,* Pinter's latest play, is a national masterpiece." Indeed the play was recognized as such by others; it received the *Evening Standard* Award for best play of 1960.

Many critics compared *The Caretaker* to Samuel Beckett's 1955 play *Waiting for Godot,* in which two tramps wait for a man they know only as Godot to arrive and give meaning and purpose to their lives. T. C. Worsley, in a 1960 review quoted by Scott, remarked, "Certainly we seem to be in Godot country," then noted that Pinter's play seems more accessible: "We are in the Beckett climate, but not the Beckett fog where everything means something else." Marowitz, who also pointed out the resemblance to Beckett's work, remarked that such a resemblance takes nothing away from Pinter: "The mark of Beckett on Pinter is dominantly stylistic; as for the subject matter, it may have a Beckettian tang to it, but the recipe is original."

Pinter's use of language in the play has also been the subject of much discussion. Playwright John Arden, also quoted by Scott, discussed language in terms of the play's "realism." According to Arden, previous realist playwrights wrote plays in which "a series of events were developed, connected by a strictly logical progression of fact, and we could be sure that anything done or said on the stage had its place in the *concrete* structure of the plot." The dialogue in Pinter's work, however, reflects a new type of realism, meandering speech that shows "not merely what [the characters] would have said if the author thought it up for them, but what they actually *did* say."

An important aspect of Pinter's dialogue for Arden was "his expert use of 'casual' language and broken trains of thought," which presents a more natural use of speech. For Marowitz, however, Pinter does not simply reflect real speech, but enhances it: "If Pinter uses tape-recorders to achieve such verisimilitude, he also edits his tapes poetically to avoid stale reproductions of life."

Other critics, however, who agreed that the dialogue is realistic, found fault elsewhere. Kenneth Tynan, writing in 1960, and quoted in *File on Pinter,* commented on Pinter's realism. "Time and again," Tynan wrote, "without the least departure from authenticity, Mr. Pinter exposes the vague, repetitive silliness of lower-class conversation." Yet Tynan suggested a certain cruelty in the quali-

Davies (Donald Pleasance) and Mick (playwright Pinter) in a scene from The Caretaker

ty of Pinter's dialogue. "One laughs in recognition," he wrote, "but one's laughter is tinged with snobbism."

Alan Brien, writing for the *Spectator* in 1960 (also quoted in *File on Pinter*) disagreed, arguing that Pinter's characters are like the members of the audience. The critic emphasized that this aspect is an improvement over Pinter's earlier plays: "His characters are now people rooted in a world of insurance stamps, and contemporary wallpaper, and mental asylums. They are still lost in mazes of self-deception, isolated behind barricades of private

language, hungry at the smell of the next man's weakness—in other words, just like us."

The Caretaker continues to be considered a classic of modern drama by most critics, but in recent years, some complaints about the play have been voiced. Kitty Mrosovsky, writing of a 1981 production and quoted in *File on Pinter,* once again compared the play to *Waiting for Godot,* but not favorably: "It has dated in a way that the earlier *Waiting for Godot* (1955) has not. . . . Not that the tramps nowadays are any fewer, nor the derelict attics with their buckets to catch the drips. But the patina of social comment can almost be peeled off the play's core, leaving at most a wry proposition about the purgatory of sharing a bedroom with your neighbor.''

Critic Elizabeth Sakellaridou, in her book *Pinter's Female Portraits,* faulted the play on feminist grounds. Sakellaridou noted that the women mentioned in the play never appear onstage, and so ''they reflect the idiosyncrasies and moods of the three male characters, and therefore, they are highly subjective creations which can hardly be identified as real people.'' Sakellaridou went on to suggest that the characterization of women in the play reflects a negative attitude in general on the part of Pinter. The text of the play, she noted, ''reveals mistrust and fear, abuse and contempt for women.''

It is not only feminists who see global problems with Pinter's play. Bernard Levin, writing of a 1977 production (quoted in *File on Pinter*), found little redeeming value in the play at all and spoke of the ''emptiness, weightlessness, and triviality'' of *The Caretaker.* ''We come out exactly the same people as we were when we entered,'' he continued. ''We have been entertained . . . we have not been bored. But we have advanced our understanding and our humanity not a whit.'' Levin further suggested that the great praise the play has received has been undeserved: ''The needle is sharp, the thread fine, the material sumptuous, the seamstress the best. But the Emperor's clothes do not exist.''

By his reference to the traditional tale of the emperor's new clothes, Levin acknowledged the high esteem in which the play is held. In spite of such criticism as his, *The Caretaker* continues to inspire numerous revivals as well as much critical attention. Although the play is not without its detractors, most critics of modern drama consider *The Caretaker* a contemporary classic.

CRITICISM

Clare Cross

Cross is a Ph.D. candidate specializing in modern drama. In this essay, she discusses Aston's motivations in his relationship with Davies.

Numerous critics have said that much of the action of *The Caretaker* is dominated by the characters' struggle for power over one another. As Mi-chael Billington remarked in his book *The Life and Work of Harold Pinter,* ''Power is the theme: dominate or be dominated.'' Pinter shows, Billington continued, ''that life is a series of negotiations for advantage in which everything comes into play.'' Indeed, in *The Caretaker,* this often seems to be the case. Davies tries to play Aston and Mick against each other as he struggles to establish a foothold in the room. Mick maintains power over Davies by physical as well as verbal assaults. And at the end of the play, Aston exerts his power by forcing Davies to leave; the struggle for power is a dominant theme in the play.

To suggest, however, as Billington and others have, that all of the characters are primarily motivated by power is an oversimplification of Pinter's play. It is true that such an assessment seems to apply to Davies. If he is to stay in the room and have Aston or Mick see to his needs and desires, he needs to gain control over them, even if he has to do so by making himself sometimes appear, not powerful, but needy. In essence, Davies cares for no one but himself and will do whatever he thinks will allow him to stay in the room. Mick, defending his territory against an intruder, attempts to control Davies primarily by physical and verbal violence. He has no real regard for the tramp. On the other hand, Mick does have at least some feeling, even if only a sense of obligation, for his brother and is, in fact, taking care of at least some of Aston's needs by allowing him to stay in the room. Although he expresses anger at his brother when he breaks the Buddha against the stove, although he tells Davies that Aston's trouble is that he does not want to work, Mick does defend Aston against Davies's cruel remarks—and he allows Aston to stay in the room. The desire for power motivates him but it is not his only motivation. Nonetheless, it does seem fair to consider the desire for power as a primary motivation for both Davies and Mick.

While Davies and Mick are dominated by their own drives for power, to suggest quite the same of Aston is to simplify his character as well as the play as a whole. Aston's attempts to care for Davies and to talk to him seem motivated, at least in part, by kindness and concern for the tramp. On the other hand, it is hard to see Aston as motivated entirely by altruism. Indeed, one could argue that Aston is kind to Davies because he wants to control him, because he wants to meet his own needs and thus is as motivated by power as are Davies and Mick. In truth, neither interpretation of Aston's character

WHAT DO I READ NEXT?

- *Waiting for Godot,* a 1955 play by Samuel Beckett, is often compared to *The Caretaker* and generally recognized—as many of Beckett's plays are—as a major influence on Pinter's style.

- *Look Back in Anger,* a 1956 play by John Osborne, is often cited as a turning point in modern British drama, the first play of the so-called ''Angry Young Men'' theatre movement. The play focuses on the struggle of a young couple, the unemployed Jimmy Porter and the wife he abuses.

- *The Birthday Party,* a 1958 play by Pinter, concerns Stanley, the only lodger in a dilapidated boarding house, who is terrorized by two mysterious men who arrive looking for him. Although this play originally received negative reviews, it is now regarded as one of Pinter's most important works.

- *Old Times,* a 1971 play by Pinter, focuses on a married couple, Deeley and Kate, who are visited by Kate's old friend Anna. The play centers on a power struggle between Deeley and Anna, each of whom wants to prove his or her possession of Kate.

- *The Bell Jar* (1963), an autobiographical novel by American poet Sylvia Plath, chronicles Plath's experience with mental illness in the early-1950s. The novel records one person's experience with mental health care and electroshock treatment in that time period.

captures the whole man. Aston does make an effort to meet his own needs but not in a cynical search for power. What Aston truly desires throughout most of the play is real contact with another human being. It is only when his efforts at connection fail that Aston exerts simple power over Davies.

In Act I, after the opening scene in which Mick looks about the dismal room, then leaves, Aston comes onstage followed by Davies. Upon entering the room, Davies begins to speak of the encounter that led Aston to bring him home. Davies was involved in some sort of scuffle at the restaurant where he was working, and Aston saw a man ''have a go'' at Davies. In relating this incident, Davies complains a great deal about his treatment at the restaurant, claiming that he was not being treated according to his station, that he was told to do work he considered beneath him.

In spite of his concern with his place in the world, however, it is clear from Davies's clothes that he is a tramp and, whether such a viewpoint is moral or not, most so-called ''respectable'' people would consider him beneath them. While many would feel sorry for someone in Davies's position, almost no one would actually take such a person home to care for him. Aston's bringing Davies home, therefore, seems an act of incredible kindness. Such kindness can also be seen to some extent in the way Aston and Davies converse. For the most part, Davies speaks and Aston listens, enduring the old man's complaints, never challenging even the most absurd of Davies's claims, such as his assertion that women have often asked him if he would like to have them look at his body. When Aston does speak to Davies, most of the time he asks questions about the old man's needs and desires.

As Act I continues, Aston makes a number of offers to Davies and these offers seem to escalate in extremity. He offers the tramp a cigarette, shoes, and money. He says he will retrieve the belongings Davies left in the restaurant. He offers to let Davies stay in his own room and even gives the tramp the keys to the house. By the end of the first act, Aston's offers of help become so extreme that they would seem incredible to most people. So unbelievable is Aston's kindness to Davies that it raises the question of motivation. It is hard to accept that a person could be that kind simply out a sense of responsibility towards one's fellow man.

There are, however, some hints that Aston may be acting from something other than kindness, may in fact be seeking to have Davies satisfy his own needs. In the first act, Aston twice tells Davies of incidents from his own life. First he tells Davies a simple story—that he went into a pub and ordered a Guinness, which was served to him in a thick mug. He tells Davies that he could not finish the Guinness because he can only drink out of a tin glass. Davies completely ignores Aston's story and immediately begins speaking about his own plans to go to Sidcup. Later, Aston tells Davies of his sitting in a cafe and speaking to a woman who, after a brief conversation, put her hand on his and asked if he would like her to look at his body. Davies responds first with disbelief, saying "Get out of it," then goes on to say that women have often said the same thing to him, not quite ignoring Aston's remarks this time, but using Aston's experience simply as a means to boast about himself.

In both cases, there is no logical prelude to Aston's stories. They seem to come out of nowhere. The most likely interpretation seems to be that Aston simply wants someone to talk to, and this interpretation seems borne out in Aston's speech in the second act in which he tells of how he was put in a mental hospital after he "talked too much." This suggests that Aston's kindness might stem from his own need to connect with a human being, any human being, even Davies. If this is the case, Davies offers no satisfaction to Aston, for the tramp is interested only in himself.

Toward the end of the first act and throughout most of the second, Aston begins to seem less motivated by simple kindness. His leaving of Davies alone in the house seems, on the face of it, an act of consideration and of trust but it is in fact somewhat ambiguous. Aston almost certainly knows that Mick may come into the house and that, if he does so, he will view Davies as an intruder. In a sense, Aston, while not at this point confronting Davies with his own power, leaves Davies in a position in which he may have to face the anger and power of Mick. Thus Aston exerts a sort of familial power over Davies.

After Mick's encounter with Davies and Aston's return to the room, Aston continues to show ambiguity in his treatment of Davies. When Mick keeps Davies's bag from him, Aston makes some attempt to get the bag back to him, but finally, he gives the bag to Mick, and it is Mick who returns it to Davies. Aston still attempts to acquire shoes for Davies, and

"IT IS ONLY POWER THAT DAVIES UNDERSTANDS"

he offers him the job of caretaker, but he complains that Davies makes noises when he sleeps. When Davies complains about the draft and rain from the open window, Aston asserts himself by telling Davies that he himself cannot sleep without the window being open.

Toward the end of the second act, though, Aston temporarily gives in to Davies on the matter of the window. He tells Davies he can "close it for the time being." In his giving in to Davies in this way, Aston may be motivated by simple kindness, or he may seek to appease Davies so that he can again attempt to talk to the man, to engage him in some sort of relationship. Again, this can be interpreted as an effort to control Davies in order to meet his own needs.

At this point in the play, it is more difficult to believe that Aston acts only from kindness. It seems possible that Aston may truly be motivated by the desire to manipulate Davies in order to use him to satisfy his own need for contact. The situation becomes more complicated, however, at the end of Act II, when Aston, in a lengthy monologue, speaks to Davies about his mental troubles. Aston tells the story of his talking too much in the cafe, of his hallucinations, his commitment, his mother's betrayal, his experience of involuntary electroshock treatments. This monologue is like nothing else in the play. Aston tells the tramp a serious story about what is almost certainly the most painful experience of his life.

Aston seems again to want someone to listen to him, and one could again argue that he simply wants Davies to meet his own needs. Such a view, however, would be too simplistic. In telling this story to Davies, Aston takes a serious risk. The social stigma attached to those who have received such treatment in a mental hospital, particularly electroshock therapy, is strong, especially in the time in which Pinter is writing. When Aston tells Davies about his hospital experience, he makes himself extremely vulnerable to the tramp. He gives Davies ammunition to use against him. This is not a man in search of power but one who desperately seeks to make real human contact.

But Aston ultimately cannot make that contact with Davies. Pinter uses lighting to illustrate this. By the end of Aston's monologue, he alone can clearly be seen; Davies stands in the shadows. This shows that no connection is made. His attempt to connect with a human being leaves him vulnerable and alone.

In the final act, Davies exploits Aston's moment of honesty. He attempts to ally himself with Mick and against Aston. Aston, once again seeming to attempt an act of kindness, continues to seek shoes for Davies, but the tramp scorns Aston's efforts to help. In fact, Davies verbally assaults Aston, insulting him, accusing him of being insane, telling Aston that he could go back into the hospital, that he could receive electroshock treatments again. It is at this point that Aston finally tells Davies he has to leave. His attempts to be kind to Davies, to connect with him, have completely failed. Even when he tells Davies to leave, however, Aston again shows kindness, offering Davies money. But still he finally and literally turns his back on Davies as he looks out the window and waits for the tramp to leave.

While it is clear that Davies, with no place to go, is alone at the end of the play, what is often overlooked is the fact that Aston is also alone. He has shown kindness to Davies. He has desperately attempted to make real human contact with him. In the end, however, Aston's desire for connection cannot be saved. It is only power that Davies understands.

Source: Clare Cross, for *Drama for Students,* Gale, 2000.

Robert Brustein

In the following essay, noted theatre critic Brustein examines Pinter's play as a work of existentialism, concluding that The Caretaker *is "a work in which existence not only precedes essence but thoroughly destroys it."*

When Harold Pinter tells us that his plays contain no meaning outside of the material itself, I think we should believe him, giving thanks for his unusual, though somewhat self-incriminating, honesty. *The Caretaker*—being little more than the sum of its component parts and dramatic values—certainly

seems totally free from either significance or coherence. In this, no doubt, it has something in common with real life. But while the work displays a surface painstakingly decorated with naturalistic details, these are so peculiarly selected that the effect is quite distorted: the play is a slice of life, sliced so arbitrarily that it has lost all resemblance to life. Because of the mystery surrounding Pinter's principles of selection, therefore, suspense is the play's greatest virtue. Pinter manipulates this with considerable skill, tantalizing us with the promise of some eventual explanation—but he stubbornly refuses to deliver. He refuses, in fact, to communicate with us at all. His language, while authentic colloquial speech, is stripped bare of reflective or conceptual thought, so that the play could be just as effectively performed in Finno-Ugric. You might say that *The Caretaker* approaches the condition of music—if you could conceive of music without much development, lyric quality, or thematic content. For the play is so scrupulously non-analytical—so carefully documented with concrete (though pointless) happenings, specific (though atypical) character details, and particularized (though unrecognizable) responses—that it goes full circle from its surface naturalism and ends up a total abstraction.

The basic anecdote is this: A slavish, peevish, vicious old down-and-out named Davies is offered lodging in a junk-filled room, part of a network of apartments waiting to be redecorated. His benefactor, the would-be decorator, is a listless, dull-witted chap named Aston, who has collected Davies in much the same impersonal way he has collected the other useless articles in the place. Aston gives Davies a bed, money, shoes, clothes, and a caretaking job, which the derelict, consumed with defenses and prejudices, accepts or rejects with alternating gratitude and grumbles. Though they live in the same room and share a quality of spiritual paralysis (Aston wants but is unable to build a tool shed; Davies is desirous but incapable of going to Sidcup for his papers), they cannot connect. Nor do they connect with Aston's brother, Mick, a mordant young entrepreneur who hardly says a word to Aston and who relates to Davies mainly by baiting him with cruel practical jokes. Following Aston's confession that shock treatments had addled his brain (a confession alien to the style of the play), Davies tries to form an alliance with Mick to evict Aston from the room. Mick first encourages Davies' scheme; then, smashing his brother's statue of Buddha for emphasis, ridicules it. After a petty altercation between the two roommates over Davies' noisy sleeping habits—which climaxes when Davies, flourishing a knife, lets slip some unfortunate remarks about Aston's "stinking shed"—Aston asks him to leave. Whimpering like a rebellious slave whipped into submission, Davies begs to be allowed to remain.

That, apart from a wealth of equally mystifying details and a few comic episodes, is the meat of the play; and I'm perspiring from the effort to extract this much coherence. One is forced to respect Pinter's command of the stage, since he has composed scenes of substantial theatrical force dominated by a compelling air of mystery, but his motive for writing the play escapes me. I would be delighted to be able to tell you that Pinter nurtures some of the seeds he plants in the work—that *The Caretaker* is about the spiritual vacancy of modern life, the inability of slave types to achieve dignity, or (favorite theme of "sensitive" contemporary playwrights) the failure of human beings to communicate with one another. But I cannot honestly conclude that it is about anything at all, other than itself. The situation, apparently ordinary, is so special, and the characters, apparently human, are so unrepresentative, that we are totally alienated from the events on the stage; and finally begin to regard these creatures as a bacteriologist might examine germ life on another planet.

For this reason, the present tendency to couple Pinter and Beckett is more misleading than it is illuminating. Pinter has obviously borrowed some of Beckett's techniques and conventions—the tramp figure, the immobility of the central characters, the repetitions in the dialogue, the occasional vaudeville stunts, the mixture of comedy and seriousness—but he has used them for totally different purposes. In *Waiting for Godot,* the action is metaphorical and universal; in *The Caretaker,* it is denotative and specific. Beckett's play reveals the feelings of a metaphysical poet about the quality of human existence. Pinter's, excluding both feeling and thought, bears almost no relation to any known form of human life, and is so impersonal it seems to have written itself. What Pinter has created, in short, is a naturalism of the grotesque wrapped around a core of abstraction—something less like Beckett than like Sherwood Anderson, though lacking the compassion of either.

The production takes full advantage of ample theatrical opportunities. Donald McWhinnie approaches the play, quite correctly, as if it were a

> WHAT PINTER HAS CREATED, IN SHORT, IS A NATURALISM OF THE GROTESQUE WRAPPED AROUND A CORE OF ABSTRACTION— SOMETHING LESS LIKE BECKETT THAN LIKE SHERWOOD ANDERSON."

perfectly conventional kitchen drama, adding a note of casual imperturbability with his direction which enhances the oddness. Brian Currah's setting—an artfully arranged hodgepodge of vacuum cleaners, lawn mowers, broken-down beds, paint buckets, and other articles of junk—provides the proper air of imprisonment. And the acting is further proof that the new English proletarian style is now more flexible than our own. Pinter, who writes succulent parts for actors, has created a really juicy character in Davies, excellently played by Donald Pleasence with a kind of shambling, sniveling, corrosive nastiness. But for me the best performance of the evening is contributed by Alan Bates as Mick, whose alternating cruelty, irony, wit, and injured innocence are etched with such assurance that one is almost convinced that there is something of consequence beneath the baffling exterior of the part.

But the surface refuses to budge. In *The Caretaker,* Pinter has gone beyond the most extreme theories of the most radical Existentialists: he has created a work in which existence not only precedes essence but thoroughly destroys it. Without some hint of the essential, all judgments must be relative, and a critic of the drama becomes as useless as those critics of Action painting who are given to analyzing their own subliminal responses to a work instead of the work itself. My subliminal response to Pinter's play was a growing irritation and boredom, somewhat mitigated by admiration for his redoubtable theatrical gifts. If these gifts can someday be combined with visionary power, beauty, heart, and mind, then we shall someday have a new dramatic artist and not just an abstract technician of striking scenes for actors.

Source: Robert Brustein, "A Naturalism of the Grotesque" in his *Seasons of Discontent,* Simon & Schuster, 1965, pp. 180–83.

Walter Kerr

Kerr offers a favorable appraisal of Pinter's play in this review, citing the play as a challenging work of theatre.

I was instantly fearful that *The Caretaker* would become popular for the wrong reasons. There was the chance, for instance, that it would be regarded as zany comedy, and forcibly laughed at. One response that is regularly made to contemporary plays of the profoundest despair is the tittering pretense that the author has carved his vast zero as a joke. This is not emptiness, the nervous laughter says, but an irresponsible playfulness. People are always mentioning the Marx brothers in connection with the "comedy" of carefully illustrated nothingness, as though we had once laughed at the Marx brothers because they struck us as irrational in the clinical sense.

Thus laughter was felt to be obligatory as three remarkable actors played out the following sequence in Harold Pinter's remarkable play. A filthy old ingrate who had been given shelter in a refuse-littered attic was offered a satchel by the vacant-eyed brother who had admitted him. Another brother, hostile for no known reason, intercepted the satchel each time it was presented. The satchel was thrust forward, snatched away, thrust forward, snatched away, thrust forward, snatched away, finally hurled to the floor in a burst of dust. The repeated gestures did have an echo of a vaudeville routine in which a chair was invariably whisked out from under the comedian as he was about to sit on it. But the routine we once laughed at had had a rationale: we understood the sequence of events, however unlikely or unlucky, that led to each experience of frustration. Here, deliberately, no causes were indicated. The bag was offered without charity and retrieved without reason. The old man's frustration was absolute; it was also—to him, as to us—incomprehensible. To laugh at it almost suggested malice. Or, at the least, the defensive sound of the giggle that is meant to ward off a threatened dissolution of the mind.

There was, further, a strong likelihood that *The Caretaker* would become necessary theatergoing merely because it was, as dramaturgy, novel, eccentric, hence a conversation piece for tired dinner tables. Three characters moved in and out of a domestic graveyard, most often with a sense of stealth, to sit and stare at one another, to recite unseeing monologues (on several occasions the listener on stage simply went to sleep, or otherwise abstracted himself), sometimes to engage in eye-to-eye conversation in which each participant pursued his own thoughts and failed to grasp the other's. All three were kept at arm's length from us, almost at species' length. The homeless old man was indecent at every turn of mind: he hesitated to use the toilet for fear the "blacks" next door might have used it; he treated the benefits doled out to him with fastidious contempt ("Them bastards at the monastery let me down"); he threatened to usurp, with a snivel and a whine, the refuge he did not deserve. The brother who was his benefactor was mindless; doctors had done something to his brain. The brother who visited came to challenge, to sneer, to torment; he was the brazen, mesmerizing pseudo delinquent none of us understands. Such sympathy as stirred in us went, by inversion, to the disreputable vagrant; horror that he was, he was recognizably human and not a robot or a Martian. But in general we were in the company of the loathsome, the lamed, and the spiteful. It was lamentably easy for so defiant a play to become, through its very violation of our ordinary tastes and our ordinary expectations, simply fashionable.

The Caretaker merited, and I think required, another kind of attention. There were two levels on which it might have been attended to, one with deep communion and hence satisfaction, one with detached but genuine curiosity.

To have been deeply satisfied, perhaps even moved as one is moved by an instant recognition of a kindred soul, it would have been necessary to share Mr. Pinter's vision of the present state of man. This vision was not reduced to a series of editorial statements; it stood as a vision, as a fluid image, as an atmosphere. But what it saw and showed us was a world wholly opaque, wholly impermeable, and, beyond the fact that we could neither see into it nor probe it with our fingers, wholly hollow. Mr. Pinter had attempted to construct, and had succeeded in constructing, a poetry of the blind: the sensed experience of a man who has suddenly lost his sight and is now in an unfamiliar room. This man gropes his way, hesitantly, talking to himself to keep himself company. There are objects about, and they can be touched when they are stumbled over; though they can be vaguely identified by cautious exploration, they remain unfriendly. There are people about, and they can be called to: but what they say is misleading because the tone of voice is not supported by the expressiveness of a face. One can guess, and do the wrong thing. One can plead, and not know when the others present are exchanging cold glances. Man— and the grimy caretaker was most nearly man in the play—is lost, rejected by what he had thought were his own kind, ousted from what he had thought was his home. Appeal is at last impossible: there are no hearts or heads to be reached.

To say that this tense, concentrated, sustained position was superbly illustrated in performance is to say too little. The play itself, given its particular insight and its precisely appropriate method of articulating that insight, must be regarded as perfect. For it to have been perfectly satisfying in the theater, however, one would have had to be ready not only to attend closely but to nod firmly and say, ''Yes, beyond doubt this is the life we live.''

Short of such utter identification, there was a second level at which the play's fascination might have been honestly felt. A playgoer might have gone to the play without having yet surrendered all hope of speaking to his fellow men, without having concluded that all dialogue is a dialogue with the figures on Easter Island, without having agreed to regard the world about him as a disarray of ripped umbrellas, broken Buddhas, and empty picture frames. It is nonetheless true that a considerable segment of twentieth-century society has so come to see the neighborhood it inhabits. The antiworld is with us, late and soon; it faces us from the paintings on our walls no less than from the increasingly impotent people within our prosceniums. What exists—in the public reality or the private mind—had better be known, whether in detachment or in surrender, whether in cool appraisal or in assent. There may have been no better way of knowing it in the early sixties than through the already cool, ruthlessly framed, astringently orchestrated survey of the wreckage called *The Caretaker*.

Source: Walter Kerr, ''*The Caretaker*'' in his *The Theatre in Spite of Itself,* Simon & Schuster, 1963, pp. 116–19.

SOURCES

Page, Malcolm, compiler. *File on Pinter,* Methuen Drama, 1993, pp. 23-25.

> MR. PINTER HAD ATTEMPTED TO CONSTRUCT, AND HAD SUCCEEDED IN CONSTRUCTING, A POETRY OF THE BLIND: THE SENSED EXPERIENCE OF A MAN WHO HAS SUDDENLY LOST HIS SIGHT AND IS NOW IN AN UNFAMILIAR ROOM.''

Sakellaridou, Elizabeth. *Pinter's Female Portraits: A Study of Female Characters in the Plays of Harold Pinter,* Macmillan, 1988, pp. 127-29.

FURTHER READING

Billington, Michael. *The Life and Work of Harold Pinter.* Faber, 1996.
> This is the first authorized biographical study of Pinter. Billington uses information gleaned from interviews with Pinter and his friends to illuminate the playwright's life and work.

Briggs, Asa. *A Social History of England: From the Ice Age to the Channel Tunnel,* Weidenfeld and Nicolson, 1994.
> This book provides a careful examination of the history of British society and contains considerable material on Postwar Britain.

Diamond, Elin. *Pinter's Comic Play,* Associated UP, 1985.
> Diamond focuses on the use of comedy in Pinter's major plays. This book includes a chapter on *The Caretaker.*

Dukore, Bernard F. *Harold Pinter,* Grove Press, 1982.
> This is a brief introduction to Pinter's major plays.

Scott, Michael, editor. *Harold Pinter: The Birthday Party, The Caretaker, The Homecoming,* Macmillan, 1986.
> This book is a compilation of numerous reviews and essays on the works cited in the title.

A Chorus of Disapproval

ALAN AYCKBOURN

1984

A Chorus of Disapproval, Sir Alan Ayckbourn's twentieth play—and one of his most successful—premiered at the Stephen Joseph Theater in the Round in Scarborough, England, in May, 1984. Following the sell-out season in Scarborough, the play opened in a large-scale production at the National Theater in London in August, 1985. The success of the play earned Ayckbourn three major British theater awards including the London *Evening Standard* Award, the Olivier Award, and the *Drama* Award.

Ayckbourn's first great success, *Relatively Speaking,* was a farce modeled on Oscar Wilde's *The Importance of Being Earnest; A Chorus of Disapproval* is not modeled on, but rather is based around, another play: John Gay's *The Beggar's Opera,* which in the play is to be performed by a local dramatic society. The play describes the ups and downs of provincial life: as the rehearsals for *The Beggar's Opera* advance, real life increasingly imitates art. As well as being a modern version of the classic "play within a play," *A Chorus of Disapproval* also explores the attraction of the theater for ordinary people, whose apparently unremarkable lives are revealed to be unexpectedly eventful.

Ayckbourn's contribution to the theater is impressive. Although his comedies were initially considered unfashionable, they have always been well-received by critics and audiences alike, all of whom

have recognized Ayckbourn's technical prowess and his unusual ability to balance comedy and pathos. *A Chorus of Disapproval,* which explores ordinary people's aspirations and disappointments, confirmed that reputation. Ayckbourn was knighted in 1987 in recognition of the extraordinary quality of his writing and his contribution to the British theatre.

AUTHOR BIOGRAPHY

Alan Ayckbourn was born April 12, 1939, in the London suburb of Hampstead. His parents divorced in 1943, and his mother, a writer of romantic fiction, later remarried. Ayckbourn grew up in Sussex, which he features as the setting for many of his plays. During high school he devoted most of his time to acting in and writing plays. At the age of seventeen he left school and started a career in the theater. After a few years working as an assistant stage manager and actor for Sir Donald Wolfit's touring company, Ayckbourn began a fruitful relationship with the Studio Theater Company in Scarborough, a small resort town in the South of England.

There, Ayckbourn worked for Stephen Joseph, an innovative stage manager who had introduced the concept of theater-in-the-round to England. (Ayckbourn modeled the character of Llewellyn in *A Chorus of Disapproval* on Joseph.) Ayckbourn soon started writing plays for the company. He left to work as a drama producer for the British Broadcasting Corporation (BBC). After Joseph's death in 1970, Ayckbourn returned to Scarborough to become the company's director of productions. He renamed the theater the Stephen Joseph Theater-in-the-Round.

In 1997, Ayckbourn fought a protracted battle with the Scarborough Town Council over funding for the faltering theater. He himself had already contributed 400,000 pounds from his own pocket, which was topped by a two million pound grant from the British National Lottery. He requested a five-year, 50,000 pound per year grant. The dispute was dubbed the battle of the "luvvies versus lavvies," because opponents of Ayckbourn's request claimed that funding the theater would necessitate closing the town's public toilets. Ayckbourn fought a public relations campaign; when he was knighted by the Queen later that year, he won the battle. The Scarborough public toilets also managed to stayed open.

Alan Ayckbourn

Ayckbourn writes light comedies about middle class morals and manners. His first major success was *Relatively Speaking,* which opened in March, 1967, around the same time that Tom Stoppard's more structurally innovative absurdist farce *Rosencrantz and Guildenstern Are Dead* opened at the National Theater. For some time, Ayckbourn's adherence to the genre of light comedy damaged his reputation in comparison to innovators such as Stoppard, Harold Pinter (*The Birthday Party*), and Joe Orton (*What the Butler Saw*). But he has always been popular with audiences, and critics have gradually come to praise his dramatic talents.

Ayckbourn has now written more plays than Shakespeare, and, according to Simon Trussler in the *Cambridge Illustrated History of the British Theatre,* his sell-out seasons at the National Theater demonstrate a box-office appeal "unequalled since Shakespeare." He has also written a great many adaptations for the stage (including an acclaimed version of Russian playwright Alexander Ostrovsky's play *The Forest* [1870] staged at the National Theater in the mid-1990s). He is also a respected director; he directed the premiere of *A Chorus of Disapproval* in 1984, and in 1987 he directed an award-winning production of Arthur Miller's *A View from the Bridge.*

PLOT SUMMARY

Act I

The structure of *A Chorus of Disapproval* exemplifies Ayckbourn's modernity: the first scene, for instance, is chronologically the last. The play begins with the tail-end of PALOS's performance of *The Beggar's Opera.* From there, the play unfolds like a cinematic flashback. The flashback structure maintains tension throughout the light-hearted ensemble piece: the audience, certain in the knowledge that the opera will be performed successfully, nonetheless fears that calamity will unfold, for after the curtain falls, Guy is abandoned by his fellow cast members.

In the second scene of Act I, Guy auditions by giving a fumbling rendition of the only song he knows, "All Through the Night." He is shown up by the director, Dafydd, who interrupts him to sing the song in Welsh. Although Guy's singing is obviously not up to standard, Dafydd immediately accepts him, partly because he is short one actor and partly because he is a warm, generous man.

During the audition, other cast members enter. A quick scene and lighting change follows, and the cast adjourns to a local pub named *The Fleece* (the name of the tavern suggests that the customers will be "fleeced" or conned out of their money). This pub parallels Peachum's tavern in *The Beggar's Opera:* indeed, the proprietor's daughter, Bridget, acts rather like Gay's Lucy, fighting with customers and stealing lovers.

Following this sociable occasion, Dafydd invites Guy home. A brief scene change finds the characters in a pleasant, comfortable living room. Dafydd offers Guy the part of Crook-Fingered Jack. Although it is only a one line part, Guy is thrilled and accepts. Then Dafydd's neglected wife, Hannah, enters. She is to play Polly Peachum in the *Opera.* Hannah has suffered in the shadow of her talkative and unobservant husband. Hannah and Guy connect emotionally—he is polite and attentive, which she appreciates, and she is sensitive about his recent loss, which he appreciates.

Another scene change finds PALOS again rehearsing. For all his enthusiasm, Dafydd is a disorganized director: the cast has only rehearsed the first fifteen pages of the script. Amidst the confusion, Guy receives an alluring invitation to dinner from the lascivious Fay, seconded by her reluctant husband, Ian. Jarvis Huntley-Pike, a jovial Northerner, persists in his mistaken assumption that Guy is a Scotsman. Meanwhile, the romantic tension between Guy and Hannah increases. The rehearsal ends with an unexpected boon for Guy: after a cast member drops out, he is promoted to the meatier role of Matt of the Mint.

The next scene is set in Fay and Ian's house. Guy arrives, assuming that he has been invited to dinner. Fay, however, has other plans. She is amused when Guy's friend arrives—a seventy-year-old woman whose presence is a considerable shock to Ian. The Hubbards, as well as the Huntley-Pikes, mistakenly think that Guy can help them in their scheme to fleece Guy's company, BLM.

The last scene of Act I, a rehearsal, is set one month after these initial scenes. Dafydd comments to Guy that "these dramatics" are "doing you good," and Guy does indeed seem more confident. The Act ends with a song from the *Opera.* Although the actresses are meant to be focused upon Crispin, who is playing Macheath, they turn to Guy. Their unconscious mistake prefigures the second act's major development: Guy's elevation to the role of Macheath.

Act II

The second act opens with a tense conversation between Guy and Hannah, conducted in a local cafe. Guy appears to have undergone something of a transformation in the last few months. He is no longer a hang-dog weakling but rather a local Lothario. He has been carrying on two affairs— one with Hannah, who is in love with him, and another with Fay, who is still trying to involve him in the BLM land scam. Hannah tries to badger Guy into choosing between her and Fay.

Suddenly, Fay appears. The cat-fight between the two women comically imitates a similar conflict between Polly and Lucy in *The Beggar's Opera.* Hannah departs in fury. Fay points out that it was she who handed Guy the role of Filch (another role upgrade), then hints threateningly that he must "come up with the goods" in return for the favor.

In the next scene, the conflict between Hannah and Fay is repeated in the struggles between Bridget, as Jenny Diver, and Linda, both of whom fight over Crispin, as Macheath. After Hannah and Linda depart the stage, Guy tries to inform Jarvis that people are scheming to profit from his land, but Jarvis is too busy telling Guy an old story about his grandfather to pay much attention.

Dafydd re-enters. He is oblivious to Guy's affair with Hannah, and, to make matters worse, confides in Guy that he is having trouble in his marriage. He complains that Hannah is "a bloody deep-freeze of a woman." However, since Guy knows that she is not, the audience is left to conclude that the fault lies with Dafydd. The scene ends in a now-familiar pattern: following Crispin's rude departure, the role of Macheath is vacant. Rebecca suggest that Guy accept it, and sure enough, he weakly agrees to step in.

A song from Guy, as Macheath, bridges the scene change to Rebecca Huntley-Pike's garden. It soon becomes clear that Rebecca is the source of the mysterious rumor about the BLM land deal. Guy is tempted to accept Jarvis's pay-off of five hundred pounds and does in fact pocket it. He is becoming more and more like Macheath.

A lighting change finds the cast involved in a final dress rehearsal. Guy changes into his costume for Macheath. The subsequent scene, in which he rejects Hannah, is in keeping with his stage character: his transformation is complete. The parting between the two lovers is repeatedly interrupted by a still-oblivious Dafydd, who is frantically trying to rig the lighting for the performance.

When Ian enters with the news that BLM is closing, all hell breaks loose. The land scam will not take place, and the disappointed cast members turn against Guy. Ian informs Dafydd of Hannah and Guy's affair, and Dafydd too turns against Guy.

The final scene of *A Chorus of Disapproval* is the last scene of *The Beggar's Opera*. The players enact the final reprieve of Macheath. The curtain falls and the actors embrace one another. But the audience, recalling the play's opening scene, knows that this scene will shortly be followed by their rejection of Guy. The ending is ambiguous—both a celebration of Guy (Macheath) and a rejection of the change he has wreaked upon their lives.

CHARACTERS

Mr. Ames

Mr. Ames is PALOS's shy piano-player. His personality is in direct contrast to Dafydd's. He only has a few lines of spoken dialogue.

MEDIA ADAPTATIONS

- *A Chorus of Disapproval* was produced as a feature film in Britain in 1989, directed by Michael Winner with a screenplay adapted by Ayckbourn and Winner. It stars Jeremy Irons as Guy, Anthony Hopkins as Dafydd, and Prunella Scales as Hannah.

Bridget Baines

Bridget is the daughter of the local publican. Bridget's official position at PALOS is stage manager and script prompt. In *A Chorus of Disapproval* she also parallels the character of Lucy, the publican's daughter in *The Beggar's Opera*. She is a rather ill-tempered young woman who manages to intimidate friends and foes alike with her physical aggression. Bridget's appearances usually center on her affair with Crispin and her hostility towards her rival, Linda. Her big scene comes in Act II, when she provokes Linda to tears.

Fay Hubbard

Fay is an attractive, sophisticated thirty-something woman. Ayckbourn describes her as "one of the local younger married jet-set." Fay calmly embarks upon an affair with Guy and lands him the part of Filch, assuming that he will then provide her with financially lucrative information about the supposed BLM land scam. She perceives their relationship as a "deal" and threatens Guy when he appears to renege on his side of it.

Ian Hubbard

Ian is an ambitious thirty-something man, married to the very attractive Fay. The couple are determined to advance in the world. Ian owns a building firm, which is his excuse for wanting to buy Jarvis's land, but it is more probable that he and the Huntley-Pikes hope to inflate the land's price and then sell it at a profit. He resigns his role as Filch in order to secure Guy's help in the scam, and reluctantly agrees to Fay's partner-swapping arrangement. When Guy misunderstands the arrangement and brings along an elderly woman friend to the Hubbard household, Ian is humiliated. He has his revenge when he reveals Guy and Hannah's affair to Dafydd in Act II.

Jarvis Huntley-Pike

"Mad" but "harmless," Jarvis owns the land that is the subject of so much wheeling and dealing in *A Chorus of Disapproval*. In his late-fifties, he is a British Northerner, prone to making bad jokes and enamored with the sound of his own voice. Jarvis's misreading of Guy—his belief that Guy is a Scotsman, based solely on the fact that when he first sees him Guy is holding a beer in one hand and a whiskey in the other—generates a good deal of humor throughout the play. Jarvis's longest appearance is in Act II, when he tells Guy a story about his philanthropic, religious grandfather, the first owner of the land, who built a cricket pitch for his workers on the land but destroyed it after he saw them playing cricket on a Sunday.

Rebecca Huntley-Pike

Rebecca is the wife of the jovial Jarvis. Younger than her husband, she shares his predilection for alcohol. Her major appearances are in the rehearsal sequence in Act I and the conversation she has with Guy in her garden in Act II. In all probability, Rebecca is the source of the rumors about BLM expanding. Just as Fay procures Guy a better part in the play, Rebecca procures him the part of Macheath. Just as Fay expects Guy to do her a favor in return, so too does Rebecca. She and her husband are nonetheless disappointed in their schemes.

Guy Jones

Guy Jones is the protagonist of *A Chorus of Disapproval*, yet he is a curiously faceless character. His chief characteristic is his passivity; in fact it is his passive acceptance of other peoples' plans for him that propels him to center stage. Guy has recently been widowed. He decides a change is in order and joins the local musical society.

Guy works for the multi-national firm BLM in "a rather small local branch in a rather obscure department called Alternative Forward Costing." Although he is clearly not a mover or a shaker, Guy's insider position within BLM makes him the focus of interest for greedy cast members.

Initially allocated a one-line part as Crook-Fingered Jack in John Gay's eighteenth-century musical *The Beggar's Opera,* Guy soon advances through the ranks, aided by recalcitrant actors and scheming actresses, until he wins the lead role of Macheath. He has a somewhat superficial affair with one of the cast members, Fay, and also embarks upon a more serious affair with his co-star, Hannah, who plays Polly. This relationship has dramatic consequences for Guy, Hannah, and her husband, Llewellyn; as the curtain falls, Guy has not only lost his job at BLM, he has also managed to alienate all of the cast members.

Dafydd ap Llewellyn

The energetic Dafydd is on-stage almost as often as Guy Jones, and although Guy is the focus of the play, Dafydd's role is in many ways far more interesting. Dafydd is a lawyer whose real passion is the theater. He longs to work with better actors than those that the local musical society PALOS provides, but he makes up for their lack of talent with his own enthusiasm.

Dafydd's passion for the theater—and his pride in all things Welsh—contrasts with his passionless marriage. Although he loves his wife Hannah, he neglects her, and their relationship is not satisfying physically. The revelation that Hannah and Guy have been having an affair is devastating to him; nonetheless, at the curtain call, he graciously thanks Guy for playing Macheath at such short notice.

Hannah Llewellyn

Hannah is married to Dafydd. A generous and loving woman and the mother of twin girls, she feels neglected and occasionally patronized by her husband. Everything in the Llewellyn household is Welsh, Hannah tells Guy in Act I, "except me."

Hannah even goes so far as to wonder if she would be missed if she died. It is these feelings of neglect that propel her into an affair with Guy, whose politeness and attentiveness are a pleasant change for her.

Hannah plays Polly Peachum in the PALOS production of *The Beggar's Opera,* and her role, as well as her marital problems, make her something of a tragi-comic figure.

At the end of the play, Hannah gambles all on Guy's love, offering to leave her marriage and her children for him, but he rejects her. It is unclear how her relationship with Dafydd will develop, but it is clear that Guy's presence in her life has changed her irrevocably.

Crispin Usher

Crispin is a tough, hostile young man who originally lands the part of Macheath in the PALOS production. Like Macheath, Crispin "runs" two women at the same time: Bridget and Linda. His big scene occurs in Act II, when he comes to blows with Dafydd, then cheerfully throws the towel in, thus leaving the company without its lead actor.

Enid Washbrook

Enid is a timid, unobtrusive, older woman, Linda's beleaguered mother.

Linda Washbrook

Linda is the daughter of Ted and Enid and has only a smidgen more character than her washed-out parents. She plays Lucy in *The Beggar's Opera* and acts out the part in real life by competing with Bridget for Crispin's affection. Unlike Bridget, who manages to match Crispin in the toughness stakes, Linda is not really up to the part nor to battles with her rival. In Act II she is flummoxed by Bridget's provocative behavior and collapses in tears.

THEMES

Change and Transformation

Ayckbourn explores the theme of change and transformation in *A Chorus of Disapproval* through the characters of Guy Jones and Hannah Lleweylln. In the very first scene of the play, Guy, as Macheath, sings about the possibility of change: "The wretch of to-day, may be happy to-morrow." After he finishes singing, the lighting alters and the action changes to backstage. The transformation is two-fold: from play-within-play to real play and from the cast's celebration to their rejection of Guy. The change in their attitude toward him—which is in fact the major theme of the play—is underlined by his costume change.

Guy's involvement in the production fundamentally transforms him. He begins the play a shy, tentative man, who seems to pale before the drive, energy, and eccentricity of his director. Ayckbourn emphasizes the contrast between the two men in the audition scene: Guy's off-key, uncertain rendition of "All Through the Night" is lost beneath Dafydd's full-throated Welsh tenor. Nonetheless, as he grows in confidence and is applauded for his skill, the experience of acting transforms Guy.

It is not simply Guy's involvement in theater that transforms him: his romantic entanglements are equally important. Although Guy is shy and tentative, he possesses a sensitive character that women find intrinsically appealing, and it is this quality that enables him to connect with Hannah. Guy's combination of good looks, weak personality, and naivete also make him appealing to the predatory Fay, while other women, such as Enid and Rebecca, find him "masculine" and "manly." Women find him attractive, although the reasons they nominate seem to have more to do with what they need and perceive than with the person Guy actually is. Even when he "plays" a romantic lead, he wears a mask that reflects others' imagination of his personality.

Hannah is meant to play the *Opera*'s romantic lead, Polly Peachum. Ayckbourn delays the introduction of Hannah partly to increase dramatic suspense and partly to surprise the audience, for Hannah seems the antithesis of Polly. Rather than being a pretty, saucy young woman, Hannah is older, wears no make-up, and is confused and flurried. But after her brief encounter with Guy, she exits on a flirtatious note, and the tone has been struck for their subsequent interaction.

Hannah's involvement with Guy transforms her. Their roles in the production enable the lovers to participate in a romance that would otherwise be barred from them, but they learn that the theater cannot offer a permanent shelter from life's problems. In fact, her affair with Guy forces Hannah to acknowledge existing problems in her life and to act upon them. In her first conversation with Guy she confesses to feeling unappreciated, a grievance that she had never previously expressed. When the curtain falls on the affair, the fantasy is over. Although Hannah offers to leave Dayfdd and her children for Guy, it is unclear whether she would actually do so. All that is clear is that she sees her marriage—and herself—in a new light. She has been irrevocably transformed.

Justice and Injustice

The opening scene of *A Chorus of Disapproval* makes clear that Guy has antagonized the cast. The

TOPICS FOR FURTHER STUDY

- Many critics feel that Dafydd's character is much more interesting for both the audience and the actor than Guy Jones's character. Do you agree?

- Given that *A Chorus of Disapproval* features a play-within-a-play, how would you approach directing it? What problems might arise in attempting to present two distinct dramatic works within one presentation?

- Do Hannah's declarations of her love for Guy ring true, or are there other conclusions you might draw about her feelings and actions?

- Compare and contrast the character of Guy Jones and Macheath (from John Gay's *The Beggar's Opera*). Both of these characters are accused of being womanizers and deceivers. Are these accurate descriptions of both men? If not, how would you characterize them, particularly their differences and similarities?

- Focus upon one theme within the play—for instance, the theme of corruption and swindling, or the theme of adulterous love—and choose an example from another medium that also explores it (for instance, a television soap opera, a newspaper report, a painting). Discuss both examples in detail; then contrast the style in which they explore the theme and the message they present to their audience.

- Ayckbourn structures the play around a flashback. What effect does the flashback structure have upon the audience watching the play? How does it effect their perception of the events that unfold and of the characters themselves?

---

play thus resembles a sort of staged detective hunt: the audience, knowing the ending, endeavors to determine how Guy misbehaved and why he is punished. By the end of the second act, those questions have been answered: Guy has strung along two women simultaneously, disappointing both of them in different ways, and he has mislead (deliberately or not) other people about their financial schemes. To an extent, the audience can only agree with Dafydd when he says, "And my one prayer is that one of these days, you'll get what's coming to you."

Yet the unexpected occurs: as the curtain finally falls, the actors embrace "their hero of the night, Guy himself." The transformation mirrors the final reprieve given to Macheath in the Opera. But this change is more than clever mimicry; Ayckbourn appears to suspend his judgment and to ask the audience to decide for themselves whether Guy should really "get what's coming" to him. Are not other characters equally culpable? Dafydd himself was muddled up in the land scam: what right does he have to cast the first stone? What of Hannah herself?

Did Guy really disappoint her, or did she, as a wife and a mother, act irresponsibly? Upon whom should the sword of justice fall? Ayckbourn is not so much undecided about these questions as he is determined to encourage his audience to think these questions through thoroughly.

The exploration of the themes of justice and injustice is not limited to Guy's bedroom antics. The parallels between the BLM land scam and the corrupt activities of the characters in *The Beggar's Opera* are too close to be coincidental. In fact, Ayckbourn makes such close parallels in order to critique contemporary middle-class aspirations. The play was written during the first years of the 1980s boom in Britain, a period in which the term "yuppie" was first coined, and Ayckbourn's depiction of social ambition and greed amongst the provincial middle classes is evidence of his sharp observation and his prescient vision. Ayckbourn does not condemn but rather draws attention to these failings in human nature, leaving his audience to decide for themselves how best to address their presence in contemporary society.

STYLE

The Balance of Comedy and Tragedy

In *The Beggar's Opera*, John Gay shows ordinary people aping the behavior of their betters. Gay's attitude is one of cynical condemnation, but Ayckbourn, writing more than two hundred years later, extends and refines his insight for a new age. It is Ayckbourn's remarkable insight that while ordinary people can fall prey to the same failings as their betters, those same lives are also filled with moments of extraordinary pathos and humor. Breadth and depth of emotion are not confined to the traditional figures of "great theater," such as kings and princes, but are rather characteristic of the human condition. Although neither Guy, Fay, nor Dafydd are "great," Ayckbourn depicts their comic and at times sad struggles with the universal experience of romantic love sympathetically. Although the audience might condemn Hannah's adultery, Guy's duplicity, and Dafydd's insensitivity toward his wife, they are also able to identify strains within their characters that are unquestionably admirable: Hannah's tenderness, Guy's sensitivity, Dafydd's passion.

Ayckbourn is held in high esteem for his ability to balance tragic subject matter with comic events. The playwright's subject matter is invariably middle-class life and marriage, explored within a traditional comic framework that relies upon the conventions of mistaken identities, misunderstandings, and precisely timed exits and entrances. However, Ayckbourn generally refuses to adhere to comic convention when ending his plays. Although the characters' amusing misconceptions are usually resolved, Ayckbourn does not offer the audience the usual happy ending that follows such clarification.

In a pattern that Ayckbourn established in his first great success, *Relatively Speaking,* and that is also evident in *A Chorus of Disapproval,* the ending of the play is ambiguous and open to interpretation. In this way he refuses to emphasize either the play's comic elements or its tragic undertones but rather tries to hold the two strands in balance.

A perfect example of Ayckbourn's ability to hold these apparently opposing elements in equilibrium is the song that opens Act II, a celebration of women sung by Crispin, as Macheath. As the song finishes, a crossfade introduces the next scene, located in a cafe. Hannah and Guy are talking over coffee and cake. It is immediately apparent that Hannah wants more from the affair than Guy is prepared to give her and that she is deeply distressed by his affair with Fay. Nonetheless, the audience's insight into Hannah's fractured emotional state is accompanied by wonderful moments of slapstick comedy, mostly focused on Dafydd's "paisley patterned" underpants that Guy mistakenly put on at Hannah's, then left at Fay's that morning. When Fay threatens Guy, emotions run full circle and the scene ends on a more serious tone. Such deft juggling of pathos and humor is typically acknowledged by critics as one of Ayckbourn's greatest talents.

The Play-within-the-Play

The device of the play-within-the-play is an ancient one, much favored by Renaissance playwrights. In William Shakespeare's *Hamlet* (1601), Hamlet hires a band of traveling players to perform a play about fratricide called "The Mouse-trap" in order to decide whether or not Claudius murdered Hamlet's father. Claudius's guilty reaction to the players' masque resolves Hamlet's doubts. Ben Jonson, a contemporary of Shakespeare, was also fond of the device. He used it in his comedy, *Bartholemew Fair* (1614), to satirize the audience's stupidity, to respond to Puritan attacks on the theater, and to celebrate the splendor and worth of the stage.

With the rise of realism and naturalism as the dominant acting and writing styles in the nineteenth century, the device fell out of use. But late twentieth-century playwrights are keen to explore the artificiality of the stage and to encourage their audience's awareness of the process of perception. They have returned the device to center-stage. In Britain, Tom Stoppard and Alan Ayckbourn have made it the centerpiece of their writing. Stoppard's *Rosencrantz and Guildenstern Are Dead* (1967), which echoes Samuel Beckett's *Waiting for Godot* (1955) and is structured around Shakespeare's *Hamlet,* hinges upon the idea of the play-within-the-play. Other Stoppard plays also rest upon the device, most notably *The Real Thing* (1982), as does his cinematic hit, *Shakespeare in Love* (1998). Likewise, Ayckbourn's first success, *Relatively Speaking* (1967), deliberately echoes the structure and themes of Oscar Wilde's *The Importance of Being Earnest* (1895).

The play-within-the-play conceit enables Ayckbourn to deepen and enrich his themes. The bare bones of the plot—Guy Jones's decision to audition for PALOS, his increasing artistic success, his romantic entanglements, his naive involvement in the BLM scheme—might be interesting in themselves. However, Ayckbourn makes these events considerably funnier and sadder by juxtaposing extracts from Gay's opera—thus by creating parallels between art and experience. Guy runs two women simultaneously, just as Macheath juggles both Polly and Lucy; the people surrounding Guy masquerade as decent and pleasant but are actually as greedy and rapacious as the thieves and con men they portray in Gay's work. Parallels between the stage and real life mean that events and characters assume a wider meaning.

Nonetheless, Ayckbourn limits the extent to which parallels between art and experience can be seen. The light-heartedness of the opera, in which a last-minute reprieve saves Macheath from the hangman's noose, contrasts to the growing seriousness of the real life company, in which Guy's antics cannot be neatly and quickly erased but are rather the cause of enduring unhappiness. Life does not always mimic art, for in life there is no god-like author to tie up loose ends and to erase blots on the copy book. What remains is the human capacity to endure, just as art also endures.

HISTORICAL CONTEXT

The Consumer 1980s and Ayckbourn as Social Critic

Britain never really recovered economically from the Second World War. Although the 1950s and 1960s were marked by full employment, wages remained low and billions of pounds were squandered in a futile effort to retain hold of rebellious British colonies like Malaysia and Burma. The economic situation splintered further in the 1970s. Crunched by a global recession and the OPEC oil crisis, inflation soared and the British economy staggered to a halt. Unemployment rose dramatically. The situation seemed to reach a crisis point during the so-called ''Winter of Discontent'' in 1978-79. Major unions launched wage claims and

went on strike; the Labor government's thin majority disappeared; and the party lost a vote of confidence in the House of Commons.

When Margaret Thatcher took the office of prime minister in 1979, she vowed to subdue the unions—which she accused of crippling industrial growth—to minimize taxation, and to woo business interests back to Britain. After a tough first few years in office, Thatcher's reign looked shaky but was secured by victory in the Falklands War (1982).

The 1980s began with a bang and ended with a whimper: the economy boomed then went spectacularly bust. While many people profited from urban expansion—which affected small businesses and the real estate market—some went under. The increasing divide between rich and poor was viewed with concern by many in Britain's artistic community, and they were joined by others who were worried about the growing domination of corporate culture at the expense of community values.

Ayckbourn's *A Chorus of Disapproval,* which is set in the fictional Welsh town of Pendon, is ostensibly removed from such concerns. But Ayckbourn's decision to concentrate upon small-town life in fact enables him to create subtle social criticism. By depicting corruption, greed, and ''insider dealing'' within a small community, Ayckbourn demonstrates that 1980s corporate culture has eaten into even the smallest and most isolated of communities.

The inclusion of material from *The Beggar's Opera* points to an unfortunate truth: greed and corruption have long been part of British culture. But the BLM land scam represents a version of these age-old traits that is particular to the 1980s. Each schemer has a different ploy: Dafydd wants to avoid paying too much for land, Ian and Fay want to buy the land at a low price and sell it at a higher price, while Jarvis and Rebecca, the owners of the land, deliberately create false information in order to sell the land in a climate of false expectations. Nonetheless, the only true profiteer in this scheme is the corporation, BLM, which decides to down-size operations, lay off employees, and thus increase its profitability.

The Changing Position of Women

Although most people tend to think about contemporary feminism as originating simultaneous to

COMPARE
&
CONTRAST

- **1984:** The British economy is just recovering from the depression of the 1970s. This new boom period is led by a group of young urban professionals, whose conspicuous consumption leads to the coining of the pejorative term "yuppie."

  Today: The British economy went through a "boom and bust" cycle in the late-1980s and early-1990s but now seems more stable. All over the world people are speculating that the "new world order" has been accompanied by a shake-down in the economic system. In 1999, Europe took its final steps towards becoming an integrated economic system, while the Dow Jones Index (the primary indicator of the U.S. Stock Market) passed the 10,000 mark.

- **1984** After the success of the Falklands War in 1982, Prime Minister Margaret Thatcher won her second general election and returned the Conservative party to power. She narrowly escapes death when an IRA bomb explodes in her hotel at a Conservative Party conference.

  Today: After Prime Minister Tony Blair's New Labor party swept to victory in 1997, thus ending fifteen years of Conservative Party rule, Britain has moved closer to union with Europe, has continued the Northern Ireland peace talks, and has become increasingly involved in European peace-keeping.

- **1984:** The situation in Northern Ireland continues to deteriorate. The British government spends billions of pounds annually on maintaining their presence in Northern Ireland. Meanwhile, the Irish Republican Army's (IRA) massive campaign for improved prisoners' rights, known as the "Dirty Protest" and the "Blanket Protest," is followed by a tragic hunger strike that results in the death of eleven IRA prisoners.

  Today: Sinn Fein (the political arm of the IRA) leader Gerry Adams negotiates a peace accord with the Irish and British governments. A Republican cease-fire in 1995 was followed by a Loyalist cease-fire that year. The cease-fires have since been broken and then resumed; likewise, the 1997 Easter Peace Agreement promised much but has, as yet, delivered little. Hopes remain high for a peace settlement in Northern Ireland.

- **1984:** Royal Academy of Dramatic Art (RADA) graduate Kenneth Branagh emerges as a major talent at the Royal Shakespeare Company when he plays the title role in *Henry V* and Laertes in *Hamlet.* The production of *Henry V* is a major new interpretation of the long-ignored play and is critically and commercially successful.

  Today: Branagh has become one of Britain's most successful actors. He founded his own theater company, The Renaissance Theatre Company, in 1987, and has also directed and starred in several films, such as *Henry V* (1988), for which he earned Oscar nominations for best director and best actor. More recently he has appeared in Woody Allen's 1998 farce *Celebrity.*

---

counter-culture movements in the late-1960s, the movement for women's rights actually dates from the late-eighteenth century. Enlightenment philosophers and pamphleteers criticized the limited application of the doctrine of human rights, as developed in the American and French Revolutions, arguing that it should not be limited to men but should also include women.

During the nineteenth century in America, women's rights advocates fought side by side with advocates of abolitionism and of temperance for societal reform. By the early-twentieth century, the suffragette movement, which fought for women's right to vote and to own property in their own name, had won victories in Australia and New Zealand, and was soon to win victories in America and

Britain. Although feminists remained active after they won the right to vote, it was not until the 1960s that the movement returned to world-wide prominence.

Change does not happen overnight, however, and society today is still struggling to absorb the ramifications of this "revolution in female consciousness." Fay and Hannah represent different positions in this period of adjustment. Neither are interested in the women's rights movements, but both women have been affected by the social changes it wrought.

Fay is a product of the sexual liberation and experimentation of the 1960s and 1970s. Confident and attractive, she casually plans to swap sexual partners and uses her sexuality as leverage in the BLM land scam. Fay is no feminist: she neither seeks equality nor urges reform. Rather, she is an individualist who makes use of her sexuality for her own profit.

Both women are married, but Hannah's marriage is light years away from Fay's. Unlike Fay, Hannah has held to the traditional ideal of marriage. She is a mother, a housewife, and a wife. But Hannah is not happy, and her affair with Guy is the catalyst that enables her to break free from a stagnant situation. For the first time she can articulate all that is wrong with her marriage—as well as all that she values in Dafydd—and to imagine the possibility of life outside the home. Should she remain with her children and husband, and if so, at what cost? Will she leave her husband, as Nora does in Henrik Ibsen's *A Doll's House* (1879)? Or will she remain to work through her problems with Dafydd?

The audience does not need to know whether or not Hannah leaves Dafydd, for what is most important is that she has undergone a radical change in perception. Like many women in the 1970s and 1980s, Hannah's first step towards an improved place in society is a reevaluation of her commitment to domesticity.

CRITICAL OVERVIEW

Ayckbourn writes out the English comedic tradition made famous by such luminaries as Oscar Wilde and Noel Coward (*Hay Fever*). However, in the late-1960s, when Ayckbourn's career took off, the comedy of manners was no longer fashionable. Critics preferred more abstract writing of the style initiated in the Postwar period by the Irish playwright Samuel Beckett (*Waiting for Godot*) and, two decades later, his British imitators Harold Pinter (*The Homecoming*) and Tom Stoppard. Ayckbourn has always been popular with audiences, and critics have also come to value his work. His knighthood in 1987 confirmed his status as one of Britain's most influential and successful playwrights.

Critical reception of *A Chorus of Disapproval*'s debut was largely positive, and it has since become known as one of Ayckbourn's best plays. In his review in the *Guardian,* Michael Billington praised the play as "a magnificent comedy," and drew attention to the intricately plotted structure of the play. But his praise for Ayckbourn was not limited to the writer's technical prowess. Billington also argued that part of the reason that the play was "heart-breakingly funny" was because Ayckbourn's characterizations were so "psychologically acute."

Irving Wardle, writing in the London *Times,* emphasized precisely this same quality in Ayckbourn's writing. His review highlighted the darker elements of the play, particularly the passive nature of Guy Jones. Wardle claimed that Ayckbourn's characterization of Guy owed a considerable debt to Russian playwright Anton Chekhov. Like the title character in Chekhov's *Uncle Vanya* (1900), Guy is "a totally passive figure who throws a surrounding and highly assertive society into turmoil. Everyone defines Guy according to their own fantasy: as a lover, a crafty businessman, a Scot, or anything else that springs to mind." In Wardle's estimation, the play owes as much to the Russian comedic tradition as it does to the British comedic tradition.

Wardle argued the case for Chekhov, but Billington, in a 1990 essay, thought more of the influence of another Russian dramatist, Nikolai Gogol. The play, Billington argued, had an "unacknowledged source: Gogol's 1836 Russian comedy, *The Government Inspector.* In that, a humble St. Petersburg clerk arrives in a small provincial town, is mistaken for the Inspector General and is enthusiastically feted to prevent him exposing the bribery and corruption that is rampant in local government." Billington added, "Guy Jones . . . is very much like Gogol's Khlestakov." Given Ayckbourn's interest and familiarity with the Russian comic tradition—he adapted *The Forest* (1870), by Russian playwright Alexander Ostrovsky, for the National Theater—either of these claims may well hold true.

Billington also discussed an element that has fascinated other critics: Ayckbourn's use of the play-within-a-play. The device allows Ayckbourn to explore the lives of provincial townspeople and to emphasize the importance of art in everyday life. Ayckbourn uses the device to demonstrate "how art consumes, shapes, and organizes life."

Billington argued that as well as foregrounding the importance of art, the device of the play-within-a-play allowed Ayckbourn to comment upon contemporary society. "Gay's *The Beggar's Opera* famously demonstrated eighteenth-century low-life aping political corruption; Ayckbourn today shows bourgeois pillars of the community jovially pretending to be highwaymen and behaving with much the same shark-like rapacity when it comes to land deals." Richard Hornby, writing in the *Hudson Review,* agreed. Ayckbourn, he wrote, targets "sexual prudery, venality, and hypocrisy." The critic pointed out that even the amusing sub-plot about the BLM land deal had a direct parallel in Gay's *Opera:* "Gay's song 'I'm Bubbled,' refers to the South Sea Bubble, the great land scheme of the time, which is reflected in the shady scheme in the outer play." Indeed, most critics found that Ayckbourn's social commentary was a light-hearted but nonetheless constant undercurrent in the play.

Critical opinion about *A Chorus of Disapproval* has been remarkably consistent: all have praised Ayckbourn's rare ability to "weave so much sadness, pathos and bitterness into a play that is still a comedy." Almost all critics commented upon Ayckbourn's technical prowess: although he is an entirely different writer from Tom Stoppard, the two are often compared for their ability to create plays whose intricate structure and complex plots reveal considerable dramatic acumen. Now that the tide has turned and critics are finally taking Ayckbourn's talents with more than a pinch of salt, they seem united in the belief that Ayckbourn's contribution to British theater has been considerable and that *A Chorus of Disapproval* is rich proof of his achievements.

CRITICISM

Helena Ifeka

Ifeka is a Ph.D. specializing in American and British literature. In this essay she argues that A

A scene from director Michael Winner's film adaptation: Guy (Jeremy Irons) enacts the role of Macheath in the play within Ayckbourn's play

Chorus of Disapproval *marries social criticism with comedy through the close parallels between it and* The Beggar's Opera.

Alan Ayckbourn has always enjoyed popularity among audiences, but for too long his critical reputation suffered under the lingering suggestion that a writer of light farce had little, if anything, to say about contemporary society. This view has been modified in recent years, although it is still rare to find criticism of Ayckbourn that takes him seriously as a social critic. Even a play like *A Chorus of Disapproval,* in which the close parallels Ayckbourn draws between his play and John Gay's *The Beggar's Opera* are a clear comment on contemporary society, is usually discussed in terms of the play's artistic merits rather than its socially critical elements. Yet it is precisely through the "artistic" elements of the play that Ayckbourn develops his subtle criticism of (prime minister) Margaret Thatcher-era Britain. The key to understanding his integration of social criticism and comedy is the close parallel Ayckbourn creates between both plays and thus between Britain in the early-eighteenth century and the late-twentieth.

WHAT DO I READ NEXT?

- *A Chorus Line* (1975) is a Pulitzer Prize-winning musical about a group of young actors and actresses struggling to make it on Broadway. The play depicts the other side of Broadway—the sacrifices and hardships people endure to make it on the stage. It is also blessed with a wonderful score. It was conceived and choreographed by Michael Bennett; lyrics were written by Edward Kleban, and the music was created by Marvin Hamlisch. It played for over fifteen years on Broadway.

- Tom Stoppard's *The Real Thing* (1982) is another example of a contemporary British play that uses the device of a play-within-a-play. Like *A Chorus of Disapproval,* it is set squarely in the world of theater, although it is concerned with successful West End theater, not provincial companies. It is also focused on love and marriage.

- Bernard Shaw's *Pygmalion* (1913) is a classic comedy about a professor, Henry Higgins, who makes a bet that he can pass off a young Cockney flower-seller, Eliza Doolittle, as a society lady by teaching her standard English and manners. While the play is light-hearted, its depiction of Eliza's rise to social acceptance, and her subsequent rebellion against the professor, offers an astute commentary on the British class system.

- *The Importance of Being Earnest* (1895), by Oscar Wilde, is a classic light farce that is structured on a series of misunderstandings. John Worthing (Jack) and Algernon Moncrieff (Algy) are two men-about-town in pursuit of Gwendolyn Fairfax (Algy's cousin) and Jack's ward, Cecily Cardew. Both men use aliases to conceal their double lives. The play showcases Wilde's exceptional wit.

- Alan Ayckbourn modeled his first successful play, *Relatively Speaking* (1967), on Wilde's *The Importance of Being Earnest.* The play is a comedy of manners and the structure also hinges on hilarious misunderstandings between the four central characters.

- *The Beggar's Opera* is a ballad opera by the eighteenth-century librettist John Gay. It was first produced in 1728, and has been popular ever since. It is a musical comedy about a group of low-life Londoners who ape the manners of the bourgeois. Macheath, the protagonist, is a master thief and lover who is betrayed by his father-in-law, Peachum but is saved by a last-minute reprieve. The German playwright Bertolt Brecht, with composer Kurt Weill, created a modern version of the opera in 1928 called *The Threepenny Opera.*

Eighteenth-century Britain was a place of tremendous change and turmoil. Following the first great national revolution in Europe, the English Civil War (1640-1646), the Protector Cromwell closed the theaters and for fourteen years the stages were silent. The Restoration era of Charles II (1660) brought many changes to British politics and also transformed the stage: Charles reopened the theaters, supported them with royal patronage, and allowed women to appear on stage. By the early decades of the eighteenth century, the theater was the most popular form of public entertainment. In a culture that lacked television or cinema and in which literacy was the exception, not the norm, the theater offered everyone, rich and poor, spectacular visual effects and gripping stories.

Meanwhile, the explosion in print culture drew more and more would-be writers to London, who churned out sensational biographies of criminals and libertines, as well as penny-poetry, popular ballads, reviews, and essays. ''Grub Street'' supported an entire culture of print-shops, taverns, and coffee-houses, and playwrights preened in its praise or withered in its contempt.

The time was ripe for a writer who could soak up the juices of popular culture and entertain his audience with a new combination of satire, pathos, and humor; John Gay proved to be just such a man. *The Beggar's Opera* was first staged at Lincoln's Inn Fields in 1728, and, as John Brewer noted in *The Pleasures of the Imagination,* the play quickly ''became the talking point of the chattering classes. . . . At a time when most productions endured for less than a dozen performances, it lasted for an unprecedented sixty-two nights in its first season.''

Gay's ballad opera was a sensation. His backers and patrons had doubted whether the unusual mixture of popular ballads and operatic arias, a love story with tales from the criminal underworld, political satire, and pomp, would appeal to audiences, but they were proved wrong. The play was not only an overnight sensation, it became the most often performed play of the century. It was revived year after year until the late-1780s, and—just as contemporary Hollywood movie-makers extend their profits by selling toy and board game ''tie-ins'' to their mass market films—so could an audience member buy house screens, fans, and playing cards decorated with music and pictures from Gay's opera. There were no ''top ten'' charts then, but the songs from the opera were widely popular and allusions to the characters and language became commonplace.

The play appealed to audiences for a number of reasons, but a primary attraction was its sly commentary on contemporary society: the corruption of government officials and parliamentarians, the aristocratic pretensions of low-life criminals, and the self-serving social-climbing of lower-middle class ''shopkeepers.'' Audiences appreciated this sly social and political satire. *The Beggar's Opera* remained popular because the text lent itself ''to topical political allusion, which the performers often provided in improvisations or elaborations on the play's text.''

Ayckbourn's decision to center *Chorus*'s depiction of the inner workings of a small town dramatic society around Gay's ballad opera is thus not insignificant. The choice of the play-within-a-play immediately begs the audience to consider carefully the parallels between themes, plot, and characters, and as well as those between early-

''FLEXIBLE ETHICS, HOLLOW RESPECTABILITY, SEXUAL PROMISCUITY—THESE ARE THE TARGETS THAT GAY SCORED THROUGH WITH HIS QUILL AND AT WHICH AYCKBOURN, TWO HUNDRED AND FIFTY YEARS LATER, ALSO AIMED HIS PEN''

eighteenth century and late-twentieth century British society.

These parallels are not always immediately apparent. In Gay's opera, Captain Macheath is a highwayman, a charismatic figure noted for his gallantry, sexual allure, and wit. Guy Jones, whose very name speaks his ''everyman'' drabness, may well be ''manly'' and ''masculine,'' but it would a long shot to call him witty, wild, or dashing. Whereas Gay's eighteenth-century hero wins favor with the audience for his daring acts, Ayckbourn's late twentieth-century anti-hero is most noticeable for his passivity. Yet American director Mel Shapiro has argued that Guy's character is open to interpretation; rather than seeing him as naive and innocent, Shapiro's lead actor believed Guy was potentially conniving, knowing, and opportunistic and played the role accordingly. To act the part of a man acting a part is a tricky feat, but such an interpretation of Guy is not uncommon, particularly since Guy clearly ''grows into'' Macheath's character during the course of the play. Such an interpretation certainly makes for a juicer role and a more complex play.

The plots of each play also seem antithetical. *The Beggar's Opera* portrays the high times and misdemeanors of a highwayman—his involvement with Polly Peachum, Lucy Lockit, and Jenny Diver, and his betrayal by the mean-hearted Peachum and by one of his one gang, Jemmy Twitcher. *A Chorus of Disapproval* seems light years away from such material: here is no London low life but rather the respectable members of a small town community whose lives, if anything, seem stultifyingly dull.

It is precisely this superficial contrast that Ayckbourn exploits so craftily in his plotting of the play. *The Beggar's Opera* is staged by a ''Beggar'' in the shadow of the gallows. The audience expects that Macheath will be hanged at the end of the play. The opening scene of *A Chorus of Disapproval* makes clear to the audience that Guy is being shunned by his fellow cast members: the entire play takes place in the shadow of this rejection. This kind of parallel between the stage and gallows was a familiar analogy in Gay's day—public executions were a popular form of public entertainment, and the throngs who gathered to gawk at the condemned man were able to buy hot cider and watch bear-baitings while they waited.

The ending of Ayckbourn's play is further evidence of the structural similarity between it and *The Beggar's Opera.* In *The Beggar's Opera,* the last scene finds Macheath imprisoned, mourned over by his paramours, and about to be executed. But—against all expectation—he is granted a last-minute reprieve by the Beggar, who, as John Brewer neatly explains, ''justifies this unexpected twist of the plot by maintaining that 'an opera must end happily' and 'in this kind of drama 'tis no matter how absurdly things are brought about'.'' Likewise, in the last scene of *A Chorus of Disapproval,* the audience expects that after the curtain falls they will witness Guy Jones being served his just deserts. On the contrary, the production is a smash, and after the performance ends ''happily and triumphantly,'' the actors ''embrace each other, most especially their hero of the night, Guy himself.''

The structural similarity of the plays emphasizes Ayckbourn's close adherence to Gay's themes. Key amongst these are the social climbing and scheming of the bored middle class and the sexual promiscuity that hides behind the facade of respectable appearances. The chief targets of Ayckbourn's criticism are the BLM land schemers—Dafydd, Fay and Ian, and Jarvis and Rebecca. Each ''interest group'' attempts to extract information illegally from Guy, offering him a ''pay-off'' as a reward for his cooperation. Dafydd is a lawyer, and when at one moment he offers Guy an ''arrangement'' for his ''help,'' then adds that Guy should not share the information because ''I'd be betraying my own client. . . [it] wouldn't be ethical,'' the audience is at once amused and repulsed by such hypocrisy. The most artful plotter of all, Rebecca, who has spread rumors about BLM in order to inflate the land's price, bribes Guy and encourages him not to ''deny the rumor.''

The punch-line to their wheeling and dealing is that BLM is in fact about to down-size, not expand, and that the whole community will feel the impact of the cuts, including, of course, Guy himself. Ayckbourn parallels Dafydd's petty corruption with Peachum's but advances Gay's original satire one step further by suggesting that in the late-twentieth century, the only fish to grow fatter from such greedy skullduggery are the big multinational corporations.

Although the chief targets of Ayckbourn's satire are the original PALOS members, it is Guy's rise through the ranks that exemplifies the cast members' self-serving approach to life. Each step up the ladder of success until he wins the dubious honor of playing Macheath is the result of a helping hand—or, more accurately, a greased palm. Innocent to the fact that Guy's sticky fingers will soon be robbing him of his own wife, Dafydd first casts Guy as Crook-Fingered Jack. The female cast members support Guy's elevation to Matt of the Mint before Fay, hoping for information about BLM, secures him the role of Filch and offers him sexual favors. Finally, Rebecca seeks to secure Guy's silent acquiescence to her rumor-mongering by winning him the role of Macheath and sweetening the deal with five hundred pounds. Guy's ''casting couch'' climb to success parallels Macheath's equally immoral rise to fame, fortune, and popularity. Both men's bubbles are pricked by the intervention of ''justice'' in the form of an avenging man (Polly's father, Peachum in *Beggar's,* and Ian and Dafydd in *Chorus*).

Too often, Ayckbourn's critics allow their interest in his comedic talents to obscure his satiric skills. Ayckbourn's social criticism is never blunt or heavy-handed, but the very faculty for which he is so often praised—his ability to unite humor and pathos—succeeds in part because of his subtle criticism of contemporary society. It is the emotional damage that results from Guy's philandering and bribe-taking, and the ethical corruption of the PALOS members' property speculation, that packs *Chorus*'s punch. Moreover, the careful accrual of parallels between Gay and Ayckbourn's play—and their societies—broadens his social criticism from one small town to British society in general. Flexible ethics, hollow respectability, sexual promiscuity— these are the targets that Gay scored through with his quill and at which Ayckbourn, two hundred and fifty years later, also aimed his pen.

Source: Helena Ifeka, for *Drama for Students,* Gale, 2000.

Stanley Kauffman

Kauffman reviews the film adaptation of Ayckbourn's play, finding that the movie version does not match the charms of the original stage play.

Alan Ayckbourn is a phenomenon. He is by far the most prolific British playwright of his time; after beginning as an actor and director (he still directs), he began writing plays in 1959 and has had 37 produced. Most of these plays by report (who could have seen them all?) are comedies on dark subjects about the English middle classes. Vis-à-vis film, Ayckbourn's career has two odd aspects. First, for all his success, no play of his has been filmed until now. Second, the play that he chose to launch his film career is, in my limited Ayckbourn experience, one of his weakest.

A Chorus of Disapproval (Southgate) is set in Scarborough, that pretty coastal town in northeast England where Ayckbourn lives and runs a theater. A young widower (Jeremy Irons) is transferred to the town by the giant company that employs him. As soon as he settles in, he reads an ad calling for performers in an amateur production of Gay's *The Beggar's Opera*. He auditions; is accepted for a one-line role; then, by a series of accidents, moves to a larger role and eventually to the lead, MacHeath. He also gets involved with two married women in the cast. And he also gets involved, though quite honestly, in a scheme to profit by a land purchase his company is supposed to make.

Amateur theatricals can be, have been, serviceable in plots as catalyst and counterpoint. But Ayckbourn, who did the screen adaptation with the director, Michael Winner, makes only routine use of the amateur show itself and no use at all of Gay's work as counterpoint. Irons gets into jams with the two women, then gets out of them: nothing is arrived at one way or another. As for the land deal, it's just plot filler, with a hint of a threat that never materializes and a finish that's quite incredible.

Incredible, too, are scenes in which the director excoriates actors in terms they have no need to endure; in which the two wives fight over Irons in a restaurant; in which wife-swapping takes place with a blatancy that makes *Oh! Calcutta!* look prim.

About the only interest in Irons's performance is in the touch of Midlands accent he gives it (his character was born in Leeds). But Prunella Scales, familiar as John Cleese's wife in the *Fawlty Towers* TV series, plays one of the smitten wives in a worn yet winning way. Anthony Hopkins plays her hus-

band, Dafydd ap Llewellyn, the director of the show, with lilting Welsh accent and bullock energy. He rams right into the part, stocky and square, squinting in his left eye, evidently portraying a man he has met somewhere along the way. The script calls for him to do things we can't believe, but he's so good that we feel it's Dafydd who is trapped in the plot, not Hopkins.

Winner, a director who started as a mediocrity 25 years ago and has since declined, is not much help. In any effective sense, the screen debut of Ayckbourn the Prolific is yet to come.

Source: Stanley Kauffman, ''Truth and Inconsequences'' in the *New Republic,* Vol. 201, no. 11, September 11, 1989, pp. 26–27.

Richard Hornby

Hornby offers a favorable review of Ayckbourn's play.

A good play that recently transferred to the West End from the National is Alan Ayckbourn's *Chorus of Disapproval*. Ayckbourn has received little serious critical attention, probably because he is so often compared to our Neil Simon. Like Simon, he writes comedies of contemporary life, and like Simon, he makes a lot of money at it, but otherwise the two are very dissimilar. Simon creates mostly eccentric characters, who are sometimes hilarious and sometimes all too predictable; Ayckbourn creates drab, ordinary characters who turn out to be oddly interesting and always funny. Simon's main source of humor is in verbal gags; Ayckbourn almost never uses them, relying instead on character and situation. Finally, Simon has little sense of dramatic structure (his main weakness), while Ayckbourn is obsessed with it; play after play involves some technical novelty, as in *The Norman Conquests,* a trilogy in which the same play is simply repeated three times in different parts of the same house; each play can be viewed independently, and differs in tone and viewpoint from the others, yet has the same six characters and follows the same events.

In *Chorus of Disapproval,* the key technical device is a play within the play; a provincial amateur drama group is performing John Gay's eighteenth-century satire, *The Beggar's Opera* (also the source for Brecht's *Threepenny Opera*). The characters, as usual with Ayckbourn, are ordinary middle-class folk, who turn out to be involved in shady business deals, personal intrigue, and sexual aggres-

> "AYCKBOURN PLAYS OFF THE
> INNER VERSUS THE OUTER PLAY
> WITH GRACE AND HUMOR; GAY'S
> PLAY IS A SEND-UP OF THE SAME
> MIDDLE CLASS ATTITUDES AND
> VALUES, PARTICULARLY SEXUAL
> PRUDERY, VENALITY, AND
> HYPOCRISY, AS ARE HELD BY THE
> CHARACTERS PLAYING THEM."

sion. A naive new member joins the troupe, who immediately project their fantasies on him; although he is just a decent, unassuming fellow with no talent, holding an unimportant job in a large corporation, they see him as a great lover, shrewd businessman, and lead performer. Seduced by two women, drawn into both sides of a dubious land scheme, he simultaneously moves up in the cast as it undergoes the attrition that is typical of amateur groups, until he is playing the lead—by which time he has lost his job, his fellow performers have developed total contempt for him, and the women have dropped him.

Ayckbourn plays off the inner versus the outer play with grace and humor; Gay's play is a send-up of the same middle class attitudes and values, particularly sexual prudery, venality, and hypocrisy, as are held by the characters playing them. Gay's song ''I'm Bubbled,'' refers to the South Sea Bubble, the great land scheme of the time, which is reflected in the shady scheme in the outer play; Macheath's having two wives reflects his offstage problem of having two mistresses. Yet ironically there is no happy ending in the main, outer play as there is in *The Beggar's Opera.* Although his plays are very funny, Ayckbourn's vision is dark; sex is an ensnarement, while idealism and decency lead merely to loss. As with Chekhov, he combines an underlying sadness with great affection for his characters, yet is unsentimental about them.

In transferring to the West End, *Chorus* took on a largely new cast, all of whom were good, and one of whom, Colin Blakely as the obsessive Welsh director of the provincial amateur theatre company,

was especially fine. Ayckbourn himself directed, as he often does (he owns his own theatre in Scarborough, where he tries out most of his plays), skillfully handling the large cast, the many set changes, and the delightful comic business.

Overall, the British theatre continues to show tremendous strength, as it has for three decades. There are problems, complaints, scandals, and colossal failures, as there always are in the theatre (if anything, these are more prevalent in its greatest periods). In New York, fewer shows open each year, major theatres lie dark for months and even years, while prices rise enormously, yet theatre people seem blandly optimistic; in London, there is an explosion of theatrical activity, and people complain constantly. It is obvious which theatre is more alive!

Source: Richard Hornby, review of *A Chorus of Disapproval* in the *Hudson Review,* Vol. XXXIX, no. 4, Winter, 1987, pp. 642–43.

SOURCES

Billington, Michael. ''Art on Sleeve'' in the *Guardian,* August 2, 1985, p. 11.

Brewer, John. *The Pleasures of the Imagination: English Culture in the Eighteenth Century,* HarperCollins, 1997, pp. 354, and 441.

Shapiro, Mel. ''Directing *A Chorus of Disapproval*'' in *Alan Ayckbourn: A Casebook,* edited by Bernard F. Dukore, Garland, 1991, pp. 173-76.

Trussler, Simon. *Cambridge Illustrated History of the British Theatre,* Cambridge University Press, 1994.

Wardle, Irving. ''Painful Laughter'' in the London *Times,* August 2, 1985, p. 15.

FURTHER READING

Billington, Michael. *One Night Stands,* Nick Hern Books, 1993.
   This collection of the *Guardian*'s famous theater critic contains a good selection from two decades of criticism.

Bloom, Harold, editor. *John Gay's The Beggar's Opera,* New York: Chelsea House, 1988.
   An excellent collection of essays on the *Opera.*

Branagh, Kenneth. *Beginning,* London: 1989.

This entertaining autobiography provides insight into Branagh's meteoric rise to fame and into the world of the London theatre.

Brook, Peter. *The Empty Space,* London: 1968.
Brook was one of the most influential theater directors in Britain in the Postwar period. He was long associated with the Royal Shakespeare Company. His directorial style showed the influences of Antonin Artaud and Bertolt Brecht. This collection of his essays offers analysis on the basic problems facing contemporary theater; the work has influenced many British and foreign directors.

Hume, Robert, editor. *The London Theater World, 1660-1800,* Southern Illinois Press, 1980.
This wide-ranging study is well-written and provides plenty of information about British theater during John Gay's lifetime, offering background with which to compare Ayckbourn's settings and environment in *Chorus.*

Everyman

ANONYMOUS

1500

Everyman was first published in England early in the sixteenth century. This English play is now thought to be based on an earlier Dutch play, *Elckerlijc,* published in 1495. It is unknown if *Everyman* was ever staged in the era in which it first appeared. The title page states ''Here begynneth a treatyse.'' This implies that the text may have been intended as reading material. Frequently, authors composed a treatise containing dialogue to create an additional emphasis on an idea, in this case a preparation for God's judgment. Such works were often created without any intention of performance. This may be true for *Everyman;* however, even if it was not performed, it is clear that the text was very popular, since there are four separate editions from the first half of the sixteenth century that have survived to this day. Frequent reprintings indicate that the text was bought and read a great deal, if not performed.

Although none of the characters in *Everyman* have any depth, the influence on later drama is especially clear when readers compare the medieval character archetypes with those created for Elizabethan drama. Christopher Marlowe's *Dr. Faustus* is often cited as an example of how the medieval morality play influenced later theatre. Marlowe's characters would be easily recognizable to anyone who had read *Everyman.* There is also the same emphasis on worldly goods and on knowledge. But Marlowe takes the ideas in *Everyman* even further and argues that even knowledge can be perverted.

But the same idea that man can seek forgiveness and salvation through contrition still appears. *Everyman* is considered one of the most accessible of the medieval morality plays because the language is closer to modern English and the story is clearly told.

AUTHOR BIOGRAPHY

Everyman is a morality play that first appeared in England early in the sixteenth century. The author is unknown, but it has been speculated by scholars that the play was written by a cleric or under the direction of the church. It is now thought to be based upon a Dutch play, *Elckerlijk* ("Everyman"), written in 1495 by Petrus Dorlandus, a Carthusian monk. Four copies of the sixteenth century editions of *Everyman* still survive, with all four published between 1510 and 1535. Although the author is unknown, the play's content, themes, and ideology reflect those of Catholic Europe. The play's emphasis on good deeds as a mechanism for salvation reflects medieval Catholic ideology.

The use of Christianity as a topic and a force behind theatre reflects a significant change from Christian opposition to early drama. Traditionally, the Catholic Church opposed the theatre because it frequently included nudity, fights with wild beasts, and because Roman sacrifice of Christians was often included as a part of pagan spectacle. An additional reason for church opposition was the use of falsehood. In drama, an actor pretends to be someone else. Although modern audiences accept this as "acting," it was interpreted by the early church to be lying. By the tenth century, drama would again become acceptable to clergy when it was reborn as liturgical drama.

The earliest liturgical dramas were included as a part of the church service and frequently took the form of a simple dialogue, often sung, between two clerics. Eventually this exchange began to include additional participants and by the thirteenth century, these dramas became a means to educate an illiterate congregation. More elaborate staging of plays began to be included in feast day celebrations, and they eventually moved from the church to the town square, which accommodated a larger audience. Eventually plays were sponsored by various guilds or trades, and they became known as miracle or mystery plays, derived from the Latin word, *minister*. By the end of the fifteenth century, these early mystery plays evolved into morality plays, of which *Everyman* is the best known.

PLOT SUMMARY

Everyman is a one-act play that begins with a Messenger announcing the play's purpose: Everyman will be called before God, and thus every man should look to the end of his life even as he begins it. The sin that initially looks sweet will eventually cause the soul to weep. Then God appears and tells the audience that man has forgotten the sacrifice that God made for them at the crucifixion. God is angry and disappointed with man, who has embraced the seven deadly sins. Since man has turned to sin, God is demanding a reckoning. He calls for Death and instructs him to seek out every man who has lived outside God's law. Death is to bring forth these men for a final reckoning. Death promises to do so and seeing Everyman, Death asks him if he has forgotten his God. Everyman is unprepared for Death and is frightened at the journey Death proposes. After warning Everyman that his judgment is at hand, Everyman asks for time to find someone to accompany him in his pilgrimage.

Everyman first sees his friend, Fellowship, with whom he has spent so much time. Initially, Fellowship says he will accompany his friend wherever he is going, but when he hears of the destination, Fellowship declines. He will offer women and good times, but he will not go on a journey to face God's judgment. Everyman is disappointed in Fellowship's response but decides that family and blood ties might make stronger companions. With this thought in mind, he approaches Kindred. It initially seems that Kindred will accompany Everyman. But when Kindred learns of the destination, he also refuses to go. Everyman is feeling increasingly isolated.

Next, Everyman turns to Goods, for whom he committed so many of the sins that weigh heavily upon him. But Goods cannot leave earth's bounds; what man acquires on earth must be left behind when he dies. Goods's role is to tempt man to sin, and so Goods will go on to the next victim, since Everyman has no further use of Goods. The betrayal of these three—Fellowship, Kindred, and Goods—makes Everyman aware that he has trusted in the wrong things.

Everyman next asks Good Deeds for help, but Good Deeds is collapsed at Everyman's feet. He is shackled by Everyman's sins and cannot help. But Good Deeds suggests that Knowledge can be of help. Knowledge takes Everyman to visit Confession, where Everyman learns that knowledge of his sins and his repentance of them is the means to find salvation. The recognition of Everyman's sins lifts the burden from Good Deeds, who can now help Everyman prepare for his journey. As he sets out on the final leg of his journey, Everyman has several additional companions to go with him. Discretion, Beauty, Strength, and the Five Wits are coming along with him, but they can only accompany Everyman for part of the distance.

Everyman receives last rites from a priest and prepares to meet Death. The audience is reminded that the priest is God's representative on earth and that man must turn to priests to help him prepare for death. As the journey continues, each of his companions leaves Everyman. Beauty is the first to go, since beauty fades quickly as man approaches death. Next Strength departs, for as man's health fades, physical strength is also lost. Next Discretion leaves, and then Five Wits abandons Everyman. Finally, Knowledge departs, and only Good Deeds remains for the final journey. An Angel greets Everyman to escort him the remainder of the way, where only Good Deeds can speak for him. At the play's conclusion a Doctor of Theology appears to remind the audience that all men must make this journey and that only their good deeds will speak for them at God's final reckoning.

CHARACTERS

Angel

The Angel appears briefly at the play's conclusion to accept Everyman into God's domain. Because of his virtue, Everyman will be accepted immediately into heaven with God.

Beauty

Beauty is one of the companions that Everyman calls forth to accompany him for part of his journey to God. And while beauty can offer some comfort to Everyman, it is the first to depart when man begins the final journey to death.

Confession

Knowledge leads Everyman to Confession. Confession represents man's best opportunity for salvation, since acknowledging Everyman's sins and asking God for forgiveness is an important element of Catholicism. Although Knowledge can accompany Everyman part way on his journey, Knowledge cannot complete the journey with him.

Cousin

When approached by Everyman, Cousin also declines to join his relative on his last journey. Instead, he states he would rather subsist on bread and water for five years than face God's judgment.

Death

Death is the means by which God will force Everyman to undertake a pilgrimage to God's forgiveness. He seeks out Everyman, whom he describes as only focused on earthly lusts and money. Death tells Everyman that he is to begin his final journey immediately and refuses an offer of riches, but Death finally allows Everyman an opportunity to prepare for his journey and to seek out a friend who might accompany him. Death is allegorical, as are all characters in this play.

Discretion

Discretion is one of the companions that Everyman calls forth to accompany him for part of his journey to God's final judgment. Discretion represents Everyman's ability to do the correct thing, to make the right choices in following God.

Doctor

A Doctor of Theology makes the final speech. He tells the audience to remember that all of Everyman's companions—Beauty, Strength, Discretion, and Five Wits—abandoned him on his final journey. It is only man's good deeds that will save him.

Everyman

Everyman is a wealthy man who is suddenly called by Death to begin his journey to God. Everyman is not ready to go, since he has not prepared for this day and has more sins than good deeds to his credit. He pleads with Death to give him a brief time to find friends who will be willing to accompany him on his pilgrimage. After being rejected by friends, family, and his own wealth,

Everyman comes to realize that he has put his faith in the wrong things. Through the guidance of Knowledge and Good Deeds, Everyman is prepared to make a final appearance before God. In the end, after all his earthly friends and companions have abandoned him, it is only his Good Deeds that speak for Everyman's worth. Everyman is allegorical and represents the choices open to all men.

Fellowship

Fellowship is the first friend that Everyman greets. Initially Fellowship is willing to help Everyman in whatever way he needs, but upon learning of Everyman's request, Fellowship is forced to deny him. The journey to face God is not one he is willing to make. Like all the other characters, Fellowship is allegorical and represents man's reliance upon earthy, transient, and superficial friendships, which are not a part of man's heavenly life. While Fellowship is Everyman's friend in drinking and lusting after women, he will not face God's judgment with his friend.

Five Wits

Five Wits are the counselors that Everyman calls forth to accompany him for part of his journey to God. The Five Wits represent man's senses and the ability to understand God's commandments and the world around him. The senses lead to reason and a way in which Everyman is able to understand and appreciate the world he inhabits.

God

God is the first character to speak and tells the audience that man appears to have forgotten the sacrifice that God made at the crucifixion. Instead, man lives in wicked sin. God, who is angry, calls Death to bring forth a reckoning of those sinners who have ignored God's mercy.

Good Deeds

Good Deeds is at first very weak and cannot rise up from the ground, since Everyman's sin keeps her bound. But she instructs Everyman to seek out knowledge for help in preparing for his journey. After Everyman has done as Knowledge instructs, Good Deeds is ready to accompany Everyman before God. It is man's good deeds that will speak for his worth at God's final judgment. Good Deeds is the only character who can accompany Everyman the entire way and, as such, is representative of

Catholic belief that it is a reliance on good deeds that will provide man with salvation before God.

Goods

Goods represents all the riches that Everyman has accumulated in his lifetime. Goods also declines to accompany Everyman on his pilgrimage, reminding him that Goods cannot leave the earthly realm (reinforcing the cliche ''you can't take it with you''). Goods also reminds Everyman that it is because of his focus on material wealth that he is now at risk before God's judgment. Goods has been lent to Everyman for only a short period of time, he tells him, and now he will move on to deceive another man. Goods is another allegorical figure that represents man's interest in riches rather than prayer.

Kindred

Like Cousin, Kindred also forsakes Everyman's pleas. He tells him he would give him a wanton woman to enjoy, but he will not accompany Everyman to answer before God. Kindred and Cousin both indicate that man cannot trust upon family to intercede before God.

Knowledge

Knowledge leads to Everyman's redemption, because it is knowledge of his sins that leads Everyman to ask for God's forgiveness. Knowledge represents a consciousness of Christianity and God's will and is the fundamental tenet of salvation. While Knowledge can lead Everyman to Good Deeds, Knowledge cannot accompany him all the way on his journey before God, indicating that learning has only limited utility in saving one's soul.

Messenger

The Messenger appears in the prologue to introduce the play and its subject matter. Messenger reminds the audience that while sin may be enjoyed during life, by the end of life, it will cause the soul to weep. The Messenger also reminds the audience that the material, transient things that man values in his corporeal existence will be worthless in the next life.

Strength

Strength is one of the companions that Everyman calls forth to accompany him for part of his journey to God. Strength will make Everyman stronger for his journey, but as he prepares for death, the strength of the body also leaves, and finally Strength is forced to abandon the final journey.

THEMES

Alienation and Loneliness

As Everyman is abandoned by Fellowship, Kindred, and Goods, he begins to feels increasingly isolated and alone. When his overtures to Fellowship are rejected, Everyman thinks that surely his family will stand by him as he faces his final judgment. Instead, what he discovers is that every man must face God's judgment alone. Earthly friendships and family are left behind in such a situation, and man is never more isolated than in facing death.

Atonement and Forgiveness

When Everyman is feeling most afraid and alone, he is given the opportunity to atone for his sins. The recognition of his sin, provided by Knowledge, leads to his meeting with Confession and to penance. The medieval Christian tradition is that man must seek atonement for earthly sins, but that God's forgiveness is always available to those who truly repent. At the end of *Everyman,* forgiveness is given freely and Everyman is prepared to meet God.

Betrayal

Everyman has placed his faith in friends and family. They have been his companions throughout life and each initially indicates their willingness to accompany him on a journey—Fellowship even vows to accompany his friend to Hell. But Fellowship and Kindred are both afraid of the real hell; both decline Everyman's invitation when they learn he is going to meet God's final judgement. This indicates that man will always be betrayed by earthly companions, since each man is ultimately selfish and must confront God alone. Their betrayal of Everyman serves a purpose, however, as their rejection forces him to search for greater truths.

Death

Death is the means by which man finally meets God. It is impending death that forces Everyman to consider his life and his accomplishments. Like most men, Everyman is unprepared for death and seeks extra time. In this respect he is like all men,

who would plead for time to make final plans and, most importantly, to make peace with God. Generally, most Christian religions suggest that death is not to be feared, but that a better, eternal existence will be known as a result of death. Still, the approach of death is often the most frightening experience that man will face. Everyman is no exception to this idea.

God and Religion

Plays such as *Everyman* are intended to help reinforce the importance of God and religion in people's lives. In this play, God represents salvation, but it is religion that provides the means to achieve that salvation. Like most drama of the medieval period, the focus of this play is how religion and a belief in God will help man overcome any travail, including death. Although God appears as a character only at the beginning of the play, his presence is felt throughout as Everyman begins to recognize his need for help beyond the earthly realm.

Good Deeds

According to Catholic belief, it is man's accounting of himself and his good deeds that will provide admittance to heaven. Thus it is only Good Deeds who can accompany Everyman on his final journey. When faced with God's judgment, man's riches, the notoriety of his friends, and the importance of his family will not speak for his worth. Only the good deeds that a man does here on earth can speak for him before God. Accordingly, good deeds is more important than faith in achieving salvation.

Knowledge

When abandoned by his friends, it is Knowledge that leads Everyman to the help he needs. It is knowledge that helps man to recognize and understand how he has sinned. It is knowledge that permits him to recognize deception and falsehoods. And finally, it is knowledge that allows Everyman to find the way to Confession and penance. If it is only his good deeds that can save man, it is knowledge that allows man to recognize the importance of good deeds in finding salvation.

Sin

Sin is the reason for this play. It is sin that angers God in the opening lines. As a theme, sin is central, since it is Everymen's sins that force his

TOPICS FOR FURTHER STUDY

- *Everyman* is an morality play. Discuss how morality plays influenced Renaissance dramas, especially those of Christopher Marlowe and William Shakespeare. You might consider either *Dr. Faustus* or *Macbeth* as examples of later morality plays.

- In what way are all the characters of *Everyman* allegorical?

- If you were staging this play, how would you costume the characters? Would you consider modern dress, something from science fiction, or do you think medieval costuming would work best? Be prepared to defend your choice as important to increasing the audience's understanding of the play.

- Research the development of medieval morality plays in England.

- Considering the roots of medieval morality plays like *Everyman,* why do you think they remain popular today? How or why does sixteenth-century religious drama speak to a modern need for religion in man's life?

- Compare *Everyman* to another readily available morality play like *The Second Shepherd's Play.* What can such plays tell us about medieval life?

- It is thought that the tenets of modern civilization have their roots in early drama. What modern values and beliefs can you identify in the ideas presented in *Everyman?*

---

final judgment. He has sinned much in his life, and the audience is told that his sins are so great that Good Deeds is immobile. Only when he can recognize and renounce his sins can Everyman be saved.

ed this drama to instruct the audience. Since few people were literate, a medieval writer could use drama to tell a story or teach a moral. The lesson in this play is how to lead a proper religious life and prepare for death and God's judgement.

STYLE

Archetype

The word archetype is generally used to describe a character who represents a pattern from which all characters or "types" are derived. The term derives from the work of Carl Jung, who expressed the theory that behind every unconscious lies the collective memories of the past. In literature, the term is often applied to a character type or plot pattern that occurs frequently and is easily recognized. In *Everyman,* Death is such a character, and the audience would immediately recognize this character and his purpose in the plot.

Audience

Authors usually write with an audience in mind. Certainly the unknown author of *Everyman* intend-

Character

The actions of each character are what constitute the story. Character can also include the idea of a particular individual's morality. Characters can range from simple stereotypical figures to more complex multi-faceted ones. Characters may also be defined by personality traits, such as the rogue or the damsel in distress. Characterization is the process of creating a life-like person from an author's imagination. To accomplish this the author provides the character with personality traits that help define who he will be and how he will behave in a given situation.

Everyman differs slightly from this definition, since each character is little more than a "type." The audience does not really know or understand the character as an individual. For instance, Fellow-ship represents little more than a quality, not an

A scene from a production staged by the Royal Shakespeare Company

individual. The audience understands that Fellowship signifies the friendships than men have while here on earth.

Drama

A drama is often defined as any work designed to be presented on the stage. It consists of a story, of actors portraying characters, and of action. But historically, drama can also consist of tragedy, comedy, religious pageant, and spectacle. In modern usage, drama explores serious topics and themes but does not achieve the same level as tragedy. In *Everyman,* drama is aligned with spectacle and is intended as a mechanism to instruct the audience on how to prepare for death.

Genre

Genres are a way of categorizing literature. Genre is a French term that means "kind" or "type." Genre can refer to both the category of literature such as tragedy, comedy, epic, poetry, or pastoral. It can also include modern forms of literature such as drama, novels, or short stories. This term can also refer to types of literature such as mystery, science fiction, comedy, or romance. *Everyman* is a morality play.

Morality Play

Following the revival of theatre in the eleventh century, the Catholic Church began to introduce brief dramatized episodes into the mass on the occasion of major festivals. These gradually developed into complete plays, performed in public places by the trade guilds, and were known as mystery plays. In some towns, there was a cycle of dramatized stories from the Creation to the Last Judgement. These were succeeded in the fifteenth century by morality plays, allegorical presentations of human vices and virtues in conflict. Among these, *Everyman* is perhaps the best known.

Parable

A parable is a story intended to teach a moral lesson. The story in *Everyman* is designed to teach people to lead a good, religious life so that they may properly prepare for death and the afterlife. The Bible is one of the most obvious sources of parables, since religion traditionally relies upon stories to teach lessons. This tradition stems from a period in which most men and women could not read, and the clergy found that stories were the most effective way to instruct moral lessons.

Plot

This term refers to the pattern of events within a play. Generally plots should have a beginning, a middle, and a conclusion, but they may also be a series of episodes connected together. Basically, the plot provides the author with the means to explore primary themes. Students are often confused between the two terms; but themes explore ideas, and plots simply relate what happens in a very obvious manner. Thus the plot of *Everyman* is how a man searches for a friend to accompany him to his final judgment. But the theme is how man can find salvation in God and Good Deeds.

HISTORICAL CONTEXT

Cultural Changes in England

The end of the fifteenth century marked the end of the medieval period in England. The sixteenth century brought with it the first of the Tudor kings and a period of relative peace following the civil wars that had plagued England during much of the preceding century. And although it was still present in smaller, yearly outbreaks, the threat of the Black Death (a plague that had killed a large portion of the European population) had finally decreased. England at the beginning of a new century was becoming a good place to live. The first of the Tudors, King Henry VII, formed alliances with neighboring countries and trade flourished in London. The cloth made from the wool of English sheep became an important commodity in Europe trading.

The ascension of commerce, however, changed the face of England. Once a predominantly agrarian culture, the cities of England—especially London—became more densely populated and urban. Farm lands were enclosed, and displaced rural families fled to the larger cities, where crowding, unemployment, and plague were a greater problem. The feudal order was ending, as well as the era of knights on horseback, who became obsolete after Henry V proved that there was a more efficient way to win a battle. Literacy increased, too, as moveable typesetting made books and other printed material more available.

Drama in the Fifteenth Century

The Renaissance began in Italy during the fifteenth century, but it did not begin in England until the early part of the sixteenth century; thus *Everyman* really represents one of the last medieval plays to be written. For the people of the medieval period, the Catholic church was the center of their lives. Its teaching guided all their actions, and its rules provided people with a pattern upon which to base all behaviors. The teachings of the church and its masses were in Latin, which few except the most learned could understand; the church held a position of authority that could not be challenged by the majority of those under its rule. Its representatives were charged with interpreting the word of God to the people, who trusted blindly in their clergy. The Catholic church still maintained a strong hold on England at the beginning of the sixteenth century. But the first stirrings of the Reformation were being felt in Europe, and by the last year that *Everyman* was reprinted, 1537, the Catholic church's rule in England had ceded to Protestantism.

Medieval drama was originally derived from church liturgy. In the ninth century, musical elaboration of the Latin liturgy began to appear as part of certain feasts. The purpose was to heighten and enhance the religious experience of the worshipers,

COMPARE & CONTRAST

- **1495:** Henry VII is king of England. Catholicism is still the religion of the country and will remain so for the next thirty years.

  Today: Because of a bloody history of oppression and suppression, anti-Catholic feelings in Great Britain have remained high since the mid-sixteenth century when Mary I had Protestants burned at the stake.

- **1495:** The Black Death (also known as the Plague), continues to claim lives. The death toll has decreased from the fourteenth century, when one-third of Europe's population died from the disease. Still, thousands will die from the Plague over the next few years.

  Today: The Plague is almost non-existent in England, although it still exists in some areas of the world. Even the American Southwest records deaths from the disease each year.

- **1495:** The Spanish Inquisition continues to persecute all ''heretics'' (those who disagree with Catholic doctrine) with religious zeal. Many are put to death for questioning the church.

  Today: Religious belief is still a significant cause of warfare and death in many countries. In

Ireland, Protestants and Catholics have begun a fragile peace. In the Middle East, religious zealotry continues to fuel terrorist actions.

- **1495:** Exploration of the New World has continued since Christopher Columbus's voyages in 1492. In the next year, England will send the first of its explorers, John Cabot, to claim land in England's name.

  Today: Modern explorers are now heading into space. Often dubbed ''the final frontier,'' space is now the region humankind is examining for possible habitation and resources.

- **1495:** A year earlier, the first English paper mills opened. This, combined, with the new moveable type presses, means that more books can be printed for at a significantly reduced cost. The movement toward literacy in England has begun.

  Today: Although it was earlier prophesied that computers and the Internet would mean the end of printed materials, books, magazines, and newspapers continue to enjoy a huge audience. Many publications are flourishing as both print and electronic media.

---

and by the tenth century, brief enactments of biblical episodes were practiced at monasteries and abbeys. The most famous was an Easter morning re-enactment of the three Marys asking for Jesus at his grave. Clerics dressed for the parts and sang the piece as dialogue, answering one another.

These ''tropes,'' as they were called, were not plays exactly, but they contained elements of drama. They had progressive plots, brief development of character, conflict, resolution, and visual spectacle. Over a period of 100 years, tropes became more elaborate and more complicated. The topics were usually biblical and the actors were clerics, monks, and choirboys. But the language was Latin rather than native languages, and the audiences were al-

most exclusively limited to those living in monastic communities.

Widespread deaths from the plague changed the nature of medieval drama and opened the way for another type of drama. When labor became scarce and expensive, people moved into the cities, which became centers of economic and cultural growth. Cycle or mystery plays evolved in towns and cities and were sanctioned by the church. Vast productions that taught Christian history and values were produced in the towns with lay-people as actors and as a part of feast day celebrations. Each guild was assigned a story, from Creation to Judgment, and each guild produced a pageant that best fit the guild's purpose. A great many of the townspeople participated as stage crew, actors, managers, and supporting cast. The audiences were large, drawn from everyone within traveling distance. Eventually, morality plays grew from this beginning. However, with the coming of the great Elizabethan theatre (the works of Shakespeare and others), morality plays disappeared as the evolving society demanded more elaborate entertainments.

CRITICAL OVERVIEW

There is no record of *Everyman* being produced on stage during the medieval period. The title page refers to the work as a treatise, and occasionally such works were fashioned as dialogues between characters. This was especially true when the author intended the work to provide a moral lesson. Whether *Everyman* was ever performed or not, it proved popular among readers, achieving four reprintings in the first years following its publication. But with the move to a Protestant religion in England—and the development of the more sophisticated Elizabethan theatre—the morality plays of the medieval period were forgotten. *Everyman* was not reprinted again until 1773 and was then regarded as an artifact of the ancient past. However, by the nineteenth century, medieval drama became an important topic of study, and eventually interest in *Everyman* surged enough to warrant a production in 1901.

In William Poel's 1901 staging in Canterbury, England, *Everyman* achieved dramatic success, according to a critic writing for the *Athenaeum,* because the play's "naive simplicity and uncompromising sincerity" had modern appeal. Although the reviewer referred to the play as primitive drama, he also found that this drama, "which seems so dull and didactic, may well have passioned our forefathers—this is, indeed, capable of passioning us." This acknowledgment of the play's strength after 500 years of dormancy must have been gratifying for the director.

Everyman, claimed the critic, had the possibility of becoming a sensation during the 1901 London theatre season. The review in the *Athenaeum* recognized that the play's focus on religion and salvation might appear quaint or dated, but the critic said that "Temptations to ridicule presented themselves, and the smile rose occasionally to the lips. It died there, and sank before the absolute sincerity of the whole. Amusement never degenerated into mockery." Accordingly, the ideas depicted in *Everyman* may have

interest and application in a more modern world. Of the staging, this critic noted that Everyman was "admirably played by a woman," although the role of God was more traditionally cast as an elderly man. Interestingly, the role of Death was played without the traditional scythe.

A review of a 1902, Manchester, England, performance cited the "amazing ingenuity, judgment and care" of the production. C. E. Montague, writing for the Manchester *Guardian,* described in detail the stage settings, which more closely approximated fifteenth-century Italian design, rather than fifteenth-century English work. Montague opined that the staging more closely reflects the ideas that Englishmen have about the fifteenth century, rather than the reality. One area deserving of praise, according to Montague, were the performances. It was a "seriousness and simplicity of method" that made the cast stand out. In dealing with such a serious topic, the cast was able to achieve "the right tragic effect of outward expression" so necessary to play the parts. Calling attention to one actor's performance, Montague noted that "the set and immobile face, level delivery, and almost unchanged position of Death were curiously effective in enhancing the solemnity of his first message to Everyman."

One negative observation in the *Guardian* review concerned the performance of Good Deeds, who Montague felt had a "rather overdone plaintiveness" and whose dialogue was sometimes not audible. In summary, however, Montague declared that the stage management was "masterly."

A New York production was also the subject of positive reviews in 1903. Elizabeth Luther Cary, writing for the *Critic,* acknowledged American audiences might be confused by a play so removed from traditional drama, but she stated that the play "seems to have aroused among its audiences a feeling in which admiration, interest, curiosity, and bewilderment are more or less evenly blended." Cary found that this production of *Everyman* was "so consistent, so simple, so genuine, so moving, and so entirely outside the bounds of modern convention [that it] is disturbing unless the tradition to which it conforms is clearly in mind." Cary pointed out that audiences must understand the play within its literary tradition.

In appraising the performances, it was the role of Everyman that earned the greatest praise from Cary. Of the actress who assumed the role, Cary said, "her interpretation is the fire of life to the naive little play which, with all its qualities, could very easily be made an affair of external and merely archaeological interest. Subtle feeling for the psychological situation raises her performance to a very high level of modern dramatic art, while the simplicity and frankness of the allegory are not sacrificed in the least degree.'' In the end, stated Cary, the ''power and charm of the acting'' dominate the performance.

In the latter half of the twentieth century, *Everyman* has achieved a level of popularity as a subject for study, particularly as interest in England's medieval period has increased. Often cited as the best representation of morality plays and of medieval drama in general, *Everyman* appears in many anthologies of drama. The play continues to be taught in college English courses and occasional productions can be found at universities.

CRITICISM

Sheri E. Metzger

Metzger is a Ph.D. specializing in literature and drama at the University of New Mexico. In this essay, she discusses how theme and character development can be employed to stage Everyman *in a manner that appeals to modern audiences.*

One of the significant problems with any modern staging of *Everyman* is that contemporary audiences have trouble appreciating the play on the same level that medieval viewers would have. The play's original audiences understood the role of religion in their lives. They believed in the reality of death, the afterlife, heaven and hell. In a period where the plague was likely to cut short life, where infant mortality was so high that people expected their children to die, and where the church could dictate behavior, the fear of death, of hell, and of Satan assumed a much larger role in life. Those factors are all much more abstract now, and modern audiences would find that fear, which Everyman experiences when faced with an unprepared death, very foreign. But the play has modern appeal, according to several writers who argue that with the correct emphasis, *Everyman* can transcend 600 years of cultural history to find a modern audience.

A successful contemporary staging of *Everyman* is possible, according to Ron Tanner in the *Philological Quarterly,* especially if the production emphasizes the irony that is present in the plot. In his essay, Tanner argued that one important key to appreciating the irony in *Everyman* is in visualizing the presentation of death. The medieval audience, Tanner noted, would have been horrified at seeing Death's approach on stage, and when Everyman attempts to bargain with or bribe Satan, the audience would have been shocked but also ''tickled'' at Everyman's nerve. Tanner argued that Everyman's ''gall is almost admirable.'' When confronted by death, Everyman says, ''thou comest when I had thee least in mind.'' This bit of irony is common to all humans, and most can appreciate Everyman's next words: ''a thousand pound shalt thou have, / And defer this matter to another day.'' To bargain with death, to attempt a bribe is what all men would have liked to do but what few would have even considered. When Everyman observes, ''I may say Death giveth no warning,'' the audience once again can laugh at Everyman's foolishness. Death gives no warning and Death takes no bribes. Every member of the medieval audience would recognize the foolishness of Everyman's words. Tanner pointed out that this irony is more evident in production than in simply reading the text, but even absent a staging, the play's humor is clearly evident in the text.

A second place where irony or humor might be emphasized in production is in the first half of the play when Everyman is searching for someone to accompany him in his journey to meet God. Certainly the play ceases to be humorous once Everyman falls victim to despair and Knowledge enters the play, but while Everyman is seeking the help of Fellowship, Kindred, and Goods, there is humor in their exchanges, humor that a modern audience can appreciate. When Fellowship offers to accompany his good friend, saying that even if ''thou go to hell, / I will not forsake thee,'' the audience understands the irony in those words.

Fellowship, who easily promises to go ''to hell'' with his friend, has in mind a more decadent location on earth. Fellowship suggests a more localized hell, one where women and drink occupy their attention. In fact, when he learns of Everyman's true destination, Fellowship admits that he is afraid of having to give an accounting to God. And when reminded by Everyman that he promised to accompany him to hell, Fellowship admits to having made that promise, and says, ''but such pleasures be set aside.'' The use of ''pleasures'' makes it clear that Fellowship intended his own definition of hell. As Tanner noted, Fellowship makes seven promises to help, each one equally elaborate, before he learns Everyman's destination.

WHAT DO I READ NEXT?

- *The Second Shepherd's Play* is one of two nativity plays that has survived from the medieval period. Both the author and the exact date of publication are unknown, but this mystery play is thought to date from the mid-fifteenth century. Like *Everyman,* it is a good example of the religious influence on early European drama.

- *The Chester Pageant of Noah's Flood* is another early English mystery play. It dates from the mid-fifteenth century and was so popular that it was still being performed late into the sixteenth century.

- *The York Cycle of the Creation and the Fall of Lucifer* is one of the earliest mystery plays. Like

many other medieval dramas, the author is unknown and the exact date of publication is also undiscovered.

- Christopher Marlowe's *Dr. Faustus* is an Elizabethan example of how morality plays influenced the drama of the late-sixteenth century. Archetype characters, though more developed than in morality plays, are still easily recognizable in this play.

- *The Chester Pageant of the Harrowing of Hell* could easily serve as a model for the last scene in *Dr. Faustus.* The descent of Christ into hell was a popular medieval legend that appeared in many of the mystery plays.

Everyman's interview with Kindred and Cousin also fails to advance his need for company on his journey. When apprised of the nature of his pilgrimage, Kindred states that he would rather exist only on bread and water for five years than face God. The speed with which he chooses a fast over facing God is humorous, since he wasted no time in making such idle promises. When faced with more pleadings from Everyman, Cousin claims to have a "cramp in my toe." His evasiveness is funny, although the audience understands that Everyman's plight is very serious. This intermingling of brief humor in the face of tragedy portends the formula that William Shakespeare would later adopt for his tragedies one hundred years later. The audience needs a few brief moments of laughter to recover from the tragedy unfolding on stage.

Another moment of laughter occurs when Everyman seeks help from Goods. By now it is clear to the audience the direction the play is taking, and the only surprise remains the means that Goods will take to avoid helping Everyman. Goods is very direct in his refusal to help; the irony comes near the end of their exchange. Goods, having told Everyman that he should have used his money to help the poor, completes his task by saying that he must be off to

deceive another just as he has deceived Everyman. He exits the stage, saying, "Have good day," as if Everyman was not facing imminent death and final judgment. Since the very next scene is an encounter with Good Deeds and a shift to more serious ideas, the audience needs this last little ironic reminder from Goods.

Another view of the play's adaptability to modern theatre is suggested by Carolynn Van Dyke in *Acts of Interpretation, The Texts in Its Contexts 700-1600,* who focused on allegory in her argument that *Everyman* can find an audience in today's students. Van Dyke pointed out that allegory offers opportunities for actors to transcend the time period in which the play is written to create a more modern and more easily appreciated representation of the central characters. She argued that the characters in *Everyman* are realistic, that "they behave like familiar individuals."

This characterization takes the characters beyond the limitations of pure allegory. Fellowship is not simply an abstract representation of Everyman's friends. He is a real character with whom the audience may identity. Friends often promise what they cannot deliver; students and audiences will

> ONE OF THE SIGNIFICANT PROBLEMS WITH ANY MODERN STAGING OF *EVERYMAN* IS THAT CONTEMPORARY AUDIENCES HAVE TROUBLE APPRECIATING THE PLAY ON THE SAME LEVEL THAT MEDIEVAL VIEWERS WOULD HAVE"

recognize that reality. Van Dyke maintained that "those characters' material forms not only represent but also redefine their names." Each character has a distinct personality or at least has the promise of a distinct personality, if given the opportunity in performance. It is actors who infuse personality into these abstract characters. "As categories and abstractions," Van Dyke noted, "they cannot be fully realized by any creature." But, she continued, "their embodiment in individual actors . . . must call upon the techniques of realistic characterization." With a skillful actor, the relationship between text, ideas, and audience can become clearer. The actor is infused with identity, and the audience has a practical application of the ideas.

Writing in *Studies in Philology,* Stanton Garner also argued that medieval morality plays must be viewed within their medium to be fully appreciated and that thus far, plays such as *Everyman* have not been valued as theatre pieces because modern audience fail to understand their correct role within the genre of drama. Although Garner was not focusing on humor, he was arguing that the visualization of characters, such as Death, is crucial to appreciating the play. Garner noted that "in performance, a stage devil is physically *there,* in real proximity to the audience, and with every gesture and movement he draws attention to his immediacy. The audience is forced to acknowledge and be aware of Death because he is not an abstract character drawn on the page. Instead, he becomes a personification of the Death that threatens all men."

Garner pointed out that this living embodiment of Death helps to suggest a world beyond the limited locations created by the words of the text. Instead of Death as an abstract concept representing a world beyond the audience's imagining, there appears on stage a form that suggests reality. Salvation ceases to be an abstract promise of the church and becomes instead, the "presence of the here-and-now." Garner made the additional observation that the audience can only understand Everyman's aloneness by seeing the play in performance. The reader understands that Everyman becomes increasingly isolated as Fellowship, Kindred, and Goods abandon him. But the audience actually sees these characters leave the stage never to return, and with each departure, Everyman becomes increasingly isolated.

Although *Everyman* proved very popular with medieval readers, there is no evidence that it was staged during that period, and records citing performance after 1600 make no mention of the play's staging. There have been, however, a number of successful productions in the twentieth century. In 1901, William Poel's staging of *Everyman* was so successful that he took it on the road in England, Scotland, and Ireland. He eventually brought the play to the United States. Its United States tour was successful enough that British productions of the play returned several more times in the next thirty years. Today, *Everyman* is occasionally staged at colleges and universities, as well as by church organizations. But these productions are either academic in nature or focused on religious ideology. Tanner, Van Dyke, and Garner have all argued that this play has value beyond such limited focus. A closer evaluation of the plot and characters would support such a move.

Source: Sheri E. Metzger, for *Drama for Students,* Gale, 2000.

David Kaula

In the following essay, Kaula, a specialist in Elizabethan literature, compares and contrasts Everyman *and Christopher Marlowe's* Dr. Faustus, *examining how well the plays translate to modern theatre and readership.*

In his recent study, *Shakespeare and the Allegory of Evil* (1958), Professor Bernard Spivack points out two related trends in the development of the English morality play during the sixteenth century: the first a change from a hero who represents all humanity to one who embodies only an aspect of humanity; the second a change from a comic to a tragic ending. Behind these changes lay the general shift from a Catholic to a Protestant theological perspective. One of the chief purposes of the older plays was to demonstrate the possibility of salvation for *all* humanity: hence the generalized hero and the happy ending. The later plays, on the other hand, were more concerned with the exceptional individual and the dilemmas he must cope with in this life rather than the next.

The various implications of this development may be seen very clearly, I think, in two plays written about a century apart, *Everyman* and Marlowe's *Dr. Faustus.* A comparison between the two is a natural, even an inevitable one to make, since both plays have as their main theme the eschatological predicament confronting every Christian individual, the choice whether to be damned or saved. Futhermore, both plays are basically concerned with only one character and his spiritual destiny; the other characters either symbolize various facets of the hero's personal conflict or are limited to strictly subsidiary roles. *Everyman* is undoubtedly the most skillful example of the morality play that has survived. T. S. Eliot claims (in ''Four Elizabethan Dramatists'') that it is perhaps the one play in which ''we have a drama within the limitations of art''— meaning, I gather, that nothing in the play is extraneous to the central homiletic purpose, that all elements of style, structure, and theme are governed by the conventions of allegory. The consistency of the form reflects the perfect clarity and oneness of belief in the playwright and his audience. By comparison, *Dr. Faustus* is an impure, hybrid play, not merely because of the revisions inflicted on it by later playwrights, but because it is transitional: it both harks back to the older drama in its use of the devices of homiletic allegory, and anticipates the fully developed tragedy of the later Elizabethans, especially in its conception of the hero.

It is in their protagonists that the two plays differ, perhaps, most obviously. Since Everyman is supposed to represent all humanity he is given no social or political identity, no attributes which would suggest that his predicament is more common to one class of humanity than another. (The only political references in the play occur in the repeated designation of God as ''Heuen Kynge'' or ''Chefe Lorde of paradyse,'' the implication being that all men, whatever their earthly status, are democratically equal before the one true monarch of the universe.) This is not to say that Everyman is merely an abstract figure, a type. He is, rather, a complete individual whose feelings as he faces death and yearns for salvation are to be understood as those of any human being caught in the same universal situation. In *Everyman* the soul, or that which unites the hero with the rest of his kind, is treated as incomparably more significant than character, or that which sets him apart. In *Dr. Faustus,* on the other hand, these

''ONE REASON THE PROCESS OF REDEMPTION FOR EVERYMAN SEEMS RELATIVELY EASY IS THAT POSITIVE EVIL DOES NOT APPEAR AS A SERIOUS IMPEDIMENT''

two aspects of the hero receive a more equal emphasis, and as the play develops a growing tension may be observed between them. As early as the opening chorus Faustus is presented as an individual set apart by the circumstances of his birth, education, and scholarly career. As he shows so clearly in his initial monologue, he is one who craves uniqueness, who longs to ''gain a deity'' and ''reign sole king of all the Provinces.'' But whatever Faustus eventually gains in distinction as a character he loses as a soul, for however cavalierly he tries to dismiss it at first he cannot escape the predicament of Everyman. All the high honor he receives for his learning and necromantic skill is ironically replaced in the end by the terrifying isolation of the final hour, when under the pressure of imminent damnation he yearns to lose all identity whatsoever and become as indistinguishable as waterdrops blended with the ocean.

The fact that Everyman, the representative individual, is saved, and Faustus, the exceptional individualist, is damned, has significant theological implications. Between the two plays falls the Reformation. Despite its several severe warnings, *Everyman* is essentially reassuring in its estimation of man's chances for salvation. Its purpose is not to terrify but to edify. ''This mater is wonderous precyous,'' says the Prologue; ''But the entent of it is more gracyous, and swete to bere aweye.'' God at the beginning speaks ruefully of His love for mankind, the sacrifice He made for them in the Crucifixion (''I coude do no more than I dyde, truely''), and His original intention that they should all be saved and share His glory. It is only because mankind is ''Drowned in synne'' that God is obliged to command Death to summon Everyman to his final reckoning. Once Everyman appears, however, he hardly bears the marks of a deep-dyed sinner. He is more like the anxious, baffled, and painfully well-intentioned hero of modern existentialist fiction. Except for the momentary truculence he shows at the outset when he asks Death what God wants with him, he never betrays any sign of wishing to resist God or question His ways, let alone aspire to a Faustian divinity. Once he realizes his spiritual danger, his faith, his will to be saved, is beyond question; and after he turns to Good Deeds and is joined by Knowledge the way to his salvation is clear.

One reason the process of redemption for Everyman seems relatively easy is that positive evil does not appear as a serious impediment. Unlike most of the other mortality plays, the world of *Everyman* is not invaded by the Devil and his ministers, the personified vices. The only obstacle to the hero's redemption is his own blindness to the true good, represented by his over-reliance on Fellowship, Kindred and Cousin, and Goods. These are not vices but mutable goods, dangerous only when their value is overestimated. (As Goods explains to Everyman, had he loved his possessions moderately and distributed alms his spiritual prospects would have been much brighter.) Death, too, is depicted as God's dignified and business-like subordinate—not the sadistic antic of the medieval *danse macabre*. The universe of *Everyman* in general is one thoroughly under the control of a benevolent deity who sees to it that the normal, repentant sinner has more than a fair chance to save himself: a universe in which the demonic is kept at a thoroughly safe distance.

Moving to *Dr. Faustus,* we are immediately impressed by the remoteness of the divine, the omnipresence of the demonic. Not only does God's benevolent protection fail to show itself as a visible reality (even the impeccably virtuous Old Man is tormented by the fiends), but God's representatives, the Good Angel and the Old Man, are heavily outnumbered by Mephistophilis, Lucifer, the Bad Angel, the Seven Deadly Sins, and an indefinite number of minor devils. The magnitude of evil represented in Faustus is far greater than it is in Everyman, for Faustus consciously wills to surmount his human limitations and rival God. This deep concern with the demonic makes Marlowe's play seem at once more primitive and more sophisticated than *Everyman:* more primitive in that it reflects that original fear of darkness and chaos which is at the core of the tragic experience; more sophisticated in that it sees the exceptionally gifted individual, the man who believes he has mastered all the known fields of human learning, as precisely the one who is most lacking in genuine self-knowledge, the most vulnerable to illicit temptation. This

concern with the potency of evil also appears in the hero's inability to repent despite his urgent desire to. Before he signs the bond Faustus suffers momentary pangs of conscience, and periodically thereafter he is moved to repent. Clearly, he is damned in the end not because of what he actually does, for his deeds are merely frivolous and self-indulgent rather than vicious, but because he despairs, because he is *convinced* that he is damned. Even as he calls on Christ in the agony of his final hour he sees only the heavy wrath of God; the one drop of blood that would save his soul unavailable to him. *Dr. Faustus* is a distinctly post-Reformation play because the hero's destiny hinges entirely on the question of faith, a question which does not enter into *Everyman* at all. This is not to say that the play is Calvinistic in its implied theology; the opportunity to renounce his bond and repent is genuinely available to Faustus to the very end, as the Old Man indicates. Nevertheless, a heavy element of spiritual predeterminism does appear in Faustus's conviction that even God's mercy is not so capacious as to embrace such a sinner as himself. Although the conviction may be illusory, it is still one of the most powerfully felt ingredients in the play.

Another significant feature of the two plays which serves to distinguish them is their treatment of time. In both plays time is to be conceived in two basic senses. First, it is a mechanically regular process, a ceaseless, irreversible flow which determines the limits of human experience but remains unaffected by it. In the second sense, it is a flexible medium which may be manipulated by man to attain his ends. The first is clock or astronomical time, the second moral time. The first is deterministic; the second involves opportunity, or man's freedom to control his own destiny.

In Everyman's progress, time in the first sense prevails momentarily but is superseded by the second. Since the play deals with the general experience of mankind, history, in the sense of what particular individuals do at a particular time and place, is almost but not entirely excluded. Only three historical events are mentioned: the Fall, the Crucifixion, and the Last Judgment—the three events which in the medieval Christian view determined the entire course of human history. The first event began history by binding man to time and mortality, the second offered him the opportunity to escape this bondage and decide his own destiny in the hereafter, the third will end all possibility of choice and so end history. Time in the first, or mechanistic, sense enters the play when Death summons

Everyman. Once the latter is fully aware of the fact that he must die, his first response is to beg for more leeway: ''Ye, a thousande pounde shalt thou haue, And thou dyfferre this mater tyll an other daye.'' But Death, immune to bribery, insists that he die that very day. After Death leaves, Everyman, alone and desperate, wishes he had never been born and shudders to think what little time he has left: ''The day passeth, and is almost ago. I wote not well what for to do.'' It is here that Everyman most closely resembles the Faustus who in his final hour curses his existence and helplessly endures the ticking away of his small stock of remaining time. After discovering the hypocrisy of Fellowship and the other worldly goods, Everyman realizes that all his life he had wasted time, that is, had misused his opportunity to prepare for the hereafter: ''Lo! now was I deceyued or I was ware; And all, I may wyte, my spendynge of tyme.'' At this point time for Everyman means finitude and the horrifying prospect of damnation.

But once he discovers a true companion in Good Deeds and receives instruction from Knowledge, Everyman is no longer obsessed with time in the negative sense. His passive waiting for death changes into a voluntary pilgrimage, a journey in which he sets his own pace and hopefully anticipates a benevolent end. What he must do is undergo the established rituals of purification: confession, penance, and the receiving of the sacraments of the eucharist and last annointing. These are rituals of renewal: they counteract the deleterious effect of time by relieving man of his bondage to his sinful past and enabling him to be ''reborn.'' The sacrament which receives the greatest emphasis in the digression on the priesthood, the eucharist, is the one which in Catholic doctrine testifies to the continual, revivifying presence of the sacred in the profane, the eternal in the temporal. Time in the latter part of *Everyman* is not negated; instead it becomes the medium of spiritual regeneration and fulfillment.

Nevertheless, as he approaches the grave Everyman is still not fully prepared to meet death. He must undergo the actual process of aging and dying, must suffer the desertion of Strength, Beauty, and his other natural attributes. In his momentary disillusionment he shows that even the penitent finds it difficult to divorce himself from the temporal and face death with equanimity. Even as he enters the grave time does not wholly cease for Everyman: he must passively but hopefully await the final event of history, the day of doom. But as the singing of the angels indicates, his ultimate redemption is no longer in doubt.

In *Dr. Faustus* references to time and eternity occur much more frequently than they do in *Everyman,* and Marlowe's treatment of time in general is more deliberate and complex. One good reason for this is that the time element is heavily stressed in the plot. Faustus has precisely twenty-four years in which to live ''in all voluptuousness.'' As his end draws nearer his obsession with time grows more intense, until at last it reaches the extremes of spiritual agony. One of the intolerable ironies which forces itself on Faustus near the end is that he has gained a limited quantity of pleasure at the cost of an eternity of pain. Another, counterbalancing irony which he fails to realize is that, given the necessary faith, he could at any moment escape his bondage to mechanistic time and enter the realm of moral time, to his ultimate redemption.

Before and during the signing of the bond Faustus naturally shows no more concern for time than he does for the spiritual consequences of his act. With what appears to be forced bravado he announces to Mephistophilis, ''Faustus hath incurred eternal death by desperate thoughts against Jove's deity''—speaking in the past tense as though the matter were final, unalterable. Having signed the pact with Lucifer, Faustus suffers his first serious misgivings after a time lapse of indefinite length, during which he has amused himself with a variety of exotic diversions. Already he has begun to despair, so profoundly that he would have killed himself ''Had not sweet pleasure conquered deep despair.'' The form his pleasure takes is significant: he has had Homer sing to him of Alexander and Oenone, and Dardanus perform duets with Mephistophilis. Faustus, in other words, seeks to escape the present with its constant flowing away of his limited stock of time by projecting himself into a remote and changeless past. The classical figures he conjures up seem seductively real at the moment, like those in a dream, but as the anachronism of Homer's singing of Alexander suggests, they are illusory; Faustus himself later admits they are not ''true substantial bodies.'' Later in this scene (II. ii in Boas's edition) Faustus again reveals his inclination to evade the present reality, together with his nostalgia for an idyllic beauty near the beginning of time, just before he is to see the pageant of the Seven Deadly Sins: ''This sight will be pleasing unto me, As Paradise was to Adam.'' The same impulse reappears with special poignancy near the end of

Faustus's twenty-four years, when he tries to find heaven and immortality in Helen's lips.

Meanwhile, the fact that time, clocktime, does flow on ceaselessly is made unmistakably clear to Faustus in the same scene in which he speaks of Homer and Alexander. When he questions Mephistophilis about the movement of the heavenly bodies the latter replies: "All move from east to west in four and twenty hours upon the poles of the world; but differ in their motions upon the poles of the zodiac." The number twenty-four should serve as an ominous reminder to Faustus, but he complacently dismisses the explanation as old hat: "These slender trifles Wagner can decide." Once the clock has announced the beginning of his final hour, however, Faustus's astronomical awareness becomes painfully acute: "Stand still, you evermoving spheres of heaven, That time may cease, and midnight never come." Looking skywards, Faustus also sees Christ's redeeming blood streaming in the firmament, but the vision is momentary. In his despair he equates the ceaseless movement of the spheres with the certainty of his damnation: "The stars move still, time runs, the clock will strike, The devil will come, and Faustus must be damn'd."

Two other significant variations on the time theme may be observed in the play. The first is the changeless state of damnation tangibly represented in Mephistophilis, who as a spirit is incapable of repentance. In his description of the nature of hell Mephistophilis indicates that while the state of damnation has no future, it does look back to a past. His greatest torment, in fact, lies in his memory of the joys of heaven and his knowledge that he will never see them again. Although Faustus at first makes light of Mephistophilis's suffering, he also realizes at the end what it means to exist without hope, without the expectation of future change. Any finite period of suffering, even ten thousand years, would be preferable to permanent exclusion from the company of the saved. As long as Faustus exists in time, however, the possibility of change is continually available to him. This is made clear through the periodic reappearance of the two angels, the first counselling hope, the other despair. When Faustus asks whether enough time remains to escape damnation, the Bad Angel answers, "Too late," the Good Angel, "Never too late, if Faustus can repent." Faustus never avails himself of the latter alternative because he cannot believe that his repentance would ever be acceptable to a deity he has so grievously affronted. He is a moral determinist

who, unlike Everyman, can think of time only as binding, not as liberating.

If time assumes a more problematic significance in *Dr. Faustus* than it does in *Everyman*, this is merely one symptom of the play's having been written in an age which was becoming increasingly sensitive to the radical distinction between the eternal and the temporal, the sacred and the profane. The distinction is most sharply focused, perhaps, in the Calvinistic conception of faith and works, which sees all of man's temporal activities as spiritually worthless, his whole salvation depending on his absolute commitment to a time-transcending deity. In less explicitly theological fashion, Marlowe and his contemporaries habitually interpreted time as a strictly negative process, the implacable destroyer of whatever man values most highly in this life—beauty, love, fame, honor. Such hostility toward the universal principle of change could arise only in a period of transition, when the medieval hunger for the changeless was still a very real and potent impulse, but when confidence in the divine was no longer firm enough to satisfy that hunger. Not that all the Elizabethans saw time as a purely negative force. A few amplified the conception of it implicit in *Everyman,* as the necessary medium or moral growth and fulfillment, the dimension through which the underlying logic of man's spiritual experience is progressively revealed and his final deliverance achieved.

O Time, thou must untangle this, not I: It is too hard a knot for me to untie.

For the most profound interpretation of time in all its aspects among the Elizabethans we must look, of course, to Shakespeare.

Source: David Kaula, "Time and Timeless in *Everyman* and *Dr. Faustus*" in *College English,* Vol. 22, No. 1, October, 1960, pp. 9–14.

Anonymous

In this 1901 anonymous review, the critic offers a mixed appraisal of a production of Everyman *by the Elizabethan Stage Society.*

To Mr. William Poel, the secretary and originator of the Elizabethan Stage Society, we are indebted for some quaint and edifying illustrations of our early stage. None of the previous experiments has had quite the value and interest of the performance given last Saturday afternoon under the shade of the venerable walls of the Charterhouse. The place was admirably suited to the entertainment, which consisted of the anonymous morality of 'Everyman' and the scene of the interrupted 'Sacrifice of Isaac' from the 'Histories of Lot and Abraham,' which is the fourth of the Chester miracle plays. That the scene was better suited than the court of Fulham Palace, which witnessed Ben Jonson's 'Sad Shepherd,' or than the halls of the various Inns of Court which have been placed at the Society's disposal, may not perhaps be said. The environment was, however, in keeping with the action, and the two were so harmonious that it became easy to conceive the mimic performance real, and to believe that we were spectators of, and almost participants in, a great historical tragedy. Tragedy indeed, in its naive simplicity and uncompromising sincerity, 'Everyman' is—that "tragedy to those who feel" which is our general lot, the great unending problem of life, responsibility, and death. There are many points from which the entertainment may be regarded, and from all it is significant. The first thing that strikes one is that the primitive drama, which seems so dull and didactic, may well have passioned our forefathers—is, indeed, capable of passioning us; the second that this particular piece, played no better and no worse than on the occasion it was, is capable, when its merits are known, of attracting all London and becoming the "sensation" of a season. Temptations to ridicule presented themselves, and the smile rose occasionally to the lips. It died there, and sank before the absolute sincerity of the whole. Amusement never degenerated into mockery.

What are the obligations of the English dramatist to the 'Elckerlijk' assigned to Peter Dorland of Diest, the Belgian mystic, the author of the 'Viola Animæ,' or to the 'Barlaam and Josaphat' of John of Damascus, we are unable to say. After the delivery of a species of prologue by a messenger, the scene, like that of 'Festus' or of one of Goethe's prologues to 'Faust,' opens in heaven with a speech from God, described in the programme by the Hebrew name Adonai, complaining of the lewdness of life of men and their neglect of His worship. Death then approaches, and is told to bid Everyman to his final pilgrimage. Everyman comes capering to his lute in festive garb and singing to his mistress. Having received from Death his instruction to prepare for immediate departure, he seeks by bribery to obtain a respite. When this effort is vain he summons Fellowship, Kindred, and Goods or Wealth; but though ready enough to accompany him to scenes of debauch or even aid him in a murder, they refuse to accompany him on so grievous a journey. Good Deeds is so weak she can neither stand nor crawl.

She is none the less helpful, and brings to him her sister Knowledge, by whom he is led to Confession. By means of penance he is then prepared for death; and after he has received the sacraments he dies penitent and pardoned, deserted by his former associates Strength, Beauty, Discretion, and Five Wits, but supported by Good Deeds, whose strength and stature are augmented, and by Knowledge.

The presentation was naturally naïve. Adonai was shown as an elderly man with a curling grey beard. Death had no scythe, but had, as in some illustrations we recall, a drum and a trumpet. He had also, it may incidentally be mentioned, a strong Scotch accent. Everyman, who was admirably played by a woman, was a bright and dapper youth in the opening scenes, and in the later presented a tragic figure. Designs for the dresses are supplied on the title-page of an edition of the morality printed by Skot, and are given in facsimile in the first volume of Hazlitt's 'Dodsley.' In preference to these, Mr. Poel has taken others from Flemish tapestries of the early fifteenth century. Whencesoever obtained, they were admirable, and the entertainment was lifelike and impressive.

No less interesting was the short scene of the attempted sacrifice of Isaac, the rhymed verses of which were well delivered. In short, we may say that a performance casting a welcome light upon the conduct of the liturgical drama is this day repeated in the court of the Charterhouse, and those who care to witness an entertainment unique in its kind are counselled to take an opportunity that most probably will not recur.

Source: Anonymous, review of *Everyman* in the *Athenaeum*, July 20, 1901, pp. 103.

SOURCES

Anonymous. Review of *Everyman* in the *Athenaeum*, July 20, 1901, p. 103.

Barnet, Sylvan, editor. *Types of Drama: Plays and Contexts,* Longman, 1997, pp. 149-51, 182-85.

Cary, Elizabeth Luther. Review of *Everyman* in the *Critic*, January, 1903. pp. 43-45.

Garner, Stanton B. Jr. "Theatricality in *Mankind* and *Everyman*" in *Studies in Philology,* Vol. 84, no. 3, Summer, 1987, pp. 277-85.

Montague, C. E. Review of *Everyman* in the *Manchester Guardian,* November 1, 1902; reprinted in *William Poel and the Elizabethan Revival,* by Robert Speaight, Heinemann, 1954. pp. 162-63.

Peek, George S. ''Sermon Themes and Sermons Structure in *Everyman*'' in the *South Central Bulletin,* Vol. 40, no. 4, Winter, 1980, pp. 159-60.

Tanner, Ron. ''Humor in *Everyman* and the Middle English Morality Play'' in *Philological Quarterly,* Vol. 70, no. 2, Spring, 1991, pp. 149-61.

FURTHER READING

Fifield, Merle. *The Castle in the Circle,* Ball State University Press, 1967.
    Fifield studies the staging of morality plays. He also offers a staging of the play using medieval production information.

Munson, William. ''Knowing and Doing in *Everyman*'' in the *Chaucer Review,* Vol. 19, no. 3, 1985, pp. 252-71.
    Munson argues that one of *Everyman*'s primary points is the assertion that struggle is as important to man as knowledge.

Speaight, Robert. ''*Everyman* and Euripides'' in his *William Poel and the Elizabethan Revival,* Heinemann, 1954.
    Speaight describes Poel's production of *Everyman* and discusses his problems with the play's theology.

Thomas, Helen S. ''The Meaning of the Character Knowledge in *Everyman*'' in the *Mississippi Quarterly,* Vol. XIV, no. 1, Winter, 1960-61, pp. 3-13.
    Thomas argues that Knowledge is a ''wisdom figure whose function it was to counsel Everyman wisely.''

Van Dyke, Carolyn. ''The Intangible and Its Image: Allegorical Discourse and the Cast of *Everyman*'' in *Acts of Interpretation, The Texts in Its Contexts 700-1600: Essays on Medieval and Renaissance Literature in Honor of E. Talbot Donaldson,* edited by Mary J. Carruthers and Elizabeth D. Kirk, Pilgrim, 1982, pp. 311-24.
    Going against the majority opinion, Van Dyke argues that the characters in *Everyman* go beyond simple archetypes to create realistic, individual characters.

Fiddler on the Roof

JOSEPH STEIN

1964

Joseph Stein's book for *Fiddler on the Roof* represents the author's best known and most successful work in musical comedy. It was one of the last big successes in an era of great musicals on Broadway. Following its debut on September 22, 1964, at the Imperial Theatre, *Fiddler* ran for 3242 performances, achieving the longest run for a musical up to that time. This success was ironic considering the play's producers' initial fears that, due to the ethnically based story, the musical might not appeal to a broad audience.

Fiddler is based on short stories written by Sholom Aleichem, a Jewish writer who wrote primarily in Yiddish. Despite the producers' reservations, a diverse audience embraced the musical, relating to its universal themes of family, love, dignity, and the importance of tradition. Many critics agreed. Theophilus Lewis, reviewing the original production in *America,* wrote, ''Joseph Stein's story has dramatic dignity, a continuous flow of humor, and episodes of pathos that never descend to the maudlin.'' While most critics generally found the musical praiseworthy on many fronts—the performances especially the original Tevye, Zero Mostel; the acting; music; choreography; and direction. Several critics, however, found the production too ''Broadway'' while others felt it was too sentimental.

Stein won three prestigious awards for *Fiddler on the Roof* in 1965: The Antoinette ''Tony'' Perry

Award for best musical, the New York Drama Critics Award, and the Newspaper Guild Award. The B'nai B'rith society also bestowed their Music and Performing Award upon Stein for his "exceptional creative achievement" in 1965.

AUTHOR BIOGRAPHY

Joseph Stein was born on May 30, 1912, in New York City, the son of Charles and Emma (Rosenblum) Stein, Polish immigrants who emigrated to the United States. Growing up in the Bronx, Stein's father read him the stories of Sholom Aleichem, a noted author of Jewish folk tales. Stein would remember these stories when he was called upon to develop the musical that became *Fiddler on the Roof.* Stein did not immediately turn to the theater, though. He attended City College, earning his B.S.S. in 1935, then his Master of Social Work from Columbia in 1937. Stein then spent six years employed as a psychiatric social worker, from 1939 until 1945.

In 1946, Stein began writing for radio. He wrote for such shows as the *Henry Morgan Show* and *Kraft Music Hall.* In 1948, he and writing partner Will Glickman began writing for the stage, contributing sketches to Broadway revues as well as whole plays and the books for musicals. Through 1958, every theatrical production Stein wrote was a collaboration with Glickman. In 1955, the duo had their biggest success with their first musical play, *Plain and Fancy.* Stein also wrote for television from 1950-62, primarily for variety shows such as *Your Show of Shows* and *The Sid Caesar Show* and specials for stars like Phil Silvers and Debbie Reynolds.

Adaptations of other people's material proved to be the highpoint of Stein's career. In 1959, he had his first solo success with an adaptation of Sean O'Casey's *Juno.* An even bigger hit was Stein's adaptation of Carl Reiner's autobiography *Enter Laughing* in 1963. The apex of Stein's stage career, however, was writing the book for the musical *Fiddler on the Roof.* Though backers were originally reluctant to produce the musical fearing it might have limited appeal, *Fiddler* went on to become a smash hit. Stein won three major awards for his effort, including the Antionette "Tony" Perry Award for best musical.

Stein continued to do well with adaptations. His next hit was the book for the 1968 musical *Zorba,* based on the novel *Zorba the Greek.* However, Stein's career was not as successful after that point, hitting a low in 1986. Stein wrote the book for the musical *Rags,* which was a continuation of the story told in *Fiddler on the Roof.* Unlike the original, *Rags* failed to catch on immediately and was a box office failure in its original five-day Broadway run. The musical did have some success Off-Broadway and in regional productions; it received a Tony Award nomination in 1987.

Stein was married to Sadie Singer until her death in 1974. The couple had three sons, Daniel, Harry, and Joshua. Stein remarried in 1976 to Elisa Loti, a former actress and psychotherapist.

PLOT SUMMARY

Act I, prologue
Fiddler on the Roof opens outside dairyman Tevye's house in the village of Anatevka, Russia, in 1905. Tevye addresses the audience, telling them that tradition keeps balance in their lives. Everyone has a role in village life, both Jews, such as matchmakers and rabbis, and non-Jews, such as the Russian officials. As long as people stay in their place and do not bother each other, Tevye says everything will be all right.

Act I, scene 1
In the kitchen of Tevye's house, his wife Golde and his daughters prepare for the Sabbath. Yente the village matchmaker comes to visit. She tells Golde that she has a husband for the eldest daughter, Tzeitel: Lazar Wolf, the butcher. Lazar is an older man, a widower. Golde is unsure about the match because Tevye wants his daughter to marry a learned man. Still, Golde agrees to arrange a meeting between her husband and Lazar.

Not knowing the details of their mother's conversation, Tzeitel's sisters tease her about Yente finding her a husband. It is implied that Tzietel is only interested in Motel, a young, impoverished tailor. Hodel, the next oldest, is interested in the Rabbi's son. The sister's sing the song "Matchmaker, Matchmaker," in which they hope to find the perfect man.

Act I, scene 2

Tevye arrives home just in time for Sabbath, the beginning of the Jewish holy day. His horse threw a shoe, and he had to make deliveries by foot. Tevye talks directly to God, saying that he wishes he was wealthy so he could better support his family. He sings the song ''If I Were a Rich Man.''

The villagers come to Tevye's house, demanding their dairy orders. One has a newspaper which says the Jews were all evicted from a nearby village. The men worry. A newcomer to the village, a young man named Perchik, tells them that they should know more about the outside world. After filling the villagers' orders, Tevye invites Perchik to stay with them for Sabbath dinner. Perchik will teach Tevye's daughters in exchange for the hospitality.

Act I, scene 3

Tevye and Perchik enter the house. The daughters greet their father enthusiastically. Motel arrives, and Golde invites him to stay for supper as well. While the daughters and guests wash up for the meal, Golde tells Tevye that Lazar Wolf wants to meet with him. Golde does not tell him why, and Tevye is convinced Lazar wants his new milk cow.

Tzeitel tells Motel that Yente had visited earlier. Tzeitel worries that a match has been made for her, but Motel assures her that he will be able to buy a sewing machine and impress her father enough to earn her hand in marriage. Tzeitel wants Motel to ask her father for permission immediately, but Motel is afraid. Still, Motel agrees to talk to him. Motel tries to bring up the subject, but the group gathers around the table to say Sabbath prayers, and he does not get a chance.

Act I, scene 4

Tevye meets Lazar at the Inn. Before Tevye comes, Lazar brags to everyone present that he will probably be married. When Tevye comes, the conversation is tense. Lazar assumes that Tevye knows what the meeting is about, but Tevye still believes the discussion regards his cow. When the truth comes out, Tevye is upset. He does not like Lazar, but he reasons that the butcher does have a steady income. Tevye agrees to the match. Lazar tells everyone around them. Even the Russians are happy for him.

Act I, scene 5

Outside of the Inn, the celebration continues. A Russian official, the constable, tells Tevye that their

Joseph Stein

district will have to undergo a ''little unofficial demonstration'' to impress an inspector who may come through. He tells Tevye as a courtesy to warn the others, because he wants no trouble between them.

Act I, scene 6

Outside Tevye's house, Perchik is giving a lesson to three of Tevye's daughters. Golde calls the girls away as they are needed to begin Tevye's work because he is still in bed. Before Hodel goes, she and Perchik talk. Perchik tells her she is smart. He dances with her in defiance of a local custom. Tevye enters followed by his wife. When Tzeitel comes out with several of her sisters, her parents tell her about the match with Lazar. While her parents, especially Golde, are happy, Tzeitel is not. She confides to her father that she does not want to marry the butcher. Tevye says he will not force her to marry.

Motel runs in, breathless. Tevye tries to brush him off, but Motel insists on offering himself as a suitor for Tzeitel. Tevye calls him crazy. Motel tells him that he and Tzeitel pledged to marry over a year ago. Though Tevye is unsure about going against tradition—particularly breaking the agreement he made with Lazar—he agrees that the tailor should marry Tzeitel.

Act I, scene 7

In Tevye and Golde's bedroom that night, Tevye tells his wife that he had a horrible dream: Lazar Wolf's first wife, Fruma-Sarah, came to Tevye and insisted that Tzeitel should not marry Lazar. Later in the dream, Golde's mother told the dairyman that Tzeitel should marry Motel. Golde is convinced then that Tzeitel should marry Motel.

Act I, scene 8

On a street in the village, people discuss the fact that Tzeitel is marrying Motel instead of Lazar. People come to Motel's shop to congratulate him. When Chava, one of the sisters, is left in charge of the shop for a moment while Motel sees to his wedding hat, several Russians block her way inside. Another young Russian, Fyedka, insists that they stop teasing her. The Russians step aside and let her pass. Fyedka compliments her, telling her he has seen her reading and admires her thirst for knowledge; he gives Chava a book.

Act I, scenes 9-10

In Tevye's yard, Motel and Tzeitel's wedding takes place.

Inside the house, the wedding reception takes place. The couple is toasted and gifts are given. Lazar stands up to congratulate them, but when Tevye interrupts him, Lazar turns angry at the fact that their agreement was broken. They argue for a while, until Perchik points out that Tzeitel wanted to marry Motel. The radical suggestion that a person's desires should take precedence over tradition disturbs the guests, especially Yente the matchmaker. Perchik continues to agitate the situation when he asks Hodel to dance. It is unheard for a man to dance with a girl at a wedding. Tevye then asks his wife to dance and soon the whole crowd is dancing with one another, save the bitter Yente and Lazar.

The reverie is interrupted by the Constable who says that the Russian officials must make their show of force that evening. Perchik tries to stop them but is clubbed down. Following the destruction, the Constable apologizes, and he and his men go to the next house. The guests begin cleaning up.

Act II, prologue

Tevye talks to heaven. It is two months later and Motel and Tzeitel are happily married, but Motel still does not have his sewing machine. Tevye asks God to send his new son-in-law a sewing machine.

Act II, scene 1

Outside of Tevye's house, Hodel and Perchik enter. Hodel is upset because Perchik is leaving for Kiev in the hopes of changing the Russian policies that resulted in the raid during Tzeitel's wedding reception. Perchik asks her to marry him and she agrees. Tevye comes in, and Perchik tells him what has been decided. Tevye says he will not give his permission. Hodel and Perchik explain that they are not asking for his permission, only his blessing. Tevye is upset but gives both his blessing and permission. He tells Golde of his decision, and she is angry at Tevye for not asking her feelings on the subject. They make up at the end of the scene, pledging their love to each other in the song "Do You Love Me?"

Act II, scene 2

In the village, Yente tells Tzeitel that she has seen Chava with Fyedka. She gives Tzeitel a letter for Hodel from Perchik. He has been arrested in Kiev. The village becomes alight with gossip about the subject. Yente blames the uproar on men and women dancing together.

Act II, scene 3

Outside of the railroad station, Hodel and Tevye wait for a train. Hodel is going to join Perchik in Siberia, where she will marry him. She wants to help him in his social activism. Tevye does not want her to go but blesses her journey just the same.

Act II, scene 4-5

It is several months later, and the villagers talk about Tzeitel and Motel's new baby.

In Motel's shop, there is a new sewing machine. The rabbi blesses it. Fyedka comes in, and everyone is silent. When he leaves, Chava follows him. Chava tells him that she is afraid to tell her family about their relationship. Tevye comes by, and he asks them to remain only distant friends. Chava tells him they still want to be married. Tevye gets angry and says no.

Act II, scene 6

Tevye pushes his cart on the road because his horse is sick. Golde finds him and tells him that Chava has left home with Fyedka. The couple were later married. Tevye says that Chava is dead to them now. He maintains this stance even when Chava arrives and pleads for her father's acceptance.

Act II, scene 7

Inside the barn, Yente finds Golde. Yente has brought two teenage boys for the remaining daughters, but Golde thinks they are too young to be married. Many villagers come into the barn followed by Tevye. There are rumors in the village. The Constable comes and tells everyone that they must sell everything and leave the village in three days. Tevye is angry but realizes the futility of fighting.

Act II, scene 8

Outside of Tevye's house, everyone is packing. The youngest daughters are going with their parents to live in America, while Tzeitel, Motel and their child will live in Poland until they have saved enough money to journey to America. Yente states that she is going to the Holy Land. Golde insists on cleaning the house before they leave. Chava comes and says goodbye. She and Fyedka are going to Cracow. Tevye gives her his blessing before she leaves, mending the rift between them. The play ends with the family leaving for their train.

CHARACTERS

Chava

Chava is the third oldest daughter of Tevye and Golde. She likes books and learning. She reluctantly falls in love with Fydeka, a Russian. When she marries him, her parents disown her. But when the Jews are forced out of the village, she visits her parents and they acknowledge her.

The Constable

The Constable is a local Russian official. Though friendly with Tevye, he follows his orders to first pillage the Jews, then force them to leave the area all together.

Fydeka

Fydeka is a young Russian man who is attracted to Chava. Noting her interest in books, he gives her a book to begin their courtship. He eventually marries her, though their union results in Chava's family disowning her. When the Russians force the Jews to leave the village, Fydeka tells Tevye and

MEDIA ADAPTATIONS

- *Fiddler on the Roof* was adapted as an immensely popular film in 1971. This version was directed by Norman Jewison and stars Topol as Tevye, Norma Crane as Golde, Molly Picon as Yente, and Rosalind Harris as Tzeitel.

Golde that he and Chava are going to Cracow because they do not want to live in a country that treats people this way.

Golde

Golde is Tevye's wife and mother of his five daughters. They have been married for twenty-five years, and she is Tevye's helpmate in life and work. She runs their home efficiently. Like Tevye, Golde wants to uphold tradition, while making sure her children are taken care of. She is the first to agree to the match between Lazar and Tzeitel and only follows her husband's lead reluctantly when he tries to go against tradition. Still, she does not want to break off relations with her daughter Chava when she marries a Russian man. Her love of family outweighs tradition in the end.

Hodel

Hodel is Tevye and Golde's second oldest daughter. Though she is a traditionalist like her parents in the beginning, she falls in love with Perchik, the radical. She breaks tradition by telling her father she is marrying Perchik and only asking for his blessing. Hodel eventually moves to Siberia to marry Perchik.

Motel Kamzoil

Motel is the impoverished tailor who is secretly engaged to Tzeitel. Though he is afraid of Tevye, he asks him for Tzeitel's hand in marriage when he learns about the match with Lazar. Motel believes that even an impoverished tailor deserves a little happiness. He turns out to be a good husband for Tzeitel. Motel desperately wants a sewing machine and eventually gets it. At the end of the play, he and Tzeitel are moving to Warsaw so they can save money and eventually emigrate to the United States.

Perchik

Perchik is a young man from Kiev with an education. Under an arrangement with Tevye, he gives lessons to the daughters in exchange for food. Perchik falls in love with Hodel and becomes engaged to her. Perchik is responsible for introducing the idea of breaking tradition into the village. He convinces Hodel to dance with him. He believes also that the villagers should have an awareness of what is going on in the outside world, especially how forces are working against Jews within Russia. Perchik is eventually arrested in Kiev and sent to Siberia, where Hodel goes to marry him.

Tevye

Tevye is the main character in *Fiddler on the Roof*. He is an impoverished dairyman and community leader with a wife and five daughters. He has a loving relationship with his family. During the play, he struggles to support them and uphold traditions. He is not inflexible, however. He agrees to let Lazar Wolf marry his eldest daughter Tzeitel as Yente the matchmaker arranged, but when she wants to marry someone else, he lets her have her way. He disowns his daughter Chava when she marries a Russian, only acknowledging her at the end of the play.

Tevye is also generous, despite his stubbornness. When he realizes that Perchik is new in town, he invites the young man to eat Sabbath dinner with his family. He also arranges for Perchik to give his daughters lessons in exchange for food. Tevye is also the contact between the Jewish villagers and the local Russian constable. Their relationship is so friendly that the Constable warns Tevye when his men must raid the Jewish community. This relationship turns sour when the Constable has to tell Tevye that the Jews must leave the village. Tevye takes his family and moves the to the United States.

Tzeitel

Tzeitel is Tevye and Golde's eldest daughter; she is about twenty years old. She is in love with Motel, the impoverished tailor, and wants to marry him. They secretly pledged to marry about a year before the play begins. When Tevye tells her of the match that has been made between her and Lazar Wolf, she begs her father not to force her into the marriage. He eventually agrees, and she happily marries the man she loves. Eventually she has a son with him. When the Jews are forced out of the village, she goes to Warsaw with her husband while they save money to move to America.

Lazar Wolf

Lazar is the local butcher and is relatively well off. A widower with no children, he asks Yente to make a match between him and Tzeitel. Though he gets Tevye to agree to the marriage, he is eventually stunned to learn that Tevye goes back on the agreement. He starts an argument over the matter at Tzeitel's wedding to Motel.

Yente

Yente is the village's matchmaker. She is a childless widow and meddles in everyone's business. She arranges the match between Lazar Wolf and Tzeitel and is appalled when Tevye allows her arrangement to fall apart. During the wedding scene, she demonstrates her loyalty to tradition by being one of only two people not to dance. At the end of the play, Yente tells Golde that she is moving to the Holy Land.

THEMES

Custom and Tradition

Tradition is central to *Fiddler on the Roof*. All of the Jewish villagers look to tradition as a guide in their lives. Tradition dictates that a matchmaker aid in the arranging of marriages, not that couples decide for themselves who and when they will to marry. Custom dictates that only men dance at weddings, not that men ask women to dance. Tradition also regulates dress, food consumption, and who can interact with whom—especially in regard to Jewish/Russian relations. While Tevye upholds these traditions to the best of his ability, the times are changing and the old way of doing things comes under repeated questioning.

Perchik is the most vocal advocate of change, arguing that people must adapt to survive in the evolving world. Yet tradition dictates an ignorance of the outside world. Perchik tries to break through this ignorance to prepare people for the worst: harassment and expulsion by the Russians.

For his part, Tevye has a soft heart for his daughters, and he ultimately makes choices that will ensure their happiness. His efforts to please his children serves as a major engine for change in the play: He will go against the tradition of arranged marriages and allow two of his daughters to select their own husbands. While he initially chaffs at Chava's choice of a Russian mate, Tevye eventually softens his stance against that union as well. By placing the needs of his family above the requirements of custom and tradition, by submitting to change and a new way of doing things, Tevye prepares his brood for the numerous changes that will confront them in the coming years.

Change and Transformation

Perchik and Tevye inevitably and sometimes unwittingly change local traditions in *Fiddler on the Roof*. When Tevye's eldest daughter, Tzeitel, tells him she does not want to marry Lazar, that she loves Motel, Tevye agrees to let her marry the poor tailor. He does this despite the fact that a match has been made by Yente and that he has made an agreement with Lazar. This goes entirely against the village's standard practice of young women marrying the men their fathers have selected for them. But to preserve a semblance of tradition, Tevye has to convince his wife Golde that Tzeitel's marrying Lazar would be wrong. He accomplishes this via a fictional dream that he relates to Golde.

Once this first change has taken place, the challenges to tradition continue, transforming Tevye's family. While Tzeitel and Motel ask Tevye's permission to marry, Hodel and Perchik only ask for his blessing. Tevye is not happy with this change in custom but agrees to it because it will make his daughter happy.

Perchik is the first to ask a woman to dance at a wedding. When he does this, most everyone follows his lead, breaking a long-standing tradition. Perchik also wants the villagers to realize that the world is changing and that the Russian czar is attacking Jewish settlements. Perchik is proven correct by the end of the play, when the local Russian officials inform the Jews that they must vacate the village in three days. This is the biggest change, for most

TOPICS FOR FURTHER STUDY

- Compare and contrast Tevye with the title character in Bertolt Brecht's *Mother Courage;* both characters struggle to survive in tough times and a harsh environment. Focus on their quests to support and guide their children.

- Research the history of the Jews in turn of the century Russia. Why was tradition—a central theme in *Fiddler on the Roof*—so important to their way of life?

- Read the short stories by Sholem Aleichem (1894's *Tevye and His Daughters*) that are the basis for *Fiddler on the Roof*. How do the demands of the short story form affect how the stories are told? How are the tales told differently on the stage?

- The title image and central metaphor of *Fiddler on the Roof*—the fiddler himself—comes from a painting by Marc Chagall. Research Chagall's background and his stylistic concerns as an artist. Compare and contrast Chagall with the Stein's play and its themes.

everyone assumed they would live their entire lives in Anatevka.

Family and Religion

In *Fiddler on the Roof*, the centers of life are family and religion. Everything Tevye does serves one or the other, often both. Tevye works as a dairyman, and he sometimes has to pull the cart himself when his horse loses a shoe or is ill. He works hard to support his wife and five daughters. Many of his personal dilemmas surround the fact that he cannot afford five dowries—let alone one. He does not know how he will marry all of his daughters off. Each of the girls, though they may defy tradition, want their father's approval. Such paternal respect is important to them. When Tevye is uncertain or feels dragged down by his weighty decisions, he looks to his God. Tevye talks directly to his deity, asking for answers to his dilemmas. The

Zero Mostel as Tevye (second from left) addresses his wife and daughters in a 1965 Broadway production

Jewish religion also serves the village at large for it is the basis of many of its traditions.

STYLE

Setting

Fiddler on the Roof is a musical comedy that takes place in 1905 in the small Russian village of Anatevka. The action of the play occurs largely in and around the home of Tevye. The kitchen, Tevye's bedroom, the front yard, and the barn are the primary locations, in addition to some brief settings in the village, including an inn, Model's tailor shop, the train station, streets, and roads. Tevye's house emphasizes his importance as the primary character as well as the centrality of the family and its traditions in the play.

Monologue

In *Fiddler on the Roof,* Tevye has two kinds of monologues: those in which he prays, talking directly to God, and those in which he directly addresses the audience. Both kinds of monologues allow Tevye to express his religious beliefs, doubts, worries, and fears. He talks about his failing horse and the problem of supplying a dowry for his five daughters. When he talks to God, especially, the importance of religion and tradition are emphasized. When he talks directly to the audience, it is usually to comment on the action of the play. The use of monologue underlines that *Fiddler on the Roof* is told from Tevye's point of view and that he is the musical's primary character.

Tevye's monologues also serve to advance the story, especially at the beginning of Act II. In this monologue, Tevye updates the audience about what has taken place since the end of Act I.

Dance

Dance is used in *Fiddler on the Roof* to underscore the themes of the play. Perchik, especially, uses dance to challenge tradition. In Act I, scene 6, Perchik makes Hodel dance with him when no one is around, though women are not supposed to dance with men. Though Hodel has been obedient before, this act—and Perchik's infectious free spirit—leads her to question traditions. During Tzeitel's wedding, Perchik asks Hodel to dance again. She agrees, which leads to all the guests save two (Lazar and Yente) breaking the tradition.

Dance is also used in other ways in *Fiddler.* When Tevye agrees that Tzeitel will marry Lazar, he dances for joy. The whole inn joins him in this dance, including some Russians. Dance primarily serves as a symbol of freedom and happiness in the play.

Symbolism

The title of the musical is derived from its most obvious symbol: the fiddler on the roof. The fiddler, as Tevye tells the audience, represents the fragile balance of life in the village. Tevye says "every one of us is a fiddler on the roof, trying to scratch out a pleasant, simple tune without breaking his neck." The fiddler appears at key moments in the play: the prologue to Act I; Act I, scene 4, when Tevye agrees to the match between Tzeitel and Lazar; when Tevye is warned about the forthcoming pogrom (assault on the Jews' property); the wedding scene, where tradition is broken and the pogrom takes place; and at the very end of the play when the family leaves for America. Then, the fiddler climbs on to Tevye's wagon, indicating that challenges will confront them where ever they go.

HISTORICAL CONTEXT

The 1960s was one of the most prosperous decades in the history of the United States. Between 1960 and 1965, low unemployment and low inflation dominated. The average worker's salary increased by one-fifth. People had more money and more things to spend it on. Still, there was some labor unrest, such as a short strike by the United Auto Workers (UAW) against General Motors in 1964. Despite such incidents, America's economic strength contributed to its position as a world leader. This position was sometimes difficult and lead to long-term problems. America renewed its commitment to prevent the communist insurgency in the small Asian country of Vietnam in 1964 by committing the first significant troop dispatches to aid the South in their battle against the Vietcong in the North. The U.S. also continued its stance in the thirty-year-long Cold War, a power stalemate with the Soviet Union that pitted the implied threat of each country's nuclear arsenal against the other (the term "Cold

War" originated from the fact that while war-like conditions existed between the two countries, the fear of nuclear devastation prevented any actual fighting or significant escalation of hostilities).

For many Americans, the world was becoming a much smaller place; improved and increasingly affordable modes of transportation made travel easier both within the North American continent and abroad. Where people could not travel, television expanded knowledge of the world at large, offering a vicarious means of global expedition. Television also opened people's eyes to the burgeoning social problems in America. This increased awareness of inequalities and injustice within their own borders motivated many people to become actively involved in the correction of such problems: activists took stands throughout the decade on such issues as civil rights, poverty, and war.

Though courts had affirmed many of the tenets of American civil rights in the 1950s, it was in the 1960s that activists fought, both passively and aggressively, for their implementation in a meaningful way; fights for equality in the workplace, in public institutions such as schools, and in other public places became widespread. In 1964, President Lyndon Baines Johnson signed the Civil Rights Act of 1964 which banned racial discrimination in public places and employment. President Johnson also lead a national war on poverty. To that end, he signed the Equal Opportunity Act of 1964 which funded youth programs, community-based anti-poverty measures, small business loans, and the creation of the Jobs Corps.

Inspired by the Civil Rights Movement, women began demanding equal rights, especially as more women entered the workplace. The feminist movement also found inspiration in such books as Betty Friedan's *The Feminine Mystique.* One reason the women's movement gained power was the introduction of the birth control pill in the early-1960s. This medication sparked the "sexual revolution" of the 1960s, enabling women (and men) to pursue sexual relationships without the risk of pregnancy.

Other social groups challenged traditional roles. Young people "revolted" in the 1960s, not just by participating in the rights movements. They protested against their parents and society's values, especially the middle- and upper-class fixation with

COMPARE
&
CONTRAST

- **1905:** There is widespread student protest against the Russian injustices, particularly educational inequality.

  1964: Students are among the first to demonstrate for greater civil rights and to speak out against American involvement in Vietnam.

  Today: While the spirit of social protest is alive and well, nation-wide mass demonstrations are less common due to less overt social injustices and the absence of a war such as Vietnam.

- **1905:** There is widespread prejudice against Jews in Russia. There are over 600 anti-Jewish riots called pogroms, many of which result in loss of property and life.

  1964: There is widespread prejudice against African Americans in the United States, especially in the South. Violence is used in an attempt to deny them such basic civil rights as equal access to public services and integrated education.

  Today: While prejudice against minorities remains, many institutional barriers have been overcome; there is significant legislation to ensure social equality. Prejudice and injustice still arise, however, as in the Los Angeles, California, riots that resulted following the acquittal of white

police officers accused of beating black motorist Rodney King.

- **1905:** By law, Jews are banned from many jobs in Russian society; they are denied positions simply because of their religion.

  1964: Civil rights legislation in the United States seeks to address hiring practices that work against African Americans and other minorities.

  Today: Conservative forces in the United States seek to rescind some aspects of the civil rights legislation, targeting Affirmative Action and other ''quota'' practices as reverse discrimination that works against qualified whites.

- **1905:** The number of Jews allowed to receive a secondary or higher education is restricted by law.

  1964: Though the American court system orders the desegregation of public schools, some state officials, especially in the South, are reluctant to follow through. Some openly defy the law.

  Today: There is a debate over the merits of integration in education. Court-mandated bussing practices—enacted to integrate schools—are phased out in some areas of the country.

---

material wealth. When the United States became more deeply involved in Vietnam, college campuses were the frequent settings for powerful antiwar demonstrations. Some young men refused to fight in a war in which they did not believe and which they felt posed no threat to the American way of life.

Despite such momentous changes in society, Broadway theater, especially the musicals of the early-1960s, targeted an older, more conservative audience. Musicals were nostalgic for the great examples of the form from the past. The year 1964 had three such productions: *Fiddler on the Roof, Hello, Dolly!,* and *Funny Girl.* Movies were the exact opposite, with many independent filmmakers

finding an outlet for their counter-culture agendas in film. The 1960s marked a significant turning point in western cinema, with many films rising to challenge the status quo; 1964 was the year that director Stanley Kubrick's landmark antiwar satire *Dr. Strangelove* debuted.

CRITICAL OVERVIEW

When *Fiddler on the Roof* had its first out-of-town try-out in Detroit, Michigan, there was debate over whether the show would ever have the mass appeal to make it to Broadway. A reviewer from *Variety* predicted it would only have a slim chance to be successful. Still, good word of mouth spread through its next stop in Washington, D.C. By the time *Fiddler* reached Broadway, it was a blockbuster hit from the first night, September 22, 1964. *Fiddler on the Roof* was the hit of the season and played on Broadway until July 2, 1972.

Still critics were unsure about the sustained appeal of such an ethnically specific play. Theophilus Lewis in *America* wrote, "Not that extravagant praise of *Fiddler* involves more than a remote risk." Nonetheless critics praised the source material, Sholom Aleichem's stories. Howard Taubman in the *New York Times* asked, "Who would have guessed that the stories of Sholom Aleichem would be suitable for the musical stage?" The reviewer in *Time* magazine said, "Paradoxically, *Fiddler*'s conscientious good taste may have robbed it of the richer seasoning of the Sholem Aleichem tale it comes from. *Fiddler* does not swell with Aleichem's yeasty joy, pain and mystery of living."

Some critics thought that *Fiddler* would save Broadway. Taubman wrote: "It has been prophesied that the Broadway musical theater would take up the mantle of meaningfulness worn so carelessly by the American drama in recent years. *Fiddler on the Roof* does its bit to make on this prophesy."

Fiddler received many rave reviews for its content. Henry Hewes in the *Saturday Review of Literature* wrote, "Joseph Stein and his collaborators have . . . arrived at a remarkably effective mixture that thoroughly entertains without ever losing a sense of connection with the more painful realities that underlie its humor, its beauty, and its ritual celebrations." Taubman argued that the play "catches the essence of a moment in history with sentiment and radiance. Compounded of the familiar materials of the musical theater—popular song, vivid dance movement, comedy and emotion—it combines and transcends them to arrive at an integrated achievement of uncommon quality."

Many of the critics who liked the play expected more from it, however. These critics believed the musical bowed too much to the cliches of Broadway. Taubman was one such critic. He wrote, "if I find fault with a gesture that is Broadway rather than the world of Sholom Aleichem, if I deplore a conventional scene, it is because *Fiddler on the Roof* is so fine that it deserves counsels towards perfection." In another review, Taubman said, "I wish it had the imagination and courage to turn away from all compromise with what are regarded as the Broadway necessities."

Several critics were not as impressed by *Fiddler on the Roof*. The critic from the *Nation* found the musical less satisfying than the source material, writing "I found it too endearing—worthy of the affection the enthusiastics had manifested. Yet thinking of it in its detail, the text lacked the full savor of the sources." Yet the critic went on to say that he changed his mind over time. Wilfred Sheed, writing in the *Commonweal,* was more harsh. He wrote, "some of the attempts to establish an atmosphere of Yiddish quaintness in *Fiddler* are pushy and overexposed and fair game for straight criticism. There is too much formula here; the village of Anatevka unburdens itself of more wry resignation in a half an hour that you'd expect to hear in a year."

Still, Sheed, like many other critics, singled out the performance of Zero Mostel, the original production's Tevye, for praise. Theophilus Lewis in *America* believed that "In human values, Tevye is a magnificent character, and Zero Mostel's portrayal is a memorable one." Taubman agreed, saying "Zero Mostel's Tevye is so penetrating and heartwarming that you all but forget that it is a performance." Mostel's Tevye has come to be regarded as the ultimate interpretation of the role.

CRITICISM

A. Petrusso

In this essay, Petrusso discusses the breakdown of tradition in Fiddler on the Roof.

In *Fiddler on the Roof,* tradition is an important theme, defining the lifestyle of Jews living in Anatevka, Russia, in 1905. As the dairyman Tevye says to the audience in the prologue to Act I, "Because of our traditions, we've kept our balance for many, many years. Because of our traditions, everyone knows who he is and what God expects him to do." Such traditions define every facet of

WHAT DO I READ NEXT?

- *Rags,* a musical written by Joseph Stein that was first produced in 1986. It continues the story of Tevye and his family upon their arrival in the United States.

- *Russia in the Age of Modernisation and Revolution 1881-1917,* published by Hans Rogger in 1983, is a history of Russia, including treatment of the Jews and the events of the Revolution of 1905.

- *Wandering Star* is a novel by Sholem Aleichem

published in translation in 1952. It concerns a Yiddish theatrical group touring Russia.

- *Life Is with People: the Culture of the Shetetl,* a nonfiction book published by Mark Zborowski and Elizabeth Herzog in 1952, describes the customs of a type of Jewish town known as a shetetl.

- *Native Land: A Selection of Soviet Jewish Writers* is a collection of short stories compiled by Chaim Beider and published in 1980.

Jewish life, including how young girls find husbands. But traditions that have not changed for many years are challenged in *Fiddler on the Roof.* Tevye, especially, is forced to accept change—as well as force change himself. Most of these changes are related to marrying off his daughters but not all. Tradition is challenged in *Fiddler on the Roof,* primarily through Tevye and his daughters.

Though Tevye claims to embrace tradition in the prologue to the first act, he regularly cuts corners. He invites change into his house in the form of Perchik, a former student from Kiev who is an outsider in the village. In Act I, scene two, the other villagers are suspicious of Perchik's warnings about the changes taking place in the world at large. While they think that Tevye's inability to make his deliveries is "bigger news than the plague in Odessa." Perchik tells them: "You should know what's going on in the outside world." Despite the villagers distrust, Tevye invites Perchik in for Sabbath supper. Further, Tevye hires him to teach his daughters, though a villager calls the thought of educating girls "radical."

There are conservative forces in Tevye's household. Golde, Tevye's wife, does not believe in women's education. When she catches Chava with a book in the first scene of Act I, she says "You were reading again? Why does a girl have to read?

Will it get her a better husband?" Later, in Act I, scene six, Golde interrupts her daughters' lessons with Perchik to have them help finish their father's work when he oversleeps.

While Tevye is a poor man who cannot afford dowries for his daughters, he wants learned men for their husbands. He agrees to Lazar's match, mostly because Lazar is a good man and relatively wealthy. However, when Tevye tells Tzeitel about the match in Act I, scene six, she begs him not make her marry Lazar. She tells her father, "Papa, I will be unhappy with him. All my life will be unhappy. I'll dig ditches, I'll haul rocks." This argument does not phase him, but when she says "Is that [an agreement] more important than I am, Papa? Papa, don't force me. I'll be unhappy all my days." His daughter's impassioned plea reaches his heart, and he agrees to dissolve his agreement with Lazar. Tevye's fondness for his daughters forces his second abandonment of tradition.

Tevye's daughters serve as some of the greatest agents of change in Stein's play. When Tzeitel believes that a match might have been made for her in Act I, scene three, she tells the man she really loves, Motel, that he must ask her father for her hand. Motel is afraid of Tevye and apprehensive because he is a poor tailor. He says that he does not feel adequate enough to ask for her hand—at least not until he gets his new sewing machine. Though Motel does not work up enough courage in this scene, he is forced to do so in Act I, scene six, when Tevye tells Tzeitel about the match with Lazar.

Tevye does not abandon tradition without an argument, however. When Motel offers himself as a prospective husband for Tzeitel, Tevye says "Either you're completely out of your mind or you're crazy. Arranging a match for yourself. What are you, everything? The bridegroom, the matchmaker, the guests all rolled into one?" When Tevye finds out that Motel and Tzeitel gave a pledge to each other over a year ago, he is outraged. In a reprise of the song "Tradition," Tevye sings incredulously "They gave each other a pledge / Unheard of, absurd / Where do you think you are? / In Moscow? / In Paris? / This isn't the way it's done / Not here, not now / Some things I will not, I cannot, allow." Despite these misgivings, Tevye sees that his daughter is happy with the poor tailor and eventually relents. In fact, Tevye goes as far as to deceive his wife in Act I, scene seven, describing a horrific dream so that this wedding can occur.

Tevye's second daughter Hodel starts out as the family's biggest keeper of tradition next to her father. Early on, when Tzeitel worries that Yente has brought a match to her mother, Hodel says, "Well, somebody has to arrange the matches. Young people can't decide these things for themselves." Hodel likes the rabbi's son. She is even the first to be suspicious when Perchik says he is a "good teacher." She replies, "I heard once, the rabbi who must praise himself has a congregation of one."

But Hodel is the first daughter to really break tradition, under Perchik's influence. In Act I, scene six, she is left alone with him for a moment. Hodel perceives she has been insulted by Perchik and immediately turns to tradition for support. She tells him, "We have an old custom here. A boy acts respectfully to a girl. But, of course, that is too traditional for an advanced thinker like you." Perchik protests several lines later, stating that "our ways are changing all over but here. Here men and women must keep apart. Men study. Women in the kitchen. Boys and girls must not touch, should not even look at each other." Perchik goes on to tell her that in the city, men and women, girls and boys can dance together. He grabs her hand and starts to dance with her. Though startled, Hodel dances along.

Later, during Tzeitel's wedding, Hodel and Perchik are public agents of change. At the recep-

> "TRADITION IS CHALLENGED IN *FIDDLER ON THE ROOF*, PRIMARILY THROUGH TEVYE AND HIS DAUGHTERS"

tion in Act I, scene ten, Perchik goes over to the women's side and asks Hodel to dance. While some villagers call this act a "sin," Tevye defends the young man's brash act. After Perchik and Hodel dance, Tevye joins in and makes Golde dance with him. Soon the rest of the village joins in, save Lazar and Yente. Both of them have suffered the most because of these breaks with tradition.

Finally, when Perchik must leave in Act II, scene one, he asks Hodel to marry him. She agrees, though it will be a hard life for her. Tevye enters and they tell him of their engagement. This break with tradition is again hard for him to understand. He believes they are asking for his permission and tells them no. Perchik tells him, "We are not asking for your permission, only for your blessing. We are going to get married." Tevye has another crisis of conscious, but he asks himself "did Adam and Eve have a matchmaker? Yes, they did. Then it seems these two have the same matchmaker." Again, when Tevye sees that one of his daughters is happy, he gives in and breaks with tradition. He allows Hodel to travel to Siberia, where she will marry Perchik. There is no wedding for him to attend, though she promises to keep one tradition and marry under a "chupa" or canopy.

Of all of Tevye's daughters, however, Chava makes the biggest break with tradition. She crosses a line that even Tevye cannot allow. In Act I, scene eight, Chava minds Motel's tailor shop for a moment. During that time, a young Russian man named Fyedka begins to talk to her. He tells her, "I've often noticed you at the bookseller's. Not many girls in this village like to read." He goes on to offer a book to her. Chava is uncomfortable with him because he is not Jewish. She does not want to take the book, but she finds herself doing so. When Motel returns, she lies to him, saying that the book is her's. By Act II, scene two, the villagers, like Yente,

A scene from a 1971 Broadway production featuring Peg Murray as Golde and Paul Lipson as Tevye

have noticed that the Russian and Chava have been spending time together.

In Act II, scene five, things come to a head. Chava tells Fyedka that she is afraid to tell anyone about their relationship. When Tevye comes by, Fyedka wants to talk to him, but Chava says that she is the one who must confront her father. She argues, ''The world is changing, Papa.'' He replies, ''No. Some things do not change for us. Some things will never change.'' Chava then informs her father that she and Fyedka want to be married. He says that he will not allow it and grows angry. By the next scene, Chava has secretly married Fyedka and begs her father to accept the union. He cannot. Tevye asks, ''Accept them? How can I accept them. Can I deny everything I believe in? On the other hand, can I deny my own child? On the other hand, how can I turn my back on my faith, my people? If I try to bend that far, I will break.'' Chava leaves with her husband, disowned. Tevye says that she is dead to him.

In the final scene of the musical, Chava comes with her husband to say goodbye following the Jews' expulsion from the village. Though Golde and Tzeitel warmly greet her, Tevye still cannot accept what she has done. Fyedka and Chava tell them that are leaving the village, too, because they do not want to be a part of this injustice. Just before the couple leaves Tevye tells Chava in a quiet way ''God be with you,'' acknowledging her and the changes in tradition that inevitably have come to his family.

Tevye and his daughters force an evolution in society's transitions which predict greater changes for their village and their country. The community of Anatevka is literally breaking down at the end of *Fiddler on the Roof* just like the traditions that fell through the course of the play. A way of life is disintegrating, making way for new traditions and mores. Stein implies that people like Tevye contribute to such a process. By being innovators, the agents of change, those involved gain the strength of character to face an uncertain future.

Source: A. Petrusso, for *Drama for Students,* Gale, 2000.

Thomas M. Disch

Reviewing a 1991 revival production of Fiddler on the Roof, *Disch finds that Stein's play still has the power to charm an audience. The critic summa-*

rized: "As of right now this is the best musical on Broadway."

Of *Fiddler on the Roof* little more need be said that it is as good as ever. The art of curatorship has rarely been exercised so scrupulously in the Broadway theater. The Chagallesque sets by Boris Aronson have been faithfully reproduced; ditto the Zipprodt costumes. The credits at the foot of the program are worth quoting in full for what they may portend for future revivals: "Original Production Directed & Choreographed by Jerome Robbins," followed in letters half that size by "Choreography Reproduced by Sammy Dallas Bayes/Direction Reproduced by Ruth Mitchell." The role of Tevye is reproduced by Topol, who, oddly, seems younger this time round than in the 1970 movie version, when he had to work at looking the age he's now achieved naturally. So, if you loved *Fiddler* in 1964, you can love it again just the same; and if you missed it then, here's your chance. Book (Joseph Stein), score (Jerry Bock) and lyrics (Sheldon Harnick) may never before have meshed with this kind of Rolls-Royce precision.

Has Time, then, played none of its usual ironic tricks on the text? Well, it does seem darker to me now, and the final curtain, with Tevye heading for the New World but leaving behind three daughters probably destined to be victims of the Holocaust, seems overtly tragic. In the movie version, by contrast, the final emphasis is that Tevye's glass is half-full rather than half-empty: America awaits him, in Technicolor. And if *Fiddler*'s a tragedy, then may it not be a tragic flaw in Tevye's character that he accedes to his daughters' determination to marry for love rather than prudentially? It's a question that makes the story a lot more interesting, though it must remain unanswerable. Everyone in the cast does a splendid job, but I won't recite the honor roll. I'll just give an unqualified recommendation. As of right now this is the best musical on Broadway.

Source: Thomas M. Disch, review of *Fiddler on the Roof* in the *Nation,* Vol. 252, no. 1, January 7/14, 1992, pp. 26–27.

Harold Clurman

While finding the show "endearing—worthy of affection," Clurman ultimately finds Stein's Fiddler on the Roof *to be less than great theatre.*

After seeing *Fiddler on the Roof* (based on some Yiddish short stories; book by Joseph Stein, music by Jerry Bock, lyrics by Sheldon Harnick) numerous members of the audience confessed (or proclaimed) that they shed tears of compassion and gratitude; others have asserted that their hearts swelled in elation, while still others were convulsed with laughter. My own reception of the show was cool.

I too found it endearing—worthy of the affection the enthusiasts had manifested. Yet thinking of it in its detail, the text lacked the full savor of its sources; the music simply followed a pattern of suitable folk melodies without adding, or being equal, to them; Jerome Robbins' choreography, though correct in its method, was not—except for two instances—as brilliant as I had expected it to be. Boris Aronson's sets did not "overwhelm" me; even Zero Mostel's performance, which cements the diverse elements and gives them a core and a shape, was open to objections. Then, too, were not those critics right, in the press and the public, who maintained there was a Broadway taint in the mixture?

Yet the longer I reflected, the greater grew my regard for the show! The steadier my effort to arrive at a true appraisal of my feelings, the more clearly I realized that the general audience reaction was justified. By a too meticulous weighing and sifting of each of the performance's components one loses sight of the whole.

The production is actually *discreet.* For a popular ($350,000) musical there is a certain modesty in its effect. The vast machinery of production—I do not refer to the physical aspects alone—which must perforce go into the making of an entertainment of this sort has by an exercise of taste been reduced to a degree of intimacy that is almost surprising.

The choreography, for example, does not attempt to electrify: though it is rather more muscular, broader and certainly less "cosy" than Jewish folk dancing tends to be, Robbins has on the whole successfully combined the homeliness of such dancing with Cossack energy. And though Aronson's sets may remind one of Chagall, they do not really attempt to achieve Chagall-like results. (Chagall's art is always more emphatically Russian or French than anything else. Whatever their subject, his paintings possess a certain opulent flamboyance that is hardly Jewish.) Aronson, faced with the need to

"SHOLOM ALEICHEM'S CHARACTERS ARE A CONCENTRATE OF MAN'S BELIEF IN LIVING WHICH DOES NOT EXCLUDE HIS INEVITABLE BEWILDERMENT AND QUESTIONING OF LIFE'S HARDSHIP AND BRUTAL CONFUSION"

move his sets rapidly, as well as to give them the atmosphere of impoverishment required by the play's environment without robbing them of a certain quiet charm, has made his contribution to the proceedings relatively unobtrusive—which a Chagall stage design never is. (There is also in Aronson's pictorial scheme a nice contrast between the ramshackle drabness of the places in which the play's characters are housed and the profuse yet delicate greenery of the natural surroundings.) Considering too the dizzying extravagance of Mostel's histrionic quality, his performance is remarkably reserved.

None of this, however, goes to the heart of the show's significance, which must be sought in its effect on the audience. That effect comes close, within the facile laughter, the snug appreciation of an anticipated showmanship, to something religious. To understand this one must turn to the play's original material: stories by Sholom Aleichem. Sholom Aleichem (pen name for Sholom Robinowitz, born in Russia in 1859, died in New York in 1916) was the great folk artist of Yiddish literature—an altogether unique figure who might without exaggeration be compared to Gogol. The essence of Sholom Aleichem's work is in a very special sense *moral*. It is the distillation of a humane sweetness from a context of sorrow. It represents the unforced emergence of a real joy and a true sanctification from the soil of life's workaday worries and pleasures. Although this blessed acceptance of the most commonplace facts of living—generally uncomfortable and graceless, to say the least—appears casual and unconscious in Sholom Aleichem, it is based on what, in the first and indeed the best of the play's numbers, is called "Tradition."

This tradition, which might superficially be taken to comprise little more than a set of obsolete habits, customs and pietistic prescriptions, is in fact the embodiment of profound culture. A people is not cultured primarily through the acquisition or even the making of works of art; it is cultured when values rooted in biologically and spiritually sound human impulses, having been codified, become the apparently instinctive and inevitable mode of its daily and hourly conduct. Sholom Aleichem's characters are a concentrate of man's belief in living which does not exclude his inevitable bewilderment and questioning of life's hardship and brutal confusion.

In the stories this is expressed as a kindness which does not recognize itself, as pity without self-congratulation, as familiar humor and irony without coarseness. This is beauty of content, if not of form. For the Eastern (Russian, Polish, Rumanian, Galician) Jews of yesteryear "would have been deeply puzzled," Irving Howe and Eleazer Greenberg have said in their admirable introduction to a collection of Yiddish stories, "by the idea that the aesthetic and the moral are distinct realms, for they saw beauty above all in behavior."

More of this meaning than we had a right to expect is contained in *Fiddler on the Roof*. Is it any wonder, then that an audience, living in one of the most heartless cities of the world at a time of conformity to the mechanics of production, an audience without much relation to any tradition beyond that expressed through lip service to epithets divested of living experience, an audience progressively more deprived of the warmth of personal contact and the example of dignified companionship, should weep thankfully and laugh in acclamation at these images of a good life lived by good people? In *Fiddler on the Roof* this audience finds a sense of what "togetherness" might signify. Without the cold breath of any dogma or didactics, it gets a whiff of fellow feeling for the unfortunate and the persecuted. It is a sentiment that acts as a kind of purification.

Is there too much "show biz" in *Fiddler on the Roof?* Undoubtedly. But apart from the fact that dramaturgic and musical equivalents of Sholom Aleichem's genius are not to be had for the asking, is it conceivable that a truly organic equivalent of the original stories could be produced in our time at a theatre on West 45th Street? The makers and players of *Fiddler on the Roof* are not of Kiev, 1905, nor do they live (even in memory) a life remotely akin to that of Tevye the Dairyman, his family and his friends, or of the author who begat them. The producers of *Fiddler on the Roof* are Broadway—as is the audience—and, in this instance, perhaps the best of it. Those who have attended some of the latter-day productions of the Yiddish stage itself will know that they too are as alien to the spirit of Sholom Aleichem as anything we see at the Imperial Theatre.

The name of Chagall has almost unavoidably come up. The nearest thing to that artist's type of imagination dwells within *Fiddler on the Roof*'s leading actor. Zero Mostel has "Chagall" in his head. Mostel's clown inspiration is unpredictably fantastic—altogether beyond the known or rational. One wishes this fantasy were allowed fuller scope in the show, even as compliments for its control are in order. For Mostel too, being part of Broadway, will fleetingly lapse into adulterations inhospitable to his fabulous talent.

Source: Harold Clurman, review of *Fiddler on the Roof* in the *Nation,* Vol. 199, no. 10, October 12, 1964.

SOURCES

Hewes, Henry. "Broadway's Dairy Air" in the *Saturday Review of Literature,* October 10, 1964, p. 33.

Lewis, Theophilus. Review of *Fiddler on the Roof* in *America,* January 2, 1965, p. 25.

Review of *Fiddler on the Roof* in the *Nation,* October 12, 1964, p. 229.

Review of *Fiddler on the Roof* in *Time,* October 2, 1964, p. 82.

Sheed, Wilfred. "The Stage: A Zero and a Cipher" in the *Commonweal,* October 16, 1964, p. 100.

Taubman, Howard. "For Better or For Worse: Unaware of Limitations Popular Musical Theater Turns to Unusual Themes—'Fiddler' Brings One Off" in the *New York Times,* October 4, 1964, section 2, p. 1.

Taubman, Howard. "Theater: Mostel as Tevye in 'Fiddler on the Roof'" in the *New York Times,* September 23, 1964, p. 56.

FURTHER READING

Altman Richard and Mervyn Kaufman. *The Making of a Musical: Fiddler on the Roof,* Crown, 1971.

> This book discusses *Fiddler on the Roof* from its conception to the original Broadway production as well as premiers in Europe and the Middle East. The evolution of the movie version is also included.

Guernsey, Otis L., Jr. *Broadway Song & Story: Playwrights, Lyricists, and Composers Discuss Their Hits,* Dodd, Mead, 1986, p. 115.

> This is an interview with Jerry Bock, Sheldon Harnick, and Joseph Stein on the creative process behind *Fiddler on the Roof.*

Rosenberg, Bernard, and Ernest Harbug. *The Broadway Musical: Collaboration in Commerce and Art,* Crown, 1971.

> This book discusses the creative and financial process of putting together a Broadway musical, including *Fiddler on the Roof* in its discussion.

Suskin, Steven. *Opening Night on Broadway: A Critical Quotebook of the Golden Era of Musical Theatre,* Schirmer, 1990.

> This book features summaries of critical response to and quotes from reviews of original Broadway productions, including *Fiddler on the Roof.*

Fool for Love

SAM SHEPARD

1983

Sam Shepard's *Fool for Love* is arguably the playwright's best known play. Focusing, as many of Shepard's plays do, on the dark side of life in the West, *Fool for Love* was first produced at the Magic Theatre in San Francisco in February, 1983, before moving to Off-Broadway at the Circle Repertory Theatre in May of that year. Shepard himself directed these original productions, winning Obie Awards for his writing and directing as well as the award for best new American play.

Critics gave *Fool for Love* mixed reviews. The play is primarily a struggle, mostly of words, between two on-again/off-again lovers, Eddie and May. By the end of the play, it is revealed that this is an incestuous relationship between half-siblings. Some of the dissenting critics found the dialogue between them, especially at the beginning of the play, to be cliched. Others believed that Shepard was covering territory and themes that he had dealt with to better effect in plays such as *Buried Child* and *True West,* adding nothing new and going nowhere fast. Critics who praised the play found the character of May to be one of the first strong, autonomous women created by Shepard. Some critics also found the device of the Old Man, a ghost-like presence on stage, to be very effective.

Most critics agreed that with this new play, Shepard continued his exploration of the mythic American West—particularly as it was portrayed in the pulp entertainment of the 1950s and 1960s—and

its extrapolation to contemporary environments and relationships. As Frank Rich wrote in the *New York Times,* "*Fool for Love* is a western for our time. We watch a pair of figurative gunslingers fight to the finish—not with bullets, but with piercing words that give ballast to the weight of a nation's buried dreams."

AUTHOR BIOGRAPHY

Shepard was born Samuel Shepard Rogers III on November 5, 1943, in Fort Sheridan, Illinois. He was the son of Samuel Shepard and Jane Elaine (Schook) Rogers. His father was an Army officer, and Shepard grew up on military bases. The family eventually settled in Duarte, California, where Shepard's father bought a farm. Shepard attended Mount San Antonio Junior College in Walnut, California, for several years, studying agriculture.

As a teenager, Shepard's home life grew increasingly difficult; his father had become an abusive alcoholic and father and son frequently were at odds. In 1963, Shepard left home for New York City, seeking work as an actor. On the bus ride to New York, Shepard changed his named from Steve Rogers, as he had been known all his life, to Sam Shepard. The next year his first play, entitled *Cowboys,* was produced. Through his work as both a writer and actor, Shepard became something of a cult celebrity in New York City's East Village in the 1960s and early-1970s.

Shepard wrote numerous Off-Broadway and Off-Off-Broadway plays (several of which won Obie Awards), several screenplays (including *Zabriskie Point,* with four others), and appeared in numerous experimental theatre productions. Many of Shepard's plays featured characters and myths culled from the vanishing American West as well as more general topics pertaining to American culture. Shepard was married in 1969 to actress O-Lan Jones, with whom he had a son, Jesse. Shepard and his family spent 1971-74 in England, where he wrote some of his best-known early plays, notably 1971's *Mad Dog Blues* and 1972's *The Tooth of Crime.*

Upon his return to the United States, Shepard's work took on new dimensions. By the late-1970s, Shepard began acting in feature films. He also continued to write important plays, many of which focused on broken families, difficult relationships between men and women, and the individual's quest for identity. In 1979, Shepard received the Pulitzer Prize for Drama for his play, *Buried Child.* Shepard's career as a movie actor also grew. He appeared in such notable films as *Days of Heaven* (1979) and *The Right Stuff* (1983). In 1983, he worked with Jessica Lange in *Frances,* becoming romantically involved with her. After divorcing his first wife, Shepard and Lange became a couple and had two children together, Hannah and Sam Walker.

The year 1983 was big one for Shepard, in addition to appearing in two high profile films and meeting his life partner, Lange, he expanded his theatrical influence considerably. He directed the original production of *Fool for Love* at Circle Repertory Company in New York City. He received two Obie Awards, one for his directing effort and the other for the best new American play. Two years later, in 1985, Shepard wrote the screenplay for Robert Altman's film adaptation of *Fool for Love* and played the role of Eddie in the film.

Since then, Shepard has continued to write and direct plays, including the 1986 family play *A Lie of the Mind.* He has also written several screenplays, including *Paris, Texas* and *Silent Tongue.* Shepard spent much of the late-1980s and 1990s acting in numerous films and television movies, including *Baby Boom, Thunderheart, Purgatory,* and *Dash & Lilly,* while experimenting with different theatrical forms including adaptation and comedy. By the late-1990s, his reputation was solidified as one of the greatest living American playwrights.

PLOT SUMMARY

Fool for Love opens in a cheap, sparsely furnished motel room on the edge of the Mojave desert. May, a woman in her early thirties, sits on the edge of the bed, staring at the floor. Eddie, a man in his late thirties, is dressed in cowboy gear and sits in a chair at the table. Eddie assures May that he is not leaving her. May accuses him of having another woman's smell on his fingers. May worries that he will erase her and threatens to kill the other woman. Eddie tries to calm her down, saying that he has come thousands of miles to see her. May still accuses him of being with a rich woman. Eddie admits he took someone out to dinner once, but May believes there is more to it.

Sam Shepard speaking at a workshop at the University of Minnesota

Eddie tries to change the subject. He tells May that he is taking her back. He bought land in Wyoming. May does not want to move because she has a job now as a cook and does not want the kind of life Eddie is offering. Eddie promises to take care of her. He rises to get his things from his car, but May is not sure. Before he gets out the door, she kisses him, then knees him in the groin. Eddie falls to the ground. She goes into the bathroom, slamming the door behind her.

Eddie lies on the floor and begins to talk to the Old Man, who has been on stage since the beginning of the play. Like Eddie, the Old Man is dressed in cowboy gear. He sits in a rocking chair, drinking whiskey. It is indicated that he is not a real person but a figment of May and Eddie's imaginations. May comes out of the bathroom and changes into a sexy red dress. She tells Eddie that she hates him and that she has someone coming to visit her. Eddie immediately becomes jealous and leaves. May pulls her suitcase out from under the bed and quickly packs it. When she hears Eddie returning, she hides it.

Eddie returns with a shotgun and some tequila. He offers May some of his alcohol, but she claims she is on the wagon. Eddie questions her about the man who will visit. Eddie tells May they will both sit and wait for him. May does not want Eddie to meet her date. May complains that Eddie has disrupted her life for far too long. Eddie reminds her that they will always be connected. May asks him to leave. Eddie calls her a traitor and leaves with his gun.

As soon as Eddie leaves, May calls out his name and sinks to the floor. The Old Man begins to tell a story that indicates that he is May's father. The story concerns a car ride the Old Man, May, and her mother took through Utah. May hears Eddie coming back, and she quickly scrambles to sit on the bed, staring at the tequila. Eddie comes in and May takes a drink. Eddie tells May that he almost left, but then he realized that May was probably making up the story about the date to get even with him. May says that she can never get even with him.

May accuses Eddie of not realizing that it is over. Eddie wants to know if she has had sex with this man yet. She does not answer him but wants to know what he plans on doing when the man comes. Eddie says that he will hurt him. May tries to leave, but Eddie grabs hold of her. May screams, and Eddie takes her inside. Eddie promises to be good and introduce himself as her cousin, not her brother. May does not want Eddie to meet the man and threatens to call off the date. Just as she is about to leave, headlights stream into the window. Eddie promises May that he will not hurt the man.

May opens the door and realizes that it is not her date because the car is a Mercedes-Benz. Eddie tells her to close the door and come back in, but May says someone in the car is staring at her. Eddie hides behind the bed. He tells May to get away from the door. The woman in the car fires her pistol at Eddie's truck, flashes her headlights, and honks continuously on her horn. May begins fighting Eddie as he drags her down to the ground. May accuses him of bringing this woman here, asserting that this is the woman she suspects Eddie of dating. Eddie forces her to stay down. The woman in the Mercedes leaves. Eddie admits that woman is crazy. May asks if he has had sex with her yet. Eddie finds that his windshield has been blown out.

May turns on the lights, but Eddie turns them off. Eddie wants them to leave. May tells him that she is not going with him. The Old Man starts to speak again, about how Eddie and May both look their mothers not like him or his family. The focus returns to Eddie, who tells May that he will not leave, and he will track her down wherever she goes. May does not believe his love will last,

because he has professed his fidelity before and left her numerous times over the past fifteen years. May tells him she does not want him anymore. Eddie tries to push her into the bathroom, but she screams. At that moment, Martin, May's date, pushes himself inside. Martin tackles Eddie and almost punches him before May stops him. Martin says he heard the screams and thought something was wrong. May introduces Eddie as her cousin. Eddie immediately contradicts her, calling her a liar and presenting himself as her half-brother.

Martin explains his tardiness. He forgot that he had to water the football fields. Martin apologizes for knocking Eddie over, saying that he thought May was in trouble. Eddie says that she is in trouble. May says that they were going to leave right before he came, but Eddie contradicts her again and continues to toy with Martin. May tries to get Martin to leave with her, but Eddie says that it would be better to stay and tell stories. May goes into the bathroom. Martin tries to leave, but Eddie stops him and slams him against the wall. Eddie tells Martin that he and May know each other from high school, that she is his half-sister. Eddie continues with his story, informing Martin that they did not know they were related until after they began a sexual relationship.

Eddie elaborates the story further, and the Old Man chimes in on the details. The Old Man had two separate lives with two women, May's mother and Eddie's mother, and he would go back and forth between them. One day, the Old Man took Eddie to May's mother's house, and that is when Eddie met May. May breaks in and tells Eddie that he is crazy and a liar. Martin tries to leave several times, but Eddie makes him stay and listen to the story. May finishes it for him, telling Martin that her mother figured out something was going on and followed the Old Man around until she found the other woman. The Old Man left both women soon after, and by this time, Eddie and May were seeing each other. May's mother tried to break them up, but it did not work. Eddie's mother eventually committed suicide. The Old Man claims not to have known this. The Old Man is appalled as Eddie and May come together and kiss.

Outside, the rich woman in the Mercedes returns and sets fire to Eddie's truck, freeing his horses. Martin informs Eddie of this, and Eddie goes out to check on it. May continues to pack. Martin offers to help May, asking if she will be going with Eddie. She says that he is already gone. May leaves the room.

CHARACTERS

Eddie

Eddie is a cowboy-type in his late thirties. He is the older half-brother of May, with whom he has had an on-again/off-again love affair for fifteen years. Eddie is a liar and unreliable. He has appeared out of nowhere, claiming to have traveled several thousand miles to see May. From the first, May accuses him of having an affair with a rich woman, which Eddie denies. Throughout the course of *Fool for Love,* May's suspicions prove correct as the rich woman shoots out Eddie's windshield, sets fire to his truck, and frees his horses. Eddie also promises to not tell Martin, a man with whom May has a date, that they are brother and sister, but Eddie does anyway. He also tells Martin about his odd relationship with his half-sister. Eddie also has a violent streak, and threatens May physically several times. He tries to control May physically and emotionally, but she does not give in. May allows Eddie to pull her down at one point, but she ultimately rises above his pettiness. Though Eddie claims to want May throughout the play, at the end, he leaves without her.

Martin

Martin is May's date for the evening. He works as a gardener and day laborer. When he first arrives, May's room is dark and she is screaming. Martin takes action, pulling Eddie off May and slamming him against the wall. When May tells Martin that Eddie is her cousin and there was nothing wrong, Martin apologizes. May has already described him as ''gentle'' and he lives up to this description. Martin does not display much shock when Eddie and May reveal the nature of their relationship. After Eddie leaves, Martin offers to help May, but she refuses.

May

May is the younger half-sister of Eddie. She is in her early thirties. May lives in the motel room where all the action of *Fool for Love* takes place. She has recently gotten a job as a cook. May has been getting on with her life after putting up with Eddie loving and leaving her for fifteen years. Eddie's return upsets May. She claims to smell another woman, a rich woman, on his fingers, and she is right. When May tells Eddie that she has a date that night, Eddie becomes jealous and finds it hard to believe. He cannot accept that May might have been with another man and has her own life.

May has not fully accepted it either. She has mixed feelings about Eddie and knows the trouble he can cause. When her date arrives, Eddie sabotages May's relationship with Martin by telling him that he and May are lovers as well as half-siblings. After Eddie leaves at the end, Martin asks May if she is going with him, but May knows Eddie and his habits too well. The half-siblings go their separate ways.

The Old Man

The Old Man is Eddie and May's father. Like Eddie, he dresses in cowboy gear. While he appears as a character on stage, the old man is actually a figment of their imaginations. During the play, the Old Man listens to the discussion between Eddie and May, occasionally commenting on what has been said. He becomes troubled when Eddie and May start talking about their affair and how the Old Man had two separate lives with their mothers. When May reveals that her mother committed suicide, the Old Man is surprised at the revelation. The Old Man only finds comfort in his imagined marriage with country singer Barbara Mandrell.

THEMES

Memories and Reminiscence

Eddie and May's joint past fuels much of *Fool for Love.* Each of them carries their own interpretation of the memory of their relationship. Eddie wants this memory to continue as reality into the future. That is why he has tracked May down to this motel room. May wants to escape the past and move on with her life as a individual. The memories seem to make this choice impossible. At the end of the play, Eddie effectively ends May's potential relationship with Martin by telling him about the roots of he and his half-sister's incestuous affair. May gets her opinion in, too, by finishing Eddie's story from her point of view. Eddie tries to use memory to try to control May, but she has grown beyond his manipulations. May has her own memories of Eddie repeatedly abandoning her; she has learned to use her bad memories of his desertions as reinforcement in refusing him.

Memory also comes into play in another way in *Fool for Love.* According to Shepard's description, the character of the Old Man is a figment of the siblings' imaginations. He is their father, but not really living in the same way they are. He is an independent reminiscence that addresses his children, primarily Eddie, as needed. The Old Man is more than a memory, however. Through Eddie and May's dialogue, the Old Man becomes upset when he learns that his memory of the past is wrong. While the Old Man knows his double life has caused his children's problematic situation, he learns that May's mother killed herself because of his double dealings. May also says some things that contradict the Old Man's memory of the past. He tries to get Eddie to make May see things his way but fails.

Sex, Love, and Passion

Many of the memories Eddie and May share are of a sexual nature. Their feelings of love, hate, and jealousy drive *Fool for Love*. Since the moment they first met, before they knew they had the same father, Eddie and May have had a mutual passion. Though Eddie claims to love May, he also is involved with another woman, "the countess" as May calls her. During the course of *Fool for Love*, this woman shoots out Eddie's windshield, sets his truck on fire, and frees his horses—all presumably crimes related to her sexual jealousy. Eddie wants to continue his affair with May—and possess her sexually as he has in the past.

May's love is much more conflicted than Eddie's. When Eddie finds out that she will have a date that evening with Martin, his passion takes on a fury not unlike the rich woman's. Eddie proceeds to destroy May's potential new love with stories of their incestuous relationship. Similarly, while May wants to move on, she also retains some of her passion for Eddie.

Such uncontrolled passion is what led to the doomed situation in *Fool for Love* in the first place. The Old Man had two separate lives with two women. He fell in love with both of them. Indeed, the Old Man inadvertently introduced Eddie to May when the Old Man felt compelled to visit May's mother one evening. The Old Man's sexual sins drove Eddie's mother to suicide and live on in his children's tortured psyches.

Family

The fact that Eddie, May, and the Old Man are immediate family adds an unusual, volatile twist to the situation in the play. Over the course of the

MEDIA ADAPTATIONS

- *Fool for Love* was adapted by Shepard for the screen in 1985. Directed by Robert Altman, the film features Shepard playing the role of Eddie and Kim Basinger as May.

drama, Shepard drops hints that May and Eddie are related. It is not until the end that Shepard reveals that they are half-siblings and the Old Man is their father. In light of this revelation, Eddie and May's relationship is all the more disturbing. Yet while this is not a normal family, there are the same kind of misunderstandings and personal dynamics that exist in normal family relationships. For example, the Old Man led a double life with two women, resulting in May and Eddie. This Old Man is supposed to be a figment of Eddie and May's conscious, yet he disappeared while Eddie and May were still in high school. He did not know about the consequences of his disappearance. Eddie's mother killed herself, and May's mother essentially shut down emotionally. This kind of pain could be found in any kind of family, let alone the unusual one found in *Fool for Love*.

STYLE

Setting

Fool for Love takes place in a motel on the edge of the Mojave Desert in California. All the action is confined to one motel room, occupied by May. It is a cheap room with faded paintings and old fashioned floors and furnishings. Adjacent to the room is a bathroom and the parking lot. The Old Man sits in a rocker inside the room, from which he can observe the proceedings and comment as necessary. Because this room is May's and a symbol of her growing sense of independence, Eddie's presence seems like an invasion as he tries to control her

TOPICS FOR FURTHER STUDY

- Explore the themes of *Fool for Love* via the two pieces of music called for in the stage directions, Merle Haggard's ''Wake Up'' and ''I'm the One Who Loves You.''

- Research the psychological implications of incest. Use your research to explore May's conflicted feelings for Eddie and Eddie's desire for May.

- Compare *Fool for Love* with *Passion,* a play by Peter Nichols which appeared at the same time on Broadway. Both plays explore sexual politics, though *Passion* is about people from the upper class. What does each play say about class and sexual relationships in this time period?

- Research the psychology of men who lead dual lives with two or more women, like the Old Man did with Eddie's mother and May's mother. Why do they make this choice? How does it affect their children?

within it and lure her out of it. May ends up leaving on her own, but the Old Man, her father, remains, as he will be part of her consciousness forever.

Sound Effects

The tensions in *Fool for Love* are economically and effectively emphasized by sound effects. Every time Eddie or May bangs into a wall, the stage directions call for it to ''boom.'' According to the stage directions, the front and bathroom doors are supposed to be specially constructed to make the boom louder when they are slammed shut. This effect underscores the volatile emotions at hand.

Eddie's other woman, ''The Countess,'' never makes a physical appearance, but her presence is made known by sound and light effects. The audience sees the head beams of her Mercedes and the sound of the car pulling up in front of May's room. The countess's anger is amplified by the sounds of her pistol shooting out the window of Eddie's truck,

her releasing Eddie's horses from their carrier, and, finally, her setting his truck on fire. These sound effects make real May's suspicions about Eddie, and, in turn, give Eddie an excuse to physically protect May from The Countess.

Monologue

Near the end of *Fool for Love,* May and Eddie each have long monologues which allow them to tell their version of their shared past. When Eddie finds himself alone with Martin, May's date, he takes the opportunity to relate his and his sister's past. Eddie does this to shock Martin, scare him away so that he can have May all to himself. Eddie tells Martin about when he first met May, not knowing that she shared the same father as he. Eddie emphasizes the fact that they were in love from that first moment onwards. May overhears this story from the bathroom and interrupts when Eddie makes this claim. Then, in her monologue, she gets the opportunity to tell her side of the story. She finishes what Eddie has started, telling Martin what happened after they met. May describes their meeting, the discovery that their father was leading a double life. Their father left both of them. Eddie's mother committed suicide, while May's mother withdrew into herself. While Eddie only sees the good in their loving, May sees the tragic swells that have touched other lives.

The Old Man does not like May's version. Yet he, too, has a monologue near the beginning of the play. He describes an incident from May's childhood when he was living with her and her mother. May was a child upset during a long car ride. The Old Man stopped near a field and walked her around in it. The cows they came across had a calming effect on the child, and May was quiet the rest of the time. The Old Man's story is the first time he acknowledges that he is May's father. It makes him seem human and compassionate, not the kind of unfeeling womanizer who would lead a dual life with two separate families.

HISTORICAL CONTEXT

In 1983, the United States was a country of contradictions. Its president was Republican Ronald Reagan, who served a total of two terms with his conservative, anti-Communist platform. Reagan was a former movie actor who often played western hero roles; his presidency was greatly informed by his persona as an actor, as he co-opted heroic cowboy rhetoric in his diplomatic dealings and made highly effective use of his television-ready talents. Reagan was also seen as family man, though he was the first president to have been divorced. Many Americans responded to Reagan's role as president, though a number of critics, finding the former thespian's politics superficial and showy, complained that the executive's position was little more than that, a role essayed by an actor.

In 1982, a five-year recession ended for the United States. While inflation in 1983 was only 3.2%, the economy was only relatively prosperous despite Reagan's promises. Reagan's government promoted supply-side economics and de-industrialization. There were many mergers and acquisitions as the government promoted deregulation for big industries. Tax cuts were given to the rich and the government spent a great deal of money building up the military (the era marked the largest peacetime growth of U.S. defense in history). The American stock market was in the midst of a bull market (a trading trend in which high optimism results in aggressive trading). While there were tax increases for social security, the wealthy had more disposable income.

Along those lines, the lifestyle of the wealthy became a popular topic for a large part of the country. Appearances were important and glitz ruled on television, movies, and books. Popular television shows included fictional soap operas such as *Dynasty* and *Dallas* and infotainment mainstay *Lifestyles of the Rich and Famous*. Material success was seen as important. Books like *Hollywood Wives* by Jackie Collins in 1983 also promoted glitzy lifestyle. In 1983, movies such as *Risky Business* and *Trading Places* promoted a ''have it all'' mentality. This consumer boom stretched to the common man but not far. David Mamet's 1983 play *Glengarry Glen Ross* showed the darker side of the pursuit of material wealth.

Common people did not do as well as their upper class counterparts. They did not benefit from economic prosperity. There was a decline in real wages. At the beginning of 1983, the number of unemployed was 11.5 million. By the end, it was about 35 million. There was more corporate uncertainty as heavy industry became deindustrialized

Kim Basinger as May in a scene from director Robert Altman's film adaptation; this scene shows May at work in the cafe, a setting that is only alluded to in the stage version

and deregulated. The homeless rate increased about 25% per year in the 1980s. There was increased violence on American streets and handgun sales boomed. There was also increased tensions between races, and child abuse became a national crisis.

Some popular musicians expressed the turmoil of middle- and lower- class life. In 1983, there was a Rock against Reagan tour, organized to protest the president's economic policies that favored the minority rich while penalizing the lower- and middle-classes. Bruce Springsteen and the E Street Band also were quite popular in the mid-1980s. Springsteen, a ''normal guy'' from New Jersey, looked and dressed like a working man. He promoted patriotism, a hot topic at the time, yet questioned America's values in songs like his 1984 hit ''Born in the U.S.A.'' Springsteen was also one of the earliest artists to use music videos to promote his songs on MTV.

Another segment of society that suffered in the 1980s were farmers. There was a serious farm crisis during this period. Farmers produced more than

COMPARE & CONTRAST

- **1983:** Cellular phone service is tested in Chicago. The bulky phones cost $3000, while monthly service fees total about $150. The target audience is businessmen who need to keep in constant touch with clients and their home office.

  Today: Cellular phone service is available throughout the United States. Palm-sized phones are available. Phones and rates are relatively inexpensive. Many people use cellular phones to keep in touch with loved ones from anywhere at anytime.

- **1983:** Early Macintosh computers are introduced. The Lisa model is the first to feature a mouse. IBM announces its development of a chip that can story 512K of memory.

  Today: Personal computers are available for under $1000. Memory capabilities can measured in the gigabytes. The mouse is obsolete on laptops, which can feature trackpads to move a cursor. With widely available access to the Internet, people can easily remain in contact with their friends and family around the globe.

- **1983:** The United States invades the island of Grenada. Marines land to protect U.S. citizens (and interests) from the Marxist government.

  Today: The United States protects its interests by participating in the NATO (North Atlantic Treaty Organization) bombing of Kosovo, among other military operations.

---

they could sell. Land prices fell sharply. Many farmers had heavy debt and numerous family farms went bankrupt. The federal government was forced to subsidize farms and farmers. In 1985, the first Farm Aid benefit concert was held to help troubled farmers pay off their debts. Several movies were also made on this subject beginning in 1984. One, featuring Shepard the actor, was called *Country.*

CRITICAL OVERVIEW

Critics of the original productions of *Fool for Love* were divided from the first. Even those that praised the play, however, qualified their kudos. For example, Jack Kroll of *Newsweek* wrote, ''It's a classic rattlesnake riff by Shepard, the poet laureate of America's emotional Badlands. *Fool for Love* is minor Shepard, but nobody can match the sheer intensity he generates in his dramatizing of lyric obsessiveness.'' Frank Rich of the *New York Times* concurred: ''*Fool for Love* isn't the fullest Shepard creation one ever hopes to encounter, but, at this

point in this writer's prolific 20-year career, he almost demands we see his plays as a continuum: they bleed together.''

Even critics who disliked *Fool for Love* found Shepard's production worthy of note. Robert Brustein, in the *New Republic,* wrote, ''There is nothing very thick or complicated about either the characters or the plot, and the ending lacks resolution. But *Fool for Love* is not so much a text as a legend, not so much a play as a scenario for stage choreography, and under the miraculous direction of the playwright, each moment is rich with balletic nuances.'' Brustein credited Shepard's direction and his actors for the success of the play. Brustein ended his review by saying they ''exalt what in other hands might have been a slight, unfinished script into an elegiac myth of doomed love.'' William Kleb of *Theater* agreed, writing ''*Fool for Love* comes across as a kind of psycho-sexual free-for-all, or nightmare, and Shepard's production magnifies and intensifies the violence of its action and imagery.''

Some critics found the expression of fury in *Fool for Love* to be problematic to the point of monotony. Walter Kerr of the *New York Times* wrote, ''Physically and mechanically the [original] production knows what it is about. I wish we did. I say it because Mr. Shepard does not *want* us ever to be certain of what his door-slamming dance of rage is meant to signify.'' Kerr went on to say, ''The evening flirts with a fundamental boredom because of a strong sense that, under the makeup, there is nobody there.'' His colleague Rich concurred, noting, ''The knockabout physical humor sometimes becomes excessive both in the writing and in the playing; there are also, as usual, some duller riffs that invite us to drift away.'' T. E. Kalem of *Time* took it a step further, writing ''Even the love play is ominous. With his cowboy spurs and boots Shepard's symbols for the untrammeled, virile male Eddie hurls himself against walls, somersaults across the floor and swings his lariat to rope in bedposts and random chairs. This is an amusing form of sexual intimidation, but it does not wholly evade silliness.''

Kalem is one of several critics who found the impact of the incest angle less than satisfying. Kalem wrote that ''in an effort to give a vivid but scarcely mind-churning work more mythic gravity, Shepard makes known long the way that the lovers are half-sister and half-brother. Somehow this lacks impact, merely suggesting that incest is the most potent brand of sibling rivalry.'' Kleb agreed: ''incest has little or no real function in the development of the central conflict of the play, and it is a matter of moral indifference not only to the characters but, here, to the playwright as well.''

Critics who found *Fool for Love* problematic believed the play meanders. Catharine Hughes in *America,* wrote: ''As in *True West,* it is the old versus the new West, lust versus love, love versus hate, with the innocent and oblivious Martin caught in the violent crossfire. And, I regret to say, it winds up going no place. Shepard seems incapable of bringing it into focus.'' John Simon of *New York* held a similar view, stating that Shepard ''makes, I regret to say, less sense of himself here than others have been known to make of him in the past, but that maybe because *Fool for Love* is a particularly opaque and inconclusive play, with the kind of open ending that does not so much make you want to speculate about it as shut the door behind it.'' Not all critics agreed, however. Rich of the *New York Times* felt that ''it could be argued, perhaps, that both the glory and the failing of Mr. Shepard's art is its extraordinary afterlife: His words often play more feverishly in the mind after they're over than they do while they're before us in the theater.''

CRITICISM

A. Petrusso,

In this essay, Petrusso compares and contrasts the play and the film version of Fool for Love.

Sam Shepard wrote the stage play for *Fool for Love* in 1983. Two years later, Shepard wrote the screenplay for the filmed version of *Fool for Love* and appeared in the movie as Eddie. Thus, Shepard was able to make his mark on two different versions of the same story. He had to meld each to the demands of their respective genres but also had a chance to expand on and explore different ideas within his core story. In this essay, the differences and similarities between the two versions will be discussed, as well as what these aspects say about the core story.

At the heart of both the film and stage versions of *Fool for Love* is the tumultuous relationship between half-siblings Eddie and May. This conflict drives the plot and is the substance of the story. Eddie and May have carried on a long-time affair. There are accusations on both sides of abandonment and disloyalty. Both versions feature the lovers' rat-a-tat arguments, their ''coming together'' and ''falling apart.'' However, the dialogue in the play seems more intense and unyielding, mostly because of the production demands. In the stage version, *Fool for Love* is performed straight through, with no intermission. There is no break from the tension, no escaping the confrontation. It is an all-out assault on the audience. In the film version, events are broken up a little more. There are breaks and pauses that last much longer because the film allows for longer silences while visual images add to or reflect on the story at hand.

The variations on *Fool for Love*'s settings enhances these differences in dialogue and intensity level. The stage requires a very static setting. In the play, Shepard confines his actions to one place, May's motel room. There is no place else to go; the setting is claustrophobic and tense. When the play opens, Eddie is already inside May's space, the confrontation is already in swing. If Shepard had broken his play up into acts or scenes, there could have been more settings, but the play's confining force would have been compromised. As it stands, Eddie is intruding in May's place and invading her life. The Old Man, their father, is present off to one side, rocking in his chair. Shepard specifically says

WHAT DO I READ NEXT?

- *True West,* a play by Shepard that was first produced in 1980. This play also concerns troubled siblings (two brothers) and their absentee father.

- *The Magic Toyshop,* a novel by Angela Carlin that was published in 1969. The story focuses on an incestuous relationship through the eyes of a teenage girl.

- *Six Characters in Search of an Author,* a play by Luigi Pirandello that was published in 1950. The drama employs a technique similar to the one used in *Fool for Love* in which an empty chair is placed outside the frame.

- *Forbidden Partners: The Incest Taboo in Modern Culture,* a nonfiction book by James S. B. Twitchell published in 1987. In this book, Twitchell explores the use of incest in art and literature in the contemporary culture of the United States.

- *Buried Child,* a play by Shepard first produced in 1978. In the play, a family secret of incest and infanticide is accidentally discovered years after the fact.

in his stage directions that the Old Man ''exists only in the minds of May and Eddie.'' The Old Man's presence is very unnatural, spiritual, when compared to Eddie's imposing, corporeal presence.

These ideas take on very different forms in the film version. The space is again confined but not merely to May's motel room. The movie uses a whole motel complex, consisting of individual, free-standing motel cabins, a restaurant/bar, a play area for children, a trailer for the Old Man, and a large parking lot. This variety of settings opens up numerous possibilities for expanded scenes. When the movie opens, Eddie is on the road and May is working in the restaurant. Eddie seems much more predatory in the movie, in part because he circles May's new life as an animal would circle its prey.

Eddie pulls into the motel complex, and May hides from him within the restaurant. Eddie goes on his way, perhaps thinking he has pulled into the wrong place but returns a short time later. By then, May has gone to her cabin and locked the front door. Then she hides in the bathroom and locks that door as well. To drive home Eddie's invasion, Shepard has the character break down May's front door. He literally invades her space in the movie.

Eddie has not only physically invaded May's space, he has also invaded her sense of security, of mental stability. The audience can see that May has a job and her own life. These facts are stated but remain questionable in the play. Eddie and May make brief mention of her car, which tipped Eddie off that he was in the right place. There is no car in the play. May seems to have moved on, left her past behind—but for one factor. In the stage play, the Old Man is confined to a rocker on one side of the stage. In the movie, he has a whole trailer to himself with remnants of his past (mostly junk) surrounding it.

At the beginning of the movie, just before Eddie comes to the complex, May watches the Old Man through a window. He watches her back. This implies that May has lived with the Old Man's presence much more than Eddie. She might have a new life, but it is lived in the shadow of the Old Man and her past. Eddie seems free of this constraint. There is nothing to indicate that the Old Man's spirit haunts Eddie the way it does May. The only moment that comes close is when the Old Man invades Eddie's space, checking out his truck while Eddie makes one of his initial confrontations with May. This detail adds a different spin on the triangle between the Old Man, Eddie, and May. The Old Man is much more mobile in the film. He walks around, sometimes hiding in corners, listening and watching events unfold.

Whether or not the Old Man is a figment of Eddie and May's imagination in the film is debatable, but Shepard uses the demands of film to enhance one mythical part of the stage version. In the play, Shepard has Eddie, May, and the Old Man each deliver a monologue that tells part of their collective story. The Old Man talks about an incident when May was a child, crying in the car during a long trip. Eddie tells the first half of the story of how he and May met. May concludes the story. These tales may or may not be true in the stage play. It is hard to tell if they are part of the mythology these characters create about themselves or actual events. In the movie, these stories are told by the same characters, but Shepard uses the visual possibilities of the genre to add to their possible reality.

Shepard enhances these stories with a theme that runs through a large part of the film. Soon after Eddie appears, he goes outside to tend to his horses. May follows him. While they are in the parking lot, a couple and a little girl drive up. The threesome is dressed in 1950s clothing. They are the Old Man, May as a child, and May's mother from decades past. The family checks into the motel. Later, the man leaves, then comes back after a short while. When the man comes back, young May is locked outside and plays on the swing set. She is retrieved by her father a short time later. Before he does so, there is a moment where the young May and the real May look at each other and hug. After the father takes the young May from the adult May, the elder woman lies down in the sand that surrounds the swing set. The Old Man comes over and tells his story about May as a child.

However, the Old Man's story, like the ones Eddie and May tell later in the film, is almost a complete contradiction of the actual events. During each flashbacks, the actual events are shown. The stories match only in places, emphasizing the mythological elements in a way the stage play could never do. For example, in the Old Man's story, he, May's mother, and May are on a car trip, but May is not crying, nor is the mother asleep as he claims. Both are wide awake and silent. The Old Man does take young May into a field filled with cows, but it does not change the child's demeanor to any noticeable degree.

Similarly, Eddie talks about the way the Old Man lived with them and the walk they took one day where he first met May. Many of the details are visually contradictory. For example, Eddie says that his father gave him the first sip of liquor after his father purchased a bottle. The visual story has the Old Man not offering his son anything. However, Eddie and his father do take a walk to a house with a red awning, and Eddie does see a young May. Of the three, May's story matches the visuals the most, implying she is the most honest of the three characters, yet her story still contains several contradictory details. May is right about the fact that Eddie's mother committed suicide, something with which Eddie agrees and the Old Man finds appalling. He cannot tolerate harsh reality as well as his children can.

The movie and the stage play diverge on ''reality'' on one, final point. Because the play's action is

> THE PLAY CANNOT MATCH THE VISUAL ELEMENTS THAT THE FILM BOASTS. ULTIMATELY, THE FILM EXPLAINS WHAT THE PLAY IMPLIES. THE PLAY'S INTELLECTUAL DEMANDS ON ITS AUDIENCE ARE MUCH GREATER. THE AUDIENCE MUST DECIDE WHAT IS TRUTH AND WHAT IS MYTH"

confined to one room, the audience does not see the Countess (Eddie's other woman) and her Mercedes-Benz nor do they see Eddie's truck and his horses. While there are sound effects to make these elements seem real, the mythical aspects of the play can casts doubts on their existence. In the movie, these elements are shown. Though mere visual representation does not validate reality, the case for the existence of these elements is stronger in the film than the play. Though the Countess does not speak a word, she does step out of a Mercedes-Benz toting a gun. Similarly, there are horses, making Eddie's claims about a new life in Wyoming seem possible. At the end of the movie, after the Countess sets fire to Eddie's truck and May packs her bags to leave, Eddie is shown riding one of his horses to catch up with the Countess. May walks down the road in the opposite direction. What is implied at the end of the stage play becomes reality in the movie.

The stage and film versions of *Fool for Love* retain many of the same story elements but use them quite differently. Each version of the story is distinct. The movie's intensity level is not as sustained as the play's because of the demands of the genre. The play cannot match the visual elements that the film boasts. Ultimately, the film explains what the play implies. The play's intellectual demands on its audience are much greater. The audience must decide what is truth and what is myth as it watches the play unfold. The movie limits possible interpretations because many points left untold in the play are fully realized. Neither version is better than the other but both show the depth of Shepard's ability as both a playwright and screenwriter.

Playwright Shepard in the role of Eddie in Altman's film adaptation

Source: A. Petrusso, for *Drama for Students,* Gale, 2000.

Gerald Weales

Weales reviews Shepard's play in this excerpt, finding the work to be "at once ambiguous and concrete" in its depiction of a strange love affair.

Shepard's new play is *Fool for Love,* which came to New York from the Magic Theatre of San Francisco in the production Shepard directed for that theater (with which he has been allied for the last few years). Not the kind of love story that Austin was trying to write, this is a Shepard love story, which

means still another confrontation, one which reveals that May and Eddie, however often they try to go their separate ways, are inextricably bound together. It is a binding which suggests that of Lee and Austin and indicates that the play, whatever its surface melodramatic plot, is about the nature—the "double nature," I suppose I should say—of love. Since May and Eddie are (or may be: evidence is always hard to verify in a Shepard play) half brother and sister, it is possible that the playwright intends the kind of split he presented in *True West,* a common personality that is at once feminine and masculine, gentle and violent, holding and escaping. I do not intend to imply that either side of these compounds be assigned solely to the man or the woman in the play. Eddie is a rodeo performer, a wanderer, who returns once again to May, who rejects him and hangs on to him, often within alternating lines.

The action takes place in Andy Stacklin's stark setting—both realistic, suggesting the cheapest kind of motel, and metaphorical—a playing area so lightly furnished that it holds little besides the bed, a table at which the characters can drink, and a host of uncontrolled emotions. It is simultaneously a trap (Shepard directed Kathy Whitton Baker's May to hug the walls as she circled like a caged animal) and a refuge, and both characters leave at the end, exiting into a blaze of light (Eddie's burning truck, set fire by an angry lover who has also shot up the motel), each going his own way but with no sense that this is other than a temporary rest before the next reunion. It is possible that their telling the story of their meeting—their high school romance, the disastrous events that followed the discovery that the father had two wives (Eddie begins, May picks it up, and the versions do not mesh)—is intended to mark a genuine change in the compulsive connection between them; but I think not, even though the Old Man, presumably the father, explains that love involves the ability to walk away, an embrace that is not a stranglehold. The Old Man is an equivocal character, a figure who sits at the edge of the stage commenting on the action, now and then accepting a drink from Eddie, a product of Eddie's imagination perhaps but one so concrete that he can eventually invade the playing area and defend his own idea of love.

Women characters—particularly mother figures—carry heavy thematic weight in Shepard plays (*Curse of the Starving Class, Buried Child*, even *True West*), usually in contrast to a male/father figure, but the roles tend to be peripheral. Not since *Cowboy Mouth* (1971) has a woman character shared the central conflict, but *Fool for Love* has more to do with a play like *True West* than it does with Shepard's work from the early 1970s. As usual with Shepard, *Fool for Love* is at once ambiguous and concrete, marvelously effective in some of its bits, a blending of the theatrical and the ideational; but occasionally, despite the intensity of the performers and the production, it seems suddenly to go languid, to trap itself in reiteration which is not the same as repetition in the best dramatic sense. Perhaps I was simply spoiled by the Steppenwolf *True West*, which kept me constantly alert, checking for booby traps in the

THIS IS A SHEPARD LOVE STORY, WHICH MEANS STILL ANOTHER CONFRONTATION, ONE WHICH REVEALS THAT MAY AND EDDIE, HOWEVER OFTEN THEY TRY TO GO THEIR SEPARATE WAYS, ARE INEXTRICABLY BOUND TOGETHER"

laughter. In *Fool for Love,* I found myself wanting to say, yes, I know.

Source: Gerald Weales, review of *Fool for Love* in the *Georgia Review,* Vol. XXXVII, no. 3, Fall, 1983, pp. 602–04.

John Simon

Despite finding Shepard's play to possess considerable theatre craft, Simon ultimately finds the work "ponderous, imponderable."

Originality may but need not be a virtue; remember original sin. It is time we stopped gushing about Sam Shepard's almost sinful originality (it amounts to no more than facility) and ask ourselves to what uses he puts it—in, say, *Fool for Love,* the current import from San Francisco's Magic Theatre, complete with his staging and cast. Since so much of Shepard's action takes place between the lines, it is good to see just what the author has in mind with his action-packed silences. And, for that matter, how he wants his often gnomic utterances to be uttered.

He makes, I regret to say, less sense of himself here than others have been known to make of him in the past, but that may be because *Fool for Love* is a particularly opaque and inconclusive play, with the kind of open ending that does not so much make you want to speculate about it as shut the door behind it. We are in a motel room on the edge of the Mojave Desert, but so underfurnished and penurious that the desert might as well be running through it. Sitting on the bed is May, a waitress or short-order cook, her head hanging down, disconsolate. Circling around her is Eddie, a rancher or stunt man in westerns, her on-and-off lover since high school fifteen years ago, and perhaps her half-brother. At the edge of the set,

"MAY AND EDDIE BOUNCE
THEMSELVES AND EACH OTHER
AGAINST THE WALLS AND FLOOR AS
IF THEY WERE BOTH PLAYERS AND
BALLS IN A JAI ALAI GAME."

where limbo seems to begin, sometimes in the action and sometimes out of it, The (their?) Old Man sits rocking and guzzling Jim Beam.

May has resolved to give up on Eddie; in fact, she would just as soon stab him to death during a kiss, but, in the event, she merely knees him in the privates. Eddie, denying her accusations that he has two-timed her with the Countess (whoever she is), tells May that, to see her, he has come thousands of miles from a Wyoming ranch he wants to buy for them to live and prosper on. They quarrel, fight, almost make love; she can't quite let him go, yet is expecting Martin, some sort of janitor or caretaker, who will take her to the movies. This arouses Eddie's jealous fury. Meanwhile the Old Man maunders on about being married to Barbara Mandrell, whose invisible picture he sees on the wall; later he reminisces about May and Eddie, suggesting he might have begotten them on two wives between whom he shuttled till he vanished altogether.

That's the play in a nutshell, though it's nuttier than this makes it sound. May and Eddie bounce themselves and each other against the walls and floor as if they were both players and balls in a jai alai game. When not tossing their bodies, they hurl recriminations and self-justifications; sometimes the Old Man interrupts with his bizarre ramblings, and sometimes the Countess, in her car in the parking lot outside (where Eddie's caravan and horses are also parked), races around beaming her headlights into the room and, if we're to believe Eddie (who is easily as tricky as Sam Shepard himself), aims to shoot them both. As it happens, she merely sets the caravan, and perhaps the horses, on fire. When Martin shows up, he becomes the fall guy for both May and Eddie, though in fact it is Eddie who falls on his behind and scoots around on it chasing Martin, which adds to the production's athleticism if not to its clarity.

Ideas—mostly old but still serviceable—float or rampage around: Old West versus New West, sex versus love, lovehate between man and woman, the disintegrating family, the innocent bystander caught in the crossfire of mighty opposites, and so on; they have all done yeoman's work in previous Shepard plays. And again, what dominates here, only more so, is the absence, the powerful absence of discipline, Shepard's besetting sin. The characters are raucously idiosyncratic, the dialogue is very much the author's eccentric and evocative own, the violence is zanily original as violence goes, but what does it all add up to? Or does it merely subtract from such better efforts as *True West* and *Buried Child*?

Shepard, moreover, has overdirected his play into frenzies of violence as well as excesses of languor, until both the pregnant silences and the abortive explosions threaten to burst the play at its seams—if only those seams could be located. For disjointedness is the order of the evening. Andy Stacklin's set is suitable and, above all, sturdy, for it has to take even more of a beating than the characters; Kurt Landisman's lighting and Ardyss L. Golden's costumes are equally apt. A fine cast, too: Ed Harris's Eddie, ominously lassoing the bedstead; Will Marchetti's Old Man, garrulous even when silent; Dennis Ludlow's Martin, his innocence painfully mauled. Best of all is Kathy Baker's May, with the face of a Mannerist angel fallen on its face, but sexier for being slightly out of whack; a voice husky with injury that plays xylophone on your spine; and a personality all silken menace, for which any panther would sell his skin. But *Fool for Love* is finally, despite moments of gallows or lariat humor, all portents—ponderous, imponderable.

Source: John Simon, "Soft Centers" in *New York,* Vol. 17, no. 24, June 13, 1983, pp. 76–77.

Edith Oliver

Calling Fool for Love *"mysterious and unsettling," Oliver offers a favorable appraisal of Shepard's play, also terming the work "as funny as anything he's ever done."*

Sam Shepard, the California (at present) spellbinder, has brought his company from San Francisco's Magic Theatre to the Circle Repertory in his new play *Fool for Love,* which he himself has directed, and which will run through June 19th. It is as mysterious and unsettling—now you see it, now you don't—as spare and, incidentally, as funny as anything he has ever done. I cannot remember being taken aback more often, at so many unpredictable moments, and I'll try, in describing it, to spoil as few of the surprises as possible. The action takes place in a motel room in California, at the edge of the Mojave Desert. A young woman, utterly deject-ed, is sitting on the edge of the bed, her head in her hands and her long hair streaming over her arms. She is called May, and across the room, sitting on a chair and looking at her, is Eddie. Watching them from a porch outside the room sits the Old Man, with a bottle of liquor. Eddie tries to talk to May but gets no reply; he tentatively walks over to her, touches her neck, and strokes her hair. She grabs his legs and refuses to let go. When he shakes free, she speaks her first words to him: "You smell. I don't need you." She accuses him of trying to erase her, and then threatens to kill him and the rich woman he has been living with. He protests that he has driven more than two thousand miles to find her, crying much of the way because he missed her so. "How many times have you done this to me?" she asks him. They stare at each other and then start to make love, but she hurts him and he falls to the floor. "You're a stunt man," she says, and exits into an adjoining bathroom. The Old Man speaks for the first time: "I thought you were supposed to be a fantasist," he says to Eddie, whereas he himself is a realist. Pointing to a nonexistent picture on a blank wall and then describing it, he remarks, "That's realism." For a while, I thought the Old Man was meant to be the dramatist's alter ego, the spinner of the plot, for he never takes his eyes off the action within the room, and he comments on it from time to time, but later in the play another possibility pre-sents itself. A fourth character, who appears about two-thirds of the way through, is a hapless young fellow named Martin, who arrives to take May to the movies and becomes, poor soul, the butt of Eddie's funniest jokes and business. A fifth charac-ter, who does not appear, is the rich woman, who drives what we are told is her huge black Mercedes-Benz back and forth in front of the motel, shining the bright headlights into the room. ("How crazy is she?" May asks. "Pretty crazy," says Eddie.)

In *Fool for Love,* Mr. Shepard, his extraordi-nary imagination in charge, probes as deeply into the two lovers and rings as many changes on them as he did with the brothers of *True West.* Like the brothers, May and Eddie lie and love and fight and struggle for command, with no victory in sight. There is a subterranean plot, and there are several of this dramatist's incomparable monologues (well, comparable perhaps to Harold Pinter's). In *Fool for Love,* no inanimate objects fly through the air, as

they did in *Curse of the Starving Class* and *Buried Child* and *True West,* but Ed Harris, the splendid actor who plays Eddie, certainly does. Stunt man indeed—he caroms off the walls and into the cor-ners, chases Martin around the room, and ends up hardly the worse for wear. (At the preview I saw, Mr. Harris was wearing an inconsequential bandage around one hand, which impeded him not at all.) As May, Kathy Baker is just as good, though less athletic, and Dennis Ludlow and Will Marchetti are fine, too, as Martin and the Old Man. Mr. Shepard is the most deeply serious humorist of the American theatre, and a poet with no use whatever for the "poetic." He brings fresh news of love, here and now, in all its potency and deviousness and foolish-ness, and of many other matters as well.

Source: Edith Oliver, review of *Fool for Love* in *New York,* Vol. LIX, no. 16, June 6, 1983, p. 110.

" MR. SHEPARD IS THE MOST DEEPLY SERIOUS HUMORIST OF THE AMERICAN THEATRE, AND A POET WITH NO USE WHATEVER FOR THE 'POETIC'

SOURCES

Brustein, Robert. Review of *Fool for Love* in the *New Republic,* June 27, 1983, pp. 24-25.

Hughes, Catharine. "The World of Sam Shepard" in *America,* November 5, 1983, p. 274.

Kalem, T. E. Review of *Fool for Love* in *Time,* June 6, 1983, p. 79.

Kerr, Walter. "Where Has Shepard Led His Audience?" in the *New York Times,* June 5, 1983, sec. 2, p. 3.

Kleb, William. "Sam Shepard's Free-for-All: *Fool for Love* at the Magic Theatre" in *Theater,* Summer-Fall, 1983, pp. 77-82.

Kroll, Jack. "Badlands of Love" in *Newsweek,* June 6, 1983, p. 90.

Rich, Frank. "Stage: 'Fool for Love,' Sam Shepard Western" in the *New York Times,* May 27, 1983, p. C3.

Shepard, Sam. "*Fool for Love*" in *Famous Plays of the 1980s,* Laurel, 1988, pp. 33-95.

Simon, John. "Soft Centers" in *New York,* June 13, 1983, pp. 76-77.

FURTHER READING

Bottoms, Stephen J. *The Theatre of Sam Shepard: Studies of Crisis,* Cambridge University Press, 1998.
   In this book, Bottoms takes a critical look at Shepard's life through his plays, including an extensive discussion of *Fool for Love.*

Brater, Enoch. "American Clocks: Sam Shepard's Time Plays" in *Modern Drama,* Winter, 1994, pp. 603-13.
   In this article, Enoch explores the critical role time plays in Shepard's *Fool for Love* and *A Lie of the Mind.*

Marranca, Bonnie, editor. *American Dreams: The Imagination of Sam Shepard,* Performing Arts Journal Publications, 1981.
   This collection of critical essays covers Shepard's career as a playwright and interviews with the playwright. The book also includes essays on directing and acting in Shepard's plays.

Rosen, Carol. "'Emotional Territory': An Interview with Sam Shepard" in *Modern Drama,* March, 1993, pp. 1-12.
   In this interview, Shepard discusses his whole career as a playwright, actor, director, and thematic concerns in plays such as *Fool for Love.*

The Foreigner

LARRY SHUE

1983

The Foreigner was first produced at the Milwaukee (Wisconsin) Repertory Theatre in January of 1983, and the boisterous laughter it created there made the play an enormous local success. Named by the American Theatre Critics Association as one of the best regional theatre plays for the 1983-1984 season, *The Foreigner* was subsequently produced Off-Broadway in November of 1984 at the Astor Place Theatre in New York City. Lukewarm responses from the critics failed to quench the play's enormous audience appeal, and as Laurie Winer reported in a 1988 *New York Times* article, "one of the few Off Broadway plays to overcome negative reviews, *The Foreigner* played 685 performances and fully recouped its $250,000 investment."

Because of the extraordinary commercial success of *The Foreigner,* Shue's other plays came to the attention of American theatre companies. His earlier farce, *The Nerd,* had gone from its successful Milwaukee production in 1981 to similarly successful productions in England. It played in Manchester in 1982 and at the Aldwych Theatre in London in 1984, where it earned more money than any other American play on the West End. Two years after Shue's death, in 1987, *The Nerd* was produced on Broadway, and eventually his more serious play, *Wenceslas Square* (1984), became popular as well. These plays are now staples of university, regional, and community theatres all over America.

In 1980, Shue studied with a theatre company in Japan. He developed the central idea for *The Foreigner* when he discovered that the Japanese would tolerate even his most bizarre behavior (because he was unaware of Japanese social customs), dismissing his inappropriate actions as the conduct of an outsider. *The Foreigner* remains Shue's most highly regarded work and is considered the most perfectly realized of his plays.

AUTHOR BIOGRAPHY

Larry Shue's promising career as a comic playwright was cut short by his untimely death in a plane crash at the age of thirty-nine. Possessed of considerable technical skill, Shue had yet to prove that his stage comedy could rise above its commercial value and express a sophisticated comic vision.

Born July 23, 1946, in New Orleans, Louisiana, Shue grew up in Kansas and Illinois, displaying an early interest in theatre; as a ten-year-old, he would create plays in his family's garage and charge a penny for admission. After participating in high school dramatics, Shue attended Illinois Wesleyan University and graduated with a B.F.A. in theatre in 1968. As an undergraduate, Shue wrote two plays produced at Illinois Wesleyan, but he began his professional theatrical life as an actor.

After serving in the entertainment division of the United States Army from 1969 to 1972, Shue continued his acting career with the Harlequin Dinner Theatres in both Washington, D.C., and Atlanta, Georgia, winning two acting awards in Atlanta in 1977.

As an actor, Shue joined the Milwaukee Repertory Theatre in Milwaukee, Wisconsin, in 1977. Two years later his one-act play, *Grandma Duck Is Dead* (1979), launched his mature playwrighting career. Shue was named Playwright in Residence for Milwaukee Rep in 1979 and his mature, full-length plays soon followed, including the two works for which he is best known—*The Nerd* (1981) and *The Foreigner* (1983)—as well as his more serious play, *Wenceslas Square* (1984). Shue's acting career also included a stint with the Berkeley Repertory company in California, some brief appearances in films, and work on the well-known television soap opera *One Life to Live.*

Shue was among fourteen people who died in a commuter plane crash near Weyer's Cave, Virginia, on September 23, 1985. The plane crashed into Hall Mountain, killing everyone aboard, as the flight approached the Shenandoah Valley airport between Staunton and Harrisonburg. At the time of his death, Shue's fortunes were clearly rising. *The Nerd* had been a phenomenal success in London, *The Foreigner* was still running in New York, and he had been commissioned by the Disney studio to write a screenplay for the latter play. He was also working on the script for a comedy series for CBS, had been commissioned to write the book for a Broadway musical based on *The Honeymooners* television series, and he was about to make his Broadway acting debut in *The Mystery of Edwin Drood.*

Many feel that had Shue lived longer he might have produced an even more impressive body of drama, both serious and comic. In a *Chicago Tribune* obituary, Richard Christiansen asserted that, at the time of his death, Shue's ''career was building to a level of international fame.''

PLOT SUMMARY

Act I, scene i

It is a stormy night in spring as two Englishmen, Staff Sergeant ''Froggy'' LeSueur and his friend Charlie Baker, enter the log cabin fishing lodge owned and operated by Betty Meeks in Tilghman County, Georgia, two hours South of Atlanta. Every year, Froggy serves as a weekend demolition instructor for the American army, and this year he has brought his shy and sad friend, Charlie, to America in an attempt to cheer him up. Back in England, Charlie's wife is apparently dying.

After they arrive, Charlie is still inconsolably sad. For twenty-seven years Charlie has been a proofreader for a science fiction magazine, and he reveals that his wife finds him so boring that she regularly cheats on him. As uncomfortably shy as he usually is talking with people, Charlie is now terrified about being left alone for three days with strangers while Froggy leads his training sessions. Froggy promises to come up with some kind of plan to keep Charlie from having to talk to people.

In a conversation alone with Betty, Froggy learns that the proprietor is in danger of losing her lodge because the county property inspector, Owen Musser, is about to condemn the building as unsafe. Betty's current guests at the lodge include Catherine Simms (heiress of a very large local fortune), Catherine's fiancé (the Reverend David Marshall Lee), and Catherine's younger brother, Ellard, who appears to be a "half-wit." If Betty has to sell the house, Catherine and David plan to buy it.

Froggy arrives at a solution to Charlie's problem. He tells Betty that Charlie is a foreigner who is ashamed of not understanding English and mustn't be spoken to. Betty is excited about meeting a foreigner, but, alone with Froggy, Charlie says he can't pull off the ruse. Froggy agrees and leaves, telling Charlie to simply explain the joke to Betty. However, Catherine comes into the room, does not see Charlie, and angrily confronts David with the news that she is pregnant. When Catherine discovers Charlie, she is outraged that anyone would eavesdrop on her "real personal conversation." Charlie is about to offer an excuse, but when Betty enters and explains that Charlie doesn't understand English (saying "an' Frog wouldn't lie to me"), Charlie feels trapped in Froggy's wild plan.

The mean-spirited Owen Musser then enters and everyone leaves but Charlie and David. Owen and David talk freely in front of the "foreigner," and thus Charlie overhears the two men's plan to buy Betty's fishing lodge and turn it into a headquarters for the Ku Klux Klan, which David jokingly refers to as a "good Christian hunt club." As long as the necessary brickwork on the foundation remains undone, the lodge will be condemned and David will use Catherine's money to buy the lodge at a bargain price. However, he must keep Ellard looking like a half-wit to keep from sharing the family inheritance; David tricks Ellard into bringing Catherine a carrot instead of a candle and leaves partially eaten apples around the house to make Ellard appear stupid.

Act I, scene ii

The following morning, Betty is trying to get the bumbling Ellard to bring sauerkraut up through the trap door from the cellar. Charlie talks to Froggy on the phone and tells him that something suspicious is going on with David and Owen. Betty is making breakfast for everyone and warns Ellard not to talk to Charlie, but Ellard becomes fascinated with the strange visitor and offers to teach Charlie some English.

Beginning to enjoy his little charade, Charlie encourages Betty's enthusiasm for entertaining a foreigner, making up silly dances and gestures for her to interpret. He also begins to sit with Catherine, listening to the bored, former debutante complain about her life. Charlie gradually falls in love with her. Ellard enters and impresses Catherine and Betty with the English he has "taught" Charlie. It is indeed "a day for surprises" as the presence of a "foreigner" has rejuvenated everyone, including Charlie himself.

Act II, scene i

Two days later, David and Owen examine materials salvaged from the burning of the Klan headquarters in Atlanta. As the two villains leave, Ellard and Charlie enter, continuing their English lessons. Catherine and Betty join the group, and Ellard relates how he and Charlie have been in Tilghman, watching the workers build the new courthouse, where Ellard is learning how to lay bricks. Froggie returns to check in on Charlie and is shocked to see that Charlie has not only continued to pretend that he is a foreigner but has prospered in the ruse.

As a lark, Froggie traps Charlie into telling a story in his foreign language, and Charlie, up to the challenge, creates a fairy-tale-like narrative that everyone seems to understand. Charlie becomes the center of everyone's attention, especially the adoring Catherine. Alone with Froggy, Charlie exults over his "adventure," thinking that he may be acquiring a "personality."

When Froggy leaves and Owen enters, Charlie discovers a way to intimidate the racist Owen, scaring him with mysterious threats that lead Owen to call Betty and David into the room. Now with an audience, Charlie also humiliates David, who is astounded when Catherine enters and announces that Ellard's success with bricklaying and teaching English to Charlie has led to her decision to share the family inheritance with her brother.

As Charlie teaches the group about his language and culture, David and Owen are made to look very stupid. Owen brandishes a knife, threatens everyone with Klan vengeance, and storms out. David follows to calm him, and the rest are left to worry about Owen's threats. Catherine is leaving a frantic message for Froggy on an answering machine just as Owen cuts the power to the lodge. All turn to Charlie for a plan.

Act II, scene ii

That evening, Charlie's plan for withstanding the Klan attack is in place, though no one is confident of its success. As the Klan marches up the hill toward the darkened lodge, Charlie rouses Betty,

Catherine, and Ellard to their battle stations. Hooded and heavily armed men crash through the door, led by Owen, who confronts Betty and Charlie, announcing the vigilante justice of the Klan. The power to the house is restored and Klansmen are sent upstairs to find Catherine and Ellard. An armed Klansman comes down holding Catherine, who says that the others captured Ellard.

Owen orders Charlie to dance on a table, but Charlie assumes a menacing posture and threatens Owen instead. Pointing his finger at one of the Klansman, Charlie seems to make the hooded figure melt into the floor, leaving only the Klan robe behind. Owen and the other terrified Klansmen bolt from the lodge. The trick is then revealed. Upstairs, Ellard had knocked out a Klansman with a croquet mallet and put on his robe. Then, standing over the trap door to the cellar, Ellard was able to "disappear" on cue.

David enters from upstairs, holding his bruised head, and Catherine discovers her fiance's villainy. But as David is backing out the door, Froggy enters, verifies that David owns the van parked outside, and blows up the van with his detonating device. Catherine announces she is going to help Betty fix up the lodge and suggests that Ellard do the brickwork.

As they are saying goodbye to Charlie, Froggy presents his friend with a telegram that makes Charlie very sad. Catherine comforts Charlie and asks him to stay. Still in "character," Charlie agrees. Froggy reveals the news to Betty: the telegram did not announce that Charlie's wife had died but that she had run off with a proctologist.

CHARACTERS

Charlie Baker

Charlie Baker is the "foreigner" of the play's title, an Englishman in his late-forties who comes to Georgia for a weekend visit with his friend, Staff Sergeant Froggy LeSueur. Initially, Charlie is extremely shy, dull, and morose as he worries about the apparently imminent death of his philandering wife. A proofreader for an English science fiction magazine, Charlie considers himself "boring" and wonders what it would be like to have a vibrant personality. At the beginning of the play, Charlie is so sad and shy that he doesn't want to speak to anyone.

When Froggy introduces him as a "foreigner" who can't speak or understand English, however, Charlie gradually discovers his hidden potential. Overhearing the plot of the Reverend David and Owen Musser to buy Betty's lodge and turn it into a meeting place for the Ku Klux Klan, Charlie ultimately leads Betty, Catherine, and Ellard in a successful fight against these villains. In helping Betty thwart David and Owen's machinations, Charlie discovers leadership skills, love, and the vibrant personality he has always craved.

Reverend David Marshall Lee

The Reverend David Marshall Lee is the fiancé of Catherine and one of the main villains, along with Owen, in the play. Pretending to be concerned about Betty and her struggling business, David secretly attempts to gain control of her lodge so he can turn it into the Tilghman County headquarters for the Ku Klux Klan. David appears to be friendly, sincere, genuinely decent, kind, and patient, and he is quite canny in carrying out his devious plot. In Act II, however, Charlie's clever taunts subtly reveal David's basic meanness.

Staff Sergeant Froggy LeSueur

Froggy is the ebullient demolition expert from the British Army who brings his friend, Charlie Baker, to Georgia for a three-day weekend. In his annual visits to the United States, Froggy has become good friends with Betty Meeks and is genuinely concerned about her welfare. When Charlie pleads for solitude during his brief stay, Froggy is caught between his loyalties to both Betty and Charlie; he hatches the plan to pass Charlie off as a "foreigner." Froggy's plan is for Betty to be charmed by the exotic visitor while Charlie gets his needed peace and quiet. In his late-forties, Froggy speaks in a Cockney dialect, is dressed in his army fatigues, and is extremely cheerful.

Betty Meeks

In her seventies and a widow, Betty Meeks is the owner and operator of the fishing lodge and resort in which the play takes place. Betty has always dreamed of traveling outside of Georgia and is quite thrilled with the prospect of having a "real, live foreigner" as her guest. Since the death of her husband, Betty has been struggling to keep her resort business alive, unaware of David and Owen's underhanded plot to gain control of it. Betty speaks with a strong Georgia accent. She talks to Charlie, "the foreigner," as if he were deaf, as if speaking louder and slower will facilitate Charlie's understanding.

Owen Musser

The racist Owen Musser is a local Georgia man who serves as the henchman for the main villain, the Reverend David Lee. After being named the property inspector for Tilghman County, Georgia, Owen has the authority to condemn Betty's fishing lodge as structurally unsafe, which would force Betty to sell and enable David Lee to purchase the lodge with the money he gains from marrying Catherine. To call Owen ''crude'' is to indulge in understatement: he is mean-spirited, ignorant, volatile, and extremely prejudiced against anyone who doesn't fit his ideal of ''Christian, white America.''

Catherine Simms

Catherine is staying with Betty at the lodge. She is engaged to the Reverend David Lee, unaware of his true, villainous character. A former debutante and the heiress of a huge fortune, Catherine is bored with life, restless, and unsure of what she wants. When she discovers in Charlie a man who is genuinely kind and really enjoys listening, she believes she has found her ideal romantic mate. Catherine is small in stature and pretty.

Ellard Simms

Ellard is Catherine's younger brother and an extremely insecure young man who is considered by others to be mentally defective. Shue describes him as ''a lumpy, overgrown, backward youth, who spends much of his time kneading something tiny and invisible in front of his chest.'' Catherine has promised to give Ellard half of their very large inheritance if he shows any signs of mental and social competence. The villainous Reverend David Lee conspires to make Ellard appear stupid in order to maintain control over all of Catherine's money, but during the course of the play Ellard proves to have both moderate intelligence and considerable courage.

THEMES

Search for Self

Though Shue's main interest in *The Foreigner* is to make his audience laugh, he is also concerned with the theme of self-awareness. Charlie, Ellard, Betty, and Catherine struggle to discover who they really are while David and Owen attempt to hide their real identities from both others and themselves. Only one character, Froggy, is quite comfortable with his sense of self.

Charlie is the most obvious example of the struggle to achieve self-awareness. Convinced at the beginning of the play that he is boring and dull, Charlie discovers not only that he has an interesting personality but that he is worthy of a woman's love. Like many insecure people, Charlie has permitted others to define the way he sees himself. His seemingly lowly proofreader's job doesn't appear exciting or even necessary by the world's standards—''I sometimes wonder whether a science-fiction magazine even needs a proofreader.''

It is Charlie's familiarity with science fiction, however, that enables him to so cleverly intimidate Owen and pull off the disappearing act that frightens off the Klan in the play's climax. In the opening scene Froggy had said ''you would've faced enemy fire with the best if you'd 'ad to,'' and it is indeed a kind of enemy fire that Charlie faces when David and Owen threaten him and his new friends. Uncharacteristically competent, calm, clever, inventive, and brave, Charlie finds a sense of self by the end of the play and earns the love of Catherine.

By way of contrast, Froggy has a strong sense of self and never questions who he is (though he is far less of a presence in the play than Charlie). Ever the competent military operative, Froggy is confident, positive, and unflappable, even when surprised. He promises that he will solve the problem with Charlie's shyness, even when he has no idea how to do so. When his plan doesn't turn out the way he anticipated, Froggy adjusts. Characteristically, he works fearlessly with explosives—''one less mountain to worry about.'' But when David first meets Froggy and addresses him as ''sir,'' the honest Froggie says, ''Don't call me sir. I ain't no bloody officer.''

Like Charlie, Ellard has serious identity problems. Considered by everyone around him to be a ''half-wit,'' Ellard has come to play the role that others have given him. For the purposes of comedy, Ellard is genuinely slow, but the play suggests that Ellard also has significant human qualities. For example, in the breakfast scene, as he first attempts to ''teach'' Charlie English, Ellard embodies both his habitual self-doubt and his genuinely indomitable nature ''But your fork—man, I wish somebody

TOPICS FOR FURTHER STUDY

- Many critics of *The Foreigner* imply that the play has only "commercial" appeal, that it is not much different from the typical television sitcom. Compare Shue's play with one or more of your favorite television sitcoms and argue for or against this assertion.

- Some critics of *The Foreigner* claim that the play reduces southerners to "politically incorrect" stereotypes. Investigate the way southerners are portrayed in both serious literature and in popular entertainment, comparing these treatments with Shue's portrayal of Betty, Catherine, Ellard, David Lee, and Owen.

- Research the history of the Ku Klux Klan in America and describe in detail the status and activity of the Klan in America in the early-1980s.

- Klanwatch, a branch of the Southern Poverty Law Center, has monitored Klan and other hate group activity since 1981. By the late-1990s, Klanwatch was aware of over 400 racist and neo-Nazi hate groups in America as well as 500 "militia" groups. Research this explosion of hate-group activities in America in the latter half of the twentieth century and discuss whether a comedy like *The Foreigner* can hope to ameliorate such a social problem.

- Research the psychological condition of shyness, bashfulness, or timidity. What causes it in real life? How does overcoming real-life shyness compare with Charlie's triumph over shyness in *The Foreigner?*

---

else'd help you with this, 'cause I don't know anything, but—I think that your fork—your fork'd be the main thing you'd use."

Betty is another who sees herself in a diminished way. Since her husband's death, Betty doesn't think of herself as being very capable, and she is all too ready to capitulate to her economic problems. But when she meets Charlie, Betty begins a process of rejuvenation that carries throughout the play. When Charlie says "thank you" to a cup of tea at their first meeting, Betty confidently assumes that she enabled him to learn his first words of English. And when Charlie tells his fractured fairy tale, Betty is convinced that she "understood practically all of it." Hauling out her harmonica after thirty years, Betty rediscovers her vitality in Charlie's presence—"he makes me feel twenty years younger" she tells Froggy; "You done saved my life when you brung him here."

Catherine is an heiress whose former debutante identity can no longer define her. Filled with self-hatred, Catherine is humiliated by her pregnancy.

She will not walk "down that aisle all ballooned up as big as a house in front of all my people" because her premarital pregnancy doesn't fit the image that was created for her by her wealthy parents. Her identity crisis is so severe she thinks "I'm just goin' nuts, I guess . . . I'm probably just ready for the funny farm." By the end of the play, however, she discovers a new self and decisively chooses Charlie as a mate and father for her child.

David and Owen fit in with the theme somewhat differently. Both have been assuming false identifies for so long that they have lost touch with any real sense of self. When David's villainy is finally discovered, Catherine demands to know why David hadn't been honest with her. The stammering reverend finally comes up with, "I wanted it to be a surprise!" The line is funny but also poignant as it reveals someone who has had all of his persona stripped away, leaving nothing but an idiotic non-sequitur as a response.

Finally, Owen serves as a contrast to Ellard; Owen is genuinely stupid but thinks of himself as intelligent. When he takes the title of Tilghman County property inspector, Owen puffs up and begins to think of himself as a worthy candidate for sheriff. But this is the same man who sees supernatural forces in lightning storms—''They'uz a man melted out thar in them hills oncet. . . . Now, that's true. They's things out thar.'' Hilarious as Owen's stupidity is, it is also an important element in the thematic issue of self-awareness.

Prejudice and Tolerance

Another theme that stands out in *The Foreigner* is the importance of tolerance; David and Owen illustrate most clearly Shue's distaste for prejudice. When Owen first meets Charlie, the concept of ''foreigner'' is enough to turn Owen into a hilariously ludicrous bigot—''well—we don't get s'many o' your kind these parts. (Rubs his chin.) Why—last time I saw a foreigner, he was wrigglin' on the end o' my bayonet.'' Owen wants to exterminate anyone who doesn't resemble ''his'' kind—''gonna wipe you all right out—all you dummy boys, black boys, Jew boys. We gonna clean up this whole country, by and by.'' And David, though a little more subtle, is similarly intolerant of anyone who doesn't resemble him. He has set out to create ''a new nation . . . a Christian, white nation . . . the most powerful Christian force on earth'' that ''could have made this country clean again! Wiped this nation clean of—(Looking at Charlie) people like him!. . . Foreigner! Jews! Catholics!''

But the theme of tolerance is also expressed through Betty, who is on the one hand a little impatient with Ellard and on the other comically sensitive to the feelings of the ''foreign'' Charlie. In the breakfast scene, Betty warns Ellard to ''behave'' himself and ''pay Charlie no mind.'' When she reenters and finds the two with juice glasses on their heads, Betty scolds Ellard but encourages Charlie to put his glass back on his head, immediately assuming that the behavior is part of Charlie's foreign culture.

She lectures Ellard on tolerance for diversity and encourages Charlie to continue what he is doing, strange as it might seem to her—''if Charlie wants to put a glass on his head, that's fine . . . that means that's what they do in his country, at breakfast time. Evidently they all put glasses on their heads. But don't let me catch you doin' it too; that looks like you're makin' fun of him. You hear?'' The situation is richly comic because Betty is so

thoroughly confused in her generosity. At the same time, Shue is reinforcing his thematic assertion that human beings must tolerate and even celebrate individual differences if the world is to survive.

STYLE

Situation

Very often a comedy will succeed because it starts with an inherently funny situation. Take for instance two very close friends being thrown together as roommates and discovering they can't live with one another because one is obsessively neat and the other is habitually messy. This is the situation in Neil Simon's, *The Odd Couple,* one of his most successful stage comedies. Simon's characters, Felix and Oscar, repeated their roles in both a movie and a long-running television sitcom and then spawned a female version of the play where all the genders of the characters were reversed.

Much of the enduring success of Simon's creation is due to the humor inherent to the initial comic situation. In fact, Simon sold the movie rights to *The Odd Couple,* even before he had written the play itself, on the basis of a thirty-two word sentence that simply described the ''situation.''

On television, ''situation comedies'' or ''sitcoms'' dominate the comic fare, and they too get their initial power from their situational concepts. For example, a visitor from outer space joins an earthly family and the *Mork and Mindy* series (1978-1982) starring Robin Williams is born. In 1972, with the United States seriously conflicted over Vietnam, a comically disparate group of battlefield surgeons in the Korean War populate the long-running *M*A*S*H* television series (1972-1983). Film director Blake Edwards created the bumbling French police inspector Jacques Clouseau and the popular ''Pink Panther'' series of films ran for three decades.

Shue's situational concept starts with a middle-aged and unusually shy British man who is whisked off for a relaxing weekend to the rural South of the United States, where he yearns to be left alone, is passed off as a foreigner, and overhears a plot against the basically good people who serve as his

A Showbill from Shue's play

hosts. When he takes advantage of his assumed role and helps save these people from the villains of the story, this man discovers a deeper identity that leads to a much happier and more productive life.

But because Shue was a gifted comic writer, this initial situation breeds equally inspired situations within the framework of the play. For example, at the breakfast table in Act I, scene ii, the shy ''foreigner'' encounters a ''slow'' and decidedly southern young man who tries to teach him English, southern style ''can—you—say—''fork''? (Holds up his fork) . . . two parts. ''Faw-werk.'' Later, the ''foreigner'' is trapped by his friend, Froggy, into telling a story in his supposedly native language, and, thinking very quickly, the foreigner makes up a hilariously fractured fairy tale, complete with wildly acted out gestures ''(Imitating with his right hand a huge, slovenly beast crashing through the forest) 'Broizhni, broizhni! Broizhni, broizhni!' Y byootsky dottsky? Hai. (Skipping in a semi-circle with his left hand.)''

Then, when given an opportunity to secretly confront the villains of the story, this same shy man, who thinks of himself as being ''dull,'' brilliantly humiliates the villains while maintaining his pose as an innocent ''foreigner:'' '''Please calm down.'

That's what he was saying, Owen. Not 'Bees come down.' I think that's good advice, too. (Owen watches Charlie like a serpent.).'' Much of the hilarity of Shue's comedy comes from clever dialogue but the driving power of the play's fun comes from ingeniously conceived comic situations.

Characterization

The wildly comic situations in *The Foreigner* work well because they are complemented by surprisingly interesting characterization. Shue's characters are not complex or profound, but they are far from the flat stereotypes that they initially appear to be. Jay Joslyn, in an essay from the *Milwaukee Sentinel,* said of Shue: even ''his villains are not stickmen. They are well observed, a subtle mixture of weakness and hatefulness.'' The villains and heroes would likely be the most melodramatic of the play's characters, but the characterization of Owen serves as a striking example of Shue's more complex comic skill.

That Owen is hateful in his melodramatic way is quite clear. When he first meets the ''foreign'' Charlie he absurdly mistakes him for a Vietnamese and taunts him with ''Well—we don't get s' many o' your kind in these parts. (Rubs his chin.) Why—last time I saw a foreigner, he was wrigglin' on the end o' my bayonet.'' Asking ''whar's your mother,?'' Owen opines that she's probably dead and that ''they's probably not enough of 'er left to spread on toast.'' Much of the comedy comes from the absurd exaggeration of Owen's venom, but the comedy is heightened because the audience has also perceived how pathetically stupid and vulnerable Owen is. When he makes his first entrance at Betty's he appears out of the pouring rain and says ''Hey, Bet. Nice weather fer eels.'' The substitution in the cliched phrase of ''eels'' for the more conventional ''ducks'' is funny but also chilling. Eels would be creatures Owen would enjoy handling. He is, himself, eel-like. But then, when Betty asks, ''Owen, what're you doin' in here,'' Owen responds in a comically literal way, focusing on the prepositional phrase, ''in here,'' and says, ''It 'uz rainin' outside.''

Owen is genuinely menacing and frightening, but he is at the same time comically superstitious, literal minded, and potentially incompetent. Any situation he is put in, like the final scene where he and his klansmen terrorize Betty and her guests, is a situation with rich comic possibilities because of the complexity in his characterization.

HISTORICAL CONTEXT

The Legacy of Vietnam

The villainous Owen Musser appears to have fought in the Vietnam War because when he first meets Charlie he taunts him by saying, "why—last time I saw a foreigner, he was wrigglin' on the end o' my bayonet." Then, asking where Charlie's mother is, Owen says, "where's she at now? Down under ground, someplace? Some foreign graveyard the hell off someplace, pushin' up—palm trees, 'er sump'm?" The slow-witted Owen probably jumps to this conclusion because "charlie" was a euphemism for the enemy Viet Cong soldiers in the conflict.

It can be assumed that Vietnam was on Shue's mind throughout his brief playwrighting career. He served in the army at the height of the Vietnam conflict, though he never fought overseas. In *Grandma Duck Is Dead,* his first play for Milwaukee Rep, a group of college students in June of 1968 are concerned with avoiding the military draft. In his production notes for the play, Shue suggests that an anti-Vietnam war song used in the Milwaukee Rep production was highly appropriate. In *The Nerd* the character Willum is a Vietnam veteran who opens his home to a man who saved his life on a Vietnam battlefield. And finally, in *Wenceslas Square,* Dooley, drafted and in the army during the Vietnam years, expresses very negative feelings about army life. One of Shue's thematic concerns in *The Foreigner* is prejudicial thinking, a distinctive part of the American Vietnam experience, and Owen's Vietnam duty has certainly fed the building inspector's preconceptions regarding "foreigners."

In 1983, the debacle of Vietnam was still a sensitive issue in America, even though nearly a decade had passed since the United States had accepted virtual defeat and withdrawn its last troops from Vietnam. Vietnam has been so traumatic an episode in American history, however, that its ghost rises even today whenever the United States is involved in foreign hostilities; in 1983 it had risen again because of American military involvement in Central America.

In March, 1983, President Ronald Reagan attempted to persuade Congress to approve $60 million in military aid to the democratic El Salvadorean government, and the news media was quick to draw parallels with the Vietnam disaster. As *Newsweek* reported in March, "Ronald Reagan, for one, raised the specter of Vietnam. 'There is no parallel whatsoever with Vietnam,' he said soothingly; then he went on to suggest that El Salvador is a bigger threat to U.S. security than Vietnam ever was." Reagan argued that El Salvadorean and Nicaraguan rebels supported by Cuba and the Soviet Union had to be stopped before the cliched domino effect jeopardized the entire region, sweeping the entire world into communism. The debate escalated throughout the year but because of the legacy of Vietnam there was no uniform enthusiasm for military intervention in Central America.

The Ku Klux Klan

For nearly 150 years, the racially supremacist agenda of the Ku Klux Klan has waxed and waned in America. In the early-1980s Klan membership had experienced another resurgence, according to an organization called Klanwatch that was created in 1981 in response to that new growth spurt. In *The Dragon and the Cross: The Rise and Fall of the Ku Klux Klan in Middle America,* Richard Tucker quoted Klanwatch figures that number Klan membership in 1981 at "an estimated eleven thousand." This membership statistic was up from a low of "about fifteen hundred in 1974." In 1965 membership "had climbed to forty-two-thousand at the height of the civil rights battles," and at one point in the nation's history there were millions of Klan members.

Founded in Tennessee in the 1860s as an innocent social club, the Klan soon shifted to a racist agenda in response to southern disaffection over the politics of post-Civil War Reconstruction. But after a period of rapid growth, the Klan's excesses led to governmental sanctions and a decline in its numbers until the major revival of the Klan after World War I. The heyday of the organization lasted from 1915 to the mid-1920s, when somewhere between three and five million Americans throughout the United States claimed membership. This version of the Klan focused first on Catholics, then on Jews and Blacks, as undesirable groups. The Klan's moralistic, white, Anglo-saxon, protestant prejudice considered these groups "foreign," not "100% Ameri-

COMPARE & CONTRAST

• **1983:** In April, Chicago elects its first black mayor, Harold Washington, in a very close race following a bitter campaign that frequently referred openly to the racial issue. Weeks before the election, incumbent Mayor Jane Byrne, a white female, announces herself as a write-in candidate, intensifying the racial overtones of the campaign.

Today: The country has considered a black candidate for the office of President of the United States. Public opinion polls in 1995 revealed that retired General Colin Powell, had he agreed to run, would have received widespread support as the first black candidate for President.

• **1983:** In October, the United States Senate votes 78 to 22 to create an annual federal holiday to commemorate the birthday of Martin Luther King, Jr., the slain black civil rights leader of the 1950s and 60s. Opposition to the motion is led by North Carolina senator Jesse Helms, and individual states are left free to decide if they will officially observe the holiday.

Today: Martin Luther King Day is widely observed throughout the United States (including North Carolina) on the third Monday in January. The observance seems generally more visible than the Presidents' Day set aside to honor the birthdays of George Washington and Abraham Lincoln.

• **1983:** Neil Simon's *Brighton Beach Memoirs* appears on Broadway as Simon attempts to shed his image as a mere "gag-man" and to portray himself as the author of more "serious" comedy. The first in an autobiographical trilogy, *Brighton Beach Memoirs* wins Simon a number of enthusiastic supporters among the critics.

Today: Simon has failed to win an enduring reputation as a "serious" artist, even though more recent plays like *Proposals* (1997) continue to promise a more "mature" and serious Simon.

---

can." But the Klan's negative publicity in the 1920s eventually caused another precipitous decline in participation and by 1930 there were only a few hundred thousand members, mostly located in the South.

Where racism persists, however, the Klan keeps at least a foothold, and the 1950s and 1960s saw another resurgence, this time smaller, less pervasive yet more violent than its historic predecessors. This "new" Klan was more focused in the South and, responding to the Civil Rights movement, was more targeted on blacks. As Tucker reported, "from 1956 to 1966, there were more than one thousand documented cases of racist terrorism, assaults, and murders committed by Klansmen and their allies."

Tucker reported that by 1988, Klan membership "had dropped again to about five thousand," but in the same year David Duke, a former "Grand Dragon" (or high level leader) of the Klan, was elected to the Louisiana state legislature, running openly as a racist and former Klansman. He lost when he ran for the United States Senate two years later but, as Tucker attested, "he managed to get 44 percent of the total vote and 60 percent of the white vote." In 1983, Larry Shue could ridicule the Klan and make the audience laugh at its silliness, but the humor was and continues to be powerful because the insupportable Klan idea refuses to die.

CRITICAL OVERVIEW

The initial production of *The Foreigner* at the Milwaukee Repertory Theatre (Milwaukee, Wisconsin) on January 13, 1983, was a huge success. The local audience was familiar with Shue's work, and this new play did not disappoint them.

When the play moved to the Astor Place Theatre, an Off-Broadway venue in New York City, on November 1, 1984, the production was directed by Jerry Zaks, and Shue himself played the role of "Froggy" LeSueur, with Anthony Heald as Charlie Baker. Heald was widely acclaimed in the title role, even by critics who disliked the play. Later in the run, when Heald took a leave of absence, Shue himself played the role of Charlie.

In a series of "preview" performances before the official opening night, New York audiences found the play as hilarious as their Wisconsin counterparts. And one evening, after the show officially opened, the boiler in the basement of the theatre burst, sending the audience outside into a freezing rain, though the playgoers refused to leave until the boiler problem was temporarily rectified and they had a chance to see the second act. The overwhelmingly positive audience response to *The Foreigner* led the show's producers to make plans to transfer the production to a Broadway theatre.

But then the critics came to review the show; reviews were less than kind. In the words of Samuel G. Freedman in a *New York Times* article entitled, "A Play Survives against the Odds," the critic found the plot "preposterous even for a farce." Though they recognized that the play generated tremendous laughter, the critics distrusted the audience response and considered the play shallow. Writing for the New York *Daily News,* Douglas Watt called *The Foreigner* "an unpalatable hash." He found the play's situations and plot contrivances arbitrary and strained, its characters stereotypical and cliched. He grudgingly admitted that "though his story is ridiculous, Shue does get off a few funny lines."

The highly influential Frank Rich, writing for the *New York Times,* called Shue's play "labored" with a "preposterous plot" based on an "incredible premise," altogether an "inane recipe." And John Simon wrote in *New York* that Shue's play was "unintelligent trash" based on "utter implausibility." Clive Barnes of the *New York Post* was a little more kind, finding the play only "somewhat flawed, and poised curiously in the disputed territory between comedy and farce." Barnes called the central premise of the play "alien corn," and he

considered the play itself "an only sporadically hilarious tale of unlikely shenanigans." John Beaufort of the *Christian Science Monitor* dismissed the play with only the mild rebuke that "accepting Charlie's adventures, even at their farcical value, demands more than a willing suspension of disbelief."

Not surprisingly, this critical response in the media hurt attendance of *The Foreigner* and a week after the official opening of the play its success was further complicated when the actress playing Betty died and had to be replaced. After the euphoria of the previews, the producers now had to consider closing the show and taking a financial loss. As Freedman recalled, "business, which had been solid during previews, immediately plummeted. In its first full week, the show grossed $9,881, well below its break-even point of $23,000. The show's cash reserve went to cover losses. A closing notice was posted backstage."

However, the company members believed in the play and took pay cuts, distributed flyers in Times Square, and met with theatre groups to revive the word of mouth the previews had initially created. Over 80,000 lapel buttons were made to advertise the show, and *The Foreigner* was finally saved by a Texas oil millionaire who saw the play, found it hilarious, and invested $60,000 in the production until the word of mouth could generate another steady audience for it. Eventually, all of these measures succeeded, the audiences returned in large numbers, and the play enjoyed an unusually long Off-Broadway run. *The Foreigner* was eventually awarded an Outer Critics Circle Award for best Off-Broadway play and productions began sprouting up all over the country. Also named one of the best plays in the regional theatre repertoire by the American Theatre Critics Association, the play even attracted the Disney empire, which bought the film rights and hired Shue to write the script.

When Shue's plane crashed, ending his personal dreams for a long playwrighting career, *The Foreigner* was a solid commercial success. Well over a decade later, the play still generates numerous high school, community, university, and regional theatre productions each year. Reviewing a 1999 community theatre production in Salt Lake City, Utah, Claudia Harris declared that *The Foreigner* "is a staple of regional and community theatre that has not worn out its welcome." The capacity of *The Foreigner* to rouse tremendous laughter has not diminished with the passage of time.

CRITICISM

Terry R. Nienhuis

Nienhuis is a Ph.D. specializing in modern and contemporary drama. In this essay he discusses the levels of comedic skill that Shue displays in The Foreigner.

There is no question that Larry Shue was capable of making audiences laugh. Fellow playwright and actor Amlin Gray reported in *A Book of Tributes* that "one night in 1981, during the paper bag scene [in *The Nerd*], a man in the audience fell out of his seat, holding his sides against the laughter that he couldn't stop, and rolled down three steps before he could recover." Richard O'Donnell, a regional actor who had performed in both *The Nerd* and *The Foreigner,* reported in *A Book of Tributes* that "the people who came to see *The Nerd* laughed so hard that at times we [the actors on stage] broke the fourth wall and laughed out loud with them." Even in Berlin, Germany, where the title of Shue's *The Nerd* was translated into "Louse in a Fur Coat" (a proverbial constant irritant) Shue's comedy left the audience "shrieking with laughter," according to a review quoted in *A Book of Tributes.* In a *Washington Post* eulogy for the playwright, David Richards quoted John Dillon, artistic director of the Milwaukee Repertory Company during Shue's tenure there, as simply saying, "his plays were always laugh machines."

Even Shue's critics had to admit that they were tickled by his work. In her *New Yorker* review of *The Foreigner* Edith Oliver was clearly lukewarm in her response to the play. She found it "funny" but also "silly." She asserted that the audience must take the premise of the play and "gulp it down." However, she concluded with the statement, "I have no critical comment to make, unless expressing enjoyment can be considered criticism. I laughed start to finish at one comic surprise after another." Three years later, while reviewing *The Nerd,* Oliver would admit that "the laughter, and not only my own [was] practically unceasing."

Though belly laughs are often seen by the general public as the very definition of great comedy, critics tend to consider uncontrollable laughter as a sign of an unsophisticated and unreflective response to a non-literary event. More cerebral twentieth century models for stage comedy would include Russian dramatist Anton Chekhov (*Uncle Vanya*), whose brilliant plays consistently straddle the line between the comic and serious, tending to elicit smiles rather than guffaws. Contemporary American playwright Neil Simon is the most commercially successful playwright of all time, but in the decades since his 1961 Broadway debut Simon has still not been able to convince critics that he is a "serious" comic dramatist. At the time of his death in 1985, Larry Shue's unquestionable skill at creating uproarious laughter had already begun to pigeonhole him as a Neil Simon-like comic playwright—one capable of eliciting laughter but not of provoking serious thought.

To some extent, of course, very intense laughter from a theatrical audience can elicit a begrudging admission that something magical might be taking place on stage. In April of 1985, a critic for *People Weekly* wrote, "if you want the final word on *The Foreigner,* a wild farce by newcomer Larry Shue, listen to the audience packed into New York's Astor Place Theatre. From start to finish the crowd yelps like hyenas." And Shue himself, quoted in the same essay, gave testimony to the redemptive potential in raucous laughter: "You have tired, neurotic people filing in," he stated, "and you have kids coming out—giggling and flirting."

The main trigger for belly laughs in the plays of Neil Simon or in many television sitcoms is the "one-liner," a piece of dialogue that surprises the audience with an unexpected twist. For example, in Simon's *The Odd Couple,* the poker players, after taking notice of Oscar's broken refrigerator, ask the difference between the brown and green sandwiches that Oscar is serving. He says of the green, "it's either very new cheese or very old meat."

Shue's comedy is similarly fueled by scintillating one-liners. For example, in the first scene of *The Foreigner,* Froggy attempts to minimize the seriousness of Charlie's wife "makin' eyes at some bloke." Froggy asks "where was it?" and Charlie answers, "the shower." Froggy's gentle questioning and the phrase, "making eyes," suggests a certain timidity in Charlie's wife, perhaps even some innocence (what kind of woman would marry a man like Charlie, after all?). The audience is led to expect that the worst-case scenario is probably a casual flirtation. However, with the image of rampant sexuality that follows, the audience has their expectations violently overturned and the result is raucous laughter.

Then, when Froggy discovers that Mary's indiscretions were more than "one little dalliance,"

WHAT DO I READ NEXT?

- *The Nerd* (1981) is Shue's other full-length farce. It focuses on the humorous attempts of a group of friends to rid themselves of an obnoxious guest (the nerd of the title).

- *Wenceslas Square* (1984) is a more serious play by Shue. It deals with political and social repression in Czechoslovakia in 1974.

- *Grandma Duck Is Dead* (1979) is the one-act play that launched Shue's playwrighting career. This comedy is set in a messy dorm room at an Illinois college in the late-1960s and was inspired by Shue's own college experiences.

- *What the Butler Saw* (1969), by British playwright Joe Orton, is a more bizarre, sensational farce that seeks to shock its audience through irreverent behavior and frequent references to sex.

- *The Odd Couple* (1965) is Neil Simon's most famous comedy, distinguished its ingenious situation and "one-liner" humor.

- *The Invisible Empire* (1986), by William Loren Katz, is a history of the Ku Klux Klan specifically designed for the student reader. An annotated bibliography describes other histories of the organization.

- *Help for Shy People and Anyone Else Who Ever Felt Ill at Ease on Entering a Room Full of Strangers* (1981), by speech communication therapist Gerald M. Phillips, explains what causes shyness and how to overcome it.

---

he asks "'ow [how] many, then?," and Charlie answers, "twenty-three." This very large number places the infidelity in another category altogether. When Froggy expresses his disbelief, Charlie says, "quite true. Actors, writers. All the glamorous professions, you see. Criminals. . . . Veterinarians." In this list of "glamorous professions" the word "veterinarians" jumps out as a particularly incongruous example and shocks the audience into yet another belly laugh.

But Shue's comedy is not sustained merely by expert one-liners. Underneath nearly all the huge laughs is a genuine interest in what it means to be human. Take, for example, the wonderfully funny "breakfast scene" where Ellard has been directed by Betty to take no notice of Charlie. Ellard's intense curiosity gets the best of him, however. As Shue comments in the stage directions, "Ellard's idea of paying Charlie no mind is to stare at him as though he were a unicorn." In the outrageously funny events that follow, it is easy to lose sight of the very powerful human dynamic at work in this scene.

Ellard's spirit has been beaten down by years of low expectations, but he still cannot resist investigating this curious phenomenon in front of him. And Charlie, who has been similarly underestimated his whole life, has come to breakfast hoping to be left alone yet initiates the contact with Ellard. Charlie begins by smiling, perhaps out of nervousness, but the stage directions then specify that Charlie "picks up his fork, examines it, [and] frowns. He looks at Ellard, questioning." This is the trigger for the entire breakfast scene, indeed for the play itself, and it is certainly not an idle gesture on Charlie's part nor is it an arbitrary one in Shue's dramaturgy. Does Charlie react to Ellard out of a genuine desire to create human contact? Or does he engages Ellard out of puckish love of play? Whatever Charlie's motive, he belies in this gesture the self-denigrating appraisal that he is "boring," just as Ellard will belie to some extent the charge that he is "stupid."

Shue's stage directions go on to specify that "Ellard looks back [to Charlie], almost responds, but decides not to. Can this stranger really not know

" SHUE'S COMEDY IS NOT SUSTAINED MERELY BY EXPERT ONE-LINERS. UNDERNEATH NEARLY ALL THE HUGE LAUGHS IS A GENUINE INTEREST IN WHAT IT MEANS TO BE HUMAN"

what a fork is? No—better to mind one's own business." If Shue were merely interested in setting up and stringing together one-liners, this kind of sensitive writing would never appear in the play. Ellard tries to ignore Charlie, as he has been ordered to but it is impossible. Charlie begins imitating Ellard's actions and soon the two are engaged in a mirror image of one another, a classic comic bit that comes alive in this scene because Shue is ultimately sensitive to the human psychology that lies beneath the laughter.

In a similar fashion, Shue creates a significant subtext for the scene in which Charlie humiliates the villainous Owen Musser. By this time in the play, the audience has clearly chosen sides. Owen is a creep and Charlie has become heroically clever—the farthest thing from a "boring" person. Charlie has begun to feel a sense of his own potential and just before Owen reenters, Charlie, alone with Froggy, realizes how easy his new sense of wit has become for him. Having survived Froggy's challenge to tell a funny story, Charlie realizes that he might have "an idea" about how to save Betty and her friends from Owen and David. When Froggy leaves with the line, "I feel a bit like Doctor Frankenstein," Charlie begins "pacing furiously," saying to himself, "Frankenstein. Yes."

The resulting scene with Owen is very funny because Owen thinks he is in control when it is the brilliant but subtle Charlie who is in the driver's seat. After Owen blasts Charlie with racist threats, Shue specifies that there be a pause before Charlie says, "brightly," "Are you happy?" This apparent non-sequitur has all the force of a one-liner but its real power comes from the complexity of the dramatic moment. Charlie is setting up Owen's destruction and the fullness of Charlie's counterattack comes as a total surprise to the audience. Aware of

Owen's superstitious nature, Charlie will confound him with words just vague enough to seem capricious but so appropriately threatening in their mysterious way that the audience can revel in Owen's intimidation and at the same time glory in Charlie's discovery of personal power.

When Owen dismisses Charlie's words as "jabberin'," Charlie shifts gears: "Hello! Goodbye! One-two-three. (Owen snorts, looks away. Pause. Different tone.) I loook tru your bones. . . . Yes. Me see. Moon get beeg. You sleep—sleep out, out. All you skin—bye-bye. I come. I look tru your bones. . . . Gonna look into your bones, when de bees come down." The humor here is based not merely on a shallow reversal of expectations but on a sense of justice and a celebration of human capabilities. Charlie has entered the play as an apparently incompetent human being, but he has since discovered powers he never knew he had. The audience laughs uproariously, in part because the comic villain has gotten his comeuppance, in part because the human potential for personal growth has been reaffirmed. Shue should not be confused with Shakespeare or Chekhov, but there is in this scene and many others in *The Foreigner* a dramatic texture that the belly laughs can often obscure.

In Laurie Winer's 1988 article in the *New York Times,* director Jerry Zaks recalled that he "had never heard of Larry Shue" when producer Jack McQuiggan sent him a copy of *The Foreigner* in 1984. "I was completely knocked out by the effortlessness of the comic writing," he stated. "It was one of those special plays where you can't wait to see where it's going, and you can't believe that it's as funny as it is." The laughs, said Zaks, "invariably come out of situation and characters, and always in a wonderfully surprising way . . . when people walked out of that theatre they were dizzy. Every night, two or three hundred people went crazy in the basement of this building, and I remember thinking that if a visitor from another planet came and saw this, it would think something very powerful had been going on."

In his final tribute to his friend, Gray said that Shue "used conventional structures as springboards, and he used them very skilfully. But sometimes all the underpinnings would just drop away and there would be a passage like the paper bag scene in *The Nerd* or the breakfast scene in *The Foreigner* that lifted off into a sublime celebration of how silly and how lovely it is to be human. Now that Larry's gone, nobody else will write these scenes, because nobody else knows how.'' And Rose Pickering, an actress in the Milwaukee Repertory Company, perhaps summed Shue up the best: ''he leaves behind a legacy in his plays, a legacy of laughter and gentle humanity that reassures all us misfits that we can fit in somewhere.''

Source: Terry R. Nienhuis, for *Drama for Students*, Gale, 2000.

Edith Oliver

Oliver praises the production of The Foreigner, *yet questions the plot's overall implausibility.*

James Agee classified certain movies as ''intelligent trash,'' a category that he neither respected nor condemned, but recognized as having its uses. At a posh London party, Sarah Bernhardt was so overcome by all that staid propriety that she whispered to a French acquaintance, ''Allons nous encanailler!'' (''Let's go make pigs of ourselves!'') In the theater, too, there is room for some slumming, which, I imagine, is what Larry Shue's *The Foreigner* means to provide. After seeing this farce by the actor-playwright, I suspect that he is quite capable of writing intelligent trash for well-bred pigs to wallow in, as the play does, at times, rise to this level. Mostly, however; it is content to be unintelligent trash.

The Foreigner brings an unlikely pair of Englishmen—''Froggy'' LeSueur, a boisterous corporal and demolition expert, and Charlie Baker, a timid, boring reserve officer, whose wife may be dying and is certainly cuckolding him, to Betty Meeker's Fishing Lodge Resort in Tilghman County, the heart of Georgia darkness. Here the smooth Reverend David Marshall Lee and his rough pal, Owen Musser, are planning to take over, with the help of the Klan, today the lodge, tomorrow America. David is about to marry the pretty but somewhat benighted ex-debutante and heiress Catherine Simms, who has a semi-idiot brother, Ellard, and a fortune with which David and Owen plan to finance the takeover of what they propose to turn into White America. Because of his extreme shyness, which makes talking to strangers agonizing, Charlie is passed off as a foreigner having no English while Froggy goes off on some demolition job. Betty, the aging proprietress, the exploited and dimly suspicious postdeb, and the rather speculative half-wit are enormously taken with the cute ''foreigner,'' who, in turn, takes to being fussed over as any lamb would to being lionized.

Now, what prevents this farce—in which, typically, bumbling good overcomes cunning but falli-

> WHAT PREVENTS THIS FARCE—IN WHICH, TYPICALLY, BUMBLING GOOD OVERCOMES CUNNING BUT FALLIBLE EVIL—FROM BEING INTELLIGENT TRASH IS ITS UTTER IMPLAUSIBILITY.''

ble evil—from being intelligent trash is its utter implausibility. What makes good farce a valid art form is its keeping a firm grip on reality no matter how much its feet may slip on banana peels. In *The Foreigner,* however, people are stupid and inept beyond any relation to reality, except when they become, equally unbelievably, improbably clever or wise. And the author cannot even make his premise seem credible enough to support the airiest of fantasies. Furthermore, his wit, despite occasional flashes, goes into lengthy eclipses during which we seem to be viewing the proceedings through smoky glass. Take this line of Catherine's to her brother: ''You couldn't catch a chipmunk if all his legs were broken and if he were glued to the palm of your hand.'' This kind of line is trying too hard. Not feeling confident that it has scored with the broken legs, it huffs on to that sticky hand in the hope of clinching a laugh, and doesn't get it in either place. Ellard replies, ''I wouldn't want him then,'' which in its pseudologic is mildly amusing; but because the big yocks have failed to come, the answer makes us conjure up in all seriousness a broken-legged beastie, and the fun turns sour.

One main source of humor in the play is the language of the nonexistent country from which Charlie claims to hail. In this double-talk, he improvises everything from badinage to lengthy anecdotes, and Froggy must fall in with it, however clumsily. The word for ''yes,'' Charlie tells us, is ''*gok*,'' and the word for ''no'' is ''*blint*''; otherwise, the lingo sounds mostly like pig Russian, and less funny than it could be. Rather more amusing is the rapid progress Charlie makes in English—as are also his recidivisms whenever it pays to act dumb—and the status of genius this confers upon him. Here the comedy is nicely abetted by a lovably ludicrous performance from Anthony Heald, who has a fine talent (as demonstrated also in *Quartermaine's*

Terms) for turning nerds into richly textured specimens insofar as this is humanly possible. That the author makes him, as he also does Ellard, in some ways too smart is not the actor's fault.

There is good work from the entire cast, which includes Sudie Bond (who had trouble with her lines), Patricia Kalember (a perfectly befogged yet sunny southern belle), Robert Schenkkan (a whited supremacist sepulcher), Kevin Geer (a nitwit quite witty in the nitty-gritty), Christopher Curry (a redneck sweaty under the collar), and the author, Larry Shue (whose Froggy is an unusually convincing portrait of a lower-class Englishman by an American actor). Karen Schulz's set, though quite adequate, bears a spine-tingling resemblance to that of *Moose Murders,* thus arousing expectations that no play, perhaps, can fulfill. Rita Ryack's costumes and Paul Gallo's lighting are highly professional, and Jerry Zaks, himself a funny actor, has directed for easygoing drollery rather than frantic farce, which would have been right had the material met him halfway. In short: the production, *gok;* the play, *blint.*

Source: Edith Oliver, review of *The Foreigner* in the *New Yorker,* Vol. 60, November 19, 1984, pp. 187–88.

John Simon

While finding that Shue's play has many humorous moments, Simon ultimately finds The Foreigner *short on actual story. The critic offers high praise for the production, however, citing the skills of the actors in particular.*

''*The Foreigner,*'' by (and with) Larry Shue, at Astor Place, is a silly, funny farce, for Shue has a truly humorous and jokey mind and the knack of turning a phrase. A British Army officer, a demolitions expert, comes to an inn in Georgia on some assignment or other, bringing with him a friend called Charlie, whom he must leave there from time to time. Charlie, a shy man, is overcome by panic at the thought of having to make conversation with strangers, so, to protect him, the officer tells the proprietress of the inn that Charlie is a foreigner unable to understand English, much less speak it. That is the premise (and basic joke) of the play, and what you do is place it on the tip of your tongue and gulp it down. Just when Charlie, alone, has decided to confess to the hoax, a sinister, two-faced minister enters, and down the stairs rushes his pretty fiancée to announce that she is pregnant. Loud, intimate conversation follows, and suddenly she notices Charlie, head in hands, and raises hell. Proprietress

reassures her that Charlie can understand nothing. In the course of the action, Charlie overhears quite a lot—there is villainy and skulduggery afoot, but the villains take no notice of him whatever. Since surprise is the essence of farce, you'll get no more from me, except that at the end the villains are thwarted, the Ku Klux Klan is turned back, and everybody good lives happily ever after.

I have no critical comment to make, unless expressing enjoyment can be considered criticism. I laughed start to finish at one comic surprise after another. Anthony Heald, that fine young actor, appeared to be having the time of his life as Charlie, and so did the late, adorable Sudie Bond as the credulous, rapt proprietress, Kevin Geer as a dim-witted handyman, Robert Schenkkan as the shifty clergyman, Patricia Kalamber as the fiancée, and Mr. Shue as the British Army officer. Jerry Zaks was the quick-witted director.

Source: John Simon, ''If the Shue Doesn't Fit'' in *New York,* Vol. 17, November 12, 1984, pp. 135–36.

SOURCES

''Audiences Have Taken a Shine to Playwright Larry Shue'' in *People Weekly,* April 8, 1985, p. 123.

Barnes, Clive. ''Funny 'Foreigner' Strikes Familiar Chord'' in the *New York Post,* November 2, 1984.

Beaufort, John. '''Foreigner' Zany Adventures in Georgia'' in the *Christian Science Monitor,* November 14, 1984.

Cherkinian, Harry. ''So Short A Time'' in *Milwaukee,* November, 1985.

Christiansen, Richard. ''Actor Larry Shue, Comedy Playwright'' in the *Chicago Tribune,* September 25, 1985.

''Farewell to the M*A*S*H Gang'' in *Newsweek,* February 28, 1983, p. 44.

Freedman, Samuel G. ''A Play Survives against the Odds'' in the *New York Times,* November 19, 1985.

Gray, Amlin. ''A Tribute'' in *A Book of Tributes* (Glen Ellyn, IL), Glen Ellyn Public Library, n.d., p. 43.

Harris, Claudia W. ''Get Acquainted with Hale's Fast and Funny 'Foreigner''' in the *Salt Lake Tribune,* January 21, 1999, B 3.

Joslyn, Jay. ''Larry Shue's Brilliant Gifts'' in the *Milwaukee Sentinel,* reprinted in *A Book of Tributes* (Glen Ellyn, IL) Glen Ellyn Public Library, n.d., p. 11.

O'Donnell, Richard. ''Real Life's Awfully Hard'' in the *Door County Advocate,* October 10, 1985.

Oliver, Edith. ''Not Much to Celebrate'' in the *New Yorker,* November 19, 1984, pp. 187-88.

Oliver, Edith. Review of *The Nerd* in the *New Yorker,* April 6, 1987, p. 81.

Rich, Frank. ''Anthony Heald in 'Foreigner''' in the *New York Times,* November 2, 1984, C 3.

''Reagan Sounds the Alarm'' in *Newsweek,* March 14, 1983, p. 16.

Richards, David. ''Stage Lights & Laughter'' in the *Washington Post,* September 29, 1985.

Simon, John. ''If the Shue Doesn't Fit'' in *New York,* November 12, 1984, p. 135.

Pickering, Rose. *A Book of Tributes* (Glen Ellyn, IL), Glen Ellyn Public Library, n.d., p. 41.

Tucker, Richard K. *The Dragon and the Cross: The Rise and Fall of the Ku Klux Klan in Middle America,* Archon, 1991, pp. 187, 192.

Watt, Douglas. ''Foreigner' Sounds Like a Lot of Nonsense Talk'' in the *Daily News,* November 2, 1984.

FURTHER READING

Gorsline, David L. *Larry Shue, An Appreciation,* http// www.geocities.com/SoHo/Studios/4753/Shue.html, July 14, 1998.

A tribute to Shue that includes biographical information not found elsewhere, along with interesting details regarding the production of Shue's plays.

''Larry Shue,'' in *Contemporary Literary Criticism,* Vol. 52, Gale, 1989, pp. 390-94.

Excerpts from twelve critical essays covering Shue's major plays, including Douglas Watt, Frank Rich, John Simon, and Edith Oliver on *The Foreigner.*

''Shue, Larry,'' in *Contemporary Authors,* Vol. 145, Gale, 1995, pp. 411-13.

An overview of Shue's life and work with biographical information, a brief summary and assessment of his plays, and a list of newspaper and magazine articles referring to Shue.

Winer, Laurie. ''Theatre Jerry Zaks, Guide to *Wenceslas Square*'' in the *New York Times,* February 28, 1988, Section 2, p. 5.

Jerry Zaks, director of the original New York production of *The Foreigner,* is quoted extensively and his comments reveal much about Shue's personality and skill as a playwright.

The Hostage

BRENDAN BEHAN

1958

Behan's absurdist tragi-comedy, *The Hostage,* was originally written in Irish Gaelic and performed in that language as *An Giall* at the Damer Hall, St. Stephen's Green in Dublin, Ireland, in 1957. Following the success of that production, Behan translated the play into English and Joan Littlewood, the innovative director of the Theater Workshop in London agreed to direct it. The premiere of *The Hostage* opened on the 14th of October, 1958, at Littlewood's Theater Royal in Stratford, London.

The Hostage received mixed reviews upon its debut, but as Littlewood's Theater Workshop became increasingly well-known and respected, interest in the original production increased. The work has subsequently become one of the pillars upon which Behan's reputation rests, and the original Littlewood production has since become recognized as evidence of the Theater Workshop's important role in Postwar British theater.

The play's structure is loose and some of the dialogue comes straight out of on-the-spot improvisations, but the basic plot revolves around the IRA's kidnaping of a British soldier. The IRA plans to use the hostage as a bargaining chip for the release of an IRA prisoner who is due to be executed in Belfast the following morning. The British soldier is held prisoner in a rough-and-ready Dublin lodging house that also functions as a brothel, and while he is held there, the prisoner's presence causes much discus-

sion about past and present Irish nationalism and Britain's involvement in colonial affairs in general.

The play is written in a non-realist style; characters frequently burst into song and sometimes into song-and-dance routines, and Behan consistently tries to undercut seriousness with humor. Littlewood tried to act and direct her plays in a way that would break down the "fourth wall" between actors and audience. It is a key text of the Absurdist theater movement, a movement that influenced later generations of playwrights such as Tom Stoppard and Harold Pinter. The play is especially important because it represents the intersection of British and Irish theater that occurred prior to the escalation of hostilities in Northern Ireland.

AUTHOR BIOGRAPHY

Brendan Behan was born February 9, 1923, in Dublin, Ireland, into a working-class Irish-Catholic family that had long been involved in the Republican movement. His father worked as a house painter, a trade in which his son also trained, and he was active within the Irish-Catholic community in Dublin as a labor leader and an Irish Republican Army (IRA) soldier. Behan's uncle Peader Kearney wrote the "Soldier's Song," which became the Irish national anthem, while his mother was also a passionate Republican.

Behan joined the Fianna, a Republican youth organization through which the IRA recruited members, and he became involved in the IRA when he was sixteen. In 1939 he was arrested in Liverpool for possession of explosives: he had planned to mount a single-man mission to blow up a British warship in the Liverpool docks. He was imprisoned for two years in a reformatory in Borstal, England, an experience that he wrote about in his memoir *Borstal Boy* (1958). Three years later, in Dublin in 1942, he was arrested again, this time for the vague crime of "revolutionary activities," and was sentenced to three years in an Irish prison. (He also served time again in England in the late-1940s.)

After his release from prison in 1945, Behan returned to his old trade of house painting and also worked as a seaman and a free-lance journalist. During this period, he began to hone his skills as a writer. He shot to fame with the Joan Littlewood production of *The Quare Fellow* in London in 1956.

Brendan Behan

The play is set in an Irish prison on the eve of a hanging. The work was followed by the even more successful production of *The Hostage* in 1958. The play is a loosely structured tragi-comedy centered around an English solider who has been kidnaped by the IRA and is being held hostage in a Dublin brothel. The success of this production had been preceded by the production in Dublin of the original Irish Gaelic version of the play, *An Gial.* Behan translated the play into English, and the text was then altered considerably by the improvisations of the Littlewood cast. Consequently the two plays differ from each other in quite important ways.

Behan's reputation is based mainly upon his two major plays and memoir, the distinction of being one of the first Irish playwrights to break into the Postwar London theater scene, and his contributions to English-language Absurdist theater. Behan was an alcoholic, and as he became more successful his drinking increased and his creativity diminished. He died from complications resulting from alcohol abuse, diabetes, and jaundice in 1964. His brothers, Brian and Dominic, are also writers. Brian has written a memoir about and a novel based on the life of his mother, Kathleen, while Dominic made his name with the anti-IRA drama *Posterity Be Damned* (1960) and several family memoirs.

PLOT SUMMARY

Act I

The Hostage takes place in 1960 in an old house in Dublin. It is owned by Pat, an old Irish nationalist and IRA soldier, and Meg, his spouse. They run it as a lodging house and brothel. Meg believes that ''the old cause [of Irish freedom] is never dead.'' Pat has an entirely different attitude. He states that ''the days of the heroes are over.'' However, by play's end, Pat is shown to be more nostalgic about the War of Independence (1919) and the Civil War (1921-23), and more nationalistic, than he at first appears.

Monsewer enters. Pat and Monsewer were comrades during the Irish Civil War. Monsewer is the real owner of the house, but because he is mentally ''distracted'' and believes that he is still fighting in the Civil War, Pat runs the house for him. Monsewer was an ''Anglo-Irishman'' who ''converted'' to the Irish cause during the First World War. He learned Irish Gaelic and fought for the IRA during the Easter Uprising ''like a true Irish hero.'' Pat, who is a ''real'' Irish man, does not understand Irish Gaelic and complains that he would need ''an Oxford University education'' to do so.

Pat and Meg continue to fight about the meaning of Irish nationalism. Colette, Mr. Mulleady, and a Russian sailor enter. Colette is a prostitute. She complains that she will not accept the sailor as a customer because he is ''a communist'' and ''it's against my religion to have anything to do with the likes of him.'' But Pat solves the matter by asking if the sailor has money. When he pulls out a ''big wad of notes,'' they all dive greedily for it. Meg comments that money ''is the best religion in the world,'' to which Pat responds, equally sardonically, ''And the best politics, too.''

Meg and Pat continue to argue about Monsewer and the Republican fondness for cultural nationalism, for ''talking Irish and only calling themselves by their Irish names.'' They crack jokes about Anglo-Irish identity and discuss the partition of Ireland in 1922 by Lloyd George and Michael Collins. Suddenly, the cast burst into song. The whole scene is a wordy, witty lesson in recent Irish history, particularly about the split within the Republican movement that resulted from the partitioning of Ireland.

Meanwhile, the hypocritical Miss Gilchrist is carrying on with the lecherous, drunken Mulleady.

The two of them piously pray for divine forgiveness for their ''fall from grace'' while continuing to fondle each other. Meg accuses Miss Gilchrist of being a ''half-time whore.'' After Miss Gilchrist exits, Pat asks people for rent, and ''the room clears as if by magic.''

Teresa, the shy, innocent maid servant, enters and informs Pat and Meg that there is ''a man outside.'' The IRA Officer and the Volunteer enter and sternly assess the house's security. The other characters exit, and Pat alone remains to talk business with them. The IRA Officer is a cold, arrogant, bureaucratic man, and soon he and Pat are arguing about their different understandings of the IRA. Pat is furious about events that happened in the past— the prioritizing of military victory over socialist reform, and his own punishment for disobeying orders—while the IRA Officer is contemptuous of the IRA's former communist membership.

After the two men settle some petty arrangements, they are interrupted by a radio announcement, to which everyone in the house rushes to listen. It is about the young IRA prisoner imprisoned in Belfast Jail, who is due to be executed the next day. The British have refused him a reprieve.

After some rambling comments about the prisoner, the room clears and Meg and Teresa start making the bed. Pat re-enters, and Meg seizes the opportunity to say that although she is sad about the prisoner's imminent execution, she is glad ''that there are still young men willing and ready to go out and die for Ireland.'' For once they agree: the prisoner, Pat says, will certainly ''be in the presence of the Irish martyrs of eight hundred years ago'' when he dies. Meg then laments that the Belfast boy will never have known any real love other than his love for Ireland.

Meg proposes some dancing to cheer everyone up, and as the cast members dance to a reel, Leslie, the British soldier, accompanied by the two IRA guards, enters. The act ends with the solider and the cast members singing an absurdist song.

Act II

Later that day, Leslie is guarded by the IRA Officer and Volunteer but not closely enough to stop him interacting with the other residents of the brothel. He scrounges a cup of tea off the inexperienced Volunteer, and as soon as the Volunteer's back is turned, ''all hell breaks loose.'' Colette offers him a free five minutes upstairs, while other characters generously produce "stout, hymn sheets, aspidistras, and words of comfort."

Pat clears them out of the room, then leaves with the Volunteer. Teresa enters with the prisoner's tea tray. They start talking. Leslie begs a cigarette off her. She produces one that Pat gave her—an early sign that the old Republican has a warm heart—then offers to go out and buy a pack of cigarettes for him. She exits. The Officer then accuses Leslie of attempting to escape (in fact he wants to go to the bathroom) and implicates Teresa. Pat assures the belligerent man that Teresa will "do nothing to bring the police here." For all of Pat's assurances, the officer is unimpressed, and the two men are once more at each other's throats.

Distracted by a street demonstration against the impending execution of the Belfast prisoner, the Officer exits and the other characters seize the opportunity to visit Leslie. Miss Gilchrist and Mulleady are the first of his visitors. They spend their time with him indulging in nostalgic praise of the British monarchy and singing songs celebrating self-love. Pat soon drives them off-stage. Teresa returns, and the young man and woman continue to exchange details about their lives, developing an intimacy that seems to be leading towards romance.

The couple are interrupted by Monsewer, who stages a mock drill, then sings a song about "the Captains and the Kings." This light interlude is disrupted by the Officer, who returns to inspect the prisoner. He then leaves, while Teresa remains, and tells Leslie about her strict Catholic convent education. In a compassionate gesture, Teresa gives the prisoner her medal of the Virgin Mary. The atmosphere changes when they sing a courtship song to each other, then suddenly leap into bed. Discovered by Meg, Teresa protests innocently that "I was just dusting."

Meg begins singing a song about the Easter Uprising, which Leslie, in a self-referential authorial aside, says was written by "Brendan Behan." During the chaos that subsequently unfolds, Pat hands Leslie a copy of a newspaper in which Leslie reads about his own capture. "'If [the Belfast prisoner is] . . . executed—the IRA declare that Private Leslie Alan Williams will be shot as a reprisal.'' The act ends with Leslie singing a bigoted, bitter, patriotic song.

Act III

Later that evening, Meg and Pat bicker about Pat's narration of his heroic past. Their disagree-

ment emphasizes the disputed nature of Irish history. Miss Gilchrist spouts pious nothings about the prisoner, to which Meg responds brusquely. Meanwhile, Leslie asks Pat why he has been captured. Pat and Meg respond promptly: there is a war on, and Leslie is a "prisoner of war." Leslie answers angrily that his capture will have no effect at all upon the British Government. He is increasingly apprehensive about his safety, for it seems certain that the British government will not negotiate with the IRA.

Pat seems to become more sympathetic towards the prisoner: he even joins in, with the other cast members, when Leslie sings a song, "When Irish Eyes Are Smiling." This moment of shared camaraderie marks their acceptance of the prisoner's humanity and heightens their concern about his imminent execution. This acceptance is emphasized by Behan in the surreal song-and-dance return in which Mulleady deserts his paramour, Miss Gilchrist, and joins Rio Rita and his transvestite lover, Princess Grace, in a song that celebrates being "queer." (Later, it appears that all three men are in fact secret government agents and are preparing to rescue the hostage.) Leslie is about to join in the song-and-dance routine but is stopped by a horrified Miss Gilchrist.

After a slight scene change, Teresa enters to find Leslie sleeping. He is bitter about his impending execution and is hostile to her, but he is terrified when she starts to leave him. They agree that if he escapes, she will come and visit him at his army barracks in Armargh. They are then interrupted by the IRA Officer. Suddenly the British police burst into the house. Mulleady reveals himself to be a secret policeman. In the confusion, Leslie is shot by British troops. The play ends with a tragi-comic lament sung by Leslie, who rises from the dead.

CHARACTERS

Colette

Colette is a younger prostitute who works in the brothel. Early in the play she complains about taking a communist as a customer.

Meg Dillon

Meg, Pat's spouse, is responsible for running the brothel. Pat claims to have found her on the street and taken her in. She shares his sardonic sense of humor and dislike of hypocrisy and is particularly critical of Miss Gilchrist's pious twittering. Meg is a romantic Irish nationalist and something of a sentimentalist: she sighs for the Irish fighting spirit of by-gone years and mourns for the Belfast prisoner. But she is also quick to point out the problem in Pat's pride in the past and his contempt for the present generation: to her, there is no difference between the two periods of fighting.

Meg and Pat spend a considerable amount of the play bickering about Irish nationalism. Their fights are a way for Behan to explore opposing points of view about the Troubles.

Miss Gilchrist

"Prim and proper" Miss Gilchrist is not a regular inhabitant of the lodging house. An acquaintance of Mr. Mulleady's, she appears with him after the two of them have been making "disgusting . . . noises" in their room together for three hours. Miss Gilchrist masquerades as an evangelical, tract-carrying Christian, but she is apparently not pure enough to resist an occasional fall from grace. In Act Two she and Mr. Mulleady sing songs in celebration of King and Country, but her alliance with him is torn asunder when he takes up with Rio Rita and Princess Grace.

Princess Grace

Princess Grace is a black sailor who is Rio Rita's boyfriend. At the play's end, he colludes with his boyfriend and Mulleady and betrays Pat and Monsewer.

IRA Officer

The IRA Officer is a schoolmaster in his working hours and a tough man in his free time. His uptight bureaucratic attitude to the provisioning and securing of the hostage reflects his schoolmaster background. Behan describes him as a "thin-faced fanatic." He shares with Miss Gilchrist a penchant for pious posturing. Pat dislikes his absolute humorlessness.

Kate

Kate is the pianist who accompanies the cast members when they sing.

Monsewer

Monsewer, who is somewhat mentally distracted, is an "Anglo-Irishman" who "converted" to the Irish cause during the First World War. He fought for the IRA during the Easter Uprising "like a true Irish hero" and learned Irish Gaelic, believing that "at a time like this, we should refuse to use the English language altogether." To him, English is the language of the oppressing nation. He is fond of parading on-stage, playing his bagpipes and ordering the brothel inhabitants to form a marching line. Monsewer's character allows Brehan to poke fun at the Anglo-Irish and their penchant for cultural nationalism, but it also allows him to examine Irish identity in general.

Mr. Mulleady

Mulleady is described in the play as a "decaying Civil Servant," and as such he is part of the small group of lodging house inhabitants who think of themselves as "genteel" (part of the lower-middle class who aspire to the values and manners of the upper class). Mulleady carries on with an equally hypocritical partner, Miss Gilchrist, and the two of them band together in Act Two to sing songs that celebrate their pro-English and pro-monarchical values. However, at the play's end, after he has informed upon Pat and Monsewer and invaded the house, he reveals himself to be a secret policeman.

Pat

Pat is the caretaker of the brothel and lodging house and an old comrade of Monsewer's. He is a tough, sardonic middle-aged "ex-hero" who fought in the Easter Uprising and the Irish Civil War. Pat initially presents himself as being unmoved by Meg's passionate proclamation that "the old cause is never dead," but it soon becomes clear that he too nurses a sentimental longing for the old days of the Easter Uprising. Pat is contemptuous of the New IRA, believing them to be bureaucratic and humorless.

Pat is present on stage for most of the play, and his comments about the Irish Republic are the linchpin of Behan's exploration of Irish nationalism. Pat's past service, and his skepticism about the IRA then and now, allow Behan to represent a nontraditional perspective of the older generation of nationalists. This serves as a contrast to Mulleady's fool-hardy romanticism and the Officer's hard-nosed Puritanism. Pat also operates as the organizer of much of the action: pushing characters off stage or calling them on.

Rio Rita

Rio Rita is a homosexual navy man. Flamboyant and witty, he spends much of his time on stage flirting with his boyfriend, Princess Grace, or avoiding paying the rent he owes Pat. At the play's end,

Rio Rita joins forces with Mulleady and betrays Pat and Monsewer to the police.

Ropeen

Ropeen is an older prostitute with pro-British sympathies who works in the brothel.

Russian Sailor

The Russian Sailor, who is Colette's customer, is actually a police spy.

Teresa

Teresa is Pat and Meg's maid servant. An orphan, she is nineteen years of age and comes from the country, where she was educated in a strict Catholic convent. She had just one other job before coming to Dublin but had to leave because "there was a clerical student in the house." She is out of her league in the lodging house and brothel, but she demonstrates her good heart by comforting Leslie. Their brief involvement represents the romanticism of Irish nationalism's blood sacrifice mythology. After Leslie is shot, Teresa mourns him and promises never to "forget you . . . till the end of time."

Volunteer

The inexperienced volunteer works as a "railway ticket-collector" to earn money and volunteers for the Cause when he can. His incompetency and soft-heartedness is a neat foil to his leader's bureaucratic attitude and toughness, and he is utterly unable to stop people visiting Leslie.

Leslie Williams

Leslie appears at the end of Act One, although his impending presence dominates much of the action prior to his appearance. Orphaned Leslie is a young British solider who is completely unprepared for his kidnaping and is genuinely ignorant about the politics of the country in which he is fighting. Initially, he does not seem to take his situation seriously: sex, cigarettes, and a "nice cuppa tea" are his main interests. However, when he learns that the Belfast prisoner will not be reprieved, he realizes he stands a good chance of being shot in retribution, and his attitude darkens. He is shot at the end of the play. His death can be interpreted in a number of ways: as evidence of British bungling, as an innocent slaughtered unjustly in a conflict about which he knew nothing, or as a dramatically just "eye for an eye."

THEMES

Irish Identity

The most important theme in *The Hostage* is Irish identity. Behan demonstrates that Irish identity is rooted in the memory of martyrdom and violence. But he also argues that Irish identity is not a concrete, easily fixed ideal but rather a confused concept. Behan explores this theme through a series of conversations between Meg and Pat.

The basic foundation of the plot, the impending execution of the IRA prisoner in Belfast, is made clear in the first seconds of stage time, and Monsewer's dirge alerts the audience to the fact that, for all the jigs and jollity, the play has a serious undercurrent and a potentially tragic conclusion. Within minutes, too, the play's central theme, the meaning of Irish identity, is made clear. Meg's opinion of the prisoner's impending death is romantically nationalist: he "did his duty as a member of the IRA," which proves beyond doubt that "the old cause is never dead." Pat opposes such nonsense: he is a realist, and to him, "the days of the heroes are over this forty years past." Prayers for Irish freedom are doomed: the island will never again be united or free of the British.

Pat and Meg's conversations are crucial to Behan's exploration of Irish identity. Their interchanges reveal that although Pat is skeptical of the IRA's present manifestation, he is unabashedly nostalgic about its past actions, particularly its role in the 1916 Easter Uprising, the War of Independence, and the Irish Civil War. To him, those events are central to recent Irish history and those were the times when "the real fighting was going on." The more Pat talks, the more it becomes clear that he is as romantic and idealistic about "the old cause" as his spouse. Why then does he deny the importance of the IRA and espouse disinterest in Irish Republicanism now?

The answer to this question is twofold. Like many Republicans, Pat finds the partitioning of Ireland an act of incomprehensible betrayal. "We had the victory—till they signed that curse-of-God treaty in London. They sold the six counties to England and Irishmen were forced to swear an oath of allegiance to the British Crown." Like many

TOPICS FOR FURTHER STUDY

- Research the Irish War of Independence and the Irish Civil War. How does Behan represent these periods of Irish history in his play? What is his view of the contemporary situation in Ireland?

- Compare and contrast the themes of *The Hostage* and *The Quare Fellow*. Why does Behan choose an impending execution as the focus point for two of his dramas?

- Discuss the role of the song-and-dance routines in *The Hostage,* asking yourself either how the routines develop existing themes within the play, or how the routines contribute to the breaking down of the ''fourth wall'' between audience and actors.

- Is *The Hostage* really an Absurdist play? If you think it is, make a case for your opinion. If you think it is not, offer another categorization of it, for instance as a political satire or a tragedy.

- Focus upon the ending of *The Hostage*. How is the audience meant to interpret the ending, given the preceding tone and events?

Republicans, Pat refused to accept the partitioning of Ireland, and ''went on fighting.'' When he was no longer able to do that, he and Monsewer established their house in Dublin as a safe-house for IRA men on the run.

But the other reason for Pat's disgust with the IRA is that the organization prioritized military action over social reform. After the Partitioning, Pat continued to work within the IRA, but his involvement in the 1925 County Kerry agricultural reform movement—in which laborers collectivized private land—finally set the seal on his alienation from the IRA, which intervened in the collectivization and court-marshaled Pat for his involvement. In the present, Pat sees similar examples of Republican narrow-mindedness and near-sightedness in the Officer's bureaucratic behavior. Pat's commitment to Irish Nationalism and to armed action against the

British is thus predicated upon a demand for immediate change in the present, or, as he says of the County Kerry movement, upon ''answers'' rather than ''questions.''

Irish history is replete with examples of heroic sacrifice for the sacred cause of liberty and of terrible suffering. Irish identity celebrates these events and almost glorifies blood sacrifice for the ''mother country.'' The most important recent example of this is the 1916 Easter Uprising, which was organized by its participants in the full and certain knowledge that they would most likely die, and which was carried out in the hope that such sacrifice would inspire the Irish people to rise up against the British. Meg's song about the Uprising in Act Two celebrates the rebel's valor. In the same Act, Pat repeatedly emphasizes that he ''lost my leg'' in the Civil War, a loss that is, to him, evidence of his commitment to the cause.

Behan suggests that the implications of the Irish valorization of sacrifice for Irish identity are profound. The cultural glorification of sacrifice and suffering means that Republicans will always have men and women willing to sacrifice their lives for the cause. Moreover, the ''eye for an eye'' mentality is deeply ingrained within Irish culture: he makes clear that the IRA are fully serious when they threaten Leslie's reprisal killing. Above all, the valorization of sacrifice and suffering means that the conflict could stretch on indefinitely, for Irish Republicanism can feed upon past and present acts of violence and suffering to sustain itself and renew its energy to continue the fight against British rule.

British Identity

Irish identity is based upon myths, symbols, and history that are particular to Ireland—the British, for example, do not share the Irish attachment to blood sacrifice or their fervent memorialization of terrible suffering. Irish identity is also based upon Irish *opposition* to Britain, and, likewise, Britain's weary contempt for the Republican movement and its prejudice against the ''drunken and unruly Irish'' is a defining element of its identity. To an extent, each countries' sense of identity depends upon the other's. Behan's decision to translate the play into English and stage it in London entailed addressing a British audience, consequently he spent a considerable amount of stage time exploring the meaning of British identity in the Littlewood production.

Behan's understanding of British identity can be seen clearly by contrasting three songs. In Act

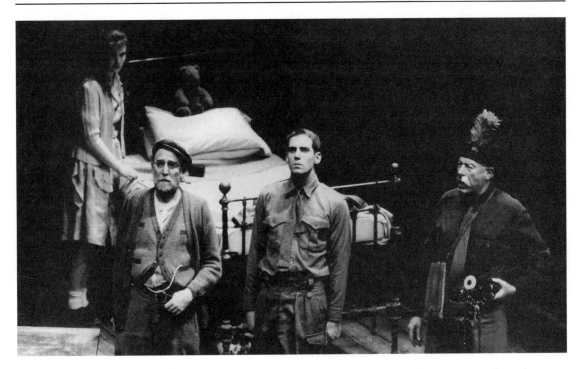

A stage production of Behan's play: Pat (Dermot Crowley), Leslie (Damien Lyne), and Monsewar (John Woodvine).

Two, Mulleady, Miss Gilchrist, and Ropeen band together with Leslie to celebrate British values. For them, British identity depends upon the royal family. Behan's mocking depiction of Mulleady ''savoring and drooling'' over a cheap tabloid report of ''the true pattern of the Queen's life'' and his other contemptuous remarks about the royal family throughout the play, indicate that he regards the monarchy as worthless. Nonetheless, to lower middle class folk such Miss Gilchrist and Mulleady who try to ape the manners and values of the upper middle class, the royal family represents the glamour, wealth, and gentility to which they aspire. These values are Mulleady's ''Bible.''

Social snobbery, religious piety, and class hierarchy are values that Mulleady and Miss Gilchrist associate with British identity—and specifically with the ''British Empire'' of which they, as Irish people, consider themselves to once have been part of, and of which they mourn the loss. Behan, however, is firmly opposed to such snobbish nostalgia, and his song satirizing their values makes clear that he believes the ''Empire'' gives nothing and takes everything while duping its loyal followers: ''Us lower middle classes. . . . Employers take us for a set of asses/ The rough, they sneer at all

attempts we make/ To have nice manners and to speak correctly/ And in the end we're flung upon the shelf/ We have no unions, [no] cost of living bonus.''

Brehan's characterization of Monsewer deepens his representation of British identity within the play. Monsewer is a complicated character: blessed with a French name, an Irish mother, and an English father, he extols the pleasures of English upper class life while nonetheless proclaiming allegiance to the Irish Republic. His six-verse song in Act Two celebrates his ''memories of summers long past.'' The British may have been defeated in the Irish War for Independence, but they can still ''do thrilling things'' on the ''playing-fields of Eton.'' Taking tea on the lawn, playing cricket, drinking port: these are some of the innocuous delights that Mulleady celebrates. But the song soon takes a darker turn. Verse three reveals the racist underbelly to the British Empire: ''in many a strange land . . . all bear the white man's burden.'' Verse four switches back into Mulleady's idealized vision of Britain, but verses five and six return to the corruption of the Empire: lost innocence (''an apple half-bitten'') and racism (''praise God that we are white'').

Such damning condemnation of British racism and imperialism is echoed finally in Leslie's song at the end of Act Two. Having suddenly come face to face with the very real danger that he will be killed and having heard the IRA Officer declare that he is, after all, living proof that Ireland is at war, the soldier bursts into a patriotic song. The song echoes Mulleady's in that it declares allegiance to King and Country and even refers to some of the famous hymns that celebrate British identity, such as "Jerusalem." But the punch comes in the last verse, when Leslie, saluting to a bugle call, declares that he wishes "the Irish and the niggers and the wogs/ Were kicked out and sent back home." Brehan's representation of British identity comes down firmly against British imperialism and racism and asks his audience to reflect critically upon their attachment to Britain.

STYLE

Setting

Behan's play is set in a run-down lodging house in Dublin. The lodging house was originally rented by Monsewer to be a safe-house for IRA soldiers on the run. However, financial constraints forced Monsewer and Pat to open the house to other people, to "all sorts of scruffy lumpers." Behan was a poet of the working-class, and he made working-class dialogue and character his forte. The setting allows him to run the gamut of characters and to exploit the comedic resources of such types. But Behan's decision is not a purely practical one: the brothel-cum-lodging house has rich symbolic resonance.

Maureen Waters has argued in *The Comic Irishman* that Behan's decision to set the play in a lodging house and a brothel demonstrates the denigration of Pat and Monsewer's Republican idealism and, indeed, of the "old Republican ideal." It might be more accurate to say that the setting represents the Treaty's prostituting of Ireland Michael Collins's decision to "sell" the six counties to England in exchange for peace in the Republic. But this reading is only persuasive if one imposes one's own feelings about prostitution upon Behan's, and there is little evidence to suggest that Behan was judgmental about the occupation. His characterizations of prostitutes are in fact reasonably sympathetic. The setting may suggest the radical possibilities of Republicanism: that its emphasis upon the unifi-

cation of Ireland and its socialist platform should mean, logically, that it reaches out to embrace society's "undesirables."

The Songs

Behan and Littlewood shared a delight in music-hall theater, and the bawdy, comic music-hall songs in *The Hostage* and their more somber Irish counterparts are an essential part of the play. The songs cue the audience to mood changes; they develop themes in lyrics rather than in action; and they provide thumb-nail character sketches more efficiently and entertainingly than expository prose.

Each act contains a mixture of songs: Act One, which begins with an Irish jig, includes Irish songs about the War of Independence and the assassination of Michael Collins; Act Two includes Meg's poignant and bitter song about the Easter Uprising, as well as Monsewer's celebration of the British aristocracy and Leslie's racist, patriotic chant; and the last Act includes a similar range of songs, one of which celebrates "queer" sexuality and another the beauty of "Irish eyes." This mixed bag of goods is as eclectic as the inhabitants of the Dublin lodging house; each song proves to be more revealing about the singer than their dialogue.

From Pat's first song about an IRA victory over the Black and Tans during the War of Independence, the audience realizes that his Republicanism, which he has only moments ago dismissed as "long over, finished and done with," is in fact alive and well, albeit rooted in the past rather than in the present. Behan offers Pat's relish in the IRA victory— "And the Irish Republican Army/Made shit of the whole mucking lot"—as one side of the Republican movement. Contrasting to it a few minutes later is Meg's romanticized Republicanism, with all its associated valorization of blood sacrifice and suffering, represented in her lament for Michael Collins: "Ah, curse the time, and sad the loss my heart to crucify/ Than an Irish son, with a rebel gun, shot down my Laughing Boy. . . . My princely love, can ageless love do more than tell to you. . . . For all you did and would have done, my enemies to destroy."

Pat and Meg's songs—and their characters— represent the two different sides of Republicanism who divided politically over Partitioning: Pat followed De Valera and joined the rebels fighting against the Treaty, but Meg's sympathies are with Collins. Thus Behan's inclusion of songs cues the audience into the political differences between Pat and Meg, into the complexities of modern Irish history, while building up, through the references to violence, tragic loss, and death, an atmosphere suggestive of impending loss.

The songs are not simply used in these ways, though; they are also very much part of Behan and Littlewood's conscious use of "alienation" effects. One of the best examples of the complex results of such techniques is the songs that Leslie sings. Leslie, as "the hostage," is the focus of much attention in the play, both from the characters and the audience. The residents seek him out because they are curious about him, and likewise the audience's attention is glued upon him whenever he is on-stage. Who is this young soldier? Does he deserve to die? Can he redeem himself in Irish eyes? Behan and Littlewood deliberately undercut the growing sympathy and empathy for Leslie at the end of Act Two. Meg's swelling chant about the sacrifice of the Easter Uprising celebrates Irish courage, condemns British cruelty, and asserts an undefeated rebel spirit. It is an impressive, passionate, and moving performance. Bare minutes later, it is Leslie's turn to sing. He has just learned he may well die. But rather than exploiting this moment for all it is worth—rather than capitalizing upon the audience's sympathy for Leslie—Behan hands him a song that slaps that sympathy in the face and, in all probability, alienates the audience altogether. "I am a happy English lad, I love my royal-ty. . . . But I wish the Irish and the niggers and the wogs/ Were kicked out and sent back home."

Behan and Littlewood's use of music-hall style songs for satiric purposes is best illustrated by comparison of Mulleady and Miss Gilchrist's songs in Act Three. The first song, sung by Mulleady, Rio Rita, and Princess Grace, cheerfully and defiantly proclaims "we're here because we're queer . . . we're queer because we're here." The underlying joke about this song is that the "queerness" is not limited to sexuality—the three men are secret policemen, and their "odd couple" union proves that political expediency can unite the most apparently opposed people, just as sexuality can be a bridge across all sorts of class and racial differences. Contrasting to this is Miss Gilchrist and Leslie's cheery music-hall style song, whose cheery tone and rhythm contrasts ironically to its grimly satiric

subject. The pious Miss Gilchrist asks in a shocked voice whether Leslie would sponge off "women's earnings," to which the disaffected working-class Leslie replies contemptuously that he would: "I'm fed up with pick and shovel/ And I'd like to try it once." Whether their topics are middle-class morality or social mores about sexuality and gender, Behan and Littlewood use the music-hall style songs to great effect to entertain their audience with strong satire.

HISTORICAL CONTEXT

Within ten years of Behan writing *The Hostage* in 1958, Ireland would be immersed in massive historical and political change. The IRA had carried out a series of low-key campaigns in the North in the 1950s, but after the hostile Protestant reaction to the Catholic civil rights campaign in 1968, the organization split into two wings, one of which decided to return permanently to "active duty" as long as Ireland remained partitioned. The violence and tragedy of the Troubles remains part of Northern Ireland to this day, although in the last five years steps have been taken towards resolution of the conflict. Although the play touches on contemporary issues, however, for the most part it is concerned with events in the recent past, particularly the Irish War of Independence, the partitioning of Ireland in 1921, and the subsequent Civil War.

The conflict between Britain and Ireland did not originate in the twentieth century but rather in the original occupation of the island by the Normans in the twelfth century, and, more particularly, by the savage invasion of Ireland by Cromwell and his subsequent suppression of Irish revolt in the seventeenth century. Resistance to British occupation was a sporadic element in Anglo-Irish relations throughout the next few centuries, and it solidified in the last decades of the nineteenth century, when Irish campaigners focused on the need for tenancy reform and Home Rule. The movement for Home Rule was defeated in the British parliament in the 1880s, but it remained a crucial element of the nationalist platform.

In the first decade of the twentieth century, Irish political nationalism was bolstered by a cultural

COMPARE
&
CONTRAST

- **1958:** Britain's continued commitment to its colonial Empire is met with widespread resistance, particularly in Malaysia and Cyprus. Nonetheless the government continues to pour funds into maintaining its presence in these countries.

  Today: Britain relinquished control over both Malaysia and Cyprus in the 1960s and handed Hong Kong back to the Chinese in 1999. Today Britain's major involvement in foreign countries is in the NATO peacekeeping force.

- **1958:** British sovereignty in Northern Ireland is largely unquestioned, except by a small minority of Republicans.

  Today: After the 1968 Civil Rights Campaign and the subsequent escalation of the British military presence in Northern Ireland, the future of British sovereignty looks uncertain, particularly when Britain is moving towards granting increased autonomy to Scotland and Wales.

- **1958:** The world watches as America battles to desegregate its public schools. The U.S. Supreme Court hands down *Brown v. Board of Education of Topeka* in 1954, ruling that "separate educational facilities are inherently unequal." Four years later the Court orders the states not to delay desegregation, Governor Faubus of Arkansas, where the conflict over Little Rock High School has already attracted world-wide media coverage, defies the Court by closing four schools and reopening them again as private schools.

  Today: After a slow and painful integration of the public system in the 1960s, the Supreme Court handed down another historic decision in 1971. *Swann v. Charlotte-Mecklenberg,* upheld a plan to accelerate integration by busing students across towns. In the 1990s, the tide turned against the practice, and the more conservative court retreated from its original position. Classroom performance and Ebonics have replaced desegregation as the key flashpoints for secondary education and race relations in America in the twenty-first century.

nationalist movement. The Gaelic League was founded to revive interest in the speaking and study of Irish, the Gaelic Athletic Association was founded to promote Irish sports, and the Irish Renaissance, supported by such figures as W. B. Yeats, John Millington Synge, and Lady Augusta Gregory, promoted Irish letters and art. Simultaneously, the Sinn Fein (the name is Gaelic for "Ourselves Alone") movement, led by Arthur Griffith, preached political self-determination, and the Irish Republican Brotherhood, a militant secret organization, began recruiting more actively.

In 1912 the third Home Rule bill was introduced into the British parliament, and the subsequent debates over it threatened to drag Ireland into civil war. The outbreak of World War I averted the impending conflict. The British prime minister, Asquith, enacted Home Rule but attached it to a Suspensory Act that delayed Home Rule until Britain was again at peace. Nonetheless, the Irish Republican Brotherhood had already made plans to take control of Ireland, and on Easter Monday, 1916, about 2,000 members of the Brotherhood seized the General Post Office and other buildings in Dublin, issued their stirring declaration of Irish independence, and organized a provisional government. Fighting continued for some weeks. The Republicans were forced to surrender and were executed, a punishment that electrified many previously apathetic Irish. Sinn Fein swept to power in the elections of 1918 and proclaimed a provisional (independent) government, and the Irish Republican Army (IRA) was organized to destroy the British administration. A large section of the Irish police resigned; the British replaced them with English recruits who became known as the Black and Tans due to the color of their temporary uniforms. There followed three years of open fighting between Irish and British forces, and in the end the British were defeated.

The conclusion of the fighting was a treaty signed on December 6, 1921, that divided Ireland into two areas: the twenty-six counties of the south became the Irish Free State, while the six northern-most Protestant-majority counties remained under direct British rule. Far from providing a solution to the conflict, the Treaty embedded hostilities still further, for a significant proportion of the Republicans opposed the partitioning of their island, and ''unification'' became the rallying cry of their campaign against partition. The split within the Republican movement over partition led to the Irish Civil War. The anti-partition faction were eventually forced to concede defeat.

The bitterness that the partitioning aroused subsided amongst much of the general population, particularly under the leadership of Edmund De Valera, one of the few surviving members of the Easter Uprising, who became leader of Sinn Fein and dominated Irish politics as Prime Minister and President for the rest of his life. In the 1930s he abolished the oath of allegiance to the crown and stopped interest payments to Britain (from loans that dated back to the late-nineteenth century). De Valera also altered Ireland's constitutional status: he abolished the office of governor general and replaced it with that of an elected president, changed the title of the Irish Free State to Eire (Ireland), and introduced a new constitution (ratified in 1937).

From the mid-1950s through to the early-1960s, the Irish government tried to control IRA raids on British army posts along the border with Northern Ireland. But the situation worsened dramatically after 1968. Catholic residents in Northern Ireland began to lobby both the Northern Irish and British governments to improve their representation and treatment in Northern society, particularly in the areas of housing and employment. In 1968 Catholics launched a major civil rights campaign that began peacefully but was met with violent resistance from the Protestant majority. British troops were called in to protect Catholic residents in Derry and Belfast, but soon the troops participated in the violence against Catholics. By the early-1970s, the IRA and armed Protestant volunteer armies such as the Ulster Freedom Fighters and the Ulster Defense Force, often helped by the Royal Constabulary and the British army, were engaged in outright civil war.

The situation began to change in the mid-1990s. Both sides have issued cease-fires at various times and have signaled their interest in advancing towards a peaceful resolution of the Troubles. However, a final resolution that is amenable to all three sides—the Republicans, the Protestant Loyalists, and the British government—has yet to come.

CRITICAL OVERVIEW

There is no unanimous critical opinion about *The Hostage,* and the seeds of critical disagreement about the play seem to have been sown in the first reviews. The play premiered in London on October 14, 1958, and the next day reviews appeared in both the London *Times* and the *Guardian* that mixed praise with condemnation.

The unnamed author of the *Times*'s review recognized Behan's comic genius and his deft characterizations. ''Meg is the shameless woman of the streets who enjoys letting herself go in a flood of patriotic rhetoric as much as she enjoys 'taking the mickey' out of rival rhetoricians,'' and ''Pat is an old man who endlessly tells steep stories of his heroic exploits in the Troubles.'' The *Times* reviewer emphasized that Behan's play was in large part successful because Behan was not afraid to poke fun at Irish character types.

However, the *Times* reviewer was unimpressed with the Littlewood-influenced structure of the play. ''It is as formless as though it were being improvised on the spur of the occasion.'' At times, he wrote, Behan's writing shows ''shamelessly loose touches.'' This criticism of the play was also voiced by Philip Hope-Wallace, in his review in the Manchester *Guardian* on the same day. Hope-Wallace was not impressed by the song-and-dance routines that dotted the play. He found them disruptive and complained that they were most inappropriate at the play's end. When Leslie rises from the dead and joins the cast members in a song, ''the shadow of drama has shrunk away, and with it any possibility of serious comment.''

Both reviewers agreed that Behan's writing was energetic and vital and they found his irreverence refreshing, but they were united in their distaste for the non-traditional style and structure of the play. Hope-Wallace went so far as to complain that the mixture of styles was a ''collision'' and ''a rout of good taste.''

The overall thrust of these reviews was echoed in much criticism of the play over the next decade. In 1962, John Russell Taylor, for instance, could not see the point of the farce, which he described as ''irrelevant.'' He too complained that the farcical moments hindered the development of the play's tragic themes. Like many critics, Taylor suspected Behan of losing control of the play: ''at times it looks like going off the rails altogether in its quest for the easy laugh.''

The play's reputation was further damaged in 1975 by an article in *Modern Drama* that compared and contrasted the original Irish version and the later English-language version. Richard Wall demonstrated conclusively that the two versions differed so substantially as to be entirely different plays, and it was clear from the tenor of his article which one he thought superior. The original version had been written for the Abbey Theater in Dublin (founded by, amongst others, the poet and dramatist W. B. Yeats, and strongly associated with the naturalism and symbolism of the Irish Renaissance) and had been funded by a grant from the Irish Gaelic League. *An Giall* was simply not as bawdy nor as comic as *The Hostage:* in *An Giall* the romance between Teresa and Leslie is ''remarkably chaste,'' and the opening is ''solemn.''

Wall argued that Behan made the changes because ''A serious play about the age-old 'Irish Question' stood little chance of notice in England in the late fifties, particularly in view of the fact that it [the original] contained no drinking except tea, no wild Irish jigs, no anti-English rebel songs and no mob scenes.'' In short, Wall felt that Behan altered the play to pander to English expectations and to engage an audience preoccupied with contemporary British domestic and international politics (thus the references to the Wolfenden Report and the Cyprus crisis).

Wall's damning declaration that the English-language version destroyed ''the integrity of the original play'' was soon picked up by other critics. In an ironic way, of course, his argument about the transformation of the original paralleled the very process of British colonization and interference in

Irish identity about which Irish nationalists had so long complained. But it also confirmed the myth of Behan's disorganization and drunkenness: witness the repeated story that while the Littlewood theater troupe were rehearsing using Behan's incomplete literal translation of the original script, the author was drinking his way through his paycheck in the pub across the road.

It was not until the late-1970s and early-1980s that the critical tide turned. The two plays, critics acknowledged, are quite different, but that fact should not subtract from the worth of either version. The original Irish version was indeed a naturalist drama, more somber in tone and certainly more concerned with the Troubles. But the English-language version had its own merits and has been celebrated by critics to this day as one of the earliest examples of English-language Absurdism in the 1950s and as one of the best productions by Littlewood's influential Theater Workshop.

The publication in 1978 of an edition of Behan's complete plays, including some little-known one-act plays for radio, vindicated Behan and Littlewood's celebrants. The collection was edited by a long-time friend and collaborator of Behan's, Alan Simpson, who directly addressed the slur that *The Hostage* was inferior to *An Giall* and dismissed the matter out of hand. Simpson argued that Behan's collaboration with Littlewood was productive, particularly for a writer who was prone to be repetitious, but also pointed out the limits of the collaboration—Behan was at times unhappy with the Theater Workshop's negative representation of the IRA.

Probably the best example of the Behan reassessment is David Krause's essay in *The Profane Book of Irish Comedy*. The essay argued that the original critical contempt for the absurdist elements of *The Hostage* were typical of middle-class prejudice against working-class theatrical forms, such as the conventions of music-hall theater, with which the working-class Behan was well versed. ''The prim people who are unamused by 'mere' farce usually complain about 'mere' music hall. It is not a foregone conclusion,'' however, ''that a dramatist who writes a farcical play in an episodic music-hall form is 'merely' having fun.'' Krause's discussion of Behan's use of farce and music-hall conventions demonstrated conclusively that Behan's repeated attempts to make the audience laugh had political and theatrical purpose. The Krause essay, and the publication of Simpson's collection and his balanced introduction to it, demonstrate that Behan is finally being appreciated on his own terms.

CRITICISM

Helena Ifeka

Ifeka is a Ph.D. specializing in American and British literature. In this essay she discusses Behan's play as an example of Absurdist theater.

Critics were at first puzzled by Brendan Behan's tragi-comedy *The Hostage.* They could not decide why Behan had created the bizarre mixture of serious themes with comic music-hall routines: was he writing in bad taste or had he simply lost control of the play altogether? They could see that the mixture had an almost Brechtian "alienation effect" upon the audience—they themselves had experienced those precise feelings of alienation and confusion while watching the play—but for what purpose? The answer would not become clear for some time: Behan had abandoned the Naturalism of Dublin's Abbey Theater and had completely bypassed the comedy-of-manners so popular at the time in favor of a cutting-edge fusion of Brechtian theater and the new Absurdist drama that was just emerging on the Continent. Like his Irish predecessors, W. B. Yeats, James Joyce, and Samuel Beckett, Behan created a form that expressed the modern moment as he saw it—chaotic, comic, incomprehensible, and tragic.

Absurdism, as a philosophy and as a theatrical form, was very much a product of the Second World War, and it is no accident that many of its principle figures, such as Albert Camus, Bertolt Brecht, and Beckett, were all active in the anti-fascist movement in the 1930s and in the Resistance in the 1940s. They were writers who had initially believed that they might make the world a better place and had hoped to use their art to resist forces that were intent on destroying workers' rights and human dignity.

But Absurdism was also shaped by the trauma, violence, and horror of the Second World War: a war in which millions of Jews were murdered (the Holocaust), in which millions of European civilians were displaced and killed, and in which totalitarian regimes (particularly the Nazi party in Germany and the Fascist party in Italy) systematically targeted intellectual and artistic dissidents. Absurdists railed in their various ways about the fundamentally mysterious and indecipherable nature of human existence—of fate, of wars, of love, and of death. Confronting the unknowable nature of the world and of human nature naturally creates intense feelings of despair, loss, bewilderment, and purposelessness. How could anyone continue life—let alone create art—after the orchestrated horror of the Holocaust? Absurdists saw little if any meaning, order, and purpose in the world. Such tremendous upheaval in experience—and in expectation of how the world should and could be ordered—had to be met with a complete reappraisal of artistic form.

This is precisely what happened. At first, the change was slow. In the midst of the War, Camus still favored the essay form for his influential *Le Mythe de Sisyphe* (1942; English translation, 1955). The traditional form of the novel still had some weight for him in 1948, when he published *The Plague,* but he had subsumed its narrative in symbolism: a damning allegory of Nazi-occupied France and the extermination of the Jews. While Camus clung to traditional form to express unconventional ideas, Beckett went the whole hog and created form that matched his meaning. In 1955, Beckett's play *Waiting for Godot* opened in Cambridge. It had been rapturously embraced by critics and audiences alike in its first (French-language) performance in Paris in 1953, and British critics were curious to see what all the fuss was about. They received it with a mixture of bewilderment, confusion, and praise. But Beckett was only moving through his first paces. As he continued to write, he pushed his stylistic innovation to its logical conclusion: one of his plays, *Breath,* contains no dialogue at all, only sound and movement.

In short, the Absurdists abandoned traditional dramatic form. Coherent dialogue went down the toilet, as did naturalist characterizations and cohesive plots. In their place were characters whose behavior and language baffled as often as they clarified, plots that are spliced up with songs, dances, *commedia dell'arte* mime sequences—forms and techniques that forcibly reminded the audience that they were no longer watching nineteenth-century drama but were facing modern angst.

Behan was not originally an Absurdist writer: Joan Littlewood made him one. Their collaboration together on *The Quare Fellow* and *The Hostage* was so unique that it is no understatement to say that

WHAT DO I READ NEXT?

- Behan's *The Quare Fellow* was his first major play and the start of his fruitful collaboration with Joan Littlewood. It was originally produced in Dublin and then adapted successfully for the London stage by Littlewood's Theater Workshop. The play is also focused upon an impending execution and explores Irish nationalism. However, it is set in a prison, and the overall tone of the play is much bleaker than *The Hostage*.

- Behan's autobiographical novel *Borstal Boy* is well-worth reading: it provides insight into the writer's life experience and a glimpse of his relaxed prose style. The autobiographical novel is based upon Behan's teenage experience in English prisons and reformatories when he was jailed for possession of explosives. The narrative is moving and humorous and describes the young narrator's transformation from his initial pose of boyish bravado to a deeper understanding of himself and his fellow prisoners.

- W. B. Yeats was Ireland's greatest poet, and his work is readily accessible in either a collected or selected edition. Of particular interest are two volumes of poetry: *The Tower* (1928) and *The Winding Stair* (1929). Both volumes contain exquisite poetic meditations upon the Easter Uprising, the War of Independence, and the Civil War. Yeats was a leading figure in the Irish Renaissance and the first Irish writer to win the Nobel Prize for Literature. He served as a senator for the Irish Free State from 1922 to 1928.

- Seamus Heaney is Ireland's best known contemporary poet. He shot to international fame with his second collection of poetry, *Death of a Naturalist* (1966), which opens with the famous poem "Digging." Heaney addresses Irish nationalism in some of his writing, but he is most interested in describing rural Ireland in all its glory and its violence.

- Bertolt Brecht was a German dramatist and poet. He emigrated to the United States then returned to Germany after the Second World War. He is most famous for developing a theory of theater that aimed to destroy the passivity of the audience that he felt was the result of naturalist drama, and instead to encourage them to be aware of the theatricality of the performance and to think critically about the issues it raised. Brecht achieved this "alienation effect" in his "epic theater" by developing a highly stylized acting style and by discarding the naturalist conception of the play and replacing it with a series of loosely connected scenes, which he connected with songs (that often commented on the plot; the technique has also come to be known as "Brechtian Theatre"). An enjoyable early example of his marriage of theory and praxis is his musical *The Threepenny Opera* (1928), an adaptation of John Gay's 1728 *The Beggar's Opera*.

- Irish playwright and poet Samuel Beckett is one of the great writers of the twentieth century. His play *Waiting for Godot* was tremendously influential in Postwar European, British, and American theater. The original French-language version of the play, *En attendant Godot,* premiered in Paris in 1953 to widespread acclaim; the English-language premiere in London in 1955 forever altered contemporary drama. Beckett's somber Absurdist play portrays two tramps, Estragon and Vladimir, who wait endlessly for a mysterious person called Godot.

Littlewood and her troupe of actors became the plays' second authors. Littlewood had a unique influence upon British and Continental theater. She was born into a working-class London family and studied for the stage at the Royal Academy of Dramatic Art. Rather than capitalizing on her success there, she turned her back on West-End theater and headed for Manchester, where she founded an amateur experimental theater group, Theater Union. The group split up during the Second World War but came together again in 1945, this time calling themselves Theater Workshop. They set up shop in London in 1953, and soon Littlewood's productions, which opened in an unfashionable part of London, were invariably so successful that they transferred to the West End (and New York and Paris). Littlewood was so committed to experimental theater that the success eventually became too much for her, and she left London for Africa and later France.

According to Behan's long-time friend and collaborator, Alan Simpson, Littlewood's work with Behan was profitable for both partners. Their first collaboration, *The Quare Fellow,* "was a turning point in Behan's career.... Littlewood and her company were in total sympathy with the play's implied condemnation of capital punishment, the morality of which was being hotly debated in Britain at that time.... This comedy-drama with its large cast of proletarian characters and no starry roles was a perfect vehicle for the group."

The production of *The Hostage* was an even more "important landmark." One of the most important aspects of the Behan-Littlewood collaboration was the use of Brechtian devices to alienate the audience and break down the fourth wall. Rather than lulling the audience into believing in the veracity of the play, Behan and Littlewood tried to keep them aware of the production's essential artificiality by throwing in asides about the author, directly addressing the audience, and breaking any build towards emotional warmth or tragedy with bawdy humor and song-and-dance routines.

The most important example of this technique is at the very center of the play: the juxtaposition between the tragic subject matter of two men facing execution and the light-hearted, farcical style in which the play is performed. This core juxtaposition is developed by frequent repetition of its basic pattern within each scene and act. Just as audience sympathy grows for the beleaguered and doomed Leslie, he bursts into a rabidly patriotic and racist song. Just as the audience becomes involved in Leslie and Teresa's tender exchanges, the couple jump into bed. Just as the audience is absorbing the full horror of Leslie's untimely death, he rises from the floor and sings to them. All these examples demonstrate the overwhelming dominance of this technique of juxtaposition in the play and its impact upon the audience, who are alienated from their

> BEHAN SOUGHT TO DO MORE THAN GIVE HIS AUDIENCE A GOOD NIGHT OUT AT THE THEATER: THAT WAS IMPORTANT TO HIM, BUT HE ALSO WANTED TO PROD THEM, CHALLENGE THEM, PROVOKE THEM, AND ABOVE ALL 'GET THEM THINKING.' THE CRAZY HUMOR OF *THE HOSTAGE*—AND MORE GENERALLY THE THEATRE OF THE ABSURD—WAS HIS MEANS TO THAT MOST SERIOUS END"

original emotions and brusquely asked to think about the action and issues more rationally. This structural juxtaposition also mirrors the play's topic: the real life North-South divide within Ireland.

Behan and Littlewood's Absurdism does not begin and end with the play's structure; on the contrary, many of the characters appear Absurdist. Mulleady, for instance, is a living demonstration of the troubling uncertainty of Irish identity. How can an aristocratic English man educated at Eton and Oxbridge and saturated in an upper class culture of high teas and after-dinner port decide to "become Irish?" Is Irish identity a coat that can be shrugged on so quickly? Can one become Irish by learning and speaking a language used only by an elite? Can language define cultural identity? These questions are crucial to any understanding of Irish identity, not only for the Irish themselves but for their near neighbors and sometime foes, the British audience to whom Behan and Littlewood were directing their production. These are the questions that they wanted their audience to ponder as they left a viewing of *The Hostage.*

Thus, to understand Behan's development as a playwright and his relationship to contemporary society and politics one must understand the influence of Absurdism upon him. Critics have often questioned Behan's politics; Alan Simpson, for instance, believed that Behan was more pro-IRA

A shot of the stage setting (the brothel) for The Hostage

than Littlewood's direction might have suggested, while others have pointed out that on-stage, his political commentary was a mixture of sharp-tongued radicalism and humane tolerance. Behan's representation of contemporary politics makes a lot more sense if he is understood to be a writer who was influenced by the style and beliefs of Absurdism. Likewise, his theatrical style and bric-a-brac form make a lot more sense if seen in the context of Absurdist drama.

Behan, together with Littlewood, was seeking to create a new form of drama that addressed and reflected the crises of his time. Moreover, he sought

to do more than give his audience a good night out at the theater: that was important to him, of course, but he also wanted to prod them, challenge them, provoke them, and above all ''get them thinking.'' The crazy humor of *The Hostage*—and more generally the theatre of the absurd—was his means to that most serious end.

Source: Helena Ifeka, for *Drama for Students,* Gale, 2000.

Robert Brustein

Brustein is one of the most respected drama critics of the late–twentieth century. In this excerpt, he appraises Behan's play as "neither serious nor even a play," instead calling the work "too disordered to support any more than a wink of solemnity."

It has been suggested that in *The Hostage* Brendan Behan is trying to "open up the stage." This is an understatement. He would like to hack the stage to bits, crunch the proscenium across his knee, trample the scenery underfoot, and throw debris wildly in all directions. Like his various prototypes—Jack Falstaff, Harpo Marx, W. C. Fields, and Dylan Thomas—Behan is pure Libido on a rampage, mostly in its destructive phase; and if he has not yet achieved the Dionysian purity of those eminent anarchists, he is still a welcome presence in our sanctimonious times. In America, comedy went underground (i.e., turned "sick") when the various humane societies built a protective wall around mankind, for an art form based on uninhibited abandon and open aggression cannot long survive the Anti-Defamation League, the N.A.A.C.P., the Legion of Decency, and *McCall's* Togetherness, not to mention those guardians of cultural virtue who now review theatre, movies, and TV for the newspapers. But Behan seems to have crossed the Atlantic without any significant accommodation to American tastes, outside of an abrupt conversion from Irish whiskey to homogenized milk. Behan is waging total war on all social institutions excepting brothels and distilleries.

For the dramatic bludgeon he has installed at the Cort is now flailing indiscriminately at everything in sight, including the British Empire, the I.R.A., the Catholic Church, the Protestant clergy, the army, the police, the F.B.I., and the D.A.R. What these disparate organizations have in common is their orthodoxy: Behan is waging total war on all social institutions excepting brothels and distilleries. But though destructive Libido can be the source of a lot of fun, it is hardly an organizing principle, so the author's assault on order leaves his play almost totally lacking in dramatic logic. Its substance is taped together with burlesque routines, Irish reels, barroom ballads, and outrageous gags (some old, some new, some borrowed, but all "blue"), while its scarecrow plot is just a convenient appendage on which to hang a string of blasphemous howlers. "This is a serious play!" screams a dour, baleful, humorless I.R.A. officer after a typical irreverency. But he convinces nobody. *The Hostage* is neither serious nor even a play. It is a roaring vaudeville turn, too disordered to support any more than a wink of solemnity.

Nevertheless, the plot—which is exhausted the moment you sum it up—does seem serious in its basic outline. Set in a Dublin brothel in modern times, the action revolves around the kidnaping, and ultimate death, of a young English soldier, taken by the I.R.A. because the British are going to execute a Belfast revolutionary. This promises an Irish political drama, and one can easily imagine how O'Casey might have interpreted the same situation. The brothel would become a symbolic Temple of Love, Life, and the Dance; the prostitutes would be "pagan girls" with ample bosoms and free, sensual natures; the comic characters would emerge as personifications of bigotry, indifference, and selfishness; the death of the boy would be an occasion for commentary on the victimization of the innocent by war; and the play would probably conclude with a vision of a better life to come.

But while Behan has turned to O'Casey for his plot outline, he does not share O'Casey's weakness for adolescent sexuality or utopian social communities. In his illogical, irresponsible view of society, in fact, he comes much closer to Ionesco; in his technique and treatment of low life, closer to the early Brecht. His whores are tough, funny, breezy hookers; the brothel is a sleazy dive run exclusively for profit ("Money is the best religion . . . and the best politics"); and the boy's death is followed immediately by his inexplicable resurrection for a final song ("O death where is thy sting-a-ling-a-ling"). As for the comics—a grotesque gallery which includes a madam and her "ponce" winging standup jokes at each other in the manner of a minstrel show; a religious eccentric goosed in the middle of her hymn by an ex-Postal clerk with a sanctified air and roaming fingers; and two pansies named Rio Rita and Princess Grace ("That's only my name in religion")—they are on stage primarily for what they can contribute to the general mayhem. For Behan's theme is "Nobody loves you like yourself," and his brothel is simply one of the last refuges of privacy where a man can pursue his pleasures and have his laughs.

On the other hand, the poignancy and desperation of the humor aptly illustrate the growing shakiness of this position as the private world becomes more and more circumscribed. Generously spread throughout the play are topical references which change with the latest newspaper headlines (a Russian sailor off the Baltica is now one of the customers in the house), anxious glances in the direction of the H-bomb ("It's such a big bomb it's after making me scared of little bombs"), and melodious admonitions to Khrushchev, Eisenhower, and Macmillan ("Don't muck about, don't muck about, don't muck about with the moon"). The forces gathering outside the brothel have now become so overwhelming that they cannot be ignored; and the violence behind Behan's farcical attitudes reveals his impotent frustration at being involuntarily implicated in the frightening activities of the great powers.

Joan Littlewood's production works hard to preserve all the wilder values of this vaudeville whirligig. The company, which has been mostly imported from her Theatre Workshop in England, is an excellent one—in the cases of Avis Bunnage, Alfred Lynch, and Patience Collier sometimes even inspired. But while Miss Littlewood has developed the appropriate Epic style, and has scrupulously tried to avoid gentility, I still don't think I've really seen the play. Perhaps English actors cannot suppress their instinctive good manners, for while the production rolls along with admirable speed and efficiency, it lacks robustness, coarseness, and spontaneity. But then only a troupe of burlesque comics endowed with the brutal wit of Simon Daedalus and the shameless vulgarity of Aristophanes could hope to catch the proper tone of this sidewinding improvisation. It is an open question whether *The Hostage* belongs on the legitimate stage at all, but considering that Minsky's is out of business, it is important to have it there. Its careless laughter is like a sound out of the past, and Behan's paean to unconditioned man is a wholesome antidote to what Orwell called "the smelly little orthodoxies that are now contending for our souls."

Source: Robert Brustein, "Libido at Large" in his *Seasons of Discontent,* Simon & Schuster, 1965, pp. 177–80

Walter Kerr

Kerr reviews The Hostage *in this excerpt, finding the play to be an entertaining and provoking experience, ultimately calling the play, "a wild night and a welcome one."*

During the first moments of *The Hostage* it was difficult to know whether author Brendan Behan was simply committing a nuisance or renewing the life of the stage. One character was heard to remark of another that he had "a face like a plateful of mortal sins," which is just how the play looked.

The curtain rose on a grinning and feverish jig which was no part of the narrative but intended

solely for the audience's macabre, and slightly startled, delectation. The jiggers included an old crone in black with her front teeth missing, an amiable ex-revolutionary with his one leg useless, a redheaded tart, a couple of homosexuals and a hymn-singer hiding behind spectacles.

When this broth settled down—though it never did settle down since all were back on their toes the minute a tinny piano chose to tinkle—we learned that we were housed in a brothel and that while a dozen raffish idlers, guzzlers, lechers, and perverts pursued their nightly devotions the seedy place was fated to become the temporary prison of a captured British soldier.

What sort of a play was this to be? We were not kept in the dark, only dizzy. When the browbeaten but ebullient inmates were not leering over the footlights to sing us a song (Mr. Behan had written outrageous lyrics for every standard sentimental song that ever dampened a pub), they were telling us jokes, right in the middle of the plot. Glancing at the unhappy prisoner, the housekeeper inquired of the officer who had brought him there:

"Have you got the place well covered, sir?"

"Yes, why?" snapped the officer.

"It might rain."

Shocked laughter from the audience. At which the officer wheeled on the customers, threatening them with a gesture. "Silence!" was his command to Broadway. "This is a serious play."

This was a serious play which had to do with the howling foolishness of bothering our heads over all our minor skirmishes and empty civil squabbles while the hydrogen bomb is waiting in the wings. The seriousness was obvious, and did not have to be stated often. ("The I.R.A. is out of date—and so is everything else.") The howling foolishness of it was given much more footage. Bouncing guards that seemed to have been borrowed from the line of ducks in a shooting gallery wheeled in and out and roundabout; for a while nobody entered except in the act of zipping his trousers, or even his kilt; tea was served, and the teabags haughtily rejected, between ballads. As the evening skipped and tugged until its seams were nearly burst, Mr. Behan seemed to be suggesting that we might just as well kick our heels, grinning, on the edge of the grave—if that's all we can think of doing.

And there was another way of looking at it. One of the things the irrepressible author may possibly have had in mind was the creation of a scatological version of *Everyman*. The soldier who was plucked from nowhere, for no reason, and promptly earmarked for Death was an ordinary young innocent, Cockney to his teeth and bewildered to his toes. Around him scampered all of the Vices contemporary man has succeeded in bringing to a pitch of refinement, each of which was prepared to make the jolliest possible case for itself. Only the Virtues were missing, which may have been Mr. Behan's method of suggesting that we are short on them. The rambunctiousness, and the savage-sweet ending (the innocent was shot, the mood sobered abruptly, then the dead man rose and joined the jig) united death and dance in an almost classic Dance of Death.

In dashing all of this off at breakneck speed, Mr. Behan was three or four persons at once. He was a kind of infant exhibitionist, proud of his never having been trained (the number of calculated shockers was enormous, and this may well have been the play with something to offend everybody). He was a random humorist, ready to borrow from absolutely anyone. (''I'm as pure as the driven snow.'' ''You weren't driven far enough.'') He was, again, a better humorist than that, an original piece of salt who might have reminded you of Mort Sahl, or the more extravagant Mark Twain, or simply of your drunken uncle who happened to be a true wit.

And he was an astonishing man of the theater. Whatever the willful excesses or woolly inspirations that overtook him, Mr. Behan could make the actors on stage blur into the folk out front with an intimacy and a dour communion that was infectious. The ribald evening was blatantly, boastfully, unself-consciously alive.

Why? The energy that stirred so mysteriously at the center of the stage, tumbling over all the usual conventions of the theater as though they were so many unimportant ninepins, came, I think, from two definable sources. One of them was the plain certainty that Mr. Behan, for all his celebrated tosspot habits, does possess the single-minded, self-generating, intuitive power of the natural-born artist. He may have neither discipline nor taste; but he has a gift that speaks, in however irresponsible and unmodulated a voice, for itself.

Nothing here should have been cohesive, and everything was. Simply, it seems never to have entered the author's head that his lapses of invention

> **THIS WAS A SERIOUS PLAY WHICH HAD TO DO WITH THE HOWLING FOOLISHNESS OF BOTHERING OUR HEADS OVER ALL OUR MINOR SKIRMISHES AND EMPTY CIVIL SQUABBLES WHILE THE HYDROGEN BOMB IS WAITING IN THE WINGS.''**

or his headlong determination to make hash of the proprieties should in any way compromise the truly lyrical or observant or just plain funny things that represented him at his individualistic best. And, somehow, they did not get in the way of our hearing ''He couldn't knock the skin off a rice pudding'' or of our exploding into laughter as a Negro boxer marched into a melee carrying an enormous placard, ''Keep Ireland black!'' The borrowed, the blue, and the Behan seemed all the same man: a gregarious and all-devouring personality shouting its own name from the Dublin chimney pots. Everything on the menu was malicious.

The second interior strength of the evening lay in director Joan Littlewood's high-powered hearing aid. Miss Littlewood's radar was able to detect, at all times, just where her author's uniqueness lived; she could hear the cockeyed private inflection that bound so much malarkey and so much inspiration together. Another director might have been frightened by the pantomime fantasy—stomping soldiers, crawling bodies, wandering shadows—that opened the second act, and so botched it. Anyone might have wondered what to do with a madman in a kilt, a spinster given to outbursts of plain chant, a frustrated lecherer who went over to the other camp, where he camped.

Miss Littlewood's assurance never faltered. She played the outrages as though they were casual commonplaces, and the casual commonplaces as though they were vaudeville routines. You were not permitted to catch your breath and consider what you had last heard: the lines and songs kept tumbling out, they came from the throat of a willful man and a witty man, one who loves to pretend to be

> " FOR IF THE PLAY, LIKE ALL ART, IS TO BE A LITTLE MORE REAL THAN REALITY, IT MUST, IN OUR TIME, BE A LITTLE MORE ABSURD THAN ABSURDITY"

wicked; and you wouldn't want to miss the rest of the nightmare party, would you?

Excesses of every kind? Yes, indeed. But a wild night and a welcome one.

Source: Walter Kerr, "*The Hostage*" in his *The Theatre in Spite of Itself*, Simon & Schuster, 1963, pp. 108–12.

John Simon

Finding influences "from Pirandello to Jean Genet," Simon offers a favorable review of Behan's play.

Of the five productions I am about to review, two were superior, one fair, and two poor. There would be nothing remarkable about this breakdown which is just what one would expect the law of averages and Broadway to produce, except for the interesting coincidence that the two good productions were, in their fashion, improvisations; that the middling one was the work of an established, respected playwright; and that the inadequate pair were both adaptations of not exactly choice novels. And as it so often happens with coincidences, this one has nothing coincidental about it. . . .

The reviewers who were vying with one another to find the source of Brendan Behan's *The Hostage* (with Brecht, I believe, getting the largest number of votes) were no less misguided than those who, sighing or snorting, announced that it was absolutely unlike anything else. *The Hostage* is distinguished by the fact that it is absolutely like every other play—all other plays that ever were, rolled into one. What a marvelous "mélange adultère de tout!" Everything is here from Pirandello to Jean Genet, from Ernst Toller to the later O'Casey, and

if anyone went looking in it for *Everyman* or Strindberg's *Damascus* trilogy, I'm sure he could find them too—just as Noel Coward, despite Behan's jibes at him, is likewise present. For this is truly a *Summa Theatrologica* for our time. And what you cannot find in the printed text is bound to be in the changes, additions, and ad libs which can be savored in the performances, whether put there by Behan, Joan Littlewood, the superbly imaginative director, or the actors themselves. I am sure that, like madras shirts, no two bleeding *Hostages* are alike.

Behan's play is about a lovable dolt of an English soldier held as hostage by some Irish Irregulars who have billeted themselves in an even more irregular Dublin establishment with a number of no less lovable Irish dolts for in- and cohabitants. If a certain Irish boy is hanged by the British in Belfast, the dopey little Cockney will be shot in Dublin. And this is the first respect in which *The Hostage* triumphs: the one kind of play it has nothing, but nothing, to do with is the Irish Patriotic Play, or even the Irish Irish Play, as once manufactured by Yeats, the young O'Casey, and the rest. If the play has any fundamental kinship with anything, it is with the *commedia dell'arte,* or its latterday avatar, the burlesque skit. Even those of its lines that are the *sine qua non* of every printed and produced version, such as Miss Gilchrist's, the "sociable worker's" remark, "I'm pure as the driven snow," to which Meg Dillon (fractured Irish for Mary Magdalen) replies, "You weren't driven far enough," smack of stage or, more precisely, barroom improvisation.

Improvisation, surely, is one of the most appropriate genres for an era of the absurd such as we are, or think we are, living in. In *The Hostage,* the dead may rise to sing a song, the pansies take over the leadership of the police, or (in the American version) a faggoty Negro boxer carry a sign reading "Keep Ireland Black." For if the play, like all art, is to be a little more real than reality, it must, in our time, be a little more absurd than absurdity. This is by no means easy to do, and various approaches have been tried: Beckett anatomizes, as it were, the interstices between events that never quite occur; Ionesco takes an impossibility, treats it as if it were the most ordinary thing in the world, and works from there; Behan keeps the audience, actors, and playwright unprepared for and flabbergasted by what happens next, and so feels that he has a working model of our world. There is even a cue for the author to appear on the stage and deliver his own immediate feelings if his intoxication is sufficient or business at the box-office insufficient. If Genet, in *The Balcony,* saw the brothel as a world in which our libidinous dreams come true, Behan, in *The Hostage,* sees the world as a brothel in which every sort of happiness is possible—except ultimate fulfillment. . . .

Source: John Simon, review of *The Hostage* in the *Hudson Review,* Vol. XII, no. 4, Winter, 1960, pp. 586–88.

SOURCES

Krause, David. "The Comic Desecration of Ireland's Household Gods" in *The Profane Book of Irish Comedy,* Cornell, 1982, pp. 105-70.

Wall, Richard. "*An Giall* and *The Hostage* Compared," in *Modern Drama,* Vol. XVIII, no. 2, June, 1975, pp. 165-72.

Waters, Maureen. "A Borstal Boy" in *The Comic Irishman,* State University of New York Press, 1984, pp. 161-72.

FURTHER READING

Behan, Brian. *With Breast Expanded,* London: 1964.
Brian Behan's biography of his charismatic and passionate mother Kathleen, who had a tremendous influence upon all her sons, including Brendan Behan.

Behan, Dominic. *Teems of Times and Happy Returns,* London: 1961.
Dominic Behan's family memoir provides an intimate glimpse of the Behan brothers' early lives.

Behan, Dominic. *My Brother Brendan,* Leslie Frewin, 1965.
An intimate biography of the playwright by his brother.

Jeff, Rae. *Brendan Behan: Man and Showman,* London, Hutchinson, 1966.
A biography of the playwright written shortly after his 1964 death.

Jesus Christ Superstar

ANDREW LLOYD WEBBER

TIM RICE

1971

Jesus Christ Superstar, a two-act rock opera, gave opera a radical facelift through its use of vibrant rock music for a solemn topic. Andrew Lloyd Webber (music) and Tim Rice (lyrics) created a new kind of Jesus, a prophet / rock star whose appeal stems as much from the crowd's energy as from his own inspirational message. The album of songs, released a year before the first stage production of the play, created a market for the dramatic version, which opened to sold-out audiences who were already familiar with its songs. The play is a baroque fusion of styles, rock rhythm with ballad narrative, dramatic characterization with rollicking choreography, and operatic star performances that together paradoxically succeed in communicating a humble theme of love and acceptance. Sacred themes are fused with ancient political history and modern sensibilities into an entirely new form of theater art. To some critics the mixture was balanced, taut, and spectacularly successful, but to others, it was a travesty. Leaving out the Resurrection was considered both blasphemous and brilliant, bringing picketers to the streets to protest the play, while critics raved its genius. Jesus is portrayed as having human qualities, doubts, and faults, yet his crucifixion becomes all the more poignant for it. The play was unique in its genesis as well, having begun its life as a record, thus putting initial emphasis on musicality over plot and staging. The first Broadway musical to have started in this way, it remains an innovative work of drama and music that has weathered well,

Andrew Lloyd Weber and Tim Rice after winning the Academy Award for best music (for their collaboration on Evita*) in 1997*

with a production nearly always taking place somewhere in the world.

AUTHOR BIOGRAPHY

The two young men from Britain had collaborated on earlier works before their successful enterprise with *Jesus Christ Superstar* and each had an impressive career in music. Andrew Lloyd Webber was born in 1948 in London of musician parents, his

father a composer and the Director of the London College of Music and his mother a piano teacher. Webber followed in their footsteps from an early age, learning the piano, French horn, and violin. By the time he was six, he was designing toy theatrical productions on the playroom floor, and at age nine he published his first composition, an opera based on Oscar Wilde's *The Importance of Being Earnest*. At twelve, he met his idol Richard Rodgers after sending him a fan letter. He attended the Guildhall School of Music and Drama and then the Royal College of Music. After one term at Oxford University, where his intention was to study architecture, he returned to London and met Tim Rice, a lover of classical music who was singing with a contemporary music group, the Aardvarks.

Rice, who was born in Amersham, England, in 1944, had attended the Sorbonne in Paris and had studied law in London, but was now a singer and lyricist, having just published his first song the year he met Webber, 1965. A mutual teacher friend asked them to collaborate on a new musical that his students could produce. The result was an early *Joseph and the Amazing Technicolor Dreamcoat,* which went on to be produced at Central Hall in Westminster. There a London *Sunday Times* drama critic praised it, and the pair repackaged the play in 1972 for the London stage, where it earned them a wider audience and still more praise.

The duo's next musical was *Jesus Christ Superstar.* Since they could not find a sponsor for a full production, they recorded one song, Judas's "Superstar," and released it to local underground radio stations in Great Britain and the United States. It became a hit single, so they recorded the entire, elaborate two-record album at great expense, making it, according to one critic, "the most expensive demo record ever." The album, too, succeeded wildly (except in Great Britain), so that with a demand waiting for them, they were able to produce the stage rock opera to sold-out crowds and mostly enthusiastic critics. The pair went on to produce more hits together, including *Evita* (1978). Webber has earned six Tony awards, four Drama Desk awards, three Grammys, and five Laurence Olivier awards, mostly for best score and best musical. In 1992 he was knighted for his service to the arts. He was the first recipient of the American Society of Composers, Authors, and Publishers Triple Play award. In 1995, Webber was inducted into the American Songwriters' Hall of Fame and also given the Praemium Imperiale Award for Music. In 1997 he was elevated to the peerage as The Lord Lloyd-Webber of Sydmonton. Tim Rice has earned Grammy, Tony, and Academy Awards for his lyrics. Rice wrote the lyrics for the Disney feature cartoon *The Lion King* and worked with Alan Menken to produce the lyrics for Disney's *Aladdin,* among others. Rice has published over 30 books on British pop music, and runs his own book publishing company, Pavilion Books, which he established in 1981. He is also the United Kingdom's chairman for Sports and the Arts. He was knighted in 1994 for his work in the arts and sports.

PLOT SUMMARY

Act I

The play opens with the actors arriving in a desert, laden with their costumes and props. In the film version, a battered bus slowly makes its way across the desert into the foreground. The actors ready themselves, slipping into costume and character, preparing to give a performance of the last seven days of Christ's life, as much for their own sakes as for the pleasure of the audience. The largest, most awkward piece to unload is the heavy wooden cross. Judas observes these preparations from afar, edgy and already aloof from the rest of the group.

Act I: Heaven on Their Minds

As Judas watches the others, he begins to formulate and to articulate to himself just what is bothering him about Jesus: his superstar status, his moving from a vehicle of God's message to a show in and of himself. The followers think "they've found a new Messiah," and Judas worries about their anger when they discover Christ is just a man. Meanwhile Jesus shares his peaceful message to an adoring crowd.

Act I: What's the Buzz

At the house of Simon the Leper, the apostles press a tired Jesus to tell them where their group will go next, to begin a political and religious revolution, demanding, "When do we ride into the Jerusalem?" The apostles fail to notice that Jesus needs to withdraw and rest, but Mary Magdalene offers solace, saying "Let me try to cool down your face a bit." Christ tells them that only Mary knows what he needs.

Act I: Strange Thing Mystifying

Judas cannot stand that Jesus lets a former prostitute ("a woman of her kind") attend to him, but Christ hurls back, "If your slate is clean, then you can throw stones / If your slate is not, then leave her alone." Mary sings "Everything's Alright," but Judas continues to prod, saying that the money for her "fine ointments . . . could have been saved for the poor." Jesus admonishes Judas and the apostles not to waste their precious time, since he knows he will not be among them for long.

Act I: This Jesus Must Die / Hosanna

The next morning, the Jewish Priests convene to decide what to do about the "rabble-rouser" whose mad mob can be seen and heard singing "Hosanna! Superstar!" in the background. Annas, father-in-law of the High Priest Caiaphas, emphasizes the danger, since the Romans, who occupy their land, will surely punish all Jews for the revolutionary behavior of one man and his band of wild followers. Caiaphas decides that "like John before him, this Jesus must die." Jesus addresses Caiaphas and the priests gently, explaining that "nothing can be done to stop the shouting," while the ecstatic followers wave palms and joyfully anticipate their triumphant entrance to Jerusalem.

Act I: Simon Zealotes

The now rather large crowd moves in choreographed rhythm with Jesus, asking to be touched, kissed, acknowledged. Simon sees that this powerful force of "over fifty thousand" has political potential. "Keep them yelling their devotion," he advises Jesus, "But add a touch of hate at Rome." Perhaps they can oust the Romans and regain their land. Jesus responds with a simple gesture of peace.

Act I: Poor Jerusalem

As Jesus begins to sing, the crowd quiets and sits in a circle around him. His song expresses his worry that his followers, although they chant their adoration, do not truly understand power and glory. The end of the song shifts inward, when he both realizes and explains that "to conquer death you only have to die."

Act I: Pilate's Dream

Pontius Pilate is a Roman Governor disturbed by a dream he has had, in which a Galilean is martyred and he, Pilate, takes the blame. Pilate is a man usually comfortable with his station and power, but the dream leaves him unsettled.

Act I: The Temple

Moneylenders, prostitutes, wine-, goat-, and carpet-sellers have taken over the temple. Christ strides up to them and angrily turns over tables, protesting, "My temple should be a house of prayer." After shouting for the "den of thieves" to "get out," Jesus sinks into a reverie, summing up his three years on earth, but even in this private moment he is besieged by the sick and poor, who crowd him until he screams at them, "Heal yourselves!"

Act I: Everything's Alright (Reprise) & I Don't Know How to Love Him

Mary Magdalene once again soothes Jesus to sleep, and then goes into her own reverie about her conflicting feelings, both platonic and romantic, for this man.

Act I: Damned for All Time

Meanwhile, Judas, in anguish but armed with resolve, offers to betray Christ's whereabouts to the priests, who give him thirty pieces of silver for his service. The priests plan to have Jesus arrested and turned over to the Romans for execution.

Act II: The Last Supper

The apostles indulge in the Last Supper as a meal and not as sacrament, until Jesus sings, "This is my blood you drink / This is my body you eat." But their blank faces tell Jesus that they will forget him after he dies. His announcement that one of them will betray him raises protests from all but Judas, who takes it up as a challenge to do so. Judas departs, the apostles drift off to sleep, and Jesus sinks into lonely contemplation. He begins to question his fate, to question God and his own earthly mission. As his resolve fades, he accuses God, "You're far too keen on where and how but not so hot on why." But getting no cosmic encouragement, he steels himself for the ordeal to come, so that he can see God at last. At the end of the scene, Judas kisses Jesus on the cheek, and Jesus asks him, "Judas, must you betray me with a kiss?"

Act II: The Arrest

As the Roman soldiers arrive to arrest Jesus, the apostles struggle awake and sleepily retrieve their swords. Jesus calms them and goes willingly with the soldiers, who shove him along. On his way, a crowd surges around him, including Annas and Judas. Some taunt, "Now we've got him," while others quiz the prisoner like copy-hungry television reporters hounding a film star, "What would you say were your big mistakes?" Caiaphas confirms the arrest with the gravity of a judge, sending the prisoner on to Pilate, who alone has the power of sentencing to death.

Act II: Peter's Denial

A maid and her grandfather recognize Peter as one of the prisoner's followers, which Peter three times denies. Mary reminds him that Jesus had predicted his behavior.

Jesus (Ted Neely) addresses his followers in a stage production of Jesus Christ Superstar

Act II: Pilate and Christ

Pilate reluctantly interviews the prisoner, realizing that he lost a measure of his control due to the crowd's zeal to kill this man. He finds Christ's calm amazing and wants not to hurt him. As a way of avoiding responsibility, Pilate then sends Christ on to King Herod (who was half Jewish), since Herod has legal jurisdiction over the Jews, ''You're Herod's race! You're Herod's case!''

Act II: King Herod's Song

King Herod is an overweight, self-indulgent, and corrupt king surrounded by sycophants and living in depraved luxury. In a tightly choreographed ragtime song and dance, he taunts Christ to perform a miracle on demand, and when Jesus does not stir, he angrily sends him away. Meanwhile, Mary and Peter sing, ''Could We Start Again, Please?''

Act II: Judas's death

Judas, wracked with guilt, accuses Annas and Caiaphas of hurting the victim he turned over to them. They repulse him, and his anguish increases as he sings an apology to Christ, shifting to his own rendition of Mary's song, ''I Don't Know How to

Love Him.'' Realizing too late his own guilt, he hangs himself. The choir chants, ''So long Judas / Poor old Judas.''

Act II: Trial before Pilate

Caiaphas brings Jesus back to Pilate for a definitive execution. Still Pilate feels it too heavy a duty, and his interview of the prisoner seems like an attempt to find any excuse to release him, ''I'll agree he's mad / Ought to be locked up / But that's no reason to destroy him.'' Jesus once again fails to supply anything but further proof of his divine immunity. Pilate agrees to flog Christ with thirty-nine lashes, an extreme torture. Afterwards, Pilate tenderly lifts the broken man, but when Jesus tells Pilate he has no power, Pilate goes into a rage and allows Christ's ''great self-destruction'' to take place.

Act II: Superstar

Judas, somehow resurrected, presides over the walk with the cross and preparations for crucifixion, assisted by three choirs of ''angels'' who sing the ''Superstar'' reprise. Judas asks Jesus whether he shouldn't have staged this show in a better era, since ''Israel in 4 B.C. had no mass communication.'' Christ dies simply, on the cross.

Act II: John Nineteen Forty-one

The show over, the actors repack and variously board the bus, some in a brisk businesslike manner and some, like Mary, casting a last wistful glance back at the set. The curtain falls.

CHARACTERS

Annas

The father-in-law of Caiaphas, Annas is a high priest ready for action. His warning that Christ's ''half-witted fans will get out of control'' (a phrase that could as easily apply to rock fans as apostles) has the desired effect on Caiaphas, convincing him to arrange the killing of this new radical religious leader, as he did John the Baptist. Annas reassures the distraught Judas that he has done the right thing by turning Jesus in; since the mob turned against Jesus, it seems clear to Annas that Judas had ''backed the right horse.'' The moral implications of Judas's act seem lost on Annas.

Caiaphas

Caiaphas is the High Priest of the Pharisees, or Jewish priests. He wants to get rid of Jesus, in fear that the Romans will punish all Jews for the ruckus caused by Christ's followers. The Jews are in a precarious relationship with Rome; the priests have to tread a middle road between pleasing the Roman government and guiding their own people by upholding Jewish law and tradition. Caiaphas cannot afford to have Jesus erode his authority with a new religion. Therefore, he decides to eliminate this new leader around whom the Jews are ''foolishly'' assembling.

Jesus Christ

The Jesus of this rock opera is as much a rock idol as he is a religious leader. He exudes peace, proclaims peace, lives peace, but is otherwise a rather human ''son of God,'' since he has human doubts. Jesus displays human emotion on several occasions: irritation at his apostles for their unceasing demands on him, anger at the merchants and moneylenders in the temple, and genuine fear and doubt just before his execution. The spell he casts over his followers comes partly from his pure simplicity and partly from their desire to adore him, make him the object of their piety; they seem to miss his point that devotion is due to God, not to him.

MEDIA ADAPTATIONS

- A re-mastered version of the original cast recording is available from MCA Records, as is the original soundtrack from the film *Jesus Christ Superstar,* starring Ted Neely (Jesus), Yvonne Elliman (Mary), and Carl Anderson (Judas). A 20th anniversary production in London is also available on CD, through RCA Records. In 1994, a group of Atlanta-based rock musicians re-recorded the work as *Jesus Christ Superstar: A Resurrection,,* with Amy Ray singing the part of Jesus. The recording is available on Daemon Records. The BBC produced a 20th anniversary radio production around 1992, but has not released the recording. The original song lyrics and music score are widely available.

One of his characteristic gestures is to stroke the cheek of his admirers, and his calm even in the face of Judas's anger is both inspirational and other-worldly, and, to Judas and Pilate, exasperating. It is his purity which prevents Jesus from recognizing that the precariousness of his political position (he is a threat to the Romans and Pharisees), more than the religious ideals he represents, that leads to his downfall. On top of his purity is another characteristic: his Superstar quality. Jesus is not just a man, but a ''happening,'' an event, a center of power around which the apostles and devout followers revolve.

Female Apostles

The wives of the apostles dance with Simon in a frenzy of devotion, and also quietly serve food and drink when the group is resting.

King Herod

Herod is a self-indulgent, half-Jewish despot who rules all of Galilee, including its captive Jews. His court consists of a corrupt band of sycophants who serves Herod's lavish tastes. Herod makes a joke of Christ, as he probably does with any serious aspect of his kingship. The whipping of Jesus at first titillates his depraved side, but when the punishment goes too far, Herod is visibly disquieted.

High Priest

See Caiaphas

Judas Iscariot

Judas is more politically astute than Jesus; he sees Jesus turning into a cult figure whom the crowd accepts as the new Messiah. Judas is too practical a man to allow the possibility to enter his mind that Jesus truly is the Messiah. He only sees that if Jesus continues his self-indulgence, he will bring trouble to himself and his followers, since the Romans and Jewish Pharisees will not abide this threat to their authority. Unlike the other actors, Judas begins the play in character: even before getting into costume, he is aloof and temperamental. His mood of impatience and frustration stems from what he sees as a good thing ''gone wrong.'' He allows his disappointment in the mission to cloud his doubts about betraying Christ. After the guards take Christ away, however, Judas realizes the enormity of his betrayal, and sees that he will for all time ''be spattered with innocent blood.'' Therefore he hangs himself, although he later appears, resurrected it seems, to sing a final tribute to Jesus Christ, Superstar.

Maid by the Fire

The young maid, sitting around a fire for warmth with her grandfather and a Roman Soldier, recognizes Peter as having been with ''that man they took away,'' which Peter denies.

Mary Magdalene

Mary is a former prostitute who has joined the band of apostles and wives and serves Jesus. In fact, her attraction to him is more than platonic; it is also the same kind of physical attraction with which she is very familiar, and yet, the combination of these attractions, along with her awe of this holy man, make her afraid of her own feelings, as she describes them in her song, ''I Don't Know How to Love Him.'' Of all of Christ's followers, Mary best understands his need to stay ''calm'' and unworried, to take time for himself and to pace himself so that he will not break down under the demands of the crowd. She is empathetic to Peter, too, even when he betrays Jesus as predicted. Mary is the female embodiment of Christ's message of love and acceptance. She gives the impression that, even more than the work of the apostles, it will be those with her faith in Jesus the man that will fuel the survival of Christianity.

Male Apostles

The male apostles follow Jesus and sing a song that indicates their awareness that they could gain a kind of immortality from their association with this leader, ''so they'll all talk about us when we die.'' They get caught up in the atmosphere of adoration, dancing and singing, not noticing that Jesus does not want such excessive devotion. The apostles seem to love the Jesus ''happening'' more than the man, although they protest their loyalty when Christ confronts them at the last supper. They also love their wine, drunkenly falling asleep just when Jesus needs them most, rousing briefly when the Roman Guard arrests him but easily talked out of fighting the guards when Jesus tells them to put away their swords.

Merchants and Moneylenders

These take over the temple to sell their wares and are dismissed by an uncharacteristically angry Jesus.

Old Man

The Maid's grandfather is the third to accuse Peter of association with Jesus, prompting Peter's third denial.

Peter

Peter is a loyal apostle who considers ridiculous Christ's prediction that he will betray him three times. But he does exactly as Jesus predicts, and when Mary points this out to him, Peter defends himself, saying that he had to lie to protect himself. However, Peter realizes the harm he has done to their cause, and he wants to turn back time, giving him a chance to protect his leader instead. He sings with Mary Magdalene ''Could We Start Again Please?''

Pontius Pilate

Pilate is the Roman Governor to whom Jesus is first brought for punishment by the Jews, and who refuses to appease the crowd, due at least in part to a dream he has had portending his own incrimination if he does. He defers by sending Jesus on to King Herod instead, on the grounds that only Herod, as King of Galilee, has the authority to condemn a Galilean to death. When the Pharisees' guards bring Jesus to Pilate for the second time, Pilate reluctantly has the young zealot flogged, as a measure to appease a crowd that could easily turn against him. Pilate endeavors to elicit any kind of concession from Christ, attempting to find an excuse to dismiss him unharmed. Pilate recognizes that he is contending not with Jesus but with the crowd demanding a crucifixion. Jesus does not play into Pilate's game; Pilate's anger gets the best of him, and he condemns Christ to die on the cross, fulfilling his prophetic dream.

Priests

The Priests are the Pharisees, who perch like vultures on the stark improvised scaffolding that serves as their temple. They are the council convened by Caiaphas to decide what to do about ''Jesusmania,'' which threatens the entire Jewish community, for the Romans do not make distinctions within the group and would punish all Jews for Christ's actions.

Roman Soldier

The Roman Soldier recognizes Peter as a friend of Christ's and prompts Peter's second denial.

Stage Manager

The stage manager sees to the unloading of props and trunks of costumes and gets the band of young actors ready to produce the play, which seems to be produced as much for their own sakes as for the viewing pleasure of the audience.

Simon Zealotes

Simon's surname Zealotes comes from the Greek word ''zeal,'' meaning enthusiastic devotion. It is Simon's ''zealous'' goal to urge the Jesus cult to revolt against Rome. He tells Jesus to turn the mass of followers against Rome so that the Jews can accomplish ousting the Romans, as well as establishing their new religion. ''There must be over fifty thousand,'' he tells Jesus, ''and everyone of fifty thousand / would do whatever you tell him to.'' Simon shows himself quick to battle in the encounter of the Last Supper, but when Jesus tells him to put away his sword, he obediently does so.

TOPICS FOR FURTHER STUDY

- How does the character of Jesus Christ respond to and reflect values prevalent in the 1970s when the rock opera was produced? How does this characterization compare to the Biblical representation of Christ?

- Is sacred or religious material appropriate for a rock opera? Why or why not?

- Research the political situation of the Jews in the time of Christ. Compare the play's portrayal of the Pharisees and the Zealots to your findings.

- Why was Herod reluctant to execute Jesus?

- Webber and Rice have been criticized for their sympathetic treatment of Judas Iscariot. How has the portrayal of Judas changed over the centuries, and what might account for any shift in sensibilities toward him?

- Why does the play leave out the Resurrection of Christ?

THEMES

God and Religion

Jesus Christ Superstar is not simply a portrayal of the historical figure of Jesus, a rabbi who promoted the idea of loving one's enemy, but an exploration of the star status of Jesus, who gathered around him a following of devoted disciples and had a timeless, worldwide impact. According to critic James R. Huffman in the *Journal of Popular Culture,* works like this one ''ask the right questions, but allow each individual to provide his own answers.'' One of the questions it asks is what kind of relationship one should have with God and/or Jesus. A range of responses is portrayed, from Mary's loyal, personal devotion that threatens to border on physical passion, to Judas's skepticism and betrayal. Mary's relationship represents the person who embraces the values of Christianity and wants a personal connection to God but cannot achieve it:

Mary doesn't "know how to love him." Judas represents the classic doubter, one who realizes too late what really matters. However, most of the followers are just part of the crowd, like the "over 50,000" that Simon Zealotes sings about. This crowd sees Christ as a fast track to salvation ("I believe in you and God, so tell me that I'm saved"). The disciples, on the other hand, are mere buffoons, more interested in their own glory than in appreciating the profound event taking place before their eyes. The line, "always hoped that I'd be an apostle, knew that I would make it if I tried" is an ironic comment on their misguided aspiration, and the lines that follow it drive the point home, "Then when we retire we can write the gospels, so they'll still talk about us when we've died." The apostles prove of little use to Jesus at the Last Supper, since they fall asleep when their leader needs them most, and then foolishly offer to fight for him once it is too late to save him. Significantly it is not the apostles or those closest to Jesus—Mary, Judas, Simon, or Peter—but the anonymous crowd whom Jesus helps, touches, and heals. Jesus thus is seen as healing others, confirming their beliefs, but not confirming those of the characters with whom the audience most identifies. Religious commitment seems simple, somehow, for others, but vexed with doubts and insecurity for oneself. In this way, *Jesus Christ Superstar* hits a nerve with its postmodern audience, many of whom share both Mary's desire for a passionate connection to a higher power and also Judas's jaundiced belief that such faith would be naive and, ultimately, misplaced. The fact that Judas later repents and discovers that Christ loved him too also resonates to the skeptic's fear of "missing out."

Doubt

Jesus himself provides an exploration of religious doubt. While his followers either accept his divinity blindly or, like Judas and the Priests, fear the political consequences of his impact while ignoring his mission, Jesus alone understands that his mission is serious and vital. In fact, he will undergo the ultimate test of faith, by willingly accepting his own death. This fate he seems to ignore until the time draws dangerously close. In this respect he is no different from any human who ignores or maintains a surface faith as long as things are going well. When Christ comes face to face with the fact that he truly must die, it shakes the foundations of his faith, and he asks himself "Why am I scared to finish what I started?" But then realizes in mid-sentence

that it is not his plan he was following but God's. Now skeptical, he demands proof and becomes angry with God when it is not given. "God, thy will is hard," he accuses his heavenly father, "But you hold every card." By the time he reaches Pilate for the second interrogation, Christ has mended his breach of faith and faces his trial with new resolve, telling Pilate, "Any power you have comes to you from far beyond. / Everything is fixed and you can't change it." Christ's acceptance of his crucifixion dissolves his doubt.

STYLE

Rock Opera

Tommy (1969), hailed as the world's first rock opera, broke with the tradition of the musical stage production by incorporating rock music into the classical opera genre. *Tommy,* an album released by The Who, told through its songs the story of a deaf mute who becomes a guru because of his pinball skill. The album was an immediate success, and was soon transformed into a live stage production that The Who took on a worldwide live tour, during which they recorded *Tommy Live* in front of record-breaking audiences. They also produced a film version, directed by Ken Russell. The rock opera is, like opera, a form that advances the plot through songs, with few or no spoken parts. The rock element pertains to the music and choreography of the piece, but in the cases of *Tommy* and *Jesus Christ Superstar,* it also contributed the theme and protagonist of the play in the form of the rock star. Operas feature both solo numbers and chorus or ensemble pieces, and both *Tommy* and *Jesus Christ Superstar* follow this pattern. The rock opera as a genre has mostly faded away, having served its purpose to broaden the definition of the musical production and of the format of the rock album. However, the brief era of rock opera resulted in a number of song cycle or "plot rock" albums (albums whose songs tell a story), such as The Kink's *Preservation Act I* and *Preservation Act II,* Pink Floyd's *The Wall,* David Bowie's *The Rise and Fall of Ziggy Stardust,* and The Beatles' *Sergeant Pepper's Lonely Hearts' Club,* paving the way for the concept rock videos of the MTV era.

Point of View

The physical and emotional perspective from which the viewer is led to view the spectacle of a dramatic production is from afar, and this is especially true when the production is a musical. When viewing a dramatic production, the audience looks onto the stage as onto a miniature world, complete with furnishings and a false horizon peeping through the window, and the viewer has the sense of being outside of the events, judging them like a god. Only at certain moments is the viewer invited into the private world of a given character, and that is when that character muses aloud in a soliloquy, sharing private thoughts as though unaware of the audience listening to every word. The character might encourage this intimacy through facing slightly offstage, in a three-quarters profile, putting the audience outside the line of vision, giving the impression that eavesdropping will not be detected. The actor might speak quietly, almost in a whisper, further indicating the privacy of his or her thoughts. At this moment, the viewer's perspective can merge with that character's perspective, such that the events are seen through that character's point of view. Usually only one or two characters' thoughts are revealed in this way, and the play may privilege one character's perspective by focusing on that person's inner thoughts more than the other's. When the production is a musical, the sense of being outside of the action is enhanced through the pageantry of the choreographed movements onstage, which are not at all like real life and thus remind the viewer of the artificiality of the performance.

Only when the characters sing a soliloquy, with a spotlight creating a temporary connection to the audience, does the viewer gain a sense of identifying with the characters. In a musical or opera, the solos shift the point of view from one soloist to another. Even though Jesus is the central character in *Jesus Christ Superstar,* the soloists, Judas, Mary, and Jesus, each have a different assessment of his mission, and the viewer's point of view shifts according to who is singing. Throughout most of the play the point of view lies outside of Jesus, in Judas's perspective, as he assesses this leader's impact on the crowd and tries to decide just how to take him. The perspective shifts to Jesus whenever he sings. Thus the viewer is led to consider not only who Jesus seemed to be to others, but what kinds of doubts and problems he himself had in his life and mission. The shifting point of view asks viewers to identify with Jesus as a man, and to identify with his followers, some of whom saw him as a superstar and others who doubted him. The fact that Christ's resurrection was excluded from the play leaves ambiguous the question which perspective to be-

lieve, thus the shifting point of view of the play contributes to the theme of doubt and faith.

HISTORICAL CONTEXT

The Biblical Story of Jesus

The story as told in the play *Jesus Christ Superstar* follows fairly closely what is known about the life and times of the historical Jesus. Jesus, a rabbi whose father apparently was a carpenter, worked for a time in that trade as well before developing a ministry based on loving one's enemy and a more holistic attachment to God than simply complying with religious law. Jesus went out to preach to the people rather than wait for them to come to him in a temple, as did most other rabbis of the time. It is speculated that Jesus was a member of the Pharisees, a progressive, democratic Jewish sect that interpreted the Torah more liberally than did the more conservative Sadducees. Jesus preached mostly in Galilee and apparently took the rather dangerous step of going into Jerusalem to preach as well, as the play delineates. Here he met with more difficult adversaries than he had in Galilee, with Jewish leaders who considered his teachings controversial and with Romans who feared a rebellious uprising. Jesus may have been a "marked man" in the sense that there were those who wanted to remove this threat to the authority of the Romans and the Pharisees, the high priests of the Jewish community. Knowing that he would not be suffered to live and preach much longer, he held a farewell meal on the eve of Passover and was arrested in the garden of Gesthemene by Roman soldiers. Jewish authorities first tried him, found him guilty of high treason (for pretending to be the Messiah, although there is no evidence that Jesus made this claim), and sent him to Pilate for execution. Nothing was recorded of him for the first forty years after his death, then the letters of the Apostle Paul (a Hellenized Jew born after the death of Jesus who introduced Christianity to the Greeks) refer to his ministry. The synoptic gospels (Matthew, Mark, and Luke) probably written after the Pauline letters, tell slightly conflicting stories, but essentially also confirm the existence of a rabbi named Jesus who was crucified under Roman law.

The Theatrical "Happenings" of the 1960s and 1970s

Theater in the 1960s and 1970s was, to use the parlance of the time, a "happening," a word that

COMPARE & CONTRAST

- **Time of Christ:** Jesus was a rabbi with a devout following, but he did not himself promote the idea of ''Christianity.'' This was a later development that arose out of the Resurrection experience and the Easter tradition that merged the legend of Jesus's rising with an ancient, existing myth of rebirth and renewal of a holy leader. Jesus was not a cult figure, but a charismatic religious leader of the Jews. Christianity during his life was neither a religion nor even a concept, although some of its precepts were developing.

  1970s: Christianity had flowered and was beginning to wilt by the time that Webber and Rice wrote their rock opera of Jesus. Although churches flourished in numbers, religious belief had eroded since the medieval period. Even so, some devout Christians were offended by Webber and Rice's portrayal of Jesus as a man with human weaknesses, while others delighted in a refreshing look on a time-warn symbol. When the album was first released, churches all over the world incorporated its songs into their services, including some catholic churches, the Pope had just recently overruled the Church's ban against playing music in services.

  Today: Christianity continues to grow across the globe, in a resurgence of fundamentalism that exists side by side with widespread secularism, atheism, and skepticism.

  Time of Christ: Women did not preach or hold any kind of office in the church, and did not attend services in the Jewish synagogue, because their presence was considered a potential distraction for male worshipers.

  1970s: The women's liberation movement sought greater equality for women in all walks of life, although actual change was slow in coming. Liberal Jewish synagogues allowed women to attend services, and a woman rabbi was ordained in 1935; however, orthodox synagogues were not as progressive.

  Today: There are women preachers in many religions, although the Catholic church still does not allow them, and liberal and reformed synagogues have female rabbis and free seating for all worshipers. Some Orthodox synagogues have recently installed special one-way screens allowing women to hear the Torah being read and to observe other services, yet remain invisible to the male worshipers.

  Time of Christ: Judaism was the religious faith of a group of persecuted people who held tightly to their customs and beliefs. It required following exacting rituals and extreme devotion.

  1970s: Judaism had become more important to Jews as a sense of shared cultural and historical experiences than a shared system of beliefs. The religion had split into four main factions (orthodox, reformed, liberal, and conservative), and many Jews did not regularly attend services.

  Today: Only about 20% of Jews attend regular synagogue services, and being Jewish still consists of one's familial cultural heritage as much or more than one's religious beliefs.

implied energy, spectacle, and significance. Beginning with *Hair* in 1967, nudity and shocking language would become commonplace in the theater, and audiences came to expect to be shocked and challenged as well as entertained. That *Jesus Christ Superstar* (1971) committed the sacrilege of conflating religion with Broadway spectacle was almost par for the course, as was its celebration of the hippie style, a style that valued the personal expression of uniqueness and freedom. There was a movement toward less formality as well as fusion with other art forms. This was experimental theater, often entailing audience participation, anachronistic costuming and props, and extending the stage to the larger world. Thus the combination of rock music with ancient, biblical themes in *Jesus Christ Superstar,* although completely unique in itself, was consistent with the prevailing mood of the theater.

CRITICAL OVERVIEW

Jesus Christ Superstar was the first Broadway musical to have begun its life as a record. The single record of Judas's song "Superstar," released in 1970, at first drew little notice from the listeners of the underground rock stations that played it, but over the next few months the song gained attention in the United States, if not in Great Britain, where it was produced. One form of this attention was pure outrage, for the song, especially when taken out of the context of the play, seemed to many religious listeners blasphemous when it asked "Jesus Christ, Superstar, do you think you're what they say you are?" Although it finally received a good response, it never rose above the top 80s in the Billboard listing. Nevertheless, the single record sold over 100,000 copies by May, 1970. Based on this success, Rice and Webber recorded the full rock opera and packaged it in a two-record boxed set purposely designed to look like other recorded operas. On October 21, 1971, the New York opening performance (on tape) of the rock opera was held in a church, coordinated with a slide presentation of religious paintings. The invited reviewers and the rest of the audience gave the record a standing ovation. Then the album was released to radio stations, whose reviewers loved it. Scott Muni of radio station WNEW called the song, "an out and out smash." By February 6, 1971, it climbed to the top of the *Billboard* list of hot songs in the United States. *Billboard* predicted, "It is destined to become one of the most talked about and provocative albums on the pop scene." Two weeks later, the albums made it to the top of *Cashbox*'s list, which hailed it as "a powerful and dynamic rock score of sweeping melodies." Jack Shadoian of *Rolling Stone* raved that "many of us rockheads . . . have been sitting around waiting for something extraordinary to happen. This is it." Although some reviewers disliked the fusion of rock sound in opera format ("When it isn't dead-boring, it's too embarrassing to hear," quipped the *Cue* reviewer), others, such as Derek Jewell of the *London Sunday Times,* saw it as

Yvonne Elliman as Mary Magdalene in a scene from the stage production

the herald to a new art form, with music "more moving that Handel's *Messiah* . . . a work on a heroic scale, masterfully conceived, honestly done, and overflowing with splendid music and apt language." The music derived its unique blend of styles from many varied sources. William Bender wrote: "Webber and Rice do not outdo the Beatles or the Rolling Stones or the Edwin Hawkins Singers, Prokofiev, Orff, Stravinsky or any other musical influence found in their work. But they have welded these borrowings into a considerable work that is their own." The record set became the best-selling two-record album of all time, grossing over $15 million in the year of its release.

The first London stage play was performed at a West End theatre with Paul Nicholson as Jesus. It ran for eight years (3,358 performances) and became West End's longest-running musical up to that point; it currently ranks as the fifth longest running musical in West End history, behind three other Andrew Webber musicals, (*Cats, Starlight Express,* and *Phantom of the Opera).* In the Spring of 1971, before the play reached Broadway, the album set had sold 2 million copies in the United States and *Life* magazine featured photos of one of the many improvised performances being staged across the country, many of which were produced in violation of the play's copyright. *Life* attributed its popularity to music and lyrics that "bridge the generation gap," being at once "both secular and reverent." The opening of the official Broadway production was delayed by sound problems, but the show, starring Ben Vereen as Judas, Jeff Fenholt as Jesus and Yvonne Elliman as Mary Magdalene, got underway to the admiration of both the critics and the public. The Broadway run took in almost $3 million, ran from 1971 to 1973, and won the 1971 Drama Desk Award.

The 1973 film version starred rock singer Ted Neely as Jesus, Carl Anderson (Ben Vereen's Broadway understudy) as Judas, and Yvonne Elliman as Mary Magdalene. Many critics panned the film; however, it won British Academy Awards for Best Sound Track and Best Cinematography and grossed more than 10 million dollars at the box office. Both the film and the stage production have enjoyed wide popularity worldwide since its release.

A twenty-year anniversary tour garnered large audiences across the United States in 1993, and London's West End produced a twenty-fifth anniversary production in 1998. James R. Huffman of the *Journal of Popular Culture* points to one reason for the play's appeal: "Works like *Jesus Christ Superstar,* which asks the right questions' but allow each individual to provide his own answers, will be appropriated by nearly all the atheist, the agnostic, and the believer. Only the indifferent will remain unimpressed; only the devout and the aesthetically critical may be offended."

CRITICISM

Carole Hamilton

Hamilton is a Humanities teacher at Cary Academy, an innovative private school in Cary, North Carolina. In this essay she discusses the portrayal of Jesus as a rock star phenomenon in Jesus Christ Superstar.

In a recent interview Tim Rice admitted that from an early age he was fascinated by the character of Judas. Without Judas, he said, there would be no Christianity, since it was Judas who directly caused Christ's martyrdom and thus gave the world a tragic heroic figure around whom a whole religion would coalesce. Rice wanted to put Judas on the stage, by taking the sketchy, known "facts" about him and hypothesizing a set of logical reasons and a psychological make-up that could have led to his devastating betrayal. That Rice succeeded in his endeavor is without question. His Judas has a clear, if not forgivable, motive, and his tale of emotional remorse and suicide ring truer to life than the dispassionate reporting of the Bible, which merely states that Judas repented and hung himself. Rice's Judas realizes that his soul is forever tarnished with his act, that his name will forever be "dragged through the slime and the mud." *Jesus Christ Superstar* begins from Judas's point of view and ends with his observations on the Christ phenomena; however, to make Judas the character come to life, Rice also needed to create a viable Jesus as his protagonist. Rice eschewed the persona of Jesus familiar in Biblical stories and the art these stories have inspired over the ages, since that persona of pure goodness makes any opponent appear foolhardy and heinous for martyring the messiah. The Jesus of familiar artistic renderings is a ghostly, divine figure, whose perfection and goodness exude through his otherworldly bearing and patient suffering with eyes confidently cast heavenward. Rice needed a different kind of Christ, a flesh-and-blood saint, an imperfect martyr, whose activities would *not* be above reproach. Therefore, to suit the Judas of his imagination, Rice created a Jesus complete with doubts and frailties, a worldly saint far removed from the ideal figure of Renaissance paintings. The Jesus in *Jesus Christ Superstar* is a fallible human.

The story of Jesus's anger at the sellers in the temple market is a commonplace; Rice has him shriek, past the edge of self-control. Rice also

WHAT DO I READ NEXT?

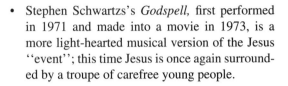

- Stephen Schwartzs's *Godspell,* first performed in 1971 and made into a movie in 1973, is a more light-hearted musical version of the Jesus ''event''; this time Jesus is once again surrounded by a troupe of carefree young people.

- The novel *Ben Hur: A Story of Christ* (1880) by Lewis Wallace, as well as the 1959 film version *Ben Hur,* starring Charleton Heston, portrays the time period from the angle of a young Jew who is sent to the galleys on a false charge, escapes, and converts to Christianity.

- *The Greatest Story Ever Told* (1949) by Fulton Oursler is a fictionalized biography of Jesus, told in a compelling style.

- *Quo Vadis* (1897) by Nobel prize winner Henry K. Sienkiewicz (translated by W. S. Kuniczak) describes the historical times, focusing on Roman culture at the time of the birth of Christianity.

- Webber and Rice collaborated one other work with a religious theme, *Joseph and the Amazing Colored Dream Coat* (1969), which they originally wrote for a children's production and revised after the success of *Jesus Christ Superstar.*

- The film version of *Tommy* (1975), directed by Ken Russell and written and performed by the rock group *The Who,* tells the story of Tommy, a deaf mute who becomes a superstar because of his skill at pinball.

---

portrays a healer who runs out of patience with the endless demands of the sick and poor, who claw at him and enclose him, chanting, ''Won't you touch, will you heal me Christ?'' The superstar Jesus also regrets having accomplished little in his life, and feels show-stopping doubt when faced with sacrificing his own life and can only rouse himself through spite and anger, ''Alright, I'll die! See how I die!'' Although fallible, Jesus is a charismatic leader, who draws to him an immense and loyal crowd. To this crowd and to his disciples, he is the messiah, the savior for whom the Jews waited for centuries, whose coming was prophesied in Isaiah and elsewhere in the Hebrew Bible. Being a charismatic savior who nevertheless grapples with human faults made Rice's Jesus a ''flesh-and-blood human being,'' as Clifford Edwards of *Catholic World* observed. Those closest to this human Jesus, such as Judas, see that he has faults and that he is not a blameless god. Mary Magdalene even momentarily wonders about falling in love with him, a speculation that seems impossible to have about the Jesus of, say, Michaelangelo's ''Pieta'' or Leonardo da Vinci's ''Last Supper.'' A flawed Jesus then, raises the possibility that he is yet another false messiah,

who will lead the Jews to destruction, not heaven. His very popularity increases the risks for the Jews if Jesus is not what he thinks he is, since, as Judas points out, the crowd is ''getting much to loud'' and ''they'll [the Romans will] crush us if we go too far.'' It is in this way that Rice's version of Jesus provides Judas with a clear and defensible motive for betrayal: to avert the wrath of the Romans, which the priests anticipate as ''our elimination because of one man.'' In this sense, Rice has fashioned the classic conflict, one that contains within it the seeds of two conflicting outcomes, a hopeful one salvation for the Jews and its opposite, their destruction.

The play opens with Judas's apprehensions, instantly shifting the focus away from cliched reverence for Christ's goodness to the more complex concern over success that might swell the unconventional rabbi's head or turn him into a ''superstar.'' Unlike Christ's other followers, who idolize a messiah as the road to their own salvation, Judas is more skeptical, and less innocent. Judas resents Mary Magdalene's use of costly ointments to soothe the tired prophet because it diverts money from the

> AS YEATS OBSERVED IN 'THE SECOND COMING,' THE RELIGIOUS CENTER DID NOT HOLD; RICE AND WEBBER SUGGEST THAT POP CULTURE AS CULTURE'S CORE CAN HOLD"

poor; possibly this symbol of messianic status (messiahs alone warranted anointment) offends him as well. Judas accuses Jesus of immodesty, chiding him that ''You've begun to matter more / than the things you say.'' Jesus is too popular, and his ''followers are blind, too much heaven on their minds'' to see the danger they are in. Caiaphas, too, objects to Christ's popularity, for it draws followers away from his sphere of control. Even so, Caiaphas begrudgingly has to admit that Jesus is a smooth operator, ''No riots, no army, no fighting, no slogans / One thing I'll say for him Jesus is cool.''

To be ''cool'' in 1960s parlance meant that one could win respect without making any overt effort. The word ''cool'' connoted being ''hip,'' or fashionable, smart, and impressive; a ''cool'' person could maintain the aura of outward calm, while generating excitement in others, like an Elvis Presley or other rock star. A successful rock star appeared disinterested while the crowd went wild. Rice's Jesus epitomizes coolness: he is a ''superstar'' with a winning style, who draws large audiences, yet his inner calm rarely ripples. As such, he inspires both jealousy and disdain from Judas, who goads himself into action by calling Jesus ''a jaded mandarin,'' a fallen idol. The Christ of *Jesus Christ Superstar* is not simply a humble saint or martyr, but a rock star, whose star status is buoyed up and defined by *and* dependent upon the crowd's enthusiasm. This novel re-fashioning of Jesus was the *coup de grace* that launched the album and later the stage production into the public eye. The concept of a rock star Jesus seemed to many a contradiction of terms, for how could a saint be hip or cool, how could a humble martyr be nonchalant or even suave? Religious leaders were affronted by the rock Jesus. It was an invasion of territory Jesus fit the mold of the classical symphony hero, but not the mold of the heathenish rock musician.

According to Reverend Billy Graham (who occasionally used the *Superstar* music in his revivals) to ignore Christ's divine status in this way ''border[ed] on blasphemy and sacrilege.'' Frank Garlock, a minister and music theory chair at Bob Jones University (a Christian school) rankled at comparisons between the *Superstar* opera and great classics of reverent music, saying ''This comparison is so ludicrous that it is absurd. The opera is certainly not talking about the Lord Jesus Christ in honor of whom Handel composed the *Messiah* and for whose glory Bach composed some of the greatest music known to man.'' Others found the comparison refreshing, as did Derek Jewel of the *London Sunday Times,* who found *Superstar* ''Every bit as valid as (and . . . often more moving than) Handel's *Messiah.''* The worlds of classic opera and rock music were as opposite as they could be: the one a marker of highbrow, conservative taste and the other a kind of ''in your face'' protest against conventionality. *Jesus Christ Superstar* offended by yoking divine content to a profane medium. It recast a revered saint as a dubious rock star, thereby presuming to raise sacrilegious rock music to the level of respectable classical music. In doing so, Rice and Webber recreated the shock and excitement that Jesus must have engendered. Jesus achieved ''star status'' in his short life; he was the Biblical equivalent of Prince, Elvis, or Madonna. Rice and Webber's use of rock music is a profound statement about the tremendous impact he must have had in Galilee. The composers of *Superstar* suggest that the Galileans responded to the Christ ''happening'' as the contemporary world would respond to the meteoric rise of a new rock superstar.

Rice explains, ''It is undeniable that Christ made more impact on people than anyone who has ever lived an impact of colossal proportions.'' They re-contextualize Christ's controversial appearance in terms that reflect modern sensibilities, thus revitalizing the worn cliche of the icon called Christ. At the same time that their Christ is brought squarely to earth, such that ''A common reaction to *Superstar* is 'It was the first time I ever thought of Jesus as a real person,' '' he is also a superhero. Although his divine status is stripped away, Christ is catapulted to superstardom. As Yeats observed in ''The Second Coming,'' the religious center did not hold; Rice and Webber suggest that pop culture as culture's core can hold. With religion shoved to the margins, the twentieth century still seeks sacred heroes. Herod speaks for the swarms of groupies who exist from show to show, waiting to bow down to the next pop hero. With Herod, the modern being beseeches each new pop star to rise beyond human frailty to star status, saying, in the words of the *Superstar* libretto, "I'm dying to be shown that you are not just any man." Perhaps, as Judas complains at the end of the play, Christ appeared in the wrong century after all; "Israel in 4 B.C. had no mass communication," no way to honor a star of Christ's magnitude. Judas chides Jesus, "Why did you choose such backward land and such a strange place?" Rice and Webber plunk him down into a happening place, and, ironically, their Christ and their Judas succeeded where their historical counterparts failed: they "reached a whole nation." However, *Jesus Christ Superstar* the rock opera reached those nations not by the path of faith but by the route of rock.

Source: Carole Hamilton, for *Drama for Students,* Gale, 2000.

Malcolm Boyd

Boyd assesses Rice and Weber's musical, basing it against traditional religious doctrine; the critic's conclusion is that the play trivializes the events of the Bible.

Can Jesus survive "*Jesus Christ Superstar*"? Sometimes it is "Love Story" in Jerusalem. Other times it is only "The Greening of the Box Office.". . . But is it a serious work of art? And how does it deal with the Passion of Christ?. . .

In a myriad of details gone wrong, the show bears little resemblance to the New Testament. Yet, what is most important, Jesus' mission got misplaced somewhere from drawing board to Star Chamber.

Is this the Jesus of a significant counter-culture? Not at all. For we see him reject the sick and distressed victims of society who come to him for help. We see a restless and tired "star" Jesus arrogantly send Judas away to do the work of betrayal. Fatigue and introspection could have legitimately been portrayed. But despair looms too centrally in Christ, conveying a sense of mission lost and purpose forgotten. (p. 1)

[There] is clearly the absence of a cross rooted in earth in "*Jesus Christ Superstar.*" Such lack of specificity leads to those quasi-religious fantasies which obliterate detailed truth. I am not one of those purists who decry the show's bypassing of the resurrection. After watching Jesus hang on a Daliesque golden triangle (an avant-garde symbol of the cross?) for a glamorous simulation of the crucifixion, I offer thanks to the pantheon of gods

Carl Anderson as Judas sings a song in the stage production

that we were indeed spared a resurrection. But in its failure to come to terms with the sacrifice of a Christ-figure, or the Passion of Christ, "*Jesus Christ Superstar*" also fails to become a seriously motivated and constructed rock opera.

It is several things: a Rockette operetta, a Barnumian put-on, a religioso-cum-showbiz pastiche, and a musicalized "Sweet Sweetback's Baadasssss Judas Song." The Jews seem to be guilty, once again, of causing Jesus' death. . . . We are thrust against energy without exuberance, torture without tragedy, in this collage-in-motion. . . . (pp. 1, 7).

> MARY MAGDALENE IS A COOL, MOD AND SINCERE CHICK WHO DIGS JESUS BUT SENSES THAT HE IS VERY DIFFERENT FROM OTHER MEN WHOM SHE HAS KNOWN."

The sharp intrusion of sex—again and again and again—into the show can only focus attention on Jesus' own sexuality. Is he Gay? Bisexual? Straight? Asexual?. . .

The sexuality of Jesus will undoubtedly comprise the Exhibit A controversy about the show. He and Mary Magdalene fondle and kiss each other; I felt an implicit acceptance of the fact that they have enjoyed intercourse. The exposure of this side of Jesus' humanity drew cheers from the audience, perhaps in reaction against the celibate Jesus of churchianity who has been used traditionally as a major argument against sex outside of (and before) wedlock as well as against homosexuality.

Jesus as a human being (as well as the Son of God) with sexual feelings may be far overdue in our puritanical, sexually hypocritical society. Yet I feel that his sexuality was not handled sensitively or with taste in this gaudily inhuman parody. . . .

The show gives us a confused, tired but plucky Jesus who is going to the cross even if it kills him. Mary Magdalene is a cool, mod and sincere chick who digs Jesus but senses that he is very different from other men whom she has known. She sings a gentle ditty about the love for him that she feels. However, it is clearly not sufficiently deep a love to bind her to him through his torture and death. . . .

Judas' feelings about Jesus provide the real basis for the utterly fictional story line that links the musical numbers. Judas feels that he is trapped in a terrible role, one scripted by God and directed by Jesus. . . . Judas' acceptance of a predestination to damnation smacks unappetizingly of Calvinism with bitters. So Judas plays a role instead of being himself.

It is an absurd irony that a simplistic success . . . has come out of the ambiguity and violent paradox of Jesus' Passion, presented here with all dimension flattened. Even the controversy of Jesus, intellectu-

ally ignored in this show, is made marketable in a plastic-ware production. It doesn't have a soul. (p. 7)

Source: Malcolm Boyd, ''*Jesus Christ Superstar*—Two Views: A Priest Says, 'It Doesn't Have a Soul','' in the *New York Times,* October 24, 1971, pp. 1, 7.

Clive Barnes

In this review of the original Broadway show, Barnes appraises the musical merits of Jesus Christ Superstar, *stating that the show had ''the best score for an English musical in years.''*

Nothing could convince me that any show that has sold two-and-one-half million copies of its album before the opening night is anything like all bad. But I must also confess to experiencing some disappointment [with] ''*Jesus Christ Superstar.*''. . .

It all rather resembled one's first sight of the Empire State Building. Not at all uninteresting, but somewhat unsurprising and of minimal artistic value. . . .

Mr. Rice's intention was clearly to place Christ's betrayal and death into a vernacular more immediate perhaps to our times. His record sales would presumably indicate his success in this aim, but he does not have a very happy ear for the English language. There is a certain air of dogged doggerel about his phrases that too often sounds as limp as a deflated priest.

It is surely unfortunate, even bathetic, to have Christ at his moment of death remark solemnly: ''God forgive them! They don't know what they are doing.'' The sentiments are unassailable, but the language is unforgivably pedestrian. . . .

The music itself is extraordinarily eclectic. It runs so many gamuts it almost becomes a musical cartel. . . . [Mr. Lloyd Webber] has emerged with some engaging numbers.

The title song, ''Superstar,'' has a bounce and exaltation to it, an almost revivalist fervor that deserves its popularity. I also much admire the other hit of the show, ''I Don't Know How to Love Him.'' This also shows Mr. Rice at his best as a lyricist, although it is perhaps surprising to find this torch ballad sung by Mary Magdalene to Jesus Christ— even a Jesus Christ Superstar. There is a certain vulgarity here typical of an age that takes a peculiar delight in painting mustaches on the ''Mona Lisa'' and demonstrating that every great man was a regular guy at heart. . . .

[This] is not an important rock score in the manner of ''Tommy'' by The Who. It is, unhappily, neither innovative nor original. . . .

For me, the real disappointment came not in the music—which is better than run-of-the-mill Broadway and the best score for an English musical in years—but in the conception. There is a coyness in its contemporaneity, a sneaky pleasure in the boldness of its anachronisms, a special, undefined air of smugness in its daring. Christ is updated, but hardly, I felt, renewed.

Source: Clive Barnes, ''Christ's Passion Transported to the Stage in Guise of Serious Pop'' in the *New York Times,* October 13, 1971, p. 40.

Clifford Edwards

Edwards offers a mixed appraisal of Jesus Christ Superstar, *complaining that the play is willing to ''raise hard questions while refusing to supply simple answers''; the critic also assesses the play as a new gospel for the counter culture of the late–1960s and early–1970s.*

[In *Superstar* the] Christ of faith gives way to the Jesus of history. Rice and Webber have acknowledged modern scholarship's discovery that the New Testament picture of Jesus is colored throughout with propagandistic interpretation more intent on convincing the reader that Jesus is the divine God-man than in giving an historically accurate picture of the flesh-and-blood man of Galilee. (p. 218)

Rice and Webber attempt to dramatize the life-style of the historical Jesus in the midst of the life-styles and forces at work around him.

Is there any value in bypassing ecclesiastical propaganda to seek out this life-style? To an emerging culture suspicious of the establishment's propaganda, it allows a new and honest attempt to stand where the first hearers did, feel for oneself the impact of the Galilean's style, and answer for oneself, ''Who do you say that I am?'' . . . *Superstar* attempts to dramatize Jesus' life-style in the midst of competing life-styles, and then leaves one with questions rather than with answers. . . . (pp. 218–19)

Although the ''opera'' has no single, obvious climax, musically and dramatically the climax seems to be Judas' disintegration and death at the beginning of record four. . . . Judas and his life-style are of special significance.

How is one to characterize this Judas? He can perhaps best be described as the ''Uncle Tom'' of the Jesus movement, the personification of a ''failure of nerve'' within the emerging life-style, a failure of nerve which turns back in fear and betrays the emerging culture to the existing power structure. . . .

"THE COMPLEXITY OF PERSONAL MOTIVES AND THE TANGLED CONSEQUENCES OF OUR ACTIONS IN REAL HISTORY BECOME EVIDENT IN JUDAS."

[The] very strength of *Superstar* is its willingness to raise hard questions while refusing to supply simple answers. The complexity of personal motives and the tangled consequences of our actions in real history become evident in Judas. No only are we uncertain of Judas' real motives and culpability, but we become aware that Judas is uncertain of his own motives. He protests too much that he is not betraying Jesus for his ''own reward.'' He sulks because Jesus does not give him his due as ''right hand man.'' At the Last Supper he seeks to blame what he is about to do on the requirements of Jesus' own ''ambition.'' Before he dies, Judas realizes that the consequences of his betrayal have been hastened along by forces beyond his own control. . . . [There] is the recognition that complex forces in society magnify the consequences of our actions, that demonic powers can be set in motion far beyond our intentions and cannot be called back. . . .

The important place given Judas in *Superstar* contributes a problematic or ambiguous quality to the ''opera,'' for who knows how far one should trust the observations of a Judas. It is this ambiguity which leads the audience toward the realization that it must arrive at its own interpretation of the figure of the Historic Jesus.

Mary Magdalene suggests the life-style described in Timothy Leary's advice: ''Turn on and drop out.'' Whether the instrument of her turning on is acid, pot, yoga, or zazen, the end result is a detached, euphoric quality. . . . Jesus accepts the Magdalene's ministrations and defends her against Judas' criticism, but her oceanic feeling that ''everything's alright'' is transcended by the passion of his own search for "truth" or "God," and by the dramatic forces already unleashed. However, as with Judas, the portrayal of the Magdalene has its complexities. In a second solo, "I Don't Know How to Love Him," she sings of her consternation that Jesus should so disturb her "cool." . . . Apparently the oceanic feeling can be shattered by an encounter with Jesus. Lest one be tempted to make too much of the Magdalene's relationship to Jesus, it should be noted that Webber and Rice have Judas wail this same love song to Jesus. For both the Magdalene and Judas, and we suppose for their spiritual descendants today, an encounter with Superstar is pictured as engendering love, fear, and mystery. . . . (p. 219)

In stripping away "the myth from the man," Webber and Rice find no profound philosopher, enlightened reformer, or heroic leader. The great strength of their portrayal of Jesus is their recognition that apart from the myth we have only the whisper of a voice and the outskirts of the life-style of a man. The triumph of *Superstar* lies as much in what Webber and Rice have not done as in what they have done. They have refused to create a fictional character to fill the void. . . .

Where does the portrayal of Jesus focus? On Jesus as a flesh-and-blood human being. Even the outskirts of Jesus' life-style reveal his real humanity. Having his face cooled "feels nice, so nice," he joins the crowd in a happy "Hosanna, Heysanna," screams at the temple merchants, and admits "I'm sad and tired" and "scared." . . . A common reaction to *Superstar* is: "It was the first time I ever thought of Jesus as a real person." The phantom-like portrayals of an otherworldly Christ on decades of funeral-home calendars and Sunday School walls apparently makes the focus on Jesus as a real person a remarkable revelation to this generation. . . .

The words he speaks are drawn largely from the Gospel pronouncements, with very few original contributions by Tim Rice. He advocates living in the present, claims that he could give "plans and forecasts" unfathomable to those around him, and admits that earlier he was "inspired" but now is "sad and tired." He defends the Magdalene, cleanses the temple, and sings "Hosanna" with the crowd one moment while screaming at it to "Heal yourselves" at another. At critical moments Rice supplies Jesus with the lines "To conquer death you only have to die," and "I look for truth and find that I get damned." These along with a Gethsemane prayer, are the closest Rice comes to providing

Jesus with a summary of his life and mission. In Gethsemane Jesus pleads: "I'd wanna know my God, . . . I'd wanna see my God," and this possibility encourages him to accept the death his God seems to require. It is suggested that his death might make all he has said and done "matter more," but its full meaning is not revealed. (p. 220)

After Judas' death, the events involving Jesus seem almost anticlimactic as he maintains a near-silence through the trials and speaks essentially the traditional words from the cross. As if to fill this vacuum, the voice of the dead Judas returns to raise the questions we might ask of Jesus. . . . (pp. 220–21)

Superstar concludes with two minutes of tranquil music ("John 19:41") suggesting the garden containing Jesus' tomb. The audience is left to decide for itself whether this is the quiet following an honest man's death or the peace of a new Eden prepared by a greater Adam for his descendants.

Superstar is a conservative attempt to express the counterculture's interest in Jesus, and its very conservatism has prepared a solid foundation for more creative and imaginative works in the future. It has avoided cliches, sentimentality, and mere fictionalizing, presenting Jesus' real humanity forcefully while allowing the audience great latitude for personal interpretation. (p. 221)

Source: Clifford Edwards, "*Jesus Christ Superstar:* Electric Age Messiah" in *Catholic World,* Vol. CCXIII, no. 1277, August, 1971, pp. 217–21.

SOURCES

Duncan, David Douglas. "*Jesus Christ Superstar*" in *Life,* Vol. 70, no. 20, May 28, 1971, pp. 20B-26.

"Jesus Christ Superstar Anniversary Page" on http://www.geocities.com/Broadway/2596/index.html, March 28, 1999.

Jewison, Norman, and Melvyn Bragg. Screenplay of *Jesus Christ Superstar,* based on the music and lyrics of Andrew Lloyd Webber and Tim Rice, Universal Pictures, April 3, 1972.

FURTHER READING

Anthem PD. "Jesus Christ Superstar" on http://www.jesuschristsuperstar.com/1998, March 18, 1999.

An Internet site promoting the 1998-1999 UK tour of the rock opera. It also includes background with audio clips of Rice and Webber describing the play's genesis.

Daemon Records. ''*Jesus Christ Superstar:* A Resurrection'' on monsterbit.com/daemon/jcs.html, March 18, 1999.

An Internet site promoting the Daemon Records recording of the songs of *Jesus Christ Superstar* and the live Seattle production of 1996.

''*Jesus Christ Superstar*'' on http://www.reallyuseful.com/Superstar/1999, March 18, 1999.

A promotional page for a theatre troupe production of *Jesus Christ Superstar* complete with play reviews and a summary of the twenty-five-year history of the rock opera.

McKnight, Gerald. *Andrew Lloyd Webber,* St. Martin's Press, 1985.

A biography of Webber's rise to fame as a composer of hit musicals.

Nassour, Ellis, and Richard Broderick. *Rock Opera: The Creation of* Jesus Christ Superstar *from Record Album to Broadway Show and Motion Picture,* Hawthorn, 1973.

A step-by-step description of the writing and publishing process of the play and film.

Walsh, Michael. *Andrew Lloyd Webber: His Life and Works: A Critical Biography,* Harry N. Abrams, 1989.

An updated biography that describes the composer's recent works as well as his early life and career.

Krapp's Last Tape

SAMUEL BECKETT

1958

In Bob Dylan's "When I Paint My Masterpiece" (1971), the speaker expresses his weariness from ages of artistic trials as well as his excitement at the prospect of creating what will be his greatest work of art:

> Oh, the hours I've spent inside the Coliseum,/ Dodging lions and wastin' time / Oh, those mighty kings of the jungle, I could hardly stand to see em. / Yes it sure has been a long, hard climb . . . / Someday, everything is gonna be smooth like a rhapsody / When I paint my masterpiece. / Someday, everything is gonna be different / When I paint my masterpiece.

Like the speaker of Dylan's song, the protagonist of *Krapp's Last Tape* is also certain that he possesses the talent to change the world with his art but the focus of Beckett's play is how Krapp's certainty is worn down to a terrible moment of doubt and despair. Krapp ultimately realizes that *nothing* will ever be different and that his masterpiece has had no effect whatsoever in the world. The fact that Krapp wasted his life in pursuit of such a grandiose "vision" (as he calls it) marks the play as one of Beckett's most ironic and chilling works.

Like all of Beckett's work, *Krapp's Last Tape* may strike the first-time viewer as odd and unsettling: there is a minimal set, no dramatic lighting cues, nothing that a theatergoer would call a traditional "plot," and only one character a character whose only conversations are with a tape recording of himself that he made thirty years ago. However, many of the play's original reviewers noted the

force that Beckett was able to contain in what initially seems like the framework (rather than the final draft) of a play. For example, writing in the *New Republic,* Robert Brustein praised Beckett's portrait of ''impotent desire'' and his ability to capture the futility of Krapp's dreams of himself as an artist; to him, Krapp is a balance of ''pathos and absurdity'' that reveals the ''vacuity'' of our human desire to achieve greatness. While other critics dismissed the play as too artificially constructed and self-conscious, many saw it as indicative of Beckett's skill as a dramatist. In recent years, a number of biographers of Beckett (by authors such as Deirdre Bair (1978), James Knowlson (1996) and Anthony Cronin (1997)) have praised *Krapp's Last Tape* as a play which explores the isolated nature of human existence while, simultaneously, avoiding (according to Deirdre Bair) ''the searing, wrenching pain and exhaustion'' of Beckett's previous work. The play remains one of Beckett's major plays (along with *Waiting for Godot* and *Endgame*) and was directed by Beckett himself on several occasions.

Samuel Beckett

AUTHOR BIOGRAPHY

Samuel Barclay Beckett was born at Cooldrinagh (his family's home) in Foxrock, a town in County Dublin, Ireland; although there is some confusion over the true date of his birth, Beckett always held that he was born on Good Friday, 13 April 1906. A talented athlete, Beckett's body developed as steadily as his mind: after completing secondary school, Beckett entered Trinity College, Dublin, where he excelled in French and Italian. In 1928, he moved to Paris to study and teach at the Ecole Normal Superieure this move to Paris was a key event in Beckett's life, for he lived the rest of it almost exclusively in France.

While in Paris, Beckett met and befriended James Joyce, the Irish poet, short-story writer, and novelist, who was then composing *Finnegans Wake,* a difficult novel that Beckett helped its author translate into French. While working with Joyce, Beckett composed ''Dante ... Bruno. Vico ... Joyce'' (1929), his first foray into criticism. His own work soon followed: ''Whoroscope'' (1930), a poem about the nature of time, *Proust* (1931) an examina-

tion of the great French novelist, and *Dream of Fair to Middling Women* (1932, published 1993), his first novel, parts of which were revised into a collection of short stories titled *More Pricks than Kicks* and published, to almost no audience, in 1934.

Trouble with publishers and sales did not dissuade Beckett, however, from further projects. In 1938 his novel *Murphy* was published to mixed reviews (it had been previously rejected by forty-two publishers). Once World War II began, Beckett found little time to write and worked with a cell of the French Resistance; he narrowly escaped capture by the Gestapo on more than one occasion. He composed much of the novel *Watt* (published 1953) during this time.

After the war, Beckett began a period of fruitful composition, writing in French and then translating his work into English. Although his first play, *Eleutheria,* was composed in 1947 but not published until after Beckett's death, his second play, *Waiting for Godot,* (published 1952, first produced 1953) proved to be Beckett's most discussed, analyzed, and talked-about work; the play concerning a pair of tramps who wait in an unspecified place for a man named Godot who may or may not exist and does not ever arrive caused great controversy when brought to the United States in 1956. His famous trilogy of novels, *Molloy, Malone Dies,* and *The Unnamable,* were also composed during this period; all three were published in English by 1958.

For the rest of his life, Beckett continued to write in French and experiment with both prose and dramatic forms. His next major play, *Endgame* (published 1957), concerns a blind autocrat, trapped in a room with his parents who reside in dustbins; *Krapp's Last Tape* depicts an old man listening to a thirty-year-old recording of himself; *Happy Days* (1961) features a woman who delivers a long monologue while simultaneously being buried up to her neck in a mound of earth. Other experimental work followed, such as the television play *Eh, Joe?* (1966), the thirty-five-seconds-long *Breath* (1970) and the novel *Mercier and Camier* (1970). In 1969, Beckett was awarded the Nobel Prize for Literature; the following year marked the publication of his *Collected Works* in sixteen volumes. During the last phase of his career, Beckett continued to intrigue (and occasionally frustrate) audiences and readers with the prose works *Worstward Ho* (1983), *Stirrings Still* (1991), and *Nohow On* (1993) and the plays *Footfalls* (1976), *Rockaby* (1981), and *Ohio Impromptu* (1981). Beckett died at home in France on December 22, 1989. He has come to be regarded as one of the giants of twentieth-century literature and, as the title of Anthony Cronin's 1996 book suggests, "The Last Modernist."

PLOT SUMMARY

The action of *Krapp's Last Tape* occurs on "a late evening in the future" in the title character's den. Specifically, the play takes place on Krapp's sixty-ninth birthday. Every year since he was twenty-four, Krapp a would-be writer who has failed as such has recorded his impressions of the previous year and then catalogued the resulting tape's number and contents in a ledger, which he keeps locked in his desk. The play depicts Krapp listening to a tape from thirty years ago (recorded when he was thirty-nine) and then recording this year's tape.

When the play begins, Krapp is sitting at his desk, consulting his watch to confirm that the exact

time of his birth is approaching this is when he will record this year's impressions. There is a great amount of silent stage business, as Krapp fumbles with the keys to his desk drawers, removes a reel of tape, opens another drawer, removes a banana and eats it. Krapp leaves the stage (as he will do several times) to drink; the audience hears a "loud pop of cork" to confirm that Krapp is consuming some sort of alcoholic beverage.

Krapp returns to his desk and consults his ledger, looking for the number of the tape that contains the recording made on his thirty-ninth birthday. He reviews his notes on the tape (as found in the ledger), loads the spools on his recorder and begins listening. The audience then learns about the thirty-nine-year-old Krapp: he was (as he is now) alone and he felt himself to be at "the crest of the wave" in terms of his talent as a writer. The voice on the tape also comments on *another* tape that the audience does not hear: this one made when Krapp was twenty-nine. At this young age, Krapp was living with a girl named Bianca a relationship that the middle-aged Krapp on the tape calls a "hopeless business." The thirty-nine-year-old Krapp mocks his younger self's resolutions to drink less and participate in a "less engrossing sexual life." The audience further learns that Krapp's father died when Krapp was twenty-nine. At this point, Krapp switches off the tape, leaves the stage, and "pops" three more corks from their bottles.

Krapp returns to his desk, singing and coughing. He turns on the tape recorder again and listens to his voice tell of the death of his mother. While Krapp's mother faced her death, Krapp sat outside her house and toyed with a dog and black rubber ball. The tape reports that his year "of profound gloom" continued, until the night Krapp "suddenly" saw "the whole thing," and had some kind of artistic "vision" at the end of a jetty. Because of this "vision," Krapp denied himself the love of an unnamed woman, to whom he said goodbye after a (presumably sexual) encounter in a boat. The older, listening Krapp becomes disgusted with the voice on the tape and switches it off. He leaves the stage for the last time to steel himself with more alcohol.

Krapp returns and is now ready to make his last tape. He begins his new recording with, "Just been listening to that stupid bastard I took myself for thirty years ago, hard to believe I was ever as bad as that." He reveals that his bowel troubles (first mentioned on the previous tape) still plague him and that he has only sold seventeen copies of his "opus magnum." His life has been reduced to that of a shut-in the only human contact he experiences is that involving Fanny, an "old ghost of a whore." Despite his desire to remain aloof from his old memories, however, Krapp begins speaking of the previously-mentioned scene in the boat. He then removes the reel from the recorder, "throws it away," and replays the tape of him describing the woman in the boat, whose love he denied in order to produce what he thought would be his masterpiece. The play ends with Krapp listening to the end of that tape, staring into silence; the tape's last words, "Perhaps my best years are gone. . . . But I wouldn't want them back. Not with the fire in me now," hang in the air as Krapp sits motionless, staring into space.

CHARACTERS

Krapp

The title character of *Krapp's Last Tape* is a disheveled and sullen man who had dreams of being a writer and creating his "opus magnum," but who instead has spent his life as a solitary and bitter failure. His only companion is, ironically, his own voice, with which he interacts throughout the play through the use of the tape recorder. His isolation is of his own choosing, however, for he is misanthropic to the point of despising even himself, as his comments to the voice on the tape reveal. As his name suggests, everything about this man, his youth, his old age, his mind, his heart, his ideas of his own talents and impending greatness amount to little more than "crap." While the scatological joke of the title may strike some readers as juvenile or in poor taste, the name is indeed quite fitting, for it unmercifully points out exactly what Krapp's ambitions have brought him. The name also alludes to the fact that Krapp complains about his bowel troubles through the entire play and eats bananas in an attempt to prevent frequent movements. Thus, a man with such a name is incapable of one of the most simple and basic human bodily functions; such an ironic situation reveals the depth of what some readers regard as Beckett's pessimism and which all readers can recognize as the irony that pervades the play as a whole.

MEDIA ADAPTATIONS

- *Krapp's Last Tape* was adapted as a film and directed by Samuel Beckett. It is available from VideoFlicks at VideoFlicks.com.

THEMES

Alienation and Loneliness

As *Krapp's Last Tape* proceeds, the viewer understands that, during the course of his life, Krapp has systematically distanced himself from the companionship and love offered by other people. At twenty-nine, Krapp lived with a woman, Bianca, whose love he later called a "hopeless business" (despite the fact that she possessed very "warm eyes.") At thirty-nine, Krapp celebrated his birthday alone in a pub, "separating the grain" of what he felt were his great thoughts from the "husks" of his less important ones. That same year, his mother died and he told his new love that "it was hopeless and no good going on." Since then, Krapp has been completely alone, except for the occasional visit from Fanny, a "bony old ghost of a whore."

Thus, Krapp's isolation is self-inflicted; while this certainly marks him as pompous (since he felt that he could not bear to have his future career as a writer interfered with by women and love), it also evokes a degree of pity for the deluded old man. Krapp's only companion is his tape recorder; the cold and mechanical nature of a *recorded* voice (as opposed to a live one) reflects his essential isolation from human companionship and emotion. To further heighten the viewer's sense of Krapp's loneliness, Beckett has him listen eagerly to the tape (in a special "listening pose") that reveals Krapp's desperation to have anyone (even himself) engage him in conversation. (Of course, Krapp *acts* as if he has no need for the rest of humanity, but his hunching over the tape recorder belie his affected haughtiness.) What ultimately gives the play its power is

TOPICS FOR FURTHER STUDY

- The American author Henry James's "The Beast in the Jungle" (1903) is a short story that examines the life of Marcher, a man very similar to Krapp. Compare and contrast the two protagonists' expectations of their futures and what these futures actually bring them.

- In what ways is Krapp an "everyman" figure? Despite the experimental nature of the play, in what ways does it offer its audience a man who is like all men and who holds many of mankind's assumptions about the self, experience and time?

- Many now-famous writers have had their diaries, journals, and letters published. Read a selection of these by a writer such as the Scottish biographer James Boswell (1740-1795) or the English poet John Keats (1795-1821) and com-

pare their understanding and examinations of their personalities with Krapp's.

- *Waiting for Godot* (1956) is Beckett's most widely-read play. Examine the ways that the play explores issues similar to ones found in *Krapp's Last Tape,* such as alienation, isolation, and the search for meaning in a disordered and chaotic world.

- Compose an essay in which you imagine what Krapp does *after* the action of the play concludes. Despite the fact that the audience knows this is his "last" tape, will he live his remaining days any differently? Or will he sink into even deeper despair? Use what Beckett tells the viewer about Krapp in the play to support your ideas.

---

that Krapp eventually sees how alien and alone he is and what a terrible mistake he made in forsaking human companionship.

Artists and Society

While some artists have become celebrities and spokespeople for their times (such as Ralph Waldo Emerson, Arthur Miller, and Norman Mailer), others (such as J. D. Salinger and Thomas Pynchon) shun publicity and prefer to let their work speak for them. Regardless of an individual writer's feelings about publicity, however, all writers share a common goal: to have their work read by as many people as possible. Seen in this light, writers are social figures whose work brings their thoughts and ideas to the general public.

Krapp, however, is a writer whose work has reached no one and whose artistic "vision" is a total failure. The "magnum opus" that he devoted his life to creating has sold only seventeen copies and Beckett gives absolutely no indication that Krapp is a Melville-like figure whose work is too

advanced or revolutionary to be appreciated in his own time. Instead, Beckett accentuates Krapp's failure as an artist through the play's setting (the austerity of which reflects Krapp's poverty), Krapp's costume (which resembles that of a clown), and his frequent "popping" of corks when he wanders offstage. Krapp's muse comes in a bottle, and the results of his "inspiration" are negligible. Despite the fact that Krapp remarks that eleven copies of his book are being sold to "circulating libraries beyond the seas" which will help him in "Getting known," the viewer understands that Beckett holds up Krapp as a man convinced of his artistic greatness but who is ignored by the very readers he needs to proliferate his ideas.

Memory and Reminiscence

Like Tennessee Williams's *The Glass Menagerie* (1944) and Arthur Miller's *Death of a Salesman* (1949), *Krapp's Last Tape* is a play that dramatizes the ways in which memories return to a character who finds these glimpses into his or her past more real and meaningful than the events of his

Edward Petheridge as Beckett's titular character in a 1999 production at the Royal Shakespeare Company Theatre

or her present life. Krapp's present life (at the age of sixty-nine) is marked by its austerity and isolation, which he attempts to momentarily dispel through the playing of a tape he recorded thirty years ago. Krapp's tape recorder is, metaphorically, a mechanical brain; as Krapp toys with its controls, the viewer sees Beckett's imitation of the ways in which we all attempt to jump from moment to moment in the scenes which constitute our memories:

> What I suddenly saw was this, that the belief I had been going on all my life, namely (*Krapp switches off impatiently, winds tape forward, switches on again*)

great granite rocks the foam flying up in the light of the lighthouse and the wind-gauge spinning like a propeller, clear to me at last that the dark I have always struggled to keep under is in reality my most (*Krapp curses, switches off, winds tape forward, switches on again*) unshatterable association until my dissolution of storm and night with the light of the understanding and the fire (*Krapp curses louder, switches of, winds tape forward, switches on again*) my face in her breasts and my hand on her.

In the above passage, Krapp is attempting to stomp down the memory of his "vision" and instead dwell on the memory of his last real relationship with another person thus, all of the "winds tape forwards" are analogous to the ways in which all people manipulate the "tape recorders" inside their minds in order to select the "segments" they want to replay. When Krapp reaches the scene of himself and the unnamed woman in the boat, the audience learns that this memory is an important one, since as soon as it is over, Krapp "*switches off, winds tape back,*" and listens to it two more times during the course of the play. As the favorite memories of a man about to die become sweeter by their heightened value as remnants of a life that is about to end, so does the part of Krapp's tape describing his last meaningful encounter with another person become the gem of Krapp's memory. It is through this "mechanical memory" and his comparing the Krapp described on the thirty-year-old tape with his sixty-nine year-old self that Krapp ultimately learns what a terrible mistake he has made in saying "farewell to love."

STYLE

Setting

Krapp's Last Tape is set in Krapp's den a room that reflects, to a large degree, Krapp himself. It is bare, save for a small table; this lack of ornament emphasizes Krapp's emotional sterility and loneliness. As he is without any human interaction, his room is without anything that suggests comfort or humanity.

More telling than the barren stage are the lighting directions given by Beckett. The table and its immediate area are bathed in "strong white light"; the rest of the stage is in darkness. The question arises here of why Beckett would want any part of the stage to be dark i.e., why not simply have Krapp's room (even if it is to remain barren) take up the entire stage? The answer has to do with how Beckett uses lighting to mirror Krapp's attempt to fend off the figurative "darkness" that surrounds him. The voice of the thirty-nine-year-old Krapp reports (in the tape to which the older Krapp listens):

> The new light above my table is a great improvement. With all this darkness round me I feel less alone. (*Pause.*) In a way. (*Pause.*) I love to get up and move about in it, then back here to . . . (*hesitates*) . . . me. (*Pause.*) Krapp.

Light and dark symbolism runs throughout the play, with light representing knowledge, life and love and darkness representing ignorance, death and isolation. Thus, Krapp attempts to remain in the "light" of what he sees as his own superiority and intellect but the darkness is always around him, almost mocking his desire to combat it. The thirty-nine-year-old Krapp reports that there was a "memorable equinox" during the past year; since the equinox is the date on which there is an equal amount of day and night, that year was one where Krapp's "light" and "dark" forces were balanced: his mother died, but he was still alive; he had a vision of his future career as an artist yet failed to sell any books; he had a lover but left her to pursue his career. *Now,* however, Krapp is thirty years older and is about to succumb to the "darkness" that surrounds him. This is accentuated in a number of ways (least of them being the play's title), such as his singing, "Now the day is over, / Night is drawing nigh-igh." By having Krapp's table where he will record his last attempt to "enlighten" himself about the meaning of his life surrounded by darkness, Beckett subtly hints at his hero's inevitable failure to combat the different forms of "darkness" that will eventually overtake him.

Costume

In the opening pages of the play, the reader learns that Krapp is dressed in "Rusty black narrow trousers too short for him," a "Rusty black sleeveless waistcoat," a "Grimy white shirt open at neck, no collar" and a "Surprising pair of dirty white boots, size ten at least, very narrow and pointed." This outfit, combined with Krapp's "White face," "Purple nose" and "Disordered gray hair" makes him appear very much like a clown. This image of Krapp accords with what the audience eventually understands to be Krapp's earnest but foolish desire to make his mark as a writer and intellectual. Some clowns provoke laughter from their smiles and buffoonery, but others work by attempting to earnestly perform some serious task with absurd results. Krapp resembles this second type of clown, as he is thoroughly convinced of his own importance and seriousness but is always undercut by his absurd appearance. The fact that Krapp eats bananas and almost trips on one of their peels adds to the audience's perception of him as a man who, despite his attempts to prove otherwise, remains clownish.

HISTORICAL CONTEXT

The 1950s is often thought of as an era where artistic expression was as "square" and as indicative of the status-quo, as the era itself is sometimes portrayed

COMPARE
&
CONTRAST

- **1950:** North Korean forces break through the 38th parallel and capture Seoul (the capital of South Korea). General Douglas MacArthur is appointed commander of UN forces in Korea. The Korean War will continue until 1953.

  Today: North Korea remains a Communist nation, with Kim Jong Il (son of previous leader Kim Il Sung) as its President.

- **1953:** Joseph Stalin dies; Nikita Khruschchev is appointed First Secretary of the General Committee of the Communist Party. Khruschchev became Chairman of Council of U.S.S.R. Ministers in 1958 and eventually took part in his famous showdown against President Kennedy (the Cuban Missile Crisis) in 1962.

  Today: Since the collapse of the Soviet Union into a number of disparate nations, the Cold War (between the Soviets and Americans) has ended, with the United States as the assumed victor in this famous war of words and wills.

- **1958:** *Krapp's Last Tape* premieres and is viewed by some as a triumph and others as a failure, in part because of the experimental nature of its form.

  Today: Although the theaters of Broadway are almost wholly occupied with commercial fare, experimental theater is thriving in other places: plays such as Aviva Jane Carlin's *Jodie's Body* (1999), in which a nude model discourses on politics, and Dare Clubb's *Oedipus* (1999), a four-hour retelling of the myth largely from the point of view of Merope (his adopted mother), challenge contemporary audiences' ideas of theater as *Krapp's Last Tape* did over forty years ago.

on television and in contemporary films. The 1950s were, in fact, an era where major innovations in every form of art were noticed by viewers, readers, and listeners alike. With the death of George Bernard Shaw (1856-1950), the type of ''well-made play'' perfected by him (one which relied on conventional forms and structures) began to be replaced in some artists' minds with more experimental forms the most famous example of which remains Beckett's own *Waiting for Godot* (1952), which many viewers found exciting, different, and unlike any play they had ever before seen.

The forms frequently employed in other genres of literature experienced similar reexaminations and revisions. In 1950, Ezra Pound's ''Seventy Cantos'' were published, which are as unlike traditional verse as *Godot* is as unlike Shaw's *Pygmalion*. In 1953, Archibald MacLeish published his *Collected Poems,* the experimental nature of which struck many readers; MacLeish was awarded the Pulitzer Prize for the volume. Vladimir Nabokov's controversial novel *Lolita* was published in 1955 and was certainly one of the most daring novels ever written;

its plot concerns a middle-aged professor's love for a twelve-year-old ''nymphet.'' Two years later, Albert Camus (1913-1960), one of the leading philosophical novelists of the era, was awarded the Nobel Prize; although he sometimes refuted the label, he is often viewed as a proponent of existentialism, a radical philosophy concerning man's inability to find truth and meaning in himself or his world. That same year marked the premiere of *Endgame,* Beckett's second theatrical triumph; like Camus, Beckett was often described as an existentialist but expressed his disdain for any labeling of himself or his art. Other experimental works of literature from this time include Jack Kerouac's novel *On the Road* (1957), published at the dawn of the ''beatnik'' movement, and Harold Pinter's *The Birthday Party* (1958), which was lauded as one of the playwright's first major successes. Gunter Grass's *The Tin Drum* (1959), a novel told from the point-of-view of a three-year-old child who decides to stop growing, was praised as revolutionary in its examination of Germany during the Hitler era. An interesting close to the era can be found in Jean-Paul Sartre's *Cri-*

tique de la dialectique (1960), in which the controversial philosopher, playwright, and novelist expressed his political philosophies that were shaped, in part, by the rise of Soviet communism in the previous decade.

Other forms of art took similar wayward routes. The visual arts were enriched by the continued work of Pablo Picasso (1881-1973), whose painting ''Massacre in Korea'' reflected the turbulence caused when North Korean forces broke through the 38th parallel and recaptured Seoul, sparking the Korean War (1950-1953). Surrealism, which attempted to revamp old forms into more dreamlike ones, blossomed: Alberto Giacometti (1933-1970) unveiled his sculpture ''Seven Figures and a Head'' in 1950, Marc Chagall (1889-1985) unveiled his painting ''The Red Roofs'' in 1954, and Salvador Dali (1904-1989) revealed ''The Lord's Supper'' in 1955. Many experimental films were also made during this time: works such as *Rashomon* (1950), *La Strada* (1954), and *The Seventh Seal* (1956) forever altered conventional cinema. Architecture, too, saw one of its most daring moments with the completion (in 1958) of Frank Lloyd Wright's Guggenheim Museum in New York City. Music also took new turns with bebop and ''cool jazz'' gaining momentum. While there were many fine works employing conventional structures and forms (such as 1953's *From Here to Eternity* and 1959's *The Miracle Worker*), the era was one where many artists Beckett among them grew dissatisfied with tradition and sought to break away from it in their own different ways.

CRITICAL OVERVIEW

Like many of Beckett's plays, *Krapp's Last Tape* was both praised and disparaged when it was first shown to British and American audiences. Writing in the *New Republic,* Robert Brustein stated that the ''haunting and harrowing'' play was Beckett's best and that it offered its viewers ''the perfect realization of Beckett's idea of human isolation.'' To Brustein, the play's greatness lay in Beckett's ability to ''sound those chords of compassion which have always vibrated quietly in his other work''; his enthusiasm for the play can be seen in his lauding the ''extraordinary economy of the writing'' and the ''absolute flawlessness of the form.'' Tom Driver, reviewing the play for the *Christian Century,* of-

fered similar praise, bluntly describing it as ''the best theatre now visible in New York.''

However, not all critics responded so favorably. Kenneth Tynan, the former manager of England's National Theater and one of the most powerful drama critics of the 1950s wrote a devastating review of the play. Written not as a traditional review, but as a parody of Beckett's style, Tynan mocked what he saw as Beckett's refusal to satisfy an audience's fundamental need for action and events in a play. The review's two ''characters,'' Slamm and Seck, make comments like, ''Nothing is always about to happen,'' and state that the play ''would have had the same effect if half the words were other words.'' Tynan's review ends with Slamm asking, ''Could you do as much?'' and Seck replying, ''Not as much. But as little.''

While Tynan was alone in his abject dismissal of the play, other critics found it another example of an experiment that failed to fulfill the basic requirements for drama. Writing in the *Spectator,* Alan Brien called both *Krapp's Last Tape* and *Endgame* ''exercises in peevish despair.'' His explanation of what he disliked about Beckett's work is representative of the way many viewers felt that Beckett's *ideas,* while interesting, were expressed in a decidedly awkward and unpalatable way: ''As the floodwaters rise he burns his bridges, scuttles his boats, punctures his water wings and tries to forget how to swim.'' (In other words, Beckett knows what constitutes ''good theatre'' but abandons these elements in an attempt to be different and ''artistic.'') Brien expands on this point by stating, ''Art is illusion and Beckett seeks to destroy even that by creating deliberately inartistic works of art.'' Clearly, Brien (like many others during Beckett's career) had a different definition of ''art'' than the playwright.

Interestingly, the critical befuddlement that greeted the play was almost predicted by Alan Schnieder, the play's New York director:

> First they say *Godot* was terrible, then when I do *Endgame* [which premiered in New York in 1958] they say, Well, *Godot* was not so bad but *Endgame* was awful. So I direct *Krapp,* and the critics say *Godot* was really good terrific but what happened to *Endgame*? And *Krapp* was really lousy. As each new play comes along, the previous ones get better while the current one is awful. Critics can't seem to comment on what's before them without dragging in the other ones and rationalizing their previous reactions.

Throughout his career, Beckett was frequently ''ahead of his audience,'' and *Krapp's Last Tape* is one of a number of works (with *Waiting fir Godot* as the most famous example) that have come to gain the critical respect it deserves only after its premiere.

Many contemporary critics prove this assertion with their open enthusiasm for the play. In his 1971 book, *All I Can Manage, More Than I Could,* Alec Reid describes what gives *Krapp's Last Tape* its power, concluding that the play is more than the enactment of a script:

> It is not the words, the movements, the sights several-ly which produce the impact; it is the new experience, evoked through their combination on stage. This process involving eye, ear, intellect, emotion, all at once, we shall call total theatre.

In her 1978 biography *Samuel Beckett,* Deirdre Bair argues that *Krapp's Last Tape* "marks a new step in Beckett's writing" in which he is able to dramatize "an overwhelming sense of emotion." James Knowlson, in his 1996 biography *Damned to Fame,* calls the play "unusual in Beckett's theatrical opus for its tender lyricism and for a poignancy that borders on sentimentality." Finally, in his 1997 study, *Beckett: The Last Modernist,* Anthony Cronin contends that many of *Krapp's* original viewers turned away out of a "refusal to face the bleakness of Beckett's vision." Thus, Alan Schneider was correct in his idea of how Beckett's work takes time to be appreciated by critics.

CRITICISM

Daniel Moran

Daniel Moran is an educator specializing in literature and drama. In this essay, he examines the ways in which Beckett's play explores a man's turning away from humanity to pursue his dreams of artistic success.

In *A Portrait of the Artist as a Young Man* (1916), an autobiographical novel by Beckett's fellow Irishman James Joyce, the reader follows the artistic awakenings of Stephen Dedalus, who, as the novel progresses, becomes increasingly certain of what he sees as his destiny to become The Great Artist. Stephen is in constant rebellion against what he sees as the "nets" that attempt to ensnare artistic expression: Catholicism, nationalism, and creative conformity. Stephen's determination to "forge in the smithy" of his soul "the uncreated conscience" of his race, however, is constantly undercut by the very things he wishes to flee: despite his disdain for the church, for example, his first great moment of inspiration owes as much to the image of the Virgin

Mary as it does to that of the peasant girl whose beauty strikes his aesthetic sensibilities. Later he admits to a friend that while he does not believe in God, he does not have the courage to *dis*believe in Him, either. Eventually, he decides that he must employ "silence, exile and cunning" if he is to escape the nets of tradition and that he must fly above the snares of Ireland. The novel ends as he leaves his homeland for Paris, where he is convinced he will be able to answer his calling.

Like Stephen, the protagonist of Samuel Beckett's *Krapp's Last Tape* was, at one time, certain that he had the makings of The Great Artist. Unlike Joyce, however, who ends his *Portrait* with the hero looking forward to his new career, Beckett begins his play with the would-be artist in his last days and informs the audience, in a number of ways, that Krapp's previous visions of grandeur were grounded more in his pompous ideas of self-importance than in any discernible vocation. As Stephen saw the need to flee from Ireland, Krapp felt a similar need to flee from his own humanity and reject the "light" of life and love. While Stephen's success as an artist is questionable (we later learn, in Joyce's *Ulysses* [1922], that he has returned to Ireland without any crowns of laurel), Krapp's failure is unmistakable: we watch him, on his sixty-ninth birthday, mechanically remember (through the playing of a tape) his former self and ultimately come to a numbing realization: he has wasted his life in pursuit of a false identity of The Great Artist that he forged in the smithy of his soul thirty years ago. As Stephen could not truly flee his home (and all its religious and political associations), Krapp learns in his last days that he was a fool to think he could have said, as he so proudly did at the age of thirty-nine, "farewell to love." His name, rather than his recorded aspirations, reveals his ultimate achievement.

While viewing the play, the audience actually meets *three* different (yet, in certain ways, similar) Krapps. The play begins with the sixty-nine-year-old Krapp on his birthday; when he listens to the tape he made of himself on his thirty-ninth birthday, we meet the "second" Krapp, who, in turn, comments on his recent replaying of the tape he made of himself at twenty-nine (the "third" Krapp). Thus, time in the play moves backwards and forwards at once, and it is through his moving back in time by listening to his past self (commenting on *another* past self) while simultaneously moving into his increasingly desolate future that Krapp eventually comes to his moment of crisis. By comparing the

WHAT DO I READ NEXT?

- *Waiting for Godot,* Beckett's 1952 play, is his most famous and widely-studied work. Its minimalist plot concerns two tramps who wait in an unnamed place for an appointment with Godot a mysterious figure who never appears but who always promises to arrive the following day.

- Like *Krapp's Last Tape,* Beckett's 1957 play *Endgame* explores the effects of isolation and the human tendency to impose order on a completely chaotic world.

- Beckett's trilogy of novels, *Molly, Malone Dies,* and *The Unnamable* (1959) are considered his greatest achievement in prose. The novels explore many of the themes found in *Krapp's Last Tape,* such as loneliness, isolation, and the creation of identity.

- James Joyce's novel *A Portrait of the Artist as a Young Man* (1916) follows the exploits and artistic awakening of Stephen Dedalus, Joyce's autobiographical counterpart. Like Krapp, Stephen is often convinced that he is destined to rise above what he sees as the ignorance of his contemporaries.

- Vladimir Nabokov's 1965 novel *Despair* follows the sinister exploits of Hermann a Krapp-like character who views himself as superior to others and who (again like Krapp) is used by his creator to comment on the issue of artistic creation.

- Perhaps the most famous American play of the twentieth century is Arthur Miller's 1949 drama *Death of a Salesman,* which treats the theme of memory and reminiscence in a way very similar to that found in *Krapp's Last Tape.*

---

three Krapps, the viewer (much like Krapp himself) eventually finds that the tapes reveal the life of a man who (by his own choice) became increasingly convinced of his own superiority over the natural desires of humanity. Unlike Joyce, who portrays the growth of his artist-hero's mind, Beckett invites the viewer to learn how his artist-hero has regressed into an absurd, clownish ghost.

To better understand how the play operates on a viewer, a brief "biography of Krapp" may clarify the reasons the older Krapps comment as they do on their younger counterparts. In his twenties, Krapp lived on Kedar Street with Bianca. He made "resolutions" to drink less and have a "less engrossing sexual life." His father died, his bowel troubles began and he sensed "shadows of the opus . . . magnum": the masterpiece he imagined he would someday write. At thirty-nine, his mother died (after a "long viduity," i.e., widowhood) which Krapp learned from watching her window from a bench outside her house. Krapp felt no sorrow ("There I sat . . . wishing she were gone") and played with a dog while his mother lay dying. The rest of that year was one of "profound gloom and indigence" until a night in March, when Krapp "suddenly saw the whole thing" and had his great "vision" of his calling and of his destiny as The Great Artist. To facilitate what he saw as his impending greatness, Krapp broke off with his current love after their final sexual encounter in a boat. At sixty-nine, Krapp has seen no artistic success: his "opus magnum" has sold only seventeen copies (netting him "one pound six and something"). He is a myopic alcoholic who stumbles about the stage yet remains convinced that his decision to forsake love in the name of his "artistry" was the correct one that is, until the end of the play. As the play's title indicates, there will be no seventieth birthday for Krapp.

Once the events in Krapp's life are understood, the viewer can then begin asking questions about why Beckett uses this particular man's life to explore the issues of disillusionment and isolation. The first question that needs to be answered is why Beckett has Krapp make these tapes in the first place the answer has to do with Beckett's showing the audience Krapp's inflated sense of his own importance (which will vanish in the play's final moments). Through some arithmetic, the viewer can deduce that since there are five spools of tape in each box and nine boxes of tapes in Krapp's desk, there are forty-five tapes in all. Krapp is sixty-nine, so he began making his annual tapes at the age of twenty-four (69-45=24). Krapp makes a new tape on each of his birthdays at the exact time of his birth, demonstrating his idea that his life is worth recording. But since many people keep diaries and journals, Krapp's tapes may not strike the viewer as particularly pompous until one begins to examine the way he guards and orders them. The tapes are all neatly arranged with their contents briefly described in a ledger that Krapp keeps, along with the tapes themselves, *locked* in his desk. Consider the idea that anyone would want (or even care) about Krapp's tapes or that they need to be catalogued for the benefit of future generations the notion is absurd. Consider also the young James Boswell, author of *The Life of Samuel Johnson* (1791), who began keeping a journal at the age of twenty-two: he records in his *London Journal* his desire to have his diaries "carefully laid up among the archives" of his family and (in an even more Krappian moment) his conviction that "there is a blossom about me of something more distinguished than the generality of mankind." Like Boswell, the youthful Krapp was convinced he would "blossom" into a figure whose life would be worth recording. Krapp uses tapes because he loves to hear the sound of his own voice (as Beckett's stage directions about the thirty-nine year-old voice suggest) and because the use of a machine (rather than pen and paper) suggests the mechanical nature of the elder Krapp. (Also note the irony of Krapp as a writer who does not actually *write* anything.) His recorder is an electric brain that he must use in lieu of actual memories, since he has become so distant from his own past and the emotional life he once possessed. Although he consults an envelope on which are scribbled his notes for this year's recording, his present ruminations are hollow and trivial.

The previously mentioned troubles with Krapp's bowels link the three Krapps together. At twenty-nine, Krapp was plagued by "unattainable laxation," at thirty-nine Krapp described himself as "sound as a bell, apart from my old weakness" and at his present sixty-nine, Krapp complains of the "sour cud and the iron stool." Krapp's lifelong constipation, however, is partly his own doing, since he

> READERS OF BECKETT MAY FIND SUCH A TOUCHING MOMENT ODD IN HIS *OEUVRE*, BUT EVEN A SAMUEL BECKETT WAS WARY OF BECOMING A KRAPP"

constantly eats bananas an old home remedy for "stopping up" the bowels. The thirty-nine-year-old Krapp reports, "Have just eaten three bananas and only with difficulty refrained from a fourth. Fatal things for a man with my condition"; the older Krapp eats two bananas before he utters a single word. Besides their association with silent-movie clowns slipping on their peels (which Krapp almost does), Krapp's eating of so many bananas is symbolic of his desire to become *emotionally* constipated and "stop up" the natural flow and release of human longings and desires. Krapp sees his intellectual "visions" as much more important than the love (or even company) of other people, and has acted accordingly, rarely leaving his room except for a single visit to "vespers" where he fell asleep. To Krapp, The Great Artist cannot be sidetracked by love and must (like Shakespeare's Lady Macbeth), "stop up / The access and passage" of emotion to his heart.

"Stopping up," however, is not the same as "wiping out," and despite Krapp's efforts to flee his own humanity, his emotions eventually do emerge, painfully, like his "iron stool." When listening to his younger self, the thirty-nine-year-old Krapp mocks his previous romance with a girl named Bianca: "Well out of that, Jesus, yes! Hopeless business." Similarly, the sixty-nine-year-old Krapp mocks the thirty-nine-year-old's farewell to the girl in the boat: "Just been listening to that stupid bastard I took myself for thirty years ago, hard to think I was ever as bad as that. Thank God that's all done with anyway." These two Krapps' jeers at their former selves are "emotional bananas" means by which the Krapp looking back on his past attempts to "stop up" any regrets he may feel. But emotions, like bodily waste, will eventually come out, and Beckett suggests as much through the two Krapps' mentioning of the eyes of the women they forsook. After mocking his previous love for

Max Wall as Krapp in a 1975 production staged at London's Greenwich Theatre

Bianca, the thirty-nine-year-old Krapp remarks (after a significant pause), ''Nothing much about her, apart from a tribute to her eyes. Very warm. I saw them again. (Pause.) Incomparable! (Pause.) Ah well.'' (The regret in Krapp's ''Ah well'' (repeated at four different times in the play) gives the lie to his presumed haughtiness.) Similarly, the same Krapp, after telling his love ''it was hopeless and no good'' going on, ''asked her to look'' at him. Krapp may fool himself, but he cannot fool the viewer, who realizes that Beckett is offering us a glimpse of a man whose emotional constipation is about to end; the ''iron stool'' of Krapp's epiphany will prove painful indeed.

Before advancing to this moment, however, one should also consider how Beckett uses light and dark symbolism to suggest Krapp's growing isolation and abandoning of his humanity. For example, as a youth, living with Bianca (whose name means ''white'' in Italian) on Kedar Street (''Kedar'' is an anagram of ''darke''), Krapp was able to fend off the ''darkness'' of isolation inherent in the world (''Kedar Street'') with his emotional attachment to another person. While his mother was dying, Krapp sat outside gazing at a ''dark young beauty'' who was ''all white and starch'' and pushing a ''big black hooded perambulator''; the chiaroscuro im-

ages here and mingling of death and birth in the ''black perambulator,'' suggests the death of Krapp's worries over his mother and the possible birth of himself as an artist. The ''little white dog'' to whom Krapp tossed a ''black, hard, solid rubber ball'' suggests a similar combination of light (life) and darkness (death); also noteworthy is the fact that this year was one with a ''memorable equinox'' (the day on which there is an equal amount of day and night) at this point, Krapp was able to ''balance'' the light and dark forces in his life.

However, the most significant and complex pairing of light and darkness occurs when Krapp's thirty-nine-year-old voice tells of his moment of supreme inspiration that he had after his mother's death:

Spiritually a year of profound gloom and indigence until that memorable night in March, at the end of the jetty, in the howling wind, never to be forgotten, when suddenly I saw the whole thing. The vision, at last. This I fancy is what I have chiefly to record this evening, against the day when my work will be done and perhaps no place left in my memory, warm or cold, for the miracle that . . . (*hesitates*) . . . for the fire that set it alight. What I suddenly saw then was this, that the belief I had been going on all my life, namely (*Krapp switches off impatiently, winds tape forward, switches on again*) great granite rocks the foam flying up in the light of the lighthouse and the wind-gauge spinning like a propeller, clear to me at last that the dark I have always struggled to keep under is in reality my most (*Krapp curses, switches off, winds tape forward, switches on again*) unshatterable association until my dissolution of storm and night with the light of the understanding and the fire

As previously mentioned, the world of *Krapp's Last Tape* is one of darkness: Krapp's vision occurred at night and is likened to a "fire" that sets his mind "alight," much as the "light of the lighthouse" offers a beacon of guidance to ships at sea. The essence of Krapp's vision here can be discerned by completing his broken off sentence: he became convinced that the "dark" he "always struggled to keep under" is, in reality, his "most " *precious ally.* Ironically, Krapp believed that his full artistic triumph would only be reached by *embracing,* rather than avoiding, the darkness of the world which explains why he then said "farewell to love" and began pursuing his dreams of being an artist. Only by confronting the essential isolation of his own existence would Krapp produce his "opus magnum." However, by embracing the darkness of the world, Krapp has produced nothing other than a small circle of intellectual light that surrounds his table; his embracing of darkness is like his constantly eating bananas: a means by which he assumes an unnatural pose in regard to the natural "light" of the world. He cannot even bear to listen to his former self describe the "vision," since he has begun to realize that his past "enlightenment" was questionable and specious. Krapp now records his tapes at night and uses them to try to fend off the encroaching darkness of total isolation and death, but as his song suggests, "Now the day is over, / Night is drawing nigh-igh." Dressed in "dirty white boots," a "grimy white shirt," black trousers and a black waistcoat, Krapp's equinox is long past.

Thus, the action of the play *begins* with its hero about to succumb to the darkness of all that he once thought would bring him success. At sixty-nine, Krapp's mind possesses no "light" of the intellect: he does not remember the definitions of words he once used ("equinox," "viduity") and instead delights in the sounds of simple words like "spool." Like the "vidua-bird," Krapp, too, is alone, living through a long, sickly and alcoholic "viduity" in which he has been widowed from the rest of humanity. However, his final moments on stage are ones where he *does* become "enlightened" to what he has done with his time on earth. While recording this year's tape, Krapp's mind takes him back to a

time when he was able to bathe in the light of humanity: he tells himself that, tonight, he will probably:

Lie propped up in the dark and wander. Be again in the dingle on a Christmas Eve, gathering holly, the red-berried. (*Pause.*) Be again on Croghan on a Sunday morning, in the haze, with the bitch, stop and listen to the bells. (*Pause.*) And so on. (*Pause.*) Be again, be again. (*Pause.*) All that old misery. (*Pause.*) Once wasn't enough for you. (*Pause.*) Lie down across her.

Krapp is at his moment of crisis: despite his attempts to mock his former selves and justify his decision to "embrace the darkness," he wishes he was alive again on a *morning* (instead of his present dark evening) and part of the human race that he once sought to avoid. Because of this realization, Krapp "suddenly bends over machine, switches off, wrenches off tape, throws it away, puts on the other, winds it forward to the passage he wants" and switches it on so he can hear again his description of his old lover's eyes. As Krapp listens, he makes no comments because his sarcasm is no match for the power of his epiphany:

I lay down across her with my face in her breasts and my hand on her. We lay there without moving. But, under us all moved, and moved us, gently, up and down, and from side to side.

Pause. Krapp's lips move. No sound.

Past midnight. Never knew such silence. The earth might be uninhabited.

Pause.

Here I end this reel. Box (*Pause. *) three, spool (*Pause.*) five. (*Pause.*) Perhaps my best years are gone. When there was a chance of happiness. But I wouldn't want them back. Not with the fire in me now. No, I wouldn't want them back.

Krapp sits motionless staring before him. The tape runs on in silence.

This, and not the "vision" he had at thirty-nine, is Krapp's true moment of enlightenment. The words about the earth being uninhabited apply to the present Krapp as well and the "fire" in him has cooled to an ember. His entire *life* has been an unwitting "opus magnum," the theme of which is that the intellect may be the superior part of man's nature, but to forsake other aspects of humanity in order to satisfy it can only result in painful isolation. Readers of Beckett may find such a touching moment odd in his *oeuvre,* but even a Samuel Beckett was wary of becoming a Krapp.

Source: Daniel Moran, for *Drama for Students,* Gale, 2000.

Arthur K. Oberg

Oberg examines the nature of self in Beckett's play, delineating the similarities between Krapp's Last Tape *and the works of Marcel Proust, a French author who greatly influenced the playwright.*

Krapp's Last Tape opens on one man alone with his own memories and desires, punctuating a monotonous present by recall of a moment-lit past. As a writer and as a man lying "propped up in the dark," Beckett makes Krapp's associations with Proust even more pointedly prominent. The situation of Krapp stocktaking and listening to old stocktakings is dependent upon the catalysts of Time, Habit, and Memory, the trinity considered by Beckett in his 1931 study of Proust. Considerations that Krapp has made and will continue to make of his life—intellectual, physical, spiritual—are rendered rememberable, if not memorable, with the aid of dictionary and tapes. Krapp now is not Krapp past nor Krapp future. Like Proust, Beckett explores the relation of the self, possessed of Memory and by Habit, within Time. What both writers explore is the mental mechanism by which that which is lost is found.

Krapp, by being able to summon and shut off mechanically his memories of things past, raises for an audience the question of whether *Krapp's Last Tape* is a parody of Proust. Certainly parody is involved. It is evident both in the general reduction of Krapp's memory process to mechanization and in the playing of particular segments of the tapes where life is seen as parodic. Also, by means of counterpointing and of juxtaposition with scenes that blatantly involve parody ("Bony old ghost of a whore"), moments that for Krapp were once memorable or incomparable are gently drawn into parody.

But if Krapp's spools of tape are meant to serve as parodies of Proust's vases, what has been neglected by critics is that Proust himself, as Beckett has pointed out, saw the parodic nature of certain memory processes, as well as of desire. Memory forms, transforms, and deforms. Joining Eliot in considering the pathos of men "mixing/Memory and desire," Beckett creates in *Krapp's Last Tape* a play that is not so much a Proustian exercise parodying Proust as an attempt to dramatize (and, hence, support) what is central in the Proustian vision.

In Beckett's study of Proust he follows through Proust's sharp distinction between the workings of voluntary and involuntary memory, associating the latter with those miraculous moments of break-

through that emerge under the breakdown of space and time. What Beckett stressed was the mystic, religious character of those past moments that involuntary memory happens upon, moments of "revelation" and "annunciation." Akin to Joycean epiphanies, it is these moments of Proustian revelation that provide the structure of *Krapp's Last Tape*. As Krapp plays back past tapes, he passes from high moment to high moment. With Krapp in control of the switch, these moments resemble a cinematic fade-in, fade-out technique. The girl on the platform, the black ball, the jetty and punt scenes blend and form an extended showing forth of charged experience from Krapp's past. But the mechanization of the mechanism of memory—by making involuntary memory voluntary—commits Krapp to the destruction of moments that refuse reduction to human control:

> But involuntary memory is an unruly magician and will not be importuned. It chooses its own time and place for the performance of its miracle. (*Proust* pp. 20–21) So that no amount of voluntary manipulation can reconstitute in its integrity an impression that the will has—so to speak—buckled into incoherence. But if, *by accident,* and given favourable circumstances (a relaxation of the subject's habit of thought and a reduction of the radius of his memory, a generally diminished tension of consciousness following upon a phase of extreme discouragement), if by some miracle of analogy the central impression of a past sensation recurs as an immediate stimulus which can be instinctively identified by the subject with the model of duplication (*whose integral purity has been retained because it has been forgotten*), then the total past sensation, not its echo nor its copy, but the sensation itself, annihilating every spacial and temporal restriction, comes in a rush to engulf the subject in all the beauty of its infallible proportion. (p. 54).

Beckett's apocalyptic language used to describe the Proustian miracle "annihilating," "rush," "engulf"—condemns Krapp in his attempts to mechanize, and thus destroy the very nature of, intense memories of lost things. Krapp's mistaken and pathetic taped past, instead of parodying Proust, relates to Proust's awareness of the dialectic of memory, in which voluntary and involuntary memory are seen as separate processes of the same mind. Beckett does not condemn voluntary memory, but rather indicates that voluntary and involuntary memory belong to different orders of experience. When, as in *Krapp's Last Tape,* voluntary memory is used, not for simple mnemonic recall, but to savor moments that refuse automatic summoning, Beckett parodies the misuse of the memory processes. Krapp's moments of visionary fire cannot be mechanically recalled without seeming perverse; for only through loss can that which was blinding, or beautiful, be found.

Beckett's understanding of the Proustian voluntary and involuntary memory allows him in *Krapp's Last Tape* to present a dramatic study of the changing and changeless self: addicted to Habit, imprisoned by Time, frightened and attracted to the possibility of release through involuntary Memory. If Krapp's spools mistakenly seek by an act of will to render the presence of the Proustian moment, Beckett is concerned with more than the parody of involuntary memory. Above all, he is concerned with the pathos of an old man, torn by memory and desire. And, in the presentation of this old man, Beckett again looks back to Proust, joining Proust in an exploration of the nature of epiphany-like moments and of desire.

Constipated in sexual and artistic performance, creative activities which Beckett significantly correlates, Krapp can find a way out of a confined, repetitive past only by reference to those miraculous moments which his tapes conclude by ossifying instead of preserving. Putting aside for a moment the wrongness of Krapp's attempt to hold what cannot be held, we may consider the nature of those moments that Krapp alternately would repeat and "keep . . . under." Associated with what only involuntary memory ought to find, the meshed moments on the jetty and in the punt provide the point toward which all of the earlier flashes of memory (the girl on the platform, the black ball) proceed and from which the rest of the play gently, and then cuttingly, falls. The confusion of the jetty-punt scenes expresses Krapp's ambivalence toward such experience; he would both replay it and switch it off just short of its consummation.

The pain that Krapp feels in a remembrance of things past cannot be separated from the pleasure it yields. Like Pozzo in *Waiting for Godot,* Krapp finds unpleasantness and pain in the act of remembering happy days. The pain is due as much to elegiac nostalgia as it is to the intensity of experiences which both annihilate and create. Momentarily, that "suffering of being" which Beckett observed in Proust overwhelms Krapp:

> Lie propped up in the dark—and wander. *Be* again in the dingle on a Christmas Eve, gathering holly, the red-berried. (*Pause.*) Be again on Croghan on a Sunday morning, in the haze, with the bitch, stop and listen to the bells. (*Pause.*) And so on. (*Pause.*) *Be* again, *be* again. (Pause.) All that old misery. (Speech italics mine)

> KRAPP FINDS UNPLEASANTNESS AND PAIN IN THE ACT OF REMEMBERING HAPPY DAYS."

The meshed jetty-punt scene establishes itself alongside other Beckett epiphany-like moments of clarity in his plays which were made possible under the regenerative workings of nature (water) and human nature (love)—the Lake Como reminiscence of Nell, Maddy's rehearsal of a honeymoon resort, Ada's recollection of a moment with Henry by the sea, Winnie's recall of "the sunshade you gave me . . . that day . . . (*pause*) . . . that day . . . the lake . . . the reeds." Winnie's moment is remarkably close to Krapp's playing of the punt scene, except that Winnie's is sanctified by drifting or floating up out of the blue. Although the result of involuntary memory, Winnie's moment shares with Krapp's moment a breakdown of syntax that signals a breakthrough of distinctions of subject and object, lover and beloved. Beckett records in both instances that rare Proustian moment of possession in which opposites are reconciled; moving and motionless, brilliant and blinding, the Proustian miracle is rendered in images of motion (rhythm) and light (fire). Harmony and enlightenment thus are suggested as epitomizing such moments.

If Beckett considered in his monograph on Proust the impossibility of complete possession, his plays at times approach "those rare miracles of coincidence, when the calendar of facts runs parallel to the calendar of feelings." Where *Krapp's Last Tape* departs from Beckett's other dramatic works is in seeking to compress, into an edited whole, those moments or fragments which formed only an infinitesimally small part of Krapp's lifetime. As a result, there is the impression of grotesque distortion of the best (or worst) moments of Krapp's life. Although dependent upon expectation, life finally is not lived from intense moment to intense moment. And the disparity between the rhythm of life lived and life remembered becomes apparent in Krapp's desperate effort to isolate those moments of "congruence" and "realisation" which punctuated eternities of loneness and loneliness and tedium.

That charged moments are transient or absolute, and cannot be kept or rendered communicable in words, is presented in *Krapp's Last Tape* in conjunction with an exploration of the nature of desire, a concern particularly central to an old man considering his younger years. In the jetty-punt scenes the Proustian miracle is specifically conceived in terms of the possibility of gratified desire leading to fulfillment (or extinction) of self. What began as a parody of the workings of involuntary memory expands into a philosophical-psychological statement that shows Beckett to be in a tradition more modern and ancient than that indicated by Proust or Bergson.

Beckett's involvement in *Krapp's Last Tape* in probing the nature of desire is very much at the human center of the play. As Beckett pursues the chances for a man's escape from sameness by means of transcendent moments, here closely connected with the momentary possession of desired object or person, he dramatizes both a particular Krapp and a generalized Everyman. What, Beckett asks, is the nature of desire? Through Krapp's playing back of old tapes, we discover not only that the Proustian moment cannot and will not be mechanized, but that the sheer nature of desire is parodic. Not only do memorable moments slip, words lose their meanings, and occasions shift context. More seriously, gaps are exposed in the fabric of desire that lend the kind of pathos to Krapp as desiring animal that Shakespeare drew from considering the human condition in his plays:

> This is the monstruosity in love, lady, that the will is infinite, and the execution confined; that the desire is boundless, and the act a slave to limit (*Troilus and Cressida* III.ii.85–88).

Krapp's derisive laughter joins laughter on tapes that reveal Krapp, younger, when he was equally caught up in the disparities of desire and execution, ideal and real object.

Krapp, by being born, is committed to the mockeries of desire. He is like the *Act Without Word I* figure for whom the carafe is always beyond reach, except that Krapp's frustration is related less to the impossibility of attainment than to the nature of desire and to that metaphysical *post coitum triste* attendant upon awareness of the incongruities of ideal and real object. By having renounced the girl in the punt, Krapp is not spared her later transformation into "bony old ghost of a whore." Significantly, Krapp's very renunciation had suggested his fear of ever having to reconcile her with the idea or the ideal of the girl in his mind.

Krapp, then, dramatizes a situation which is inescapable as long as man desires. But his situation is complicated and intensified by his desiring in the face of depleted powers and by his attempting to keep what is not allowed. Love song and swan song, *Krapp's Last Tape* is Krapp's farewell to love and to life. But in waiting for the day to be over, which his song has soured and secularized, Krapp edits his life against the coming of night and compounds parody with pathos. Part voyeur, self-therapist, and old man, Krapp attends upon a world of diminished capacities and lost connections. Erections now are difficult for him, and keys and envelopes have been reduced to the function of locking up bananas and serving as space for jottings. There is no appointment for Krapp to keep except to wait for the night of which he so brokenly sings.

Frustrated and mocked by desire, Krapp's birthday becomes a celebration of his approaching death. Associating sex, sickness, and death, Beckett merges a remembered child nurse with Krapp's mother's sick nurse, relates the punt scene to both sexual intercourse and death, and has Krapp pun on "crutch" as crutch and crotch. And the philological affinity of "viduity" and "vidua-bird" is used to point up an association of sex with death. Pathetic and parodic, life would not be equal to desire even if sickness and death could be eliminated.

If Beckett's consideration in *Krapp's Last Tape* of the nature of desire is both Proustian and more general than Proust, so does his dramatization of Krapp as desiring, old man remove him from indebtedness to specific antecedents. A large part of the power behind *Krapp's Last Tape* derives from its giving the impression of what it is like to grow old and yet to keep on desiring, to seek to break time's tedium by resort to an occasionally illuminated past. Krapp's situation joins him to Yeats's aging man poems, to Eliot's "Gerontion," and to Frost's protagonist in "An Old Man's Winter Night."

Beginning as a Proustian work, *Krapp's Last Tape* evolves into a dramatization of an aging, desire-ridden man, into a play that leaves the job of positing antecedents or placing it in a contemporary context (the significance of pause, the undercutting of vision come to mind) farther and farther behind. Like any major literary piece, *Krapp's Last Tape* both has origins and is originless. Krapp's "P.M.s" come out of the oldest and most recent questionings of the nature of desire and of those intense moments which man is neither fated nor allowed to keep. *Post meridiem. Post-mortem. Krapp's Last Tape* expresses the parody and pathos of desire in an aging man for whom a decrease in erections is not accompanied by a decrease in desire.

Source: Arthur K. Oberg, ''*Krapp's Last Tape* and the Proustian Vision,'' in *Modern Drama,* Vol. 9, no. 3, December, 1996, pp. 333–38

Henry Hewes

Hewes reviews a production of Krapp's Last Tape, *finding the play to contain a ''passion for life and a robust poetry'' that the critic found lacking in Beckett's other plays, notably* Endgame *and* Waiting for Godot.

As a man who found ''*Waiting for Godot*'' exasperating and ''*Endgame*'' stifling, it is a joy to report that Samuel Beckett's newest effort lets loose a passion for life and a robust poetry that were deplorably manacled in the aforementioned plays. Titled ''*Krapp's Last Tape,*'' this short character study begins unpromisingly as we watch a filthy old man rummaging about his disordered, dimly lit room. Too much time is taken for us to see the suggestion that man is an animal torn between primitive satisfactions (represented by a drawer in which Krapp keeps a supply of bananas) and intellectual ones (represented by a second drawer in which Krapp keeps his last spool of unrecorded tape). But from the moment Krapp puts away a banana he has started to eat and decides to listen to a particular tape in his vast collection of reminiscences recorded over a forty-year period (here we willingly allow Mr. Beckett the poetic license of pretending that tape recorders were in use many years before 1946, when they actually were put on the market), the play acquires energy and dramatic tension.

It is not a man revisiting his real past as Emily did in ''Our Town,'' but a man revisiting his past as he recalled it in shorter retrospect. Moreover this man is not the depressed, half-alive specimen that squirmed on the microscope slide in Mr. Beckett's other plays. He is a man of extraordinary acuity, sensitivity, and vigor. And finally Krapp has an honesty that permits him to share his human weaknesses with the audience. At one point in the tape he is playing he hears his younger self launch into some romantic overstatement of life's meaning which makes him furious with himself, and he rushes to push the button that will allow him to skip that painful portion. On another occasion, as he is listening with more ease to the old tape, he belatedly hears himself use the word *viduity*. In disbelief he replays the sentence again, angrily stops the ma-

chine, rushes to get a dictionary and looks the word up. In this sequence, Mr. Beckett has not only been eminently theatrical, but he has also demonstrated for us the wonder and greatness of language, which most of us must use too pedestrianly.

A little later he skips too far along the tape and comes in at the end of what appears to be a juicy description of a love affair. As the tape moves on into a calmer philosophical postmortem, Krapp jumps with comic, understandable fervor to the rewind button. The description, when we do hear it, is richly poetic, and puts us all to shame for the relative poverty of our own experiences. We feel this poverty both in our depth of feeling and in our unwillingness to treat it with the importance and beauty it has to offer.

At the end of the play Krapp is left with his arms about the tape recorder, an old man clutching the heat of life with an appreciation that has grown proportionately with his diminished power to live it.

The performers are excellent. This applies to both the faithful tape recorder and to Donald Davis, who give us the old Krapp in character, and the young Krapp in a pre-recorded voice that sounds a little like Orson Welles. Director Alan Schneider and designer William Ritman have used the stage imaginatively. Behind the lighted foreground they have created a darkness into which Krapp can take mysterious excursions whose purpose is suggested only by the sound of a cork being pulled out of a bottle. The end result is a rich half-hour in which Mr. Beckett happily emerges as closer to Dylan Thomas than to the intellectual stunt man he has previously appeared.

Source: Henry Hewes, ''It's Not All Bananas'' in the *Saturday Review,* Vol. 43, no. 5, January 30, 1960, p. 28.

SOURCES

Bair, Deirdre. *Samuel Beckett,* Harcourt Brace Jovanovich, 1978, pp. 491, 514-15.

Beckett, Samuel. *Krapp's Last Tape,* in *Krapp's Last Tape and Other Dramatic Pieces,* Grove Press, 1957, pp. 7-28.

Boswell, James. *Boswell's London Journal 1762-1763,* Mc-Graw-Hill, 1950, p. 161.

Brien, Alan. Review of *Krapp's Last Tape* in the *Spectator,* November 4, 1955.

Brustein, Robert. Review of *Krapp's Last Tape* in *Samuel Beckett: The Critical Heritage,* edited by Lawrence Graver and Raymond Federman, Routledge & Kegan Paul, 1979, pp. 192-93.

Cronin, Anthony. *Samuel Beckett: The Last Modernist,* HarperCollins, 1997, p. 481.

Dylan, Bob. ''When I Paint My Masterpiece,'' Big Sky Music, 1971.

Knowlson, James. *Damned to Fame: The Life of Samuel Beckett,* Simon and Schuster, 1996, p. 397.

Reid, Alec. *All I Can Manage, More Than I Could,* Grove Press, 1971, p. 21.

Tynan, Kenneth. Review of *Krapp's Last Tape* in *Samuel Beckett: The Critical Heritage,* edited by Lawrence Graver and Raymond Federman, Routledge & Kegan Paul, 1979, pp. 189-92.

FURTHER READING

Graver, Lawrence and Raymond Federman, editors, *Samuel Beckett: The Critical Heritage,* Routledge and Kegan Paul, 1979.

The entire volume is a collection of original reviews of Beckett's work; the section on *Krapp's Last Tape* features both a positive and negative review.

Knowlson, James. *Damned to Fame: The Life of Samuel Beckett,* Simon and Schuster, 1996.

Knowlson's exhaustive biography explores the ways in which Beckett's life in Ireland and France affected his work. Knowlson also treats Beckett's service to the French Resistance in great detail.

Knowlson, James, editor. *The Theatrical Notebooks of Samuel Beckett Volume III: Krapp's Last Tape,* Grove Press, 1992.

This volume features the entire text of *Krapp's Last Tape* as well as a facsimile of Beckett's notebook in which he kept his ideas (written in French) about how he wanted the play to be directed and performed.

O'Brien, Eoin. *The Beckett Country,* The Black Cat Press, 1986.

This is a large collection of photographs of the Irish locales that influenced Beckett's work; there are several images in the collection that surface in *Krapp's Last Tape.*

The Night of the Iguana

TENNESSEE WILLIAMS
1961

Tennessee Williams's *The Night of the Iguana* is the last of the distinguished American playwright's major artistic, critical, and box office successes. First performed on December 28, 1961, on Broadway in the Royale Theatre, *The Night of the Iguana* won Williams his fourth New York Drama Critics Award. Like other plays by Williams, *The Night of the Iguana* focuses on sexual relationships and odd characters, including one crippled by his desires, the Reverend Shannon. Indeed, in retrospect, many critics see *The Night of the Iguana* as the link between stylistic eras (early/middle to late) for Williams. They argue that Williams reveals more of himself in this play than his previous work. Indeed, unlike many of Williams's plays *The Night of the Iguana* ends on a positive, hopeful note. However, some contemporary critics of the original Broadway production found the play lacking form and derivative of Williams's earlier successes, such as *A Streetcar Named Desire*. There has also been a lingering controversy over what the iguana, mentioned in the title, represents. The iguana, which spends most of the play tied up on the edge of the veranda, is seen as a symbol for a number of things, including freedom, what it means to be human, and Shannon. As an unnamed critic in *Time* magazine wrote, ''Purists of the craft may object that, strictly speaking, *The Night of the Iguana* does not go anywhere. In the deepest sense, it does not need to. It is already there, at the moving, tormented heart of the human condition.''

AUTHOR BIOGRAPHY

Williams was born Thomas Lanier Williams on March 26, 1911, in Columbus, Mississippi. He was the son of Cornelius Coffin and Edwina (maiden name, Dakin) Williams. Williams's father, a traveling salesman, was rarely home for Williams and his elder sister Rose. The children and their mother lived with her parents in Tennessee until 1918. That year, Cornelius Williams moved the family to St. Louis when he was hired as the sales manager for a shoe company. Williams began writing as a child, publishing poetry in his junior newspaper. In high school, he published short stories in national magazines.

After graduating from high school in 1929, Williams entered the University of Missouri, Columbia. Williams considered becoming a journalist, but he was forced to leave after two years due to financial hardship caused by the Great Depression. Williams went to work at his father's employer, the International Shoe Company, where he was miserable. Williams returned to college for a year at St. Louis's Washington University, before being forced to drop out again. Williams finally finished his degree at the University of Iowa in 1938.

Williams had begun writing plays as early as 1935, producing them locally. He dubbed himself Tennessee Williams in 1939, based on a nickname he acquired at Iowa for his Southern accent. Based on a group of his plays, Williams won the Group Theater prize in 1939. This led to wider recognition as well as a Rockefeller Fellowship in 1940. Williams made his living writing, even spending a half a year as a screenwriter for MGM in 1943. The experience and form did not suit him, and Williams turned to plays full time by 1944.

In 1944, Williams wrote *The Glass Menagerie* which firmly established his literary reputation. He won numerous accolades for the play, which had some basis in Williams's own life. Between 1944 and 1972, Williams produced over a dozen plays, many of which were extremely successful. Williams won the Pulitzer Prize for drama twice, the first for what many critics consider his best play, 1947's *A Street Car Named Desire,* and the second for 1955's *Cat on a Hot Tin Roof.* Williams called his style ''poetic naturalism''—referring to the poetic edge present in his style of dramatic realism. Williams's last big hit in this vein was 1962's *Night of the Iguana.*

After *Iguana,* Williams's plays differed in form and content, and many were not critically acclaimed nor commercially successful; many were seen as derivative of his earlier work. Williams suffered a mental collapse in the late 1960s, spending several weeks in a psychiatric hospital. His last minor success was in 1972 with *Small Craft Warnings.* Williams continued to write plays as well as novels and short stories, until his death on February 24, 1983.

PLOT SUMMARY

Act I

The Night of the Iguana opens at the Costa Verde Hotel in Mexico. The hotel's proprietress, Maxine Faulk, greets her old friend, an expelled minister named Reverend T. Lawrence Shannon, as he pants his way into the hotel. Maxine tells him that her husband, Fred, has died recently. Shannon, a tour director, is distressed and has the key to his tour bus hidden in his pocket. He wants the tour to stay here because he is afraid of losing his job and he is on the verge of collapse. The reason for Shannon's distress is revealed: His tour group consists of 11 young Baptist music teachers and he has had sexual intercourse with one of them. Everyone has found out about the liaison, including the head of the group, Miss Fellowes.

Miss Fellowes gets off the bus and confronts Shannon. She insists on using the hotel's telephone to report Shannon to her local authorities and his employer. Maxine tries to give Shannon her dead husband's clothing and put him into her husband's old room. Maxine gets her employees to take the women's luggage off the bus, as Shannon has requested. Miss Fellowes returns and continues to argue with Shannon about his conduct and the tour. When she learns about the luggage, she insists that it be returned to the bus. Maxine tries to get Shannon to give up the key but he won't hear of it.

In the meantime, Hannah Jelkes, an artist of about 40 years of age, has appeared at the hotel and asked Shannon about rooms for herself and her elderly grandfather, a poet of minor reputation known as Nonno; he informs her that there are vacancies. When she returns with the old man, Maxine only gives them rooms when Shannon insists. However, they have no money to pay, because they usually work for their funds among hotel patrons: she as a character sketch artist, and he reads poems. After Maxine tells them they can stay for one night, Hannah confides in Shannon that her grandfather is not well and might have had a slight stroke. Shannon helps Hannah into her room, and Maxine returns, jealous of the attentions Shannon has paid to Hannah.

Act II

At the hotel several hours later, Maxine confronts Hannah. Maxine attempts to get Hannah and her grandfather to move to a boarding house, but Hannah makes herself useful then tries to sell her jade. Their conversation is interrupted by the return of Shannon and some other guests. Hannah asks Shannon about the boarding house, and he tells her it is unsuitable. Their conversation is interrupted by the entrance of Charlotte, the young woman with whom Shannon had a liaison. Shannon hides and Hannah covers for him. When Charlotte figures out that he is in his room, Shannon comes out. Charlotte tells him that they must get married, but Shannon informs her that he does not love anyone. Miss Fellowes approaches, prompting Charlotte and Shannon hide. Again, Hannah covers for them, but Miss Fellowes finds Charlotte and drags her away.

Shannon emerges wearing his minister's frock. Hannah helps him with the collar, then sketches him. Shannon tells her he has been on "sabbatical" from his church for a year, because he had sexual intercourse with a Sunday school teacher and then committed an act of heresy. He was kicked out of his church and then sent to an asylum. Hannah decides to try to sell her paintings to the Baptist teachers and leaves Shannon in charge of her grandfather. In the meantime, some of the employees return with an iguana, which is tied to the veranda to be fattened for eating. Maxine enters and offers drinks to Shannon, who refuses.

Nonno takes a fall in his room, and Shannon quickly helps him up and brings him out. He begins to recite a poem when Hannah returns and helps him when his memory falters. Nonno finishes and Hannah makes him sit down, though he loudly asks about how much money they have made. Shannon helps her deal with him, calming the old man down and directing attention away from the situation. They sit down to eat, and Nonno blesses the food when prompted by Shannon. Nonno shows his dementia as Hannah explains that her grandfather was a minor poet. Maxine appears with a liquor cart, and she and Shannon get into a shoving match with it after Maxine insults Nonno. Shannon leaves mo-

Tennessee Williams

mentarily, and Maxine and Hannah argue. Hannah threatens to leave, even though a storm is coming. Maxine tells her to stay away from Shannon, though Hannah denies there is any attraction. Shannon returns, and Maxine brings the liquor cart to other guests. Shannon tells Hannah she is a lady after she gives him one of her last cigarettes after he asks for it. Hannah tells him that she wishes she could help him, and he is touched. She retrieves her paintings, and they watch the storm as it hits.

Act III

This act opens in the same place, several hours later. Shannon is in his room writing a letter to his Bishop when Maxine interrupts. Maxine tells him that she is considering moving back to the United States. She also tries to coerce him to stay at the hotel with her. He leaves to mail his letter himself when he sees the Baptist teachers gathered around the bus. Jake Latta, a man from the tour company, is with them. Jake approaches Shannon and Maxine and informs Shannon that the group of Baptist teachers will now be combined with Jake's tour group. Jake demands the key, but Shannon will not give it up. Jake believes Shannon has gone crazy. The key is finally taken from Shannon by force, and he demands severance pay. Jake leaves, taking the tour group with him.

Shannon almost follows, but Maxine makes him stay. After Maxine leaves to collect her fees from the group, Shannon nearly chokes when his cross and chain get caught on something. Hannah rescues him, but he tries to leave again. Maxine returns and has Shannon tied up to control his ''crackup.'' At Shannon's request, Hannah talks to him. She also makes him poppyseed tea. He is upset about the sketch she drew of him and because she refuses to untie him. He is cruel to her, suggesting that she should add hemlock to Nonno's tea, and while she is bothered by it, she knows why he is acting this way. Though she still will not untie him, she does light a cigarette for him and put it in his mouth. The cigarette falls underneath him and he begins to panic. While Hannah tries to retrieve it, Maxine returns and is angered by the scene. She again tries to intimidate Hannah. Shannon promises to sleep with Maxine later if she will untie him. Satisfied, she leaves to attend to other guests.

Shannon manages to free himself from the rope and immediately heads to the liquor cart. Hannah tells him that she too nearly suffered a breakdown and survived by endurance and a will to keep on going. She also is determined to stay at the hotel. Hannah convinces him to drink a cup of poppyseed tea when he asks her about her love life. She tells him that she has had two encounters and has learned to accept what she cannot improve. Shannon tries to touch her, but she tells him to back away. Shannon tries to get her to travel with him, but she refuses this request as well. She decides to pack her things for tomorrow when the iguana's movements become loud and bother her. She asks Shannon to cut it loose. He complies after much discussion. Nonno calls her, informing her that he has finally finished his poem. Maxine returns and is upset to find that Shannon is untied. Shannon agrees to stay with Maxine. Hannah sits with Nonno, who has just died.

CHARACTERS

Jonathan Coffin

Jonathon Coffin is the elderly grandfather of Hannah Jelkes. He is nearly 98 years ''young'' and a minor poet. With his granddaughter, he travels around the world, paying his way by reciting poems to hotel guests. Coffin is somewhat senile, very hard of hearing, and uses a wheelchair and a cane to get around. His dementia increases during the night at the Costa Verde. Coffin manages to finish one last

poem before he dies at the end of *The Night of the Iguana*.

Maxine Faulk

Maxine is the middle-aged padrona of the Costa Verde Hotel. She has recently been widowed; her husband Fred has died. Even before his death, Maxine was sleeping with other men, mostly local boys. Maxine is an old friend of Shannon's. Though he is suffering from mental collapse, she tries to ply him with rum-cocos in an attempt to get him under her control, sexual and otherwise. Shannon resists for the most part. Maxine is extremely jealous when Hannah arrives and bonds with Shannon. Maxine does not want Hannah and her grandfather to stay, but Shannon convinces her to change her mind. Maxine confronts Hannah over the connection she sees between Hannah and Shannon, but Hannah dominates the conversation. In the end, Maxine gets her way, and Shannon agrees to stay at the hotel indefinitely with her.

Judith Fellowes

Judith Fellowes is the leader of the group for which Shannon is acting as tour guide. She is very angry at Shannon for his involvement with one of her charges and reports him to his superiors.

Charlotte Goodall

Charlotte is the young girl whom Shannon has sex with on the tour. She is very much in love with him and wants to get married.

Grandpa

See Jonathan Coffin

Hannah Jelkes

Hannah Jelkes is a middle-aged spinster from New England. She seems about 40, but could be a few years older or younger. She travels the world with her elderly grandfather, Jonathon Coffin, a poet. Together they stay in hotels and pay their way via their respective artistic skills; Hannah is an artist who paints watercolors and sketches people in charcoal and pastels. Hannah and her grandfather stay at the Costa Verde Hotel out of desperation: they are nearly penniless. In fact, Maxine does not want them to stay, but Shannon convinces her otherwise. While at the hotel, Hannah does not sell any art, but her calm serenity helps Shannon through his breakdown. She works as the opposite of Shannon in many ways. For example, she has only had two sexual encounters in her life, yet has a greater understanding of herself and life than Shannon. Though Shannon wants them to travel together, Hannah refuses, telling him to stay with Maxine. At the end of the play, Hannah is left alone when her grandfather dies and her future is uncertain.

Nonno

See Jonathan Coffin

Reverend T. Lawrence Shannon

Reverend Shannon is the central character in *The Night of the Iguana.* He is a middle-aged minister who lost his church when he had an improper relationship with a Sunday school teacher. Shannon becomes a tour guide, leading groups in many different countries. He leads his current group to the Costa Verde Hotel after he has sex with one of his young charges. Shannon suffers a crisis verging on breakdown at the hotel. He refuses to let the group leave, fearing he will lose his job. To that end, he holds the key to the bus in his pocket. Maxine backhandedly tries to help him, by tempting him with alcohol and sex. Shannon finds his salvation in Hannah, who helps him face himself and his problems. Shannon ends up letting the group go, by force, but symbolically frees himself when he frees the iguana tied up by the veranda. At the final curtain, it is implied that Shannon will stay at the hotel with Maxine and help her run the establishment.

MEDIA ADAPTATIONS

- *The Night of the Iguana* was adapted as a film in 1964. This version was directed by John Huston and starred Richard Burton as Shannon, Ava Gardner as Maxine, and Debra Kerr as Hannah.

Shannon is not the only character driven by lust. Maxine also engages in numerous affairs—and did so while married to her now-deceased husband. When Shannon arrives at the hotel, she immediately begins trying to seduce him with her body and rum-cocos. She wants to control Shannon through sex. Maxine becomes extremely jealous when Shannon shows interest in Hannah, the spinster from New England. Unlike Maxine and Shannon, Hannah is not motivated by sexual desire. She has only had two sexual encounters in her life. Hannah helps Shannon through his crisis, but refuses his sexual advances. After the worst has passed, Shannon decides to stay and live with Maxine, seemingly the only option, sexual or otherwise, that he has left open.

THEMES

Sex and Sexual Desire

Many of the characters and much of the plot of *The Night of the Iguana* is driven by the desire for and the consequences of sexual relations. Shannon is the primary focus of these tensions. He is a minister who has lost his church, and a tour guide who, during the course of the play, loses his group and his job. In both instances, Shannon acted inappropriately towards a young woman. In the latter, for example, Shannon had sex with a young Baptist girl who was part of the group he was leading. Maxine, the padrona of the hotel, tells Shannon that many of his problems stem from the fact that his mother caught him masturbating as a child and beat him because she believed it was wrong. She believes that Shannon gets back at her by engaging in such behaviors.

Alienation and Loneliness

Underlying the theme of sex and sexual desire, is alienation and loneliness. Both Maxine and Shannon fear being alone, in their own way, while Hannah has a seemingly secure relationship with her grandfather that prevents true alienation from the world. Maxine desperately wants Shannon to stay with her and help her run the hotel that her recently deceased husband left her. She tries everything in her power to control him: leaving her shirt half open; plying him with rum-cocos, knowing he has a problem with alcohol; tying him up when he seems really crazy. She wins in the end because Shannon is just as alone as she is. He lost his church and his status as minister long ago. His job is not conducive to forming positive long-term relationships: the groups come and go, and he is left alone. Shannon has no real friends except Maxine and her now-dead husband. They join forces at the end because this is the only solution to their loneliness.

TOPICS FOR FURTHER STUDY

- Research the history of American and German expatriates in Mexico during World War II. Why were people like Shannon, Hannah, and Maxine drawn there?

- Compare and contrast Shannon with another sexual character, Stanley Kowalski from Tennessee Williams's play *A Streetcar Named Desire.* Why are both emotional cripples? How do they deal with their sexual desires?

- Explore the psychology behind Shannon's story of his mother and how it affects the sexual choices he makes with women.

- Research the iguana and its habits. What does the animal's characteristics add to its symbolic meaning in *The Night of the Iguana?* Where else has the iguana been used in art?

Hannah's fortunes turn counter to Maxine and Shannon's. Hannah's only companion is her elderly grandfather, the poet Jonathon Coffin. The old man is practically senile and requires her constant care. But, unlike Shannon and Maxine, Hannah is not really lonely. She has someone to take care of, someone who loves and depends on her. While she may be sexually alienated, she is not lacking what seems to be a permanent human relationship. However, Hannah's grandfather is old, and he dies at the end of play. Having already refused Shannon's offer to be traveling companions, Hannah has a future as uncertain as Shannon's was at the beginning of *The Night of the Iguana.*

Permanence

Each of the characters in *The Night of the Iguana* lack permanence. Only Maxine desires it from the beginning, in her quest to convince Shannon to stay with her to run the hotel. The fact that the play is set in a hotel—a place filled with temporary residents—epitomizes this condition. Shannon has lived a transitory life since he was expelled from his

church. Being a tour guide involves dealing with different groups of people, leaving him little opportunity for a lasting relationship. Even when Shannon tries to make a connection—by sleeping with one of his tourists—it is an impermanent gesture. He does not want to marry the girl, though she wants so marry him. Shannon refuses Maxine's sexual overtures throughout the play for similar reasons: he almost fears permanence. Hannah and her grandfather live an analogous life. Though they have an unspecified home base in New England, they choose to travel the world, living in hotels. They pay their way by selling Hannah's art and reciting Nonno's poetry to hotel patrons. They are an independent entity that does not seek or embrace permanence, except in each other. But even this situation is only temporary. Jonathon Coffin dies at the end of the play, leaving Hannah in a situation that is even less permanent than it was before. There is no indication of her next move, but Shannon chooses to embrace permanence by staying with Maxine and running the hotel.

STYLE

Setting

The Night of the Iguana is a drama set in Mexico in 1940. All the action takes place in one location: the veranda of the Costa Verde Hotel and several rooms that open up on to it. The veranda serves as a passageway between guests' rooms and the beach, and many characters walk through. The veranda also has several components key to the story: the hammock, the railing, and its underside. The hammock is Shannon's favorite spot and where he is placed when he is tied up. Shannon's cross gets caught in the railing, and he is nearly choked to death. The iguana is tied up underneath the veranda, thrashing about, until Shannon frees him. The rooms that open up on the veranda are separate cubicles with screen doors. During the night scenes, when the veranda is illuminated, the action inside the rooms is highlighted. Such illumination and separation, which occurs primarily in the second half of the play, emphasizes the loneliness of the room's occupants.

Symbolism

The events in *The Night of the Iguana* are underscored by symbols. The most prominent is found in the title: the iguana. The iguana is caught by local boys who work at the hotel and tied up underneath the veranda for fattening. When the time is right, the local boys will kill and eat the animal. This does not happen, however. By the end of the play, Shannon has cut the reptile loose, at the request of Hannah. The iguana could represent a number of things. Many critics believe that it represents Shannon, who is also tied up during the course of the play. Like the animal, Shannon is straining against the bonds of society and fighting a losing battle. The iguana could also be seen as a symbol of the human condition. There are other symbols at work in the play. The spook that Shannon claims is following him can be seen as his conscience. The rum-cocos, which Maxine constantly tries to push on Shannon, are a symbol of her sexuality. The storm that threatens throughout the play parallels Shannon's life-changing dilemma.

Costumes

Several of the characters in *The Night of the Iguana* are described wearing specific kinds of clothing that underscore their actions. In Act II, Shannon dons his long-unused minister's shirt and collar, as well as a cross. He wants to symbolically reconnect with his past as well as prove to the tour group that he was once a minister, but the button on the collar is so worn that it immediately pops off. He cannot even wear the garb. Later, he nearly chokes himself to death on the cross. At the end of the play he gives Hannah his cross to fund her journey back to the United States.

At the same time Shannon puts on his minister's clothes, Hannah emerges from her cubicle wearing an artist's smock with a silk tie. It is carefully daubed with color to complete the look of a working artist. Hannah wears this smock when she tries to convince hotel patrons to allow her to sketch them for a fee. It makes her look "authentic," though she is an artist no matter what she wears. The outfit defines her for others, rather than for herself. Unlike Shannon, she is fairly secure in her identity. Costumes also define Maxine who wears a half-unbuttoned shirt when she first sees and tries to seduce Shannon.

HISTORICAL CONTEXT

The early 1960s marked a transitional time in American history. In 1961, for example, President Dwight

A still from director John Huston's film adaptation of William's play: the Reverend (Richard Burton) and Maxine (Ava Gardner)

D. Eisenhower left office. The new president was the youthful, more liberal John F. Kennedy. Change was not limited to the United States: political and cultural turmoil could be found worldwide and the United States was often involved.

One of the biggest threats to the American mainland in the 20th century was Cuba after Fidel Castro rose to power. In 1961, the United States cut off diplomatic relations with Cuba. Cuban exiles, backed by the American government, led an invasion into Cuba at the Bay of Pigs—the operation was a dismal failure. The Soviet Union, the United States' most formidable enemy, placed missiles aimed at the United States in Cuba. The Soviets later remove their missiles from the island after the Cuban Missile Crisis of 1962. The Soviet Union and the United States eventually began discussing disarmament in Geneva later in the decade.

In the early 1960s, the United States also became involved in the on-going conflict in Vietnam. Military aid and advisors were sent to American allies in the region. By the end of the decade this involvement would become extremely controversial and create a rift in American society.

COMPARE
&
CONTRAST

- **1940:** The United States watched the beginnings of World War II and considered intervention. Eventually the country was drawn into the conflict.

  1961: The United States watches the beginnings of the Vietnam conflict. Eventually, the country was drawn into the war.

  Today: While there are no widespread wars, the United States retains a position as the world's peacekeeper and considers intervention in numerous localized conflicts.

- **1940:** The growth of war-related industry drew nearly 12 million women in the workforce. However when the war ended, women's pay went down and they earned much less than men.

  1963: The beginnings of the modern feminist movement take root, with the publication of Betty Friedan's *The Feminine Mystique.*

  Today: Women struggle to balance the demands of work and home life. There is still a significant disparity in pay: women earn much less than men for the same work. The feminist movement is on the decline.

- **1940:** Some methods of birth control have been available for several years, though many are still restricted. Attitudes towards sex are becoming more liberal.

  1961: The birth control pill is introduced, giving women more control than ever over their bodies.

  Today: Birth control has become even more convenient. Devices such as Norplant can be inserted into a woman's arm and work for up to six months.

- **1940:** Nazi Germany forces the beginnings of Jewish repression. This takes many forms in different countries, including restriction of movement and denial of basic human rights. The Auschwitz concentration camp is built.

  1961: Nazi official Adolph Eichmann is convicted in Israel for his role in the death of six million Jews during World War II.

  Today: Efforts to keep alive the memory of the Holocaust are widespread. Movies on the topic, such as *Schindler's List* and *Life is Beautiful,* are popular and win numerous awards.

Despite these conflicts, the United States became dominant in the political and cultural climates of the world. The economy boomed, and American businesses grew rapidly at home and abroad. Americans were prosperous. Disposable goods were developed and the youth market boomed. While America developed a reputation for technical innovation (for example, Telstar, a satellite owned by AT&T transmitted television signals for the first time), the Soviet Union put the first man, Yuri Gagari, in space in 1961. Such incidents drove home the fear that the American education system was not up to the demands of the modern society that was emerging.

One of the biggest changes in the United States concerned women. There was mounting tension due to the schism between women's traditional roles and changing society. More women entered the workforce, many of whom were married. During World War II, many women joined the workforce to support the war effort as many men went off to fight in the war. When men returned home, they took back most of the jobs, but women continued to work, though only part-time or in traditional women's professions. By 1960, 36% of women were in the workforce, accounting for 32% of total workers. The feminist movement gained momentum when Betty Friedan published *The Feminine Mystique* in 1963. In this book, she argued that women should seek self-fulfillment. Though they may have found such fulfillment in the workforce, they were still responsible for the majority of household chores.

The lives of women did not only change in the workforce. Women's fashion also became looser. In the 1960s, it became acceptable for women to wear pants in more formal social situations for the first time. In general, women dressed less formally overall, and younger women embraced fashion that changed from season to season. Women also married at a later date, and the divorce rate grew. There was more sex outside of marriage, and premarital sex became more common. In 1961, the birth control pill became available on the open market, making contraception easier than it had ever been for both single and married women. Such changes marked the emergence of modern society in America.

CRITICAL OVERVIEW

Many critics believe that *The Night of the Iguana* was Tennessee Williams's last great play. Howard Taubman of the *New York Times* writes, ''For Mr. Williams, *The Night of the Iguana* marks a turning point. When compared with the best of the preceding plays, this work of subtle vibrations reflects a profound change. It goes beyond the elimination of the explosive and shocking gestures, which have given some of the other works the fillip of being sensational and scandalous, and reaches into the playwright's attitude towards life.'' A concurring critic, Harold Clurman of *The Nation,* finds Williams's writing to be superb. He says, ''The writing . . . is lambent, fluid, malleable and colloquially melodious. It bathes everything in glamour.''

Numerous critics believe the character of Hannah is key to the play's success. An unnamed critic in *Life* argues, ''*The Night of the Iguana* is Williams's best play in many seasons, and Hannah drives home—more explicitly than any of his other characters ever has—the heart of his writing.'' Taubman agrees when he writes, ''No character of Mr. Williams' invention has had the heartbreaking dignity and courage of Hannah Jelkes. . . .'' Even an unnamed critic in *Time,* who calls the plot ''sketchy,'' finds something to like. This critic writes, ''It is Hannah's kindness to be cruel.''

The other main character, the fallen Revered Shannon, is seen by most critics as more typical of Williams, but he still has some distinctive attributes. Clurman of *The Nation* argues that ''There is very

little indulgence in the portrait of Reverend Shannon.'' Glenn Embrey in his essay ''The Subterranean World of *The Night of the Iguana,*'' believes Shannon's fate defines him quite differently than other tortured souls in Williams's plays. He writes, ''The main character of *The Night of the Iguana* seems to escape the violent fate usually in store for Williams's heroes. True, desire has been ruining Shannon's life for the past ten years, but at the climax of the play he manages to form what promises to be a lasting sexual relationship with a mature woman. This optimistic ending appears to make *Iguana* very different from the serious plays that precede it; for the first time hope breaks across Williams's bleak world.''

One source of controversy among critics is the function and power of the minor characters. Some see the group of German tourists who pop in and out of the story as extraneous. These critics believe the Germans serve no real function in the plot but to give it a sense of time and some comic relief. Other critics like them for their reactions to the main plot.

Some critics dislike the play overall, but find moments of merit. Richard Gilman in *The Commonweal* writes ''The talk is that the play is Williams's best since *Cat on a Hot Tin Roof,* and the talk, for once, is right. But it seems doubtful that is right for the best reasons. . . . [T]wo things have mostly been ignored. The first is that *The Night of the Iguana* perpetuates nearly all of Williams's failings as a dramatist. . . .'' Similarly, an unnamed critic in *Newsweek* writes ''At no time does *Iguana* achieve the single, dramatic clap of thunder that will clear the troubled air. . . .''

Other critics who dislike the play find it too similar to previous plays written by Williams. Robert Brustein in *The New Republic* writes ''In *The Night of the Iguana,* Tennessee Williams has composed a little nocturnal mood music for muted strings, beautifully performed by some superb instrumentalists, but much too aimless, leisurely, and formless to satisfy the attentive ear. . . . [H]e has explored this territory too many times before—the play seems tired, unadventerous and self-derivative.'' John McCarten of *The New Yorker* finds fault in the use of the characters. He writes ''The Williams genius for making assorted bizarre types believable is in evidence, all right, but our interest in them is aroused only sporadically.'' Later in his article, Brustein of *The New Republic* writes, ''let us put down *The Night of the Iguana* as another of his innumerable exercises in marking time.''

CRITICISM

A. Petrusso

In this essay, Petrusso examines the so-called "happy" ending of Williams's play via the motivations of its three main characters.

One source of controversy among critics of Tennessee Williams's *The Night of the Iguana* is the decision of Reverend T. Lawrence Shannon to stay at the hotel with Maxine Faulk at the end of the play. Glenn Embrey, in his essay "The Subterranean World of *The Night of the Iguana*," argues "the ending isn't as believable as it is formally pleasing and optimistic. Even according to the overt level of drama, the ending sounds suspiciously like the product of wishful thinking. For one thing, it comes rather suddenly and unexpectedly; an hour's exposure to human compassion, a cup of poppy tea, and a bit of Oriental wisdom hardly seem sufficient to eradicate habits and attitudes hardened over ten years." Embrey misses the undercurrents of the play. Shannon has no choice but to stay at the hotel, and the events of the play—particularly his interaction with Hannah, which leads to personal growth—make the decision seem like the right one. By looking at each corner of the primary character triangle—Shannon, Hannah, and Maxine Faulk, the hotel owner—the reasons for Shannon's decision and the seemingly happy ending become much more clear.

When Shannon arrives at the hotel at the beginning of Act I, he is a desperate man looking for a friend; that friend is Fred Faulk, Maxine's husband. Unfortunately, Fred is recently deceased, and Maxine is more interested in a companion to keep her company and help her run the hotel than in being Shannon's friend. Shannon's problems are numerous. Ten years earlier, he was an Episcopalian minister leading a church in Virginia. He was locked out of his church after he seduced (or was seduced by, according to Shannon) a Sunday school teacher and gave a sermon the following Sunday that was full of heresy. Shannon became a tour guide, traveling around the world. Over the years, he continued to lose jobs as he acted inappropriately towards female clients. He comes to the Costa Verde Hotel while working for Blake Tours, the only company he has not been fired from. But he has recently seduced (or been seduced by) Charlotte, a sixteen-year-old Baptist school teacher, who was a member of his latest tour group. The head of Charlotte's group, Miss Fellowes, has found out about the affair

and is furious. Costa Verde is to be Shannon's refuge from this storm. He is not altogether mentally well, and he keeps the key to the bus in his pocket so the group has to stay there while he sorts out this mess. His intentions are not clearly thought out.

Shannon places the blame for his problems on everyone but himself. He believes he is followed by a "spook"—his past which haunts him. He does not even take responsibility for the seductions: he blames the girls for the affairs. He does this despite the fact that after at least two of these sexual encounters he hits the women involved, perhaps an acting out of his own guilt. Shannon is a weak man who constantly associates with weak, immature women. He is fundamentally lonely as well. By leading tour groups, he makes few real, long-term connections with people. Tourists come and go, and he never sees them again. Shannon is desperate for real contact, but does not have the means or the capacity to find it. He has to stay in control, but he cannot do it very well. When he first arrives at the hotel, Maxine immediately tries to control him and make him into Fred by putting him into Fred's clothing and Fred's room. Shannon pulls away from these offers; He is not ready to accept such a fate just yet.

Soon after Shannon's arrival, Hannah Jelkes appears, trying to find rooms for herself and her elderly grandfather, the minor poet Jonathon Coffin. The first person she meets is Shannon, who helps convince Maxine that they should stay, if only for one night. Hannah is the opposite of every woman with whom Shannon has had any type of relationship—she is a New England born and bred spinster, about 40 years of age. In many ways, Hannah has been and still is as desperately lonely as Shannon, but she handles it with serenity. Unlike Maxine, she does not try to seduce him from the first. Instead, she wants to help him. Hannah is a saint, the answer to prayers Shannon should have said.

Hannah does for Shannon what Maxine (and apparently the young women he has slept with) could never do: give of herself unconditionally in a helpful, non-sexual manner. For example, she covers for him when Miss Fellowes and Charlotte are looking for him. But one event is particularly telling. Near the end of Act II, while engaged in conversation with Shannon, Hannah reaches into her pocket for her cigarettes. She only has two left, and returns the packet to save the smokes for later. Shannon asks for a cigarette, and Hannah selflessly gives him the packet. He throws them away and

WHAT DO I READ NEXT?

- *Cat on a Hot Tin Roof,* a play by Tennessee Williams first performed in 1955, also concerns a character, Brick, who is plagued by self-deception of a sexual nature.

- *The Male Experience,* a nonfiction book published by James A. Doyle in 1983, explores male psychology, focusing on their sexuality and masculinity.

- ''The Night of the Iguana,'' in *One Arm, and Other Stories,* is a short story by Tennessee Williams published in 1948. The play is based on this story, though many of the elements are very different.

- *The American Expatriate: No Land's Man,* a nonfiction book published by John Fowles in 1964, discusses Americans living and working in foreign countries, including Mexico.

- *Our Lady of Babylon,* a novel published by John Rechy in 1996, explores relationships between the sexes, women's sexual behavior, and sex roles in history.

---

gives her a tin of better quality cigarettes. Shannon questions her about the act, but Hannah does not think the moment is much of anything. She tells Shannon, ''Aren't you making a big point out of a small matter?'' Shannon replies, ''Just the opposite, honey, I'm making a small point out of a very large matter.'' This event gives Shannon hope and a certain closeness with the serene woman.

In the events that follow at the end of Act II and throughout Act III, Hannah continues to bolster Shannon's sense of self and give him life-changing advice. She tolerates his histrionics. To help Shannon help himself, Hannah has him help Nonno (her grandfather) on several occasions. She gets Shannon to admit that what he did to those girls in his charge was wrong, though he denies it to almost everyone else. After Shannon is tied up for fear that he might hurt himself, Hannah is the only one he will speak to calmly. She tells him, without judging him, that he is enjoying the penance involved in being tied up on the hammock, suffering like Christ for his sins. No one else, not even Maxine, can tell him such things.

Hannah takes it further. She even admits that she respects him—something that no one to that point has said. This gives him the strength soon after to break out of the ties that bind him. Hannah also feels sympathy, even empathy for his loneliness, which he fully appreciates. One piece of advice that she gives to him is ''Accept whatever situation you cannot improve.'' This advice changes the course of his life, though he does not realize it at that moment. Because of this connection, Shannon wants to travel with Hannah, but she refuses the offer. She is only there to help, not serve as a crutch. She only asks that he free the iguana, as she has freed him. She can only give so much of herself.

Shannon logically turns to Maxine, the woman who has pursued him from the moment he set foot in the hotel. Maxine is the opposite of Hannah in many ways, though they share common traits. She, too, is desperate, but is sexually aggressive and insulting to Shannon. As mentioned earlier, Maxine tries to literally get Shannon to take the place of her dead husband by giving him Fred Faulk's shoes, clothing, and room. Knowing that Shannon has had problems with alcohol in the past, she continually tries to get him to drink rum-cocos, which he always turns down. Maxine wants to control him, but her methods alienate Shannon. Maxine does not respect Shannon for much of the play, yet she admits at the beginning of Act III ''it's . . . humiliating—not to be . . . respected.'' Further, Maxine senses the connection between Shannon and Hannah and is extremely jealous. Maxine wants to be rid of her rival, but she has met her match in Hannah. Even Shannon points out that she will not win such battles.

> **"** SHANNON HAS GROWN DURING THE PLAY AND BECOME A MAN THAT UNDERSTANDS HIMSELF. AT LEAST HE HAS MORE AT THE END THEN HE DID AT THE BEGINNING OF *THE NIGHT OF THE IGUANA,* WHICH IS ABOUT AS HAPPY AS THE ENDING GETS"

When Shannon threatens to get totally out of control, Maxine is the one who has him tied up. She says that she has dealt with his breakdowns before and threatens to send him to the nuthouse. Yet despite such problems and Maxine's own flaws, by the end of the play she is exactly what Shannon needs. She is the rest of his cure, the part that Hannah cannot provide. After Hannah has refused him and he has set the iguana free, Maxine can finally give him that rum-coco. She can finally get him to go swimming with her, something he has also refused to do. Maxine is aware of his past, but now that Shannon has been able to give up control—free his iguana as it were—he can live with it.

Shannon stays at the Costa Verde not just because he has nowhere else to go (he gave his crucifix with an amethyst in it to Hannah to provide for her return to the States), but because the hotel is the sight of his healing. Shannon will get what he needs there: a cure for loneliness, mature sexual companion or companions, a stable place to live. It makes sense as he has examined his soul and may be still vulnerable to the world. He also has no money or job, and there may be a warrant for his arrest in Texas. The hotel and Maxine are about the only place Shannon can safely live in. Hannah's protection was only short term. This ending is not necessarily the "positive" one that some critics make it out to be. Shannon has lost everything and is living with a woman who has been both mean and helpful to him. His future has numerous uncertainties: How long will the relationship with Maxine last? Will he have another breakdown? If nothing else, Shannon has grown during the play and become a man that understands himself. At least he has more at the end

then he did at the beginning of *The Night of the Iguana,* which is about as happy as the ending gets.

Source: A. Petrusso, for *Drama for Students,* Gale, 2000.

Michael Tueth

Tueth reviews a 1996 revival production of Williams's play. Comparing the 1961 play to recent revivals of other playwrights' works, the critic found Night of the Iguana *to have weathered the decades quite well, calling it a "beautiful and compassionate play."*

The American theater is now at the stage of maturity in which a theater season needs to include some revivals of what might be considered American classics. Not all such revived plays bear up well under the test of time. For instance, two recent Broadway revivals of popular plays by William Inge, "Picnic" and "Bus Stop," have come across almost as period pieces from the pre-sexual-revolution era of the 1950's. Tennessee Williams, however, seems to be faring much better, especially in one current production.

The Night of the Iguana, which opened in 1961, is generally considered to be Williams's last Broadway success. It enjoyed considerable attention at the time, running for almost a year and winning the Drama Critics Circle Award for Best Play and a Tony award for its leading actress, Margaret Leighton. A popular film version followed in 1964, starring Richard Burton, Deborah Kerr and Ava Gardner. It has now returned to Broadway at the Roundabout Theater, starring Cherry Jones, who won the Tony Award and several other honors as Best Actress last season in another Broadway revival, "The Heiress." Also in leading roles are the Chicago actor William Petersen and the Broadway and Hollywood actress Marsha Mason. The production is in the reliably sensitive hands of Robert Falls, who guided a juicy revival of another Williams play last season, "The Rose Tattoo."

The story is set in the jungle, the lush tropical setting of a Mexican tourist hotel—but also in the tangled, interior landscape of Williams's favorite people, his company of the lost, lonely and frightened. The Rev. T. Lawrence Shannon (Petersen), an Episcopalian priest who has been locked out of his church for his heretical views of God and his behavior with young women of his congregation, now leads bus tours through "God's landscape."

A scene from the film: Shannon (Burton) orders Charlotte (Sue Lyons) out of his room

Suffering from fever, nervous exhaustion and the threats of his angry customers, he has guided his tourists to a hotel run by his old friend, Maxine Faulk (Mason), a brassy, recently widowed woman. Soon after his arrival, he meets Hannah Jelkes (Jones), a New England spinster who travels about with her 97-year-old philosopher-poet grandfather. Psychologically they are all at the end of their rope, like the iguana that Maxine's Mexican houseboys have caught and tied up until they can slaughter it for dinner. They spend one night together fighting off their demons and maneuvering for new chances at life.

William Petersen's portrayal of the priest emphasizes his erotic helplessness and the pain of his doubts about God, whom he calls "his oblivious majesty." Marsha Mason wisely avoids too much "earth-mother" posturing, conveying instead a sexual playfulness and genuine concern, as a woman who realizes that she misses her deceased husband more than she suspected and now sees an attractive replacement in their old friend, Shannon. Cherry Jones's controlled movement and diction first express the necessary self-reliance and desperate discipline of her situation, then the bravado of a poker-game bluffer and eventually a heart as vulnerable

and knowing as Maxine's and as hungry and frightened as Shannon's.

The first act can be a bit off-putting simply because of its noise. Petersen, as Shannon, has the opportunity to express anxiety about his fate, regret for his misbehavior and doubts about divine benevolence, but he insists on declaiming all of these matters at top volume. Also the grandfather is supposed to be so hard of hearing that Hannah and others have to shout much of their dialogue toward him. The arguments between Shannon and the lady-tourists, too, could be played more lightly (and more quietly). They have much more comic potential than is exploited in this production. Newcomer Paula Cale, as the young tourist currently infatuated with Shannon, exhibits every nervous quality and none of the charm of a 16-year-old girl, adding to the general mayhem and prompting one to ask how someone even as confused as Shannon could succumb to her whining and twitching. Finally, the presence of German tourists at the hotel (the action of the play is set in 1940), as examples of the Nazi master-race mentality to contrast with the fragile human beings who fascinate Williams, serves mostly to provide a series of interruptions. Someday perhaps a director will feel free to eliminate these

> THIS IS NOT ABOUT LIFE IN
> 1940 OR 1961 OR 1996. THIS PLAY
> IS TIMELESS IN ITS EXPRESSION OF
> OUR DEEPEST YEARNINGS FOR
> CONNECTION, FOR ASSURANCE, FOR
> HOPE AND MAYBE EVEN FOR GOD."

caricatures from this otherwise beautiful and compassionate play.

Act two is the payoff in this production, to which perhaps the noise of Act One is a necessary prelude. Shannon is eventually strapped into a hammock to prevent him from committing suicide, and Hannah prepares him some poppy tea. It is night, the tourists have departed, a lightning-storm has ended, and the place has quieted down. There then ensues a soul-baring conversation between these two lost travelers that expresses for the spell-bound audience every hope and fear Williams sought to examine in his whole dramatic career. Their intimate conversation becomes a duet of longing and questioning, culminating in the classical benevolence of Hannah's observation, ''Nothing human disgusts me unless it's unkind, violent.'' The spiritual ''one-night stand'' of the minister and the spinster achieves the kind of universal sympathy for our wounded lives that we have always found in great theater.

This is not about life in 1940 or 1961 or 1996. This play is timeless in its expression of our deepest yearnings for connection, for assurance, for hope and maybe even for God.

Source: Michael Tueth, ''Return of the Iguana'' in *America,* May 4, 1996, pp. 24–25.

Richard Gilman

In this essay, Gilman reviews a 1962 production of Williams's play, stating calling it the playwright's best work since Cat on a Hot Tin Roof. *Gilman concludes that* Night of the Iguana*'s better points make up for Williams's less stellar dramatic offerings.*

By now it should be clear that Tennessee Williams' real subject is the painfulness (not the tragedy) of

existence, and the fate of human dignity (not of the soul) in the face of suffering. It should also be clear that however neurotic Williams himself may be and however widely neurosis enters into and affects his work, there is little point in looking for the roots of his art, and less in searching out the meaning of any particular play, on one or another categorical Freudian plot of ground; because to Williams *everything* is painful—sexuality, touch, communication, time, the bruteness of fact, the necessity to lie, the loss of innocence. And finally it should be clear that toward his material Williams has alternately been elegist, soothsayer, mythmaker, immolator, exorcist or consoler—none of the incarnations final and no one incarnation carried through to finality.

Unfortunately, nothing is clear. The state of Williams criticism is a jungle, in which every hot opinion flourishes. You may find the three or four or seven critics you most respect each sending up a different species of leaf. No American playwright, except possibly O'Neill, has been so much praised or damned for the wrong reasons, just as none has so successfully (and to the exacerbation of the problem) straddled the popular and elite camps. And no playwright has so helped to muddy his work's image by coyness, obfuscatory pronouncements, false modesty and inability to accept that when you eat the cake it is gone.

Thus Williams' new play came to us and was greeted with the familiar irrelevancies and extraneous considerations, and the familiar embarrassment. It was dismal to read his breast-beating acceptance of the Chicago critics' unfavorable notices. (The Chicago critics indeed! Can anyone imagine Brecht, O'Casey, Giradoux or even O'Neill deferring to Claudia Cassidy?) And now that the supreme court has reversed the verdict, what has the playwright to say? What, for that matter, does the new verdict, the New York talk, have to tell us about ''*The Night of the Iguana?* ''

The talk is that the play is Williams' best since ''*Cat on A Hot Tin Roof,*'' and the talk, for once, is right. But it seems doubtful that it is right for the best reasons or that it tells the whole story. In the general eagerness to rediscover a humane or optimistic or elegaic or non-apocalyptic Williams, the Williams of ''*Streetcar*'' and ''*The Glass Menagerie,*'' two things have mostly been ignored. The first is that ''*The Night of the Iguana*'' perpetuates nearly all of Williams' failings as a dramatist; the other is that the renewal, the moving up from the depths of ''*Sweet Bird*'' and ''*Period of Adjust-*

ment," is precisely of a kind to throw light on what those weakness are.

Essentially, it is the never-settled dilemma of what kind of playwright to be. The problem divides here into three. The decor: a detailed, exact reproduction of a seedy Mexican hotel near Acapulco, circa 1940; realism at the zenith (flakiness of walls, lushness of vegetation, *real* rain), yet also attempts at "poetic" atmosphere, suggestions of symbolic values. The text: an amalgam of hard realism, expert and winning, and sloppy lyricism; the dialogue used conflictingly to advance the plot or create character or establish vision or as abstract self-sufficiency. The structure: two nearly separate plays, a first act of tedious naturalism filled with supererogation and subsidiary characters of strictly commercial lineage (a Nazi family, a lesbian, Mexican boys lounging darkly); and a second wherein much is stripped away and a long central anecdote with its attendant effects rests securely on a base of true feeling and dramatic rightness.

The anecdote, neither so long nor nearly so shocking as that in "*Suddenly Last Summer,*" but having much the same purpose, to establish and compel assent to the play's central difficult proposition, is only partly detached from the main flow of action, struggling to issue from it, correct it, illuminate it and give it permanence. It is an example of what Williams does best, as so much of the earlier business exemplifies what he does worst.

Told by a forty-year-old woman who has lived a life of celibacy while shepherding, on a nomadic, Vachel Lindsay-like existence, her aged grandfather, a minor poet who will read his work for coins and is fighting against failing powers to complete his last mysterious poem, a prayer for courage, the story constitutes a revelatory experience to set against the despair over the inexorability of erotic compulsion with which the play is otherwise largely concerned. There is a possibility that it would lose much of its splendor without the incandescent purity of Margaret Leighton's performance as the woman, but one tends to think that it would be hard to destroy.

What is so new in it, and in the play, for Williams, is the announcement of chastity as a possibility, as well as unromantic pity for the sensually driven. For the man to whom it is told, and who exists on the stage as wound for Miss Leighton's ministrations and arena for her victory (sadly, he is played unclearly and with spurious force by Patrick O'Neal), is an Episcopalian priest who has been

> "NO AMERICAN PLAYWRIGHT, EXCEPT POSSIBLY O'NEILL, HAS BEEN SO MUCH PRAISED OR DAMNED FOR THE WRONG REASONS."

defrocked for committing "fornication and heresy in the same week" and has become a tourist guide in Mexico, where he maintains an unbroken line of lust and self-pity.

At the play's end he is not healed nor are his circumstances altered—his last act is in fact to accept ruefully his condition, marked out for him by the person of the female hotel-owner, a woman of absolute appetite and primitive sensuality—acted with great gum-chewing, buttocks-wriggling, nasty élan by Bette Davis. But what has happened to him, and to the audience whose surrogate he is as Val or Brick or Chance Wayne could not be, not even Blanche or Maggie, is that there is now a sense of destiny continued under a placating star, that the painfulness of what we are and are driven to do is eased by being faced and by being given a counter-image, tenuous but lasting; and the whole thing has managed to work because for once there are no false moves, no violence seeking meaning but exhausting it, no orgasmic aspirations and no proliferation from a center without its own center.

It is almost enough to compensate for all those other things, that ephemeral, debased theater, that Williams hasn't yet ceased to give us. Indeed, as memory pares away the inessential, it does compensate.

Source: Richard Gilman, "Williams as Phoenix" in the *Commonweal,* Vol. LXXV, no. 18, January 26, 1962, pp. 460–61.

Robert Brustein

While Brustein says that Williams's play offers some enjoyment, he ultimately finds Night of the Iguana *to be "too aimless, leisurely, and formless to satisfy" a discerning theatregoer.*

In *The Night of the Iguana,* Tennessee Williams has composed a little nocturnal mood music for muted strings, beautifully performed by some superb instrumentalists, but much too aimless, leisurely, and formless to satisfy the attentive ear. I should add that I prefer these Lydian measures to the unmelodious banalities of his *Period of Adjustment* or the strident masochistic dissonances of *Sweet Bird of Youth;* for his new materials are handled with relative sincerity, the dialogue has a wistful, graceful, humorous warmth, the characters are almost recognizable as human beings, and the atmosphere is lush and fruity without being outrageously unreal (no Venus flytraps snapping at your fingers). With this play, Williams has returned once again to the primeval jungle, where—around a ramshackle resort hotel near Acapulco—the steaming tropical underbrush is meant to evoke the terrors of existence. But he has explored this territory too many times before—the play seems tired, unadventurous, and self-derivative. Furthermore, the author's compulsion to express himself on the subjects of fleshly corruption, time and old age, the malevolence of God, and the maiming of the sensitive by life has now become so strong that he no longer bothers to provide a substructure of action to support his vision. *The Night of the Iguana* enjoys no organizing principle whatsoever; and except for some perfunctory gestures towards the end, it is very short on plot, pattern, or theme.

One trouble is that while Williams has fully imagined his *personae,* he has not sufficiently conceived them in relation to one another, so that the movement of the work is backwards towards revelation of character rather than forwards towards significant conflict. ''The going to pieces of T. Lawrence Shannon,'' a phrase from the play, might be its more appropriate title, for it focuses mainly on the degradation and breakdown of its central character—a crapulous and slightly psychotic Episcopalian minister, very similar to the alcoholic Consul in Malcolm Lowry's *Under the Volcano.* Thrown out of his church for ''fornication and heresy''—after having been seduced by a teenage parishioner, he refused to offer prayers to a ''senile delinquent''—Shannon now conducts guided tours in Mexico, sleeping with underage girls, coping with hysterical female Baptists, and finding evidence of God in thunder, in the vivesection of dogs, and in starving children, scrabbling among dungheaps in their search for food. Other characters brush by this broken heretic, but they hardly connect with him, except to uncover his psychosexual history and to expose their own: The Patrona of the hotel, a hearty lecherous widow with two Mexican consorts, out of *Sweet Bird of Youth;* Hannah Jelkes, a virgin spinster with a compassionate nature, out of *Summer and Smoke;* and Nonno, her father, a ninety-seven-year-old poet—deaf, cackling, and comatose—out of *Krapp's Last Tape.* The substance of the play is the exchange, by Hannah and Shannon, of mutual confidences about their sexual failures, while the Patrona shoots him hot glances and the poet labors to complete his last poem. When Shannon goes berserk, and is tied down on a hammock and harassed by some German tourists, the iguana is hastily introduced to give this action some larger symbolic relevance: the lizard has been tied under the house, to be fattened, eaten, and to have its eyes poked out by native boys. Persuaded by Hannah to be kinder than God, Shannon eventually frees the iguana, tying its rope around his own neck when he goes off, another Chance Wayne, to become one of the Patrona's lovers. But though Shannon is captured, Nonno is freed. Having completed his poem about ''the earth's obscene corrupting love,'' he has found release from such corruptions in death.

The materials, while resolved without sensationalism or sentiment, are all perfectly familiar: the defeated perverse central character, punished for his perversity; the Strindbergian identification of the human body with excrement and defilement; the obsessively sexual determination of every character. But by keeping his usual excesses to a minimum, Williams has provided the occasion for some striking performances. Margaret Leighton, especially, has endowed the stainless Hannah with extraordinary sensibility and tenderness, plumbing depths which Williams himself has been unable to reach since his earliest work. Bette Davis, playing the Patrona in flaming red hair and blue jeans, bats her pendulous lids on her laugh lines and is always on the surface of her part, but she is still a strongly felt personality; Alan Webb's Nonno is humorously senescent; and Patrick O'Neal plays Shannon with suppressed hysteria and a nagging, relentless drive which sometimes reminds one of Fredric March. Always on hand to produce rain on the stage, Oliver Smith has stifled his passion for opulence in the setting, within which this gifted ensemble seems to find its way without directorial eyes (Frank Corsaro's name is still on the program but I detect his influence only in a couple of Method Mexican extras).

For all its virtues, though, the play is decidedly a minor opus. A rich atmosphere, a series of languid scenes and some interesting character sketches are more than Williams has offered us in some time, but they are still not enough to sustain our interest through a full evening. Perhaps Williams, identifying with Nonno, has decided to think of himself as only "a minor league poet with a major league spirit," and there is enough fatigue in the play to suggest that, again like Nonno, he feels like "the oldest living and practicing poet in the world." But even a minor poet fashions his work with more care and coherence than this; even an aged eagle occasionally spreads its wings. I am inclined to persist in my heresy that there is at least one more genuine work of art left in Williams, which will emerge when he has finally been able to objectify his personal problems and to shape them into a suitable myth. Meanwhile, let us put down *The Night of the Iguana* as another of his innumerable exercises in marking time.

Source: Robert Brustein, "A Little Night Music," in the *New Republic,* Vol. 146, no. 4, January 22, 1962, pp. 20, 22–23.

> **WHILE WILLIAMS HAS FULLY IMAGINED HIS *PERSONAE,* HE HAS NOT SUFFICIENTLY CONCEIVED THEM IN RELATION TO ONE ANOTHER."**

"The Violated Heart" in *Time,* January 5, 1962, p. 53.

Williams, Tennessee. *The Night of the Iguana,* in *Three by Tennessee,* Signet Classic, 1976, pp. 1-127.

SOURCES

Brustein, Robert. "A Little Night Music," in the *New Republic,* January 22, 1962, pp. 20-23.

Clurman, Harold. A review of *The Night of the Iguana,* in the *Nation,* January 27, 1962, pp. 86-87.

Embrey, Glenn. "The Subterranean World of *The Night of the Iguana,* " in *Tennessee Williams: A Tribute,* University Press of Mississippi, pp. 325-40.

Gilman, Richard. "Williams as Phoenix," in the *New Republic,* January 26, 1962, pp. 460-61.

McCarten, John. "Lonely, Loquacious, and Doomed" in the *New Yorker,* January 13, 1962, p. 61.

Taubman, Howard. "Changing Course: Williams and Rattigan Offer New Styles," in the *New York Times,* January 7, 1962, sec. 2, p. 1.

"Tennessee in Mexico" in *Newsweek,* January 8, 1962, p. 44.

"Tough Angel of Mercy" in *Life,* January 22, 1962, pp. 67, 70.

FURTHER READING

Boxill, Roger. *Modern Dramatists: Tennessee Williams,* St. Martin's Press, 1987.
  This book covers Williams's career as a playwright, focusing on his major plays, including *The Night of the Iguana.*

Hardison Londre, Felicia. *World Dramatists: Tennessee Williams,* Frederick Ungar Publishing, 1979.
  This book critically discusses each of Williams's plays in-depth and includes a chronology of his life.

Hayman, Ronald. *Tennessee Williams: Everyone Else is an Audience,* Yale University Press, 1993.
  This is a critical biography of the playwright, covering his entire life and career.

Williams, Dakin and Shepherd Mead. *Tennessee Williams: An Intimate Biography,* Arbor House, 1983.
  This is a biography of the playwright, written by his younger brother.

Oh Dad, Poor Dad, Mamma's Hung You in the Closet and I'm Feelin' So Sad

ARTHUR KOPIT

1960

Arthur Kopit wrote *Oh Dad, Poor Dad, Mamma's Hung You in the Closet and I'm Feelin' So Sad* while he was studying European theater on a post-graduate travel scholarship earned at Harvard. His aim was to enter the work in a school playwriting contest, never anticipating that it would bring him worldwide acclaim at the age of twenty-three. As its subtitle indicated, he wrote the play as a parody—''a pseudo-classical tragifarce in a bastard French tradition''—in the new, avant garde French theater of Arthur Adamov, Eugene Ionesco, and Samuel Beckett. It was this subgenre of the theater that, in 1961, Martin Esslin labeled the Theatre of the Absurd.

Kopit's work won both the contest and an undergraduate production at Harvard. The play created such a stir that it was moved into a Cambridge, Massachusetts, commercial house, the Agassiz Theater, where it garnered very positive reviews. The favorable notices attracted the attention of the Phoenix Theatre in New York, a major Off-Broadway house that staged alternative theater works. The play opened there on February 26, 1962, running for 454 performances, an extraordinary achievement for an unknown playwright with no previous New York production credits. The work also won both the Vernon Rice and the Outer Circle Awards.

The offbeat, dysfunctional characters—especially Madame Rosepettle and her son, Jonathan—caused some critics to complain about a lack of

serious purpose in the play as well as its derivative elements, but the farcical and fanciful treatment of an overly-protective, domineering mother and her neurotic son gave New York and European audiences little pause. Most commentators could not argue with success and found the play a engaging spoof of everything from Tennessee Williams's *Rose Tattoo* to Freudian psychology.

Although Kopit, like Edward Albee (*Who's Afraid of Virginia Woolf?*), was initially tagged an absurdist, his subsequent work showed him to be capable of a wide variety of theatrical styles. A careful craftsman, over his career he has experimented widely with both form and content, establishing himself as one of the most diverse and innovative playwrights that America has produced. *Oh Dad* remains a psychedelic romp, a popular chestnut for small theaters and repertory groups both at home and abroad. It can be argued that the play's characters lack psychological complexity but most viewers agree that they are unforgettable.

Arthur Kopit

AUTHOR BIOGRAPHY

Arthur Lee Kopit was born in New York City on May 10, 1937, son to George and Maxine Dobin Kopit. He grew up in Lawrence, on Long Island, where his father worked as a jewelry sales manager. After graduating high school in 1955, he entered Harvard University on an engineering scholarship; but he was also interested in the arts, and after his first year he became involved in Harvard's Dunster House Drama Workshop. He had seven of his plays produced there, directing six of them himself and winning two playwriting prizes. He graduated from Harvard *cum laude* in 1959.

Kopit's earliest professional works—mostly one-acts—were parodies and tragicomic or black farces, prefiguring the play which solidified his reputation, *Oh Dad, Poor Dad, Mamma's Hung You in the Closet and I'm Feelin' So Sad* (1960). After being staged at Harvard and a local commercial theater and later in London, *Oh Dad* began a New York run of 454 performances at the Phoenix Theatre on February 26, 1962. The play subsequently enjoyed a successful tour of the United States and Europe.

On the basis of *Oh Dad*, critics identified Kopit as a promising absurdist playwright, a judgment that, given Kopit's great diversity, proved to be both premature and too restrictive a label. With the bow

of *Indians,* first produced in London by the Royal Shakespeare Company in 1968, Kopit gave notice that his work defied categorization. A protest play, *Indians* simultaneously debunks the American myths created to vindicate both the massacre of native Americans and the Vietnam War, using Buffalo Bill's Wild West Show as its central metaphor.

Again, with *Wings* (1978), Kopit demonstrated that he was too much an innovator to be bound to a particular dramatic movement or subgenre. The work first appeared as a radio play, from research undertaken after Kopit's father had a debilitating stroke. It was refashioned for the stage, becoming what many consider the writer's best and most original work. It is almost a monologue, a dramatization of a stroke victim's inner struggle to cope with the loss of coherent speech. Concurrent with his work on *Wings,* Kopit began teaching as a playwright in residence, first at Wesleyan and thereafter at other universities in New York and New England.

Throughout his career, Kopit has shown that he is one of the most careful and deliberate craftsmen in the American theater. He is also one of its most inventive and far-ranging playwrights. In addition to a variety of stage plays, many of which reflect an abiding interest in history and contemporary social problems, he has written librettos for musicals and diverse works for radio and television, including documentary mini-series. His grants and awards include a Vernon Rice Award (1962), Outer Circle Award (1962), American Academy Award (1971), CBS Fellowship (1976), Italia Prize (1979), and an Antionette (Tony) Perry Award (1982).

PLOT SUMMARY

Scene I

Oh Dad opens in a luxurious hotel suite in the Caribbean Port Royale hotel. A squad of bellboys scurry in, bearing the exotic belongings of Madame Rosepettle and her son, Jonathan. Two bring in a coffin and, confused by Madame Rosepettle's directions, pull the handles off and dump the coffin on the floor.

Madame Rosepettle begins issuing orders with a wilting, supercilious sneer. She also begins an endless litany of complaints with both the hotel's personnel and the accommodations. She directs two bellboys to put the coffin in the master bedroom, next to the bed, while other bellboys continue carting in more things, including two black-draped Venus flytraps, a dictaphone, and mourning drapes. When the Head Bellboy asks where to put the dictaphone, she scoffingly remarks that any nincompoop would know where.

Bristling at the Madame's contempt, the Head Bellboy at first tries to be tactful, but as she grows more insulting, he demands her respect. Madame Rosepettle, however, quickly reduces him to compliant jelly. She is, she reminds him, a very rich Tourist, greatly outranking him. She sends him off to hang the drapes on the windows in the master bedroom, then tells Jonathan to remind her to have him fired. Jonathan, variously called Edward, Albert, and Robinson—names belonging to his deceased father—dutifully begins taking notes on a pad.

More bellboys enter with chests containing Jonathan's stamp and coin collections. When Madame Rosepettle asks Jonathan where he wants his things, he is barely able to stutter out an answer, using instead his trembling "paw" to direct the bellboys. The Head Bellboy, without tools to hang the drapes, re-enters and apologizes. Madame Rosepettle pulls a hammer and nails from her large purse and sends him back. After complaining about

the poor service, she begins tipping the bellboys with coins randomly selected from Jonathan's collection. She also presents Jonathan with a 1572 Javanese Yen-Sen, proclaiming it the rarest of all coins, if only because none were ever minted.

Hearing the hammer beating in the master bedroom, the Madame recalls cavorting to the sound of a pneumatic drill in Buenos Aires and begins dancing around the room. She stops when other bellboys carry in Jonathan's trunk of books. They open it, depositing hundreds of books on the floor. Jonathan falls on them voraciously, stuttering out the names of famous writers and reading from their works "in wild abandon."

Rosalinda, Madame Rosepettle's silver piranha, is carted in next. When the fish's bowl is uncovered, the widow uses a pair of tongs to extract from it the skeleton of the fish's last meal, an alley cat. Madame Rosepettle complains that Rosalinda must be fed pedigreed Siamese cats, preferably warm and cuddly kittens. Then, before dismissing the completely cowed bellboys, Madame Rosepettle asks about a large, 187-foot yacht she has spied in the harbor, learning that it belongs to one Commodore Roseabove. Finally, after speaking affectionately to her little fish, she begins recording her memoirs on the dictaphone as Jonathan slips off to the balcony to look down on a carnival now heard in the street.

Scene II

It is two weeks later. In the suite, Jonathan is talking with Rosalie, two years his senior but dressed "in a sweet girlish pink." She asks why he can not go out. He haltingly explains that he has duties, that he must stay to feed the Venus flytraps. She presses him further, and he explains that he has at least gone out to the balcony and watched her, which encourages her to make him tell her more. She learns that he has watched her through a homemade telescope, fashioned from a blowgun and some lenses used to examine his stamps. Rosalie tries to look through the telescope but sees nothing on the horizon, prompting Jonathan to respond that the failure to see anything is what his mother calls "a Lesson in Life."

When Jonathan admits to spying on Rosalie and the children after whom she looks, the girl explains that she is their baby sitter. She tries to entice Jonathan to visit her after the children are asleep, but she only sets him to trembling and stuttering incoherently. He explains that he has too much to do inside. He admits that Madame Rosepettle locks him in, but he says that it is only for his own good.

When a cuckoo clock sounds, Jonathan tries to usher Rosalie out. He begins to panic when it sounds again and urges Rosalie to leave before it is too late. Delaying, she makes him promise to call. Terrified, Jonathan pleads with her to go, then suddenly collapses, confessing that he loves her. The cuckoo clock goes completely haywire as Madame Rosepettle enters from the master bedroom, demanding to know why Rosalie is still around.

When Rosalie accuses Madame Rosepettle of eavesdropping, the older woman calls the babysitter a slut, denouncing her for playing a sexual variation of blind man's bluff with one of the older children in her charge. She tries to make Rosalie leave, but the girl begins asking the Madame why she treats her son as she does, questioning the mother as to why she let Rosalie visit Jonathan in the first place. Madame Rosepettle admits that she wanted to let Jonathan see what Rosalie was really like, then once again tries to get the girl to leave.

Madame Rosepettle insists that Rosalie is unworthy of Jonathan, who is "as white as fresh snow" (while Rosalie is "tainted with sin"). The girl finally leaves. Before she does, however, Jonathan pleads with Rosalie to return another time, and she and Madame Rosepettle go to their respective doors, leaving Jonathan alone in the center of the room.

Scene III

It is night, a week later. Jonathan, alone, sits in a chair near Rosalinda, the fish. Exotic carnival sounds invade the room, and Jonathan jumps up to shut the French windows but the panes come alive and sway with the music before crashing on the floor. Jonathan moves to the balcony, past the two growing Venus flytraps that begin to growl and lunge at him.

Madam Rosepettle and Commodore Roseabove waltz into the room under a follow spot. They dance around the table, stopping momentarily as he romantically pleads for her hand and she, coyly at first, resists. The intoxicating interlude is fleeting, for Madame Rosepettle takes charge and makes a mockery of the Commodore's suite. She spins him around, makes him dizzy, then violently kisses him, making him gasp for air. He tries to sit down at the table, but his chair suddenly pulls out from under him.

Finally seated, he attempts love overtures again. He pours champagne, but when the pair clink their glasses in a toast, the glasses break. Madame Rosepettle snaps her fingers, and a waiter appears from the shadows with another table, complete with tablecloth, candles, glasses, and a bucket with champagne.

Madame Rosepettle admits that the Commodore's money is attractive, but she complains that he is "a bit too bulky" to make him worth her while. Then she begins a long, meandering confessional, explaining her dark views on life and love. She tells Roseabove that she had killed her husband and now carts him about like a trophy. He grows apprehensive and wants to leave, but she insists that he remain to listen to her "bedtime story." She divulges that she only slept with her husband once, a union that produced Jonathan. She also reveals that she spied on her husband, trying to understand him, more like a specimen than a human. She also admits that she hid Jonathan from him. She almost gleefully recounts, too, that Mr. Rosepettle had died and lain next to his last mistress for six hours without her knowing the difference. Horrified, Roseabove tries to escape, but the door knob comes off in his hand. He is able to crawl out only after Madame Rosepettle mocks him, sending him back to the "world waiting to devour those who trust in it; those who love."

Madame Rosepettle then prepares for her nightly beach outing and exits, leaving Jonathan alone. He appears from behind the Venus flytraps, which, even larger now, threaten to snatch and devour him. He deftly evades them but accidentally jars the table and starts up the dictaphone. In panic, he retrieves a fire axe from a glass case and attacks and destroys the plants. As he turns next to the fish, Rosalie enters followed by drunken bellboys. She is dressed garishly, in a girlish, pink party dress, complete with crinolines. She commands Jonathan to put down the axe, for a moment thinking that he has killed his mother. But, after smashing the bowl and killing the fish, he explains that Madame Rosepettle would not let him see Rosalie again or even communicate with her by mail. Rosalie tires to get him to run off with her, but he is terrified at the prospect of actually leaving the suite. She then tries to entice him into the master bedroom, but he is very frightened. She goes in the room, pulls the black drapes from the windows, and gets on the bed, inviting him to join her.

When Jonathan finally enters the room, she begins to undress, but after he sits down, the closet door suddenly opens and the corpse of Mr. Rosepettle drops on the bed. Rosalie stuffs it back in the closet and continues with the seduction, but the body tumbles out again. Rosalie simply shoves it onto the floor. Jonathan begins to respond, but when she admits to having seduced all kinds of men, he is repulsed. He smothers her to death with her skirt, then begins burying her body under a funeral mound consisting of his stamps, coins, and books. Horrified by what he has done, he tries to run out, but his father's dead hand grabs one of his ankles and he falls to the floor. He manages to free himself and retreat to the balcony as his mother returns

Disheveled and sand-covered, Madame Rosepettle briefly and triumphantly describes her sand-kicking interference with moonlit lovers but soon discovers the dead fish and destroyed plants. She spots Jonathan and asks for an explanation. He merely scans the sky with his telescope, spotting a plane and waving at it. She goes into the master bedroom, trips over the corpse of her deceased husband, and discovers Rosalie. At the curtain, more insistently, she once again demands an explanation. Jonathan has none to offer.

CHARACTERS

Albert

See Jonathan Rosepettle

Edward

See Jonathan Rosepettle

Head Bellboy

The Head Bellboy, holding the rank of lieutenant, is in charge of a platoon of bellboys. He takes issue with Madame Rosepettle's lack of respect for his position when, in the opening scene, she repeatedly insults him as he and his troop escort her, Jonathan, their luggage, and menagerie into their suite in the Port Royale hotel. After she reminds him that she is a well- heeled tourist and that she can get him another stripe, he immediately becomes her creature, contrite and meekly obedient. He is the first victim of the overbearing and outlandishly capricious Madame Rosepettle.

Robinson

See Jonathan Rosepettle

Rosalie

Rosalie is a combination baby sitter and nanny for a dozen children left in her charge by wealthy parents who travel about and periodically send her an addition to the tribe. She is two years older than Jonathan but in terms of experience might as well be twenty years his senior. Although she is decked out in pink and white girlish innocence, she has had many sexual encounters (if her claims are to be believed). Madame Rosepettle proclaims that Rosalie has even sexually dallied in the bushes with the oldest of the male children that she supervises.

Madame Rosepettle hopes to quell Jonathan's interest in Rosalie by allowing the girl to pay him a visit, assuming that Rosalie will reveal herself to be well-used baggage, but matters do not quite work out as Madame Rosepettle expects. In their initial meeting, against all odds, Rosalie and Jonathan become intrigued with each other. She finds in him a new challenge, a timid and frightened youth who desperately needs to get out from under his mother's dominance.

It becomes Rosalie's mission to liberate Jonathan and thwart the will of Madame Rosepettle by seducing him. Later, visiting the suite on the sly, her seduction is interrupted in the most macabre sequence in the play, when the corpse of Jonathan's father falls out of the closet on top of her. Rosalie pays with her life for her sexual advances after admitting to Jonathan that she is no innocent. What hope there might be for freeing Jonathan from his mother's smothering control ends up under a mound of books, stamps, and coins on Madame Rosepettle's bed.

Commodore Roseabove

A wealthy yachtsman, owner of the largest yacht in the Caribbean, Commodore Roseabove is a dissipated playboy with romantic designs on Madame Rosepettle. During her stay in the luxurious Port Royale hotel, he wines and dines her but to no avail.

The Commodore only appears in the final scene of the play, when Madame Rosepettle makes a shambles of his suite. He tries to ply her with champagne, music, and endearing words, but she turns the affair into a travesty by blocking all his overtures of love. As she confesses her feminine shortcomings and carnivorous motives, he grows increasingly wary and finally terrified. She quite literally wants his heart but not the rest of him, though what she would do with his heart, short of feeding it to one of her pets, remains a mystery. In any case, she watches him crawl through the door after having reduced him to a weak, stuttering fool, a pathetic "nothing," in Madame Rosepettle's view. The Commodore may have risen above the rank and file, but the domineering and emasculating Madame Rosepettle easily turns him into an incompetent old codger.

Jonathan Rosepettle

Son to Madame Rosepettle and Albert Edward Robinson III, deceased, Jonathan suffocates from overprotection. His mother's conviction that he should remain a total innocent, pure as snow, has reduced him to a stammering, trembling neurotic, full of abnormal fears and thinly veiled hostilities.

Madame Rosepettle keeps Jonathan locked up in their hotel suite along with her menagerie of omnivorous pets. Convinced that he is destined for some unspecified greatness, she encourages him to learn about the world from its coinage, its stamps, and its books, not from experiencing it firsthand. He is extremely curious, however, and spends time out on the balcony, looking through his home-made telescope and watching the people celebrating life in the street below.

Under his mother's tutelage, Jonathan has become wary of others, suppressing all his instinctive longings, including sexual needs. He is challenged by Rosalie, who, by Madame Rosepettle's design, visits Jonathan. His mother knows that Jonathan has been watching Rosalie through his telescope and assumes that Rosalie, in person, will offer bracing evidence of her immorality, turning Jonathan against her and women in general. But Jonathan is attracted to Rosalie, and though his fears render him almost helpless, he manages to stammer out his interest in her and pleads with her to return.

During her second visit, however, things go wrong. Rosalie begins an aggressive seduction routine, coyly enticing Jonathan onto Madame Rosepettle's bed in the suite's master bedroom. When she admits that she has engaged in sexual adventures with others, confirming what Madame Rosepettle had said about her, Jonathan smothers Rosalie with her skirt and then buries her under his stamps, coins, and books.

Madame Rosepettle

Madame Rosepettle is a highly eccentric and extremely wealthy matron, mother to Jonathan and widow to Albert Edward Robinson Rosepettle III.

MEDIA ADAPTATIONS

- *Oh Dad* was adapted to film in 1967 under the play's full title. Directed by Richard Quine, it starred Rosalind Russell, Robert Morse, Barbara Harris, Hugh Griffith, Jonathan Winters, Lionel Jeffries, and Cyril Delevanti. The film is available on videocassette.

Presumably, she is in mourning. She dresses in black and carries her husband's coffin with her as she treks around the Caribbean with her son and their odd assortment of belongings and pets.

From the outset, it is clear that Madame Rosepettle is in charge. As a nightmarish variation on the "Ugly American" tourist, she barks out intimidating orders and threats, cowering the horde of hotel bellboys who carry the Rosepettle's strange possessions into their regal suite. When the Head Bellboy tries to protest her lack of respect for his rank, she quickly transforms him into a humble and compliant underling by reminding him that she is the "Tourist," the one with the money, the one who must be obeyed.

The Madame carries the same sort of impatient authority into her relationship with Jonathan, whose development she attempts to shape by sequestering him in their hotel suite and strictly controlling his activities. She allows him to read, play with his stamps and coins, and tend to her bizarre pets: the pair of man-eating Venus flytraps and the silver piranha, Rosalinda. In the process of shaping her son for some destined but undetermined greatness, she has reduced him into a frightened, timid, and extremely insecure human specimen. She is, in brief, the overly-protective mother gone amok.

Madame Rosepettle is also the castrating female gone manic. She treats the idea of love between men and women as a sickness needing a cure. Her favorite pastime is to patrol the beach at night, kicking sand on those passionate souls that she finds necking in the moonlight. When she is wooed by

Commodore Roseabove, she suggests that she is willing to accept his proffered heart if he is willing to cut it out and give it to her. In her confessional, she admits that she spent only one night with her husband, the ugly man she married when she was twenty-eight and still a virgin. She also extinguishes the Commodore's romantic designs on her by revealing her utter contempt for the simple male breed, the easily manipulated and abused fools about whom she has nothing good to say. She even confesses her belief that men are hers to kill, as she killed her husband, whose body she keeps in the closet like a trophy. The frightened Commodore with the long yacht is lucky to escape with his life.

Madame Rosepettle's driving purpose in life is to protect her son from such unpleasantries as sex. In order to stem Jonathan's burgeoning interest in Rosalie, she pays the girl to visit Jonathan, convinced that the girl will reveal that she is little more than a slut. That does not happen right away, however, and Jonathan's interest in Rosalie increases. His mother's view of Rosalie seems vindicated in the girl's later visit with Jonathan, when she tries to seduce him admits that she has been promiscuous in the past. Rosalie at least evidences a spunk that challenges Madame Rosepettle's authority, but all ends badly when Jonathan chokes her to death and Madame Rosepettle is left demanding to know just what the death of her pets and Rosalie's book-stamp- and coin-buried body all means.

THEMES

Absurdity

As Kopit indicated in the subtitle of *Oh Dad, Poor Dad, Mamma's Hung You in the Closet and I'm Feelin' So Sad,* he was influenced by the ''bastard French tradition,'' meaning the plays of the avant garde Parisian dramatists, some of whom, like Beckett and Ionesco, were expatriates living in France. Elements of the absurd include highly exaggerated, dysfunctional familial relationships, which is most notably present in the play in the maltreatment of Jonathan by his mother, whose overprotectiveness is simply destructive.

There are many other absurdist elements in the tragic or black farce, however. Among them are the surrealistic, nightmarish motifs, including the ever growing Venus flytraps and the body of Mr.

Rosepettle, which not only falls out of its closet at a most inconvenient time but also, momentarily, comes to life to grab Jonathan's ankle and trip him. There are also the absurdist anomalies, like the haywire cuckoo clock that sounds not to measure regular time units but to reflect human moods, as do the growling Venus flytraps, gleefully gulping piranha, and the dancing French windows. There are, too, the lapses into pure nonsense, like the comic bits in which Madame Rosepettle produces a hammer from her purse or explains that a 1572 Javanese Yen-Sen that she gives to Jonathan for his collection is the rarest of all coins because it was never minted at all, and that, in fact, she had made it herself. Like most of the absurdists, Kopit attempts to show that language and logic are both inadequate and unreliable tools in human discourse, more likely to mask honesty than reveal it.

Obedience

Jonathan Rosepettle's obsessive fears arise from his total obedience to his mother and her tyrannical control of him. He is a devastating caricature of the dutiful son, locked away from the outside world that his mother believes would corrupt him and turn him into another despicable man. His repressed hatred for her emasculating authority starts to well up in him, but he is so afraid of her that the most he can manage is an attack on her pets, surrogate targets that in the most primitive sense embody what she herself is: a man-eating carnivore.

With the squad of bellboys who first accompany the Rosepettles into their suite, Madame Rosepettle issues orders like a military drill instructor, with mocking comments on the inadequacies of the staff and whispered promises to see them all dismissed. Her wealth cowers them, and they hop about like Keystone cops under her wilting barrage of threats and enticements. Although the segment is humorous, it is also an indictment of the incivility and thoughtlessness of the idle and capricious rich, those who abuse the authority that wealth affords them.

Death

A common feature in the Theatre of the Absurd is a farcical treatment of both death and the dead, matters that are normally treated with solemn reverence. It is their disrespectful and at times zany approach to such things that explains these plays' paradoxical description as tragifarces. In a very twisted sense, *Oh Dad* is a threnody (a dirge or lamentation of loss). Initially, Madame Rosepettle is decked out in mourning black. She and her son accompany the coffin of her departed husband in something like a funereal procession. She even totes around black drapes, used to cover the windows in the master bedroom, where she keeps Albert Edward Robinson Rosepettle III's remains in the closet, as if the suite somehow serves as a transitional mortuary for the yet to be buried corpse.

The atmosphere, however, is outlandishly irreverent. The coffin no sooner enters the suite than it is dropped unceremoniously on the floor. The widow grieves not a jot, and before the play draws to an end, Mr. Rosepettle's corpse tumbles twice from the closet and is finally kicked to the floor as Rosalie tries to seduce Jonathan. Rosalie's own death and burial on the bed under a mountain of stamps, coins, and books is merely dark slapstick, more funny than shocking or serious. Death in *Oh Dad* wears a clown's face and makes audiences laugh, if at times uncomfortably.

Alienation and Loneliness

Sequestered in the hotel suite by his mother, Jonathan's sole companions are his mother's pets and his books, stamps, and coins. She deliberately cuts him off from the outside to ensure that he will remain innocent and pure. His is an enforced alienation. He begins to experience some natural though terribly confused longings, but until Rosalie appears in the suite, he is restricted to observing life vicariously, looking off the balcony and reading his books. He is otherwise afraid, having bought into his mother's jaded view of the world, especially her attitude towards love, which she finds repulsive. His hope is Rosalie, in whom he takes an interest. Madame Rosepettle's own sexual frigidity—passed on to Jonathan—wins out in the end, however, and he smothers the girl to death. Madame Rosepettle's triumph seems complete, though she herself seems unable to find the meaning of the bizarre situation at the play's end.

Rites of Passage

Oh Dad plays off against a traditional sexual rite of passage into adulthood, both parodying the process and aborting it. Jonathan's initiation into the joys of sex is initiated by Rosalie, but because Madame Rosepettle's has instilled her warped world view in Jonathan, the process ends badly, with

TOPICS FOR FURTHER STUDY

- Research Off-Broadway Theater and its significance for young, experimental playwrights in the 1960s and 1970s.

- Identify the "bastard French tradition" named by Kopit and its influence on the playwright as evidenced by *Oh Dad*.

- Investigate and compare the treatment of dysfunctional families in *Oh Dad*, Edward Albee's *Who's Afraid of Virginia Woolf?*, and one other American play identified as belonging to the Theatre of the Absurd.

- Investigate the techniques of parody and relate your findings to Kopit's purpose, techniques, and characterizations in *Oh Dad*.

- Research the assaults on American "momism" that preceded Kopit's depiction of Madame Rosepettle in *Oh Dad*, using Philip Wylie's *A Generation of Vipers* (1942) as a resource.

Rosalie's seriocomic death. All hope for Jonathan's sexual maturation seems to die with her, whatever the implied aftermath to the situation that exists at the play's end.

Victim and Victimization

Madame Rosepettle is a power figure, an emasculating and demanding woman who tolerates no ideology save her own. She is a victimizer, and everyone else in the play is her victim, even her deceased husband. Her chief victim is, however, is Jonathan, whom she browbeats unmercifully. From the outset, it is clear that she has reduced him to a terribly insecure, frightened, and emotionally arrested youth incapable of functioning without her.

Commodore Roseabove is also a victim, as is the Head Bellboy. The former is quickly put in his proper, subservient place by Madame Rosepettle, who has not a shred of respect for any male. Roseabove has the temerity to romance the frigid widow, for which he is both savagely mocked and terrorized. Indirectly, Rosalie is also the woman's victim, for it is Madame Rosepettle's aberrant views infecting Jonathan that lead him to kill the girl.

STYLE

Setting

Although the immediate setting of *Oh Dad* is an elegant suite in a luxurious resort hotel, the exotic sounds and lights of the world outside invade the room and suggest both an exotic and romantic atmosphere. It is the world of Port Royale, the Caribbean city that exists only in fantasy. The location throbs with the sounds of a life denied to Jonathan, who is locked away from it.

The light, music, and other sounds awaken in Jonathan some primitive longings. Madame Rosepettle's warping influence on his psyche has been so total, however, that he is terrified at the prospect of doing anything more than watching life pass by him from a distance. She intends to keep in a world of ''light,'' beyond ''the world of darkness,'' the ''sex-driven, dirt-washed waste of cannibals eating each other up while they're pretending they're kissing.''

Absurdism

Although in part a parody, Kopit's play also makes use of absurdist drama. For example, language falters, making communication difficult, particularly for Jonathan, who stammers and stutters his way through the play. Characters are also dysfunctional and exaggerated types. Madame Rosepettle is a monster of maternalism, for example, while Jonathan, her victim, is a hyperbolic bundle of inhibitions and fears. There is also an irreverent treatment of serious matters, especially love and death. Havoc is played with logic as well, when, for example, the stuffed body of Jonathan's father momentarily comes to life, or when the Venus flytraps start growing at an unnatural rate.

Black Humor

A specific quality of much absurdism in both drama and fiction is black humor, evoked in places in which grotesque elements commingle with serious concerns—especially death. The bellboys who carry in the coffin of Madame Rosepettle's dead

husband comically pull its handles off and drop it on the floor, and later, while Rosalie is attempting to seduce Jonathan, Rosepettle's corpse becomes a macabre Jack-in-the-box, interrupting the seduction by falling twice from the closet on top of the pair.

Parody

Kopit parodies other playwrights in *Oh Dad*, especially Tennessee Williams. Madame Rosepettle's long confessional in the third scene is a send up of confessionals made by tormented females in Williams's plays—Blanche DuBois in *A Streetcar Named Desire,* for example. In his bizarre use of ''rose'' in all the characters' names, including Rosalinda, the fish, Kopit also takes comic swipes at another Williams play, *The Rose Tattoo.* Presumably, Kopit is also taking an irreverent swipe at the heavy-handed Freudian underpinnings of much realistic drama, especially Eugene O'Neill's *Long Day's Journey into Night* (1956).

Femme Fatale

Rosalie is a comically distorted familiar type, the *femme fatale,* a female character who brings misfortune, often death, to men. Rosalie attempts to seduce Jonathan, an ironically fatal enterprise, as it ends up costing Rosalie—not Jonathan—her life. She is bundled in the robes of girlish innocence, a frilly, pink party dress that suggests that she is a young innocent; this presentation is comic misdirection, since, as she finally admits to Jonathan, she has already had many sexual encounters.

Grotesque

Among the grotesque elements of *Oh Dad* is Madame Rosepettle's menagerie of pets. These are not warm and cuddly animals but rather malicious creatures, like the piranha Rosalinda, that eat such traditional pets. Rosalinda's favorite meal is a fresh Siamese kitten. The other pets, two large Venus flytraps, grow enough in size to threaten Jonathan or any other man—much like Madame Rosepettle herself. These omnivorous pets seem ideally suited to the woman, for, metaphorically speaking, she is on a mission to chew up and spit out any male she meets.

Pathetic Fallacy

Madame Rosepettle's pets are animated and endowed with human-like responses, expressing a consciousness of what is happening around them.

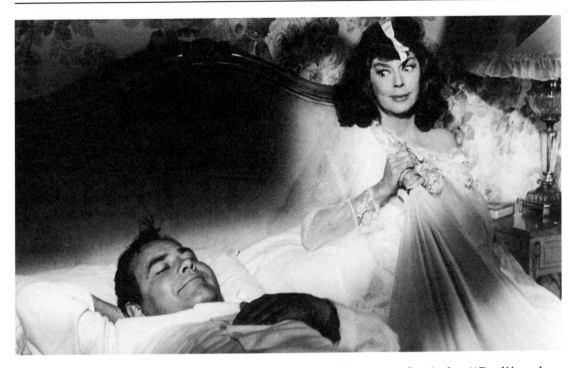

A scene from the film adaptation starring Jonathan Winters as the titular "Dad" and Rosalind Russell as Madame Rosepettle

For example, the Venus fly traps growl and bob and weave like fighters when Jonathan tries to cut them to pieces with an axe. When he turns the axe on the mocking, giggling Rosalinda, the fish screams in terror. Even Madame Rosepettle's dictaphone comes to life on its own when Jonathan jars the table on which it rests, issuing a "strange noise" before "speaking" in Madame Rosepettle's voice.

Satire

Through the two main characters in *Oh Dad*, Madame Rosepettle and her son, Jonathan, Kopit satirizes the sexual mores of what the avant garde in the early-1960s viewed as an "uptight" America. Both are bizarre exaggerations. Madame Rosepettle is the chaste and moral matron turned into an emasculating monster, while Jonathan is the protected son reduced to a neurotic mess, full of inhibiting fears of natural desires. They provide a mordant commentary on middle-class, sexual morality, and the destructive potential of such trappings.

Symbolism

Kopit's play is rife with symbolism. Madame Rosepettle's pets are vivid representations of the woman's omnivorous nature. Just as the pets literal-

ly devour living things, the Madame symbolically devours men; she has more than likely killed her husband, and she has "devoured" any shred of independence that Jonathan may have had. The recurrent use of the word "rose" in many characters' names also serves an ironic, symbolic purpose. A rose is typically associated with love and purity. Yet none of the characters named after the flower are even remotely connected to such concepts. Rosalie, while making a superficial attempt to appear pure, is actually something of a sullied tramp. Commodore Roseabove, while professing to "love" the Madame, is really after sex. Rosalinda, the piranha, is a carnivorous killer of cuddly kittens. And Madame Rosepettle, whose name most explicitly evokes the flower ("rose" "petal"), exhibits behavior in direct contrast to the common ideals associated with the rose.

HISTORICAL CONTEXT

The 1960s was a decade of tremendous turmoil and change in the United States. It was a Cold War decade, a period in which the threat of a nuclear

COMPARE
&
CONTRAST

- **1960s:** The Cold War and the threat of communism looms large in the American consciousness throughout the decade, cresting during the Cuban missile crisis of 1963.

  Today: The Cold War threat has largely evaporated with the dissolution of the Soviet empire. There remain communist strongholds, including China, North Korea, and Cuba.

- **1960s:** The Civil Rights Movement begins, struggling against segregation and social injustice. The decade will also see the flowering of the women's and gay rights movements.

  Today: Some now say that the Civil Rights Movement has gone too far, particularly in quota and set aside programs, called reverse discrimination by their critics. However, statistics argue that Black Americans still have a long way to go to achieve social justice and a fair share of the economic largess of the country. Similarly, while women, gays, and minority groups such as Native Americans and Chicanos have made some progress towards achieving social justice and equitable treatment, none has seen its goals completely met.

- **1960s:** The Theatre of the Absurd in the early-1960s offers a fresh theatrical perspective. The new, shocking, and perplexing drama is an important catalyst in the rise of the experimental Off-Broadway movement.

  Today: Works by first generation absurdist playwrights like Ionesco and Beckett are now considered classics, and although the techniques and some of the themes of the Theatre of the Absurd have left an indelible mark on drama, its most famous pieces are now more venerated than imitated.

---

holocaust seemed almost probable, especially after the Bay of Pigs fiasco, a failed attempt to assassinate Cuba's communist leader Fidel Castro, in 1961. At that time, Castro put Cuba firmly in the Soviet camp. Billboards across America reminded people that Communism was only ninety miles off the Florida coast. When the Soviets put missiles in Cuba, the greatest crisis of the Cold War met the administration of President John F. Kennedy head on.

Despite Cold War fears, when Kennedy took office as the country's thirty-fifth president, there was hope for a new government that would redress domestic social problems, including racial unrest and poverty, and achieve justice for all Americans. The hope seemed to end with Kennedy's assassination on November 22, 1963, despite the fact that his successor, President Lyndon B. Johnson, committed himself to securing passage of much of the civil-rights legislation first proposed under the Kennedy Administration. Still, a darker mood settled on the country, leading to new demonstrations, including Martin Luther King, Jr.'s civil rights march on Selma, Alabama, in 1965, and new outbreaks of violence, including the Newark, New Jersey, race riots of 1967.

By the mid-1960s, the U.S. was also bogged down in Vietnam, fighting a war that for many Americans seemed both strategically unwarranted and morally reprehensible. Along with racial problems, the war divided the country and led to unrest and open dissent that coincided with the rise of a counter-culture with its memorable "make love, not war" slogan and uninhibited sex and open use of illicit drugs like LSD and marijuana. In the last year of the decade, 300,000 young people gathered at Woodstock, a music festival in upstate New York, to celebrate life and hope for peace. In that same year, 1969, Chicago police gunned down Black Panthers Fred Hampton and Mark Clark, and Neil Armstrong became the first man to tread on the moon.

The divisiveness of the 1960s produced terrible violence, including more assassinations. Besides

John Kennedy, the decade claimed the lives of important leaders Malcolm X, Martin Luther King, Jr., and Robert Kennedy. There was senseless violence abroad as well. In 1968, American soldiers killed five-hundred unarmed Vietnamese men, women, and children in the Vietnamese peasant village of My Lai. The violence continued into 1970, when four students protesting the Vietnam War were gunned down by the Ohio National Guard at Kent State University.

The violence was partly prompted by changes threatening the establishment, much of it springing from Vietnam War dissent and a quest for racial justice. However, other movements emerged in the 1960s that forced the nation to reassess its values and social mores. Almost single-handedly, with her publication of *The Silent Spring* in 1962, Rachael Carson launched the environmental movement, resulting in, among other things, the Clean Air Act of 1963. Three years later, in 1966, the National Organization for Women (NOW) was organized to promote women's rights. The American Indian Movement's foundation followed in 1968, fighting for the rights of Native Americans. The next year, 1969, at a bar in New York, the so-called Stonewall Rebellion initiated a crusade for gay rights and equality before the law.

Culturally, the 1960s were also a decade of great change. Rock music became the most popular form, turning artists like the Beatles, the Rolling Stones, Jimi Hendrix, Janis Joplin into icons for a generation. Film also evolved into a social voice, as independent productions such as *Easy Rider, Medium Cool,* and *Zabriskie Point* spoke directly to the youth culture. In theater, the Off- and Off-Off-Broadway movements were thriving, introducing important new voices like Edward Albee, Sam Shepard, and Kopit. Dramatic works like the rock-musical *Hair* (1968) broke down barriers against such things as on-stage nudity and obscene language and openly assaulted the values of the establishment. In general, the arts reflected the new political and social currents and helped foster change.

CRITICAL OVERVIEW

Kopit's *Oh Dad* has the distinction of being a relatively rare phenomenon: an extremely successful first work staged in New York by a new and virtually unknown playwright. When *Oh Dad* opened at New York's Phoenix Theatre on February 26, 1962, beginning a run of 454 performances, it already had a production history, both in the United States and abroad. In fact, the play was published in 1960, the same year in which it was first staged at Harvard and then, professionally, at the Agassiz Theatre in Cambridge, Massachusetts. It was during it's run at the Agassiz that it came to the attention of the staff of the Phoenix. Before the Phoenix mounted its extremely successful production, however, the work had already been staged in London, where it was directed by Frank Corsaro and starred Stella Adler as Madame Rosepettle.

In the New York staging, directed by Jerome Robbins, an experienced cast headed by Jo Van Fleet as Madame Rosepettle, Austin Pendleton as Jonathan, and Barbara Harris as Rosalie kept audiences delighted, making it a major box-office success. It also garnered the Vernon Rice and Outer Circle Awards, both significant honors.

Still, the play proved to be something of an embarrassment for some commentators, though none of them had enough influence to put out the Phoenix's lights in the critical first month of the production. Some of the critical reception placed Kopit's play at the center of a minor controversy lying at the base of Martin Esslin's brief observations on the work in his landmark study *The Theatre of the Absurd.* For Esslin, *Oh Dad* illustrated "how difficult it seems in America to use the convention of the Theatre of the Absurd," as if, like fine French wines, the techniques of the absurd dramatists simply did not travel well, as if, in fact, such techniques lost their serious purpose in America.

For many hostile critics, Kopit's play simply lacked the metaphysical implications of the European brand of absurdism, its apocalyptic vision and existential ennui, thereby turning (in their estimation) *Oh Dad* into superficial silly-putty, a watered-down variation on the genre, or what a reviewer in *Theatre Arts* termed "theatre of the absurd, junior grade." To the *Commonweal*'s Richard Gilman, in trying to emulate the masters of the Theatre of the Absurd, Kopit produced an example of "the merely foolish," a work in which "there is no sense of ideas at work and there is assuredly nothing metaphysical, and nothing mysterious." A similar complaint was made by Robert Brustein in the *New Republic,*, who claimed that with Kopit's play "the avant-garde fashion turns chi-chi." In imitating the avant-garde dramatists, stated Brustein, the playwright "tends to reduce the Absurd to the ridiculous."

Even in some favorable assessments of *Oh Dad* Kopit is warned of the risks of imitation. The *New York Times*'s Howard Taubman, who saw Kopit's potential as "an important playwright," opined that the day must come when "imitators of a fashionable style are revealed as charlatans," a time of judgment when "an all-encompassing revulsion may set in." The critical caveat often made is that Kopit should strive to be less derivative, particularly as the fashionable string of the Theatre of the Absurd was quickly playing itself out. Yet, at the same time, Kopit was praised for his comic genius, something that is purely instinctive and can not be derived, even in parody. Despite the luggage Kopit borrowed from the Theatre of the Absurd, many critics, like Priscilla Buckley in the *National Review,* found him "a truly original and comic playwright."

In *Oh Dad* Henry Hewes of the *Saturday Review* saw a play "full of opportunity for stage fun." While admitting that Kopit's technique is borrowed, the critic also found great originality in the playwright's subject and theme, "the area he so brilliantly, entertainingly, and cruelly explores." For Hewes, the play was the best thing seen at the Phoenix in several seasons.

If some critics at the time viewed *Oh Dad* as a rather sophomoric romp and Kopit himself as a sort of artistic *enfant terrible,* the playwright's succeeding works, beginning with *Indians* (1968), quickly forced some re-assessments and from some of the original nay sayers, including Brustein, a begrudging apology. Fears that Kopit's parodic pilfering from absurdists and other dramatists, including Tennessee Williams, would turn him into a theatrical flash in the pan were quickly dispelled. The playwright simply set out in new directions, as he has done throughout his career; he has repeatedly proven himself one of the most innovative and experimental playwrights in American theater and one of its most deliberate and careful craftsmen. *Oh Dad* is still viewed as a play that shows the dramatist's great comic promise, creative elan, and failsafe theatrical sense. It is also a play that, like Rosepettle's corpse, keeps popping up on stage.

CRITICISM

John W. Fiero

Fiero is a retired Ph. D. and former teacher of drama and playwriting at the University of Southwestern Louisiana. In this essay he examines Oh Dad *as parodic satire using the techniques of what Kopit himself, in the play's subtitle, called "a bastard French tradition."*

More than any other commercially successful American play identified with the Theatre of the Absurd, Arthur Kopit's *Oh Dad, Poor Dad, Mamma's Hung You in the Closet and I'm Feelin' So Sad* exemplifies a widely-held belief among experimental playwrights: the social and political climate of America in the early-1960s was inhospitable to the reputed nihilism underlying the tragic farces of European playwrights of the absurd like Samuel Beckett, Arthur Adamov, and Eugene Ionesco. What was clearly missing in the post-World War II American consciousness was the pervasive existential despair and pessimism left in the wake of the war's death and destruction—a condition from which the civilian United States was largely insulated but from which most Europeans had been unable to escape or hide.

Although not expressed in such terms, that view seems to lie behind much of the criticism directed at American artists influenced by the European avant garde. For Richard Gilman, writing in *Commonweal,* what distinguished "the absurd from the merely foolish" was, in the final analysis, a sense of the absurd "in a metaphysical and not just a behavioral sense." Kopit's *Oh Dad* seemed to exemplify the problem for some early commentators, who claimed that although the playwright successfully aped the manner of the "bastard French tradition" in the play, he did so superficially, achieving form without substance, shock without meaning, and laughter without reflection. The *New Republic*'s Robert Brustein, for example, opined that Kopit merely evidenced "a desire to join a parade rather than to communicate a unique vision," a deficiency that tended only "to reduce the Absurd to the ridiculous."

The point, to a degree, is justly made. The world most often evoked by European absurdists, especially Beckett and Ionesco, is either a desolate or senseless world or sometimes both, as it is in Beckett's *Waiting for Godot* (1952) and *Endgame* (1957). In this world, humanity seems like it is being herded towards the mass grave of an extermination camp, where naked bodies are dumped to tumble over each other like discarded manikins. It is a world in which life or death become indifferent choices, for it is less a world than a spiritual void,

WHAT DO I READ NEXT?

- Philip Wylie's *Generation of Vipers* (1942) offers a jaundiced view of the American values, institutions, and traditions, including what he calls ''momism,'' the hypocritical American mother, and sexual mores.

- Terance McNally's *And Things That Go Bump in the Night* (1964) is a play that, like *Oh Dad,* has absurd, nightmarish elements and deals with a dysfunctional family.

- Edward Albee's plays *The American Dream* (1961) and *Who's Afraid of Virginia Woolf?* (1962) are contemporaries of *Oh Dad* and invite comparison with Kopit's play in respect to both theme and technique.

- Arthur Adamov's absurdist plays *Les Retrouvailles* (''The Recovered,'' 1952) and *Comme Nous Avons Ete* (''As We Were,'' 1953), like Kopit's *Oh Dad,* examine the theme of destructive parental control.

---

one in which, as in Ionesco's *The Lesson* (1950), authority has devolved into a mere exercise of brutal, dehumanizing, and meaningless power exercised over and over.

Kopit's *Oh Dad* does seem far removed from that sort of apocalyptic vision. Still, the playwright never indicated that his purpose in constructing the play was to present such a world. Moreover, he does not try to convey a sense that the world that he does create is *the* world, that it is a microcosmic representation of humanity's common plight in a purposeless universe. He simply uses absurdist techniques in a parody that approaches burlesque— though a parody deliberately more of manner than of matter. His purpose is not in the least metaphysical; it is, first and foremost, satirical. That was Kopit's choice, and it seems only fair to approach his work on his own terms.

And *Oh Dad* is pungent and savage satire. Madame Rosepettle is almost pure caricature, a monster mother who turns her child into a neurotic bundle of fears that bar any progress he might otherwise make towards maturity. She is an outrageous, otherworldly character, but she is very, very funny. Furthermore, Kopit's lack of metaphysical concerns not withstanding, in the figures of Madame Rosepettle and Jonathan as well as the plot of *Oh Dad* the playwright does in truth address at least some of the same thematic concerns of first-genera-

tion Theatre of the Absurd writers. As Doris Auerbach pointed out in *Sam Shepard, Arthur Kopit, and the Off Broadway Theater,* like Ionesco, Kopit spoofs the tendency of social-thesis drama to lean too heavily on psychological plausibility and confirms that language is more often than not a barrier to human communication.

Like Arthur Adamov, another bona fide charter member of the Theatre of the Absurd, the playwright also attacks the overly-protective mother who tries to keep her son from experiencing a mature, sexual relationship with a member of the opposite sex. Kopit rolls two stereotypes into the single figure of the widow Rosepettle, however, for she is also a frigid, castrating bitch goddess, incapable of any normal kind of love. Her favorite pastime, besides measuring yachts (a blatant symbol for the male genitalia she wishes to destroy), is to patrol resort beaches with a large flashlight to find lovers to annoy by kicking sand on them. She despises sex as something dirty and unwholesome, and, if she could, she would rid the world of its blight. Her strategy in Jonathan's case is to frustrate his procreative instincts by keeping the nasty world of sex beyond locked doors and filling his mind with her poisonous ideas.

Kopit uses parody trenchantly, depicting the destructive effect of such excessive parental control and violent anti-sexuality through hilarious exaggeration. Yet it is precisely this hilarity that gives some critics pause in considering the play. There is about *Oh Dad* a comic gusto that blunted and disguised the work's serious assault on the American Mom, a figure that since the 1960s has been roasted to pieces, even in the holiest of holies, television sitcoms (see Peg Bundy, the inept nurturer of *Married with Children*). When Kopit took on the maternal archetype in 1960, she still had her sacrosanct image largely in tact, modern psychology (ie, psychoanalyst Sigmund Freud's Oedipal theories) notwithstanding.

The result seems to have been a discomforting uneasiness in the laughter Kopit evoked in his play. Somehow it did not seem quite right to find Madame Rosepettle and her antics as funny as they appear. Some reviewers even seemed guilty of some critical misdirection, finding the chief fun in the play in its spectacle and giving almost exclusive credit to the production cast and technicians for the play's popular success. Gilman, for example, while admitting that the staged play had "engaging moments," claimed that they were "more a matter of performances and decor than of any intrinsic excellence." "Verbally," for the critic, the play had "almost no existence at all."

A playwright's contributions to a play are not limited to its words, however. Kopit's imaginative vision included all the major non-verbal elements and special effects. These, clearly tied to his text, are not a production staff's invention. Furthermore, they have a definite organic function, particularly Madame Rosepettle's bizarre pets—an outlandish extension of the woman's own all-consuming nature; the pets are omnivores ready to pounce on and devour any victim, including Jonathan. The creatures are not present simply "to hide the thinness and immaturity of the play," as Brustein claimed.

Moreover, as Harold Clurman argued in the *Nation,* the shocking subject—the castrating, overly-protective mother—is blunted by being "masked in extravagant paradox, magical (visual) stage tricks and festively macabre color."

The play, after all, is not just parody and satire, it is also a nightmarish fantasy with many surrealistic elements. There is even a cartoon quality to the work, at least until Madame Rosepettle begins her rambling confessional to the Commodore in the last scene of the play. The action even seems "framed" by the play's non-verbal elements: the garish, psychedelic colors that intrude from outside with neon intensity and the exotic music with its primitive beat that suggests a torrid world beyond the cage in which Jonathan is held, a virtual prisoner of his mother's misanthropy.

The action, always bordering on lunacy, also has a cartoon-like illogicality. Things happen for which there is no plausible explanation. There is, for example, the body of Mr. Rosepettle, that falls from the master bedroom closet at the most inopportune moment, not just once but twice, and then, briefly but conveniently (or perhaps inconveniently), seems to come to life, strangely reanimated. Coffin handles and door knobs come off and a chair suddenly moves from under a would-be sitter as if some puckish and invisible gremlin were playing devious tricks for its own perverse delight.

Most of all, there is the animation of non-human entities: the Venus flytraps, Rosalinda the piranha, a cuckoo clock, and even windows frames. In their behavior, they all exhibit human traits. For example, in the last scene, quite inexplicably, the plants start expanding, growing from flytraps into mantraps trying to snatch and devour Jonathan. Here and elsewhere probability simply goes by the boards, as it always has in the loony-bin world of cartoons and, it should be added, in the absurd world of Ionesco, at least in a play such as *Amedee, or How to Get Rid of It* (1954), a play in which a corpse expands and threatens to shove the living characters into the wings.

As Auerbach noted, these cartoon elements offer a "perfect parody" of an absurdist strategy, the tendency to externalize inner, subconscious realities in outward projections exhibiting the irrationality of dream and fantasy, much in the manner of surrealism. Rosalinda and the plants, argued Auerbach, "concretize the dangers of maternal love and the unresolved Oedipal conflict."

A scene from director Richard Quine's film adaptation of Kopit's play

Kopit may have had no metaphysical row to hoe in *Oh Dad,* but he did have a serious purpose. In "The Vital Matter of Environment," an article he wrote for *Theatre Arts* before the play opened in London in 1961, he lamented the fact that the American playwright had to work in a "creative environment" that was inimical to innovation. Moreover, he insisted that theater in America had "been singularly outstanding in its inability to assimilate traditions," unlike theater in Europe.

In creating *Oh Dad,* Kopit was attempting to assimilate the new tradition of the European avant garde, fitting it to a theme relevant to his own creative environment. He was also countering what he called "a Puritan-influenced attitude toward the theatre" in America, the strong current against which the Off-Broadway, alternative theater movement was resolutely moving.

It is ironic that the prevalent American optimism of the early-1960s began eroding soon after the successful New York run of *Oh Dad* ended. Images of senseless and violent death—whether in Dallas (the assassination of President Kennedy) or Saigon (the first stirrings of the Vietnam War)—courtesy of the evening television news, began putting the country much closer to the heart and soul of the absurd.

For Kopit, however, it was a bit too late. The absurd had in fact become passe and had jumped from the fringe into the mainstream. Kopit, with a seemingly bottomless bag of new tricks, absorbed what he had learned through parodic imitation and simply moved on, becoming over his long career one of the most diverse and innovative playwrights in the American theater.

Source: John W. Fiero, for *Drama for Students,* Gale, 2000.

Arthur Ballet

Ballet provides an overview of Kopit's farce in this essay, explicating the plot and offering a brief history of the play's creation.

The setting is a lavish suite in a Caribbean hotel, where Madame Rosepettle, her son Jonathan, and her dead husband (in a coffin) as well as their very large, carnivorous plants and assorted treasure, have ensconced themselves. Entering their restricted quarters is Commodore Roseabove, who attempts to court Madame Rosepettle, followed by Rosalie, who seduces and tries to free the imprisoned Jonathan from his mother. In addition to this collection of characters, there are a platoon of bellboys as well as Rosalinda, the rare (and talking) goldfish, which apparently eats cats voraciously.

> *OH DAD, POOR DAD,* REMAINS
> A FUNNY, SOMETIMES SURPRISING
> AND STARTLING REACTION BY A
> YOUNG WRITER AGAINST PARENTAL
> DOMINATION."

This peculiar, not to say zany, ménage has intimations of something more, and in the 1960's it seemed very avant-garde to some scholars and no doubt to much of its Broadway audience. A number of writers put the play into the absurdist camp, and perhaps it belongs there still, but for all those dark implications it seems to have settled into being accepted simply as a "farce in three scenes", which is all that Mr. Kopit claims for it.

Jonathan, a stuttering, frightened young man, lives out his meager life by looking out at the world through binoculars, and he sees a world, into which his mother has forbidden him to venture. And then Rosalie enters: vamp and liberator who comes over to flirt and eventually lure Jonathan into bed in the very room where Dad is stuffed in the closet. The goofy actions of the beginning of the play in time give way to both long monologues and to some serious (or at least gruesome) goings on. The plants, for example, must not be put "close together . . . they fight". Jonathan is terrified, it would seem with good reason, of everything and everyone, especially of Mother, the indomitable Madame. Exaggeration, of course, is the manner in which the play is cast, but at its heart there is a reality which is both recognizable and horrifying.

Jonathan tries to avoid this reality by constantly having "so much to do". There is here, it seems, an echo of Tennessee Williams's *The Glass Menagerie* and of its pathetic Laura. Instead of a unicorn to keep him from truly experiencing life, Jonathan has his stamps, his plants to feed, his coins to examine, and above all his spying on Rosalie, the baby-sitter across the street. He will do almost anything to avoid facing the facts of his closed world. When he is asked why he never goes out, he responds, "Because Mother locks the door".

Not surprisingly, Rosalie notices that "there's something very strange here". This is not a normal family by any standard, and the farce challenges the concept of "normality" and effectively exposes major eccentricities which may be funny to the outsider but terribly destructive to the intimates. Madame Rosepettle philosophizes that, in any event, "life is a lie" and that one must be very careful, for life " isn't what it seems"—implicating both the shenanigans on stage and in the audience's world in her comment.

Audiences today may find the play nothing more than an undergraduate prank by Arthur Kopit, who has since moved on to more serious theatre writing. But *Oh Dad, Poor Dad,* remains a funny, sometimes surprising and startling reaction by a young writer against parental domination. "True love" in the form of the alluring Rosalie, who may be an innocent or may be a slut, liberates the young Jonathan (perhaps, by extension, all youngsters) from the mad, material restrictions of his mother. When the outraged Madame Rosepettle discovers the seduction of her son, she announces that "this place is a madhouse" and she is quite right. By the end of the play Jonathan, the sweet *naif,* has destroyed the plants, the goldfish, his own hopes for liberation, *and* poor Rosalie, leaving Madame Rosepettle asking: "What is the meaning of all this?"

Source: Arthur Ballet, *Oh Dad, Poor Dad, Mamma's Hung You in the Closet and I'm Feelin' So Sad"* in *The International Dictionary of Theatre,* Volume 1: *Plays,* edited by Mark Hawkins-Dady, St. James Press, 1992, pp. 567–68.

Robert Brustein

In this short essay, Brustein examines Kopit's dramatic career as of 1966. In addition to discussing the playwright's other work to date, he touches on the significance of Oh Dad.

Kopit also borrows avant-garde techniques without adding anything original of his own, but whereas Schisgal wants to entertain the middle classes, Kopit wants to ridicule them: his short pieces are semi-disguised acts of aggression against the very, domestic values Schisgal celebrates. Kopit's derision, however, is often combined with petulance, and since it is primarily aimed against overprotective mothers and insensitive fathers, it hardly seems very daring or brave. There is something a little juvenile about Kopit's writing; for him, the theater is mainly a medium for pranks, an intention he suggests in his looping, longitudinal titles. In his most notorious work, *Oh Dad, Poor Dad, Mamma's Hung You in the Closet and I'm Feelin' So Sad,* the title is ultimately the most revealing part of the play, since it sums up this author's major characteristics: his Oedipal fixation, his hatred of maternal women, his skittishness, his black humor, and, especially, his nostalgia for childhood. The play itself is an exercise in the absurdist mode which borrows freely from various avant-garde styles, blends in the fruity atmosphere of a Tennessee Williams play, and comes off as a curious mixture of satire, irony, fantasy, and farce. Kopit is most interesting when he is most outrageous—the funniest scene in the play concerns a young boy and girl prevented from making love by a corpse which keeps falling on top of them—but aside from this brief necrophiliac episode and a few other isolated passages, the play fails to rise above a certain brittle archness.

The two short plays that follow this famous sketch are also limited by deficiencies in attitude and feeling. *Sing to Me Through Open Windows* is a fantasy of childhood about a sensitive boy, a cute clown, and a wise old man which is embarrassing in its cloying sentimentality: the sort of thing that appeals to drama coaches in boys' camps and elocution schools. *The Day the Whores Came Out To Play Tennis,* though facile in its satire, is a better work, and its basic notion—that a group of prostitutes should attempt to wreck a country club by hitting tennis balls against it—is wacky enough to promise real amusement. But once again, the author is unable to sustain his action or to find a meaningful target for attack: the crude manners of wealthy country club Jews are hardly a universal subject for satire. Kopit has wit, a good sense of the bizarre, and a developing satirical talent, but he is still impeded by a certain undergraduate peevishness and cuteness.

Source: Robert Brustein, ''Arthur Kopit'' in *Modern Occasions,* selected and edited by Philip Rahv, Farrar, Straus, and Giroux, 1966, pp. 133–34.

Alan Lewis

In this excerpt from his book, Lewis discusses the unique nature of Kopit's play, noting in particular its ''grotesque, surrealist attack on sex, mother, and the devouring female.''

Arthur Kopit, a recent Harvard graduate, created a sensation with his first play *Oh Dad, Poor Dad, Mamma's Hung You in the Closet, and I'm Feeling So Sad,* which is subtitled ''A Pseudoclassical Tragifarce in a Bastard French Tradition.'' A fortunate combination of circumstances also helped in the success of his first venture. Jerome Robbins, well-known choreographer, directed the play and achieved movement close to modern ballet, which

> KOPIT'S DERISION IS OFTEN COMBINED WITH PETULANCE, AND SINCE IT IS PRIMARILY AIMED AGAINST OVERPROTECTIVE MOTHERS AND INSENSITIVE FATHERS, IT HARDLY SEEMS VERY DARING OR BRAVE.''

the play required. Josephine Van Fleet, a resourceful actress, romped through the leading role with bravura vindictiveness, ably assisted by Barbara Harris, a rising talent in the American stage and the most successful of the recent graduates from the little theatres.

The play is unique for many reasons. It is a grotesque, surrealist attack on sex, mother, and the devouring female. The characters are comic-strip exaggerations, symbolic and ludicrous on the level of a grand hoax or a sophomoric parody of Tennessee Williams, Ionesco, and all avant-garde writers. On stage, it is a technician's delight, with its Venus's-flytraps that grow larger and the piranha fish which has spoken lines, doors that open and close on their own power, chairs that slide away or remain fixed, and a corpse that embraces the young Rosalie as she attempts her seduction of Jonathan.

Kopit's titles for his earlier student plays were preparations for the long-winded nonsense of this fantasy of cannibalism and mockery of romance. The names of many of the characters begin with the prefix Rose. Madame Rosepettle says she wanted her husband to be ''Mine, all mine—mine to love, mine to live with, mine to kill; my husband my lover my own . . . *my very own.*'' She achieved her purpose by murdering him, and now drags his corpse around with her on her travels as a physical symbol of her triumph. She keeps her son Jonathan at the perpetual age of ten, warding off the destroying problems of growing up. She amuses herself by kicking sand in lovers' faces on the beach, and lures Commodore Roseabove into a disillusioning and embarrassing tête-a-tête. Rosalie, a constant teenager, tries to win possession of men by being all sex. She would seduce Jonathan and free him from his mother's hold so that she can possess him complete-

❝ THE CHARACTERS ARE
COMIC-STRIP EXAGGERATIONS,
SYMBOLIC AND LUDICROUS ON THE
LEVEL OF A GRAND HOAX."

ly. The women do not always triumph. In the end, as Rosalie manages to get Jonathan on his mother's bed, the father's corpse hops out of the closet, falls between them, and raises a dead hand in warning to Jonathan. Rosalie is suffocated under the stamp and coin collection.

The form of the play is a single conceit developed in multiple ramifications, a succession of tricks which grow thin and repetitious. Madame Rosepettle essays a serious explanatory note, which sounds hollow when surrounded by the high jinks that keep the play bubbling. Instead of confessing on a couch to her analyst, Madame Rosepettle confesses on her feet to her captive lover:

> "... it is I who have saved him [her son]. Saved him from the world beyond that door. . . . A world waiting to devour those who trust in it . . . A world vicious under the hypocrisy of kindness, ruthless under the falseness of a smile. . . . A Leave my room and enter your world again, Mr. Roseabove—your sex-driven, dirt-washed waste of cannibals eating each other up while they pretend they're kissing. Go, Mr. Roseabove, enter your blind world of darkness."

The play is far too discursive, and incompatible with Rosalie's more direct, "Take off your clothes. . . . Drop your pants on top of him [your father], then you won't see his face."

As a first play, *Oh Dad, Poor Dad* was a lighthearted contribution on a much overworked theme. It perhaps would have been better as a long, concentrated, one-act play. A college-boy hoax on the present trend of being anti-woman, anti-sex, and anti-life can be amusing for a short time. Kopit now faces the tensions imposed on the writer of a first-play success. He wrote two short one-acters, *The Day the Whores Came Out to Play Tennis* and *Mhil'daiim,* which were scheduled for production at the University of Minnesota but withdrawn when the issue of obscenity was raised. When presented at the Actors Studio, they elicited little enthusiasm. Another full-length play, *Asylum or What the Gentlemen Are Up To Not to Mention the Ladies,* which

he describes as a sinister comedy dealing with the transformation of a man from sanity to insanity, has had production problems and has been withdrawn by the author for further revisions.

Kopit's first efforts are insufficient for definitive judgment. If he can sustain the macabre laughter at the expense of our sacred cows, he may become a valued demonic clown, but he is too preoccupied with his personal and seemingly sensational rebellion.

Source: Alan Lewis, "New-Play Madness and Some New Voices" in his *American Plays and Playwrights of the Contemporary Theatre,* Crown (New York), 1965, pp. 200–02.

SOURCES

Brustein, Robert. "The Absurd and the Ridiculous" in the *New Republic,* Vol. CXLVI, March 19, 1962, p. 31.

Buckley, Priscilla L. "Well Now, Let's See . . ." in the *National Review,* Vol. XII, June 6, 1962, p. 416.

Clurman, Harold. Review of *Oh Dad* in the *Nation,* Vol. CXCIV, March 31, 1962, p. 289.

Gilman, Richard. "The Stage: The Absurd and the Foolish" in the *Commonweal,* Vol. LXXVI, April 6, 1962, pp. 40-41.

Hewes, Henry. "The Square Fellow" in the *Saturday Review,* Vol. XLV, March 17, 1962, p. 35.

Review of *Oh Dad* in *Theatre Arts,* Vol. IL, May, 1962, p. 61.

Taubman, Howard. "One Work at a Time" in the *New York Times,* March 11, 1962, p. 1.

FURTHER READING

Auerbach, Doris. *Sam Shepard, Arthur Kopit, and the Off-Broadway Theater,* Twayne, 1982.
    Besides offering useful critical analyses of Kopit's early work, especially *Oh Dad, Indians, The Day the Whores Came Out to Play Tennis,* and *Wings,* this study has an important chapter surveying the history of the Off-Broadway Theatre.

Bordman, Gerald. *American Theatre: A Chronicle of Comedy and Drama, 1930-1969,* Oxford University Press, 1996.
    This work documents the production history of American theater over four decades and provides a good survey of the dramatic milieu in which Kopit and other early American absurdists wrote. For Bordman, the American theater went into a decline in the 1960s, after having passed through "Golden" and "Silver" periods.

Esslin, Martin. *The Theatre of the Absurd,* 3rd edition, Peregrine, 1987.

> Important chapters on the absurdity, tradition, and significance of the absurd remain mandatory for an understanding of the aims and methods of those writers lumped under the absurd rubric by Esslin. In ''Parallels and Proselytes,'' Esslin gives Kopit early notice as an American example, along with Edward Albee and Jack Gelber.

Kopit, Arthur. ''The Vital Matter of Environment'' in *Theatre Arts,* Vol. XLV, April, 1961, pp. 12-13.

> In this brief article, Kopit offers important insights into the state of the American commercial theater—its ''inability to assimilate traditions'' and its lack of invention. Although not an artistic manifesto, the article reveals the playwright's mind set at the time *Oh Dad* was being readied for its London production.

Little, Stuart W. *Off Broadway: The Prophetic Theater,* Coward, McCann, & Geoghegan, 1972.

> Little's study is a documentary history and useful guide to the Off-Broadway movement from 1952-1972, the period during which Kopit rose to prominence.

Wellworth, George. *The Theater of Protest and Paradox,* New York University Press, 1964.

> This study discusses the new, alternative theater of the 1950s and early-1960s and is valuable for its coverage of the early critical responses to *Oh Dad.*

Peter Pan

SIR J(AMES) M. BARRIE
1904

Peter Pan, which was alternately titled "The Boy Who Would Not Grow Up," was first performed in London, England, on December 27, 1904, at the Duke of York Theatre. It has since become one of the most widely performed and adapted children's stories in the world. It is also Barrie's best-known work, though he was a prolific author writing in a number of genres. Critics believe that one reason *Peter Pan* was successful from the first is that Barrie combined fantasy and adventure in a way not done before. The play offers a fresh means of storytelling that appeals to both adults and children. While children enjoy the imaginative story and flights of fancy, adults can relate to Peter Pan's desire to forego mature responsibilities and live in the moment. Roger Lancelyn Green wrote in his book *Fifty Years of Peter Pan:* "*Peter Pan* is the only children's play that is also a great work of literature."

The text of the play has evolved since it was first performed in 1904. The original stage production of *Peter Pan* was only three acts. Barrie let the story grow through several novels and different versions of the stage play to arrive at a standardized text by 1928. The playwright claimed that he did not remember writing the play, which began as a backyard amusement for some of his young friends. After its London debut, *Peter Pan* became an annual Christmas event in that city's theater district for several decades. The play has also been adapted into a musical stage version as well as several different kinds of movies. Ironically, considering the play's

prominent theme of motherhood, Peter Pan is tradi-tionally played by a young woman, while Nana the dog is usually played by a man in a dog suit.

AUTHOR BIOGRAPHY

J. M. Barrie was born on May 9, 1860, in Kirriemuir, Scotland, a village located in the Lowlands. He was the son of a poor weaver, David, and his wife, Margaret Ogilvy Barrie. Barrie was the second youngest of ten children and one of only several to survive infancy. Barrie's mother ensured that he received an education, and the playwright eventual-ly received his M.A. from Edinburgh University in 1882. After Barrie's elder brother and Margaret Barrie's favorite son died when Barrie was six, he took it upon himself to take his brother's place. The author's relationship with his mother was unusually close and was often based in a fantasy world due to Margaret's bedridden condition. Barrie's complex relationship with his mother is thought by many to be the inspiration for the mother-worship that critics feel is central to *Peter Pan.*

Barrie began his writing career as a journalist soon after graduation from Edinburgh, first in Nottingham, then back in Scotland, and finally, London. In the late-1880s, Barrie published several novels and short stories. His first bestseller was 1891's *The Little Minister.* In that same year Barrie began writing plays and playlets, beginning with a one-act burlesque entitled *Ibsen's Ghost, or, Toole up to Date.* After successfully turning *The Little Minister* into a play in 1897, Barrie focused almost exclusively on the theatre. From 1901 until 1920, he wrote one play per year. One of Barrie's most famous plays during this period was 1902's *The Admirable Crichton,* a combination of fantasy and social commentary. These same elements were em-ployed in Barrie's best–known work—and his only play intended explicitly for a young audience— *Peter Pan,* first produced in 1904.

The play had its roots in a novel Barrie pub-lished in 1902, *Little White Bird,* written for some young friends of Barrie, the Davies. Barrie met the family in London's Kensington Gardens in 1897 and was immediately enamored with the three young boys, George, Jack, and Peter, as well as their mother, Sylvia. Barrie befriended the family, spend-ing considerable time with them over the years (the head of the Davies household, Arthur Davies, did not always like the situation but tolerated it nonethe-

J. M. Barrie

less). Barrie worshiped Sylvia much like he did his own mother. This relationship was developed to the exclusion of Barrie's wife, the actress Mary Ansell, whom he had married in 1894. They divorced in 1909, their marriage apparently unconsummated. In many ways, Barrie was like Peter Pan, a man who had not fully matured.

After *Peter Pan* and several novelizations of the story, Barrie continued writing notable plays. Most were adult dramas and comedies that fre-quently played with fantasy, including *Dear Brutus* (1917). Barrie's success as a playwright allowed him to be generous with funds, and he gave often to individuals as well as important causes. Barrie ceased to write plays until a year before his death when he suddenly produced two Biblical dramas. Barrie died on June 19, 1937, in London.

PLOT SUMMARY

Act I

Peter Pan opens in the nursery of the Darling family household in Bloomsbury, London. The family is somewhat impoverished, employing Nana, a Newfoundland dog, as the three children's nurse.

When the play's action begins, Nana is putting the youngest Darling child, Michael to bed, while Mrs. Darling prepares to go out for dinner with her husband. Wendy and John, the eldest and middle, respectively, play at being their parents for her. While Nana sees to the children. Mrs. Darling confides to her husband that she saw the face of a little boy at the window trying to get in and that she has seen it before. She almost caught him once but only managed to snare his shadow, which she has kept rolled up in a drawer. Mrs. Darling also describes a ball of light accompanying him.

Mr. Darling declares that he is sick of Nana working in the nursery and takes her to be tied up in the yard. Wendy hears Nana's barking, noting that the sound is one of danger and warning, not unhappiness. Despite her reservations about leaving her brood, Mrs. Darling tucks the children in bed and departs, turning out their light as she goes. Right after she leaves, Tinkerbell and Peter Pan enter, looking for Peter's shadow. Peter finds the shadow but cannot reattach it. His efforts awaken Wendy. She learns that he does not have a mother and that she must never touch him. She finally realizes that he cannot reattach his shadow, and she sews it back on for him. She tries to kiss him, but he is ignorant of this simple display of affection. Instead, he gives Wendy an acorn button which she puts around her neck. He tells her about fairies and the Lost Boys and introduces her to Tinkerbell.

Peter reveals that none of the Lost Boys have mothers, so he comes to the Darling children's window to hear their stories and relate them to his friends. Wendy says that she knows lots of stories, so Peter teaches her how to fly so she can come to Never Land and tell stories to the Lost Boys. She insists that her brothers learn to fly as well, though Peter is not as interested in teaching them. Peter blows fairy dust on them and the children fly away to Never Land. Mr. and Mrs. Darling come home to find their children's beds empty.

Act II

In Never Land, the Lost Boys wait for Peter to return. They discuss their fear of pirates and how they do not remember their mothers. The pirates approach, lead by Captain Hook, and the boys hide in the trees. Captain Hook orders his crew to look for the boys, especially their leader, Peter Pan, because he cut Hook's arm off and the Captain wants revenge. Hook decides to catch the boys by leaving poisoned cake out that will kill them. Tiger Lily and her band of Indians make a brief appearance, and they see the pirates. They decide that they will scalp them when they catch them.

Following the pirates' departure and Peter and the Darling children's arrival, the Lost Boys emerge from their hiding places. Tinkerbell tricks the boys into shooting an arrow at Wendy. Wendy falls to the ground and seems dead. Peter lands. Wendy is very much alive: the arrow hit the acorn button Peter gave her. Tinkerbell is unhappy to learn that Wendy is alive, and Peter sends her away.

Peter decides that they will build a house around the still-prostrate Wendy. While Peter and the Lost Boys gather material, Michael and John land. They cannot believe where they are, and Peter shortly employs them in the building of their house. Once the structure is built around her, Wendy wakes up. Everyone begs her to be their mother. After a moment of hesitation, she agrees and begins to tell them the story of Cinderella.

Act III

Peter and the boys play in the Mermaid's Lagoon, trying unsuccessfully to catch a mermaid to show Wendy. Peter tells Wendy about Marooners' Rock, where sailors are left to die by drowning in the tide. The boys sense danger, and they all hide underwater. Two of Hook's pirates show up with a captive Tiger Lily and her Indians. They leave their captives on the rock. Peter imitates Captain Hook's voice and tells the pirates to untie their prisoners. The pirates follow his orders and release Tiger Lily, but the real Captain Hook arrives.

Hook tells his pirates that the boys have found a mother and that all is lost. One of Hook's men suggests that they capture Wendy and all the boys, kill the boys, then make Wendy their mother. Hook learns of the voice, Peter's, that commanded them to free Tiger Lily and communicates with it. Peter tells Hook that he is Hook. The real Hook asks many questions, but cannot figure the situation out. Finally, Peter tells Hook who he is, and leads an attack on the pirates. All the boys, except Peter, manage to capture the pirates dinghy and float away. Wendy and Peter are left stuck on the rock. The tide starts to come in, and Wendy makes her escape by holding on to the tail of a kite. Peter stays behind, hiding in a floating bird's nest.

Act IV

All of the children manage to make it back to their underground home. Tiger Lily and her Indians guard the children from the pirates above ground.

Wendy has done the laundry and is serving the boys, save Peter, a pretend meal, as is done in New Land. The boys bicker among themselves, and it is revealed that Wendy regards Peter as the father of the bunch.

Peter returns and greets the Indians, thanking them for guarding his home. While the boys get ready for bed, Peter is concerned that it is only "pretend" that he is the father. When Wendy questions him, he tells her that he feels like her son, not the father to her mother. The boys return and under Wendy's orders, climb into bed. The story she tells them is about her own home—her father, mother, and Nana—and her brothers immediately recognize it. Wendy ends the story by saying that she knows the mother is leaving the window open for the children, hoping they will return and fly through it. But when she implies that she and her brothers will eventually return, Peter is unhappy. Despite this, Wendy decides that they will return to their parents. She asks Peter to make the appropriate arrangements.

Tinkerbell is to guide the Darlings home, but she tries to refuse the task. The boys beg Wendy not to leave, but she quiets them by telling them to come back with her. Her parents, she is sure, will adopt the Lost Boys. Peter refuses to join them, though Wendy wants him to come along as well. As Tinkerbell leads them away, the Pirates attack the Indians, many of whom perish. Hook's crew takes Tiger Lily and several others prisoners. Hook has other pirates wait, and when Peter is deceived into believing the attack is over, everyone leaves. Captain Hook is right there and everyone, except Peter who is asleep, has been captured. Tinkerbell wakes Peter and tells him what has happened. Peter vows to rescue Wendy.

Act V, scene 1

On the pirate ship, Hook is happy, convinced that Peter is dead from the poison he left. Hook calls up the prisoners, telling them that six will walk the plank but two can become his cabin-boys. The boys refuse to work for him, and Wendy is brought up to witness their deaths.

Unbeknownst to Hook, Peter is swimming the waters around the ship, pretending to be a crocodile (the animal Hook most fears). Tinkerbell's light flits around, distracting the pirates, while Peter climbs aboard and hides in the cabin. Hook orders one of his men to fetch the cat, but the pirate does not return for he is killed in the cabin. Hook sends

several other men inside, and they are all killed. This scares the pirates and they believe they are doomed. The boys are driven into the cabin, Peter releases their manacles, and they find hiding places from which to attack.

Hook decides to throw Wendy overboard to change their luck. Peter reveals himself then, and the boys attack. The battle finally comes down to Peter and Hook in a sword fight. When that reaches a stalemate, Hook arranges for the ship to be blown up in two minutes. Peter finds the bomb in time. Hook is finally defeated and eaten by a crocodile.

Act V, scene 2

In the Darling household nursery, Mrs. Darling waits for her children's return. Mr. Darling and Nana have switched places for his earlier actions which led to the loss of their children. Peter precedes the children and convinces Tinkerbell to bar the window to the nursery shut so the children will think they are unwanted. When he hears Mrs. Darling's sorrow, he opens the window again, and the children return. Michael and John are momentarily disoriented but decide to creep into bed. The family reunites, then brings the rest of the Lost Boys into the house.

Peter calls Wendy, and Mrs. Darling offers to adopt him, too, but he refuses. Mrs. Darling offers that Wendy can visit Peter once a year for spring cleaning.

CHARACTERS

Mr. George Darling

Mr. Darling is married to Mary Darling and is the father of the Darling children. A childish man, he is rather brusque to his children and Nana. Mr. Darling tries to trick Michael into taking his medicine by not taking his own. He also insists on tying up Nana outside which leads to Peter Pan taking the children to Never Land. Mr. Darling does pay the price in the end: he is forced to live in Nana's kennel while the children are missing. He is remorseful for his actions and is happy when they return.

John Darling

John is the middle Darling child. When *Peter Pan* opens, he does not like girls nor does he want to bathe. He plays house with his sister Wendy and

MEDIA ADAPTATIONS

- *Peter Pan* was adapted as a silent film in 1924. This version was released by Paramount and was directed by Herbert Brenon. It starred Betty Bronson as Peter Pan, Mary Brian as Wendy, and Virginia Brown Faire as Tinkerbell.

- An full-length animated version was filmed in 1953. Released by Disney, it was directed by Clyde Geronimi and Wilfred Jackson. It featured the voices of Bobby Driscoll as Peter Pan, Kathryn Beaumont as Wendy, and Hans Conreid as both Captain Hook and Mr. Darling.

- A live television version was performed on NBC in 1955, then done again live in 1956. Both versions featured Mary Martin as Peter Pan, Kathleen Nolan as Wendy, and Cyril Ritchard as Captain Hook.

- A made-for-television adaptation was shown on NBC in 1976. It featured Mia Farrow as Peter Pan and Danny Kaye as Captain Hook.

- An animated television series based on the stage play was shown in syndication in 1990. Known as *Peter Pan and the Pirates,* it featured the voice of Tim Curry as Captain Hook and Jason Mardsen as Peter Pan.

only responds positively when she announces their child is a boy. When Peter comes, John is excited to learn to fly and go to Never Land to fight pirates. Still, he is the first to want to go home when Wendy tells her story about their parents. John has a sense of pride about his heritage. He refuses to be a pirate when he learns he would have denounce the British king.

Mrs. Mary Darling

Mrs. Darling is the loving mother of the Darling children. Where her husband loses his temper, she is patient and kind with both George and the children. Mrs. Darling is the first to have noticed Peter Pan's face in the window and fears for her children's safety. She is devastated when her worst fears are confirmed and is ecstatic when they return.

Michael Darling

Michael is the youngest of the Darling children and the littlest when the arrive in Never Land. He is obstinate and does not want to go to bed or take his medicine. When Peter comes into their nursery, he is the first to fly. During the battle on the pirate ship, Michael kills a pirate. When they finally return home, Michael is slightly confused as to who his mother really is and he is also disappointed to find that his father is smaller than the pirate he killed.

Wendy Darling

Wendy Darling is a young girl for whom Peter Pan shows great affection. She is the eldest child of Mr. and Mrs. Darling. Wendy likes to play house, even before Peter convinces her to fly to Never Land. She is a fairly obedient and helpful child, mindful of her responsibilities. For example, Wendy helps her father get Michael to take his medicine and is quick to point out when her father tries to cheat. When Peter finds his shadow in a drawer and cannot reattach it, Wendy solves the problem and sews it back on for him. In Never Land, Wendy takes the role of the Lost Boys' mother very seriously, though she says she has no experience. She does her best to fulfill the role, but when she realizes how much her absence must hurt her own mother, she insists on returning home bringing along the Lost Boys so they can be adopted.

Wendy is also patient and kind. She tries to teach Peter about kissing but does not embarrass him when it is obvious he does not know what she is talking about. When Peter is uncomfortable about being the boys' father, Wendy accepts this, too. Wendy also has a whimsical side: she desperately wants to catch a mermaid.

First Twin

See The Lost Boys

Captain Jas Hook

Captain Hook is a pirate who lives in Never Land. He is the mortal enemy of Peter Pan because Peter severed his arm in a battle and fed it to a crocodile. Hook spends the play trying to enact revenge on Peter Pan and the Lost Boys. When one of his pirate band learns that Peter has Wendy, he captures her, hoping to make her the mother for the ship. Hook also succeeds in capturing the Darling brothers and the Lost Boys, but when Peter and Hook fight their final battle, Hook loses and is eaten by a crocodile.

Hunkering
See The Lost Boys

The Lost Boys

The six Lost Boys live in Never Land, and include Peter Pan among their number as their leader. They are boys who had fallen out of their carriages when their nurses were not looking. No one claimed them and after seven days, they were sent to Never Land. Since they have no mother, they are excited by Wendy's presence and do everything to please her. Following Peter's lead, they also defend her. When given the opportunity to go home and be adopted by the Darling family, they return to England.

Nana

Nana is dog employed as a nurse in the Darling household. She gives the children their medicine, puts them to bed, and tends to their needs much like a human nanny.

Nibs
See The Lost Boys

Peter Pan

Peter Pan is the ageless boy who is at the play's center. He ran away from home when he found out what kind of responsibilities he would have as an adult. He does not want to grow up at all. As the captain of the Lost Boys, however, he does lead them and tell them stories. He also takes it upon himself to find them a mother, which he does in bringing Wendy to Never Land. Despite his actions to the contrary, Peter professes his disdain for responsibility. When Wendy sets him up as the Boy's father, he does not want the position. He tells Wendy that he looks upon her as his mother also.

Peter's refusal to grow up also affects his memory. He cannot remember incidents for very long after they happen. He is also ignorant of basic human interactions such as kissing and tells Wendy he can never be touched. But Peter is not afraid to fight. When Tiger Lily is in jeopardy, he saves her.

When Wendy and the Lost Boys are captured by Captain Hook, he battles and saves them. For the most part, however, Peter is content to play his pipes and make merriment.

Second Twin
See The Lost Boys

Slightly
See The Lost Boys

Tootles
See The Lost Boys

Tiger Lily

Tiger Lily is an Indian who leads a tribe of men in Never Land. She is a friend of Peter Pan's. When he rescues her from Captain Hook, she repays the favor by guarding his underground home.

Tinkerbell

Tinkerbell is a fairy who is the size of a fist. She got her name because she mends fairy pots and kettles. She appears as a ball of light who can dart quickly around rooms, and speaks only in bells. She is attached to Peter Pan, and follows him around everywhere. Tinkerbell is rather jealous of Wendy and tries to subvert the affection Peter Pan shows for her. She also risks her life for Peter, swallowing poison meant for him.

THEMES

Sex Roles

Sex roles, especially motherhood, are explored in *Peter Pan.* Peter convinces Wendy to come to Never Land so she can see a mermaid, but he really wants her to act as a mother to himself and the Lost Boys. She is to tell them stories, like her own mother tells to her. Though Wendy admits she has no experience playing a mother role, she imitates her own mother's behavior and manages to win the boys over.

Peter is unwilling to play father to Wendy's mother, however. He will accept the role if it is just ''pretend,'' but he is unwilling to accept actual

TOPICS FOR FURTHER STUDY

- Compare and contrast the standardized dramatic text of *Peter Pan* (1928) with any of the novelizations of the Peter Pan story that Barrie wrote. How do the demands of the different literary forms affect the basic plot?

- Research societal attitudes towards women and motherhood in turn-of-the-century England. How do these attitudes compare with the depictions of women in *Peter Pan?*

- The rights to *Peter Pan* have been owned by Disney for a number of years. Research how the character and the story have been modified, particularly in reference to Disney's immensely popular animated adaptation, since the debut of the stage play in 1904.

- Compare and contrast the character of Wendy Darling in *Peter Pan* with Alice in Lewis Carroll's children's fantasy book *Alice's Adventures in Wonderland.* How are their experiences in a fantastic land similar? Different? How does the fact that these characters are female affect their fantastic experiences?

responsibility. Though the exact role of ''father'' is not clearly defined in the play—Mr. Darling is more of a temperamental child than a nurturing, paternal figure—Peter is only willing to serve as the primary defender of the Lost Boys' home, little more. He is more concerned with adventure, having fun, and fighting pirates—aspects that conveniently fit into his role as a protector. Peter does not understand what being a father means. John tells the other Lost Boys at one point, ''He did not even know how to be a father till I showed him.'' Peter tells Wendy, in roundabout fashion, that he only knows how to be a son, which frustrates other characters such as Tiger Lily.

Duty & Responsibility

Duty and responsibility—or a lack thereof—drive the actions of many characters in *Peter Pan.*

Peter Pan wants to avoid all adult responsibility and goes to great lengths to achieve this goal. He refuses to play father to Wendy's mother, uncomfortable even when pretending the role. In the end, when Wendy and her brothers decide to go back home, Peter will not let himself be adopted by the Darlings as the other Lost Boys are. If he went back, he would eventually have to grow up, assume responsibility, and become a man. This is unacceptable to Peter so he stays alone in Never Land, and Wendy comes back annually to do his spring cleaning. Despite his fear of adulthood, Peter does his duty as captain of the Lost Boys and protector of Wendy (and Tiger Lily). He rescues all of them from Captain Hook's band of pirates. He can only be responsible in these types of situations.

Conversely, Wendy, Tiger Lily, and even Captain Hook exhibit a sense of responsibility. When each is in a leadership role—be it mother, Indian chief, or head pirate—they act as their duties require them. Even the Lost Boys fulfill their responsibilities as followers of Peter. But only Wendy has a duty-related dilemma. She realizes that she is a daughter. As eldest child and the one who led her brothers away to Never Land, Wendy comes to understand that her own parents might need their children. Wendy must fulfill her role as daughter and go back home because other people, besides the Lost Boys and Peter Pan, need her. She solves her dilemma by inviting everyone to come and live with the Darling family.

Good and Evil

In *Peter Pan,* the lines between good and evil seem clearly drawn on the surface. Peter, the Lost Boys, Wendy, and her brothers, as well as Tiger Lily and the Indians, are on the side of good. Captain Hook and his pirates are evil. They are pirates, an occupation that requires certain antisocial, criminal behaviors. Yet the distinction between good and evil is not as clearly defined as it initially appears. The Indians are after scalps when they encounter the pirates. Employing methods of questionable honor, Peter does lead Wendy and her brothers away from their home. Tinkerbell is jealous of Wendy and while she does heroically save Peter, she also tries on several occasions to cause Wendy considerable harm.

The antagonists of *Peter Pan* are more distinctly ''bad,'' but they are also not as clearly developed as Peter, the Darling children, or the Lost Boys. In their limited time on stage, they are only shown scheming or fighting. Yet there is indication that they have more rounded characters. Like Peter and the Lost Boys, they also desire a mother, suggesting that much of their behavior might be tempered by a female influence. Yet because Barrie took more time in developing his protagonists, their motivations, while still essentially good, are more complex than Hook and the Pirates'.

STYLE

Setting

Peter Pan is a children's fantasy/adventure set in turn-of- the-century London and an imaginary place called Never Land. The action that takes place in London is focused in the nursery of the Darling household, located in the borough of Bloomsbury. Never Land is an island, and the action in these scenes takes place in the forest, including shelters both above and below ground; there is also a lagoon where mermaids swim. The other Never Land location is Captain Hook's pirate ship, the Jolly Roger, where the play's climactic battle takes place. These diverse settings emphasize the difference between reality and fantasy. Though the Darling household has a dog for a nanny (a slightly fantastic notion), the household is predominantly rooted in sober reality; order prevails within the home. In Never Land, there is no mature authority so the island features forest, lagoons, and pirate ships—things that appeal to a child's sense of adventure and fun. There is very little order or responsibility; the Lost Boys and the pirates are dutiful followers of their respective leaders, but there is little organization beyond obedience on the field of battle.

Special Effects

Peter Pan features numerous special effects to emphasize the fantastic elements, especially of the otherworldly Tinkerbell and Peter. Tinkerbell is a fairy. In the earliest productions, she was not played by a person but was merely a lighting effect (some latter-day productions have employed an actor to portray Tinkerbell, mostly informed by Walt Disney's animated adaptation of the play which depicted the fairy as an actual, tiny person). Tinkerbell often appeared as a ball of light created by light hitting an angled mirror, her voice a splash of bells. As little more than light and sound effects, Tinkerbell could appear otherworldly to the audience, able to flit

about the stage very quickly. Like the fairy, Peter exhibits extra-human characteristics: he is able to fly, he is ageless, and much about his person defies reason—such as his shadow being detached from his body.

The special effects are an essential part of Barrie's play and a primary reason for its popularity among generations of audiences. For a production to be effective, the play must realistically present such things as Peter flying, a dog that acts human, and a magical fairy. Most productions of *Peter Pan* employ some type of wire and pulley system that enables stagehands to lift the actors off the ground and move them about as if they are flying. Nana the dog-nanny is frequently played by a human in costume. Various lighting and sound effects are used to convey Tinkerbell's presence and fairy-like abilities. If properly executed, these effects heighten the sense of fantasy and fun in the play.

Foreshadowing: Mother's Instinct

When the dramatic technique of foreshadowing is used in Barrie's play, it is most often in conjunction with mothers and mothering; maternal insights usually telegraph important events in the play. Mrs. Darling had previously seen Peter in the window when tucking her children into bed and reading them stories. She is reluctant to go out to dinner with her husband in Act I because of what she has seen. Her worst fears are realized when Peter does come back for his shadow and convinces the children to come to Never Land. When Wendy assumes the role of mother to the Lost Boys and her own little brothers, she, too, develops a mature instinct. While telling her "children" a story about her home, she realizes, with the help of John, that her mother probably misses her and that they must return home.

HISTORICAL CONTEXT

At the turn of the twentieth century, Great Britain was a formidable world power, controlling territory on nearly every continent. Queen Victoria ruled the country from 1837 until her death in 1901, and her influence on Great Britain was still felt in 1904 though her son Edward VII was on the throne. The Edwardian era was extravagant for those with money, but the difference between the rich and the poor was a sharply divided line. Though the United

An example of the special effects used to heighten the stage presentation: Peter (Mary Martin) takes flight (with the aid of a cable and harness) in a battle with Captain Hook

States was still a developing nation, its industrial power gave it a burgeoning reputation.

While London was the center of several international markets, including currency and commodities, there was economic doubt and tension after years of prosperity due to the Industrial Revolution of the late-nineteenth century. Certain commodities suffered while others prospered. Farmers who grew grains did not do as well as dairy or fruit farmers. Industry moved towards consolidations and concentrations of power, but exports continued to fall. Still, London was the capital of finance and banking, and this market made up for the overall trade deficits in other areas. The national average income continued to increase, but the gap between classes continued to grow.

Despite wage increases, there was a movement among laborers in Great Britain to organize. Both skilled and unskilled workers joined unions in record numbers to address their concerns. Many labor leaders professed socialist and Marxist beliefs. A political party often sympathetic to many of the concerns of workers and lower classes was the Liberal party. When they won parliamentary control in 1906, they addressed many social reform

concerns. They made free meals available to poor schoolchildren and founded a medical service to address those children's health concerns. Still, poverty was widespread in England, with one study showing that 27% of the population of York lived below the poverty line.

One source of controversy in both Great Britain and the United States was the use of child labor in factories and mills. In the United States there was a call for regulations on the number of hours a child could work as well as a call for mandatory attendance at school. In 1904, the National Child Labor Committee was formed in the United States. The first child labor law was passed in the United States in 1908.

Women also worked in these factories and rarely received the same wages as men; women's job opportunities were limited to certain sectors as society still believed a woman's place was in the home. Some women in the United States demanded the right to vote to address these and other concerns while others organized their own unions and formed other groups to promote their agendas, which often focused on social welfare. The Women's Trade Union League (WTUL) was formed in the United

COMPARE
&
CONTRAST

- **1904:** Child labor is common in both the United States and Great Britain but is a source of controversy. Legislation is proposed to regulate it, including laws that would require children to spend a certain amount of time in school.

  Today: Child labor in American and England is highly restricted. Still, several American companies, including Nike, employ factories in developing countries to manufacture their goods at an extremely low cost. These factories often use child labor in sweatshop-like conditions.

- **1904:** People flying in airplanes is an almost unheard-of concept. The Wright brothers made their first successful flight in 1903.

  Today: Commercial air travel is common all over the world. Thousands of flights span the globe daily.

- **1904:** Women comprise nearly one-third of the workforce in the United States. They are confined to certain jobs, mostly of a domestic nature, and receive low pay.

  Today: Women comprise approximately half the workforce in the United States. While job opportunities are available in nearly every field, on average women make less than 80% of their male counterparts.

- **1904:** Education has only recently been made compulsory in the United States and is still not required in Great Britain.

  Today: Education, at least to age 16, is mandated by law in the United States and Great Britain.

States in 1903. A similar voting and social reform-minded organization was formed that same year in Britain. Called the Women's Social and Political Union, its leadership called for violent acts against unsympathetic forces and hunger strikes among its members to dramatize its message.

CRITICAL OVERVIEW

When *Peter Pan* was first produced in London in 1904, it was an immediate success. Though it broke box-office records, its producers were unsure if the play would be successful at all because it was so unlike anything that had been staged before. Barrie was regarded as a genius in his day, not just for the childlike insights that inform *Peter Pan* but also for a number of the other plays the prolific author wrote. Max Beerbohm, writing in the *Saturday Review,* said: "I know not anyone who remains, like Mr. Barrie, a child. It is this unparalleled achieve-

ment that informs so much of Mr. Barrie's later work, making it unique. This, too, surely is what makes Mr. Barrie the most fashionable playwright of his time. Undoubtedly, *Peter Pan* is the best thing he has done—the thing most directly from within himself. Here, at last, we see his talent in its full maturity."

Contemporary critics noted that the play has appeal for both children and adults. A reviewer from the *Illustrated London News* wrote: "There has always been much in Mr. Barrie's work, of the child for whom romance is the true reality and that which children of a larger growth called knowledge. Insofar as the play deals with real life, we think it a bit cruel."

Many critics praised Barrie for not condescending to children, for dealing frankly with the cruelties of real life. In his book *The Road to Never Land: A Reassessment of J. M. Barrie's Dramatic Art,* R. D. S. Jack argued, "*Peter Pan,* by highlighting the cruelty of children, the power-worship of adults, the impossibility of eternal youth, the inadequacy of narcissistic and bisexual solutions, presents a very harsh view of the world made palatable by humour and held at an emotional distance by wit and the dream.'' Jack concluded, ''*Peter Pan* addresses children but it treats childhood neither sentimentally nor as a condition divorced from adulthood.''

Other critics have found that some aspects of *Peter Pan* are overly sentimental, especially those scenes taking place in the Darling household. Defensive of such accusations, Roger Lancelyn Green, in his *Fifty Years of Peter Pan,* wrote: ''Sometimes, be it admitted, he [Barrie] approached perilously near the borderlands of sentimentality: such moments are seized upon with uncritical zeal as examples of typical Barrie, and the whole condemned for the occasional blemish.''

Peter Pan has also been examined by critics more closely from other angles. In *The Road to Never Land,* Jack explored *Peter Pan* in terms of a Barrie-created mythology. He wrote: ''Barrie was intent on devising a structure which combined the demands of an artificial, perspectivist creation-myth with those of a drama addressing both adults and children.''

Others have used psychological approaches to understand *Peter Pan* and what the play says about its author. Many critics believed that Barrie himself did not want to grow up and that the play is an extension of his own experiences. Green wrote in *J. M. Barrie: A Walck Monograph,* that ''all of Barrie's life led up to the creation of Peter Pan, and everything that he had written so far contained hints or foreshadowings of what was to come.'' Critics have explored Barrie's complex relationship with the Davies family and his own mother, seeking to understand his motivations in the creation of *Peter Pan.*

Several critics have focused specifically on the themes of motherhood that pervade the play, arguing that Barrie idealizes mothers to a fault while fathers are portrayed as unloving. John D. Shout in *Modern Drama,* believed that Barrie used *Peter Pan* to further an agenda. He wrote, ''*Peter Pan* may have come to life as a bunch of tales to beguile Barrie's young friends the Davies boys, but it ended up much more a sequence of object lessons for young women, and a far more artful set of lessons than the old manuals since the women are paying attention and can hardly suspect that they're being preached to.'' In the same essay, Shout added, ''adult males in this play are simply cowards or cads which only serves further to elevate the women.''

This dichotomy continues to be a source of critical debate regarding *Peter Pan.*

CRITICISM

A. Petrusso

In this essay, Petrusso discusses the idealized depiction of women—and the unfavorable depiction of adult men—in Barrie's play.

Many critics have argued that *Peter Pan* idealizes women, especially in their roles as mothers. By idealize, critics mean Barrie oversimplifies them, seeing them only as mothers rather than well-rounded human beings. While Barrie does idealize women, the female characters are not so simple. By looking at the main female characters, how they are idealized, and the development of their roles within the play, it becomes clear that they are complex idealizations. Barrie emphasizes this complexity by contrasting the women with his less favorable depictions of adult males; the men in his play are silly and in dire need of mothering.

Mrs. Mary Darling is the most idealized female character in *Peter Pan.* She is the epitome of motherhood. She has sacrificed her wedding dress to make coverlets for her children's beds. She dislikes going out or socializing, preferring to stay at home with her children. When she has to go out, as she does in Act I for her husband's job, she is reluctant to leave and believes that something is wrong. She even acts like a mother to her husband. When he cannot tie his tie, she does it for him, soothing his anger like she would a small child. In Act V, scene ii, when the children return home, she agrees to adopt all the Lost Boys and even offers to adopt Peter. When Peter refuses, she will not allow Wendy to go back with him to Never Land but only to visit once a year to do his spring cleaning.

Mrs. Darling is the baseline for women in *Peter Pan.* She could be no more perfectly written for such a role: she is polite and giving, without faults, desires, or ambitions, except those that relate to her children.

In many ways, Wendy is her mother's daughter. About eight- or ten- years-old, Wendy likes to play house with her brother John. When her father tries to convince her brother Michael to take his medicine, she is the one to immediately help him deal with the situation. After Peter Pan enters the

WHAT DO I READ NEXT?

- *Mary Rose* is a play written by Barrie in 1920. It concerns a woman who has returned home after living among fairies.

- *Charlotte's Web,* written by E. B. White in 1952, is a children's novel that also deals with motherhood (in this case a spider who nurtures a young pig) as well as the perils of maturity.

- *The Little White Bird; Or, Adventures in Kensington Gardens,* a novel written by Barrie in 1902, is a precursor to the story of *Peter Pan.*

- *Androcles and the Lion,* a 1913 play by George Bernard Shaw, is a children's farce that was written as a direct response to *Peter Pan.*

- *The Peter Pan Syndrome: Men Who Have Never Grown Up* (1983) is a nonfiction book by Dan Kileya. It is a psychological analysis of males in the United States.

---

nursery and explains the situation with his shadow, Wendy solves the problem and sews it on for him. Wendy is a junior version of Mrs. Darling.

But when Wendy is in Never Land, she proves that she is more than a petite version of her mother. She does act as mother to the Lost Boys—though she admits "I am only a little girl; I have no real experience"—though her actions are not solely motivated by the interests of her "children." She wants to swim with mermaids, though Peter warns her they like to drown children. In Act IV, Peter becomes uncomfortable with being the father to Wendy's mother, even if it is only pretend. Wendy knows there is more to these kinds of relationships, a fact unclear in the depiction of Mrs. Darling. When Wendy asks Peter, "What are your exact feelings for me, Peter?," he replies, "Those of a devoted son." This upsets Wendy, but she cannot tell him what she wants him to be exactly because "It isn't for a lady to tell." This statement reveals Wendy's desires—as well as an understanding of the mores in male/female interactions—in her relationship with Peter.

In Never Land, women, including Wendy, are allowed to be more complex, perhaps because it is a fantasy land that exists outside of the rigid social conventions of England in the early-twentieth century. Tiger Lily is a prime example of Never Land's

empowered females. Though she is a minor character, Tiger Lily is not a mother or surrogate nurturer; she is an Indian leader, the daughter of an Indian chief. Barrie describes her as "the belle of the Piccaninny tribe, whose braves would all have her to wife, but she wards them off with a hatchet." In Act II, when she learns pirates are in the area, she wants to attack them and collect their scalps. They lose this battle, and Tiger Lily nearly dies in the process. Peter Pan steps in and saves them, and Tiger Lily and her men act as guards to the underground home of Peter, Wendy, and the Lost Boys.

These are not the typical acts of a woman (let alone a mother) in this time period. Like Wendy, Tiger Lily wants Peter to be fulfill a relationship with her other than as a son. Peter tells Wendy of the similarity, reporting that "Tiger Lily is just the same; there is something or other she wants me to be, but she says it is not my mother."

Tinkerbell, the fairy, is more like Tiger Lily than Mrs. Darling or Wendy. Though in the earliest stage production Tinker Bell was no more than a reflection off a piece of glass, she nevertheless has a multi-faceted personality. Her primary loyalty is to Peter Pan, and she does not want anyone to interfere with it. Unlike any other female character in *Peter Pan,* Tinkerbell displays jealousy, especially towards Wendy, and acts on it regularly. She pulls

> AS MUCH AS BARRIES IDEALIZES WOMEN, HOWEVER COMPLEXLY, PETER PAN ULTIMATELY REJECTS FULL-TIME MOTHERING"

Wendy's hair and tricks the Lost Boys into shooting Wendy with an arrow. Even when Wendy wants to go back home, Tinkerbell is reluctant to aid her in any way. Also, whenever Peter, or anyone else for that matter, says something that Tinkerbell thinks is stupid, her response, in the fairy language, always translates as "you silly ass." Like Tiger Lily, Tinkerbell also exhibits considerable bravery, swallowing the poison intended for Peter at the end of Act IV. Also like Tiger Lily, the fairy has an occupation that is not directly related to motherhood. Tinkerbell is so named, as Peter explains to Wendy, "because she mends the fairy pots and kettles."

The primary female characters in *Peter Pan* are not merely idealized stereotypes. They are much more, albeit in the safety of a fantasy world. Though this aspect implies that "real" women do not act this way, there is another angle in which to explore Barrie's idealization of women: via their male counterparts in the play. Barrie's women are defined by what his men are not. The adult males in *Peter Pan* need women and make them look like the paragons of sensibility, adding a luster to their ideal portrait.

Both Mr. Darling and Captain Hook are rather childish and incompetent in their own way. Mr. Darling is easily frustrated over such simple acts as tying his tie. A little later in the same act, he is desperate to get his son Michael to take his dose of medicine. While telling Michael to be a man, Mr. Darling proceeds to fake taking his own bitter medicine in an attempt to trick the child into swallowing his. It does not work, and Mr. Darling's other children catch him in the lie. Mr. Darling continues to try to deceive his children, trying to turn his cowardice into a joke by putting some of the potion in Nana's bowl. Mr. Darling's frustrations come to head, and he finally insists on locking Nana

outside like a "proper dog." This leads directly to Peter Pan leading the children away from home and into Never Land.

Mr. Darling is glib, heartless, and immature, quite the opposite of his wife. Though he feels repentant enough to live in Nana's dog kennel the whole time the children are gone, he suggests in Act V, scene ii, that they close the nursery window. This is significant for this is the window through which the children left, and Mrs. Darling believes, correctly, they will come back. Mr. Darling fails to comprehend such a notion and, on the whole, does not understand much of anything.

Captain Hook is a bit more perceptive than Mr. Darling, but he lives in the fantasy world of Never Land. Barrie describes him as courageous with but two exceptions, "the sight of his own blood, which is thick and of an unusual color" and crocodiles. Because of a previous battle with Peter, Hook has a hook in place of one of his hands. Like Mr. Darling, Hook's plans are based on trickery. He wants to kill the Lost Boys by poisoning some cake and leaving it out for them. This plan fails because of Wendy's mothering. Indeed, when Hook finds out that Peter and the Lost Boys have a mother in Wendy, he plans on capturing them, killing the boys, and making her the pirates' mother. Hook's desire is that of a boy, not the grown man he is appears to be. The Captain is also easily tricked by Peter on a number of occasions, making him more like a boy than a man.

If these are adult male role models, it is no wonder that Peter Pan has no desire to grow up. He is already more of a man than either of them, in a way. He wins battles, defends his home, and goes on adventures. But as much as Barries idealizes women, however complexly, Peter Pan ultimately rejects full-time mothering. He refuses to be adopted by the Darlings and the ideal mother, Mary. No matter how idealistic Barrie's depiction of women may be, though, the fact that Peter rejects such domesticity undercuts his message in a very profound way.

Source: A. Petrusso, for *Drama for Students,* Gale, 2000.

John Bemrose

In this review of a 1987 revival production of Peter Pan, *Bemrose examines the prevailing fascination with Barrie's character and his exploits. The critic terms the playwright's tale as timeless and, of*

A scene from the immensely popular animated version of Barrie's play

this production, states "this Peter Pan *generates magic" and "compels belief."*

Peter Pan, the boy who refused to grow up, has flourished in the hearts of children and adults since he first took flight 83 years ago. The stage and book versions, written by Englishman J.M. Barrie, have never been entirely out of fashion. But now a new generation is learning to love Peter Pan—and his struggle with the villainous Captain Hook. For many Canadians, the highwater mark of the current revival is the Shaw Festival's spectacular production at Niagara-on-the-Lake, Ont., which opened

Aug. 14. But publishers, too, have been getting in on the action. Montreal's Tundra Books has just released *The Eternal Peter Pan,* the first volume of a trilogy of Pan-related books. As well, the rights to Barrie's drama and novel, now held by a London children's hospital, become public next year—giving added momentum to rumors that Hollywood director Steven Spielberg is planning a film version starring Michael Jackson. It all confirms Barrie's genius in finding a theme that has caught the imagination of four generations.

That theme is simple: growing up is not as wonderful as adults sometimes pretend. Peter Pan

> **"** THAT THEME IS SIMPLE: GROWING UP IS NOT AS WONDERFUL AS ADULTS SOMETIMES PRETEND."

has seen the writing on the wall—the dull jobs and bored faces of so many grown-ups—and he wants no part of it. In the book version, his quixotic revolt is frequently overburdened by Barrie's ponderous commentary. But the play sticks economically to the story line, a virtue wonderfully enhanced by the Shaw's magnetic production. Its *Peter Pan* has more gusto than an old Errol Flynn adventure film.

It also has the nerve to look into the darker corners of Barrie's vision—his references to death and the sadness of growing old—from which more saccharine versions, from Broadway and Hollywood, have tiptoed away. Most important, this *Peter Pan* generates magic—the result of a successful melding of astounding technical effects and old-fashioned acting skill. Only the most thoroughgoing cynic would be bothered by a glimpse of the wires holding up Peter and his fellow fliers: this *Peter Pan* compels belief.

In the past the roles of Peter and his band of followers, the Lost Boys, have frequently been played by mature actresses. Other versions have featured children in those parts. But director Ian Judge has opted for an all-adult cast of both sexes, a tack that simultaneously ensures strong acting and infectious comedy. To watch Ted Dykstra as the toddler Michael Darling, hugging his Teddy Bear and moving about on all fours, is to be struck by both the latent infantilism of adults and the charm of children.

When Michael and his two siblings fly to Never-Never Land, where Wendy (Marti Maraden) is to take care of Peter's tribe of orphans, the audience gets its first glimpse of designer Cameron Porteous's wizardry. Not only do Peter (Tom McCamus) and the Darling children levitate; their beds do too, turning into clouds as the miniature lamplit city of London revolves below.

The technical sleight of hand, however, never overwhelms Barrie's attempts to reveal the world of the imagination—Peter's kingdom. It is a place where evil men are more comic than dangerous. The Shaw's artistic director, Christopher Newton, returns to the stage as a deliciously frightening Captain Hook, swaggering, sulking and muttering dark piratical oaths (''Bicarbonate of soda!'') with relish.

As the hero, McCamus is at once ethereal and boyish. He also has just the right touch of coldness. Peter, after all, is not human like the others. He can remain a child forever, but in his immortality he can never know what it is to have a fully human heart.

Source: John Bemrose, ''The Peter Pan Principle'' in *Maclean's*, Vol. 100, no. 35, August 31, 1987, p. 127.

Kappo Phelan

Phelan reviews a 1950 revival of Barrie's play, finding that the work holds the same appeal for him as an adult as it did when he first viewed it as a youngster. He offers a positive review of this production, praising the principle actors for their skill.

I would feel a good deal safer dealing with this review of the Barrie classic if I had managed to get a child to go with me. As a matter of fact I did vainly try to seize a child, with somewhat mixed results. My first (progressive) nephew had the chicken-pox, and the school in which my second (progressive) nephew abides, refused to release him in mid-week. Thirdly, the daughter of one of my best (Jungian) friends flatly refused to go, although her little brother, aged four, kept shouting into the telephone, ''Peter Pain! Peter Pain! Me. Me.'' Needless to say, I gave up on that one.

The reason for all this benevolence was frankly in the interests of criticism as well as curiosity. Admitting, as I must, to a real nostalgia for Eva Le Gallienne's distinguished and absolute production of the play in the early thirties, it seemed to me I ought to temper possible prejudice with some outright junior reaction. Failing this conspiracy however, I might as well confess to having had a very good time at the present Lawrence-Stevens production. The business adds up, surprisingly, to fair Broadway. There is, in the person of Boris Karloff, the very best Captain Hook imaginable; there is, in Jean Arthur, an intriguing Peter; there is an enchanting Nana (you remember the sheepdog nurse) played by Norman Shelly; there is one excellent Ship set by Ralph Alswang; and there is music by Leonard Bernstein which is up-to-the-minute and sensitive, saving only those moments when he descends into radio solos with interpolated lyrics of his own. And finally there is, alas, our ridiculous system of re-hearsal-time which literally forces a show as techni-cally complicated as this one before the public before it can possibly be ready.

One can only suppose that Wendy Toye, the choreographer, must be even now delivering a few honest war-whoops to her Indians, and that she is also removing her Pirates from the chi-chi ballet class into some degree of grrr. Again, someone or other must be working to pull the grand final battle up into a real fight rather than a romp. But by far the most serious difficulty will be that the vaunted flying devices do not work invisibly, a circumstance which puts a grave kink in a good many of the lines of the play, not to say its point. All of the wires are visible against the backdrop and the costumers have not managed to conceal that lump between the shoulder blades of the air-borne children which makes them look like ill-managed puppets. I don't know how the wonderful Shultz Family got away with these impossibilities for Maud Adams and the other American productions, but certainly someone ought to find them and ask immediately. It's impor-tant. In a play that is all illusion, surely the illusion ought to be delivered; particularly a play for child-ren. I daresay there will be some people who will be gratified that their offspring will not now be hurling themselves from the window on nothing but faith. But think of the questions these worthies are going to have to answer: why? why? why? Think of the explanations: it's a joke and yet not a joke; it's only a play; no, it isn't a lie.

I must say the parental tone of this account is tedious even to me. But I can't escape it now and it's good to be able to close on an encouraging note. Miss Arthur's job is a subtle achievement. Her Peter is certainly a boy: he is lithe, fresh, knobby, cropheaded, laughing, clever. And astonishingly enough, he is the opposite of romantic. The actress seems to rely on remoteness far more than the swaggering *bruhaha* that the part also provides. Somehow or other, she is playing it as *all Pan,* a true sprite, elusive as a snowflake. It is true she has no trouble vanquishing Mr. Karloff; we watch her doing it. But in the end, it seems to me it is Mr. Karloff, with his ruffles, his inky cloak, his rolling r's, his grand style, who really wins. I don't earnest-ly think anyone under ten is going to emerge from this version of Barrie wanting to wander off and be a Lost Boy. I think everyone is going to want to play Captain Hook from now on.

Source: Kappo Phelan, review of *Peter Pan* in *Common-weal,* Vol. LII, no. 5, May 12, 1950, pp. 127–28.

Robert Hatch

Hatch reviews a 1950 revival production of Peter Pan *for which new songs were composed by Leonard Bernstein. While finding the actors to be skillful, the production design imaginative, and Barrie's text to be as appealing as ever, the critic was less than pleased with the new musical num-bers, finding their presence superfluous to the en-joyment of the tale.*

Considering the perishability of fantasy, the low esteem in which whimsy is now held and the knowing smiles of the recently analyzed, it must require a good deal of courage to offer ''*Peter Pan*'' today. Peter Lawrence and R. L. Stevens, producers of the current Jean Arthur-Boris Karloff revival, are suitably rewarded for their daring—they seem to have a hit on their hands.

But having taken the plunge with Barrie, it is too bad that the present backers then lost their nerve a bit and decided to help him along with a few ideas of their own. They engaged Leonard Bernstein to write ''additional'' lyrics and music, and hired a small male ballet troupe to fill out what they must have regarded as a thin evening. But the foxy Barrie needs no plumber's helpers, and ''*Peter Pan*'' is not thin; the additions merely slow up the action, clutter the stage with a number of unemployed merrymakers and from time to time overpower the innocence of the play with a ''production number'' vulgarity. Bernstein's contributions are the more unfortunate because they are the more obtrusive. His songs are not only unwanted; with one or two possible excep-tions they are strikingly inferior. In particular, ''Who Am I,'' inflicted on Wendy, who is otherwise touchingly played by Marcia Henderson, is a stale and cynical song-mill concoction. The settings, to get the rest of the trouble out of the way, are heavily jocose in the Disney toadstool manner and the mermaids are from Minsky.

Against these very real obstacles, Jean Arthur and Boris Karloff lead an admirable cast to trium-phant success. It is astonishing that anyone today can be as beguiling a Peter as Miss Arthur. She plays the part with wonderful taste, neither kidding the sentimentality being seduced by it. She is frank-ly boyish, embarrassed and unembarrassing, evi-dently enjoying herself enormously. I cannot make comparisons because. I did not see Maude Adams or even Marilyn Miller or Eva Le Gallienne in the role, but Miss Arthur is the right Peter for 1950. She lets Barrie the cuteness and confines herself to the matter-of-fact business of flying through space and conversing with fairies.

Karloff in the dual role of father and pirate builds his share of the evening almost to co-star stature. It is much too late discover that the dreadful Mr. Karloff is a fine comic, but his fastidiously bloodthirsty Captain Hook will be convincing proof for anyone who may have missed ''Arsenic and Old Lace.'' The lost boys of The Never Land are an engaging sandlots group, Joe E. Marks is ridiculously sprightly as Smee, the timid pirate, and Norman Shelly produces an air of lunatic solicitude in Nana, the children's St. Bernard nurse. His crocodile is a little dispirited, but it is a thankless role.

Despite its age and despite the meddling of well-meaning friends, ''*Peter Pan*'' is as shrewd and winning entertainment as Broadway is apt to offer this year, but it would be bad luck to see it on a night when either Miss Arthur or Karloff missed the performance.

Source: Robert Hatch, ''Barrie Wins Through'' in the *New Republic,* Vol. 122, no. 19, May 8, 1950, pp. 20–21.

SOURCES

Barrie, James. *Peter Pan, Or, the Boy Who Would Not Grow Up,* Scribner, 1928.

Beerbohm, Max. ''The Child Barrie'' in the *Saturday Review,* January 7, 1905, pp. 13-14.

Green, Roger Lancelyn. *Fifty Years of Peter Pan,* Peter Davies, 1954, pp. 2, 155.

Green, Roger Lancelyn. *J. M. Barrie: A Walck Monograph,* Henry Z. Walck, 1960, p. 34.

Jack, R. D. S. *The Road to the Never Land: A Reassessment of J. M. Barrie's Dramatic Art,* Aberdeen University Press, pp. 167-68, 170.

Review of *Peter Pan* in *The Illustrated London News,* January 7, 1905.

Shout, John D. ''From Nora Helmer to Wendy Darling: If You Believe in Heroines, Clap Your Hands'' in *Modern Drama,* 1992, p. 360.

FURTHER READING

Barrie, James. *Margaret Ogilvy,* Scribner, 1896.
  This is a biography Barrie wrote about his mother. It offers considerable insight into the playwright's psyche as well as the roots of his fascination with motherhood.

Birkin, Andrew. *J. M. Barrie and the Lost Boys: The Love Story That Gave Birth to Peter Pan,* Clarkson N. Potter, 1979.
  This book details the complex relationship between Barrie and the Davies family. It features pictures, letters, and other primary source information.

Jack, R. D. S. ''The Manuscript of *Peter Pan*'' in *Children's Literature,* 1990.
  This article discusses the original manuscript of *Peter Pan* and the evolution of the basic story.

Walbrook, H. M. *J. M. Barrie and the Theatre,* F. V. White & Co., 1922.
  This book offers both analyses of Barrie's plays, including *Peter Pan,* and background information on Barrie and his work.

The Piano Lesson

AUGUST WILSON

1987

The Piano Lesson is the fourth of August Wilson's cycle of plays about the African American experience in the twentieth century. It opened at the Yale Repertory Theater in 1987, and, later, on Broadway, to great success.

The play was inspired by Romare Bearden's painting *Piano Lesson*. It is set in Pittsburgh in 1936 and focuses upon the relationship between the Charles siblings, Berniece and Boy Willie, who clash over whether or not their family's piano should be sold. In the mid-nineteenth century, when the Charles family were slaves, two members of the family were sold by their owners, the Sutters, for a piano. Subsequently, a master-carpenter in the Charles family was ordered by the Sutters to carve the faces of the sold slaves into the piano. He did that and more: he carved the family's entire history into the piano. The instrument was later stolen by Berniece and Boy Willie's father, who was then killed by the Sutters in retribution.

The play explores African Americans' relationship to family history, particularly to the history of their slave ancestors. While Wilson's cycle of plays is set during the twentieth century, all of his plays explore the legacy of slavery and the roots of American racism—this play is as concerned with the Ante-bellum period as it is with America during the Great Depression.

Wilson presents the Charles' different attitudes towards their family history in a naturalistic style:

the dialogue accurately reflects everyday dialect, and the action is interwoven with scenes of people preparing meals, hot-combing hair, and bathing. The play's central metaphor, the piano, dominates this structure, while Wilson's inclusion of ghosts and spirits demonstrates his diverse cultural and literary influences. Although a few critics were critical of his mixing of styles and traditions, the majority applauded his imaginative fusion of African, American, and African-American traditions.

The Piano Lesson won Wilson his second Pulitzer Prize and confirmed his status as one of America's most important and innovative living playwrights.

AUTHOR BIOGRAPHY

Wilson was born Frederick August Kittel in 1945 in Pittsburgh, Pennsylvania. He grew up in a racially diverse working class neighborhood, the Hill, where he lived with his mother and five siblings. His mother, a single parent, worked as a domestic to support her six children. Her own mother, Wilson's grandmother, had walked from North Carolina to Pittsburgh in search of better opportunities. Wilson's mother remarried when he was still young, and the family moved to a white suburb. Wilson met persistent racism in the schools he attended there, and at fifteen he was frustrated enough by this prejudice to leave school and educate himself at the local library. There, he read ''anything'' he wanted to, and educated himself about the Afro-American literary tradition by reading works by Ralph Ellison, Langston Hughes, Countee Cullen, and Arna Bontemps, amongst others. Their example inspired him to write poetry and short fiction.

Wilson was active in the Civil Rights Movement of the 1960s, particularly the Black Power movement, and one of his contributions to the movement and to his community was to co-found Black Horizon on the Hill, a community theater set up in 1968. Like many community theaters founded during this period, Black Horizon on the Hill aimed to increase political awareness and activism in the local community while also encouraging the development of local talent. Here Wilson premiered his first one-act plays.

In the late-1970s, Wilson moved from Pittsburgh to St. Paul, Minnesota, where his plays finally attracted widespread critical attention. Wilson's se-

rious theatrical debut was *Black Bart and the Sacred Hills,* a drama written in 1977 and performed in 1981. His first big hit was *Ma Rainey's Black Bottom* (1984), which was workshopped at the National Playwright's Conference before playing at the Yale Repertory Theater and later opening on Broadway. This play was followed by two acclaimed dramas, the Pulitzer Prize-winning *Fences* (1985) and *Joe Turner's Come and Gone* (1986).

These three plays form part of Wilson's ambitious series of dramas about African-American experience during the twentieth century (his aim is set a play in each decade of the century). The fourth play in this cycle, *The Piano Lesson* (1987), is set in the 1930s and explores the different attitudes of a brother and sister to their family inheritance, a piano for which their ancestors were sold and which is engraved with their ancestors' images. *The Piano Lesson*'s combination of comedy and tragedy garnered Wilson another Pulitzer Prize and confirmed his reputation as one of America's most important and innovative playwrights.

Wilson's earliest writing was poetry, and his training in this field is still evident in his writing, which showcases the lyricism of African-American speech patterns and language and blends naturalist structure with devices that originate in black spiritualism. His social criticism also makes his writing especially rich, while his naturalism makes him heir to a tradition that includes such American greats as Arthur Miller and Tennessee Williams—a tradition that he has adapted to include powerful representations of African-American experience.

PLOT SUMMARY

Act I

The action takes place in the kitchen and parlor of the house where Doaker Charles, his niece, Berniece, and her eleven-year old daughter, Maretha, live. Boy Willie, Berniece's brother, has just arrived from down South with his friend Lymon. The two men have stolen a truck and have hauled a load of watermelons in it. They plan to sell the melons and split the profits evenly. Lymon is in trouble with the sheriff back home and announces that he plans to stay in Pittsburgh, but Boy Willie insists that he will return South.

Boy Willie greets his uncle Doaker exuberantly, and although it is only five o'clock in the morning, he soon raises the whole household from sleep. Soon the audience learns that Boy Willie's motives for driving to Pittsburgh are by no means innocent. He plans to take the family heirloom, an antique piano, from Berniece and sell it—whether she agrees or not. Boy Willie believes that the profits from this sale, together with those from the melons, will enable him to buy land from the Sutter family and set himself up as an independent farmer. He complains that Berniece never uses the piano and uses this observation to justify the sale. His complaint is crucial to later developments in the play, particularly the final scene.

During Act One, scene one, the audience meets Berniece and her daughter Maretha. Berniece is hostile to Boy Willie, who she believes is responsible for the death of her husband, Crawley, three years ago. She has just had a great shock: she claims she saw Sutter's ghost standing at the top of the steps. The audience has just learned that Old Man Sutter fell down a well three weeks ago. Boy Willie says she is dreaming. (However, later in the play the audience learns that Doaker saw Old Man Sutter's ghost before they arrived, just three days after he died, and in the third act Sutter's ghost appears again.)

Berniece is being courted by an old acquaintance of Boy Willie's, Avery, who, like him, used to work and plant the land but has now moved North. Avery has become a preacher and is trying to raise funds to build a church. Avery recounts a dream he had to Billy Willie and Lymon. Boy Willie is more interested in finding out from Avery the name of the antiques dealer who wants to buy the piano. As the scene ends, Boy Willie asks Berniece directly about the dealer, thus revealing to her his plan to sell the piano. She immediately announces that she ''ain't selling that piano. If that's why you come up here you can just forget it.'' The scene is set for their confrontation over their heritage.

In Act One, scene two, much of the mystery surrounding the piano is explained. The greater part of this scene is played out between Doaker and his older brother, Wining Boy, and their nephew Boy Willie. Wining Boy and Doaker reminisce about their old loves. They are interrupted by the arrival of Boy Willie and Lymon, who have been trying to sell their truck-load of watermelons. Inevitably, talk turns to Boy Willie's schemes to buy the Sutter land (which Doaker claims ''ain't worth nothing no

August Wilson

more'') and to sell the piano. Doaker decides to give Boy Willie a lesson: ''See, now . . . to understand why we say that . . . to understand about that piano . . . you got to go back to slavery time. See, our family was owned by a fellow named Robert Sutter,'' the grandfather of the recently diseased Old Man Sutter.

Robert Sutter decided to buy his wife, Miss Ophelia, a piano for their wedding anniversary. Since Sutter had no cash, he traded ''one and a half niggers'' for the piano, selling Doaker's grandmother (also called Berniece) and his father (then a young boy). However, Miss Ophelia began to miss her slaves, ''so she asked to see if maybe she could trade back that piano and get her niggers back.'' The offer was refused. Doaker's grandfather, also called Boy Willie, was a master carpenter; Sutter ordered Boy Willie to carve pictures of his wife and son into the piano legs, so that Miss Ophelia could have ''her piano and her niggers too.'' Boy Willie did just that: but he also carved other images from the family history into the piano—''the story of our whole family,'' as Doaker relates.

After the Civil War, the Charleses were freed and became share-croppers for the Sutters. Berniece and Boy Willie's father, Papa Boy Charles, decided to steal back the piano, believing that ''as long as

Sutter had it . . . he had us. . . we was still in slavery.'' The family managed to obtain the piano, but Papa Boy Charles was killed in retribution, burnt to death by a lynch mob in the train (the ''Yellow Dog'') on which he was attempting to escape. The murder set off a series of mysterious deaths (the latest of which is Old Man Sutter's) that are supposedly caused by the ''Ghosts of the Yellow Dog.''

Act One, scene two, ends with Berniece and Boy Willie fighting about the piano and about Boy Willie's role in Crawley's death. Berniece emphasizes the pain the piano caused her widowed mother. Suddenly, Maretha screams—she too has seen Old Man Sutter's ghost.

Act II

In Act Two, scene one, Wining Boy cons Lymon and Boy Willie, who have sold their melons and are flush with cash, into buying some second-hand clothes.

In scene two, Avery repeats his proposal of marriage to Berniece, who refuses to consider it seriously before Avery has established his church. She points out that she, as a woman, is subject to unfair standards: ''You trying to tell me a woman can't be nothing without a man. But you alright, huh? You can just walk out of here without me—without a woman—and still be a man. . . . Everybody telling me I can't be a woman unless I got a man.'' The scene ends with Berniece asking Avery to return the next day to exercise Sutter's ghost and bless the house. Avery promises to do so.

Scene three is split into two halves. In the first half, Boy Willie comes home with a woman he has picked up, Grace, but the two of them are thrown out by Berniece, who complains that their behavior is not appropriate since Maretha lives in the house. In the second half, Lymon arrives and talks to Berniece. He compliments her on her nightgown and gives her a bottle of perfume. They kiss, before Berniece departs. This scene and the previous one with Avery suggest that Berniece is beginning to put Crawley in the past and move forward. It is also a humorous contrast to Berniece's restrictive behavior in the previous scene.

In the last scene in the play, Lymon and Boy Willie try to remove the piano from the house, but Berniece threatens them with Crawley's gun. At this climatic moment, Avery appears. He begins his ceremony to exorcize Sutter's ghost and bless the house. Sutter's ghost is heard, and Boy Willie starts wrestling with it. Avery despairs of healing the family, saying, ''Berniece, I can't do it.'' Suddenly, ''Berniece realizes what she must do.'' She begins to play the piano, calling on her ancestors to help her. The song works: the ghost is exorcized, Boy Willie returns to the room. He leaves peacefully, saying as he does, ''Hey Berniece . . . if you and Maretha don't keep playing on that piano . . . ain't no telling . . . me and Sutter both liable to be back.''

CHARACTERS

Avery

Avery was one of Boy Willy's acquaintances down South but like so many other southern African-Americans he migrated to the North. He now works in Pittsburgh as an elevator operator. Avery has also become a preacher and is trying to raise funds to build a church. His dream of becoming a preacher and ministering to a congregation represents one of the traditional ways in which African Americans rose to prominence within their communities and reminds the audience of the importance of religion within African-American culture.

Avery's dream includes Berniece: he courts her and hopes that she will agree to marry him and play piano for the church congregation. But when Avery repeats his proposal of marriage to Berniece in Act Two, scene two, she refuses to talk about it seriously. Instead, she asks him to return the next day to exercise Sutter's ghost and bless the house. Avery promises to do so. Avery's exorcism ceremony is unsuccessful, however. It is up to Berniece to call upon another spiritual source—the power of her ancestors—to rid the family of Sutter's presence.

Berniece Charles

Berniece, Boy Willie's sister, long since left the South for Pittsburgh. There she married Crawley and had a daughter, Maretha. Widowed for three years, she works as a domestic to support her small family. Recently, an old acquaintance from down South, Avery, has begun to court her; however, Berniece is very ambivalent about his interest. She feels angry that her family and friends are pressuring her to marry again: ''Everybody telling me I can't be a woman unless I got a man.''

Berniece's attitude toward the piano is also profoundly ambivalent. On the one hand, she is fiercely protective of it and refuses to allow Boy Willie to sell it. She also encourages Maretha to play the piano. On the other hand, she refuses to play the piano herself, claiming that she only played it while her widowed mother was alive out of respect. After her mother's death, she ceased to play it because she was bitter about the pain it had brought the family.

In the last scene in the play, Lymon and Boy Willie attempt to remove the piano, but Berniece threatens them with Crawley's gun. The potentially tragic confrontation between sister and brother diffuses when Sutter's ghost appears. While Boy Willie tries to wrest it physically from the house, Berniece turns to the past—to African-American spiritualism—to exorcize its presence. The siblings' joint battle with the past thus reconciles them in the present.

Boy Willie Charles

Boy Willie is Berniece's brother and Doaker's nephew. Unlike them, he has remained in the South, farming the land that their family worked for generations. He dreams of raising enough cash to buy land from the diminished Sutter family so that he can become an independent farmer rather than a debt-ridden share-cropper. Boy Willie plans to raise the cash by selling a load of watermelons and the family piano, which he part owns with Berniece. To this end, he travels North to Pittsburgh.

Berniece refuses to sell the piano, however, and there are additional troubles in the past that divide brother and sister. During Boy Willie's last visit, he was involved in an illegal racket and fell into trouble with the local police. He lied to Berniece's husband, Crawley, about the racket; Crawley tried to protect him from the police and was killed. Boy Willie departed hastily. His grieving, hostile sister is thus doubly opposed to his plan to part with the family legacy.

Boy Willie complains that Berniece never uses the piano, and he uses this observation to justify his decision to sell it. His complaint is a good example of his pragmatic approach to life: why should not an unused piano be sold to purchase productive land? But it does no justice to Boy Willie's character to describe him as simply interested in ''getting ahead.'' Boy Willie reverences the family past in a different way from Berniece. He seeks to revitalize the land worked by his enslaved ancestors and to make that land finally theirs by owning and working it himself. Moreover, he seeks to educate his niece, Maretha, about her background, believing that pride in the past will help her hold her head high.

Doaker Charles

Doaker is Berniece and Boy Willy's uncle. He is a dignified, wiser older man who used to earn his living building and working the railroads and now works as a railroad cook. If Boy Willie and Berniece are two out-of-kilter wheels, their uncle Doaker is the frame that holds them together. He is the play's chief story-teller: in fact, he does a better job of remembering and narrating the family history than either Berniece or Boy Willie.

It is through Doaker that the audience learns about the importance of the piano: ''See, now . . . to understand about that piano . . . you got to go back to slavery time.'' Doaker's description of the piano's place in their family history is powerful stuff, and although he plays a neutral role in the siblings' dispute, his narration of the story suggests that he sides with Berniece.

Maretha Charles

Maretha is Berniece's eleven-year-old daughter. She is mainly important because Berniece and Boy Willy clash about how she should be raised. Should she be told her family's history, particularly the history of the piano that her mother is encouraging her to play, or should she be encouraged to forget it and thus be freed from the ''burden'' of the past? The resolution of this question has particular importance because Maretha, as the next generation of the family, represents the future of not only her own family but of the African American people.

Wining Boy Charles

Wining Boy is Doaker's brother and thus Boy Willie and Berniece's uncle. He is a failed musician and gambler, by turns charming and affectionate, at others, selfish and irresponsible. As his name implies, he is something of a ''wino''—a heavy drinker—and also something of a ''whiner''—a bluesman.

In Act One, scene two, Wining Boy reminisces about old times with Doaker. He also succeeds in conning money from Lymon and Boy Willie, both of whom are flush with cash after selling their watermelons. His role in the play is not critical but in some ways his presence is a reflection upon the present fate of the piano: the failure of the music within.

Grace

Grace's appearance on-stage is brief. She and Boy Willie have a brief encounter in the living room before Berniece, outraged, orders them to stop or leave the house. They leave.

Lymon

Lymon is Boy Willy's friend from "down South." He is in trouble with the local sheriff back home and has traveled North with Boy Willy to escape prosecution and to sell their truck load of watermelons. Lymon plans to stay in Pittsburgh. It is, however, his first time in the North, and for much of the play he is more concerned with exploring the dazzling city lights than with selling the watermelons and finding a job.

His inexperience and naivete provides much humor in Act Two, scene one, when Wining Boy cons him into parting with six hard-earned dollars for a cheap suit, shirt, and pair of shoes. His naivete is also apparent in Act Two, scene three, when he tells Berniece that Boy Willie picked up the woman Lymon had been angling after.

During this scene, Lymon compliments Berniece on her nightgown and gives her a bottle of perfume. They kiss. Their brief intimacy suggests that Berniece is melting the barriers she erected after Crawley's death; this prefigures the play's positive resolution.

THEMES

Past and Present

Wilson's cycle of plays concentrates on African-American experience during the twentieth century, but they are all also focused—in either direct or indirect ways—upon the experience of slavery.

The Charles family in Wilson's play is almost a textbook example of the southern black experience in the nineteenth and twentieth century, and it is certain that Wilson intended his characters to be representative of that history. After the emancipation of the slaves in 1863, most ex-slaves remained on the land, renting from their former masters as tenant-farmers (sharecroppers). The returns from their labor were low, the risks of natural disasters were high, and the costs of living were artificially inflated because it was mainly whites who owned the stores at which blacks bought and sold their goods. Many sharecroppers were locked into a cycle of debt to their former masters and lived in grueling poverty. This paucity and debt were compounded further by white hostility.

The promises of the Reconstruction Era were cut short, and the introduction of "Jim Crow" laws that segregated whites and blacks confirmed the enduring influence of American, and particularly southern, racism. The accelerating industrialization of the North in the last decades of the nineteenth century promised workers higher wages, improved work conditions, and a better standard of living. Many rural blacks migrated North, and when demand for labor peaked during and after World War One this steady flow North became a torrent.

In the play, the Charles family were once owned by the Sutters and worked the Sutter land as slaves. After emancipation, they remained on the same land but became sharecroppers for the Sutters, renting the land from their former masters and working it for themselves. Finally, a part of the family migrated North to Pittsburgh, leaving only Boy Willy behind.

Boy Willie refuses to abandon the land and migrate North. His dream of finally owning, rather than renting, the Sutter land, is an extraordinary anomaly, and it reflects Wilson's own curiosity about what "the fabric of American society would be like if blacks had stayed in the South and somehow found a way to develop [economically] and lock into that particular area." His father's desire to reclaim the piano is later paralleled in Boy Willie's desire to remain on the land. Both father and son believe that reclaiming the heritage of slavery—and transforming it through labor and ties of affection—will alter their relationship to their family and to their history.

Boy Charles believed that the piano symbolized "the story of our whole family and as long as Sutter had it . . . we was still in slavery." Boy Willie also tries to alter the family's relationship to their slave history—to break the bond of master and

TOPICS FOR FURTHER STUDY

- Wilson was inspired to write *The Piano Lesson* by Romare Bearden's painting *Piano Lesson.* Examine the painting, then consider the symbolism of the piano in the play, particularly the carvings on it. Compare and contrast the painting and the play in terms of their representation of art in African-American life.

- Research the Great Depression and Franklin D. Roosevelt's New Deal in 1930s America, then, using your research, consider Wilson's representations of poverty and opportunity in *The Piano Lesson.*

- Research the Great Migration of southern African-Americans to the urban North. Then, using your research, discuss Wilson's speculation about what might have happened if more African-Americans had stayed on in the South and found a viable way to work the land. Do you think this might have been possible, and what kinds of social changes would have to have taken place to make this work?

- Why is Sutter's ghost haunting the Charles family, and how convincing is its unseen presence on-stage?

- Consider one or more of the following examples of Wilson's use of language in *The Piano Lesson* and, using examples, demonstrate how it contributes to the power and believability of the play: black dialect, metaphor, lyricism.

- Using examples from the text, identify what you believe is the play's central message and consider its importance today.

---

slave, of owner and renter, by becoming an owner himself, the master of the very land that the Charles family has worked for so many generations.

The central conflict in the play, the battle over the future of the piano, is generated by Boy Willie's desire to transform the past by altering the present. However, the battle takes place precisely because the piano's history is so important: each family member has strikingly different responses to its past. In part, then, the piano's lesson is a lesson about the past: history can sound dramatically different depending upon *who* is telling a story and *why* they are telling it. Understanding this lesson is crucial to understanding contemporary race relations in America and the extraordinary divide between black and white experience in the past.

Just as the play's central conflict originates in Boy Willie's desire to remake the past, so too can the conflict be resolved only by Berniece's decision to return to the past. When her mother died, Berniece refused to perform the "ancestor worship" that her mother had demanded of her (playing the piano to invoke, and also to honor, the blood sacrificed for it). Ironically, Berniece's attitude towards the piano is now almost as pragmatic as Boy Willie's: both of them see it as "a piece of wood."

But when Avery's Christian exorcism fails, Berniece returns to her mother's ritual practices in order to save her brother and to exercise Sutter's ghost. She plays the piano and calls upon the spirits of the dead to help her. Wilson describes her actions as "a rustle of wind blowing across two continents," and her plea to her ancestors and her gratitude at their help recalls African rituals of ancestor worship. The piano's lesson, then, is also a lesson that asks African Americans to value family ties and to acknowledge their personal involvement in the legacy of slavery.

The American Dream

One of the themes that Wilson explores in all of his plays is the conflict between the American dream and African-American experience of poverty and racism. In *The Piano Lesson* each of the central characters has a different vision of their future, and the contrast between then defines Wilson's exploration of the barriers African Americans faced in achieving the American dream.

The phrase "the American dream" describes the belief in the possibility of advancement in American society: an immigrant who arrives at Staten Island with nothing in his pockets can, with hard work, eventually earn and save enough to enable him to buy and own his own house and to live in reasonable prosperity. Boy Willie's dream of owning his own land resembles the traditional American dream.

Avery also has a dream, but it differs markedly from Boy Willie's. Avery has "been filled with the Holy Ghost and called to be a servant of the Lord." He now works in his spare time as a preacher while trying to raise funds to build a church. Both Avery's dream of becoming a preacher and ministering to a congregation, and Boy Willie's dream of becoming a farmer and owning his own land, represent two key elements of African-American experience— religion and the land. Likewise, Avery's ecstatic religious language is the other side of the black southern dialect in which Boy Willie speaks.

Their dreams represent two ways blacks could "make it" in this period; however, there were other possibilities for economic advancement. The character of Wining Boy represents another of the few avenues of advancement traditionally open to blacks: music. Wilson explored this path in the first play in his cycle, *Ma Rainey's Black Bottom* (1984), and his critique of white exploitation of black musical talent in that play is echoed in his characterization of Wining Boy, a failed "recording star," a piano player whose luck has run out. Not everyone, however, is lost to the lure of hope: while Berniece is pragmatic about her own position in society, she nonetheless nurtures the dream that her daughter will advance socially by becoming a piano teacher, while Lymon, too, hopes to make it in the big city.

Perhaps the most important dream in the play, however, is Papa Boy Charles's dream that possession of the piano will alter the family's relationship to their past. His dream of removing the piano from Sutter's house and restoring "the story of our whole family" to his kin is accomplished at the cost of his life. The Sutters's murder of Boy Charles reiterates their past violence to the Charles family. Moreover, the "liberation" of the piano and the murder of Boy

Charles on the railway (a powerful symbol of escape and liberation for blacks, because it was one of the routes North used by fugitive slaves) occurs on the Fourth of July. Wilson thus points to the original limits of the American Revolution—in which white citizens won freedom from British tyranny while maintaining their own tyranny over black slaves— and the limits of its rhetoric for African Americans living in the segregated 1930s.

STYLE

Naturalism

Naturalism is often confused with realism; however, although the two styles both represent "real life," there are important differences between them. Naturalist writers were influenced by scientific and evolutionary theories of human character and of social interaction. One of the central motifs of Naturalist writing is the individual's struggle to adapt to an often hostile environment. Indeed, most Naturalist writers emphasize their characters' environment to such an extent that it becomes an integral element in their narratives. Moreover, their protagonists usually belong to a less fortunate class than their middle-class audience or readership, and the description of their struggle to survive and succeed against all odds usually allows the writer the opportunity to make powerful social criticism.

Wilson is considered a Naturalist playwright *par excellence.* Although the play's conflict is triggered by Boy Willie's sudden appearance, the drama unfolds during the Charles family's everyday activities. Doaker describes precisely what kind of "ham hocks" he wants Berniece to buy, and he shares with her and the audience his plans to cook "cornbread and . . . turnip greens." When Avery arrives to propose to Berniece, she is busy heating up water for her evening bath. The final climatic argument between Berniece and Boy Willie occurs while Berniece is combing her daughter's hair. These kinds of details are the staple of Naturalism: they foreground the everyday experiences of the characters while deepening the veracity of the characterizations.

Like many American Naturalist dramas—Eugene O'Neill's *Long Day's Journey into Night,* for example—the action of *The Piano Lesson* takes place over a short period of time: from Thursday morning to Friday evening. The brevity of the plot's span intensifies the drama of the events that unfold, while the kinds of detail described above allow the audience an extraordinarily intimate glimpse of the family's life. The *brevity* of the time frame is an implicit contrast to the *length* of the family's history; this contrast emphasizes the Charles' inherent problems in relating to and narrating their family history, since, when their family were illiterate slaves, they relied upon storytelling, music, and art, rather than writing, to recite and remember their joys and sorrows.

The African Tradition: Ancestor Worship and Storytelling

In the final scene, Wilson describes Berniece's decision to play the piano as a "rustling of wind blowing across two continents." The playwright himself merges two different cultural traditions within the play, the African and the American, and seems to suggest that this melding of cultures is essential to African-American identity.

Ancestor worship is integral to African religious practice, and the spirits of the ancestors are believed to be able to influence people's lives and cause good or bad events, depending upon whether the spirits are malevolent or benevolent. In fact, although ancestor worship is premised upon respecting and honoring the dead, the practice also ensures that spirits will remain benevolent and will protect the worshipers from malevolent forces. Neglect of the spirits removes their protection and may even incur their wrath.

The piano is the Charles' family totem: it visibly records the lost lives of Berniece and Boy Willie's ancestors, and it is the only tangible link remaining between past and present. Their ancestors' spirits coalesce in the piano, which is precisely why Berniece's mother, Mama Ola, polishes it, prays over it, and asks her daughter to play it. She keeps the shrine to her ancestors clean and pure and maintains her link with them by praying and playing it.

Berniece refuses to play the piano after her mother's death because she "don't want to wake them spirits." Consequently, "they never be walking around in this house." However, her refusal to honor the piano in the ways her mother has taught her means she has abandoned her African heritage

and "disrespected" her family history. Berniece comes to realize that her neglect has allowed the Charles' to be persecuted by Sutter's ghost. When Berniece finally starts playing again and calls upon her ancestors' spirits, she affirms the importance of maintaining African cultural practice and of honoring the history of slavery.

The other important African cultural practice in *The Piano Lesson* is storytelling. Again, this is a cross-cultural practice, but one that is particularly important to African Americans, who were denied formal education and literacy skills even after Emancipation. Slaves created or adapted songs and relied upon community storytelling to remember their heritage and history. Two scenes in particular hinge upon African-American storytelling.

Avery's dream, which he narrates in Act One, scene one, reflects the importance of the Book of Revelations and of the scriptural promise of redemption to African-American Christianity. His narration of the story is a testimony to his conversion experience and displays the speech patterns of evangelical preachers. His dream is influenced by the New Testament story of Christ's birth as well as by Old Testament stories of prophets being called and chosen by God. But Avery has cast these traditions in an African-American context: the pilgrimage begins in a "railway yard," the three wise men become "three hobos" (who are reminiscent of the murdered hobos on the Yellow Dog), and he strongly emphasizes the ecstatic elements of the experience.

An even more important story is told in the next scene by Doaker, the de facto patriarch of the Charles family. Doaker uses the call and response structure that is common to African ritual practice and to evangelical preaching: "'I'm talking to the man . . . let me talk to the man. . . . Now . . . am I telling it right, Wining Boy?' 'You telling it.'" He also uses rhythm to great effect by pausing throughout his story and repeats certain phrases to intensify its drama. Doaker's story is the core of the play: it reveals the importance of the piano, and he is shown to be the one family member who still honors the ancestors' spirits by telling their stories.

Many of the other characters tell stories about themselves during the play, a practice that emphasizes Wilson's belief in the importance of the oral tradition to African-American identity. Storytelling keeps the past alive in the present, for it establishes the individual's connection to their personal and cultural history. Survival depends upon the continuation of this practice across the generations: in the final scene of the play, Boy Willie begins to teach Maretha her family stories. He insists that if she knows about and celebrated her history, it will dramatically improve her self-esteem: she "wouldn't have no problem in life. She could walk around here with her head head high. . . . She [would] know where she at in the world."

HISTORICAL CONTEXT

Slavery and Reconstruction

The widespread importation of slaves to America began in the 1690s in Virginia. Although slaves had been imported earlier than this, it was in the 1690s that indentured servants, who sold themselves to masters for contracts of five to eleven years in exchange for the price of their passage from England or Ireland to America and the cost of their keep during their indenture, were increasingly replaced by permanently enslaved laborers. Contrary to popular misconception, the colonists actually preferred indentured servants to slaves, for the latter were a more expensive investment. But after six decades of migration, there were simply not enough English, Irish, and Scots migrants to meet the colonists' demand. The foundation was set for slavery in America: the kidnaping of human beings, their transportation from Africa to Jamaica, the West Indies, and North America, their forced labor in those colonies and later generations' inheritance of their parents' enslaved status.

It was the rhetoric of the American Revolution (1775-1783) that for the first time forced Americans to reconsider their attitudes towards slavery: the Revolution's expressions of freedom and equality for all men was contradicted by the existence of an enslaved underclass. Some southerners and northerners briefly entertained emancipating the slaves (and repatriating them to Liberia or settling them in an empty part of America), but these schemes were soon abandoned.

During the ante-bellum period (the era before the American Civil War) strong opposition to slavery developed in the North. Partly in response to abolitionist attacks and partly as a result of the growing racism within southern society, southern slave-owners and apologists for slavery began to offer the public "scientific" and "philosophical" defenses of slavery.

As the decades rolled by, the gulf between the defenders and the opponents of slavery widened, although there was considerable overlap in misconceptions about blacks between the more conservative of the abolitionists and their opponents. The growing tension within society about slavery came to a head in the American Civil War (1861-1865). Should slavery be extended to the newly settled states of Kansas and Missouri? Should slavery be abolished in the southern states? What kind of labor system would replace it and would the agrarian South still be able to function economically, particularly in competition with the more industrialized North? What would happen to the emancipated slaves?

Although slavery was the key issue dividing the North and South, Abraham Lincoln prioritized maintaining the American union of states above all else. The Emancipation Proclamation issued on January 1st, 1863, emancipated slaves in the southern states; congress passed the thirteenth amendment in 1865, thus emancipating all remaining slaves.

The North's triumph over the South in the Civil War and its determination to help the emancipated African Americans adjust to their new position in society soon subsided under a growing wave of conciliatory action and nostalgic sentiment for the South. The promises of the Reconstruction Era (1865-1876)—the dream of better treatment of and opportunity for blacks, and the possibility of integration and reconciliation between the races—were quickly cut short. Republican presidents adopted a conciliatory approach to the southern leadership. All hope of establishing a truly egalitarian society in the South was destroyed in the 1880s and 1890s when southern legislatures successively introduced the "Jim Crow" segregation laws that disenfranchised blacks and made true civil rights impossible.

During and after the Reconstruction, southern blacks struggled to define their new place in society. Although there had always been a small but significant free black population in America who enjoyed better educational and occupational possibilities than their enslaved brethren, most ex-slaves were trained for nothing but rural labor. The choices facing them were limited: they could either leave the land and work in urban factories or they could remain on the land as sharecroppers. Many chose to remain, but in the boom years of the 1910s and 1920s, and during and after World War I (1914-

COMPARE
&
CONTRAST

- **1936:** President Franklin D. Roosevelt is elected for a second term by a massive majority. He wins every state but Virginia and Maine. Congress is 80% Democrat. Roosevelt's unprecedented victory depends upon a big swing in the black voting population from the Republicans to the Democrats.

1987: Ronald Reagan is serving his second term in office. He had been reelected in 1984 by the greatest Republican landslide in U.S. history, having won in forty-nine states. Nonetheless, during his seventh year in office he attracts severe criticism for his involvement in the Iran-Contra Affair and his veto of the Clean Water Act.

Today: President Bill Clinton was reelected to office in November, 1996, with 49% of the vote, the first Democrat since Roosevelt to be reelected. However, his second term in office is marred by the Whitewater investigation and the Monica Lewinsky scandal.

- **1936:** Eight million people are unemployed and the economy is in deep recession. Roosevelt's New Deal offers support to the unemployed and attempts to boost the economy with public works programs and support for farmers.

1987: The 19th of October is "Black Monday" on Wall Street: a massive slump in share prices of over 20%. The crash is the worst in the history of the New York Stock Exchange, and the decline in stock prices is nearly double the 1929 plunge.

Today: Contrary to all predictions, the American economy continues to boom. The collapse of the Japanese and Mexican markets only affected the New York Stock Exchange briefly. The Dow Jones Index passed the 10,000 mark for the first time in January of 1999, the bull market continues to grow, and the unemployment rate is the lowest in forty years.

- **1936:** Eugene O'Neill becomes the first American playwright to win the Nobel Prize for Literature.

1987: August Wilson becomes the first African-American playwright to win the Pulitzer Prize for Drama, with his play *Fences*. In the same year, Rita Dove, an African-American poet, wins the Pulitzer Prize for Poetry for her collection *Thomas and Beulah*.

Today: African-American writers continue to accrue honors nationally and internationally. African-American novelist Toni Morrison became the first African American to win the Nobel Prize for Literature in 1994, and August Wilson won the Pulitzer Prize for Drama for a second time in 1990.

1919) in particular, there was a mass exodus of southern blacks to the northern cities.

America in the 1930s

The 1930s were characterized by severe economic depression in America and abroad. The Great Depression had its roots in Britain and America's punitive reparations policy after their victory in First World War, in technological advances that increased output and profits but made many workers redundant, and in depressed agricultural, mining, and textile markets. Stock-market speculation only concealed the weaknesses eating away at America's economic heart. The stock market crash of 1929 did not trigger the Depression but rather was a response to and a confirmation of existing problems within the market and the international banks.

From 1929 to 1932, unemployment in America rose from about 1.5 million to about 15 million. On the land, in the early-1930s, good weather produced an over-supply in agricultural produce, but people in the cities went hungry. By the mid-1930s, drought and bank foreclosures had driven farm prices down by more than 50% and many tenant-farmers were forced off their land. Agricultural laborers, many of whom were black southerners, were as badly hit as factory workers in the city, who, like them, joined millions of others in the bread lines (welfare handouts for those who could not afford to buy food).

Nonetheless, President Herbert Hoover's administration maintained an attitude of stoic indifference, believing that "market forces" would solve the escalating crisis—a proclamation that proved false. In March, 1933, Franklin D. Roosevelt was elected to the presidency. He immediately began implementing his "New Deal" reform plan: relief for the unemployed, fiscal reform, and stimulus measures to boost economic recovery. Roosevelt owed his election success in part to African Americans' desertion of the Republicans—the party of Abraham Lincoln, which they had traditionally supported—for Roosevelt's party, the Democrats. Both Roosevelt's New Deal and African Americans' switch in political allegiance transformed twentieth-century American politics. In subsequent decades, the struggle for African-American civil rights would be closely related to the politics of the Democratic Party.

CRITICAL OVERVIEW

August Wilson's *The Piano Lesson* won a Pulitzer Prize before opening on Broadway, an honor that is indicative of the almost unanimous praise critics showered upon the play. Yet the drama still attracted its fair share of negative criticism, some of which came from privileged onlookers who had witnessed its transformation over three years of extensive workshopping. Wth the exception of these few hostile voices, however, most critics greeted the play with strong applause.

William A. Henry III, writing for *Time,* stated that the play was Wilson's "richest yet," a sentiment echoed by many other critics, including the *New York Post*'s Clive Barnes, who called it "the fourth, best, and most immediate in the series of plays exploring the Afro-American experience during this century." However, one or two critics failed to join this chorus of approval. Robert Brustein, a prominent director and reviewer for the *New Republic,* issued a damning attack of the play, arguing in detail that it was "the most poorly composed of

Wilson's four produced works." John Simon, writing in *New York,* joined Brustein when he complained that the play was an unwieldy mixture of farce, drama, and Broadway musical. Simon's attack was deemed by many as unwarranted, since laughter and tragedy walk hand in hand in many of the great tragedies (such as Shakespeare's *Hamlet, King Lear,* and *Macbeth*).

Henry, in his largely positive review of the play, did acknowledge that Wilson had blurred genre boundaries by mixing tales of the supernatural with "kitchen-sink realism." This, in fact, was an element of the play to which many critics had a mixed response. Was it necessary, they asked, to hear the sound of a toilet flushing off-stage, or to watch Berniece washing with "real" water in a sink? Wilson's decision to mix genres irritated Brustein and Simon in particular: Brustein called the supernaturalism "ludicrous" and "forced," while Simon asked, "why, in this day and age, bring in ghosts at all?"

Looking at the larger critical picture, however, these critics seemed to have missed the point: Wilson's mixing of genres is natural for a playwright who seeks to represent dual cultural traditions in one form and on one stage, and his inclusion of a supernatural sub-plot reflects African-American culture in the 1930s, not white American culture in the 1980s. Indeed, Michael Morales, in *May All Your Fences Have Gates: Essays on the Drama of August Wilson,* argued that the supernatural element of the play is crucial to Wilson's representation of African-American history.

Many critics were fascinated, and rightly so, by the play's central symbol, the piano. Barnes called the musical instrument "a living symbol of the family's past—its slavery and its escape, its blood and its tears. . . . The piano is . . . an heirloom of tragic memory and meaning." Frank Rich, writing in the *New York Times,* discussed the piano's symbolism in detail. He emphasized the instrument's bountiful but painful heritage: "Sculptured into its rich wood are totemic human figures whose knifedrawn features suggest both the pride of African culture and the grotesque scars of slavery." "The siblings at center stage" inherit both "the pride and scars," and the piano is their key to their reconciliation with their family history and their identity as African-Americans. *Time*'s Henry concluded his evaluation of the play by stating, simply and powerfully, "the musical instrument of the title is the most potent symbol in American drama since Laura Wingfield's glass menagerie"—a reference to Tennessee Williams's play *The Glass Menagerie.*

The most negative criticism came from critics who suggested that Wilson's success depended on his ability "to stimulate the guilt glands of liberal white audiences." The *New Republic*'s Brustein dismissed Wilson's previous plays and added that he found little "power or poetry" in *The Piano Lesson.* Brustein felt that any comparisons between Wilson and Shakespeare or O'Neill were ridiculous. Wilson had "limited himself" to exploring "the black experience" whereas O'Neill "wrote about the human experience."

Not satisfied with producing this nonsensical and rather insulting distinction between general human experience and black experience, Brustein continued in a similar vein: "Still, enough radical vapor floats over the bourgeois bolster and upholstered couches [of the play] to stimulate the guilt glands of liberal white audiences. Unable to reform the past, we sometimes pay for the sins of history and our society through artistic reparations in a cultural equivalent of affirmative action." Brustein's statements suggest, falsely, that white audiences lack the ability to appreciate artistic representations of experience other than their own and also ignore the black audience attending Wilson's plays; moreover, his statements suggest that he has misinterpreted the reconciliatory message of the play's ending.

Simon displayed a similar hostility to Wilson's success in his review of the play. He attacked it for having too many sub-plots, for mixing genres, and for being repetitive: "it is sincere but overcrowded, overzealous, and, without quite knowing where it is headed, repeats everything three or four times." But he saved his most damning criticism for his last lines. Simon argued that the play was essentially a product of "two years of testing and rewriting at five leading university and commercial theaters": in short, that it owed as much to the skills of professional theatre craftspeople as it did to Wilson himself. "Less favored, nonminority practitioners," he claimed, would not have enjoyed such help.

Simon and Brustein's attacks on Wilson's talent and on the merits of *The Piano Lesson* are not typical of the overall criticism of the play, but they do represent the kinds of criticism, illogical though

A Playbill for Wilson's play

they may seem, that Wilson, as an African-American playwright writing about African-American experience, has had to face. Most critics, however, are not encumbered by such blinkers. They can appreciate that Wilson, far from wanting to stick to strict definitions of what constitutes a "proper" realist play or "real" human experience, is an artist interested in inventing new forms and voices as much as he is in connecting to voices and traditions from the past.

CRITICISM

Helena Ifeka
Ifeka is a Ph.D specializing in American and British literature. In this essay she argues that Wilson's plays are an eloquent form of social protest and public education.

August Wilson's Pulitzer Prize-winning play (his second) *The Piano Lesson* demonstrates that commercially successful theater can be an eloquent

WHAT DO I READ NEXT?

- Immanu Amiri Baraka (formerly LeRoi Jones) is an African-American playwright whose writing encompasses be-bop poetry and black nationalist plays. His plays *Dutchman* and *The Slave Ship* (1966) are important examples of black nationalist writing. Wilson produced all of Baraka's plays when he was working at the Black Horizons Theater.

- Arthur Miller's *Death of A Salesman* (1949) is one of the most famous plays of the twentieth century. This Pulitzer Prize-winning drama exemplifies the "well-made" play of the realist tradition, in which escalating tensions concentrated around the central protagonist unfold neatly scene by scene before reaching a dramatic conclusion. In this case, the central protagonist is the failed sales- and family man, Willy Loman, whose sons Biff and Happy are unable to fulfill his thwarted dreams. Wilson's play *Fences* has been compared to *Death of A Salesman,* although Wilson has stated that he is not familiar with it.

- Tennessee Williams's Pulitzer Prize-winning play *Cat on a Hot Tin Roof* (1955) depicts the bitter family tensions that originate in failed marriages, repressed sexuality, and the desire to control a southern plantation. The play is an excellent example of American naturalism.

- Booker T. Washington's classic autobiography *Up from Slavery* (1901) defined a generation.

Washington was born into slavery on a Virginia plantation; freed at fifteen, he taught himself to read, then walked almost 500 miles to attend a vocational training institute. He was later selected to head the Tuskegee Insitute in Alabama. Although Washington was criticized in his own time and later for his cautious approach to race issues, at the time he was the black community's most well-known and influential leader.

- Langston Hughes was one of the major figures of the Harlem Renaissance, the flowering of African-American creativity in the first few decades of the twentieth century. Hughes's superb poetry collection, *The Weary Blues* (1926), which includes the famous poem "The Negro Speaks of Rivers," launched his career and introduced audiences to a new style of poetry that was based on jazz rhythms and black idiom. The first volume of his autobiography, *The Big Sea* (1940), provides a fascinating insight into his life in America and Europe during the 1920s.

- Frederick Douglass, a nineteenth-century African-American abolitionist, published his autobiography, *A Narrative of the Life of Frederick Douglass,* in 1845. It describes his life as a slave and his escape to freedom. Douglass agitated for the abolitionist cause, organized black garrisons during the Civil War, and served his people in public office during the Reconstruction period.

---

vehicle for social protest and public education. Wilson's early involvement in the Black Power movement and in black community theater, and his ambitious plan to write a cycle of plays about African-American life in the twentieth century, are proof of his desire to "alter the relationship between blacks and society through the arts." His representation of black suffering, coupled with his celebration of black resistance and endurance, offers his audience a new representation of African-American history.

In the late-1960s, artists involved in counterculture movements resurrected the theater as a forum for political protest and a vehicle for social change. Many artists saw community theater as a means to reach out to their community and educate and politicize them. Wilson participated in the Black Power movement in the early-1960s and, like many artists during this period, he saw writing as a means to bring about social change. In 1968 Wilson cofounded the Black Horizons Theater in his home-suburb of the Hill in Pittsburgh.

Wilson found community theater at Black Horizons and, later at the Science Museum of Minnesota, a challenging experience. Throughout the 1970s he directed and wrote short plays for both these organizations, in the process perfecting his craft. Wilson was not content to remain involved in community organizations, however. He wanted the professional advice and support of the National Playwrights Center, and, after they rejected his plays several times, he finally won them over. The Center accepted a draft of *Ma Rainey's Black Bottom,* a play that became Wilson's first commercial hit.

Wilson's shift from community theater to the comparative profitability of Broadway was either hailed as progress for black audiences and artists or seen as him selling-out to white expectations and commercial incentives. But close examination of Wilson's oeuvre reveals that he maintained his original ideal: to educate his audience and to contribute positively to the African-American identity.

Wilson's aesthetics are founded on a belief in the African-ness of black Americans and upon an emphasis upon reclaiming black history. He stated in an interview conducted shortly after the completion of *The Piano Lesson* (reprinted in *In Their Own Words: Contemporary American Playwrights*) that he hopes a viewer will ''walk away from my play, whether you're black or white, with the idea that these [characters] are Africans, as opposed to black folks in America.'' Such an aim is in keeping with the black nationalist movement, which emphasizes the African roots of African Americans and the importance of African culture in sustaining generations of slaves. Wilson's inclusion of African cultural and religious practices in his plays—Gabriel's ritual dance in *Fences,* Berniece's appeal to her ancestors' spirits in *The Piano Lesson*—is just one way in which he emphasizes the ethnic roots of African Americans and rewrites their history from a black perspective.

Emphasizing such an African perspective necessarily involves recovering and re-examining black history in America. But Wilson's desire to reclaim African-American history is complicated by the fact that many African Americans were long denied the literacy and education enjoyed by most white Americans. Not only did this mean that early black writers such as the poet Phyllis Wheatley and the abolitionist Frederick Douglass struggled against great odds to write, it also meant that until recently African-American history was mainly located in oral forms, such as spirituals, jazz songs and the blues, trickster

> *THE PIANO LESSON* DEMONSTRATES THAT COMMERCIALLY SUCCESSFUL THEATER CAN BE AN ELOQUENT VEHICLE FOR SOCIAL PROTEST AND PUBLIC EDUCATION"

stories, visions, conversion experiences, and folk tales. Wilson's decision to include some of these forms in his plays evidences his commitment to valuing the diverse sources of black history and his desire to celebrate black cultural achievement.

Equally significant is Wilson's project of writing a play about African-American experience for each decade of the twentieth century. Wilson skillfully integrates sociological research into the fabric of each play, while exploring an issue that he sees as characteristic of the decade as a whole. In *The Piano Lesson,* the decade in question is the 1930s, and the issues that Wilson fixes upon are the relationship of urban blacks to their past as slaves and the Great Migration of southern blacks to the cities of the North. In effect, each play is a new installment in a new history of the African-American people.

The Piano Lesson is set in a period with which many audience members are at least superficially familiar, for the Great Depression's impact upon generations of Americans was so wrenching that to this day mention of it conjures up vivid images of gaunt faces and soup kitchens. But Wilson offers audiences a story that has not been told as often as it might have been: the story of black American experience during the Depression.

While poor blacks and whites alike experienced tremendous hardship during the 1930s, black poverty differed from white poverty in significant ways. The relatively recent resettlement of millions of blacks to urban northern centers during and after the First World War had produced enormous upheaval in kin networks, tension that was exasperated by the fact that almost all migrants moved into urban slums in the inner city. Nonetheless, the promise of steady income and improved living conditions in big cities like New York, Chicago,

Detroit, Philadelphia, and Pittsburgh continued to draw black migrants North.

The Piano Lesson dramatizes the moment of migration and represents the city's temptations: Lymon is attracted to Pittsburgh because of the possibility of finding good work, meeting attractive women, and living the "good life." Avery's decision to abandon the South and his subsequent success in Pittsburgh exemplifies a successful migration.

The play is subtly didactic: it encourages the audience to re-think American history by asking them what might have happened if more blacks had stayed on the southern land, and it encourages black Americans to value their own history of suffering and resistance under slavery. Wilson believes, as he stated in *In Their Own Words,* that "blacks do not teach their kids … that at one time we were slaves." This history must be told: "It is the crucial and central thing to our presence here in America." To this end, in the play the Charles family come to accept the burden of the past that the piano represents. The faces of their ancestors carved into the piano represent the family's loss and suffering, but the artistry of the carvings also testifies to their ancestor's achievements. Similarly, the terrible loss that Boy Charles's death brings to the family is balanced by the beauty of the music that the stolen piano gives the family.

While Wilson never sounds a strident call to arms, his representation of the history of black protest encourages the audience to value it and supports contemporary black protest. The examples given above, for instance, are testimony of the family's endurance of hardship and of their maintenance of their identity, but they are also testimony to the family's *resistance* to their bonds: Doaker's grandfather, Boy Willie, breaks his master's orders and creates an artwork that is testimony to *his* bonds of affection, rather than his mistress's, and Boy Charles's decision to steal the piano strikes another blow against the Sutters's—and white—oppression. Indeed, the play includes several important examples of blacks carving (literally and figuratively) out their own space in a hostile white world, such as Avery's attempt to found his own black church and Boy Willie's attempt to reclaim the land on which his ancestors slaved.

Wilson's essentially positive project of valuing black history, even its most terrible and painful elements, is also apparent in his representation of the richness of African-American culture. *The Piano Lesson* is typical of his plays in that he touches upon all of the central elements of African-American culture. Avery's character speaks to the importance of religion in African-American life, "our saving grace," while Berniece's call to her ancestors speaks to the continuing influence of African belief in "ancestor worship … ghosts, magic, and superstition." Wining Boy represents the black tradition of the blues, while Berniece's management of her household acknowledges women's role in the black family's resilience in the face of great adversity. Last but not least, the dialect in which the characters speak is not only realistic but also a showcase to the unique contribution African Americans have made and continue to make to American English.

Wilson's journey from community theater in the Hill to commercial success on Broadway has been a long one, but *The Piano Lesson* shows that his original belief in the playwright's potential to "alter the relationship between blacks and society" remains unshaken. He still seeks to reach out to and educate his audience, to encourage them to re-think their present and their past and to offer black audiences voices with which they can identify.

Not only does Wilson continue to use the theater as a form of public education, he also continues to use it as a form of social protest. *The Piano Lesson* mourns black suffering under slavery and its impact three generations later on the descendants of those slaves. But, like all social protest, the play harnesses the energy of anger and grief in order to change the present: the play's conclusion asks black Americans to honor their ancestors' history and their own painful inheritance.

Source: Helena Ifeka, for *Drama for Students,* Gale, 2000.

Richard Hornby

In this excerpt, Hornby review Wilson's play. While finding that the work does not hold the same appeal as the playwright's previous efforts, the critic lauds Wilson for his "vividness of characterization."

August Wilson's *The Piano Lesson* is set in the 1930s, continuing his chronicle of black life in America during each decade of the past hundred years. A family in Pittsburgh owns an antique piano, which originally belonged to the master of their ancestors in the days of slavery. The widowed young matron of the family, Berniece Charles, wants to keep the piano; her brother, Boy Willie, wants to sell it to help buy a piece of land in the

South that was originally part of the plantation on which the family were slaves. The piano is covered with carvings made by their great-grandfather, depicting the family history.

The Piano Lesson is thus not only a historical play, but also a play about a family trying to come to grips with its own history. The controversy over selling the piano is not just a simple conflict between sentimentality and practicality. The piano is a symbol for Berniece, but an empty one. She will not even play it; her daughter, Maretha, picks at it in desultory fashion. On the other hand, for Boy Willie, selling the piano is not just a means of getting some cash. Buying a hundred acres of the old plantation is a way of getting control over the family's terrible past. The land for him functions as the carvings on the piano did for his great-grandfather. Taking something that belonged to the master and making it into his own is a means to power, a way to go on record and be somebody, an ultimate triumph over white oppression.

The first act of *Piano Lesson* is talky and slow, with lengthy exposition about half-a-dozen unseen characters that is more suited to a novel than to a play, but in the second act the pace quickens. As the conflict between brother and sister approaches tragedy, the tone of the play becomes crazily comic, as when Berniece comes down the stairs with a gun in her pocket, while carefully wiping her hands on a dish towel. Boy Willie's repeated attempts to steal the piano from the living room are thwarted by the sheer bulk of the thing, a piece of business that manages to be both highly symbolic and hilarious. The mystical overtones that occur in all of Wilson's work are more explicit than usual, with apparent visitations by a ghost from the family past, which is finally exorcised.

Ultimately, *The Piano Lesson* is not as tightly written as Wilson's *Fences* or *Joe Turner's Come and Gone,* but he remains unmatched today for vividness of characterization, richness of background, sensitivity to American history, and use of poetic imagery. Motifs of ghosts (showing the influence of Ibsen and O'Neill), music, land, wood, and travel are gracefully woven into the naturalistic façade, in a way no other American playwright has done since Tennessee Williams.

Lloyd Richards directed superbly, as he has with all of Wilson's other plays. The players, from that small group of serious black American actors who are an unacknowledged national treasure, were all wonderful. Charles S. Dutton failed to get a Tony

> TAKING SOMETHING THAT BELONGED TO THE MASTER AND MAKING IT INTO HIS OWN IS A MEANS TO POWER, A WAY TO GO ON RECORD AND BE SOMEBODY, AN ULTIMATE TRIUMPH OVER WHITE OPPRESSION."

Award for his Boy Willie, but he deserved one for his inventive, varied, graceful, energetic, driven performance. (There was no timid underplaying here!) Dutton, a graduate of the penitentiary and the Yale Drama School, has a past of his own that he has exorcised.

Source: Richard Hornby, "The Blind Leading the Blind" in the *Hudson Review,* Vol. XLIII, no. 3, Autumn, 1990, pp. 471–72.

Mimi Kramer

While finding much to recommend in The Piano Lesson, *Kramer also found the playwright's conclusion to be somewhat obscure.*

The interior of the newly restored and rechristened Walter Kerr Theatre (it was formerly the Ritz), where August Wilson's "The Piano Lesson" opened last week, is truly exquisite. I have an idea that parts of Wilson's play must be exquisite, too. Unfortunately, I found it difficult to see past the head of the extremely tall man sitting in front of me. Offhand, I can think of no playwright whose work is harder to appreciate in such a situation. Wilson is unusual among contemporary playwrights in that he writes for the proscenium stage. His plays tend to present two juxtaposed areas—the adjoining rooms of a recording studio, or the world within someone's back yard and the world outside it, or a boarding house where people stay briefly and the city of roads and bridges that carry them away—and you have to be able to view the whole stage to get the full effect of what is happening there.

In the case of "The Piano Lesson," which takes place in the house of a black family in Pittsburgh in 1936, the stage is divided into two rooms (evoked by E. David Cosier, Jr.): a living room,

> IF A MAN CARVES PICTURES OF HIS WIFE AND SON ON A PIANO, TO WHOM DO THE PICTURES BELONG: THE ARTIST OR THE MAN WHO OWNS THE PIANO AND ONCE OWNED THE WIFE AND SON? WHICH IS MORE IMPORTANT, THE FUTURE OR THE PAST?"

where the piano in question sits, and where the person who wants to sell it does most of his talking; and a kitchen, where people mostly talk about why it couldn't or shouldn't or won't be sold. There are some spell-binding scenes in ''*The Piano Lesson*''—like the one in which a man sits in the living room talking about his hands while in the kitchen a woman goes through the elaborate process of taming her little girl's hair with a hot comb and grease. What the man is talking about—working to produce something that white men will own—goes back to slavery. What the woman is doing—using her hands to make her daughter conform to white fashion—looks toward the future. Because of where the actors were placed in this sequence, something of its meaning came across to me. But most of the important scenes in Act I—like the one in which a room comes alive with the movement of men singing a work song, and the one in which we hear the history of the piano—take place on the right side of the stage, the side that this very tall man and I were sitting on. I would have gone back the next night, but I quailed at the prospect of sitting through Charles S. Dutton's performance again.

Dutton is the central character, Boy Willie, whose arrival and departure frame the play, and Dutton's performance, which could all too easily win him a Tony Award (it seems calculated to), and which has already won the actor praise, is, I think, terribly damaging to the delicate structure of Wilson's play. Like the performances that Lloyd Richards—who directed ''*The Piano Lesson*''—elicited from James Earl Jones, Mary Alice, Courtney Vance, and Frankie Faison in Wilson's ''*Fences*,'' it is essentially a bid for attention. It's not so much stagy as self-conscious; indeed, self-consciousness is virtu-

ally its only quality. Stagy acting is what Maggie Smith does so well in ''Lettice & Lovage''—projecting the mannerisms of someone who doesn't behave the way real people behave. What Dutton is doing is stagy only in the sense that you know (because something in the actor's bearing or timing or intonation tells you) when a big line is coming up; for the rest, it's projected realism: the simulation of a feeling—anxiety, say, or indignation—at such a pitch that the audience is constantly aware of watching the performance of an actor in a play.

What impresses people about this sort of acting may be its effortfulness. In Mr. Dutton's case, effort means speed. Dutton bursts onto the stage at the beginning of the play acting at such a level of hysteria that his performance has nowhere to go; his character talks incessantly, compulsively, and Dutton delivers practically every speech with the unvarying, frenzied purposefulness of a crazed auctioneer. He induces a sort of delirium, so that by the end of the evening it's impossible to focus on anything Boy Willie is saying.

To be fair, it's hard to know how else an actor could approach the role. ''*The Piano Lesson*'' is a play that desperately wants cutting, and Boy Willie has most of the long speeches. Yet Dutton's performance isn't about subtlety, and all the rest of the performances are, as is the play. With the exception of ''*Fences*,'' all Wilson's plays are subtle: they explore complex ideas by constructing around some aspect of the experience of black Americans an intricate system of theme and imagery. If ''*Fences*'' was Wilson at his least interesting, that's because it was linear: its eponymous image meant basically the same thing to all the characters. The central object in this play—the piano, a beautifully carved upright, decorated with faces and scenes—means something different to everyone. To Boy Willie, who wants to use money from the sale of the piano to buy the land his family worked as slaves and sharecroppers, the piano means the future and his spiritual emancipation. To his widowed sister Berniece (S. Epatha Merkerson), whose father died stealing it from the man who owned it, the piano means a heritage of grief, bitterness, and women without men. To Berniece's would-be suitor, Avery (Tommy Hollis), the piano represents the baggage of sorrow he wants her to relinquish. For Berniece and Boy Willie's uncle, Wining Boy (Lou Myers), a former recording artist, the piano was once a living and is now a burden, and to Boy Willie's friend Lymon (Rocky Carroll), an interloper, it's just a good story. To Doaker (Carl Gordon), the head of the household, whose grandfather carved pictures of his wife and son on the piano for the slave owner who sold the wife and son in order to buy it, the piano embodies the family's history—symbolically and in concrete terms.

If a man carves pictures of his wife and son on a piano, to whom do the pictures belong: the artist or the man who owns the piano and once owned the wife and son? Which is more important, the future or the past? How do you measure the abstract value that one person puts on an object against the practical use to which another person can put it? And what is the best way of making your way in a world in which whatever you make with your hands belongs to someone else? Wilson never answers any of these questions. Instead, he tacks on an ending that takes refuge in mysticism and melodramatic event—a tendency of his. Like the stages for which he writes them, all Wilson's plays are divided in two—between earth, represented by women and home, and mysticism, embodied in the men who travel around in a world no part of which, they feel, can ever really be theirs. And mysticism always wins out. Usually, though, some marriage between the two forces has been effected in the audience's mind by means of music. "O Lord Berta Berta O Lord gal well, go 'head marry don't you wait on me," sing the men in the kitchen. "I am a rambling gambling man," sings Wining Boy, pounding the piano. "I've travelled all around this world." And later he sings, "It takes a hesitating woman wanna sing the blues," while Doaker makes up a song out of the names of the towns on the Katy line. All the music in "*The Piano Lesson*" is about travelling man and hesitating woman—except for the prayer that Berniece improvises to resolve the conflict and bring the play to a close.

I suspect that at one time Wilson had it in mind to include in the play an actual piano lesson. Wilson said in a recent *Times* interview that the play was inspired by a painting of "a young girl at the piano, with a woman standing behind her who seems to be admonishing her to learn her scales." I think this image got translated into that wonderful hair-fixing scene, in which Berniece stands behind her daughter, Maretha (Apryl R. Foster), who is seated. At one point, the child tries to play the Papa Haydn piece out of the Thompson piano primer; in disgust, Wining Boy pushes her away and launches into some boogie-woogie. But there isn't a piano lesson in the literal, down-to-earth sense. It's clear that by the time Boy Willie departs Wilson wants us to feel that the piano has taught him something—or

that he's learned something about it—but the precise message of Wilson's mystical ending is obscure to me.

Source: Mimi Kramer, "Traveling Man and Hesitating Woman" in the *New Yorker,* April 30, 1990, pp. 82–83.

William A. Henry III

Henry reviews a 1989 Chicago performance of the The Piano Lesson, *finding much to recommend in the play's content and the production.*

The piano in Doaker Charles' living room is a family heirloom, and like most heirlooms it is prized more than used, its value measured less in money than in memories. For this piano, the Charles family was torn asunder in slavery times: to acquire it, the white man who owned them traded away Doaker's grandmother and father, then a nine-year-old. On this piano, Doaker's grieving grandfather, the plantation carpenter, carved portrait sculptures in African style of the wife and son he had lost. To Doaker's hothead older brother, born under the second slavery of Jim Crow, the carvings on the piano made it the rightful property of his kin, and he lost his life in a successful conspiracy to steal it.

Now, in 1936, it sits admired but mostly untouched in Doaker's house in Pittsburgh, and it threatens to tear the family apart again. Boy Willie Charles, son of the man who stole the piano, wants to sell it and use the proceeds to buy and farm the very land where his ancestors were slaves. Boy Willie's sister Berniece denounces as sacrilege the idea of selling away a legacy her father died to obtain.

That is the premise of *The Piano Lesson,* which opened last week at the Goodman Theater in Chicago. The lesson of the title—an instruction in morality rather than scales or fingering—makes the work the richest yet of dramatist August Wilson, whose first three Broadway efforts, *Ma Rainey's Black Bottom, Fences* and *Joe Turner's Come and Gone,* each won the New York Drama Critics Circle prize as best play of the year. The fact that producers are not shoving each other in haste to bring *Piano Lesson* to Broadway, especially in a season when the Tony Awards are likely to be given to mediocrities by default, underscores the all but defunct place of serious drama in our commercial theater.

Piano Lesson debuted more than a year ago at the Yale Repertory Theater, where Wilson has launched all his plays. In that production, the work seemed an intriguing but unpolished amalgam of kitchen-sink realism (there is literally one onstage) and window-rattling, curtain-swirling supernaturalism. Not much of the actual text has changed. But at the Goodman the play confidently shuttles spectators between the everyday present and the ghostly remnants of the past, until ultimately the two worlds collide. The first glimpse of the spookily poetic comes before a word is spoken, when a shaft of white light illumines the piano, which by itself plays an eerily cheerful rag.

The other major change since Yale is the recasting of Boy Willie with Charles S. Dutton, who gives a performance as energized as his Tony-nominated Broadway debut in *Ma Rainey,* Puffing his cheeks, waving his arms, hopping around like Jackie Gleason in a one-legged jig, the burly Dutton seems a rustic buffoon. But when conversation turns to conflict, his jaw tightens and the clowning stops. In Boy Willie, Dutton and Wilson achieve that rarity in literature, a truly common, ordinary man of heroic force.

The rest of the cast is equally fine, notably S. Epatha Merkerson as Berniece and Lou Myers as the dissolute uncle Wining Boy, who leads family members in musical interludes that include a haunting, African-influenced chant. Director Lloyd Richards needs to tinker with the ending, a sort of exorcism in which a sudden shift from farce to horror does not quite work. But already the musical instrument of the title is the most potent symbol in American drama since Laura Wingfield's glass menagerie.

Source: William A. Henry III, "A Ghostly Past, in Ragtime" in *Time,* Vol. 133, no. 5, January 30, 1989, p. 69

SOURCES

Barnes, Clive. "*Piano Lesson* Hits All the Right Keys" in the *New York Post,* April 17, 1990.

Brustein, Robert. "The Lesson of *The Piano Lesson*" in the *New Republic,* Vol. 202, no. 21, May 21, 1990, pp. 28-30.

Henry, William A., III. "A Ghostly Past, in Ragtime" in *Time,* Vol. 133, no. 5, January 30, 1989, p. 69.

Hill, Holly, K. A. Berney, and N. G. Templeton, editors. *Contemporary American Dramatists,* St. James Press, 1994.

Morales, Michael. "Ghosts on the Piano: August Wilson and the Representation of Black American History" in *May All Your Fences Have Gates: Essays on the Drama of August Wilson,* edited by Alan Nadel, University of Iowa Press, 1994, pp. 105-15.

Rich, Frank. "A Family Confronts Its History in August Wilson's *Piano Lesson*" in the *New York Times,* April 17, 1990, p. C13.

Simon, John. "A Lesson from Pianos" in *New York,* Vol. 23, no. 18, May 7, 1990, pp. 82-83.

FURTHER READING

Genovese, Eugene D. *Roll, Jordan, Roll: The World the Slaves Made,* [New York], 1974.
> Genovese's exhaustive account of slave culture can be used as a source book for focused research. It provides detailed background for the culture in which Wilson's character live in the 1930s.

Honey, Maureen. *Shadowed Dreams: Women's Poetry of the Harlem Renaissance,* 1989.
> This valuable collection of women's poetry from the Harlem Renaissance also includes a readable introduction to the period.

Morgan, Edmund S. *American Slavery American Freedom: The Ordeal of Colonial Virginia,* [New York], 1975.
> This ground-breaking work of scholarship outlines the economic basis to the development of slavery in colonial Virginia and its connection to white citizens' increasing equality.

Nadel, Alan, editor. *May All Your Fences Have Gates: Essay on August Wilson,* University of Iowa Press, 1994.
> This collection of essays on Wilson's major plays is a good source for secondary criticism on the playwright.

Raboteau, Albert J. *Slave Religion: The "Invisible Institution" in the Ante-bellum South,* 1979.
> Raboteau uses a rich variety of sources for his fascinating investigation into slave religion. His study also includes interesting discussion of slave religion in other colonies, such as the West Indies, and of African religious practice.

Savran, David. *In Their Own Words: Contemporary American Playwrights,* Theatre Communications Group, 1988, pp. 288-306.
> Savran includes an informative interview with Wilson in this collection, which he recorded in New York just after the completion of *The Piano Lesson.*

R.U.R.

KAREL CAPEK
1921

When Karel Capek's *R.U.R.* (the acronymic title is short for "Rossum's Universal Robots") was first performed in 1921, it became a major international success and made Capek an internationally known playwright. Although *R.U.R.* may appear slightly dated nearly eighty years later, the concerns expressed by the playwright are still interesting to modern audiences, and the play is still performed in regional theatres. Capek's drama is also responsible for coining a new word, "robot," which became an important fixture of Hollywood films, especially the B-films of the 1950s. The word "robot" is derived from the Czech word *robota,* meaning forced labor, but it was the topic of the play, that technology can imperil the world, that made the play controversial.

The problems this play deals with are not the realities of everyday life; instead Capek is exploring the larger issues of the human condition. With technology booming immediately after the end of World War I, *R.U.R.* touched on the concerns of many people. The idea of a utopian society to replace the one fractured by the horror of the first World War was especially appealing to audiences, some of whom were deeply disturbed by Capek's vision of how technology might be misused. Capek's concerns about the dehumanization of man through technology provides the central core of this play, and it is this motif that warns of the destructive force of technology.

Although contemporary assessments of Capek's play frequently cite the stereotypical nature of the characters, there is enough depth to them to involve an audience, and this involvement is one of the play's strengths. At performances of *R.U.R.,* audiences and critics were both fascinated with the idea of non-humans that appeared human and terrified at the implications for human destruction at the hand of technology. These two reactions led to the play's success.

AUTHOR BIOGRAPHY

Karel Capek was born in January, 1890, in Male Svatonovice, a small village in northeastern Bohemia, an area that is now Czechoslovakia. Capek, the youngest of three children, was a sickly child, but by all accounts, he had a happy childhood, largely because of the influence of his older brother, Josef, who was also his best friend. Capek began writing poetry and fiction in high school, and after graduation, Capek began publishing stories, illustrated by Josef, in Czech newspapers. After studying in Prague, Berlin, and Paris, Capek earned a doctorate at Prague's Charles University in 1915. Even while at school, Capek and his brother continued to write, publishing their first book, a collection of tales, in 1916. Capek worked as a journalist and as a tutor, and he was intensely interested in the subject of Czech nationalism, often writing on that subject for his newspaper articles. His first play, *The Outlaw,* was produced in 1921. Capek fell in love with a young actress, who was an understudy in that play, but his poor health prevented them from marrying until 1935. *R.U.R.,* Capek's second play, was an enormous success, establishing Capek as an international playwright. During the next few years, Capek was very active, writing *From the Insect World* and *The Makropoulous Secret* in 1922. *Adam the Creator* was written with his brother, Josef, in 1927.

Although he was very successful as a playwright, Capek also turned his attention to novels. He published a succession of novels, including *The Absolute at Large* (1922), *Krakatit* (1924), *Hordubal* (1933), *Meteor* (1935), *An Ordinary Life* (1936), and *War with the Newts* (1937). Although he began his career as a successful playwright, it is as a science fiction writer that Capek is best known. His science fiction novels explore the possible misuse of technology, and while he did not oppose technology, Capek was concerned about man's ability to consider all of the implications of such advances. Capek briefly turned again to theatre in 1937, with *The White Plague* and *The Mother* (1938).

Capek was opposed to Nazism, and both he and his brother were warned to leave Prague as the threat of World War II became a reality. Both declined, and Capek died of pneumonia just three months before the Nazis invaded Prague. Hitler's troops did not know of Capek's death when they came to his house to arrest him. Josef was arrested and sent to a concentration camp where he later died. Karel Capek is considered one of Czechoslovakia's foremost writers. He not only championed freedom, but his contributions to literature are amongst the most important in Czech history.

PLOT SUMMARY

Act I

The play opens with Domin dictating letters to his typist, Sulla. The setting is a small island, although its precise location is not clear. A visitor is announced, and Helena Glory enters. She claims to have come to inspect the facility and leads Domin to believe that she is there as a representative of her father, the president. She is introduced to Sulla and cannot believe that she is a robot. After careful questioning of the young female robot, Helena insists that Sulla must be human. Domin offers to dissect Sulla, and Helena is aghast that Sulla would be so readily sacrificed. Hearing that she is present, Busman, Hallemeier, Gall, Fabry, and Alquist rush in. At first, Helena mistakes them for robots and tells them that she is there to save them from exploitation. She is embarrassed to learn that they are managers and doctors at the site. A discussion about the manufacturing of robots ensues, and the audience learns that robots are extremely cheap to manufacture, that they can do any type of work more cheaply than man, and that R.U.R. envisions a world where robots will produce vast quantities of food and goods, thus replacing human workers. This society is meant to sound like another Eden, but it raises questions about slavery, especially when it is revealed that the robots occasionally suffer breakdowns, that they are soon to have pain receptors, and that their human creators see themselves as gods capable of replicating creation. The men all invite Helena to lunch with them and all but Domin exit to prepare the meal. He immediately professes his love and asks Helena to marry him. After a passionate kiss, she is assumed to have agreed.

Act II

It is ten years later and it is clear that Domin is very worried about the news from abroad. There have been no boats, mail, or telephone calls in several days. The last news was of revolts by the robots. All the men have brought gifts to Helena to celebrate the ten years that she has been on the island. Through conversations between Helena and her servant, Nana, the audience learns that both women are very afraid of the robots, that even the dog and other animals sense something unnatural. A robot, Radius, has rebelled. He was designed by Dr. Gall to have a better brain than most robots, and he is not satisfied to take orders any longer. After being examined by Dr. Gall it becomes clear that Radius has become human-like in many ways. Dr. Gall wants to have him destroyed, but Helena insists that he be spared. The audience learns from Dr. Gall that the plan for the future is to build robots who would be individually designed for each country, some black, some white, some Asian. Wanting to put an end to the robots' manufacture, Helena and Nana burn old Rossum's manufacturing notes. When the plant managers and doctors enter, it is revealed that they were saving Rossum's notes as a trump card to control the robots. Before Helena can reveal that she burned them, a ship arrives in the harbor. Although, the men think it is the mail-boat, in reality it is the robots spreading word of a universal revolt. Before the human inhabitants can seek escape on a waiting gun boat, the robots seize control of the boat and surround the house.

Act III

It is later the same day. Domin, Helena, Gall, Hallemeier, Fabry, Busman, Alquist, and Nana are prisoners, surrounded by the robots who will attack at any moment. The group discusses using old Rossum's formula to buy their escape, but then it is revealed that Helena burned it. Gall confesses that he has been building robots with souls for nearly three years, and Helena admits that she asked him to do so. He has built nearly 300 of the improved or changed robots, and it is presumed that these are the leaders of the rebellion. In making the robots like men, Gall has given them the ability to hate just as

Karel Capek

men hate. Busman sits down to balance his accounts, seemingly in denial at the crisis that looms just outside, as the rest of them discuss the morality of what they have created and discuss possible ways to escape. Finally, Busman runs outside to negotiate with the robot leader, Radius. Busman thinks that he can buy escape with a bribe of billions of dollars in profits. He dies when he touches the electrified fence. Domin takes Helena to another room as the house is attacked. As this act ends, Gall, Hallemeier, and Fabry are murdered, and Alquist is sentenced to a lifetime as a slave to the robots.

Epilogue

It is one year later. Alquist is hard at work trying to recreate the formula that will make more robots. He has had no success. There are no more humans alive on the earth, and robots, who have only a short life span, are dying off. Soon the earth will be devoid of life. Radius and a group of robots enter and threaten Alquist, but he still cannot create more robots. Radius is so desperate that he is willing to sacrifice himself to dissection if Alquist could learn something from it. After explaining that he is not a scientist and refusing to dissect the robots, Alquist collapses. Two robots enter, Primus and Helena. Their conversation reveals that each is capable of great emotion and desire. Animals are no longer afraid of them and both have an appreciation for beauty that other robots lack. When Alquist awakens, he realizes that the two are different. Helena begins to cry when she thinks Primus is in danger and Primus attempts to defend Helena. Alquist sees in the two robots a possible future for the world, and calling them the new Adam and Eve, he dismisses them and tells them to go forth into the world. The play ends on this note of hope.

CHARACTERS

Mr. Alquist

Alquist is an architect and the Head of the Works Department at R.U.R. He is older and a traditionalist. He reveals in Act II that he prays that the manufacture of robots will cease and that the world will return to the way it once was. Alquist sees the manufacture of robots as a profitable venture that is evil at its core. He escapes death because Radius pronounces a sentence that Alquist should finish out his life as a laborer, a slave for the robots. In the Epilogue, Alquist tries unsuccessfully to recreate the formula to create more robots. At the play's conclusion, he finds that there are two robots who have become humans and Alquist sends them out to repopulate the earth.

Consul Busman

As the General Business Manager at R.U.R., Busman is concerned with the bottom line. When Miss Glory asks about giving the robots a soul, Busman replies with estimates of increased cost. He anticipates that eventually robots will replace all workers and that the cost of manufacturing goods will decrease steadily. When the robots attack, Busman continues working on his accounts, almost in denial. Busman decides that he can buy the humans' freedom, but when he goes to speak to the robots, he touches the fence and is electrocuted.

Harry Domin

Domin is the General Manager at R.U.R. Domin is an idealist who envisions that robots will help create a paradise on earth for man, who will have robots to do the work and free man to simply enjoy life. He envisions men as the new gods with a world to rule and robots as the servant class. At their first meeting, Domin claims to have instantly fallen in love with Helena Glory and asks her to marry him. In the end, Domin is murdered by the robots.

Mr. Fabry

Fabry is the Engineer General, Technical Controller of R.U.R. Like almost everyone else, Fabry is murdered during the robot rebellion.

First Robot

This robot is one of the group in the Epilogue who demands that Alquist create more robots.

Dr. Gall

Dr. Gall is head of the Physiological and Experimental Department at R.U.R. When the play opens, he is working on giving the robots pain receptors so that they will be more careful and less likely to damage themselves. When the robots revolt, Dr. Gall reveals that he changed the robots, made them more human he actually made them better than human. During the revolt, Gall, too, is murdered by the robots.

Helena Glory

Helena is the daughter of the President. She initially meets Harry when she comes to inspect the R.U.R. factory. On her first visit to the factory, Helena is aghast to discover that the robots, which appear so human to her, are treated as mindless drones. Even ten years after her marriage to Domin, Helena cannot be at ease amongst the robots. She pleads with Gall to make them more human, to give then each a soul. In the rebellion that follows, she is murdered by the robots.

Dr. Hallemeier

Dr. Hallemeier is head of the Institute for Psychological Training of Robots. Hallemeier tells Miss Glory that the robots are not capable of love. According to him, they have no soul or passion or will of their own. He tells Miss Glory that occasionally the robots suffer from something called "robot's cramp," a breakdown in their mechanism that resembles rebellion. In the revolt, Hallemeier is murdered by the robots.

Helena

Helena is a robot. Dr. Gall created her in Helena Glory's image, but she is only a poor copy of the original. In the Epilogue, Helena the robot is revealed to be human-like. She is one of the last robots created by Gall, and she is capable of love and emotions. Alquist sees her as the next Eve.

Marius

Marius is a robot. He works at the plant office for Domin.

Nana

Nana is Miss Glory's servant. She has come to the island to take care of Helena, who wants a human being to be close to her and not a robot. She helps Helena burn the formulas and is murdered with everyone else.

Primus

Primus is a robot, created on the same day as the robot Helena. When Alquist threatens to dissect Helena, Primus comes to her defense. Alquist realizes that Primus is human and thinks that he has discovered the next Adam, who with his Eve will repopulate the earth.

Radius

Radius is a robot in charge of the library. In Act II, he appears to be the latest victim of "robot cramp." Radius has a better brain than most other robots and he does not want to take orders. He tells Helena Glory that he wants to be a master and give orders. After an examination by Dr. Gall, it is revealed that Radius's attack is not the typical "robot cramp." Instead, it appears that he has become more human. When all the robots rebel, it is Radius who leads them. In the Epilogue, Radius realizes his folly in murdering his creators. He demands that Alquist create a formula to make more robots, and is willing to sacrifice himself to aid in the research.

Second Robot

This robot is one of the group in the Epilogue who demands that Alquist create more robots.

Servant

In the Epilogue, the servant waits upon Alquist, who has been trying to recreate the formula.

Sulla

Sulla is a robot; she functions primarily as Domin's secretary or typist. She appears like any other young woman, and is so convincing that Helena Glory cannot, at first, accept that Sulla is not human.

Third Robot

This robot is one of the group in the Epilogue who demands that Alquist create more robots.

THEMES

Anger and Hatred

When the robots rebel and attack, it is revealed that at Helena's suggestion, Dr. Gall has given the robots a soul and has given them the ability to appreciate their condition. But in making them more human-like, Gall has also given them the ability to hate, just as humans are capable of hating. Since the robots are treated like insignificant and expendable creations, they soon learn to hate their creators and all humans. They are without a conscience and can hate and kill at will.

Class Conflict

With the creation of robots, the earth is divided into two classes: those who have control and those who are controlled. The robots form this latter class, which is designed to be exploited. The robots are little more than slaves who are expected to work until they can work no longer, a period of about twenty years. They are designed and treated as though they have no feelings, no needs, and no expectations. The robots' builders envision the humans as a kind of aristocracy, superior to the robots they control. As is the case in all feudal societies, eventually the peasants or slaves revolt and murder their masters.

Duty and Responsibility

As the creators of a new life form, the robot creators have a responsibility for how their creations are used, but in this case, the builders see the robots only in terms of exploitation and greed. The builders will sell their robots to whomever orders them and has the cash to pay. They ignore the moral implications of what they have done, preferring to isolate themselves on the island. When the robots rebel, rather than stop selling the robots and explore possible solutions, the manufacturers continue to sell robots. When it becomes clear that humanity is in real danger, their only thought is for their own escape.

TOPICS FOR FURTHER STUDY

- Discuss the ending of the play. Do the new Adam and Eve signify a hopeful ending? Why or why not?

- Capek clearly had concerns about the possible misuse of technology. Discuss whether you think his concerns were justified.

- Capek's robots created a new idea that has spawned many robots since these early creations. Trace the evolution of robots in Hollywood films.

- Cloning raises many of the same questions that Capek was concerned about in this play. Investigate the ethical concerns that modern scientists and religious leaders have about creating life.

Human Condition

This play explores the human condition and envisions a scenario where man destroys himself through greed. Technology, which offers the opportunities to solve many of the world's problems, is used to create a slave race, who will perform all the labor while another group becomes richer. In response, humans become expendable and cease to reproduce. Evolutionary theory argues that survival is a function of the species best able to adapt. In the New World order, it is the humans who serve no purpose. This bleak vision of humanity is off-set at the play's ending when two of the robots offer the opportunity to create a new human race.

Individual vs. Machine

In this play, the conflict focuses on who will survive, the humans or the robots. In a real sense, when the manufacturers give the robots souls and the ability to feel, they create individuals where machines previously stood. This leads to thinking as individuals, including the desire to have control. In a sense, this play proves that the individual is superior to the machine, since as machines, the

robots could be controlled. But given the ability to think, they become individuals and superior beings.

Prejudice

One of the plans to control the robots involves creating robots to fit national or local standards instead of universal models. When discussing how this plan will work, the manufacturers reveal their own prejudices, since they see that certain "races" of robots will be built to hate other "races" of robots. The ensuing conflict will prevent the robots from uniting against humans. It is a plan to build in racial prejudice in a creation that would naturally not have that ability.

Revenge

The robots are a downtrodden group, who when they finally understand that they are slaves, seek revenge against their builders. They envision themselves as superior to humans and become so caught up in their revenge that they forget that humans hold the key to their existence. It is a symbiotic relationship, one that is forgotten by the robots. Revenge becomes more important than survival.

Science and Technology

Capek's play focuses on the dangers of technology. While new discoveries offer the best hope for curing disease and easing human existence, it also presents risks if not used correctly. The greed of those who use technology without regard for the consequences is at the center of this play. At the play's conclusion, two robots have become human and offer hope for the continuation of mankind on earth. But Primus and Helena also illustrate that it is not technology that offers the answers (Alquist cannot make new robots or modify the old), but it is human survival that matters if man is to succeed.

STYLE

Audience

Authors usually write with an audience in mind. Capek intended *R.U.R.* as a way to awaken audiences to the possible threat of technology. His concern about the fate of humanity is transmitted to the audience as they watch and listen to the drama unfold.

Character

The actions of each character are what constitute the story. Character can also include the idea of a particular individual's morality. Characters can range from simple stereotypical figures to more complex multi-faceted ones. Characters may also be defined by personality traits, such as the rogue or the damsel in distress. ''Characterization'' is the process of creating a life-like person from an author's imagination. To accomplish this the author provides the character with personality traits that help define who he will be and how he will behave in a given situation. Domin is an idealist. The audience learns this through speeches that he makes, especially his visions of an utopian society.

Drama

A drama is often defined as any work designed to be presented on the stage. It consists of a story, of actors portraying characters, and of action. But historically, drama can also consist of tragedy, comedy, religious pageant, and spectacle. In modern usage, drama explores serious topics and themes but does not achieve the same level as tragedy.

Genre

Genres are a way of categorizing literature. Genre is a French term that means ''kind'' or ''type.'' Genre can refer to both the category of literature such as tragedy, comedy, epic, poetry, or pastoral. It can also include modern forms of literature such as drama novels, or short stories. This term can also refer to types of literature such as mystery, science fiction, comedy or romance. *R.U.R.* is science fiction.

Plot

Generally plots should have a beginning, a middle, and a conclusion, but they may also sometimes be a series of episodes connected together. Basically, the plot provides the author with the means to explore primary themes. Students are often confused between the two terms; but themes explore ideas, and plots simply relate what happens

in a very obvious manner. Thus the plot of *R.U.R.* is the story of the creation of robots and the robot revolt that destroys almost all of mankind. But the theme is that of greed and technology out of control.

Setting

The time, place, and culture in which the action of the play takes place is called the setting. The elements of setting may include geographic location, physical or mental environments, prevailing cultural attitudes, or the historical time in which the action takes place. The locations for *R.U.R.* are on an island. They include the offices of the plant, Domin and Helena's home, and the plant laboratory. The action occurs over a period of eleven years.

HISTORICAL CONTEXT

The end of World War I brought many changes to Europe, Russia, and the United States. The years of war had been hard on many countries. Because of severe famine, Russia had signed a peace treaty and withdrawn from the war earlier than other countries. The Russian Revolution and the assassinations of the Romanovs did little to improve life for its citizens. Life was not much better in post-war Europe or America. The Spanish flu of 1918 left more than twenty million dead, and the war had been responsible for another eight and a half million deaths. The war had inflicted more than one hundred billion dollars worth of damage, and many countries were in serious debt. A year after the war ended a scientist finally succeeded in splitting an atom, opening the way for greater, more dangerous discoveries. Technology was allowing faster automobiles, new highways, and faster transportation. The first non-stop flight from North America to Ireland was completed in June 1919, and airplanes, which had proved very efficient during the war, were promising to provide a way to make the world smaller. Thus, when Capek began writing *R.U.R.*, the world seemed a dangerous and destructive place.

If technology was offering the promise of a better life, it was also promising a new level of destructiveness. The war effort had led to larger bombs and the development of gas weapons. The

COMPARE
&
CONTRAST

- **1921:** The first aircraft carrier is commissioned.

  Today: During periods of threatened conflict, aircraft carriers supply off-sea staging areas for bombing runs. They greatly add to a country's ability to wage war.

- **1921:** The Russian economy collapses, and Russian sailors attempt a bloody and unsuccessful mutiny.

  Today: The economy of what was once the Soviet Union is in disarray, creating increased risk from an unpaid military establishment.

- **1921:** Poliomyelitis (polio) is widespread in North America; it attacks U.S. Secretary of the Navy, Franklin Delano Roosevelt, and will leave him crippled for life.

  Today: Polio is almost completely eradicated due to immunizations, but as each disease is cured, new ones appear to take its place.

- **1921:** Famine kills 3 million Russians, and corpses are piled twenty feet high waiting for burial.

  Today: Famine continues to be a leading cause of death in the world as a result of weather disasters, such as hurricane Mitch, which destroyed much of Central America, and droughts which leave many starving in Africa.

- **1921:** The Autobahn opens in Germany, and thousands of miles of new surfaced highways are built in the United States to accommodate the increase in automobiles since the end of the war.

  Today: Citizens in both Europe and the United States take for granted the ready availability of automobiles and easy transportation that a major highway system offers.

Germans had developed a weapon so efficient that it could be used against a city from a distance of more than seventy-five miles. They used ''Big Bertha'' on Paris, and within three months, the bombardment had killed more than a thousand people. The weapon was inaccurate, but Paris was a large city and hard to miss. This new weapon showed that technology could be used to kill and from a distance, thus depersonalizing the process. War casualties, as a result of all this new technology, demonstrated just how fragile the human body really was. The sheer number of deaths and the severity of wounds shocked citizens, soldiers, and governments on both sides. In addition, soldiers fell victim to disease. The flu epidemic was so severe it was compared to the fourteenth-century plagues that killed one third of Europe's population. More importantly, the flu epidemic illustrated that while technology had made advances in killing people more efficiently, it had still not found a way to save their lives. It was a sobering lesson for human beings to learn.

If the war had horrified men, the need to find a way to prevent another war motivated leaders to seek other solutions. After five months of work, a treaty was forced upon the Germans that resulted in severe penalties and terrible financial hardship. Boundaries were redrawn and new countries created. The League of Nations was formed to settle disputes, but famine, poverty, and a decaying economic picture led to a shaky peace. This atmosphere forms the backdrop of *R.U.R.* Wars continue to be fought, but now robots sustain the casualties, which makes it even easier to continue the fighting. Leaders continue to look to better technologies to use against their enemies, and robots provide that technology. But just as the flu epidemic proved that technology and science had limits, *R.U.R.* proves that technology can create new and greater problems even as it makes life easier. Domin's desire to see robot labor eliminate famine with a plentiful harvest reflects the hunger that gripped much of the world in the years following the war. *R.U.R.* looks

A scene from a production of Capek's play

to the future and finds that answers may not be found easily in a laboratory.

CRITICAL OVERVIEW

Although printed reviews of *R.U.R.* are not readily available, there are a number of indications that the play was well received and that it enjoyed international success when it opened in the Czech National Theatre in 1921. It was equally successful when produced in Europe, Asia, and North America, opening on Broadway in 1922. At its premiere, audiences were both fascinated at the promises offered by technology and horrified at its potential for destruction. The play's success stemmed from the public's current interest in technology. Technological advances promised an easier life, one filled with more leisure time. The image on stage, of robots engaged in menial, mindless work, was appealing. Capek's lead character, Domin, suggests a utopian dream is possible. He envisions a world without hunger and with enough free labor to provide for all man's needs. Domin tells the audience of a future filled with freedom and a cornucopia of plenty, and then, the play's last three acts shatter that hope. For the audience, this turn of events is a graphic reminder that while technology may make man's life easier, it presents incredible risks far beyond what man can imagine or foresee. The play leaves the audience feeling conflicted between optimistic hopes for the future and pessimistic fears for that same future's troublesome potential.

With the play's success, Capek also found himself acclaimed an international success. This added to the reputation of the newly created Czech Republic. Although the play helped to establish Capek's reputation, he was disappointed that audiences and critics focused on the robots and not the social commentary their actions were intended to suggest. When Helena sees a robot for the first time, she cannot accept that it is real. The audience reacts just as strongly to the idea that robots might appear alive, function as humans, but need no subsistence or money to live. That they feel no pain and can express no opinions or desires also made them unique from mankind. But then the audience receives an abrupt reminder that slave labor has its price, and the horror of war is revisited in the theatre. The audience is also reminded that humanity comes with a price after all, it is the robots infusion with human-like traits that leads to the annihilation of mankind. Capek was so disappointed in the critics and audience's focus on robots instead of his social ideology that he later refused to see the play in performance. That *R.U.R.* is best remembered as the source of the word "robot" would only demonstrate to Capek that his play was a failure with regard to achieving the effect he had intended.

R.U.R. is considered the most successful of Capek's dramas. Its themes, the fate of man and the loss of man's humanity to technology, became a staple of his other works. The move from drama to fiction was a successful one for him, and Capek is best known for his science fiction novels. He did not oppose technology, but he was concerned that men had not given enough consideration to its potential misuse. For example, scientists succeeded in splitting the atom in 1919, and Capek, understanding the negative and dangerous potential of atomic energy, uses that destructive potential in *The Absolute at Large* (1922) and *Krakatit* (1924). He was not a realist focusing on man's ordinary dilemmas; instead Capek found expression in archetypal characters thrust into extraordinary situations. Capek's

novels and dramas are important as a contribution to Czech's literary reputation, but more importantly, they are important as an expression of Capek's concern for the survival of humanity. His work had relatively little influence on the future development of Czech theatre, since Capek's greatest focus was on fiction and not drama. In fact, his brother Josef's theatre designs had a more lasting influence, but *R.U.R.* continues to be performed in regional theatres where it persists in provoking discussions about technology, humanity, and greed.

CRITICISM

Sheri E. Metzger,

Metzger is a Ph.D., specializing in literature and drama at the University of New Mexico. In this essay, she discusses the theme of creation and the responsibility of the creator in R.U.R.

In *R.U.R.,* Karel Capek comes very close to echoing the ideas first explored by Mary Shelley a hundred years earlier in *Frankenstein* (1818). Like Shelley, Capek is also asking man to consider the ramifications of science. It is not simply whether man can achieve something through technology, but whether he *should* that interested Shelley. It is the question with which Capek struggled as well. The creature that Victor Frankenstein builds is meant to prove that its creator can supplant God, that God has become redundant. The creature is bigger than man, and illustrates Frankenstein's belief that he can create a man who is superior to that which God has created. Old Rossum has a similar goal. His robots are tireless workers, demanding little, but with the capacity to be stronger and faster, more efficient than the model created by God. But as both authors prove, creation is not without responsibility.

Even before Dr. Gall humanizes the robots, there were problems that signaled the failure of Rossum's creation. The robots appeared to be prone to suffering some sort of breakdown, which the plant has labeled "robot cramp." There is no acknowledged awareness that this may prove serious, and in fact, the breakdowns are dismissed as insignificant. Rossum has created something that appears human, feels human, and sounds human, but he stops short of creating humanity. However, on the surface, his creations seem to prove that man can conquer science. Rossum apparently never considers the potential for misuse, nor does he foresee that in the future man might modify his creation and create a new kind of robot. Greed motivates mass-production of the robots and their sale to any outlet with enough money. The goal of creating a labor saving substitute for man leads to the creation of quasi-men with orders to kill. And still, those who manufacture this new weapon accept no responsibility for its use. But the real creator of the robots is Dr. Gall who, through love, is motivated to create robots with souls. It never occurs to either Dr. Gall or Helena that they are creating life and that when life is created, someone has to assume responsibility for assimilating that life into society. It is the point that Old Rossum missed as well.

In a similar fashion, Victor Frankenstein misses that point when he creates his creature. He envisions himself as a replacement for God, as with his creation of a life, that God has been rendered unnecessary. As the robot's creators will learn a hundred years later, a new creation needs someone to acculturate this new life into the world. Frankenstein's creature is abandoned to find his own way, and left alone, he finds that murder is the only way to force his creator into assuming a responsible role. Of course even murder does not shock Victor, who escapes into fainting spells, illness, and sleep, rather than face what he has created. Of course, none of the plant managers at Rossum's Universal Robots feign illness when the first reports begin to surface of the robots' murderous spree; instead they continue to mass-produce their robots and accept orders and collect money. Still, they recognize the danger as they plot their escape on a waiting gun ship. Even as the robots besiege their last refuge, Busman escapes into his accounts, and the managers and scientists escape into a celebration of Helena's ten years on the island. None of the robot's creators appears willing to deal with the tragedy that is unfolding, and none will take responsibility to end it. Even when it has become clear that they may be the last of the humans to exist in the world, their only thought is to their own personal survival.

Frankenstein's creature is different from the robots in that he does not appear ordinary. He is human, but not human enough to be mistaken as such, as are the robots in Capek's play. James Naughton points out that Frankenstein's creature is really an ancestor to the robots. The purpose of the robots is different than that of the creature. Frankenstein has no role planned for his creature;

WHAT DO I READ NEXT?

- Mary Shelley's *Frankenstein* (1818) evokes many of the same issues about human responsibility as does *R.U.R.* This novel also deals with questions about the future of humanity and asks serious questions about man's humanity to man.

- *Prometheus Bound,* written by Aeschylus in the fifth century B.C., is an example from classical literature that explores how man deals with fate and with man's inhumanity toward man.

- In *The Insect Play,* written in 1922, Capek uses insects to represent man's vices and weaknesses.

- *War With the Newts* (1937) is often considered to be Capek's best novel. In this novel, man is challenged by that which he has created, just as in *R.U.R.*

- Eugene O'Neill's *Dynamo* (1929) examines a man's obsession with technology and a machine he has created.

there is no purpose to its formation, except to prove that it can be done. In contrast, Rossum has an idealistic purpose: the robots can be used to serve mankind. But, as Naughton observes, both creations are biological and not mechanical. This renders their creators god-like, since only God can create man. And while the creators have formed a biological being, they have themselves become mechanical and less human. Naughton states that "man is mocked, victimised and degraded by depersonalised, mechanistic man-made civilisation." But it is not the robots that have mocked man and mechanized his world; it is man who creates and then abandons responsibility that mocks himself and transforms humanity into machinery. When Busman attempts to use all the money the company has accumulated to pay for his escape and the others hope to buy their freedom by selling the robot formula, their actions demonstrate how dehumanized the creators have become. Similarly, when Victor Frankenstein allows his family to be murdered rather than speak

> IN *R.U.R.*, KAREL CAPEK COMES VERY CLOSE TO ECHOING THE IDEAS FIRST EXPLORED BY MARY SHELLEY A HUNDRED YEARS EARLIER IN *FRANKENSTEIN*"

out, he gives voice to the dehumanization of his actions.

Another creation, from the sixteenth century, designed to serve man was the Golem of Jewish legends. Although his purpose was intended to be noble (the Golem was to save the Jews from pogroms), like the robots, the Golem proved difficult to control. The Golem was also human in appearance and made from earth and other biological components. He was not mechanical; thus, once again, the creator, Rabbi Loew, is supplanting God to form a man. Loew's intent was worthy, but, as is the case with Frankenstein and Rossum, he failed to accept responsibility for his creation. Norma Comrada argues that there are many similarities between the Golem and Rossum's robots, and she points that these similarities include elements of Adam's creation. This reminder of man's creation by God suggests "a challenge to and competition with a higher power." But Comrada argues that there is another, more significant connection between robots and Golem. She quotes a Capek interview from 1935, where the playwright stated that "the Robot is the Golem made flesh by mass production." And yet, the robots are very different from the Golem: they never make claims to spiritual purpose and they are not designed to protect man, only to do his work. And they come to represent man's greed at its most offensive.

In this respect, the purpose of robots differs significantly from the other two earlier creation stories. Rabbi Loew never seeks any money for his creation, and Frankenstein never seeks to profit from his creature, in fact disclaiming knowledge of its existence. Only the robot's creators realize that capitalism and economic profit are the important by-products of supplanting God. This changes the emphasis of the play back to the actions of the humans and away from the robots. And there is every reason to think that is what Capek intended.

The robots proved to be both frightening and captivating when first introduced. They also provided the genesis for hundreds of robots and films that followed. The robots were so successful that their original purpose was forgotten. Capek is often quoted as saying that he wanted the play to focus on humanity, but, instead, it spawned an industry of robotic clones. William Harkins quotes Capek as saying that *R.U.R.* was "the worst of all his plays, one which he no longer wished to see on the stage." And Comrada says that Capek, "had become increasingly alarmed by the manner in which robots were perceived and portrayed in plays, films, and stories in various parts of the world." Naughton also quotes Capek as stating that *R.U.R.* "was concerned, 'not with Robots, but with people.'" He wanted to be able to say, "It was a great thing to be a man." But instead, his play questions the goodness of man. At the conclusion of Merritt Abrash's comparison between the 1923 translation of *R.U.R.* and a 1989 translation, Abrash points out that the new translation provides a clearer understanding of the role Capek intended for the robots. Abrash says that by restoring nearly twenty-five percent of preciously deleted text, the robots are diminished into just another plot device. Instead, the plot shifts its focus back to the humans, as Capek intended. The play then becomes a study in human behavior, since Abrash points out that the play becomes important when readers understand that it is not about how robots behave as robots, but about how robots behave when they become human that matters. In fact, the play is also about how humans behave when they abdicate responsibility for humanity. It is in their role as creators of men that humans fail. Capek was not opposed to science, but he was concerned with man's ability to control what he had created. His modern day creation story illustrates that responsibility for science continues to be as important as scientific discoveries it unearths.

Source: Sheri E. Metzger, for *Drama For Students,* Gale Group, 2000.

Ludwig Lewisohn

Lewisohn reviews the 1922 London production of R.U.R., *terming the production a success as both a work of ideas and an entertaining evening of theatre.*

There are two kinds of notions in the world. There is the kind that hits you between the eyes; there is the kind that irradiates the soul. Thus there are two kinds of art. There is the art that dazzles and grows dark; there is the art that shines calmly and forever. It would be a sorry sort of affectation to deny one's natural interest in the merely striking and merely dazzling, especially when it is implicated with powerful forces beyond itself. But it is healthy and necessary to keep the difference in mind. I do not at all blame the Theater Guild for producing "R.U.R." by the Czechish playwright Karel Capek, especially in view of the quality of the production; I think it well for both the directors of the Guild and for ourselves to remember and, for a space, to realize the precise quality of the drama in question. The central idea has violence rather than creative energy. Punch is not power any more than a pine torch is a star. Punch, indeed, commonly goes with a lack of power. And the lack of authentic power in the central idea of "R.U.R." is borne out by the execution, which is a strange mixture of wavering brilliance and mere confusion.

What is Capek after? What, in plain language—everything worth saying can be said thus—does he want to tell? Something like this: An industrial civilization with its power concentrated in the persons of the captains of industry and war wants hands not minds, helots not men. It is secure and powerful in the measure in which the proletariat is degraded, insensitive, supine. That is obviously true and was worked out long ago in a melodramatic but quite telling way by Jack London in one of his not altogether deservedly forgotten books. Now, Capek's argument runs on, if ever this industrial civilization does succeed in reducing the proletariat to the level of mere mechanical helots, then the death of civilization will be upon us. For when these helots revolt they will destroy all things and values that represent the spirit of man. The squint at Russia is obvious; the complete absurdity of the argument equally so. For on the one hand we have the assumption that men can be reduced to the level of mere machines which, in the nature of things, would not revolt at all; on the other hand we are told that these helots will revolt against slavery, oppression, their own soulless estate, which at once reinvests them with all the passions, powers, and thoughts from which the triumphs of civilization—St. Peter's and the Divine Comedy and the Ninth Symphony—draw their origin.

In order to project his argument pictorially and dramatically Capek uses what may be called the Golem-Frankenstein device. Rossum, a great physiological chemist, invents a method of manufacturing man-like creatures who make good workers and soldiers but are without passions or self-originating

> "CAPEK'S ARGUMENT RUNS ON, IF EVER THIS INDUSTRIAL CIVILIZATION DOES SUCCEED IN REDUCING THE PROLETARIAT TO THE LEVEL OF MERE MECHANICAL HELOTS, THEN THE DEATH OF CIVILIZATION WILL BE UPON US."

thoughts. These "robots" are manufactured, bought, and sold as workers and, finally; as cannon-fodder. They soon vastly outnumber mankind whose birth-rate declines to nothing since men cannot compete in cheapness or usefulness with the robots. They revolt —this is the central absurdity—slaughter all men left, but are doomed to extinction in their turn since the secret of their manufacture is lost. This ending, which might be called logical were not the whole thing the reverse, is furthermore stultified by an epilogue in which a male and female robot suddenly become human and enter, a queer Adam and Eve, the dusty paradise left them.

There can be no question but that behind the play, as well as in a hundred details of the execution, a high and powerful passion, a far from ignoble imagination have been at work. "R.U.R." is no ordinary work, Capek's no ordinary talent or intelligence. I have been at some pains to point out the brittleness of the argument, the confusion of the symbolism, because this brittleness and this confusion are very characteristic of a good deal of the minor serious drama of the hour. These plays come with an intellectual and poetic gesture which, upon analysis, is seen to be merely a gesture. Their turbid symbolism and specious arguments are in danger of making many people undervalue the literature which is humbler and truer, more concrete, and for that very reason more significant; not spectacular but sound.

Whatever the play has of imagination, weirdness, beauty, horror is fully expressed if not indeed heightened by the settings, costumes, acting, directing at the Garrick. As an example of the art of the theater the production is exquisite in skill, sensitiveness, in the unemphatic completeness of its command of all the resources of that art. It deserves the utmost admiration and the closest attention; the play deserves the nine days' wonder of the proverb.

Source: Ludwig Lewisohn, "Helots" in the *Nation,* Vol. 115, no. 2991, November 1, 1922, p. 478.

Anonymous

In this review of the London debut of Capek's play, the critic finds the dystopian drama to be "an exciting, thrilling play, which everyone will enjoy."

R.U.R. can hardly be better described than by its own subtitle, "A Fantastic Melodrama." Here and there the fact of its projection into the future, its touches of genuine satire, its digressions into speculation, make one mistake it for a play of ideas. Then it seems disappointing, and we perceive the thin places in plot and characterization. Especially did it seem a "let down" to me, for I have had the pleasure of watching some of the rehearsals of Mr. Karel Capek's other piece, *The Insect Play,* which Mr. Playfair produces at the Regent on May 5th. Here the satire is vivid, and the humour light and delicate. In fine, it is in comparison with *The Insect Play* that we see what is wrong with *R.U.R.,* though it may be that *R.U.R.* will be esteemed the more taking piece. *R.U.R.* has much of the character of an early work. Its whole attitude is tentative and it takes obvious refuge in action and excitement from the difficulties both of sustained characterization and reflection. There is little character drawing in it. All the people are types, somewhat hazily conceived. The exasperating *ingénue.* Helena Glory, is the least successful, and they range up to Dr. Gall (head of the psychological department of Rossum's Universal Robots) and Emma, Helena Glory's servant, and Jacob Berman, the chief cashier. But really it is a quibble to draw attention to these faults of the play, for once grant that it is to be melodrama, and not a play of ideas, it is extraordinarily good, and holds the spectators from beginning to end. The actual story also is a genuine effort of the imagination.

An old scientist has found out not merely how to produce life, but how to make tissues which can be infused with the life that he has made. He tries to imitate nature and makes an artificial dog. "That took him several years," explains one of the characters, sarcastically, "and resulted in a sort of stunted calf which died in a few days." Then he tried to make a man. But his nephew was a man of very different ideals. He saw that there was money in the idea. He saw that, given a slight twist, the formula would produce not men, but "Robots," living,

intelligent, working machines. Young Rossum goes over the human anatomy and cuts out everything that is "unnecessary." A weaver does not need to play the piano and feel joy or sorrow; or love or hate. Young Rossum, then, produces Robots. The factory is a going concern. Helena Glory comes to the island where the R.U.R. factory is situated on behalf of a sentimental "League of Humanity," who are shocked at the material way in which Robots are looked upon. She sentimentalizes over their hard lot (they are sent back to the stamping mills and ground if they show any signs of inefficiency) and ends by marrying the General Manager, Harry Domain. But Dr. Gall is a scientist and missionary, and carries on the tradition of old Rossum rather than young Rossum. He pushes forward. He endows the Robots with pain, so that they shall not be careless and break their limbs. This is the beginning of the end. Pain proves the beginning of some sort of consciousness. Ten years after the opening scene of the play the Robots are turning upon the men who have made them and conquering the world, for men have ceased to be born, and the Robots now outnumber the human beings by a hundred to one. A thrilling scene ensues in which the humans are besieged by the Robots, and finally overwhelmed, only one man surviving. But the secret of making Robots has been lost through the sentimental action of Helena Glory, who, before the catastrophe, has burned the formula.

Power has made the Robots still more like human beings. They only last twenty years, and their leaders are in agony lest the race of Robots should die out. They are machines and the formula has gone. But the anxiety, in its turn, has had its effect upon them, and the play ends with a young Robot and Robotess going out into the world suffering from new and unaccountable symptoms, such as inability to live without each other, willingness to sacrifice everything for the other's welfare, laughter and a quickened heart-beat. A new Adam and Eve have come back to the world.

An exciting, thrilling play, which everyone will enjoy. But the glamour over, to return to its faults. The part, played by old Rossum's formula is ludicrously like that of the "marriage lines" in the old-fashioned Lyceum melodrama. The tragedy is made to turn on their burning by the impulsive sentimental young wife, who has got them out of the strong box where they are kept. Now, Robots are supposed to be turned out by the hundred-thousand. Imagine a play in which the tragedy depends on Mr. Ford losing the formula for his motors! Manufacture in bulk would so patently involve at least some hundred printed copies of the formula that this flaw is worrying, and gives far more sense of unreality than a mere synthetic man. The second drawback is the extremely tiresome character of Helena Glory, played by Miss Frances Carson, whose pretty looks could do no more than make her bearable. The men characters all have a certain touch of imaginative largeness about them. Harry Domain, the manager, wants to make Robots so as to free the human race from the grind of monotonous labour. Dr. Gall is a scientist with enthusiasms. The half-comic cashier is yet a man not without grandeur and a sense of the hugeness of the machine for which he works. But Helena Glory is of the past; she is told nothing about the revolution, and her ten-year anniversary is being celebrated with pearl necklaces, cyclamens and so forth all through the exciting part. Her characteristic speech is, ''Oh, Harry, I don't understand!'' She would seem out of place in modern London, she is two or three centuries behind the life of the factory between 1950 and 1960. She interrupts the adventure story in the most exasperating way. The adult playgoer will feel almost a schoolboy irritation at the way in which she interferes with our enjoyment of the revolution scene, and in the way in which she is always on the stage. In exasperation we remember that she does not even fulfil the one function of the harem woman; she is childless. All this would be bearable if she were not so constantly in evidence.

Mr. Basil Rathbone looked very handsome as Harry Domain, but acted stiffly. Mr. Brember Wills's acting as Alquist, in the last act was too much reminiscent of his performance in *Heartbreak House.* Mr. Leslie Banks as a Robot, and Miss Beatrix Thomson as a Robotess, were admirable, and the entrance of the Robots at the end was most striking; indeed, I wish we could see more of them—they are really alarming and convincing monsters. I am sorry that Miss Olga Lindo, as Helena II., the Robotess through whom love comes back into the world, should have modelled her costume on the tradition of the opera stage, hair down, backward tilted pose and white nightgown. The result is that to most people she does not look nearly so attractive as Sulla, the unemotional Robotess.

May I compliment the Reandean management on their news-sheet and programme, of which I had not previously seen a number? The cover of it is delightful, with its harmonious printing, and the contents are quite amusing.

Source: Anonymous, review of *R.U.R.* in the *Spectator,* Vol. 130, no. 4949, May 5, 1923, pp. 755–56.

POWER HAS MADE THE ROBOTS STILL MORE LIKE HUMAN BEINGS.''

SOURCES

Comrada, Norma, ''Golem and Robot: A Search for Connections'' in the *Journal of the Fantastic in the Arts,* Vol. 7, nos. 2-3, 1996, pp. 244-54.

Day, Barbara. ''R.U.R'' in the *International Dictionary of Theatre* Volume 1: *Plays,* edited by Mark Hawkins-Dady, St. James Press, 1992, pp. 695-96.

Day, Barbara. ''Karel Capek'' in the *International Dictionary of Theatre* Volume 2: *Playwrights,* edited by Mark Hawkins-Dady, St. James Press, 1992, pp. 162-65.

Drake, William, ''Karel Capek,'' in *Contemporary European Writers,* John Day, 1928, pp. 310-16.

Harkins, William E. ''The Real Legacy of Karel Capek'' in *The Czechoslovak Contribution to World Culture,* edited by Miloslav Rechcigl, Jr., Mouton & Co., 1964, pp. 60-67.

Naughton, James D., ''Futurology and Robots: Karel Capek's *R.U.R.* '' in *Renaissance and Modern Studies,* Vol. XXVIII, 1984, pp. 72-86.

FURTHER READING

Abrash, Merritt, ''*R.U.R.* Restored and Reconsidered'' in *Extrapolation: A Journal of Science Fiction and Fantasy,* Vol. 32, no. 2, Summer 1991, pp. 184-92.
    This article offers a comparison between translations and suggests that in early translations as much as twenty-five percent of the text was censored to removed suggestive sexual or political content.

Harkins, William E., *Karel Capek,* Columbia University Press, 1962.
    This is the only book-length biography of Capek in English. It contains a lengthy discussion of his works as well.

Kussi, Peter, editor. *Toward the Radical Center: A Karel Capek Reader,* Catbird Press, 1990.
    This is a collection of essays about Capek's work and also contains a new translation of the play.

Suvin, Darko. *Metamorphoses of Science Fiction,* Yale University Press, 1979.
    This book discusses the development of science fiction as a genre and Capek's place within the genre.

A Taste of Honey

SHELAGH DELANEY

1958

When Shelagh Delaney began working on *A Taste of Honey,* she intended the material to be a novel; but instead, in what has become a very famous story, Delaney became disgusted at the lack of substance found in plays currently being produced for the stage and decided to rework her fledgling novel into a play. It took her two weeks. *A Taste of Honey* opened at the Theatre Royal, Stratford East in London on May 27, 1958. On February 10, 1959, Delaney's play moved to Wyndham's Theatre in London's West End, and on October 4, 1960, the play opened on Broadway at New York City's Lyceum Theatre. Delaney's play opened to mixed reviews. In many cases, her characters were praised for their honest, realistic voices. The play was also singled out for its accurate depictions of working class lives.

Yet there was also concern that too much praise for the play's nineteen-year-old author would make it difficult for her to ever create another hit play, the theory being that early success might prove so intimidating that she could never live up to her first accomplishment. In a sense, this is what happened, since Delaney never wrote another play that achieved the success of *A Taste of Honey.* However, this first play did earn several awards, including the Charles Henry Foyle New Play award in 1958 and the New York Drama Critics Award in 1961. The film version won the British Academy Award for best picture in 1961 and a best supporting actress award for Dora Bryan. The film also won two additional

awards at the Cannes Film Festival in 1962 for best actor (Murray Melvin) and best actress (Rita Tushingham). Much of the credit for the play's success is attributed to Joan Littlewood, whose experimental Theatre Workshop first received and produced the play.

AUTHOR BIOGRAPHY

Shelagh Delaney was born November 25, 1939, in Salford, Lancashire, England. Her father, a bus inspector, and her mother were part of the English working class, the social group that informs of her writing. Delaney attended Broughton Secondary School but began writing even before she completed her education. She had no further interest in formal education, and after she left school, she held a number of jobs, including salesgirl, usherette, and clerk.

A Taste of Honey was produced when Delaney was eighteen-years-old. Although this play was originally being written as a novel, it was rewritten as a play in response to Delaney's dissatisfaction with contemporary theatre. Delaney felt that she could write a better play, with more realistic dialogue, than the plays that were currently being staged. *A Taste of Honey* became an unexpected hit, winning several awards both as a play and later as a film. Delaney followed with another play, *The Lion in Love,* two years later (1960). She did not write another play for nearly twenty years.

Instead, Delaney focused on short stories, *Sweetly Sings the Donkey* (1963); screenplays, *Charlie Bubbles* (1968) and *The Raging Moon* (1970); and television plays, *Did Your Nanny Come from Bergen?* (1970), *St. Martin's Summer* (1974), and *Find Me First* (1979). In 1979, Delaney again wrote for the theatre when she adapted *The House That Jack Built,* a BBC television script she had written in 1977. Delaney followed this stage work with two radio plays, *So Does the Nightingale* (1980) and *Don't Worry about Matilda* (1981). After another television play, *Rape* (1981), Delaney was asked to write a screenplay based on the true story of a women who was executed for murder. This work became the film *Dance with a Stranger* (1985). Delaney has also contributed articles for the *New York Times Magazine,* the *Saturday Evening Post, Cosmopolitan,* and *Evergreen Review.*

Shelagh Delaney

Delaney's first play proved a difficult act to follow, and none of her subsequent work received the same critical acclaim that greeted *A Taste of Honey,* although her collection of short, autobiographical stories, *Sweetly Sings the Donkey,* was considered a critical success. Delaney believes in social protest and has not been afraid to speak out on the need for a more realistic theatre, one that depicts the working class environment of many British citizens. Delaney lives in London, where she was made a fellow of the Royal Society of Literature in 1985.

PLOT SUMMARY

Act I, scene i

The act opens with Helen and Jo in the process of moving into their new flat. It is cold, squalid, and damp. Helen is sick with a cold, but not too sick to engage in bickering conversation with her daughter, Jo. The two squabble effortlessly over minor issues, such where the heat is located, making coffee, or even how often to bathe. In the midst of this activity, Helen's boyfriend, Peter, enters. He is much younger than Helen. It becomes clear that Helen has moved to hide from Peter, who is very surprised to learn that Helen has a daughter. Failing to engage the older women in sex, Peter asks Helen to leave with him and get a drink. He also asks her to marry him, but is it unclear if he is actually serious about marriage or simply trying to get Helen to sleep with him. When Helen continues to insist that she is too ill to go out, Peter finally leaves. Helen tells Jo to leave the unpacking, since everything is best hidden in the dark. The scene ends with their exiting to go to bed.

Act I, scene ii

The scene opens on Jo and a young black man. He is walking her to her door and stops to kiss her. He asks her to marry him, and when she realizes he is serious, Jo says yes. The Boy pulls from his pocket a ring, but it is too large for Jo's finger, and so, she places the ring on a ribbon and ties it about her neck. The Boy is in the navy and will soon be leaving for six months at sea. After he leaves to go out with his friends, Helen begins to quiz Jo about why she looks so happy. Jo and Helen begin speaking of Jo's father, and the audience learns that many years earlier, Helen's husband had divorced her because he was not the father of the child (Jo) that Helen was expecting.

Helen tells Jo that she is going to marry Peter. At Jo's shocked exclamation that he is much younger, Helen reminds her daughter that at forty, she is scarcely old and dried up. Peter enters, and the moment Helen leaves to dress, he and Jo begin to argue. When Helen enters again, she tells Jo that Peter has bought a house in which they will live. As soon as Helen leaves again, Jo begins to go through the photos in Peter's wallet, accusing him of having many girlfriends. When Helen enters again, they all begin arguing, and finally Helen and Peter leave, and Jo begins to cry. The Boy enters and begins to sooth Jo. In her loneliness, she invites him to stay with her during the Christmas holidays.

The lights fade down and Helen enters with an assortment of boxes containing her wedding clothes. She finds the ring that The Boy gave Jo and seizes it, complaining that Jo is ruining her life in choosing marriage at such a young age. After Jo asks her, Helen begins to tell Jo about her father, whom Jo learns was an idiot. Jo immediately begins to worry that she has inherited her father's weak mind, and Helen recounts that Jo was the result of one brief encounter with a man whom she really did not know. The act ends with Helen rushing out to her own wedding.

Act II, scene i

It is summer, about six months later. The scene opens with an obviously pregnant Jo entering with her friend Geof. He has been evicted from his apartment, probably because he is homosexual. He needs a place to stay, and Jo invites him to stay in the apartment. Geof wants to take care of her, and over the coming month, he does just that, cleaning and preparing for the coming baby. Jo is full of emotions, hating the idea of love and motherhood but at the same time needing someone to love her. She calls Geof her big sister, and he is very tolerant of her mood swings. He has also been supporting her, paying the rent and buying food.

Geof very much wants to be a father to Jo's coming child. He is genuinely fond of Jo and is even willing to accept a heterosexual lifestyle if it means he will have a place in Jo's and the baby's future. Goef tries to kiss Jo and asks her to marry him, but she rejects his advances, saying she hates sex. Geof tells Jo that he would sooner be dead than leave her, and they agree that he can stay; they will continue together as they have for the past month. Helen enters. Geof has sent for Helen, reasoning that Jo really needs her mother. But he fails to understand the sordid nature of their relationship. Helen is angry that Jo is pregnant and tells her that everyone is calling her a whore. After some angry, harsh, and accusatory words are exchanged, Jo threatens to jump out the window if Helen does not leave. In the silence that follows, Jo sends Geof to make coffee, and Helen continues to bully Jo.

Helen tries to leave Jo some money, and just as she is ready to leave, Peter enters. He is as loud and obnoxious as he was six months earlier, and he is drunk and abusive. He begins to berate Helen, saying he married his mother, an old bag, by mistake. A clearly embarrassed Helen tries to silence him, but Peter lets slip that he has been chasing young women. Helen is upset. Peter stumbles and passes out. In a few moments he is back on stage, looking slightly more sober. Peter refuses to allow Helen to bring Jo back to their home, and although Helen hesitates about leaving Jo, she runs out after Peter. As the scene ends, Jo is once again alone with Geof, and Peter has taken the money that Helen intended to leave for Jo.

Act II, scene ii

It is a few months later, and Jo's baby is due any day. Geof is cleaning, as Jo sits watching him. As they begin to talk, it becomes clear that Jo is worried

A scene from the film adaptation of Delaney's play, starring Rita Tushingham as Jo (left) and Dora Bryan as Helen

that her child will be like her own father, the village idiot. But Geof tells her that Helen undoubtedly lied about Jo's father. Jo is once again emotional, and when Geof suggests that she begin preparing for the baby, Jo insists she intends to kill it. Geof has made a cake and as they prepare to celebrate the end of his schooling and exams and the coming baby, Helen walks in, loaded with packages. Jo and Helen immediately begin to argue over whether Jo will go to the hospital to have the baby. Jo insists she will have her baby in the apartment.

Helen insults Geof, and he leaves. Jo chastises Helen for being rude to Geof, but she seems not to have noticed. Within moments, Helen is forced to admit that Peter has thrown her out and run off with a younger woman. Jo leaves to go lie down, and Geof enters with a bag of food. Helen is assuming a motherly role, insisting on cleaning and caring for Jo. Although she readily admits that she never remembers Jo when she's with a man, Helen's new single status has reminded her of her daughter and impending grandchild. Even though Jo wants Geof to be with her when the baby comes, Helen has sent him away. Jo finally tells her mother that the baby will be black, and a shocked Helen suggests they drown the child or give it away. The play ends with

Helen rushing off stage to find a bar and a drink but promising that she will be back.

CHARACTERS

The Boy

The Boy is a black sailor who appears briefly, professing love for Jo. He asks her to marry him and gives her a ring. They spend a week together during Christmas, but then he leaves for a six month tour at sea. The Boy never reappears in Jo's life and does not know that she is carrying his child.

Helen

Helen is described as a semi-whore who drinks too much. As the play opens, she has a cold and has moved herself and daughter into a chilly, squalid flat. Helen is young, barely forty. She has been married and divorced, but her daughter, Jo, is the result of a brief affair with another man. Helen has been involved with many men, and she has not been any kind of real mother to Jo, who appears to desperately need maternal guidance. Helen thinks first and foremost of her own pleasure. She chooses

MEDIA ADAPTATIONS

- *A Taste of Honey* was adapted as a film in 1961, earning popular success and a number of critical awards. The film stars Rita Tushingham, Robert Stephens, Dora Bryan, Murray Melvin, and Paul Danquah. The director was Tony Richardson, who also adapted the screenplay with Delaney.

to marry Peter, perhaps because she loves him, but also because he has money to keep her. When Peter finally throws Helen out for a younger woman, she goes back to Jo, suddenly remembering that Jo is her daughter. Jo accuses Helen of never really being a mother to her. And, indeed, it appears that Helen is incapable of thinking of anything except her own needs.

Geof

See Geoffrey Ingram

Geoffrey Ingram

Geof is a homosexual art student and friend of Jo's. His landlady has thrown him out on the street, and he begins to care for Jo, sleeping on her couch. Geof genuinely loves Jo. He is perhaps the only person who completely loves and cares for her. Geof tolerates Jo's emotional outbursts and even tries to reunite her with her mother, but he discovers that Helen is too self-centered to ever love anyone but herself. Geof also offers Jo financial support, paying the rent, buying food, and performing domestic tasks like cleaning and cooking. Although Helen turns up repeatedly, whenever she happens to remember that she has a daughter or needs a place to go, it is Geof who is the steadying influence in Jo's life.

Jimmie

See The Boy

Jo

See Josephine

Josephine

Jo is Helen's daughter. She never knew her real father, but she does know that Helen's husband divorced her after she became pregnant with another man's child. Jo has many questions about her real father, but she is upset to learn that he was probably mentally deficient, an ''idiot,'' according to Helen. Jo is in love with a young black sailor. He arrives to comfort her after Helen leaves to marry Peter. The two spend a few brief days together, and after he has left for a six month tour at sea, Jo discovers that she is pregnant.

Jo has never experienced the love of a mother. She has been repeatedly abandoned by Helen, who did not want a child and has never assumed any responsibility or care for Jo. Jo is not at all sure that she wants the child she is expecting, nor is she sure what she will do with it when it appears. However, by the end of the play, it appears that Jo has rejected her mother's life for the stability that her friendship with Geof offers.

Peter Smith

Peter is about ten years younger than Helen. He fancies himself quite a lady's man, carrying photos of many old girlfriends in his wallet. He drinks too much, as does Helen. Peter is as self-centered as Helen, first begging her to marry him and then chasing other women. Peter is cruel and rude, caring little for anyone's feeling. He treats Jo, the daughter of the woman he professes to love, as a troublesome irritation to be gotten rid of. When Peter throws Helen out, it comes as no surprise to anyone involved.

THEMES

Alienation and Loneliness

Jo has essentially been abandoned by her mother. This has been a life-long pattern, but it becomes overwhelming when Helen moves her daughter to a new flat just before Christmas and then leaves almost immediately with her boyfriend. Jo's loneliness directly leads to her pregnancy. When her mother, Helen, leaves with Peter, Jo dissolves into tears. The young black man, who professes to love her, appears, and Jo invites him to stay with her for the Christmas holidays. In the previous scene, Jo is resistant to any intimacy with this young man, who is leaving for a six-month tour at sea with the navy. But when he appears later at her flat, Jo is so overwhelmed with loneliness that she throws away her future plans for work, right along with her inhibitions.

Duty and Responsibility

Helen has a duty to care for her daughter, but she assumes no responsibility for her actions nor does she assume the mother's role. Helen is ready to run off with a man, quite literally, at a moment's notice. She never considers what will happen to her child. And it becomes clear as the play progresses that this has been a frequent occurrence in Jo's life. Helen has never considered her daughter's feelings or assumed any responsibility for her care. Jo is expected to care for herself, and apparently she has done so for some time before the play opens. Helen thinks so little of her child that she never even tells the men with whom she is involved that she has a daughter. This means that Jo has no model for motherhood on which to base her own behavior. This is an issue of the last act when Jo struggles with her impending motherhood and her ambivalence over having a child of her own. There is ample evidence that, with her child, Jo will repeat the cycle of neglect that Helen started.

Friendship

Geof proves his worth as a friend through the efforts he makes to care for Jo. As her only friend, he moves in when she most needs help. Because she does not want anyone to see her, Jo cannot work, and thus, she has no funds with which to pay for rent and food. Geof needs a place to stay, having been evicted because he is homosexual, and Jo offers him her living room couch as a bed. Geof becomes Jo's only friend. He pays the rent and buys and prepares the food. His friendship extends to an attempted reunion between Jo and her mother—though Geof fails to realize the extent of Helen's selfishness. He is the only person who unconditionally loves Jo. Geof offers her loyal, generous friendship, something she has never known and is not quite sure how to accept.

Mother and Daughter Relationship

A central theme in this play is the nature of mother/daughter love. In the case of Helen and Jo, there seems to be no real parent/child relationship in the traditional sense. Helen does not act like a mother, nurturing and caring for her child. Jo does not act like a child, respecting and obeying her parent. In fact, Jo does not address Helen as "mother," preferring to call her by her given name. Jo

TOPICS FOR FURTHER STUDY

- Discuss the interracial love affair between Jo and the character known as The Boy. In view of her mother's reaction at the end of Act II, how much of a factor was race in choosing him as a date and later as a lover?

- Research the economic conditions of working class women in northern England during the twentieth century. What opportunities existed for women in the working class?

- Helen is described as a semi-whore. Discuss the depictions of women's lives and the poverty of the setting. According to late twentieth-century standards, would Helen still be described in this manner? Do you think that attitudes toward sexuality have changed that dramatically in the last forty years?

- Jo has some artistic talent and Geof is attending art school. Late in the play, the audience learns that Jo is able to earn some money touching up photos. Investigate the opportunities for aspiring artists. What kinds of jobs are available and how difficult is it to earn a living?

addresses her mother as "Helen" as a form of disrespect.

For her part, Helen has often hid the fact that she even has has a daughter, perhaps in the hopes of creating an illusion of youth for herself. Jo is abandoned by her mother whenever a better opportunity—usually a man with money—comes along. It is clear from her behavior that Jo desperately needs a mother. In the terms of a nurturing parent, Geof is the closest thing Jo has.

Pride

Jo has so much pride that she will not leave her flat once her pregnancy becomes evident. She certainly must be aware that she is the object of neighborhood gossip, but Jo refuses to face or acknowledge this negative attention. Staying a prisoner in her flat means that she cannot work, and so, she has no way to earn money and support herself. Pride is also an element of Helen's character: she is willing to push her illegitimate grandchild in a pram down neighborhood streets but when she discovers that the child is black, has too much pride to be seen with this particular child. Jo's pregnancy by a black man is not really a racial issue, rather it is a class issue. Jo and Helen may be poor, working class people, but Helen considers the black father to be from a class below their working class status. As such, Helen rejects Jo's unborn child, even offering to drown it or give it away, rather than be seen with it. Helen's misplaced pride permitted her to remain in a relationship with a man who mocked, humiliated, and eventually threw her out of his home, but this same pride causes her to reject her own grandchild, who is not deemed suitable.

The kind of pride exhibited in *A Taste of Honey* is not the positive kind that enables a character to rise above adversity. Rather, the misplaced dignity that Jo and Helen exhibit serves to chain them to their cycle of misery. They are too blinded by their skewed standards to break free of the confines of their existence.

STYLE

Angry Young Men

"Angry Young Men" was the label given to a group of British writers—notably playwright John Osborne—of the late-1950s, whose work expressed bitterness and disillusionment with Postwar English society. A common feature of their work is the antihero, a flawed, often abrasive character who rebels against a corrupt social order and strives for personal integrity. Delaney did not set out to become a part of this group, but when her play was produced, many critics saw her work as a protest against working class poverty and the hopelessness of a social system that confined people by status or class.

There are elements of the "Angry Theatre" in Delaney's play, notably its working class setting. But her characters are ultimately unmotivated. There is no sense that either Jo, Helen, or even Geof has an agenda to change the world, to correct the injustices of their existence. Unlike Jimmy Porter in Osborne's *Look Back in Anger,* Delaney's characters let life pass them by without attempting change, without lashing out, rebelling at their unfavorable

situations. As Delaney frequently stated, however, her intention was to illuminate the working class in her play, to strive for realism. She was not angling for inclusion in the Angry Theatre.

Audience

The people for whom a drama is performed. Authors usually write with an audience in mind; however, Delaney is said to have written for actors, whom she felt were being given little enough to do in contemporary productions. One interesting aspect of *A Taste of Honey* is that Delaney frequently has her characters address the audience directly. In this sense she enables the actors to more fully realize their characterizations—engage in a kind of faux dialogue with "real" people (the audience). The technique also allowed the original audiences, many of whom had little contact with the social strata depicted in the play, a closer interaction with the working class.

Character

A person in a dramatic work. The actions of each character are what constitute the story. Character can also include the idea of a particular individual's morality. Characters can range from simple stereotypical figures to more complex multi-faceted ones. Characters may also be defined by personality traits, such as the rogue or the damsel in distress. "Characterization" is the process of creating a lifelike person from an author's imagination. To accomplish this the author provides the character with personality traits that help define who he will be and how he will behave in a given situation.

Genre

Genres are a way of categorizing literature. Genre is a French term that means "kind" or "type." Genre can refer to both the category of literature such as tragedy, comedy, epic, poetry, or pastoral. It can also include modern forms of literature such as drama novels or short stories. This term can also refer to types of literature such as mystery, science fiction, comedy, or romance. *A Taste of Honey* is generally classified as a realist, modern drama.

Plot

This term refers to the pattern of events. Generally plots should have a beginning, a middle, and a conclusion, but they may also sometimes be a series of episodes that are thematically linked (a technique frequently employed by German playwright Bertolt Brecht). Basically, the plot provides the author with the means to explore primary themes. The plot of *A Taste of Honey* is how Jo comes learns to live with her mother's abandonment, while finding the strength to survive. The theme of the play is the nature of the mother/daughter relationship.

Setting

The time, place, and culture in which the action of the play takes place is called the setting. The elements of setting may include geographic location, physical or mental environments, prevailing cultural attitudes, or the historical time in which the action takes place. The setting for *A Taste of Honey* is a run-down flat in a poor neighborhood. The action occurs over a nine to ten month period, roughly the gestation period for Jo's child.

HISTORICAL CONTEXT

England in the mid- to late-1950s was still feeling the effects of World War II. The bombing of London—the "Blitz" as it was often called—began September 7, 1940, and continued throughout the war. Children were sent out into the countryside for safety, and women in their twenties became eligible for the draft. Rationing of food, fuel, and other essentials needed for the war was common place. By 1944, Germany's secret weapon, the V2 ballistic missile began targeting London, intensifying the damage from years of earlier bombing. When the war ended, American soldiers returned home to a country that had suffered little damage within its borders.

Britain, on the other hand, had suffered greatly during the war and rebuilding would take a very long time. Rationing continued long after the end of the war. People needed homes as well as buildings in which to work and pray and, once again, enjoy life. The rebuilding of Britain's less tangible assets would take a long time, also. The war had intensified feelings about loyalty and betrayal, innocence and corruption, commitment and abandonment. The

results of the Blitz and the images of the Holocaust had horrified Britains, but their endurance and survival had also strengthened the British resolve to reclaim their lifestyle.

In America, the suffering brought about by the Great Depression and World War II ended in the Postwar boom of the 1950s. With the exception of minorities, notably black Americans, the 1950s were economically successful. But this was not the case in England, where huge numbers of the population were on relief, the British government's form of welfare. There was great despair over the future and society seemed brutal and mechanistic. This was especially true of the country's industrial heartland. One response to this feeling of despair was evident in the literature of the late-1950s. A group of young writers from this period were labeled "Angry Young Men" because their writings were filled with protest, bitterness, and anger at the social values that still prevailed in Britain.

Authors such as John Osborne, Kingsley Amis (*Lucky Jim* [1954]), Alan Sillitoe (*Loneliness of the Long Distance Runner* [1960]), and John Braine (*Room at the Top* [1957]) created the antihero as the protagonist of their works. These antiheroes were young people who could see that the upper classes had no desire to share the wealth or a willingness to help the lower classes achieve success. Osborne, and writers like him, viewed the upper classes and the institutions they had established with disdain. Delaney was hailed as a member of this group when *A Taste of Honey* was produced, although she was less concerned with social change than in creating realistic characters.

For the first time, the working class was finding a voice in England's literary works. These writers were not hailing from Britain's upper classes or from the genteel South. This new breed of writer understood the working class and asked "what is real?" Their response was that for the majority of Britains, poverty, dead-end jobs, and basic survival were "real." While life for the upper classes quickly returned to normal in the Postwar years, life for the workers did not improve; England, as a victorious nation, should have prospered across its classes, yet only a small minority were benefitting during this period.

English laborers could look to America and see that the middle class were prospering, pursuing the

COMPARE & CONTRAST

- **1958:** An English Roman Catholic economist, Colin Clark, condemns birth control. Clark argues that although population growth places difficult demands on agrarian societies, it also provokes greater efforts in the fields of industry, commerce, political leadership, and science.

  Today: Birth control continues to be a politically charged issue, with murders, bombings, and increasing violence emerging as an increasingly frequent image in protests against abortion.

- **1958:** Agatha Christie's *Mousetrap* is the longest running play in British history, with over 2000 performances. Terrance Rattigan's *Variations on a Theme,* which opened on May 8, is credited as the play whose lack of content inspired Delaney to write *A Taste of Honey.*

  Today: Both *Mousetrap* and *A Taste of Honey* continue to be produced in regional theatre, but *Variations on a Theme* has achieved no lasting notoriety.

- **1958:** The Clean Air Act, passed in 1956, goes into effect. It represents Britain's efforts to cut down on deaths in London and in England's industrial cities, where many deaths are thought to be caused by the polluted air from factories and coal-burning furnaces.

  Today: Automobiles still cause pollution, but contamination from the burning of coal is significantly diminished. Britain continues its cleaning of public buildings, which for many years have been covered in the black soot left by burning coal.

- **1958:** For the first time, the British government allows women to sit in the House of Lords.

  Today: With a woman, Margaret Thatcher, having served several years as Prime Minister, women in Britain's Parliament are no longer considered novel or unusual.

"American Dream." Jobs were plentiful and wages were increasing. Workers were buying automobiles and homes and the furniture to fill them. But in England, there was little hope for the future unless the working class could find a voice. The dramas and novels of protest advocating social changes offered working class Britains a voice. Despite Delaney's protestations that she was not a member of the Angry Theatre, her play nonetheless raised awareness of the plight of the lower classes.

CRITICAL OVERVIEW

When *A Taste of Honey* opened on Broadway in October, 1960, most critics seemed more taken with the author's age than with her play. Almost every review commented upon Delaney's age, and a few upon her six foot height, but few endorsed the rousing success that the British critics bestowed upon the play. Most New York critics, instead, praised the cast and director, offering mixed praise for the play's content. These critics took a wait and see attitude toward Delaney's future prospects as a successful playwright.

In his review of *A Taste of Honey,* the *New York Time*'s Howard Taubman stated that the play was "an evocation of disenchantment done with touching honesty." Taubman cited the play's honesty and "plainness of truth" as strengths of the writer, whom, he stated has a way of telling a story that is "modest, almost muted." Much of Taubman's praise, however, was directed toward the performers, especially Joan Plowright as Jo, who the critic felt "captures the shell of cynicism that the girl has grown to shield herself from her hopelessness."

Dora Bryan as Helen in a scene from the film adaptation

Plowright provided a performance that Taubman called, "haunting." Of the playwright, Taubman noted that "the Lancashire lass may grow more optimistic as she grows older." Taubman, however, did not see Delaney's pessimism as a deterrent, finding in her play, "the redeeming savor of truth."

John McClain, writing for the *American Journal,* also found the honesty of the characters an important element of the play. McClain stated that Delaney "has not written a drama of any great significance, but she has a beautiful ear for dialogue and an amazingly uncluttered feeling for the people with whom she has grown up in her little Lancashire

town." Delaney's ability to bring truth to her characters' voices is a strength, although that does not entirely make up for the lack of purpose in her play, according to McClain. Although Delaney's work lacks a political or sociological agenda, McClain pointed out that the play "is written with such obvious sincerity and familiarity, and it is so well played, that it becomes a very touching experience in the theatre." As did other reviewers, McClain also admired Plowright's performance as a highlight of the play.

Richard Watts Jr. also offered a strong endorsement in his review for the *New York Post.* Of the characters, Watts stated that they "have a warm-blooded reality about them which reveals the young authoress as a dramatist who knows how to fill a play with recognizable and vivid human beings." Of the playwright, Watts praised Delaney and stating that "she knows how to create characters throbbing with life, she can build a dramatic situation with honesty and expertness, she writes a simple but vigorous prose and she has a compassion that is wry, unsentimental and always believable. Without sacrificing her status as a realist, she can bring fresh imagination to the drabness of her narrative. Her drama has perhaps its weaker moments, but it rarely ceases to be effective." Watts's enthusiasm for Delaney, having referred to her as exhibiting "compassionate candor . . . [and] frank and explicit realism," was also extended to Plowright's performance, which he calls, "deeply moving."

Plowright was also a major strength of the play, according to the *New York World Telegram*'s Frank Aston, who said that Plowright's is a "bravura" performance. Once again, as did other reviewers, Aston cited Delaney's honesty and reality in creating these characters and dialogue. But in the end, it was Plowright's skill as an actor that carried the show, providing "a moving experience."

Some reviewers offered a more mixed assessment of Delaney's play, including Walter Kerr of the *New York Herald Tribune.* Kerr disputed the realism of Delaney's dialogue, saying that "her people talk most strangely . . . they rap out words and phrases that now and then suggest they've all been given an aborted college education." But Kerr did think that Delaney created interesting characters, of whom all "pretensions to dignity" have been removed. *A Taste of Honey,* according to Kerr, "doesn't taste like honey, it tastes like vinegar spiced with ginger."

A less favorable review was provided by John Chapman in the *Daily News.* Chapman began by noting that Delaney's play made news in the London theatrical world, that the young playwright was hailed as "a fresh, forceful new talent." But Chapman disagreed with this assessment. While he felt that Delaney "has a fine ability for creating believable characters [and] good skill at keeping them alive," the critic ultimately complained that her play is without any real purpose. Clearly disappointed that Delaney did not live up to her advance notices, Chapman complained that he "could not become emotionally involved in it [the play]."

Robert Coleman of the *New York Mirror* had similar reactions to Delaney's work. Coleman also observed that a playwright should have "something important to say." In a review that actually called Delaney names, Coleman referred to her as "a snarling, cynical young Englishwoman" who wrote "an ode to misery."

Slightly twenty years later, *A Taste of Honey* enjoyed a major revival, first appearing Off-Broadway and a few months later, on Broadway. Once again, the reviews were very mixed. In the *New York Times,* Frank Rich offered a mostly favorable review, saying of Delaney's play that "it holds up better than most plays of England's look-back-in-anger period." Rich complimented Delaney, saying "she looks at a miserable world with charity and humor." However, Rich's greatest kudos went to Amanda Plummer as Jo. Similar to the play's earlier production, it was the actress playing Jo who captured the hearts and imaginations of the reviewers.

John Beaufort provided a positive review in the *Christian Science Monitor.* Beaufort praised the honesty of Delaney's play, calling it "no nonsense realism, and deeply genuine compassion." But a less favorable criticism was offered by the *Daily News*'s Douglas Watt, who said "the flavor's just about gone" on this twenty-year old play, which "hasn't worn very well." Watt argued that "the crudeness and contrived cheekiness of the dialogue stand out awkwardly, and the overall craftsmanship is negligible."

Within a few months of its Off-Broadway opening, Delaney's play moved to Broadway, where once again the critics were divided on the play's merits. In *Time,* T. E. Kalem called *A Taste of Honey* "taunt, vital, moving and funny." He reserved his greatest admiration for Plummer, however, saying that she "invests [Jo] with an unfaltering pulse beat of humanity" Jack Kroll of *Newsweek,* also found Plummer "unforgettable" in a performance that is "the making of an actress."

Plummer also received the only compliments to be found in Clive Barnes's review in the *New York Post.* Barnes, who found Delaney's play a bore, did find Plummer "radiant." Barnes's opinion of the 1981 revival was that "the boredom has intensified." Despite such mixed criticism, many have opined that credit must be given to Delaney for creating such a vivid protagonist. These critics argue that without the playwright's creative skills, actresses such as Plowright and Plummer would not continue to be singled out for praise.

CRITICISM

Sheri E. Metzger

Metzger is a Ph.D. specializing in literature and drama at the University of New Mexico. In this essay, she discusses the disparity in the critical assessment of Shelagh Delaney's A Taste of Honey.

Critics greeted the Broadway premier of *A Taste of Honey* with conflicting critiques. Many reviewers found the plot pointless and boring, while others found it honest and real, with wonderful authentic dialogue. It is worth considering what elements of Shelagh Delaney's play created such a diverse reaction. The New York critics were prepared to like Delaney's play, since they had received advance word from the English press that the young playwright was, as John Chapman of the *Daily News* reported, "a fresh, forceful new talent." But as were many critics in the New York theatre world, Chapman was disappointed to find that *A Taste of Honey* had no purpose, no idea, no emotional pull that commanded interest. Why this huge disparity between the British critics and the New York ones? It is possible that there is no concrete answer to that question, but it is worth considering why the same plot and characters are capable of engendering such different reactions.

Delaney's play appeared on the British stage only a year after John Osborne's *Look Back in Anger,* and the British critics were quick to put Delaney in the same class as other literary protesters—such as Osborne—who were seeking political and social change. But Delaney's writing was not motivated by such ideals. She has stated that her intent was to create realism, to bring the voices of the working class into the theatre; she did not have a political agenda to promote. As Susan Whitehead noted in *Concise Dictionary of British Literary Biography,* the British critics acclaimed Delaney's play as one which would "interpret the common experiences of today." Delaney's play offered something to the working class audience, whose existence the British theatre community had just discovered. The work was also heralded as providing "all the strength and none of the weaknesses of a pro-

nounced, authentic local accent." For British audiences, Delaney offered the opportunity to see and hear a way of life different from that of most audience members.

And for those viewers who were of the working class, this play allowed them to remember how very lucky they were compared to the characters portrayed on the stage. While Delaney might describe the play as representing authentic working class dialogue and situations, in fact, Helen is described as a semi-whore, and Jo is described first as a student and then later as largely unemployed as she hides in her flat. Neither appears to be working class. But what Delaney did bring to the stage, Whitehead noted, is "a badly needed influx of new ideas from the provinces." These ideas included the use of music and a dance-hall atmosphere and the artifice of having a character address the audience, in asides. While critics are notoriously captivated by the idea of something new and different, with "innovative" too often substituted for "content," in this case, it seems that it was largely the British critics who provided enthusiastic approval for Delaney's *A Taste of Honey.*

The American critics greeted the Broadway debut of this play with a more tempered enthusiasm. Indeed, several disliked the play. Of those who did find something to recommend in Delaney's work, critics often qualified their review to note that, while the play lacked purpose and or plot, the performances of the leading actresses helped to offset the defects in Delaney's writing. For the New York critics, few of whom even mentioned anything new or innovative in Delaney's play, the idea of a working class audience seemed to hold little attraction. In reviews of *A Taste of Honey,* the New York critics focused largely on the cast, especially on the actresses playing Jo and Helen. In many cases, critics either ignored the problems with the play's content, glossed over the character inadequacies, or narrowly focused their reviews to the performances of the actors.

And yet, the lack of content in the plays performed in the contemporary theatre is the very reason Delaney gave for writing the play. According to Whitehead, Delaney says that "she saw Margaret Leighton in Terrance Rattigan's *Variation on a Theme.* She [Delaney] told one interviewer: 'It seemed a sort of parade ground for the star . . . I think Miss Margaret Leighton is a great actress and I felt she was wasting her time. I just went home and

WHAT DO I READ NEXT?

- Tillie Olsen's ''I Stand Here Ironing'' (1961) is a short story about the relationship between mother and daughter and the effects that poverty and a working class life can have on two people.

- *Saturday Night and Sunday Morning,* by Alan Sillitoe, is a novel about Britain's working class life.

- John Osborne's *Look Back in Anger* (1957) is a play that offers an antihero, Jimmy Porter, on the verge of the middle class but aware that the upper class can squash his climb up at any moment.

- Carolyn Kay Steedman's *Landscape for a Good Woman: A Story* (1987) is about growing up working class in England and the struggle for survival.

- D. H. Lawrence's *Sons and Lovers* (1913) is set in the factory town of Nottinghamshire, a coal mining village. This novel is considered one of the first British novels to focus on working class life.

---

started work.''' It would turn out that this is the same complaint that New York critics leveled toward Delaney's work. Chapman's enjoyment of Joan Plowright's performance as Jo, as well as that of Andrew Ray's as Geof, was tempered by his disappointment in the material provided to them.

Chapman complained that both actors' performances were commendable, except that, ''in the end, he [Ray] doesn't know what do about the situation—and neither do I and neither did the author.'' Several other New York critics complained that the play was boring; crude, contrived, and of negligible craftsmanship; offered nothing to say, was an ode to misery, cynical, a thin script, and without purpose; and that it did not prove much. These are completely opposing views than those offered by the British critics. American reviewers were expecting something more from Delaney's play.

What should have occurred on stage was a more defined plot, driven by ideas and purpose. For example, early in Act I, Helen implies that she and Jo have moved to this shabby flat to get away from Peter, whom she later accuses of having followed her. He wants to marry her, but Helen gives no reason for her flight from her boyfriend—nor is there any obvious reason presented to reinforce Peter's desire to marry her. He shows Jo multiple photos of women he carries in his wallet implying

that he is involved with them. So why is he so ardently pursuing the middle-aged Helen? It makes no sense, and indeed, within months, he has once again taken up with other women and thrown Helen out. There are other holes as well, including why the black sailor would give Jo an engagement ring, promise her love and marriage, and then simply disappear. Men often promise love and marriage to secure sex, but they rarely spend money on a ring for just that purpose.

There is also a potential plot in the relationship between Jo and Helen, but Delaney barely touches upon the possibilities. As William C. Boles noted in *Text and Presentation,* there are many similarities between mother and daughter, including the fact that Jo is repeating much of her mother's history: she is working in a bar, turning to sex out of loneliness, conceiving a child as a result of her first sexual experience, enduring pregnancy under severe economic hardship. But Delaney never really develops these or any of the plot's other narrative possibilities. Instead, the audience is left to wonder what purpose Delaney intends in creating these people.

In his book *The Angry Theatre: New British Drama,* John Russell Taylor explored some of the problems presented in Delaney's work. Taylor singled out several serious problems, including the

---

lack of ideas or purpose that the American critics noted. According to Taylor, Delaney's play "has no 'ideas' which can be isolated and considered as such apart from their dramatic context." That is, it is difficult to define any theme significant enough for discussion. There is no appreciable depth for either actor or audience to explore, and, as Taylor observed, "if one tries to read the play away from the theatre, without attributing to its characters the *personae* of the actors who originally played them, it is virtually non-existent."

Interestingly enough, Taylor thought the play worked in spite of this very significant problem. The critic argued that "in the theatre . . . it has the unique power of holding us simply as a tale that is told, and the words the characters are given to speak take on, when spoken, a strange independent life of their own." Taylor was saying that it is the actors who made the play work for him and that the material was less important than the actors' ability to deliver the lines.

An assessment of other reviews, however, indicates that many critics disagreed with Taylor. Another point that Taylor made is that the relationship between Jo and Helen seems believable, but it is also, as he noted, "completely impossible." Here, Taylor offered a contradiction that cannot be explained. The critic attempted to explain this by saying that Jo creates her own little world and that in spite of her misery, she also makes no effort to move beyond that small space. It is true that plays need to be seen and heard on stage to be properly appreciated and understood, but at the same time, no play should be so dependent on an actor that it cannot be appreciated without that performance.

Delaney has said that she wrote *A Taste of Honey* in two weeks. Perhaps an extra week or two of development might have allowed for some greater depth and purpose in this play's construction.

Source: Sheri E. Metzger, for *Drama for Students,* Gale, 2000.

G. J. Ippolito

In this essay, Ippolito examines Delaney and her play within the context of her contemporaries, notably John Osborne, Peter Shaffer, and Jean Genet.

Contemporary serious dramatists fall into two broad structural groups: experimenters in form and traditional naturalists. On one side we find such playwrights as Edward Albee, Eugene Ionesco, Samuel Beckett, Jack Gelber, and Jean Genet; and on the other, Peter Shaffer, Arnold Wesker, John

> FOR BRITISH AUDIENCES, DELANEY OFFERED THE OPPORTUNITY TO SEE AND HEAR A WAY OF LIFE DIFFERENT FROM THAT OF MOST AUDIENCE MEMBERS"

Osborne, and—surprisingly—twenty-two-year-old Shelagh Delaney, whose first play has had an enormously successful career on the professional stage since its first production, when she was eighteen. The structural distinction is an academic one; both groups of dramatists are desperately concerned with the same twentieth-century problem: man's inability to communicate with man; and each seems to use the same icon, images, and basic symbols. The icon is the fundamental if despairing honesty of the pervert and the social rebel and the essential deceitfulness of the conformist; the images deal with the delusive qualities of time, experience, social institutions, and religious and sometimes political dogmas; the basic symbols are the whore, the homosexual, the frustrated *mater-familias,* the drug addict, the confused, or uncommitted young adult.

We should have expected Miss Delaney, in her youth and comparative innocence, to experiment rampantly, to reject the traditional forms of dramatic communication, to seek for models among the caustic obscenities of Genet or the surrealistic redundancies of Beckett or Ionesco. Instead, she is among the dramatic communicants who express modern anxiety in comparatively old-fashioned or academic dramatic forms; she seems to have chosen to rank herself with such dramatists as Osborne and Shaffer who employ dramatic techniques which are cousin-germain to those of Brieux, Shaw, Pinero, and Terence Rattigan; this, however, is not enough to bring her to our attention. It is her recent success on Broadway and in London that forces her upon our notice and scrutiny.

It is too early to assess the young Miss Delaney's position in the drama either as the exponent of one sort of dramatic expression or the other, but her success in the East End of London, the West End, and on Broadway, makes clear at least the attraction these elements at modern American and European drama have for writers. We must examine her play,

Murray Melvin as Geof (on right) and Jo in a scene from director Tony Richardson's adaptation of A Taste of Honey

A Taste of Honey, with these symbols and forms of contemporary drama in mind.

By her own confession, Miss Delaney is a neophyte in the theatre, unpractised and unsophisticated; however, she is exasperated both by the inarticulate and the excessively articulate practitioners of drama who play at writing about modern problems or placating the contemporary lares and penates. It is not clear whether her impatience is directed toward Ionesco's ilk or Rattigan's. She set out to write *A Taste of Honey* in order to express her own view of her generation, and with the panache of a novice poker player she succeeded brilliantly in dealing herself a full house.

A Taste of Honey, in its present Broadway production, directed by Tony Richardson and George Devine, designed by Oliver Smith, and acted by Angela Lansbury, Joan Plowright, and Andrew Ray in the principal roles, is amusing, touching, lit with occasional flashes of optimism, darkened with irony and despair, alternately sophomoric and mature in its language, and cluttered with meretricious but effective theatrical tricks. Its success on Broadway is no surprise, for the play contains those elements most likely to appeal to a popular audience: a sensational theme, a "distinguished" cast, and a kind of vulgar, outspoken humor which flatters the self-styled broad-minded; moreover, it comes to the hub of American professional theatre at the heels of some of the most widely applauded and well-attended British plays of recent seasons, *Look Back in Anger, Five Finger Exercise,* and *Irma la Douce.* Osborne, Shaffer, and the English adapters of Breffort's French musical revue, More, Heneker, and Norman, prepared the Broadway audience for a play which takes homosexuality, sexual promiscuity, prostitution, and social irresponsibility for granted as the furniture of the twentieth century. More significantly, the play has also made an enormous appeal to the intellectual brigade who, like Miss Delaney, accept unblinkingly the sordid agglommeration of characters and ideas contained within the play as the undeniable sign of the *zeitgeist.* This joint approval of Miss Delaney's play testifies that the problems she writes about are not merely intellectual considerations but pervading conditions, and that her concern with the treatment of these problems is not a youthful pose but an honest preoccupation. The things she writes about are the facts of life in this decade at least of the twentieth century; and the lexicon of images, icon, characters, symbols is the accepted if not the only possible means of conveying the facts.

The central figure of the play is Jo, young, confused, searching for some sort of creative foothold in life, through whose tentative contacts with other characters in the play—her mother, Helen; her lover, the Negro sailor; her friend, the homosexual Geof; and her mother's alcoholic husband, Peter— Miss Delaney presents a world of sterile or warped human relationships. Jo is the Everywoman of this world. Whatever Jo attempts in her efforts to bring life into the cramped and squalid world she lives in meets with frustration. She brings tulip bulbs into the flat, they do not grow; she draws pictures with a talent even her mother grants her, they remain unseen, uncommunicating; she enters into a love affair with a Negro sailor who leaves her pregnant with a child doomed to an outcast's life. Her periodic efforts at organizing herself, her flat, and her personal relationships with Geof or her mother end in failure.

It is in the interacting relationships between Jo and her mother and Jo and Geof however, that Miss Delaney drives home the central point of the play: Jo's taste of honey, her brief experience with love, only serves to emphasize the remoteness of one human being from another. If they do not selfishly deprive one another of warmth and sympathy, the moves they make toward love are abortive. The mother-daughter relationship in the play shows this clearly: Helen takes off whenever mother-love, the most reiterated twentieth-century middle-class virtue, becomes too exacting or threatens her comfort. Helen's attitude toward love in general is that it is a physical convenience: "It wasn't his nose I was interested in," she says of an old lover. Helen is a curiously contradictory character, whose inconsistencies are seemingly rooted in life and in literature: she accuses her daughter of selfishness, yet behaves selfishly herself, selfishly and unforgivably. She has a clear, realistic view of life, and the necessity to observe the traditions, and yet leads a questionable life herself. On one hand, Miss Delaney presents us with a human being, and on the other with a symbol.

Geof also reflects this inconsistency; significantly it is he who provides Jo with the most prolonged and unwavering sympathy and devotion of any of the characters in the play, precisely at the time when she most crucially needs it. She is in hiding from society, waiting for her baby, anxious about its possible insanity, and frightened of what is to come. He loves Jo and offers to marry her. The one character who offers Jo a chance at stability, a sociable conformity, and an emotional steadiness, Geof is ironically the character who, because he is

> JO'S TASTE OF HONEY, HER BRIEF EXPERIENCE WITH LOVE, ONLY SERVES TO EMPHASIZE THE REMOTENESS OF ONE HUMAN BEING FROM ANOTHER."

homosexual, cannot succeed in giving her any of this. As a result, his love for her is futile, and foreordained to sterility. He too is a compound; in part drawn from life, in part a symbol.

Jo moves between these characters, alternately affected by them and detached from them. She comments upon the society of these people not as if they touched her, but in the manner of a curiously amused, laconic sociologist: of her mother's and Peter's engagement, "I should have thought their courtship had passed the stage of symbolism;" of the children in the neighborhood, "It's their parents' fault. There's a little boy over there and his hair, honestly, it's walking away. And his ears. Oh! He's a real mess! He never goes to school. He just sits on that front doorstep all day. I think he's a bit deficient . . . His mother ought not to be allowed;" of life, "It's not [simple], it's chaotic—a bit of love, a bit of lust and there you are. We don't ask for life, we have it thrust upon us." Even when she is frightened, hurt, angered by what she sees or what happens to her, her sense of humor, even of detachment, certainly of resignation, remains: to Geof: "You've got nice hands, hard. You know I used to try and hold my mother's hands, but she always used to pull them away from me. So *silly really.* She had so much love for everyone else, but none for me;" of her birth, "A frolic in the hay loft one afternoon. You see her husband thought sex was dirty, and only used the bed for sleeping in. So she took to herself an idiot. She said he'd got eyes like me . . . He lived in a twilight land, my daddy. The land of the daft." Jo, too, is both character and symbol—the uncommitted, unresolved young adult, separating herself from her actions, only tentatively claiming that a thing is right or wrong.

Shelagh Delaney seems to maintain a stronger, healthier, more humanistic point of view than her contemporaries of either dramatic camp in her treatment of these symbols. Genet's homosexuals in a play such as *Death Watch* are nihilistic, anti-human, or to use Sartre's word, "de-real." Maurice and Lefranc symbolize destructive impulses of which Genet seems to be a perverse partisan; they are not human but incarnate intellectual concepts of a complex, depraved view of man and the theatre. They have in common with Geof an underlying sense of sterility and impotence, but unlike him they are without hope; they repel, he attracts sympathy: hence, he has greater tragic connotations. Similarly with the whore: Irma in *The Balcony* is without illusions, fidelity, a sense of shame; she shares this with Helen, whom Miss Delaney tentatively designates a semi-whore in the *dramatis personae.* However, Irma like Maurice and Lefranc is not a character rooted in humanity but an allegoric device to embody a corrosive view of a society founded on self-willed, hypocritical illusions; the whore-house she governs is the world, modern Europe, modern civilization, where she panders to the desire of these illusions. Helen panders only to herself; she achieves her impact on the audience by way of her human failings, not as an intellectualized, "de-real" symbol. She, like Geof, connotes a great deal more than Genet's figures.

Peter Shaffer and John Osborne share Miss Delaney's view of this generation; a contrast between them and her is perhaps fairer than that between her and Genet; they are closer to her in age, and the England they write about is essentially the same. Both these men are more polished literary craftsmen than she; Osborne has an ear for dialog which snaps with verisimilitude, Shaffer's prose is more elegant, precise, and evocative of complex states of mind within his characters than Miss Delaney's is at this stage. Moreover, their plays are more directly related to a social and historical point of view. Osborne sets his plays, *Look Back in Anger* and *The Entertainer,* in an England which suffers by a sentimental comparison with the good old days of the Edwardians and from an outdated system of class distinctions. The lack of communication between his characters, their frustrations in human affairs, seem to stem as much from the conflicts of class mores as from any inherent human disabilities. Alison, Helena, Cliff, and Osborne's angry young Everyman, Jimmy Porter, seem to fail as much through class differences as through anything else. Although Miss Delaney's play is set in a slum, class and social distinctions, the England of the past as it is seen by the present, do not operate in her play. A minor sociological failing in character motivation perhaps, but it results in characters who, like Jo,

seem to command more maturity and tragic consequence than the mewling, puking Porter. Nonetheless, the same protest is there against a world where communication between human beings is seemingly doomed, for whatever reason, to failure or to half-hearted, unsatisfactory compromise. Moreover, some of the same symbols seem to operate; the relationship between Cliff, Jimmy, and Alison is ambiguous. Cliff's devotion to Porter has understated homosexual elements in it; his sympathy for Alison cannot provide any help for her; the destructive love which Jimmy and Alison bear for one another results in a miscarriage which makes her barren. Human beings, proclaims Jimmy, "all want to escape from the pain of being alive. And, most of all, from love."

Shaffer's *Five Finger Exercise* is set in an upper middle class household; his characters' inability to communicate also stems in part from class or social distinctions. The difference of experiences between father and son, husband and wife, as the family moves from one social level to a higher, contributes to their individual isolation. Again the basic symbols are there: the mother, unhappy in her marital situation, looks for love and sexual gratification where it is impossible to find it; the son senses his own love for the German tutor, whose pathetic attempts at achieving some permanent relationships with human beings are countered either with uncomprehending rebuff or misunderstanding sympathy. Shaffer's characters are more complex than Miss Delaney's; they are better educated, more subtly articulate, but also less capable than Jo of detaching themselves from their predicament. This middle-class English family is a torture rack of poses, misunderstood feelings, repressed emotions, self-imposed isolation. Shaffer's characters are not so different from Miss Delaney's, but Shaffer's greater maturity gives his characters larger, more human dimension. However, because they are so much a part of the middle class, whereas Miss Delaney's are *not* of the lower class, they lack her universality.

Miss Delaney's characters seem to contain greater symbolic values than either Shaffer's or Osborne's, although she is more nearly aligned to their tradition than she is to Genet's, Albee's, or Ionesco's. The historic or social background against which Shaffer and Osborne place their characters tends to limit their symbolic significance while it enriches their human values. They seem frailer, weaker, more individual than Delaney's Jo, Helen, or Geof—who are in part romanticized versions of the symbols which the experimental dramatists use in their dramatic allegories, and in part extremely humane portraits of very human types.

Source: G. J. Ippolito, ''Shelagh Delaney'' in *Drama Survey,* Vol. 1, no. 1, May, 1961, pp. 86–91

John McCarter

Calling Delaney's play ''very special,'' McCarter offers a favorable review of A Taste of Honey, *offering particular praise for the playwright's sharply drawn characters.*

The origins of ''*A Taste of Honey,*'' which is now at the Lyceum, have the flavor of a fairy tale. The author of the play, Shelagh Delaney, is an English girl from the North Country, and a couple of years ago, while she was working as an usher in a Manchester theatre, she decided that she was wasting her time lighting people to seats so that they might behold dramas of no merit whatever. Miss Delaney, then nineteen, accordingly proceeded to write a drama of her own, and, having done so, dispatched the script to Joan Littlewood, who runs the Theatre Workshop, in Stratford. Miss Littlewood, whom you will recall as the highly capable director of ''The Hostage,'' put Miss Delaney's work into rehearsal almost immediately, and it presently came about that ''*A Taste of Honey* '' moved from Miss Littlewood's experimental theatre to the more commercial environs of London's West End, where it played for over a year. Obviously, Miss Delaney's coach was not going to turn back into a pumpkin, and so David Merrick, an American producer who likes to gamble when somebody else has shuffled the deck to his advantage, has brought the play to Broadway.

What Miss Delaney has wrought is something very special. Unless you have led a life much less sheltered than mine, you will probably find it hard to take her characters in stride. The central figures in ''*A Taste of Honey*'' are a sleazy whore and her love-starved young daughter; among their associates are a one-eyed lecher who fancies Mother, a Negro sailor who has his way with Daughter, and a homosexual who serves as a sort of handmaiden to the girl when she is quick with the Negro's child. All this no doubt sounds quite sordid, and during much of the first act, when Miss Delaney is establishing the personalities of the mother and daughter and sketching in their life in a horrible flat in a Lancashire industrial town, you may well begin to think that you are in for something pretty bad. But let me assure you that you are not, for Miss Delaney

soon demonstrates a remarkable knack for involving you emotionally with her strange quintet. They may be a tawdry lot, but when the author gets them into motion you can hear a heartbeat. ''*A Taste of Honey*'' isn't long on plot—the crux of the matter is the daughter's dilemma after the sailor has impregnated her and gone off to sea—but if the playwright's tailoring is somewhat haphazard, there is nothing shoddy about her cloth.

As directed by Tony Richardson and George Devine, the performers in ''*A Taste of Honey*'' are completely satisfactory. In the role of the mother, Angela Lansbury is at once appalling and appealing, and Andrew Ray, as her lover, has a seedy insouciance. In his brief appearance as the colored sailor, Billy Dee Williams is a plausible sort, and Nigel Davenport, who plays the homosexual, exhibits both wit and resourcefulness as he excites our sympathy even while he outrages our ethics. But it is to Joan Plowright, who portrays the daughter, that the highest praise is due, for she galvanizes every scene in which she appears. Oliver Smith has provided a properly squalid setting for the play, and the production is helped along by an instrumental quartet headed by Bobby Scott, who composed the incidental music.

Source: John McCarter, ''Lancashire Lass'' in the *New Yorker,* Vol. XXXVI, no. 35, October 15, 1960, p. 73.

Mollie Panter-Downes

Panter-Downes calls A Taste of Honey *''remarkable'' and lauds the play for its precise characterizations and ''bitingly frank domestic dialogue.''*

A remarkable new play is coming to Wyndham's Theatre on February 10th, after having a three-week refresher return run at the Theatre Royal, Stratford (the East End Stratford-atte-Bowe, not Shakespeare's home), where it was first put on, with resounding success, last May. The play is the Theatre Workshop production of ''*A Taste of Honey,*'' by a tall, good-looking nineteen-year-old Lancashire girl, Shelagh Delaney. Stratford has been for the last six years the permanent home of the Theatre Workshop, and, like the Lyric, in Hammersmith, and the Royal Court, in Sloane Square, is the London equivalent of Off Broadway. It is farther off Shaftesbury Avenue than either of the others, but, like them, it is the home of consistently intelligent theatre, and has a highly individual producer, Joan Littlewood. Miss Delaney, who used to work in a Lancashire factory before she started writing, knocked off ''*A Taste*'' in two weeks flat. It has won her, to date, an Arts

Council bursary of a hundred pounds and the Charles Henry Foyle New Play Award for 1958, besides rounds of applause from the critics. She is an original, exuberant writer, with a wonderful ear for a theatrical line. Her play takes place entirely in a scruffy bed-sitting room in her known Lancashire world, inhabited by a middle-aged tart called Helen and her daughter Jo, and later (after the mother has gone off with a well-heeled admirer) by the girl and a homeless art student, who live in a sort of pathetic, platonic babes-in-the-wood relationship after he has drifted in to anchor on her sofa. Jo is now pregnant by a colored sailor, who never makes good his promise to come back for her, and the second and best half of the play is the touching, funny, often bitingly frank domestic dialogue between her and the sofa's lodger, who maternally shoulders the cooking and scrubbing, insists on her drinking milk and reading a baby-care manual, soothes her out of her nightmare fears of inherited insanity, and is himself helped to escape from homosexuality. The play ends tragically, as might be expected. In the roles of the daughter and the boy, Frances Cuka and a thin, pale young actor named Murray Melvin are perfect.

Source: Mollie Panter-Downes, review of *A Taste of Honey,* in the *New Yorker,* Vol. XXVI, no. 51, February 7, 1959, pp. 86, 89.

SOURCES

Aston, Frank. Review of *A Taste of Honey* in the *New York World Telegram,* October 5, 1960.

Barnes, Clive. Review of *A Taste of Honey* in the *New York Post,* May 6, 1981.

Beaufort, John. Review of *A Taste of Honey* in the *Christian Science Monitor,* May 6, 1981.

Boles, William. "'Have I Ever Laid Claims to Being a Proper Mother?' The Stigma of Maternity in Shelagh Delaney's *A Taste of Honey*" in *Text and Presentation,* Vol. 17, 1996, pp. 1-5.

Chapman, John. Review of *A Taste of Honey* in the *Daily News,* October 5, 1960.

Coleman, Robert. Review of *A Taste of Honey* in the *New York Mirror,* October 5, 1960.

Kalem, T. E. Review of *A Taste of Honey* in *Time,* July 6, 1982.

Kerr, Walter. Review of *A Taste of Honey* in the *New York Herald Tribune,* October 5, 1960.

Kroll, Jack. Review of *A Taste of Honey* in *Newsweek,* July 20, 1981.

McClain, John. Review of *A Taste of Honey* in the *New York Journal American,* October 5, 1960.

Rich, Frank. Review of *A Taste of Honey* in the *New York Times,* April 29, 1981.

Taubman, Howard. "Theatre without Illusion" in the *New York Times,* October 5, 1960.

Taylor, John Russell. "Way Down East: Shelagh Delaney" in *The Angry Theatre: New British Drama,* revised edition, Hill and Wang, 1969, pp. 117-40.

Watt, Douglas. Review of *A Taste of Honey* in the *Daily News,* April 29, 1981.

Watts Jr., Richard. Review of *A Taste of Honey* in the *New York Post,* October 5, 1960.

Whitehead, Susan. "Shelagh Delaney" in *Concise Dictionary of British Literary Biography,* Vol. 7: *Writers after World War II, 1945-1960,* Gale, 1991.

FURTHER READING

Campbell, Louise. *Coventry Cathedral: Art and Architecture in Postwar Britain,* Clarendon Press, 1996.
 While this book focuses on only one building, its construction represents many of the important Postwar ideas and forces found in architectural building in the 1950s and 1960s in England and Europe.

Ellis, Peter Berresford. *A History of the Irish Working Class,* by Pluto Press, 1996.
 This book provides an examination of the how the working class in Ireland has been shaped by economic, political, and social factors.

Jones, Gareth Stedman *Language of Class,* Cambridge University Press, 1984.
 This book is a collection of essays by a British social historian that discusses the nature of class consciousness and central issues of Britain's working class.

Taylor, John Russell. *The Angry Theatre: New British Drama,* Hill and Wang, 1969.
 This book provides biographies of playwrights and a discussion of their individual works.

Throop, Elizabeth A. *Net Curtains and Closed doors: Intimacy, Family, and Public Life in Dublin,* Bergin & Garvey, 1999.
 This book focuses on the family life and the influences of religion, society, English Colonialism.

'Tis Pity She's a Whore

JOHN FORD

1633

First published in 1633, *'Tis Pity She's a Whore* is perhaps the most popular and frequently performed play by John Ford, whom many scholars consider the last major dramatist of the English renaissance.

As a dramatist, Ford faced a difficult challenge. He wrote *'Tis Pity She's a Whore* during the reign of King Charles (hence the term "Carolinian") and worked to entertain audiences who had grown up on some of the greatest plays in the English language, those of Jonson, Marlowe, and Shakespeare, among others. According to some critics, since audiences thought they had already seen everything, it was incumbent on Ford to try to show them something they had not seen. This in part accounts for the extreme behavior we see in the characters in Ford's plays.

'Tis Pity She's a Whore tells the tale of an incestuous love between Giovanni and his sister Annabella that ends in disaster and death. Set in Parma, Italy, the story takes place against a background of lust, vengeance, and greed that serves as a critique of contemporary culture and morality.

Ford's interest in aberrant psychology figures prominently in many of his plays. Influenced by the renaissance psychology of Robert Burton's *Anatomy of Melancholy,* Ford created characters with powerful emotions, strong intellects, and unbridled appetites.

Critics have noticed the parallels between Ford's *'Tis Pity She's a Whore* and Shakespeare's *Romeo and Juliet*: both plays feature young lovers, forbidden love, a meddling nurse and friar, and a tragic ending—though Ford's incestuous lovers added an extra twist not found in Shakespeare's play. While some scholars criticize the violence in Ford's plays as excessive, others praise him for realistically portraying profound—if disturbing—psychological truths.

AUTHOR BIOGRAPHY

John Ford, the second son of Thomas and Elizabeth Ford, was born in Ilsington, Devonshire, England, in 1586. The Fords were an old, well-to-do country family. While there is little information about Ford's early life, it is known that he attended Exeter College, Oxford, from 1601-1602. At the age of sixteen, in 1602, he was admitted to London's Middle Temple, where he studied law for several years, though there is no record of his having been called to the bar. The inns of court served as law schools as well as residences for young gentlemen, who also learned there the fine points of fashionable city and court life. During the years of Ford's residence, such major literary talents as dramatists John Marston and William Davenant, and metaphysical poet Thomas Carew were affiliated with Middle Temple. Literary scholars believe Ford circulated among them, and through them knew poet John Donne's family.

Between 1606 and 1620, Ford wrote several prose works, including *Love Triumphant* (1606), *The Golden Mean* (1613), and *A Line of Life* (1620). During his dramatic apprenticeship, he wrote and contributed to as many as eighteen plays, though seven have been lost.

Ford's period of major collaboration, from 1621 to 1625, included writings with various playwrights. He worked with Thomas Dekker on *The Fairy Knight* (1624), *The Bristow Merchant* (1624), and *The Sun's Darling* (1624). Ford, Dekker, and Rowley composed *The Witch of Edmonton,* which was produced at the Phoenix Theatre in 1621, while Ford, Dekker, Webster, and Rowley authored the now-lost *A Late Murder of the Son upon the Mother; or, Keep the Widow Waking* (1624).

Working independently, Ford wrote his major plays after 1625. He wrote for several theatri-cal companies, including the King's Men at the Blackfriars and the Queens' Men and Beeston's boy-company at the Phoenix.

Robert Burton's enormous *The Anatomy of Melancholy,* a Renaissance treatise detailing classical ideas about "humour" psychology, influenced Ford's first independent play, *The Lover's Melancholy* (1629). His other major dramatic works include *Love's Sacrifice* (1633), *The Broken Heart* (1633), *Perkin Warbeck* (1634), and *The Lady's Trial* (1638).

Ford's interest in aberrant psychology figures prominently in many of his plays. In general, his most successful characters evidence dignity, courage, and endurance in the face of suffering. Though Ford's plays deal with controversial themes such as incest and torture, he does so without being judgmental, neither condoning nor condemning, but rather, striving to offer an understanding of what a person experiencing such actions might think or feel.

Dating the performance history of *'Tis Pity She's a Whore* proves difficult. Published in 1633, the play's title page indicated that it had been "Acted by the Queenes's Maiesties Seruants, at The Phoenix in Drury-Lane." Quite logically, then, critics believe the play to be performed after the founding of the Queens' company in 1626 and before its publication in 1633. Though published late in Ford's career, however, some critics believe it may be the first play he wrote alone.

The details surrounding Ford's death remain unknown, though most critics believe he died shortly after the 1639 publication of *The Lady's Trial.*

PLOT SUMMARY

Act I, scene i

The Friar and Giovanni discuss Giovanni's incestuous love for his sister, Annabella. The friar, formerly Giovanni's teacher when he studied at the university of Bologna, warns him of the seriousness of his sin, but Giovanni claims his passion remains beyond his control. The Friar believes that Giovanni, a good student of logic, uses logic to prove something sinful to be virtuous. The friar warns him that others who used logic "to prove / There was no God . . . / Discover'd . . . the nearest way to hell."

When Giovanni begs for his advice, the Friar urges him to fast and pray, which Giovanni agrees to try, though it fails to rid him of his incestuous love. He believes himself fated to love his sister and to pursue her love.

Act I, scene ii

Grimaldi and Soranzo are both wooing Annabella. Soranzo believes that Grimaldi is speaking badly about him to their mutual love. For this reason, he urges his servant, Vasques, to insult Grimaldi and pick a fight. Grimaldi refuses, recognizing the dishonor of dueling with someone of a lower social class, but Vasques presses his case and a duel ensues. As Vasques bests Grimaldi, Florio and Donado break up the fight. Soranzo explains his grievance against Grimaldi, all of which Annabella and Putana, her tutoress, witness. They compare Annabella's various suitors, and Putana indicates she prefers Soranzo, though Annabella reveals no preference.

Bergetto, Donado's foolish nephew, and his servant Poggio enter, and it is revealed that Bergetto too seeks Annabella's hand. The scene ends as Giovanni enters and, after a soliloquy which reveals his incestuous infatuation, confesses his love to his sister Annabella. She replies that she loves him too, saying ''Love me or kill me, brother'' and they go off to consummate their incestuous relationship.

Act I, scene iii

Florio, Annabella's father, discusses with Donado, Bergetto's uncle, Annabella's possible marriage with the foolish Bergetto. Florio looks favorably on Bergetto's money but admits the choice lies with Annabella, saying ''My care is how to match her to her liking.'' After Florio leaves, Bergetto and his servant Poggio enter, talking nonsense about a magical mill and strange horse. Bergetto's gullibility is revealed when he explains that he believes this nonsense to be true, because the barber swore so. Florio has sent Bergetto off to woo Annabella, but instead of winning her love, Bergetto shows himself to be a fool. Florio suggests he will write a love letter from Bergetto to Annabella, sending it along with a jewel.

Act II, scene i

Giovanni and Annabella, having made love, enter as though coming from their chamber. Giovanni discusses her possible marriage, while she replies that ''all suitors seem to my eyes hateful.'' He leaves and Putana enters. When Annabella confesses her incest with Giovanni, Putana condones it, explaining that ''if a young wench feel the fit upon

her, let her take anybody, father or brother, all is one.''

Florio enters with Richardetto and his niece Philotis, who carries a lute. Richardetto pretends to be a doctor from Padua because he suspects his wife Hippolita of being unfaithful—she has been conducting an affair with Soranzo. Richardetto sent word of his death, then returned in disguise to witness his wife's behavior; the reason for Richardetto's disguise is not disclosed in this scene, however. He introduces his niece to Annabella, who leaves to have a conference with Florio, her father.

Act II, scene ii

Soranzo enters, reading a book about love and pondering his affection for Annabella. Hippolita, Richardetto's wife, and Vasques enter. Soranzo breaks off his affair with Hippolita. While her husband lived, Soranzo promised that in the event of her husband's death, he would marry Hippolita. Now, however, hearing reports of Richardetto's death, Soranzo reneges on his vow. Furious, Hippolita offers to reward Vasques financially and sexually if he helps her take her revenge on Soranzo. The servant pretends to agree.

Act II, scene iii

Richardetto explains to his niece Philotis that he has disguised himself as a doctor to discover his ''wanton'' unfaithful wife Hippolita's ''lascivious riots'' with Soranzo.

After Philotis leaves, Grimaldi tells Richardetto of his love for Annabella, and Richardetto informs him that Soranzo stands in his way. Richardetto, pretending to be a doctor, offers to supply poison to help Grimaldi kill his rival, an action that would also serve Richardetto's vengeful feelings toward Soranzo.

Act II, scene iv

Donado, Bergetto, and Poggio enter, discussing the love letter designed to help Bergetto win Annabella's love. Bergetto, however, insists not only on writing his own letter, but also reading it to Annabella. Donado forbids this, and Bergetto and Poggio go off to see the fantastic horse which the barber described to him earlier.

Act II, scene v

The Friar listens to Giovanni's confession of incest with his sister and tells him his actions threaten ''eternal slaughter'' (damnation). Giovanni wittily misuses logic in an argument that proves his incestuous love to be virtuous. The Friar condemns his former student's misuse of reason, and urges Giovanni to persuade his sister to marry another man. When Giovanni refuses, the Friar asks permission to talk with Annabella and, if he cannot convince her of the sinfulness of her relationship, at least to hear her confession.

Act II, scene vi

Donado hands Annabella a letter, with a jewel enclosed, which he has written, though the letter appears to be from his foolish nephew Bergetto. Annabella refuses the jewel, but Donado urges her to accept it; she then refuses the proposal of matrimony. She indicates that she gave Giovanni the ring her dead mother intended as a gift for her husband.

Bergetto and Poggio enter. Bergetto explains how he was beaten in a fight, aided by the "doctor" Richardetto, and flirted with by his niece Philotis. When Donado informs Bergetto that Annabella has refused him, he says, "what care I for that? I can have wenches enough in Parma for half-a-crown apiece."

Donado, Bergetto, and Poggio exit as Giovanni enters. Florio explains his pleasure that Annabella has refused Bergetto, as Florio prefers Soranzo. Left alone, Giovanni, jealous, orders Annabella to return Bergetto's jewel.

Act III, scenes i-iii

Bergetto tells Poggio that he will woo Richardetto's niece and "beget a race of wise men and constables."

Florio offers Annabella to Soranzo, encouraging their marriage. Soranzo swears he loves Annabella, but she says she loves another, "as the fates infer." She prefers to remain unmarried, but she promises that if she does marry, it will be to Soranzo. Annabella swoons and Florio sends for a doctor.

Putana tells Giovanni that Annabella's not sick, but pregnant with his child and experiencing morning sickness. To protect her virtuous reputation, she must be kept from the doctor.

Act III, scenes iv-v

The "doctor" Richardetto pretends Annabella's sickness is due to eating melons, but Florio knows what he implies when he urges her marriage to Soranzo.

Giovanni brings the Friar to see Annabella, to hear her confession. Florio urges the Friar to convince her to marry.

The "doctor" Richardetto gives Grimaldi the poison with which to kill Soranzo, who prepares to marry Annabella.

Richardetto prepares to marry Philotis to Bergetto for his money.

Act III, scenes vi-vii

The Friar meets with Annabella, describing to her the horrors of hell and urging her repentance. He tells her to break off her relationship with her brother and to marry Soranzo. She agrees. Giovanni looks on distraught as Annabella agrees to wed Soranzo.

Grimaldi enters, prepared with his poisoned rapier to murder Soranzo, when Bergetto and Philotis also enter. Grimaldi, mistaking Bergetto for Soranzo, stabs him fatally.

Act III, scenes viii-ix

Vasques informs Hippolita of Soranzo's impending wedding. She offers Vasques an erotic reward for his help in revenging herself on his master, Soranzo.

The officer investigating Bergetto's murder tells Florio and Richardetto that he saw the murderer, whom they identify as Grimaldi. Grimaldi tells the Cardinal of his mistake, however, and the Cardinal offers him papal protection.

Act IV, scene i

At the wedding feast, Giovanni refuses the drink a toast to celebrate Annabella's marriage with Soranzo. Hippolita, disguised as a local maiden, enters with a group of ladies, who dance in celebration. Hippolita reveals herself and offers a toast to the newlyweds. She intends to offer Soranzo a poisoned cup, but Vasques, Soranzo's loyal servant, switches the cups. Hippolita drinks the poisoned wine and dies.

Act IV, scene ii

Richardetto laments his wife's death but expects justice to punish Soranzo as well, for "there is One / Above begins to work." He orders his niece Philotis to return to Cremona and enter a convent as a nun.

Act IV, scene iii

Soranzo, realizing Annabella is pregnant, confronts her and demands the name of her lover. She refuses, and they argue. Vasques enters, calms his master and secretly councils him to plot revenge and let him discover the child's father. Annabella believes Soranzo and kneeling, begs his forgiveness.

Vasques convinces Putana that Soranzo will forgive Annabella if he knows her lover's name, and Putana reveals that Giovanni is the child's father. The Banditti enter and take Putana away to blind her.

Act V, scene i

Annabella repents and prays for someone to appear to hear her confession, just as the Friar passes. She gives him a letter to bring to Giovanni, "bid him read it and repent" and tells him that, because Soranzo has discovered the truth, Giovanni's life is in danger.

Act V, scene ii

Soranzo and Vasques plot revenge against Annabella; they plan to have the Banditti murder her and Giovanni.

Act V, scene iii

The Friar gives Giovanni Annabella's letter, written in her blood, which warns her brother that their secret has been discovered.

Vasques enters to invite Giovanni to Soranzo's birthday party. The Friar warns Giovanni not to attend, but he insists he will go. The Friar decides to leave Parma.

Act V, scene iv

Soranzo and Vasques plan to allow Giovanni to encounter Annabella in Soranzo's bedroom, then, hoping to catch them in the act of love-making, to have them killed by the Banditti.

Act V, scene v

Lying in bed, Giovanni talks with Annabella. Realizing the impossibility of their situation, he kills her and exits with her body.

Act V, scene vi

At Soranzo's party, Giovanni enters with Annabella's heart on his sword. He kills Soranzo, then fights the Banditti. Giovanni, wounded by Vasques, dies. Donado describes this turn of events

as a "Strange miracle of Justice," but instead of punishing Vasques for plotting Giovanni's murder, the Cardinal banishes him. The Cardinal then confiscates all the "gold and jewels, or whatsoever . . . to the Pope's proper use." Richardetto puts aside his disguise and reveals himself. The Cardinal describes Annabella with the words of the title, "'Tis pity she's a whore," making no mention of Giovanni's role in the incestuous affair.

CHARACTERS

Annabella

Florio's daughter, in love with her brother, Giovanni. In the course of her affair with Giovanni, she becomes pregnant and agrees to marry Soranzo to cover her transgression. Annabella confesses her incest to the Friar and writes a repentant letter to Giovanni. Soranzo discovers her pregnancy and vows to revenge himself on Annabella and her brother Giovanni at his birthday party. Before he can, however, Giovanni murders his sister, kills Soranzo, and dies fighting Vasques.

Bergetto

Donado's nephew, Bergetto is dense and vulgar. Much of the play's comic relief comes from his efforts to sue for marriage with Annabella. He is murdered by Grimaldi, who mistakes him for Soranzo.

Friar Bonaventura

A friar and Giovanni's professor when he studied a the university. Bonaventura urges Giovanni to fight his incestuous feelings for his sister. When Bonaventura eventually encounters Annabella, he convinces her to repent and to break off the erotic relationship with her brother. When Giovanni refuses to listen to his advice, Bonaventura leaves.

The Cardinal

Nuncio to the Pope, the Cardinal protects Grimaldi though he knows he's guilty of Bergetto's murder. At the play's end, the Cardinal confiscates the lovers' property in the name of the church.

Donado

A citizen of Parma, Donado is Bergetto's uncle. He hopes to marry his foolish nephew with Annabella by writing a love letter for him, but Bergetto insists on writing—and reading—his own letter. When

MEDIA ADAPTATIONS

- The 1973 film version by Giuseppe Patrone Griffi, released by London's Miracle Films, stars Oliver Tobias. While not an entirely faithful adaptation of the play, the film does retain the spirit of Ford's original.

- In 1962, BBC radio's Third Programme presented a radio version of the play.

- The BBC produced a second radio adaptation on Radio 3 in 1970.

- Roland Joffe directed an adaptation of the play for BBC2 television in 1980. Joffe's adaptation portrays Giovanni and Annabella, somewhat sympathetically, as rebels and condemns the hypocrisy of the mercantile, courtly, and religious society in which they live.

Bergetto's wooing fails and she rejects him, he seems unfazed and goes off to find prostitutes.

Florio

A citizen of Parma, father to Giovanni and Annnabella. While he seems to have his children's best interests at heart, telling a friend that he will not force Annabella to marry someone she does not want to, his ideas of "what is best" for his daughter are ultimately financial rather than emotional.

Giovanni

The son of Florio, Giovanni loves his sister, Annabella. They have an incestuous affair, by which she becomes pregnant. To conceal her affair, she agrees to marry Soranzo. In the end, Giovanni murders Annabella, enters Soranzo's birthday feast with her heart on his sword, and fights the Banditti and Vasques, who ultimately kills him.

Grimaldi

A Roman gentleman who loves Annabella, he conspires with Richardetto to murder Soranzo with a poisoned rapier. Richardetto, disguised as a doctor, agrees to help Grimaldi. Richardetto, who knows his wife Hippolita is having an affair with Soranzo, hopes to get revenge on his wife's lover. When they carry out their plot, however, Grimaldi mistakenly kills Bergetto instead of Soranzo. He escapes justice for this crime when the Cardinal grants him immunity.

Hippolita

Richardetto's unfaithful wife who is having affair with Soranzo. When rejected by Soranzo, she plans revenge with the help of his servant Vasques, offering him the reward of sexual favors and wealth for his help. In the event, he betrays her and remains loyal to his master Soranzo. Hippolita ends up killed when Vasques hands her the poisoned cup she intended for Soranzo.

Philotis

Richardetto's naive, subservient niece, she obeys her uncle in everything. First, he hopes she will marry Soranzo, then, he decides she must enter a convent. Without protest, she agrees.

Poggio

Bergetto's relatively loyal servant, Poggio seems to be smarter than his master, which under the circumstances is not that difficult. Also providing comic relief, he accompanies Bergetto on his fanciful adventures.

Putana

Annabella's tutoress, she accepts the news of her mistress's affair with her brother agreeably, saying she believes it is acceptable to have affairs with brothers, fathers, or anyone if the mood strikes. Tricked by Vasques into revealing the paternity of Annabella's child, he has her bound and blinded.

Richardetto

Hippolita's husband and Philotis's uncle, Richardetto disguises himself as a physician in order to uncover his wife's infidelities with Soranzo. He plots with Grimaldi to help him murder Soranzo. His motivation is revenge for Soranzo's affair with Hippolita, but Richardetto, cold and calculating, does not get very upset when his wife dies.

Soranzo

A nobleman in love with Annabella, Soranzo is having an affair with Richardetto's wife Hippolita. Soranzo marries Annabella, discovers she's pregnant by her brother, and plans revenge for this humiliation. Before he can punish them, however, Giovanni kills Soranzo at his birthday party.

Vasques

Soranzo's loyal servant and formerly servant of his father, Vasques proves central to his master's plan for revenge. Vasques pretends to plot with Hippolita to help her revenge herself on Soranzo in exchange for her money and sexual favors, but in the end he remains loyal to his master. He lies to Putana to discover the identify of the father of Annabella's baby, then has Annabella's tutoress bound and blinded. At the play's end, the Cardinal exiles him instead of punishing him for his role in the plans for revenge and murder.

THEMES

Marriage

'Tis Pity She's a Whore's action revolves around love and marriage, though for Ford, the two are not necessarily synonymous. Florio indicates that his daughter Annabella may choose any suitor she loves. He encourages her match with Soranzo, however, for financial reasons rather than emotional ones. The same seems true of Richardetto, who hopes to marry his niece Philotis to Donado's foolish but wealthy nephew Bergetto. Again, his aim is marriage not for love but for money. Ironically, the close family ties of the only two people who do seem to love each other—Giovanni and Annabella—prevent their incestuous love from being validated by society in marriage.

Love

The play presents examples of many kinds of love. First, the obviously forbidden but powerful incestuous love—which may be better described as lust—between Giovanni and Annabella. Next is the adulterous love between Soranzo and Hippolita. Richardetto does not seem like either a loving husband or caring ward for his niece. His wife Hippolita's love for Soranzo turns to murderous revenge. Her extreme passions lead to disaster, foretelling the play's ending and the destruction of Giovanni and Annabella.

The play also offers examples of love for financial reward, a kind of mercenary love. Gimaldi and Bergetto want to marry Annabella, primarily for her money. Bergetto shows the presence of bawdy love in his discussion of prostitution. Finally, Soranzo

and Giovanni, among other characters, discuss the ideals of "Neoplatonic" and "Courtly Love." Their understanding of the ideals of love function ironically to elucidate their imperfect characters. Soranzo is overheard reading a courtly love sonnet, subsequently revealing that his attitudes toward love are not in the least courtly. Giovanni's disingenuous arguments in favor of consummating his incestuous relationship with his sister stem in part from Neoplatonic ideas.

Justice

As in any story of crime and punishment, law and justice figure prominently in Ford's tragedy. Complicating things here, though, is the fact that while the lovers may be wrong, no one else in their world seems right. The play offers no ethical standard or admirable role model. It is impossible not to see the irony when, at the play's end, Donado describes the tragic turn of events as "strange miracle of justice." After all, Annabella, who has repented, has been murdered. Vasques, who plotted the lovers' murder, is freed by the Cardinal, who also grants a reprieve to Grimaldi, whom he knows to be guilty of murder. The Cardinal then confiscates the lovers' property. While in the first act, the Friar says that "heaven is just," there appears to be little justice in the world Ford presents.

Religion

Religion in the sense of sin and ethics plays a central role in the play, though religion as spirituality seems to offer no solutions to the lovers' problems. While Bonaventura, the Friar, appears a relatively positive figure, his prayers and advice seem largely ineffectual and go unheeded by all save Annabella. Religion condemns the lovers' actions, but the Friar's advice offers little help and the actions of the other clerical figures seem overtly hypocritical—the Cardinal offers sanctuary to Grimaldi, a known murderer, and at the play's end, takes possession of the lovers' land in the name of the church. Overall, the play reveals religion not as spiritual and ethical but as worldly and corrupt.

STYLE

Revenge Tragedy

As the name implies, a Revenge Tragedy is a play in which desire for revenge results in tragedy. Made popular in the Elizabethan period with plays

TOPICS FOR FURTHER STUDY

- Ford's play can be read as a commentary on the corruption of the court and courtiers of his time. Analyze the play's themes and characters in the context of late-Renaissance history. What do you believe Ford is saying about the politics of early-seventeenth century Britain? About contemporary kingship? Love? Ethics?

- While it seems to some readers that Giovanni and Annabella freely choose to consummate their incestuous love, others believe—as does Giovanni himself—that they are fated to do so. Do you believe the lovers actions to be the result of free will or determinism? Cite evidence from the play to support your position.

- While some may condemn the lovers' actions, it is possible to partially sympathize with their plight. After all, they seem to exist in a world without ethical values: family, court, and church seem corrupt and greedy. In a world without ethics, where can individuals go to decide what is right and wrong, how to live their lives?

- The case can be made that Ford's dramatic literary style resembles the baroque style evident in the fine arts of the period. Research of the art history of the time will reveal many examples of these stylistic resemblances. You might begin with artists like Bernini, Carvaggio, and Gentileschi. Compare their visions with Ford's.

- How do Ford's representations of incest compare with contemporary accounts? You might research psychologists or sociologists working with sexually abused children and compare their experiences with those related by Ford. In what ways does he present an accurate picture? What important details does he omit?

---

like Thomas Kyd's *Spanish Tragedy,* a sophisticated example of the form is Shakespeare's *Hamlet.* This dramatic subgenre is modeled on the Roman plays of similar themes, particularly the tragedies written by Seneca.

Courtly Love

The concept of courtly love first appears in the medieval period in the poetry of the Provencal troubadour poets. The idea is for the lover to woo the most worthy woman in the land, though this often was the queen or wife of a powerful man. Scholars debate as to whether this love ever was consummated, but an elaborate code of erotic language and practices grew up around it. The stereotypes of lovers losing sleep and appetite, are found in courtly love. A medieval example is *Sir Gowain and the Green Knight,* in which the lord's wife attempts to seduce Sir Gowain. Other examples are the various Arthurian romances and sonnet sequences by such renaissance writers as Sidney, Surry, Wyatt, Shakespeare, and Spenser.

Neoplatonism

Neoplatonism refers to elaborations of Greek philosopher Plato's ideas which develop from late classicism into the nineteenth century. Though complicated, in general they suggest (1) that this physical world is not real but a fallen reflection of an ideal world of ''Forms'' which exists beyond it; and (2) that a relationship exists between beauty and ethics, that the reason humans seek beauty in this physical world is because it reminds them of the good they experienced in the ideal world. Examples of these notions pervade Medieval, Renaissance, Neoclassical, and even Romantic philosophy and literature.

The Four Humours

According to Humour psychology, the balance of four bodily fluids determines human personalities. Unusual or ''humourous'' people have an imbalance in either blood, phlegm, yellow bile, or black bile. Too much blood makes a person sanguine, happy and amorous; yellow bile makes a person choleric, stubborn, and impatient; too much phlegm results in a phlegmatic personality—dull and cowardly; while excesses of black bile made a person melancholy, introspective, and sentimental.

Robert Burton, whose *Anatomy of Melancholy* explores the relationship between love and the humours, strongly influenced Ford. The theory also aids in the categorization of various Renaissance characters (in Shakespeare, for example, Hamlet is melancholy, Hot Spur is choleric, etc.). In time, the Comedy of Humours developed, which pokes fun at characters driven by one aspect of their personalities, resulting in the meaning of the word humor today.

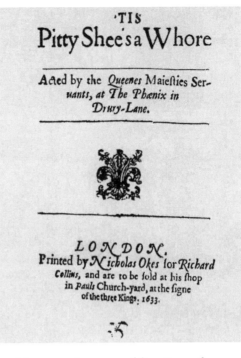

The title page from a publication of John Ford's 'Tis Pity She's a Whore

HISTORICAL CONTEXT

When Ford's drama is read, there is frequently the suspicion that the playwright is exaggerating, that no society could be as unstable and corrupt as that of the Parma he depicts. While parts of the play—particularly Annabella's death at the end—seem extravagant (and, as some critics might say, "baroque"), the historical moment which produced Ford's dramas was a contentious one. To better understand the reign of King Charles I, who ruled when Ford wrote his "Caroline" dramas, a history of England's earlier kings is necessary.

When Henry VII died in 1509, he left England on relatively sound financial footing, but his son, Henry VIII, through expensive foreign wars and uninhibited personal spending, began the dangerous trend of running a deficit. The question arose as to who would pay off the deficit. Those paying the increased taxation soon wanted more say in how the king spent their money. By the seventeenth century, a split developed between the king and elements of the landed classes—the land owners represented in Parliament—that, during the reign of King Charles I, resulted in civil war in 1642 and the king's beheading in 1649.

During this tempestuous period, when people discussed political theory, it frequently took the form of a debate between Royalism and Republicanism. The Royalists believed in monarchical ab-

solutism (the absolute power of the king), while Republicans, influenced by the relatively democratic examples of classical Athens and contemporary Italian city states like Florence, Sienna, and Venice, argued for a balance of power between the executive branch—the king—and the legislature—the Parliament—in a form of representative democracy. Interest in Italy in part accounts for Ford's setting the play in Parma.

Religion complicated these economic and political considerations. In 1517, Martin Luther's "Wittenberg Theses" began the Protestant Reformation, which lead to breaks with the Catholic Church. In 1534, Henry VIII himself broke with Rome (the seat of the Catholic Church), primarily because of the Pope's failure to annul the king's childless marriage to Catherine of Aragon. In the 1534 Act of Supremacy, Henry VIII declared himself the head of the English Church. Religion remained a divisive issue, though, as Henry's son Edward VI continued England's move toward Protestantism, a trend violently reversed after his death by the Catholic Queen "Bloody" Mary.

In 1558, Queen Elizabeth took the throne, steering a militantly centrist path between English Catho-

COMPARE
&
CONTRAST

- **1633:** The wealthy have more access to official outlets of justice like the law courts than the poor. Wealth is no guarantee of power, though, and court politics play a significant role in who receives punishment for which crime. For the poor, riots offer the most popular means of protesting issues like rising food prices or rent. Since Britain will not have a police force until the mid-nineteenth century, vigilantism and revenge are popular avenues to justice.

  Today: Revenge still remains a prominent theme in popular books and films, particularly those featuring a vigilante hero or heroine. Generally, however, most people tend to believe in institutional justice, expecting that the courts will decide on issues of crime and punishment. This in part accounts for the popularity of films and television shows about police departments or lawyers.

- **1633:** The church did not officially define and

condemn incest until the thirteenth century, but because large families shared small quarters and often beds, incest still occurred. In Britain, however, as many as 60% of the boys and 75% of the girls between puberty and adulthood grew up living with employers, relatives, or family connections rather than with their parents. This may have been one way of minimizing the temptation to commit incest.

Today: Incest is viewed as a form of child sexual abuse often related to broader family problems. Most sexual abusers were themselves abused as children; while as adults they may be sexual predators, as children they were victims. This does not mitigate their offense, but it does help psychologists treat sexually abused children in hopes of helping them avoid abusing their own children when they become adults.

---

lics and traditional "High Church" Anglicans on one hand, and reformist "low church" Dissenters and Puritans on the other. While all these religious issues seem complicated, they help explain Ford's negative representations of the Catholic Friar and Cardinal. It also helps explain why within the play, religion itself—about which different people may hold different beliefs—fails to offer any absolute standard of ethical conduct.

Ford himself was born in 1586, one year before Protestant Elizabeth's execution of Catholic Mary Queen of Scots and two years before Protestant England's invasion by Catholic Spain's Armada. In 1601, when Ford was just fifteen, the rebels involved in Essex's rebellion against Elizabeth captured one of Ford's relatives. After the queen's death and the coronation of James I in 1603, Ford and his fellow law students would have followed the trial of Sir Walter Raleigh. This grossly unfair proceeding, actually a referendum on Raleigh's

belligerent aggression toward Catholic Spain in the New World, ended with his execution in 1618. In 1605, Catholic conspirators involved in the Gunpowder Plot attempted to blow up the king and Parliament.

Decker Roper provided another example in which the history of the moment is not much stranger than the fiction of Ford's drama. The new Earl of Essex married Francis Howard, but the marriage was annulled to enable Frances to marry the Earl of Somerset, a favorite of King James. Thomas Overbury, who attended the Middle Inns with Ford and who condemned these actions, found himself imprisoned in the Tower, where Somerset and his new wife poisoned him. Some think Ford contributed to a collection of elegiac poetry marking Overbury's death.

The religious and political conflicts of Ford's day prove as dramatic as his fiction. While critics have not been able to identify exact historical sources for Ford's characters, the anxieties about marriage and power, about religion and ethics, about the nobility and the wealthy bourgeoisie play significant roles in 'Tis Pity She's a Whore.

CRITICAL OVERVIEW

As might be expected of a play that deals with incest, critical response to Ford's drama was often intense. Contemporary critical views that paint 'Tis Pity She's a Whore as decadent or psychological follow the opinions of two important nineteenth century critics, William Hazlitt and Charles Lamb, according to Mark Stavig in John Ford and the Traditional Moral Order. For Hazlitt, Ford was "a decadent romantic who delighted in melodramatic plots, licentious scenes, and revolt against the established moral order." Lamb focused less on Ford's ethics, believing that "at his best he is a profound and objective analyst of human behavior who portrays a higher morality that stresses the elevating effect of love and the nobility of endurance in time of adversity."

It is easy to see why the Hazlitt school sees Ford as decadent. After all, most critics believe 'Tis Pity She's a Whore to be the first play in English to take incestuous lovers as its main protagonists and treat them with some sympathy. The question becomes, why does Ford choose this kind of subject matter? In The Problem of John Ford, H. J. Oliver believed that after generations of powerful drama, Elizabethan and Jacobean audiences (those who lived during the reigns of Queen Elizabeth and King James) had become jaded to the dramatic conventions of the time, requiring Caroline dramatists (who wrote during the reign of King Charles) to present bolder plots and characters. "That is why the Caroline dramatist turned more and more for his subject matter to the daring, the immoral, the unnatural; that is partly why Ford, among others, sought subjects like incest and adultery and was content to have Giovanni appear with Annabella's bleeding heart on his dagger."

Elizabethan dramatists influenced the writers who came after them, and William Shakespeare's influence looms large in Ford's major dramas, particularly Othello, King Lear, and Romeo and Juliet. In 'Tis Pity She's a Whore, the accidental murder of the foolish Begatto instead of Soranzo is reminiscent of Hamlet's accidental killing of the foolish Polonius instead of Claudius. Hamlet has the opportunity to kill Claudius as he prays for forgiveness but does not, wanting instead to enact his revenge at a moment when the murderer's sins on his soul will damn him to hell. A similar action occurs at the end of Ford's drama, when Soranzo allows Giovanni to be alone with Annabella, hoping they will act lustfully and then be killed by Soranzo in the midst of an incestuous act.

To many critics, though, 'Tis Pity She's a Whore seems in many ways an incestuous retelling of Romeo and Juliet. Comparing the two plays, many of the same characters and conflicts arise: young lovers, forbidden love, a meddling nurse and friar, and tragedy all around.

Paul Cantor wrote in the Dictionary of Literary Biography, "Ford takes the potentially hackneyed theme of star-crossed young lovers and gives it a new twist by making the Romeo and Juliet of his play brother and sister." One difference, though, is that "Annabella's father, unlike Juliet's, makes it clear that he will not force her into a marriage against her wishes." Because contemporary society is largely a world which endorses marriage for love, "Ford must search for a form of love that will not have the endorsement of society," in this case, incest. Other critics believed that Annabella's father Florio only gives lip-service to her marrying for love, for he actually urges her to love the richest and most socially elevated suitor, Soranzo.

As indicated above, popular demand in part explains Ford's technique of offering controversial reworkings of familiar plots. Cantor wrote that "Ford's attraction to normally taboo themes, such as incest, may be accounted for by his need to get the attention of audiences who thought they had already seen everything there was to see on the stage." Another reason Ford may have selected such controversial subject matter for his dramas is that such powerful characters and emotions allowed him to explore the sometimes dark and dangerous depths of the human psyche. This generally follows the Lamb school's opinion of Ford, a dramatist who to Leech reveals a "preoccupation with strange and perilous human conduct."

This moral interrogation and psychological introspection seems a product of the times. In Elizabethan and Jacobean, F. P. Wilson wrote that what "distinguishes the Jacobean age from the Elizabethan is its more exact, more searching, more detailed inquiry into moral and political questions and its interest in the analysis of the mysteries and perturbations of the human mind.'' As Oliver noted, ''inquiry, analysis—these interest the Jacobean writers, these rather than incident.''

What audiences see in 'Tis Pity She's a Whore, according to Clifford Leech in John Ford, is that Ford ''had a profound understanding of suffering, and an ability to present it in dramatic poetry; he had a deep interest in abnormal conditions of the mind . . . he had a high ideal of human conduct, a reverence for love and fidelity and the relation of man and women in true marriage.''

This understanding and reverence leads Ford to allow ''Giovanni to make an unusually spirited and eloquent defense of forbidden love,'' according to Cantor. ''Moreover, Giovanni and Annabella are by far the most vibrant characters in the play, and, even though their love destroys them, there are strong suggestions that they have in the process attained an intensity of experience from which the crassly conventional characters in the play are barred.'' So the line separating the rewards and evils of the lovers' incestuous transgression becomes blurred; physically and emotionally, their love offers powerful satisfactions, but society sees it as sinful and it precipitates their mutual destruction. That society, though, is emotionally decadent, morally corrupt, and spiritually bankrupt. The play offers not positive example of true love or happy marriage.

This raises points of similarity between Ford's play and Marlowe's Doctor Faustus, wrote Cantor. In both plays, ''the protagonists are overreachers and perish in their attempt to go beyond the limits of normal humanity, but the forces which oppose them in the scheme of the play hardly have a solid moral basis in their opposition, being involved as they are in a shabby web of sexual intrigue and assassination plots.''

What then does a viewer make of Ford's dramatic choices? Is he presenting audiences with a decadent world in order to endorse or condemn adherent behavior? Another way to ask this question is: what did Ford really believe? Derek Roper, in his introduction to the play, traced Ford's ideas to his early writing, which reveal three tendencies: ''romantic and Platonic love, a Calvinistic kind of Protestantism, Stoic beliefs and the cult of honour.'' All of these concepts figure prominently in the characters and conflicts in Ford's later dramas.

In John Ford, Leech usefully identifies the playwright's debt to Queen Henrietta Maria's cult of Platonic Love. According to Leech, Ford saw Platonic love as a logical impossibility, realizing that ''the courtly code was at odds with human nature and its demands . . . Ford's plays are commonly studies of a passion which is inclusive and destructive. . . . His lovers may talk of their passion in ideal terms, but there is always in them a full drive toward coition: it is this which commonly destroys them.''

For Stavig, a reading of Ford's early works offers insight into his Christian humanist morality. Ford's writings, drawing heavily on the classical ethics of such writers as Aristotle, Cicero, Plutarch, and Seneca, urges people to trust virtue more than fortune. Ford's stoicism demands a balance between reason and passion, with love being the most difficult passion to control. Roper, however, warned about the difficulty in ascertaining Ford's beliefs, as opposed to those of his characters. ''His dedications may suggest some sympathy for those noblemen who felt deprived of their rightful influence in government by royal favorites; and some plays show admiration for aristocratic attitudes, particularly dignified defeat.''

Finally, several critics praised Ford's use of language and skillful creation of poetry itself. Leech for one believed that Ford wrote ''in a time when poetic drama was in decay, and he shows what could be done by a playwright whose purpose needed poetry but would have been ruined by an ostentatious display of the merely 'poetic.''' Poet T. S. Eliot, writing in Selected Essays, continued in this strain, admiring Ford's poetry, particularly ''that slow solemn rhythm which is Ford's distinct contribution to the blank verse of the period. . . . The varieties of cadence and tone in blank verse are none too many, in the history of English verse; and Ford, though intermittently, was able to manipulate sequences of words in blank verse in a manner which is quite his own.''

CRITICISM

Arnold Schmidt

In this essay, Schmidt examines ethics, particularly in regard to the concepts of incest and greed, as they are presented in Ford's play.

In many ways, Ford's play is a difficult one with which to come to terms. On one level, that of plot, it seems rather obvious and scandalous at that. The play tells the tale of Giovanni and Annabella, a

WHAT DO I READ NEXT?

- Christopher Marlowe's *Doctor Faustus* (1594) tells the tragic tale of a gifted man who rejects social and moral boundaries and ends in destruction. In the same way that Giovanni flaunts social mores and commits incest with his sister, Faustus sells his soul to the devil in exchange for forbidden knowledge and power. Both plays critique the ideal of Renaissance individualism; in both, excessive independence and intellectual pride lead to death.

- *Mathilda* (written in the nineteenth century but first published in 1959) a short novel by *Frankenstein* author Mary Shelley, also treats the incest theme boldly, though the act itself remains unconsummated. The novel tells the story of a father whose wife dies and who begins to have erotic feelings for his daughter, who reminds him so much of his dead wife. Fearing he may succumb to temptation, he leaves the daughter and dies.

- Director John Sayles offers another representation of incest in his 1995 film *Lone Star*. Sayles tells the story of policeman investigating a murder which may have been committed by his father, a former police officer. Here, though the incest is consummated, its significance becomes symbolic of relationships between the United States and Mexico.

- Other Renaissance revenge tragedies. These plays, as their name suggests, begin with a deed—a crime or injustice—which must be revenged. The most famous of these are Shakespeare's *Hamlet* and Thomas Kyd's *Spanish Tragedy,* though there is also what critics call the "Tragedy of Blood" seen in Webster's *The Duchess of Malfi,* and *The White Devil.*

---

brother and sister, who consummate an incestuous relationship which ultimately destroys them, as well as others. Problems for the audience arise when we start to consider the characters' actions in the context of the play itself. For one thing, while the lovers may appear to be villains—after all, their actions are condemnable—the play offers heroes. No character seems entirely worthy of our admiration, and even those who have some good qualities—Friar Bonaventura, for example—remain ineffectual and unable to change things for the better. Most of the other characters are greedy and unscrupulous, even murderous! How then are we to understand the meaning of transgression and ethics in Ford's play?

We can begin by considering *'Tis Pity She's a Whore* in light of Aristotle's theory of tragedy, as laid out in his *Poetics.* By now, his theory may be familiar: tragedy tells the story of the fall of a socially or morally elevated person, through a combination of fate and flaw. The "tragic flaw" may be

desire for power, as in Shakespeare's *Macbeth,* which leads the title character and his wife to murder and destruction; or revenge, as in such "revenge tragedies as Thomas Kyd's *Spanish Tragedy,* or Shakespeare's *Hamlet.* Giovanni's tragedy, however, more closely resembles that of Sophocles's *Oedipus Rex,* whose intellectual pride leads him to believe that he can outsmart the Fates and avoid his destiny of murdering his father and marrying his mother. A closer parallel, though, might be Christopher Marlowe's *Doctor Faustus,* in which the highly educated doctor sells his soul to the devil in exchange for greater knowledge and power.

While Giovanni believes his predicament to be the product of his fate, he actually seems to use fate as an excuse to justify his tragic flaws of uncontrollable lust and intellectual pride. A brilliant student trained in logic, Giovanni's scholastic intellect leads him to atheism. In a conversation with Annabella, Giovanni reveals how his faith in reason has under-

---

> ALL OF THE CORRUPTIONS IN FORD'S PLAY SHARE ONE THING IN COMMON: THEY ALL PREFER MATERIAL GAIN TO EMOTIONAL CONNECTION"

mined his religious faith: "The schoolmen teach that all this globe of earth / Shall be consum'd to ashes in a minute / . . . But 'twere somewhat strange / To see the waters burn: could I believe / This might be true, I could believe as well / There might be hell or Heaven." We see that he has faith, not in the power of God but the power of reason, which leads him to atheism, pride, and, ultimately, death.

In part, Giovanni's problems stem from his wilful misreading of Renaissance ideas about Platonic love, which posits an equality between the beautiful and the good. Things that seem physically beautiful on the surface merely manifest a deeper, spiritual goodness. This explains our attraction to physical beauty: we seek the beautiful as a way of reaching the good. Consider the ideas presented in one of the most influential Renaissance texts, Baldesar Castiglione's broadly Neoplatonic *The Courtier:* "Gracious and sacred beauty is the supreme adornment of everything; and it can be said that in some manner the good and the beautiful are identical . . . the proximate cause of physical beauty is . . . the beauty of the soul. . . . Therefore beauty is the true trophy of the soul's victory."

Giovanni's inability to control his lust, as Castiglione might explain, lies in the fact that the largely reasonable soul finds itself trapped in the "earthly prison" of the body. There, "deprived of spiritual contemplation, the soul cannot of itself clearly perceive the truth when it is carrying out the duties of governing the body," which can be manipulated by passion. Beauty attracts admiration, but "the mind is seized by desire for the beauty which it recognizes as good." Guided by the senses, the body "falls into the gravest errors" and mistakenly believes that beauty results from the beautiful body, rather than the ethical soul within. By the play's end, the unrepentant Giovanni still has not learned this lesson, though Annabella has come to associate beauty and ethics, saying, "Beauty that clothes the outside of the face / Is cursed if it be not cloth'd in grace."

Earlier in the play, Giovanni and Annabella make this mistake, justifying their error by believing that Fate has created their tragic situation. As Giovanni says, denying at least in part the truth, "'tis not, I know, / My lust, but 'tis my fate that leads me on." While their mutual attraction may have been fated, though, their acting on that attraction clearly requires at least in part some exercise of free will. Fate drives their love, but they make the disastrous choice of consummating it. As the earlier Castiglioine writes, while young lovers may fall victim to their passions, the desires of "mature lovers . . . [are] guided by rational choice . . . [and so] possess completely the beauty they love."

Giovanni and Annabella's immaturity prevents them from restraining their unreasonable passion. Worse, where Giovanni's reason should control his passion, instead his reason makes matters worse. In his initial discussion with Friar Bonaventura, Giovanni justifies the superiority of incestuous love over socially accepted forms of affection. He says, "Say that we had one father, say one womb / . . . gave both us life and birth; / Are we not therefore each to other bound / So much the more by nature, by the links / Of blood, of reason—nay, if you will have't, / Even of religion." Giovanni's intellectual pride drives him to employ logic and argument to justify his incestuous desires, rather than to inhibit them.

Giovanni's misuse of "natural" reason to justify his "unnatural" love for his sister raises the play's key issue: what might the incest itself symbolize? If love in the broadest sense indicates a relationship of connection and responsibility, then there are resemblances between and among the various kinds of love: parental love of children, filial love of siblings, erotic love, and the "love" of a ruler for his people. Considering the play in the context of contemporary events sheds light on the significance of the "unnatural" in social relations.

First, how does Ford represent the love of parents for children? While some critics believe Annabella's father Florio truly wants her to marry for love and happiness, others argue that he merely offers lip-service to a love match, actually urging her union with the richest and most socially elevated suitor, Soranzo. Significantly, Ford's play dramatizes the conflict between romantic marriage for love and mercenary marriage for profit. Overall, marriage seems a poor option of Annabella, whose bad luck leads to being pursued by a host of undesirable suitors: the unfaithful Soranzo, the cowardly Grimaldi, and the foolish Bergetto. Only Giovanni, her brother, seems to love her truly, and society prohibits their attractions. And Florio is not the only parent urging marriage on a child for solely monetary gain. Donado too actively tries to marry Annabella to Bergetto, whom he knows to be a fool.

Throughout the play, reason is the target and paradox the tool, as the foolish act reasonably and the reasonable act foolishly. Bergetto, whose uncle wants him to marry for money, is refused by Annabella, but he says he can buy women any time he wants—he speaks truly about loveless mercantile matrimony, which, like prostitution, exchanges money for sex. Her uncle, who prefers she marry the honorable Soranzo, is foolish were he to know what we the audience knows, that Soranzo is unfaithful and vindictive. Throughout the play, however, Ford presents examples of tainted love: Hippolita's for Soranzo is adulterous, Hippolita's offer of sex as payment to Vasques resembles prostitution. Grimaldi's woos Annabella primarily because of money. The only love that seems true, at least in part, is that between Giovanni and Annabella; though incestuous, it is, after all, based on a long-term friendship, real emotional contact, and passion.

The "unnatural" love of Giovanni and Annabella extends, at least symbolically, to the corrupt love of parents for children, which they express solely in terms of monetary gain, rather than emotional happiness. We can extend that metaphor even further and see that corruption disrupted the "natural" relations people had from the Middle Ages come to expect between their court and their king. As we will see, due to the Carolinian court's corruption, the ideal courtier did not receive reward, while the well-connected, manipulative one did.

According to D. M. Loades's *Politics and the Nation, 1450-1660,* by the early-seventeenth century, a "'conspiracy of rich men' now consisted in the swarm of favourites and parasites who swarmed around the king ... the court in many respects resembled a market [for royal patronage], where prices and profits were both high and the competition fierce and unscrupulous." It is this courtly world which Ford satirizes: corrupt, mercenary, unethical. Though these groups of influential men did not make up political "parties" in the modern sense, they did create a divisive sense of "faction"—high church, low church, old money, and new—among the courtly classes. These divisions ultimately contributed to the civil war in 1640 and King Charles's beheading in 1649.

As we have seen, when parents urge their children to marry, not for happiness, but for money, those parents violate their responsibility and corrupt their love. The same seems true when the court reeks of corruption and the king rewards, not good deserving men, but those with political connections. All of these corruptions of paternal, filial, and social "love" are "unnatural" in that they violate the "natural" emotional, ethical connections and responsibilities each love requires. In this way, they resemble incest, which some might say also violates the "natural" order.

As Derek Roper pointed out in his introduction to *'Tis Pity She's a Whore,* the play's "overt narrative . . . tells of the downfall of two guilty lovers, but inscribed within this narrative is another telling of the destruction of love and trust in a world where such things are rare." While the play does not forgive the lovers' incest, it emphasizes the corruption of the society which condemns the lovers. Parma's commercial interests, personified by Donado and Florio, behave in a greedy and underhanded manner. The noble classes, represented by Richardetto, Soranzo, and Grimaldi, also appear vain and manipulative. Members of the clergy fare little better. Because of Grimaldi's court connections, the Cardinal hypocritically protects the Roman, who has just committed murder. At the play's end, when the Cardinal condemns the lovers' incest as sinful, he also takes their property.

All of these corruptions share one thing in common: they all prefer material gain to emotional connection. As merchants, nobles, clergy, or parents, they consistently value money over love. If marriage for money is a form of socially sanctioned prostitution, on what ethical basis can a hypocritical and mercenary society condemn true love that is incestuous? While the play certainly does not justify incest, it does challenge the conventional organization of social and sexual relations. Giovanni and Annabella's love may be called sinful and lust, but they willingly face social condemnation in order to consummate it. Through seriously flawed, in some ways they seem superior to those around them who never act for love but only for material gain.

Source: Arnold Schmidt, for *Drama for Students,* Gale, 2000.

Robert Brustein
Brustein is one of the best-known theatre critics of the late twentieth century. In this essay, he

reviews a 1992 production of Ford's play. While finding that there is much to recommend in the production, the critic ultimately finds fault with director Joan Akalaitis's efforts to contemporize the play.

JoAnne Akalaitis's first production as the New York Public Theater's artistic director displays her virtues in abundance—alas, the defects of those virtues too. Her version of John Ford's *'Tis Pity She's a Whore* is undeniably terrific to look at. Set in Fascist Italy during the '30s, the production has a design by John Conklin that proves to be the best performance on stage—a compound of futurist and surrealist elements that ravish your eye while demonstrating how easily art can become a slave to tyranny. As interpolated cries of "Duce" fill the air and posters extolling God, Country, and Family materialize between the Roman arches of the stage, Conklin rolls out huge cutouts of a child's hands, anonymous nude women, and tearful faces inspired by de Chirico, Marinetti, Dali, and other artists of the time.

Akalaitis shows no squeamishness about exploring the sanguinary aspects of *'Tis Pity*—a repertory staple in Artaud's Theater of Cruelty. Her finest moment, along with the blinding of Putana, is the culminating blood bath, when Giovanni, arriving with his sister's heart impaled upon his dagger, participates in another three or four deaths, including his own. The stage is literally awash in gore, the impact so full of horror that, for once in the history of this play, the audience refrained from laughing.

She is less successful in extracting the theme of the work, which is offered as an object lesson in the brutalization of women by macho males (including Giovanni—who writes an anti-female obscenity in blood on the wall of Annabella's room). Women are certainly treated badly in *'Tis Pity,* but so is everyone. Ford wrote this incestuous version of *Romeo and Juliet* less to make a feminist point than to demonstrate (years in advance of Nietzsche and Dostoyevsky) that when God is dead, anything is possible. The abnormal love of Giovanni and Annabella is about the only redeeming feature in a world of social, political, and religious corruption, and when he takes her life at the end, Giovanni is taking the only course left to him, monstrous though it is.

Missing from Akalaitis's interpretation is not only Giovanni's towering intellect (the Friar de-

scribes him as a "miracle of wit"), but his motivating narcissism. He loves his sister largely because she's his twin—as one commentator says, they make love in a mirror and take identical vows. As played by Val Kilmer, however, he is simply an edgy, sulky, shambling boy, while Jeanne Tripplehorn's Annabella, befitting her victim status, is too subdued. Neither of these characters evokes much pathos, though the greatness of the play lies in the way the playwright redeems their corruption from an even more corrupt time. Their last scene together has virtually no love, warmth, or reconciliation, when it should be breaking your heart. Because these are actors well trained for the stage (and not just for close-ups in *The Doors* and *Basic Instinct*), one has to conclude that Akalaitis has misdirected them, especially since virtually all the other roles—with the intermittent exceptions of Erick Avari's Vasques and Jared Harris's Soranzo—are indifferently performed. No one on stage reveals an interior life, and the comic scenes are execrable. "This part has been scurvily played," says one of the characters about another in the play, and he might have been indicting almost the entire cast.

Still, the event is well worth seeing just for the brilliance of its colors and the boldness of its approach. Akalaitis may be wrongheaded and reductive to make this great seventeenth-century classic conform to contemporary feminist views, but the force of her commitment and her remarkable imagination must compel respect. Much more thought, preparation, and sweat went into the making of this blood-soaked masterpiece than hasty opinions can do justice to.

Source: Robert Brustein, review of *'Tis a Pity She's a Whore* in the *New Republic,* Vol. 206, no. 19, May 11, 1992, pp. 32–33.

Mimi Kramer

Kramer reviews a 1992 production of 'Tis Pity She's a Whore, *which updates the setting to Fascist Italy. The critic offers praise for the cast and production as well as for the director's interpretation of Ford's portrayal of male and female values.*

The production of John Ford's "'Tis Pity She's a Whore" that opened at the Public Theatre the first week of April, directed by JoAnne Akalaitis, is surprisingly engrossing. Like the production of "Pericles" that Michael Greif directed earlier this season, it features a company of capable actors, two able stars, a consistent vision of the play, and a couple of tour-de-force performances from actors in secondary roles. The stars in this instance are Val Kilmer and Jeanne Tripplehorn, who play the siblings Giovanni and Annabella—Giovanni being the young man who, against some of the best advice in Jacobean tragedy, enters into an incestuous relationship with his sister at the beginning of the play and, at the end of it, appears at a banquet with her heart on a stake.

Mr. Kilmer, who played Jim Morrison, the lead singer for the Doors, in Oliver Stone's movie of that title, also played a rock star in one of those Abrahams/Zucker spoofs. An actor like that, who knows how to play a rock star's temperament—whether in earnest or in jest—as opposed to one who merely possesses a rock star's temperament (like the young actors in the Brat Pack school), isn't a bad bet to play a Jacobean revenge hero. Callowness and a deceptive air of durability are the key here, for Giovanni is Hamlet without a conscience or an intellect. Watching him in the grip of something larger and stronger than himself, we have to believe that he thinks he is in control.

In the case of Annabella, we have to believe that she could go from thinking incest unthinkable to thinking it no big deal, and in very short order. If Annabella is too degenerate or too simple, her seduction will fail to be interesting, and that's why it isn't a bad idea, either, to cast an actress who knows how to play a victim without playing a sap. Miss Tripplehorn, who appears in the controversial date-rape scene in the new slasher movie ''Basic Instinct,'' and who got browbeaten and slathered with Vaseline in the last John Shanley play at the Public, manages to seem both intelligent and vulnerable. Watching Mr. Kilmer come on to her, you feel that if he were your brother you'd put out, too.

Unlike Mr. Kilmer, Miss Tripplehorn has trouble with the poetry, but she makes intelligible a particular brand of female naïveté, which the play, especially in Ms. Akalaitis's production, proves to be about. Yes, Jacobean revenge tragedy amounts to little more than a seventeenth-century version of ''Basic Instinct,'' but even cheap thrills command a subtext, and Ms. Akalaitis's production suggests that the subtext of Ford's play is the phenomenon we call sexual harassment—the process by which predatory men prevail with women by trading on the very customs and laws that make women feel safe. In Ford's play, women of all sorts (vulgar, innocent, elegant, corrupt) are turned against and

> THE ABNORMAL LOVE OF GIOVANNI AND ANNABELLA IS ABOUT THE ONLY REDEEMING FEATURE IN A WORLD OF SOCIAL, POLITICAL, AND RELIGIOUS CORRUPTION.''

punished for allowing themselves to be seduced—punished by the very men who lured them into their beds or their confidence. What this production skillfully brings out is that Giovanni's seduction and murder of Annabella—the play's paradigm for feminine trust elicited and betrayed—has more to do with sexual politics than with sex.

Ms. Akalaitis has updated the play to the Fascist Italy of the nineteen-thirties, to create the sense of an ossified, decadent, and repressive moral order, and in dealing with the violence she has opted for all-out realism, which is the only way to approach these plays. John Conklin's scenic design employs an idea of art-through-the-ages: a system of de Chirico archways, in which characters can eavesdrop or take shelter from the rain; sculpture fragments—a foot, an armless statue—that prefigure some of the violence; scenes in the Mannerist style appearing aloft behind a scrim; a Dadaist design on the cyclorama; and, here and there, surrealist distortions of humanity.

I liked Erick Avari's Alan Rickman turn in the Iago role, and Deirdre O'Connell's Putana and Ross Lehman's Bergetto—particularly the way their performances marshalled contempt, affection, and pity. Less popular with me were the dumb-show wedding at the beginning of Act II and the poisoning scene—two sequences that find Ms. Akalaitis up to her old pseudo-avant-garde tricks (twitching and slo-mo). I could also have done without Jan A. P. Kaczmarek's incessant electronic music and Daniel Oreskes' Mussolini impression, and without Jared Harris, who plays Soranzo—or, anyway, without his bluster and mannerisms and speech impediment. And Ellen McElduff's portrayal of Hippolita as a raving, scheming villainess—which is how she is described—seemed at variance with Ms. Akalaitis's insightful interpretation: the whole point is that

> IN FORD'S PLAY, WOMEN OF ALL
> SORTS (VULGAR, INNOCENT,
> ELEGANT, CORRUPT) ARE TURNED
> AGAINST AND PUNISHED FOR
> ALLOWING THEMSELVES TO BE
> SEDUCED."

what the men say of the women and what we see of them are two different things.

Source: Mimi Kramer, "Victims," in the *New Yorker,* Vol. 68, April 20, 1992, pp. 78–79.

Sharon Hamilton

In this essay, Hamilton examines a particular facet of Ford's play that she feels many critics ignore: the nature of the relationship between Soranzo and Annabella.

'Tis Pity She's a Whore (1633), John Ford's tragedy of brother-sister incest, is his best known work. Yet in the welter of commentary on the play, critics have ignored a puzzling taunt that the heroine flings at her newlywed husband. The situation is briefly this: in order to conceal the fact that she is carrying her brother Giovanni's child, Annabella has been compelled to marry the rake Soranzo. He knows nothing of her condition and is delighted at her sudden acceptance of his proposal. But Ford wastes no time in showing that the match is unhappy. In their first scene together after the wedding banquet, Soranzo comes in dragging Annabella by the hair, shouting insults and brandishing his sword. He describes her adultery in extravagant and graphic terms: she is a "strumpet, famous whore," entirely given up to her "hot itch and pleurisy of lust" (IV.iii.1–8; all quotations are from the Regents Renaissance Drama text, edited by N. W. Bawcutt). What enrages Soranzo is not only that he has purchased damaged goods but that he is the dupe chosen to conceal their true worthlessness: "could none but I/Be picked out to be cloak to your close tricks,/Your belly-sports?" (11.10–12). Now Annabella expects him to pretend to be "the dad/To all that gallimaufry that's stuff'd/In thy corrupted, bastard-bearing womb" (11.12–14).

But Annabella is undaunted. She tells him in no uncertain terms how little he means to her:

> had not this chance fall'n out as't doth, I never had been troubled with a thought That you had been a creature . . .

It would be hard to think of a more devastating dismissal of Soranzo's human worth. Yet instead of stopping there, she adds with still greater scorn: "but for marriage,/I scarce dream yet of that" (11.46–49). This is an odd thing to say to one's legal spouse, and it points up a larger problem of interpretation: how has Soranzo discovered the truth? Annabella is obviously pregnant; a bit later in the scene, the lewd servant Vasques marvels at the "quickness" of her "stomach's" swelling (11.169–72). But since the marriage took place so soon after Annabella realized her condition, why doesn't he assume that the child is his? One explanation is the technical one that the time scheme of the play is indefinite; there is no sure measure of how many months pass between II.vi, when the incestuous love is apparently only a few days old, and III.ii, when Annabella feels the first symptoms of pregnancy. A more intriguing possibility is that Annabella and Soranzo have never consummated their marriage. In fact, Annabella's taunt makes sense only if she is equating "marriage" with consummation. What is clearly implied is that out of revulsion or spite, Annabella has not kept her marriage bargain.

A likely setting for the quarrel is just after Annabella has refused Soranzo once again—he enters "unbrac'd." In his notes to the Penguin edition, *John Ford: Three Plays,* Keith Sturgess reminds us that this term usually signified "mental turmoil," but he too thinks that in this case it is meant to indicate that Soranzo has just gotten out of bed (p. 369). He even speculates that Ford originally intended this scene to take place on the wedding night, although he notes the problems in chronology that this reading would entail. In any case, it is at this point that Soranzo is struck for the first time by his bride's swollen shape. He has put up with a good deal from her. Vasques recalls her "scurvy looks," and "waspish perverseness and loud fault-finding," all of which, he claims, Soranzo bore meekly (11.166–69). The discovery of Annabella's infidelity wounds Soranzo at his most vulnerable point: his pride of possession. He has purchased a "most precious jewel" (IV.i.10) perversely determined to shine only for another man's pleasure.

Source: Sharon Hamilton, "Ford's *'Tis a Pity She's a Whore*" in the *Explicator,* Vol. 37, no. 4, Summer, 1979, pp. 15–16

SOURCES

Cantor, Paul A. "John Ford" in the *Dictionary of Literary Biography,* Volume 58: *Jacobean and Caroline Dramatists,* edited by Fredson Bowers, Gale, 1987, pp. 91-106.

Eliot, T. S. "John Ford" in *Selected Essays,* Faber and Faber, 1934, pp. 193-204.

FURTHER READING

Leech, Clifford. *John Ford,* Longmans, Green, 1964.
Leech usefully situates Ford's dramatic achievement within the historical context of the Jacobean and Caroline theatre traditions. He sees Ford as influenced by Fletcher and earlier dramatists, and identifies a debt to Queen Henrietta Maria's cult of Platonic Love.

Oliver, H. J. *The Problem of John Ford,* Melbourne University Press, 1955.
Offering a fine overview, Oliver opens with chapters discussing Ford's times, non-dramatic writing, and collaboration before spending a chapter on each of the major plays. A good place to begin research.

Roper, Derek. Introduction to *'Tis Pity She's a Whore,* Manchester University Press, 1997.
This is an excellent edition of the play, with extensive notes and scholarly apparatus, a twenty-two page introduction, and a bibliography for additional research.

Sensabaugh, G. F. *The Tragic Muse of John Ford,* Benjamin Blom, 1944.
Sensabaugh's influential work reads Ford's drama in the context of Renaissance thinking about ambition, science, and individualism. Particularly good are his discussion of Robert Burton's *Anatomy of Melancholy* and his ideas about humour psychology.

Stavig, Mark. *John Ford and the Traditional Moral Order,* University of Wisconsin Press, 1968.
Stavig offers strong introductory chapters on Ford's world and ideas, with a chapter on each of the major plays, including *'Tis Pity She's a Whore.* Stavig relies on Burton and other sources for outlining a series of character and personality types, which he believes appear in Ford's dramas.

Glossary of Literary Terms

A

Abstract: Used as a noun, the term refers to a short summary or outline of a longer work. As an adjective applied to writing or literary works, abstract refers to words or phrases that name things not knowable through the five senses. Examples of abstracts include the *Cliffs Notes* summaries of major literary works. Examples of abstract terms or concepts include "idea," "guilt" "honesty," and "loyalty."

Absurd, Theater of the: See *Theater of the Absurd*

Absurdism: See *Theater of the Absurd*

Act: A major section of a play. Acts are divided into varying numbers of shorter scenes. From ancient times to the nineteenth century plays were generally constructed of five acts, but modern works typically consist of one, two, or three acts. Examples of five-act plays include the works of Sophocles and Shakespeare, while the plays of Arthur Miller commonly have a three-act structure.

Acto: A one-act Chicano theater piece developed out of collective improvisation. *Actos* were performed by members of Luis Valdez's Teatro Campesino in California during the mid-1960s.

Aestheticism: A literary and artistic movement of the nineteenth century. Followers of the movement believed that art should not be mixed with social, political, or moral teaching. The statement "art for

art's sake" is a good summary of aestheticism. The movement had its roots in France, but it gained widespread importance in England in the last half of the nineteenth century, where it helped change the Victorian practice of including moral lessons in literature. Oscar Wilde is one of the best-known "aesthetes" of the late nineteenth century.

Age of Johnson: The period in English literature between 1750 and 1798, named after the most prominent literary figure of the age, Samuel Johnson. Works written during this time are noted for their emphasis on "sensibility," or emotional quality. These works formed a transition between the rational works of the Age of Reason, or Neoclassical period, and the emphasis on individual feelings and responses of the Romantic period. Significant writers during the Age of Johnson included the novelists Ann Radcliffe and Henry Mackenzie, dramatists Richard Sheridan and Oliver Goldsmith, and poets William Collins and Thomas Gray. Also known as Age of Sensibility

Age of Reason: See *Neoclassicism*

Age of Sensibility: See *Age of Johnson*

Alexandrine Meter: See *Meter*

Allegory: A narrative technique in which characters representing things or abstract ideas are used to convey a message or teach a lesson. Allegory is typically used to teach moral, ethical, or religious lessons but is sometimes used for satiric or political purposes. Examples of allegorical works include Edmund Spenser's *The Faerie Queene* and John Bunyan's *The Pilgrim's Progress.*

Allusion: A reference to a familiar literary or historical person or event, used to make an idea more easily understood. For example, describing someone as a ''Romeo'' makes an allusion to William Shakespeare's famous young lover in *Romeo and Juliet.*

Amerind Literature: The writing and oral traditions of Native Americans. Native American literature was originally passed on by word of mouth, so it consisted largely of stories and events that were easily memorized. Amerind prose is often rhythmic like poetry because it was recited to the beat of a ceremonial drum. Examples of Amerind literature include the autobiographical *Black Elk Speaks,* the works of N. Scott Momaday, James Welch, and Craig Lee Strete, and the poetry of Luci Tapahonso.

Analogy: A comparison of two things made to explain something unfamiliar through its similarities to something familiar, or to prove one point based on the acceptedness of another. Similes and metaphors are types of analogies. Analogies often take the form of an extended simile, as in William Blake's aphorism: ''As the caterpillar chooses the fairest leaves to lay her eggs on, so the priest lays his curse on the fairest joys.''

Angry Young Men: A group of British writers of the 1950s whose work expressed bitterness and disillusionment with society. Common to their work is an anti-hero who rebels against a corrupt social order and strives for personal integrity. The term has been used to describe Kingsley Amis, John Osborne, Colin Wilson, John Wain, and others.

Antagonist: The major character in a narrative or drama who works against the hero or protagonist. An example of an evil antagonist is Richard Lovelace in Samuel Richardson's *Clarissa,* while a virtuous antagonist is Macduff in William Shakespeare's *Macbeth.*

Anthropomorphism: The presentation of animals or objects in human shape or with human characteristics. The term is derived from the Greek word for ''human form.'' The fables of Aesop, the animated films of Walt Disney, and Richard Adams's *Watership Down* feature anthropomorphic characters.

Anti-hero: A central character in a work of literature who lacks traditional heroic qualities such as courage, physical prowess, and fortitude. Anti-heros typically distrust conventional values and are unable to commit themselves to any ideals. They generally feel helpless in a world over which they have no control. Anti-heroes usually accept, and often celebrate, their positions as social outcasts. A well-known anti-hero is Yossarian in Joseph Heller's novel *Catch-22.*

Antimasque: See *Masque*

Antithesis: The antithesis of something is its direct opposite. In literature, the use of antithesis as a figure of speech results in two statements that show a contrast through the balancing of two opposite ideas. Technically, it is the second portion of the statement that is defined as the ''antithesis''; the first portion is the ''thesis.'' An example of antithesis is found in the following portion of Abraham Lincoln's ''Gettysburg Address''; notice the opposition between the verbs ''remember'' and ''forget'' and the phrases ''what we say'' and ''what they did'': ''The world will little note nor long remember what we say here, but it can never forget what they did here.''

Apocrypha: Writings tentatively attributed to an author but not proven or universally accepted to be their works. The term was originally applied to certain books of the Bible that were not considered inspired and so were not included in the ''sacred canon.'' Geoffrey Chaucer, William Shakespeare, Thomas Kyd, Thomas Middleton, and John Marston all have apocrypha. Apocryphal books of the Bible include the Old Testament's Book of Enoch and New Testament's Gospel of Peter.

Apollonian and Dionysian: The two impulses believed to guide authors of dramatic tragedy. The Apollonian impulse is named after Apollo, the Greek god of light and beauty and the symbol of intellectual order. The Dionysian impulse is named after Dionysus, the Greek god of wine and the symbol of the unrestrained forces of nature. The Apollonian impulse is to create a rational, harmonious world, while the Dionysian is to express the irrational forces of personality. Friedrich Nietzche uses these terms in *The Birth of Tragedy* to designate contrasting elements in Greek tragedy.

Apostrophe: A statement, question, or request addressed to an inanimate object or concept or to a nonexistent or absent person. Requests for inspiration from the muses in poetry are examples of apostrophe, as is Marc Antony's address to Caesar's corpse in William Shakespeare's *Julius Caesar*: ''O, pardon me, thou bleeding piece of earth, That I am meek and gentle with these butchers!. . . Woe to the hand that shed this costly blood!. . . ''

Archetype: The word archetype is commonly used to describe an original pattern or model from which all other things of the same kind are made. This term was introduced to literary criticism from the psychology of Carl Jung. It expresses Jung's theory that behind every person's ''unconscious,'' or repressed memories of the past, lies the ''collective unconscious'' of the human race: memories of the countless typical experiences of our ancestors. These memories are said to prompt illogical associations that trigger powerful emotions in the reader. Often, the emotional process is primitive, even primordial. Archetypes are the literary images that grow out of the ''collective unconscious.'' They appear in literature as incidents and plots that repeat basic patterns of life. They may also appear as stereotyped characters. Examples of literary archetypes include themes such as birth and death and characters such as the Earth Mother.

Argument: The argument of a work is the author's subject matter or principal idea. Examples of defined ''argument'' portions of works include John Milton's *Arguments* to each of the books of *Paradise Lost* and the ''Argument'' to Robert Herrick's *Hesperides.*

Aristotelian Criticism: Specifically, the method of evaluating and analyzing tragedy formulated by the Greek philosopher Aristotle in his *Poetics.* More generally, the term indicates any form of criticism that follows Aristotle's views. Aristotelian criticism focuses on the form and logical structure of a work, apart from its historical or social context, in contrast to ''Platonic Criticism,'' which stresses the usefulness of art. Adherents of New Criticism including John Crowe Ransom and Cleanth Brooks utilize and value the basic ideas of Aristotelian criticism for textual analysis.

Art for Art's Sake: See *Aestheticism*

Aside: A comment made by a stage performer that is intended to be heard by the audience but supposedly not by other characters. Eugene O'Neill's *Strange Interlude* is an extended use of the aside in modern theater.

Audience: The people for whom a piece of literature is written. Authors usually write with a certain audience in mind, for example, children, members of a religious or ethnic group, or colleagues in a professional field. The term ''audience'' also applies to the people who gather to see or hear any performance, including plays, poetry readings, speeches, and concerts. Jane Austen's parody of the gothic novel, *Northanger Abbey,* was originally intended for (and also pokes fun at) an audience of young and avid female gothic novel readers.

Avant-garde: A French term meaning ''vanguard.'' It is used in literary criticism to describe new writing that rejects traditional approaches to literature in favor of innovations in style or content. Twentieth-century examples of the literary *avant-garde* include the Black Mountain School of poets, the Bloomsbury Group, and the Beat Movement.

B

Ballad: A short poem that tells a simple story and has a repeated refrain. Ballads were originally intended to be sung. Early ballads, known as folk ballads, were passed down through generations, so their authors are often unknown. Later ballads composed by known authors are called literary ballads. An example of an anonymous folk ballad is ''Edward,'' which dates from the Middle Ages. Samuel Taylor Coleridge's ''The Rime of the Ancient Mariner'' and John Keats's ''La Belle Dame sans Merci'' are examples of literary ballads.

Baroque: A term used in literary criticism to describe literature that is complex or ornate in style or diction. Baroque works typically express tension, anxiety, and violent emotion. The term ''Baroque Age'' designates a period in Western European literature beginning in the late sixteenth century and ending about one hundred years later. Works of this period often mirror the qualities of works more generally associated with the label ''baroque'' and sometimes feature elaborate conceits. Examples of Baroque works include John Lyly's *Euphues: The Anatomy of Wit,* Luis de Gongora's *Soledads,* and William Shakespeare's *As You Like It.*

Baroque Age: See *Baroque*

Baroque Period: See *Baroque*

Beat Generation: See *Beat Movement*

Beat Movement: A period featuring a group of American poets and novelists of the 1950s and 1960s—including Jack Kerouac, Allen Ginsberg, Gregory Corso, William S. Burroughs, and Lawrence Ferlinghetti—who rejected established social and literary values. Using such techniques as stream of consciousness writing and jazz-influenced free verse and focusing on unusual or abnormal states of mind—generated by religious ecstasy or the use of drugs—the Beat writers aimed to create works that were unconventional in both form and subject matter. Kerouac's *On the Road* is perhaps the best-known example of a Beat Generation novel, and Ginsberg's *Howl* is a famous collection of Beat poetry.

Black Aesthetic Movement: A period of artistic and literary development among African Americans in the 1960s and early 1970s. This was the first major African-American artistic movement since the Harlem Renaissance and was closely paralleled by the civil rights and black power movements. The black aesthetic writers attempted to produce works of art that would be meaningful to the black masses. Key figures in black aesthetics included one of its founders, poet and playwright Amiri Baraka, formerly known as LeRoi Jones; poet and essayist Haki R. Madhubuti, formerly Don L. Lee; poet and playwright Sonia Sanchez; and dramatist Ed Bullins. Works representative of the Black Aesthetic Movement include Amiri Baraka's play *Dutchman,* a 1964 Obie award-winner; *Black Fire: An Anthology of Afro-American Writing,* edited by Baraka and playwright Larry Neal and published in 1968; and Sonia Sanchez's poetry collection *We a BaddDDD People,* published in 1970. Also known as Black Arts Movement.

Black Arts Movement: See *Black Aesthetic Movement*

Black Comedy: See *Black Humor*

Black Humor: Writing that places grotesque elements side by side with humorous ones in an attempt to shock the reader, forcing him or her to laugh at the horrifying reality of a disordered world. Joseph Heller's novel *Catch-22* is considered a superb example of the use of black humor. Other well-known authors who use black humor include Kurt Vonnegut, Edward Albee, Eugene Ionesco, and Harold Pinter. Also known as Black Comedy.

Blank Verse: Loosely, any unrhymed poetry, but more generally, unrhymed iambic pentameter verse (composed of lines of five two-syllable feet with the first syllable accented, the second unaccented). Blank verse has been used by poets since the Renaissance for its flexibility and its graceful, dignified tone. John Milton's *Paradise Lost* is in blank verse, as are most of William Shakespeare's plays.

Bloomsbury Group: A group of English writers, artists, and intellectuals who held informal artistic and philosophical discussions in Bloomsbury, a district of London, from around 1907 to the early 1930s. The Bloomsbury Group held no uniform philosophical beliefs but did commonly express an aversion to moral prudery and a desire for greater social tolerance. At various times the circle included Virginia Woolf, E. M. Forster, Clive Bell, Lytton Strachey, and John Maynard Keynes.

Bon Mot: A French term meaning "good word." A *bon mot* is a witty remark or clever observation. Charles Lamb and Oscar Wilde are celebrated for their witty *bon mots.* Two examples by Oscar Wilde stand out: (1) "All women become their mothers. That is their tragedy. No man does. That's his." (2) "A man cannot be too careful in the choice of his enemies."

Breath Verse: See *Projective Verse*

Burlesque: Any literary work that uses exaggeration to make its subject appear ridiculous, either by treating a trivial subject with profound seriousness or by treating a dignified subject frivolously. The word "burlesque" may also be used as an adjective, as in "burlesque show," to mean "striptease act." Examples of literary burlesque include the comedies of Aristophanes, Miguel de Cervantes's *Don Quixote,,* Samuel Butler's poem "Hudibras," and John Gay's play *The Beggar's Opera.*

C

Cadence: The natural rhythm of language caused by the alternation of accented and unaccented syllables. Much modern poetry—notably free verse—deliberately manipulates cadence to create complex rhythmic effects. James Macpherson's "Ossian poems" are richly cadenced, as is the poetry of the Symbolists, Walt Whitman, and Amy Lowell.

Caesura: A pause in a line of poetry, usually occurring near the middle. It typically corresponds to a break in the natural rhythm or sense of the line but is sometimes shifted to create special meanings or rhythmic effects. The opening line of Edgar Allan Poe's "The Raven" contains a caesura following "dreary": "Once upon a midnight dreary, while I pondered weak and weary. . . ."

Canzone: A short Italian or Provencal lyric poem, commonly about love and often set to music. The *canzone* has no set form but typically contains five or six stanzas made up of seven to twenty lines of eleven syllables each. A shorter, five- to ten-line "envoy," or concluding stanza, completes the poem. Masters of the *canzone* form include

Petrarch, Dante Alighieri, Torquato Tasso, and Guido Cavalcanti.

Carpe Diem: A Latin term meaning "seize the day." This is a traditional theme of poetry, especially lyrics. A *carpe diem* poem advises the reader or the person it addresses to live for today and enjoy the pleasures of the moment. Two celebrated *carpe diem* poems are Andrew Marvell's "To His Coy Mistress" and Robert Herrick's poem beginning "Gather ye rosebuds while ye may. . . ."

Catharsis: The release or purging of unwanted emotions— specifically fear and pity—brought about by exposure to art. The term was first used by the Greek philosopher Aristotle in his *Poetics* to refer to the desired effect of tragedy on spectators. A famous example of catharsis is realized in Sophocles' *Oedipus Rex,* when Oedipus discovers that his wife, Jacosta, is his own mother and that the stranger he killed on the road was his own father.

Celtic Renaissance: A period of Irish literary and cultural history at the end of the nineteenth century. Followers of the movement aimed to create a romantic vision of Celtic myth and legend. The most significant works of the Celtic Renaissance typically present a dreamy, unreal world, usually in reaction against the reality of contemporary problems. William Butler Yeats's *The Wanderings of Oisin* is among the most significant works of the Celtic Renaissance. Also known as Celtic Twilight.

Celtic Twilight: See *Celtic Renaissance*

Character: Broadly speaking, a person in a literary work. The actions of characters are what constitute the plot of a story, novel, or poem. There are numerous types of characters, ranging from simple, stereotypical figures to intricate, multifaceted ones. In the techniques of anthropomorphism and personification, animals—and even places or things—can assume aspects of character. "Characterization" is the process by which an author creates vivid, believable characters in a work of art. This may be done in a variety of ways, including (1) direct description of the character by the narrator; (2) the direct presentation of the speech, thoughts, or actions of the character; and (3) the responses of other characters to the character. The term "character" also refers to a form originated by the ancient Greek writer Theophrastus that later became popular in the seventeenth and eighteenth centuries. It is a short essay or sketch of a person who prominently displays a specific attribute or quality, such as miserliness or ambition. Notable characters in literature include Oedipus Rex, Don Quixote de la Mancha, Macbeth, Candide, Hester Prynne, Ebenezer Scrooge, Huckleberry Finn, Jay Gatsby, Scarlett O'Hara, James Bond, and Kunta Kinte.

Characterization: See *Character*

Chorus: In ancient Greek drama, a group of actors who commented on and interpreted the unfolding action on the stage. Initially the chorus was a major component of the presentation, but over time it became less significant, with its numbers reduced and its role eventually limited to commentary between acts. By the sixteenth century the chorus—if employed at all—was typically a single person who provided a prologue and an epilogue and occasionally appeared between acts to introduce or underscore an important event. The chorus in William Shakespeare's *Henry V* functions in this way. Modern dramas rarely feature a chorus, but T. S. Eliot's *Murder in the Cathedral* and Arthur Miller's *A View from the Bridge* are notable exceptions. The Stage Manager in Thornton Wilder's *Our Town* performs a role similar to that of the chorus.

Chronicle: A record of events presented in chronological order. Although the scope and level of detail provided varies greatly among the chronicles surviving from ancient times, some, such as the *Anglo-Saxon Chronicle,* feature vivid descriptions and a lively recounting of events. During the Elizabethan Age, many dramas— appropriately called "chronicle plays"—were based on material from chronicles. Many of William Shakespeare's dramas of English history as well as Christopher Marlowe's *Edward II* are based in part on Raphael Holinshead's *Chronicles of England, Scotland, and Ireland.*

Classical: In its strictest definition in literary criticism, classicism refers to works of ancient Greek or Roman literature. The term may also be used to describe a literary work of recognized importance (a "classic") from any time period or literature that exhibits the traits of classicism. Classical authors from ancient Greek and Roman times include Juvenal and Homer. Examples of later works and authors now described as classical include French literature of the seventeenth century, Western novels of the nineteenth century, and American fiction of the mid-nineteenth century such as that written by James Fenimore Cooper and Mark Twain.

Classicism: A term used in literary criticism to describe critical doctrines that have their roots in ancient Greek and Roman literature, philosophy, and art. Works associated with classicism typically exhibit restraint on the part of the author, unity of design and purpose, clarity, simplicity, logical organization, and respect for tradition. Examples of literary classicism include Cicero's prose, the dramas of Pierre Corneille and Jean Racine, the poetry of John Dryden and Alexander Pope, and the writings of J. W. von Goethe, G. E. Lessing, and T. S. Eliot.

Climax: The turning point in a narrative, the moment when the conflict is at its most intense. Typically, the structure of stories, novels, and plays is one of rising action, in which tension builds to the climax, followed by falling action, in which tension lessens as the story moves to its conclusion. The climax in James Fenimore Cooper's *The Last of the Mohicans* occurs when Magua and his captive Cora are pursued to the edge of a cliff by Uncas. Magua kills Uncas but is subsequently killed by Hawkeye.

Colloquialism: A word, phrase, or form of pronunciation that is acceptable in casual conversation but not in formal, written communication. It is considered more acceptable than slang. An example of colloquialism can be found in Rudyard Kipling's *Barrack-room Ballads:* When 'Omer smote 'is bloomin' lyre He'd 'eard men sing by land and sea; An' what he thought 'e might require 'E went an' took—the same as me!

Comedy: One of two major types of drama, the other being tragedy. Its aim is to amuse, and it typically ends happily. Comedy assumes many forms, such as farce and burlesque, and uses a variety of techniques, from parody to satire. In a restricted sense the term comedy refers only to dramatic presentations, but in general usage it is commonly applied to nondramatic works as well. Examples of comedies range from the plays of Aristophanes, Terrence, and Plautus, Dante Alighieri's *The Divine Comedy,* Francois Rabelais's *Pantagruel* and *Gargantua,* and some of Geoffrey Chaucer's tales and William Shakespeare's plays to Noel Coward's play *Private Lives* and James Thurber's short story ''The Secret Life of Walter Mitty.''

Comedy of Manners: A play about the manners and conventions of an aristocratic, highly sophisticated society. The characters are usually types rather than individualized personalities, and plot is less important than atmosphere. Such plays were an important aspect of late seventeenth-century English comedy. The comedy of manners was revived in the eighteenth century by Oliver Goldsmith and Richard Brinsley Sheridan, enjoyed a second revival in the late nineteenth century, and has endured into the twentieth century. Examples of comedies of manners include William Congreve's *The Way of the World* in the late seventeenth century, Oliver Goldsmith's *She Stoops to Conquer* and Richard Brinsley Sheridan's *The School for Scandal* in the eighteenth century, Oscar Wilde's *The Importance of Being Earnest* in the nineteenth century, and W. Somerset Maugham's *The Circle* in the twentieth century.

Comic Relief: The use of humor to lighten the mood of a serious or tragic story, especially in plays. The technique is very common in Elizabethan works, and can be an integral part of the plot or simply a brief event designed to break the tension of the scene. The Gravediggers' scene in William Shakespeare's *Hamlet* is a frequently cited example of comic relief.

Commedia dell'arte: An Italian term meaning ''the comedy of guilds'' or ''the comedy of professional actors.'' This form of dramatic comedy was popular in Italy during the sixteenth century. Actors were assigned stock roles (such as Pulcinella, the stupid servant, or Pantalone, the old merchant) and given a basic plot to follow, but all dialogue was improvised. The roles were rigidly typed and the plots were formulaic, usually revolving around young lovers who thwarted their elders and attained wealth and happiness. A rigid convention of the *commedia dell'arte* is the periodic intrusion of Harlequin, who interrupts the play with low buffoonery. Peppino de Filippo's *Metamorphoses of a Wandering Minstrel* gave modern audiences an idea of what *commedia dell'arte* may have been like. Various scenarios for *commedia dell'arte* were compiled in Petraccone's *La commedia dell'arte, storia, technica, scenari,* published in 1927.

Complaint: A lyric poem, popular in the Renaissance, in which the speaker expresses sorrow about his or her condition. Typically, the speaker's sadness is caused by an unresponsive lover, but some complaints cite other sources of unhappiness, such as poverty or fate. A commonly cited example is ''A Complaint by Night of the Lover Not Beloved'' by Henry Howard, Earl of Surrey. Thomas Sackville's ''Complaint of Henry, Duke of Buckingham'' traces the duke's unhappiness to his ruthless ambition.

Conceit: A clever and fanciful metaphor, usually expressed through elaborate and extended comparison, that presents a striking parallel between two seemingly dissimilar things—for example, elaborately comparing a beautiful woman to an object like a garden or the sun. The conceit was a popular device throughout the Elizabethan Age and Baroque Age and was the principal technique of the seventeenth-century English metaphysical poets. This usage of the word conceit is unrelated to the best-known definition of conceit as an arrogant attitude or behavior. The conceit figures prominently in the works of John Donne, Emily Dickinson, and T. S. Eliot.

Concrete: Concrete is the opposite of abstract, and refers to a thing that actually exists or a description that allows the reader to experience an object or concept with the senses. Henry David Thoreau's *Walden* contains much concrete description of nature and wildlife.

Concrete Poetry: Poetry in which visual elements play a large part in the poetic effect. Punctuation marks, letters, or words are arranged on a page to form a visual design: a cross, for example, or a bumblebee. Max Bill and Eugene Gomringer were among the early practitioners of concrete poetry; Haroldo de Campos and Augusto de Campos are among contemporary authors of concrete poetry.

Confessional Poetry: A form of poetry in which the poet reveals very personal, intimate, sometimes shocking information about himself or herself. Anne Sexton, Sylvia Plath, Robert Lowell, and John Berryman wrote poetry in the confessional vein.

Conflict: The conflict in a work of fiction is the issue to be resolved in the story. It usually occurs between two characters, the protagonist and the antagonist, or between the protagonist and society or the protagonist and himself or herself. Conflict in Theodore Dreiser's novel *Sister Carrie* comes as a result of urban society, while Jack London's short story "To Build a Fire" concerns the protagonist's battle against the cold and himself.

Connotation: The impression that a word gives beyond its defined meaning. Connotations may be universally understood or may be significant only to a certain group. Both "horse" and "steed" denote the same animal, but "steed" has a different connotation, deriving from the chivalrous or romantic narratives in which the word was once often used.

Consonance: Consonance occurs in poetry when words appearing at the ends of two or more verses have similar final consonant sounds but have final vowel sounds that differ, as with "stuff" and "off." Consonance is found in "The curfew tolls the knells of parting day" from Thomas Grey's "An Elegy Written in a Country Church Yard." Also known as Half Rhyme or Slant Rhyme.

Convention: Any widely accepted literary device, style, or form. A soliloquy, in which a character reveals to the audience his or her private thoughts, is an example of a dramatic convention.

Corrido: A Mexican ballad. Examples of *corridos* include "Muerte del afamado Bilito," "La voz de mi conciencia," "Lucio Perez," "La juida," and "Los presos."

Couplet: Two lines of poetry with the same rhyme and meter, often expressing a complete and self-contained thought. The following couplet is from Alexander Pope's "Elegy to the Memory of an Unfortunate Lady": 'Tis Use alone that sanctifies Expense, And Splendour borrows all her rays from Sense.

Criticism: The systematic study and evaluation of literary works, usually based on a specific method or set of principles. An important part of literary studies since ancient times, the practice of criticism has given rise to numerous theories, methods, and "schools," sometimes producing conflicting, even contradictory, interpretations of literature in general as well as of individual works. Even such basic issues as what constitutes a poem or a novel have been the subject of much criticism over the centuries. Seminal texts of literary criticism include Plato's *Republic,* Aristotle's *Poetics,* Sir Philip Sidney's *The Defence of Poesie,* John Dryden's *Of Dramatic Poesie,* and William Wordsworth's "Preface" to the second edition of his *Lyrical Ballads.* Contemporary schools of criticism include deconstruction, feminist, psychoanalytic, poststructuralist, new historicist, postcolonialist, and reader- response.

D

Dactyl: See *Foot*

Dadaism: A protest movement in art and literature founded by Tristan Tzara in 1916. Followers of the movement expressed their outrage at the destruction brought about by World War I by revolting against numerous forms of social convention. The Dadaists presented works marked by calculated madness and flamboyant nonsense. They stressed total freedom of expression, commonly through primitive displays of emotion and illogical, often senseless, poetry. The movement ended shortly after the war, when it was replaced by surrealism. Proponents of Dadaism include Andre Breton, Louis Aragon, Philippe Soupault, and Paul Eluard.

Decadent: See *Decadents*

Decadents: The followers of a nineteenth-century literary movement that had its beginnings in French aestheticism. Decadent literature displays a fascination with perverse and morbid states; a search for novelty and sensation—the ''new thrill''; a preoccupation with mysticism; and a belief in the senselessness of human existence. The movement is closely associated with the doctrine Art for Art's Sake. The term ''decadence'' is sometimes used to denote a decline in the quality of art or literature following a period of greatness. Major French decadents are Charles Baudelaire and Arthur Rimbaud. English decadents include Oscar Wilde, Ernest Dowson, and Frank Harris.

Deconstruction: A method of literary criticism developed by Jacques Derrida and characterized by multiple conflicting interpretations of a given work. Deconstructionists consider the impact of the language of a work and suggest that the true meaning of the work is not necessarily the meaning that the author intended. Jacques Derrida's *De la grammatologie* is the seminal text on deconstructive strategies; among American practitioners of this method of criticism are Paul de Man and J. Hillis Miller.

Deduction: The process of reaching a conclusion through reasoning from general premises to a specific premise. An example of deduction is present in the following syllogism: Premise: All mammals are animals. Premise: All whales are mammals. Conclusion: Therefore, all whales are animals.

Denotation: The definition of a word, apart from the impressions or feelings it creates in the reader. The word ''apartheid'' denotes a political and economic policy of segregation by race, but its connotations— oppression, slavery, inequality—are numerous.

Denouement: A French word meaning ''the unknotting.'' In literary criticism, it denotes the resolution of conflict in fiction or drama. The *denouement* follows the climax and provides an outcome to the primary plot situation as well as an explanation of secondary plot complications. The *denouement* often involves a character's recognition of his or her state of mind or moral condition. A well-known example of *denouement* is the last scene of the play *As You Like It* by William Shakespeare, in which couples are married, an evildoer repents, the identities of two disguised characters are revealed, and a ruler is restored to power. Also known as Falling Action.

Description: Descriptive writing is intended to allow a reader to picture the scene or setting in which the action of a story takes place. The form this description takes often evokes an intended emotional response—a dark, spooky graveyard will evoke fear, and a peaceful, sunny meadow will evoke calmness. An example of a descriptive story is Edgar Allan Poe's *Landor's Cottage,* which offers a detailed depiction of a New York country estate.

Detective Story: A narrative about the solution of a mystery or the identification of a criminal. The conventions of the detective story include the detective's scrupulous use of logic in solving the mystery; incompetent or ineffectual police; a suspect who appears guilty at first but is later proved innocent; and the detective's friend or confidant— often the narrator—whose slowness in interpreting clues emphasizes by contrast the detective's brilliance. Edgar Allan Poe's ''Murders in the Rue Morgue'' is commonly regarded as the earliest example of this type of story. With this work, Poe established many of the conventions of the detective story genre, which are still in practice. Other practitioners of this vast and extremely popular genre include Arthur Conan Doyle, Dashiell Hammett, and Agatha Christie.

Deus ex machina: A Latin term meaning ''god out of a machine.'' In Greek drama, a god was often lowered onto the stage by a mechanism of some kind to rescue the hero or untangle the plot. By extension, the term refers to any artificial device or coincidence used to bring about a convenient and simple solution to a plot. This is a common device in melodramas and includes such fortunate circumstances as the sudden receipt of a legacy to save the family farm or a last-minute stay of execution. The *deus ex machina* invariably rewards the virtuous and punishes evildoers. Examples of *deus ex machina* include King Louis XIV in Jean-Baptiste Moliere's *Tartuffe* and Queen Victoria in *The Pirates of Penzance* by William Gilbert and Arthur Sullivan. Bertolt Brecht parodies the abuse of such devices in the conclusion of his *Threepenny Opera.*

Dialogue: In its widest sense, dialogue is simply conversation between people in a literary work; in its most restricted sense, it refers specifically to the speech of characters in a drama. As a specific literary genre, a ''dialogue'' is a composition in which characters debate an issue or idea. The Greek philosopher Plato frequently expounded his theories in the form of dialogues.

Diction: The selection and arrangement of words in a literary work. Either or both may vary depending on the desired effect. There are four general types of diction: "formal," used in scholarly or lofty writing; "informal," used in relaxed but educated conversation; "colloquial," used in everyday speech; and "slang," containing newly coined words and other terms not accepted in formal usage.

Didactic: A term used to describe works of literature that aim to teach some moral, religious, political, or practical lesson. Although didactic elements are often found in artistically pleasing works, the term "didactic" usually refers to literature in which the message is more important than the form. The term may also be used to criticize a work that the critic finds "overly didactic," that is, heavy-handed in its delivery of a lesson. Examples of didactic literature include John Bunyan's *Pilgrim's Progress,* Alexander Pope's *Essay on Criticism,* Jean-Jacques Rousseau's *Emile,* and Elizabeth Inchbald's *Simple Story.*

Dimeter: See *Meter*

Dionysian: See *Apollonian and Dionysian*

Discordia concours: A Latin phrase meaning "discord in harmony." The term was coined by the eighteenth-century English writer Samuel Johnson to describe "a combination of dissimilar images or discovery of occult resemblances in things apparently unlike." Johnson created the expression by reversing a phrase by the Latin poet Horace. The metaphysical poetry of John Donne, Richard Crashaw, Abraham Cowley, George Herbert, and Edward Taylor among others, contains many examples of *discordia concours.* In Donne's "A Valediction: Forbidding Mourning," the poet compares the union of himself with his lover to a draftsman's compass: If they be two, they are two so, As stiff twin compasses are two: Thy soul, the fixed foot, makes no show To move, but doth, if the other do; And though it in the center sit, Yet when the other far doth roam, It leans, and hearkens after it, And grows erect, as that comes home.

Dissonance: A combination of harsh or jarring sounds, especially in poetry. Although such combinations may be accidental, poets sometimes intentionally make them to achieve particular effects. Dissonance is also sometimes used to refer to close but not identical rhymes. When this is the case, the word functions as a synonym for consonance. Robert Browning, Gerard Manley Hopkins, and many other poets have made deliberate use of dissonance.

Doppelganger: A literary technique by which a character is duplicated (usually in the form of an alter ego, though sometimes as a ghostly counterpart) or divided into two distinct, usually opposite personalities. The use of this character device is widespread in nineteenth- and twentieth- century literature, and indicates a growing awareness among authors that the "self" is really a composite of many "selves." A well-known story containing a *doppelganger* character is Robert Louis Stevenson's *Dr. Jekyll and Mr. Hyde,* which dramatizes an internal struggle between good and evil. Also known as The Double.

Double Entendre: A corruption of a French phrase meaning "double meaning." The term is used to indicate a word or phrase that is deliberately ambiguous, especially when one of the meanings is risque or improper. An example of a *double entendre* is the Elizabethan usage of the verb "die," which refers both to death and to orgasm.

Double, The: See *Doppelganger*

Draft: Any preliminary version of a written work. An author may write dozens of drafts which are revised to form the final work, or he or she may write only one, with few or no revisions. Dorothy Parker's observation that "I can't write five words but that I change seven" humorously indicates the purpose of the draft.

Drama: In its widest sense, a drama is any work designed to be presented by actors on a stage. Similarly, "drama" denotes a broad literary genre that includes a variety of forms, from pageant and spectacle to tragedy and comedy, as well as countless types and subtypes. More commonly in modern usage, however, a drama is a work that treats serious subjects and themes but does not aim at the grandeur of tragedy. This use of the term originated with the eighteenth-century French writer Denis Diderot, who used the word *drame* to designate his plays about middle- class life; thus "drama" typically features characters of a less exalted stature than those of tragedy. Examples of classical dramas include Menander's comedy *Dyscolus* and Sophocles' tragedy *Oedipus Rex.* Contemporary dramas include Eugene O'Neill's *The Iceman Cometh,* Lillian Hellman's *Little Foxes,* and August Wilson's *Ma Rainey's Black Bottom.*

Dramatic Irony: Occurs when the audience of a play or the reader of a work of literature knows something that a character in the work itself does not know. The irony is in the contrast between the intended meaning of the statements or actions of a character and the additional information understood by the audience. A celebrated example of dramatic irony is in Act V of William Shakespeare's *Romeo and Juliet,* where two young lovers meet their end as a result of a tragic misunderstanding. Here, the audience has full knowledge that Juliet's apparent ''death'' is merely temporary; she will regain her senses when the mysterious ''sleeping potion'' she has taken wears off. But Romeo, mistaking Juliet's drug-induced trance for true death, kills himself in grief. Upon awakening, Juliet discovers Romeo's corpse and, in despair, slays herself.

Dramatic Monologue: See *Monologue*

Dramatic Poetry: Any lyric work that employs elements of drama such as dialogue, conflict, or characterization, but excluding works that are intended for stage presentation. A monologue is a form of dramatic poetry.

Dramatis Personae: The characters in a work of literature, particularly a drama. The list of characters printed before the main text of a play or in the program is the *dramatis personae.*

Dream Allegory: See *Dream Vision*

Dream Vision: A literary convention, chiefly of the Middle Ages. In a dream vision a story is presented as a literal dream of the narrator. This device was commonly used to teach moral and religious lessons. Important works of this type are *The Divine Comedy* by Dante Alighieri, *Piers Plowman* by William Langland, and *The Pilgrim's Progress* by John Bunyan. Also known as Dream Allegory.

Dystopia: An imaginary place in a work of fiction where the characters lead dehumanized, fearful lives. Jack London's *The Iron Heel,* Yevgeny Zamyatin's *My,* Aldous Huxley's *Brave New World,* George Orwell's *Nineteen Eighty-four,* and Margaret Atwood's *Handmaid's Tale* portray versions of dystopia.

E

Eclogue: In classical literature, a poem featuring rural themes and structured as a dialogue among shepherds. Eclogues often took specific poetic forms, such as elegies or love poems. Some were written as the soliloquy of a shepherd. In later centuries, ''eclogue'' came to refer to any poem that was in the pastoral tradition or that had a dialogue or mono-

logue structure. A classical example of an eclogue is Virgil's *Eclogues,* also known as *Bucolics.* Giovanni Boccaccio, Edmund Spenser, Andrew Marvell, Jonathan Swift, and Louis MacNeice also wrote eclogues.

Edwardian: Describes cultural conventions identified with the period of the reign of Edward VII of England (1901-1910). Writers of the Edwardian Age typically displayed a strong reaction against the propriety and conservatism of the Victorian Age. Their work often exhibits distrust of authority in religion, politics, and art and expresses strong doubts about the soundness of conventional values. Writers of this era include George Bernard Shaw, H. G. Wells, and Joseph Conrad.

Edwardian Age: See *Edwardian*

Electra Complex: A daughter's amorous obsession with her father. The term Electra complex comes from the plays of Euripides and Sophocles entitled *Electra,* in which the character Electra drives her brother Orestes to kill their mother and her lover in revenge for the murder of their father.

Elegy: A lyric poem that laments the death of a person or the eventual death of all people. In a conventional elegy, set in a classical world, the poet and subject are spoken of as shepherds. In modern criticism, the word elegy is often used to refer to a poem that is melancholy or mournfully contemplative. John Milton's ''Lycidas'' and Percy Bysshe Shelley's ''Adonais'' are two examples of this form.

Elizabethan Age: A period of great economic growth, religious controversy, and nationalism closely associated with the reign of Elizabeth I of England (1558-1603). The Elizabethan Age is considered a part of the general renaissance—that is, the flowering of arts and literature—that took place in Europe during the fourteenth through sixteenth centuries. The era is considered the golden age of English literature. The most important dramas in English and a great deal of lyric poetry were produced during this period, and modern English criticism began around this time. The notable authors of the period—Philip Sidney, Edmund Spenser, Christopher Marlowe, William Shakespeare, Ben Jonson, Francis Bacon, and John Donne—are among the best in all of English literature.

Elizabethan Drama: English comic and tragic plays produced during the Renaissance, or more narrowly, those plays written during the last years of and few years after Queen Elizabeth's reign. William Shakespeare is considered an Elizabethan dramatist in the broader sense, although most of his work was produced during the reign of James I. Examples of Elizabethan comedies include John Lyly's *The Woman in the Moone,* Thomas Dekker's *The Roaring Girl, or, Moll Cut Purse,* and William Shakespeare's *Twelfth Night.* Examples of Elizabethan tragedies include William Shakespeare's *Antony and Cleopatra,* Thomas Kyd's *The Spanish Tragedy,* and John Webster's *The Tragedy of the Duchess of Malfi.*

Empathy: A sense of shared experience, including emotional and physical feelings, with someone or something other than oneself. Empathy is often used to describe the response of a reader to a literary character. An example of an empathic passage is William Shakespeare's description in his narrative poem *Venus and Adonis* of: the snail, whose tender horns being hit, Shrinks backward in his shelly cave with pain. Readers of Gerard Manley Hopkins's *The Windhover* may experience some of the physical sensations evoked in the description of the movement of the falcon.

English Sonnet: See *Sonnet*

Enjambment: The running over of the sense and structure of a line of verse or a couplet into the following verse or couplet. Andrew Marvell's "To His Coy Mistress" is structured as a series of enjambments, as in lines 11-12: "My vegetable love should grow/Vaster than empires and more slow."

Enlightenment, The: An eighteenth-century philosophical movement. It began in France but had a wide impact throughout Europe and America. Thinkers of the Enlightenment valued reason and believed that both the individual and society could achieve a state of perfection. Corresponding to this essentially humanist vision was a resistance to religious authority. Important figures of the Enlightenment were Denis Diderot and Voltaire in France, Edward Gibbon and David Hume in England, and Thomas Paine and Thomas Jefferson in the United States.

Epic: A long narrative poem about the adventures of a hero of great historic or legendary importance. The setting is vast and the action is often given cosmic significance through the intervention of supernatural forces such as gods, angels, or demons. Epics are typically written in a classical style of grand simplicity with elaborate metaphors and allusions that enhance the symbolic importance of a hero's adventures. Some well-known epics are Homer's *Iliad* and *Odyssey,* Virgil's *Aeneid,* and John Milton's *Paradise Lost.*

Epic Simile: See *Homeric Simile*

Epic Theater: A theory of theatrical presentation developed by twentieth-century German playwright Bertolt Brecht. Brecht created a type of drama that the audience could view with complete detachment. He used what he termed "alienation effects" to create an emotional distance between the audience and the action on stage. Among these effects are: short, self-contained scenes that keep the play from building to a cathartic climax; songs that comment on the action; and techniques of acting that prevent the actor from developing an emotional identity with his role. Besides the plays of Bertolt Brecht, other plays that utilize epic theater conventions include those of Georg Buchner, Frank Wedekind, Erwin Piscator, and Leopold Jessner.

Epigram: A saying that makes the speaker's point quickly and concisely. Samuel Taylor Coleridge wrote an epigram that neatly sums up the form: What is an Epigram? A Dwarfish whole, Its body brevity, and wit its soul.

Epilogue: A concluding statement or section of a literary work. In dramas, particularly those of the seventeenth and eighteenth centuries, the epilogue is a closing speech, often in verse, delivered by an actor at the end of a play and spoken directly to the audience. A famous epilogue is Puck's speech at the end of William Shakespeare's *A Midsummer Night's Dream.*

Epiphany: A sudden revelation of truth inspired by a seemingly trivial incident. The term was widely used by James Joyce in his critical writings, and the stories in Joyce's *Dubliners* are commonly called "epiphanies."

Episode: An incident that forms part of a story and is significantly related to it. Episodes may be either self-contained narratives or events that depend on a larger context for their sense and importance. Examples of episodes include the founding of Wilmington, Delaware in Charles Reade's *The Disinherited Heir* and the individual events comprising the picaresque novels and medieval romances.

Episodic Plot: See *Plot*

Epitaph: An inscription on a tomb or tombstone, or a verse written on the occasion of a person's death. Epitaphs may be serious or humorous. Dorothy Parker's epitaph reads, "I told you I was sick."

Epithalamion: A song or poem written to honor and commemorate a marriage ceremony. Famous examples include Edmund Spenser's

"Epithalamion" and e. e. cummings's "Epithalamion." Also spelled Epithalamium.

Epithalamium: See *Epithalamion*

Epithet: A word or phrase, often disparaging or abusive, that expresses a character trait of someone or something. "The Napoleon of crime" is an epithet applied to Professor Moriarty, arch-rival of Sherlock Holmes in Arthur Conan Doyle's series of detective stories.

Exempla: See *Exemplum*

Exemplum: A tale with a moral message. This form of literary sermonizing flourished during the Middle Ages, when *exempla* appeared in collections known as "example-books." The works of Geoffrey Chaucer are full of *exempla*.

Existentialism: A predominantly twentieth-century philosophy concerned with the nature and perception of human existence. There are two major strains of existentialist thought: atheistic and Christian. Followers of atheistic existentialism believe that the individual is alone in a godless universe and that the basic human condition is one of suffering and loneliness. Nevertheless, because there are no fixed values, individuals can create their own characters—indeed, they can shape themselves—through the exercise of free will. The atheistic strain culminates in and is popularly associated with the works of Jean-Paul Sartre. The Christian existentialists, on the other hand, believe that only in God may people find freedom from life's anguish. The two strains hold certain beliefs in common: that existence cannot be fully understood or described through empirical effort; that anguish is a universal element of life; that individuals must bear responsibility for their actions; and that there is no common standard of behavior or perception for religious and ethical matters. Existentialist thought figures prominently in the works of such authors as Eugene Ionesco, Franz Kafka, Fyodor Dostoyevsky, Simone de Beauvoir, Samuel Beckett, and Albert Camus.

Expatriates: See *Expatriatism*

Expatriatism: The practice of leaving one's country to live for an extended period in another country. Literary expatriates include English poets Percy Bysshe Shelley and John Keats in Italy, Polish novelist Joseph Conrad in England, American writers Richard Wright, James Baldwin, Gertrude Stein, and Ernest Hemingway in France, and Trinidadian author Neil Bissondath in Canada.

Exposition: Writing intended to explain the nature of an idea, thing, or theme. Expository writing is often combined with description, narration, or argument. In dramatic writing, the exposition is the introductory material which presents the characters, setting, and tone of the play. An example of dramatic exposition occurs in many nineteenth-century drawing-room comedies in which the butler and the maid open the play with relevant talk about their master and mistress; in composition, exposition relays factual information, as in encyclopedia entries.

Expressionism: An indistinct literary term, originally used to describe an early twentieth-century school of German painting. The term applies to almost any mode of unconventional, highly subjective writing that distorts reality in some way. Advocates of Expressionism include dramatists George Kaiser, Ernst Toller, Luigi Pirandello, Federico Garcia Lorca, Eugene O'Neill, and Elmer Rice; poets George Heym, Ernst Stadler, August Stramm, Gottfried Benn, and Georg Trakl; and novelists Franz Kafka and James Joyce.

Extended Monologue: See *Monologue*

F

Fable: A prose or verse narrative intended to convey a moral. Animals or inanimate objects with human characteristics often serve as characters in fables. A famous fable is Aesop's "The Tortoise and the Hare."

Fairy Tales: Short narratives featuring mythical beings such as fairies, elves, and sprites. These tales originally belonged to the folklore of a particular nation or region, such as those collected in Germany by Jacob and Wilhelm Grimm. Two other celebrated writers of fairy tales are Hans Christian Andersen and Rudyard Kipling.

Falling Action: See *Denouement*

Fantasy: A literary form related to mythology and folklore. Fantasy literature is typically set in non-existent realms and features supernatural beings. Notable examples of fantasy literature are *The Lord of the Rings* by J. R. R. Tolkien and the Gormenghast trilogy by Mervyn Peake.

Farce: A type of comedy characterized by broad humor, outlandish incidents, and often vulgar subject matter. Much of the "comedy" in film and television could more accurately be described as farce.

Feet: See *Foot*

Feminine Rhyme: See *Rhyme*

Femme fatale: A French phrase with the literal translation "fatal woman." A *femme fatale* is a sensuous, alluring woman who often leads men into danger or trouble. A classic example of the *femme fatale* is the nameless character in Billy Wilder's *The Seven Year Itch,* portrayed by Marilyn Monroe in the film adaptation.

Fiction: Any story that is the product of imagination rather than a documentation of fact. characters and events in such narratives may be based in real life but their ultimate form and configuration is a creation of the author. Geoffrey Chaucer's *The Canterbury Tales,* Laurence Sterne's *Tristram Shandy,* and Margaret Mitchell's *Gone with the Wind* are examples of fiction.

Figurative Language: A technique in writing in which the author temporarily interrupts the order, construction, or meaning of the writing for a particular effect. This interruption takes the form of one or more figures of speech such as hyperbole, irony, or simile. Figurative language is the opposite of literal language, in which every word is truthful, accurate, and free of exaggeration or embellishment. Examples of figurative language are tropes such as metaphor and rhetorical figures such as apostrophe.

Figures of Speech: Writing that differs from customary conventions for construction, meaning, order, or significance for the purpose of a special meaning or effect. There are two major types of figures of speech: rhetorical figures, which do not make changes in the meaning of the words, and tropes, which do. Types of figures of speech include simile, hyperbole, alliteration, and pun, among many others.

Fin de siecle: A French term meaning "end of the century." The term is used to denote the last decade of the nineteenth century, a transition period when writers and other artists abandoned old conventions and looked for new techniques and objectives. Two writers commonly associated with the *fin de siecle* mindset are Oscar Wilde and George Bernard Shaw.

First Person: See *Point of View*

Flashback: A device used in literature to present action that occurred before the beginning of the story. Flashbacks are often introduced as the dreams or recollections of one or more characters. Flashback techniques are often used in films, where they are typically set off by a gradual changing of one picture to another.

Foil: A character in a work of literature whose physical or psychological qualities contrast strongly with, and therefore highlight, the corresponding qualities of another character. In his Sherlock Holmes stories, Arthur Conan Doyle portrayed Dr. Watson as a man of normal habits and intelligence, making him a foil for the eccentric and wonderfully perceptive Sherlock Holmes.

Folk Ballad: See *Ballad*

Folklore: Traditions and myths preserved in a culture or group of people. Typically, these are passed on by word of mouth in various forms—such as legends, songs, and proverbs— or preserved in customs and ceremonies. This term was first used by W. J. Thoms in 1846. Sir James Frazer's *The Golden Bough* is the record of English folklore; myths about the frontier and the Old South exemplify American folklore.

Folktale: A story originating in oral tradition. Folktales fall into a variety of categories, including legends, ghost stories, fairy tales, fables, and anecdotes based on historical figures and events. Examples of folktales include Giambattista Basile's *The Pentamerone,* which contains the tales of Puss in Boots, Rapunzel, Cinderella, and Beauty and the Beast, and Joel Chandler Harris's Uncle Remus stories, which represent transplanted African folktales and American tales about the characters Mike Fink, Johnny Appleseed, Paul Bunyan, and Pecos Bill.

Foot: The smallest unit of rhythm in a line of poetry. In English-language poetry, a foot is typically one accented syllable combined with one or two unaccented syllables. There are many different types of feet. When the accent is on the second syllable of a two syllable word (con- *tort*), the foot is an "iamb"; the reverse accentual pattern (*tor* -ture) is a "trochee." Other feet that commonly occur in poetry in English are "anapest", two unaccented syllables followed by an accented syllable as in inter-*cept*, and "dactyl", an accented syllable followed by two unaccented syllables as in *su*-i- cide.

Foreshadowing: A device used in literature to create expectation or to set up an explanation of later developments. In Charles Dickens's *Great Expectations,* the graveyard encounter at the beginning of the novel between Pip and the escaped convict Magwitch foreshadows the baleful atmosphere and events that comprise much of the narrative.

Form: The pattern or construction of a work which identifies its genre and distinguishes it from other genres. Examples of forms include the different genres, such as the lyric form or the short story form, and various patterns for poetry, such as the verse form or the stanza form.

Formalism: In literary criticism, the belief that literature should follow prescribed rules of construction, such as those that govern the sonnet form. Examples of formalism are found in the work of the New Critics and structuralists.

Fourteener Meter: See *Meter*

Free Verse: Poetry that lacks regular metrical and rhyme patterns but that tries to capture the cadences of everyday speech. The form allows a poet to exploit a variety of rhythmical effects within a single poem. Free-verse techniques have been widely used in the twentieth century by such writers as Ezra Pound, T. S. Eliot, Carl Sandburg, and William Carlos Williams. Also known as *Vers libre.*

Futurism: A flamboyant literary and artistic movement that developed in France, Italy, and Russia from 1908 through the 1920s. Futurist theater and poetry abandoned traditional literary forms. In their place, followers of the movement attempted to achieve total freedom of expression through bizarre imagery and deformed or newly invented words. The Futurists were self-consciously modern artists who attempted to incorporate the appearances and sounds of modern life into their work. Futurist writers include Filippo Tommaso Marinetti, Wyndham Lewis, Guillaume Apollinaire, Velimir Khlebnikov, and Vladimir Mayakovsky.

G

Genre: A category of literary work. In critical theory, genre may refer to both the content of a given work—tragedy, comedy, pastoral—and to its form, such as poetry, novel, or drama. This term also refers to types of popular literature, as in the genres of science fiction or the detective story.

Genteel Tradition: A term coined by critic George Santayana to describe the literary practice of certain late nineteenth-century American writers, especially New Englanders. Followers of the Genteel Tradition emphasized conventionality in social, religious, moral, and literary standards. Some of the best-known writers of the Genteel Tradition are R. H. Stoddard and Bayard Taylor.

Gilded Age: A period in American history during the 1870s characterized by political corruption and materialism. A number of important novels of social and political criticism were written during this time. Examples of Gilded Age literature include Henry Adams's *Democracy* and F. Marion Crawford's *An American Politician.*

Gothic: See *Gothicism*

Gothicism: In literary criticism, works characterized by a taste for the medieval or morbidly attractive. A gothic novel prominently features elements of horror, the supernatural, gloom, and violence: clanking chains, terror, charnel houses, ghosts, medieval castles, and mysteriously slamming doors. The term "gothic novel" is also applied to novels that lack elements of the traditional Gothic setting but that create a similar atmosphere of terror or dread. Mary Shelley's *Frankenstein* is perhaps the best-known English work of this kind.

Gothic Novel: See *Gothicism*

Great Chain of Being: The belief that all things and creatures in nature are organized in a hierarchy from inanimate objects at the bottom to God at the top. This system of belief was popular in the seventeenth and eighteenth centuries. A summary of the concept of the great chain of being can be found in the first epistle of Alexander Pope's *An Essay on Man,* and more recently in Arthur O. Lovejoy's *The Great Chain of Being: A Study of the History of an Idea.*

Grotesque: In literary criticism, the subject matter of a work or a style of expression characterized by exaggeration, deformity, freakishness, and disorder. The grotesque often includes an element of comic absurdity. Early examples of literary grotesque include Francois Rabelais's *Pantagruel* and *Gargantua* and Thomas Nashe's *The Unfortunate Traveller,* while more recent examples can be found in the works of Edgar Allan Poe, Evelyn Waugh, Eudora Welty, Flannery O'Connor, Eugene Ionesco, Gunter Grass, Thomas Mann, Mervyn Peake, and Joseph Heller, among many others.

H

Haiku: The shortest form of Japanese poetry, constructed in three lines of five, seven, and five syllables respectively. The message of a *haiku* poem usually centers on some aspect of spirituality and provokes an emotional response in the reader. Early masters of *haiku* include Basho, Buson,

Kobayashi Issa, and Masaoka Shiki. English writers of *haiku* include the Imagists, notably Ezra Pound, H. D., Amy Lowell, Carl Sandburg, and William Carlos Williams. Also known as *Hokku*.

Half Rhyme: See *Consonance*

Hamartia: In tragedy, the event or act that leads to the hero's or heroine's downfall. This term is often incorrectly used as a synonym for tragic flaw. In Richard Wright's *Native Son,* the act that seals Bigger Thomas's fate is his first impulsive murder.

Harlem Renaissance: The Harlem Renaissance of the 1920s is generally considered the first significant movement of black writers and artists in the United States. During this period, new and established black writers published more fiction and poetry than ever before, the first influential black literary journals were established, and black authors and artists received their first widespread recognition and serious critical appraisal. Among the major writers associated with this period are Claude McKay, Jean Toomer, Countee Cullen, Langston Hughes, Arna Bontemps, Nella Larsen, and Zora Neale Hurston. Works representative of the Harlem Renaissance include Arna Bontemps's poems "The Return" and "Golgotha Is a Mountain," Claude McKay's novel *Home to Harlem,* Nella Larsen's novel *Passing,* Langston Hughes's poem "The Negro Speaks of Rivers," and the journals *Crisis* and *Opportunity,* both founded during this period. Also known as Negro Renaissance and New Negro Movement.

Harlequin: A stock character of the *commedia dell'arte* who occasionally interrupted the action with silly antics. Harlequin first appeared on the English stage in John Day's *The Travailes of the Three English Brothers.* The San Francisco Mime Troupe is one of the few modern groups to adapt Harlequin to the needs of contemporary satire.

Hellenism: Imitation of ancient Greek thought or styles. Also, an approach to life that focuses on the growth and development of the intellect. "Hellenism" is sometimes used to refer to the belief that reason can be applied to examine all human experience. A cogent discussion of Hellenism can be found in Matthew Arnold's *Culture and Anarchy.*

Heptameter: See *Meter*

Hero/Heroine: The principal sympathetic character (male or female) in a literary work. Heroes and heroines typically exhibit admirable traits: idealism, courage, and integrity, for example. Famous heroes and heroines include Pip in Charles Dickens's *Great Expectations,* the anonymous narrator in Ralph Ellison's *Invisible Man,* and Sethe in Toni Morrison's *Beloved.*

Heroic Couplet: A rhyming couplet written in iambic pentameter (a verse with five iambic feet). The following lines by Alexander Pope are an example: "Truth guards the Poet, sanctifies the line,/ And makes Immortal, Verse as mean as mine."

Heroic Line: The meter and length of a line of verse in epic or heroic poetry. This varies by language and time period. For example, in English poetry, the heroic line is iambic pentameter (a verse with five iambic feet); in French, the alexandrine (a verse with six iambic feet); in classical literature, dactylic hexameter (a verse with six dactylic feet).

Heroine: See *Hero/Heroine*

Hexameter: See *Meter*

Historical Criticism: The study of a work based on its impact on the world of the time period in which it was written. Examples of postmodern historical criticism can be found in the work of Michel Foucault, Hayden White, Stephen Greenblatt, and Jonathan Goldberg.

Hokku: See *Haiku*

Holocaust: See *Holocaust Literature*

Holocaust Literature: Literature influenced by or written about the Holocaust of World War II. Such literature includes true stories of survival in concentration camps, escape, and life after the war, as well as fictional works and poetry. Representative works of Holocaust literature include Saul Bellow's *Mr. Sammler's Planet,* Anne Frank's *The Diary of a Young Girl,* Jerzy Kosinski's *The Painted Bird,* Arthur Miller's *Incident at Vichy,* Czeslaw Milosz's *Collected Poems,* William Styron's *Sophie's Choice,* and Art Spiegelman's *Maus.*

Homeric Simile: An elaborate, detailed comparison written as a simile many lines in length. An example of an epic simile from John Milton's *Paradise Lost* follows: Angel Forms, who lay entranced Thick as autumnal leaves that strow the brooks In Vallombrosa, where the Etrurian shades High over-arched embower; or scattered sedge Afloat, when with fierce winds Orion armed Hath vexed the Red-Sea coast, whose waves o'erthrew Busiris and his Memphian chivalry, While with perfidious hatred they pursued The sojourners of

Goshen, who beheld From the safe shore their floating carcasses And broken chariot-wheels. Also known as Epic Simile.

Horatian Satire: See *Satire*

Humanism: A philosophy that places faith in the dignity of humankind and rejects the medieval perception of the individual as a weak, fallen creature. "Humanists" typically believe in the perfectibility of human nature and view reason and education as the means to that end. Humanist thought is represented in the works of Marsilio Ficino, Ludovico Castelvetro, Edmund Spenser, John Milton, Dean John Colet, Desiderius Erasmus, John Dryden, Alexander Pope, Matthew Arnold, and Irving Babbitt.

Humors: Mentions of the humors refer to the ancient Greek theory that a person's health and personality were determined by the balance of four basic fluids in the body: blood, phlegm, yellow bile, and black bile. A dominance of any fluid would cause extremes in behavior. An excess of blood created a sanguine person who was joyful, aggressive, and passionate; a phlegmatic person was shy, fearful, and sluggish; too much yellow bile led to a choleric temperament characterized by impatience, anger, bitterness, and stubbornness; and excessive black bile created melancholy, a state of laziness, gluttony, and lack of motivation. Literary treatment of the humors is exemplified by several characters in Ben Jonson's plays *Every Man in His Humour* and *Every Man out of His Humour.* Also spelled Humours.

Humours: See *Humors*

Hyperbole: In literary criticism, deliberate exaggeration used to achieve an effect. In William Shakespeare's *Macbeth,* Lady Macbeth hyperbolizes when she says, "All the perfumes of Arabia could not sweeten this little hand."

I

Iamb: See *Foot*

Idiom: A word construction or verbal expression closely associated with a given language. For example, in colloquial English the construction "how come" can be used instead of "why" to introduce a question. Similarly, "a piece of cake" is sometimes used to describe a task that is easily done.

Image: A concrete representation of an object or sensory experience. Typically, such a representation helps evoke the feelings associated with the object or experience itself. Images are either "literal" or "figurative." Literal images are especially concrete and involve little or no extension of the obvious meaning of the words used to express them. Figurative images do not follow the literal meaning of the words exactly. Images in literature are usually visual, but the term "image" can also refer to the representation of any sensory experience. In his poem "The Shepherd's Hour," Paul Verlaine presents the following image: "The Moon is red through horizon's fog;/ In a dancing mist the hazy meadow sleeps." The first line is broadly literal, while the second line involves turns of meaning associated with dancing and sleeping.

Imagery: The array of images in a literary work. Also, figurative language. William Butler Yeats's "The Second Coming" offers a powerful image of encroaching anarchy: Turning and turning in the widening gyre The falcon cannot hear the falconer; Things fall apart. . . .

Imagism: An English and American poetry movement that flourished between 1908 and 1917. The Imagists used precise, clearly presented images in their works. They also used common, everyday speech and aimed for conciseness, concrete imagery, and the creation of new rhythms. Participants in the Imagist movement included Ezra Pound, H. D. (Hilda Doolittle), and Amy Lowell, among others.

In medias res: A Latin term meaning "in the middle of things." It refers to the technique of beginning a story at its midpoint and then using various flashback devices to reveal previous action. This technique originated in such epics as Virgil's *Aeneid.*

Induction: The process of reaching a conclusion by reasoning from specific premises to form a general premise. Also, an introductory portion of a work of literature, especially a play. Geoffrey Chaucer's "Prologue" to the *Canterbury Tales,* Thomas Sackville's "Induction" to *The Mirror of Magistrates,* and the opening scene in William Shakespeare's *The Taming of the Shrew* are examples of inductions to literary works.

Intentional Fallacy: The belief that judgments of a literary work based solely on an author's stated or implied intentions are false and misleading. Critics who believe in the concept of the intentional fallacy typically argue that the work itself is sufficient matter for interpretation, even though they may concede that an author's statement of purpose can be useful. Analysis of William Wordsworth's *Lyri-*

cal Ballads based on the observations about poetry he makes in his "Preface" to the second edition of that work is an example of the intentional fallacy.

Interior Monologue: A narrative technique in which characters' thoughts are revealed in a way that appears to be uncontrolled by the author. The interior monologue typically aims to reveal the inner self of a character. It portrays emotional experiences as they occur at both a conscious and unconscious level. images are often used to represent sensations or emotions. One of the best-known interior monologues in English is the Molly Bloom section at the close of James Joyce's *Ulysses*. The interior monologue is also common in the works of Virginia Woolf.

Internal Rhyme: Rhyme that occurs within a single line of verse. An example is in the opening line of Edgar Allan Poe's "The Raven": "Once upon a midnight dreary, while I pondered weak and weary." Here, "dreary" and "weary" make an internal rhyme.

Irish Literary Renaissance: A late nineteenth- and early twentieth-century movement in Irish literature. Members of the movement aimed to reduce the influence of British culture in Ireland and create an Irish national literature. William Butler Yeats, George Moore, and Sean O'Casey are three of the best-known figures of the movement.

Irony: In literary criticism, the effect of language in which the intended meaning is the opposite of what is stated. The title of Jonathan Swift's "A Modest Proposal" is ironic because what Swift proposes in this essay is cannibalism—hardly "modest."

Italian Sonnet: See *Sonnet*

J

Jacobean Age: The period of the reign of James I of England (1603-1625). The early literature of this period reflected the worldview of the Elizabethan Age, but a darker, more cynical attitude steadily grew in the art and literature of the Jacobean Age. This was an important time for English drama and poetry. Milestones include William Shakespeare's tragedies, tragi-comedies, and sonnets; Ben Jonson's various dramas; and John Donne's metaphysical poetry.

Jargon: Language that is used or understood only by a select group of people. Jargon may refer to terminology used in a certain profession, such as computer jargon, or it may refer to any nonsensical

language that is not understood by most people. Literary examples of jargon are Francois Villon's *Ballades en jargon*, which is composed in the secret language of the *coquillards*, and Anthony Burgess's *A Clockwork Orange*, narrated in the fictional characters' language of "Nadsat."

Juvenalian Satire: See *Satire*

K

Knickerbocker Group: A somewhat indistinct group of New York writers of the first half of the nineteenth century. Members of the group were linked only by location and a common theme: New York life. Two famous members of the Knickerbocker Group were Washington Irving and William Cullen Bryant. The group's name derives from Irving's *Knickerbocker's History of New York*.

L

Lais: See *Lay*

Lay: A song or simple narrative poem. The form originated in medieval France. Early French *lais* were often based on the Celtic legends and other tales sung by Breton minstrels—thus the name of the "Breton lay." In fourteenth-century England, the term "lay" was used to describe short narratives written in imitation of the Breton lays. The most notable of these is Geoffrey Chaucer's "The Minstrel's Tale."

Leitmotiv: See *Motif*

Literal Language: An author uses literal language when he or she writes without exaggerating or embellishing the subject matter and without any tools of figurative language. To say "He ran very quickly down the street" is to use literal language, whereas to say "He ran like a hare down the street" would be using figurative language.

Literary Ballad: See *Ballad*

Literature: Literature is broadly defined as any written or spoken material, but the term most often refers to creative works. Literature includes poetry, drama, fiction, and many kinds of nonfiction writing, as well as oral, dramatic, and broadcast compositions not necessarily preserved in a written format, such as films and television programs.

Lost Generation: A term first used by Gertrude Stein to describe the post-World War I generation of American writers: men and women haunted by a sense of betrayal and emptiness brought about by the destructiveness of the war. The term is commonly applied to Hart Crane, Ernest Hemingway, F. Scott Fitzgerald, and others.

Lyric Poetry: A poem expressing the subjective feelings and personal emotions of the poet. Such poetry is melodic, since it was originally accompanied by a lyre in recitals. Most Western poetry in the twentieth century may be classified as lyrical. Examples of lyric poetry include A. E. Housman's elegy ''To an Athlete Dying Young,'' the odes of Pindar and Horace, Thomas Gray and William Collins, the sonnets of Sir Thomas Wyatt and Sir Philip Sidney, Elizabeth Barrett Browning and Rainer Maria Rilke, and a host of other forms in the poetry of William Blake and Christina Rossetti, among many others.

M

Mannerism: Exaggerated, artificial adherence to a literary manner or style. Also, a popular style of the visual arts of late sixteenth-century Europe that was marked by elongation of the human form and by intentional spatial distortion. Literary works that are self-consciously high-toned and artistic are often said to be ''mannered.'' Authors of such works include Henry James and Gertrude Stein.

Masculine Rhyme: See *Rhyme*

Masque: A lavish and elaborate form of entertainment, often performed in royal courts, that emphasizes song, dance, and costumery. The Renaissance form of the masque grew out of the spectacles of masked figures common in medieval England and Europe. The masque reached its peak of popularity and development in seventeenth-century England, during the reigns of James I and, especially, of Charles I. Ben Jonson, the most significant masque writer, also created the ''antimasque,'' which incorporates elements of humor and the grotesque into the traditional masque and achieved greater dramatic quality. Masque-like interludes appear in Edmund Spenser's *The Faerie Queene* and in William Shakespeare's *The Tempest*. One of the best-known English masques is John Milton's *Comus*.

Measure: The foot, verse, or time sequence used in a literary work, especially a poem. Measure is often used somewhat incorrectly as a synonym for meter.

Melodrama: A play in which the typical plot is a conflict between characters who personify extreme good and evil. Melodramas usually end happily and emphasize sensationalism. Other literary forms that use the same techniques are often labeled ''melodramatic.'' The term was formerly used to describe a combination of drama and music; as such, it was synonymous with ''opera.'' Augustin Daly's *Under the Gaslight* and Dion Boucicault's *The Octoroon, The Colleen Bawn,* and *The Poor of New York* are examples of melodramas. The most popular media for twentieth-century melodramas are motion pictures and television.

Metaphor: A figure of speech that expresses an idea through the image of another object. Metaphors suggest the essence of the first object by identifying it with certain qualities of the second object. An example is ''But soft, what light through yonder window breaks?/ It is the east, and Juliet is the sun'' in William Shakespeare's *Romeo and Juliet*. Here, Juliet, the first object, is identified with qualities of the second object, the sun.

Metaphysical Conceit: See *Conceit*

Metaphysical Poetry: The body of poetry produced by a group of seventeenth-century English writers called the ''Metaphysical Poets.'' The group includes John Donne and Andrew Marvell. The Metaphysical Poets made use of everyday speech, intellectual analysis, and unique imagery. They aimed to portray the ordinary conflicts and contradictions of life. Their poems often took the form of an argument, and many of them emphasize physical and religious love as well as the fleeting nature of life. Elaborate conceits are typical in metaphysical poetry. Marvell's ''To His Coy Mistress'' is a well-known example of a metaphysical poem.

Metaphysical Poets: See *Metaphysical Poetry*

Meter: In literary criticism, the repetition of sound patterns that creates a rhythm in poetry. The patterns are based on the number of syllables and the presence and absence of accents. The unit of rhythm in a line is called a foot. Types of meter are classified according to the number of feet in a line. These are the standard English lines: Monometer, one foot; Dimeter, two feet; Trimeter, three feet; Tetrameter, four feet; Pentameter, five feet; Hexameter, six feet (also called the Alexandrine); Heptameter, seven feet (also called the ''Fourteener'' when the feet are iambic). The most common English meter is the iambic pentameter, in which each line contains ten syllables, or five iambic feet, which individually are composed of an unstressed syllable followed by an accented syllable. Both of the following lines from Alfred, Lord Tennyson's

"Ulysses" are written in iambic pentameter: Made weak by time and fate, but strong in will To strive, to seek, to find, and not to yield.

Mise en scene: The costumes, scenery, and other properties of a drama. Herbert Beerbohm Tree was renowned for the elaborate *mises en scene* of his lavish Shakespearean productions at His Majesty's Theatre between 1897 and 1915.

Modernism: Modern literary practices. Also, the principles of a literary school that lasted from roughly the beginning of the twentieth century until the end of World War II. Modernism is defined by its rejection of the literary conventions of the nineteenth century and by its opposition to conventional morality, taste, traditions, and economic values. Many writers are associated with the concepts of Modernism, including Albert Camus, Marcel Proust, D. H. Lawrence, W. H. Auden, Ernest Hemingway, William Faulkner, William Butler Yeats, Thomas Mann, Tennessee Williams, Eugene O'Neill, and James Joyce.

Monologue: A composition, written or oral, by a single individual. More specifically, a speech given by a single individual in a drama or other public entertainment. It has no set length, although it is usually several or more lines long. An example of an "extended monologue"—that is, a monologue of great length and seriousness—occurs in the one-act, one-character play *The Stronger* by August Strindberg.

Monometer: See *Meter*

Mood: The prevailing emotions of a work or of the author in his or her creation of the work. The mood of a work is not always what might be expected based on its subject matter. The poem "Dover Beach" by Matthew Arnold offers examples of two different moods originating from the same experience: watching the ocean at night. The mood of the first three lines— The sea is calm tonight The tide is full, the moon lies fair Upon the straights. . . . is in sharp contrast to the mood of the last three lines— And we are here as on a darkling plain Swept with confused alarms of struggle and flight, Where ignorant armies clash by night.

Motif: A theme, character type, image, metaphor, or other verbal element that recurs throughout a single work of literature or occurs in a number of different works over a period of time. For example, the various manifestations of the color white in Herman Melville's *Moby Dick* is a "specific" *motif,* while the trials of star-crossed lovers is a "conventional" *motif* from the literature of all periods. Also known as *Motiv* or *Leitmotiv.*

Motiv: See *Motif*

Muckrakers: An early twentieth-century group of American writers. Typically, their works exposed the wrongdoings of big business and government in the United States. Upton Sinclair's *The Jungle* exemplifies the muckraking novel.

Muses: Nine Greek mythological goddesses, the daughters of Zeus and Mnemosyne (Memory). Each muse patronized a specific area of the liberal arts and sciences. Calliope presided over epic poetry, Clio over history, Erato over love poetry, Euterpe over music or lyric poetry, Melpomene over tragedy, Polyhymnia over hymns to the gods, Terpsichore over dance, Thalia over comedy, and Urania over astronomy. Poets and writers traditionally made appeals to the Muses for inspiration in their work. John Milton invokes the aid of a muse at the beginning of the first book of his *Paradise Lost:* Of Man's First disobedience, and the Fruit of the Forbidden Tree, whose mortal taste Brought Death into the World, and all our woe, With loss of Eden, till one greater Man Restore us, and regain the blissful Seat, Sing Heav'nly Muse, that on the secret top of Oreb, or of Sinai, didst inspire That Shepherd, who first taught the chosen Seed, In the Beginning how the Heav'ns and Earth Rose out of Chaos. . . .

Mystery: See *Suspense*

Myth: An anonymous tale emerging from the traditional beliefs of a culture or social unit. Myths use supernatural explanations for natural phenomena. They may also explain cosmic issues like creation and death. Collections of myths, known as mythologies, are common to all cultures and nations, but the best-known myths belong to the Norse, Roman, and Greek mythologies. A famous myth is the story of Arachne, an arrogant young girl who challenged a goddess, Athena, to a weaving contest; when the girl won, Athena was enraged and turned Arachne into a spider, thus explaining the existence of spiders.

N

Narration: The telling of a series of events, real or invented. A narration may be either a simple narrative, in which the events are recounted chronologically, or a narrative with a plot, in which the account is given in a style reflecting the author's artistic concept of the story. Narration is sometimes used as a synonym for "storyline." The recounting of scary stories around a campfire is a form of narration.

Narrative: A verse or prose accounting of an event or sequence of events, real or invented. The term is also used as an adjective in the sense "method of narration." For example, in literary criticism, the expression "narrative technique" usually refers to the way the author structures and presents his or her story. Narratives range from the shortest accounts of events, as in Julius Caesar's remark, "I came, I saw, I conquered," to the longest historical or biographical works, as in Edward Gibbon's *The Decline and Fall of the Roman Empire,* as well as diaries, travelogues, novels, ballads, epics, short stories, and other fictional forms.

Narrative Poetry: A nondramatic poem in which the author tells a story. Such poems may be of any length or level of complexity. Epics such as *Beowulf* and ballads are forms of narrative poetry.

Narrator: The teller of a story. The narrator may be the author or a character in the story through whom the author speaks. Huckleberry Finn is the narrator of Mark Twain's *The Adventures of Huckleberry Finn.*

Naturalism: A literary movement of the late nineteenth and early twentieth centuries. The movement's major theorist, French novelist Emile Zola, envisioned a type of fiction that would examine human life with the objectivity of scientific inquiry. The Naturalists typically viewed human beings as either the products of "biological determinism," ruled by hereditary instincts and engaged in an endless struggle for survival, or as the products of "socioeconomic determinism," ruled by social and economic forces beyond their control. In their works, the Naturalists generally ignored the highest levels of society and focused on degradation: poverty, alcoholism, prostitution, insanity, and disease. Naturalism influenced authors throughout the world, including Henrik Ibsen and Thomas Hardy. In the United States, in particular, Naturalism had a profound impact. Among the authors who embraced its principles are Theodore Dreiser, Eugene O'Neill, Stephen Crane, Jack London, and Frank Norris.

Negritude: A literary movement based on the concept of a shared cultural bond on the part of black Africans, wherever they may be in the world. It traces its origins to the former French colonies of Africa and the Caribbean. Negritude poets, novelists, and essayists generally stress four points in their writings: One, black alienation from traditional African culture can lead to feelings of inferiority. Two, European colonialism and Western education should be resisted. Three, black Africans should seek to affirm and define their own identity. Four, African culture can and should be reclaimed. Many Negritude writers also claim that blacks can make unique contributions to the world, based on a heightened appreciation of nature, rhythm, and human emotions—aspects of life they say are not so highly valued in the materialistic and rationalistic West. Examples of Negritude literature include the poetry of both Senegalese Leopold Senghor in *Hosties noires* and Martiniquais Aime-Fernand Cesaire in *Return to My Native Land.*

Negro Renaissance: See *Harlem Renaissance*

Neoclassical Period: See *Neoclassicism*

Neoclassicism: In literary criticism, this term refers to the revival of the attitudes and styles of expression of classical literature. It is generally used to describe a period in European history beginning in the late seventeenth century and lasting until about 1800. In its purest form, Neoclassicism marked a return to order, proportion, restraint, logic, accuracy, and decorum. In England, where Neoclassicism perhaps was most popular, it reflected the influence of seventeenth- century French writers, especially dramatists. Neoclassical writers typically reacted against the intensity and enthusiasm of the Renaissance period. They wrote works that appealed to the intellect, using elevated language and classical literary forms such as satire and the ode. Neoclassical works were often governed by the classical goal of instruction. English neoclassicists included Alexander Pope, Jonathan Swift, Joseph Addison, Sir Richard Steele, John Gay, and Matthew Prior; French neoclassicists included Pierre Corneille and Jean-Baptiste Moliere. Also known as Age of Reason.

Neoclassicists: See *Neoclassicism*

New Criticism: A movement in literary criticism, dating from the late 1920s, that stressed close textual analysis in the interpretation of works of literature. The New Critics saw little merit in historical and biographical analysis. Rather, they aimed to examine the text alone, free from the question of how external events—biographical or otherwise—may have helped shape it. This predominantly American school was named "New Criticism" by one of its practitioners, John Crowe Ransom. Other important New Critics included Allen Tate, R. P. Blackmur, Robert Penn Warren, and Cleanth Brooks.

New Negro Movement: See *Harlem Renaissance*

Noble Savage: The idea that primitive man is noble and good but becomes evil and corrupted as he becomes civilized. The concept of the noble savage originated in the Renaissance period but is more closely identified with such later writers as Jean-Jacques Rousseau and Aphra Behn. First described in John Dryden's play *The Conquest of Granada*, the noble savage is portrayed by the various Native Americans in James Fenimore Cooper's "Leatherstocking Tales," by Queequeg, Daggoo, and Tashtego in Herman Melville's *Moby Dick*, and by John the Savage in Aldous Huxley's *Brave New World*.

O

Objective Correlative: An outward set of objects, a situation, or a chain of events corresponding to an inward experience and evoking this experience in the reader. The term frequently appears in modern criticism in discussions of authors' intended effects on the emotional responses of readers. This term was originally used by T. S. Eliot in his 1919 essay "Hamlet."

Objectivity: A quality in writing characterized by the absence of the author's opinion or feeling about the subject matter. Objectivity is an important factor in criticism. The novels of Henry James and, to a certain extent, the poems of John Larkin demonstrate objectivity, and it is central to John Keats's concept of "negative capability." Critical and journalistic writing usually are or attempt to be objective.

Occasional Verse: poetry written on the occasion of a significant historical or personal event. *Vers de societe* is sometimes called occasional verse although it is of a less serious nature. Famous examples of occasional verse include Andrew Marvell's "Horatian Ode upon Cromwell's Return from England," Walt Whitman's "When Lilacs Last in the Dooryard Bloom'd"— written upon the death of Abraham Lincoln—and Edmund Spenser's commemoration of his wedding, "Epithalamion."

Octave: A poem or stanza composed of eight lines. The term octave most often represents the first eight lines of a Petrarchan sonnet. An example of an octave is taken from a translation of a Petrarchan sonnet by Sir Thomas Wyatt: The pillar perisht is whereto I leant, The strongest stay of mine unquiet mind; The like of it no man again can find, From East to West Still seeking though he went. To mind unhap! for hap away hath rent Of all my joy the very

bark and rind; And I, alas, by chance am thus assigned Daily to mourn till death do it relent.

Ode: Name given to an extended lyric poem characterized by exalted emotion and dignified style. An ode usually concerns a single, serious theme. Most odes, but not all, are addressed to an object or individual. Odes are distinguished from other lyric poetic forms by their complex rhythmic and stanzaic patterns. An example of this form is John Keats's "Ode to a Nightingale."

Oedipus Complex: A son's amorous obsession with his mother. The phrase is derived from the story of the ancient Theban hero Oedipus, who unknowingly killed his father and married his mother. Literary occurrences of the Oedipus complex include Andre Gide's *Oedipe* and Jean Cocteau's *La Machine infernale,* as well as the most famous, Sophocles' *Oedipus Rex.*

Omniscience: See *Point of View*

Onomatopoeia: The use of words whose sounds express or suggest their meaning. In its simplest sense, onomatopoeia may be represented by words that mimic the sounds they denote such as "hiss" or "meow." At a more subtle level, the pattern and rhythm of sounds and rhymes of a line or poem may be onomatopoeic. A celebrated example of onomatopoeia is the repetition of the word "bells" in Edgar Allan Poe's poem "The Bells."

Opera: A type of stage performance, usually a drama, in which the dialogue is sung. Classic examples of opera include Giuseppi Verdi's *La traviata,* Giacomo Puccini's *La Boheme,* and Richard Wagner's *Tristan und Isolde.* Major twentieth- century contributors to the form include Richard Strauss and Alban Berg.

Operetta: A usually romantic comic opera. John Gay's *The Beggar's Opera*, Richard Sheridan's *The Duenna,* and numerous works by William Gilbert and Arthur Sullivan are examples of operettas.

Oral Tradition: See *Oral Transmission*

Oral Transmission: A process by which songs, ballads, folklore, and other material are transmitted by word of mouth. The tradition of oral transmission predates the written record systems of literate society. Oral transmission preserves material sometimes over generations, although often with variations. Memory plays a large part in the recitation and preservation of orally transmitted material. Breton lays, French *fabliaux*, national epics (including the Anglo- Saxon *Beowulf,* the Spanish *El Cid,* and the Finnish *Kalevala*), Native American myths and legends, and African folktales told by plantation slaves are examples of orally transmitted literature.

Oration: Formal speaking intended to motivate the listeners to some action or feeling. Such public speaking was much more common before the development of timely printed communication such as newspapers. Famous examples of oration include Abraham Lincoln's ''Gettysburg Address'' and Dr. Martin Luther King Jr.'s ''I Have a Dream'' speech.

Ottava Rima: An eight-line stanza of poetry composed in iambic pentameter (a five-foot line in which each foot consists of an unaccented syllable followed by an accented syllable), following the abababcc rhyme scheme. This form has been prominently used by such important English writers as Lord Byron, Henry Wadsworth Longfellow, and W. B. Yeats.

Oxymoron: A phrase combining two contradictory terms. Oxymorons may be intentional or unintentional. The following speech from William Shakespeare's *Romeo and Juliet* uses several oxymorons: Why, then, O brawling love! O loving hate! O anything, of nothing first create! O heavy lightness! serious vanity! Mis-shapen chaos of well-seeming forms! Feather of lead, bright smoke, cold fire, sick health! This love feel I, that feel no love in this.

P

Pantheism: The idea that all things are both a manifestation or revelation of God and a part of God at the same time. Pantheism was a common attitude in the early societies of Egypt, India, and Greece—the term derives from the Greek *pan* meaning ''all'' and *theos* meaning ''deity.'' It later became a significant part of the Christian faith. William Wordsworth and Ralph Waldo Emerson are among the many writers who have expressed the pantheistic attitude in their works.

Parable: A story intended to teach a moral lesson or answer an ethical question. In the West, the best examples of parables are those of Jesus Christ in the New Testament, notably ''The Prodigal Son,'' but parables also are used in Sufism, rabbinic literature, Hasidism, and Zen Buddhism.

Paradox: A statement that appears illogical or contradictory at first, but may actually point to an underlying truth. ''Less is more'' is an example of a paradox. Literary examples include Francis Ba-

con's statement, ''The most corrected copies are commonly the least correct,'' and ''All animals are equal, but some animals are more equal than others'' from George Orwell's *Animal Farm.*

Parallelism: A method of comparison of two ideas in which each is developed in the same grammatical structure. Ralph Waldo Emerson's ''Civilization'' contains this example of parallelism: Raphael paints wisdom; Handel sings it, Phidias carves it, Shakespeare writes it, Wren builds it, Columbus sails it, Luther preaches it, Washington arms it, Watt mechanizes it.

Parnassianism: A mid nineteenth-century movement in French literature. Followers of the movement stressed adherence to well-defined artistic forms as a reaction against the often chaotic expression of the artist's ego that dominated the work of the Romantics. The Parnassians also rejected the moral, ethical, and social themes exhibited in the works of French Romantics such as Victor Hugo. The aesthetic doctrines of the Parnassians strongly influenced the later symbolist and decadent movements. Members of the Parnassian school include Leconte de Lisle, Sully Prudhomme, Albert Glatigny, Francois Coppee, and Theodore de Banville.

Parody: In literary criticism, this term refers to an imitation of a serious literary work or the signature style of a particular author in a ridiculous manner. A typical parody adopts the style of the original and applies it to an inappropriate subject for humorous effect. Parody is a form of satire and could be considered the literary equivalent of a caricature or cartoon. Henry Fielding's *Shamela* is a parody of Samuel Richardson's *Pamela.*

Pastoral: A term derived from the Latin word ''pastor,'' meaning shepherd. A pastoral is a literary composition on a rural theme. The conventions of the pastoral were originated by the third-century Greek poet Theocritus, who wrote about the experiences, love affairs, and pastimes of Sicilian shepherds. In a pastoral, characters and language of a courtly nature are often placed in a simple setting. The term pastoral is also used to classify dramas, elegies, and lyrics that exhibit the use of country settings and shepherd characters. Percy Bysshe Shelley's ''Adonais'' and John Milton's ''Lycidas'' are two famous examples of pastorals.

Pastorela: The Spanish name for the shepherds play, a folk drama reenacted during the Christmas season. Examples of *pastorelas* include Gomez

Manrique's *Representacion del nacimiento* and the dramas of Lucas Fernandez and Juan del Encina.

Pathetic Fallacy: A term coined by English critic John Ruskin to identify writing that falsely endows nonhuman things with human intentions and feelings, such as "angry clouds" and "sad trees." The pathetic fallacy is a required convention in the classical poetic form of the pastoral elegy, and it is used in the modern poetry of T. S. Eliot, Ezra Pound, and the Imagists. Also known as Poetic Fallacy.

Pelado: Literally the "skinned one" or shirtless one, he was the stock underdog, sharp-witted picaresque character of Mexican vaudeville and tent shows. The *pelado* is found in such works as Don Catarino's *Los effectos de la crisis* and *Regreso a mi tierra.*

Pen Name: See *Pseudonym*

Pentameter: See *Meter*

Persona: A Latin term meaning "mask." *Personae* are the characters in a fictional work of literature. The *persona* generally functions as a mask through which the author tells a story in a voice other than his or her own. A *persona* is usually either a character in a story who acts as a narrator or an "implied author," a voice created by the author to act as the narrator for himself or herself. *Personae* include the narrator of Geoffrey Chaucer's *Canterbury Tales* and Marlow in Joseph Conrad's *Heart of Darkness.*

Personae: See *Persona*

Personal Point of View: See *Point of View*

Personification: A figure of speech that gives human qualities to abstract ideas, animals, and inanimate objects. William Shakespeare used personification in *Romeo and Juliet* in the lines "Arise, fair sun, and kill the envious moon,/ Who is already sick and pale with grief." Here, the moon is portrayed as being envious, sick, and pale with grief—all markedly human qualities. Also known as *Prosopopoeia.*

Petrarchan Sonnet: See *Sonnet*

Phenomenology: A method of literary criticism based on the belief that things have no existence outside of human consciousness or awareness. Proponents of this theory believe that art is a process that takes place in the mind of the observer as he or she contemplates an object rather than a quality of the object itself. Among phenomenological critics

are Edmund Husserl, George Poulet, Marcel Raymond, and Roman Ingarden.

Picaresque Novel: Episodic fiction depicting the adventures of a roguish central character ("picaro" is Spanish for "rogue"). The picaresque hero is commonly a low-born but clever individual who wanders into and out of various affairs of love, danger, and farcical intrigue. These involvements may take place at all social levels and typically present a humorous and wide-ranging satire of a given society. Prominent examples of the picaresque novel are *Don Quixote* by Miguel de Cervantes, *Tom Jones* by Henry Fielding, and *Moll Flanders* by Daniel Defoe.

Plagiarism: Claiming another person's written material as one's own. Plagiarism can take the form of direct, word-for- word copying or the theft of the substance or idea of the work. A student who copies an encyclopedia entry and turns it in as a report for school is guilty of plagiarism.

Platonic Criticism: A form of criticism that stresses an artistic work's usefulness as an agent of social engineering rather than any quality or value of the work itself. Platonic criticism takes as its starting point the ancient Greek philosopher Plato's comments on art in his *Republic.*

Platonism: The embracing of the doctrines of the philosopher Plato, popular among the poets of the Renaissance and the Romantic period. Platonism is more flexible than Aristotelian Criticism and places more emphasis on the supernatural and unknown aspects of life. Platonism is expressed in the love poetry of the Renaissance, the fourth book of Baldassare Castiglione's *The Book of the Courtier,* and the poetry of William Blake, William Wordsworth, Percy Bysshe Shelley, Friedrich Holderlin, William Butler Yeats, and Wallace Stevens.

Play: See *Drama*

Plot: In literary criticism, this term refers to the pattern of events in a narrative or drama. In its simplest sense, the plot guides the author in composing the work and helps the reader follow the work. Typically, plots exhibit causality and unity and have a beginning, a middle, and an end. Sometimes, however, a plot may consist of a series of disconnected events, in which case it is known as an "episodic plot." In his *Aspects of the Novel,* E. M. Forster distinguishes between a story, defined as a "narrative of events arranged in their time- sequence," and plot, which organizes the events to a ''sense of causality.'' This definition closely mirrors Aristotle's discussion of plot in his *Poetics*.

Poem: In its broadest sense, a composition utilizing rhyme, meter, concrete detail, and expressive language to create a literary experience with emotional and aesthetic appeal. Typical poems include sonnets, odes, elegies, *haiku,* ballads, and free verse.

Poet: An author who writes poetry or verse. The term is also used to refer to an artist or writer who has an exceptional gift for expression, imagination, and energy in the making of art in any form. Well-known poets include Horace, Basho, Sir Philip Sidney, Sir Edmund Spenser, John Donne, Andrew Marvell, Alexander Pope, Jonathan Swift, George Gordon, Lord Byron, John Keats, Christina Rossetti, W. H. Auden, Stevie Smith, and Sylvia Plath.

Poetic Fallacy: See *Pathetic Fallacy*

Poetic Justice: An outcome in a literary work, not necessarily a poem, in which the good are rewarded and the evil are punished, especially in ways that particularly fit their virtues or crimes. For example, a murderer may himself be murdered, or a thief will find himself penniless.

Poetic License: Distortions of fact and literary convention made by a writer—not always a poet—for the sake of the effect gained. Poetic license is closely related to the concept of ''artistic freedom.'' An author exercises poetic license by saying that a pile of money ''reaches as high as a mountain'' when the pile is actually only a foot or two high.

Poetics: This term has two closely related meanings. It denotes (1) an aesthetic theory in literary criticism about the essence of poetry or (2) rules prescribing the proper methods, content, style, or diction of poetry. The term poetics may also refer to theories about literature in general, not just poetry.

Poetry: In its broadest sense, writing that aims to present ideas and evoke an emotional experience in the reader through the use of meter, imagery, connotative and concrete words, and a carefully constructed structure based on rhythmic patterns. Poetry typically relies on words and expressions that have several layers of meaning. It also makes use of the effects of regular rhythm on the ear and may make a strong appeal to the senses through the use of imagery. Edgar Allan Poe's ''Annabel Lee'' and Walt Whitman's *Leaves of Grass* are famous examples of poetry.

Point of View: The narrative perspective from which a literary work is presented to the reader. There are four traditional points of view. The ''third person omniscient'' gives the reader a ''godlike'' perspective, unrestricted by time or place, from which to see actions and look into the minds of characters. This allows the author to comment openly on characters and events in the work. The ''third person'' point of view presents the events of the story from outside of any single character's perception, much like the omniscient point of view, but the reader must understand the action as it takes place and without any special insight into characters' minds or motivations. The ''first person'' or ''personal'' point of view relates events as they are perceived by a single character. The main character ''tells'' the story and may offer opinions about the action and characters which differ from those of the author. Much less common than omniscient, third person, and first person is the ''second person'' point of view, wherein the author tells the story as if it is happening to the reader. James Thurber employs the omniscient point of view in his short story ''The Secret Life of Walter Mitty.'' Ernest Hemingway's ''A Clean, Well-Lighted Place'' is a short story told from the third person point of view. Mark Twain's novel *Huck Finn* is presented from the first person viewpoint. Jay McInerney's *Bright Lights, Big City* is an example of a novel which uses the second person point of view.

Polemic: A work in which the author takes a stand on a controversial subject, such as abortion or religion. Such works are often extremely argumentative or provocative. Classic examples of polemics include John Milton's *Aeropagitica* and Thomas Paine's *The American Crisis.*

Pornography: Writing intended to provoke feelings of lust in the reader. Such works are often condemned by critics and teachers, but those which can be shown to have literary value are viewed less harshly. Literary works that have been described as pornographic include Ovid's *The Art of Love,* Margaret of Angouleme's *Heptameron,* John Cleland's *Memoirs of a Woman of Pleasure; or, the Life of Fanny Hill,* the anonymous *My Secret Life,* D. H. Lawrence's *Lady Chatterley's Lover,* and Vladimir Nabokov's *Lolita.*

Post-Aesthetic Movement: An artistic response made by African Americans to the black aesthetic movement of the 1960s and early '70s. Writers since that time have adopted a somewhat different tone in their work, with less emphasis placed on the disparity between black and white in the United States. In the words of post-aesthetic authors such as Toni Morrison, John Edgar Wideman, and Kristin Hunter, African Americans are portrayed as looking inward for answers to their own questions, rather than always looking to the outside world. Two well-known examples of works produced as part of the post-aesthetic movement are the Pulitzer Prize-winning novels *The Color Purple* by Alice Walker and *Beloved* by Toni Morrison.

Postmodernism: Writing from the 1960s forward characterized by experimentation and continuing to apply some of the fundamentals of modernism, which included existentialism and alienation. Postmodernists have gone a step further in the rejection of tradition begun with the modernists by also rejecting traditional forms, preferring the anti-novel over the novel and the anti-hero over the hero. Postmodern writers include Alain Robbe-Grillet, Thomas Pynchon, Margaret Drabble, John Fowles, Adolfo Bioy-Casares, and Gabriel Garcia Marquez.

Pre-Raphaelites: A circle of writers and artists in mid nineteenth-century England. Valuing the pre-Renaissance artistic qualities of religious symbolism, lavish pictorialism, and natural sensuousness, the Pre-Raphaelites cultivated a sense of mystery and melancholy that influenced later writers associated with the Symbolist and Decadent movements. The major members of the group include Dante Gabriel Rossetti, Christina Rossetti, Algernon Swinburne, and Walter Pater.

Primitivism: The belief that primitive peoples were nobler and less flawed than civilized peoples because they had not been subjected to the tainting influence of society. Examples of literature espousing primitivism include Aphra Behn's *Oroonoko: Or, The History of the Royal Slave,* Jean-Jacques Rousseau's *Julie ou la Nouvelle Heloise,* Oliver Goldsmith's *The Deserted Village,* the poems of Robert Burns, Herman Melville's stories *Typee, Omoo,* and *Mardi,* many poems of William Butler Yeats and Robert Frost, and William Golding's novel *Lord of the Flies.*

Projective Verse: A form of free verse in which the poet's breathing pattern determines the lines of the poem. Poets who advocate projective verse are against all formal structures in writing, including meter and form. Besides its creators, Robert Creeley, Robert Duncan, and Charles Olson, two other well-known projective verse poets are Denise Levertov and LeRoi Jones (Amiri Baraka). Also known as Breath Verse.

Prologue: An introductory section of a literary work. It often contains information establishing the situation of the characters or presents information about the setting, time period, or action. In drama, the prologue is spoken by a chorus or by one of the principal characters. In the "General Prologue" of *The Canterbury Tales,* Geoffrey Chaucer describes the main characters and establishes the setting and purpose of the work.

Prose: A literary medium that attempts to mirror the language of everyday speech. It is distinguished from poetry by its use of unmetered, unrhymed language consisting of logically related sentences. Prose is usually grouped into paragraphs that form a cohesive whole such as an essay or a novel. Recognized masters of English prose writing include Sir Thomas Malory, William Caxton, Raphael Holinshed, Joseph Addison, Mark Twain, and Ernest Hemingway.

Prosopopoeia: See *Personification*

Protagonist: The central character of a story who serves as a focus for its themes and incidents and as the principal rationale for its development. The protagonist is sometimes referred to in discussions of modern literature as the hero or anti-hero. Well-known protagonists are Hamlet in William Shakespeare's *Hamlet* and Jay Gatsby in F. Scott Fitzgerald's *The Great Gatsby.*

Protest Fiction: Protest fiction has as its primary purpose the protesting of some social injustice, such as racism or discrimination. One example of protest fiction is a series of five novels by Chester Himes, beginning in 1945 with *If He Hollers Let Him Go* and ending in 1955 with *The Primitive.* These works depict the destructive effects of race and gender stereotyping in the context of interracial relationships. Another African American author whose works often revolve around themes of social protest is John Oliver Killens. James Baldwin's essay "Everybody's Protest Novel" generated controversy by attacking the authors of protest fiction.

Proverb: A brief, sage saying that expresses a truth about life in a striking manner. "They are not all cooks who carry long knives" is an example of a proverb.

Pseudonym: A name assumed by a writer, most often intended to prevent his or her identification as the author of a work. Two or more authors may work together under one pseudonym, or an author may use a different name for each genre he or she publishes in. Some publishing companies maintain ''house pseudonyms,'' under which any number of authors may write installations in a series. Some authors also choose a pseudonym over their real names the way an actor may use a stage name. Examples of pseudonyms (with the author's real name in parentheses) include Voltaire (Francois-Marie Arouet), Novalis (Friedrich von Hardenberg), Currer Bell (Charlotte Bronte), Ellis Bell (Emily Bronte), George Eliot (Maryann Evans), Honorio Bustos Donmecq (Adolfo Bioy-Casares and Jorge Luis Borges), and Richard Bachman (Stephen King).

Pun: A play on words that have similar sounds but different meanings. A serious example of the pun is from John Donne's ''A Hymne to God the Father'': Sweare by thyself, that at my death thy sonne Shall shine as he shines now, and hereto fore; And, having done that, Thou haste done; I fear no more.

Pure Poetry: poetry written without instructional intent or moral purpose that aims only to please a reader by its imagery or musical flow. The term pure poetry is used as the antonym of the term ''didacticism.'' The poetry of Edgar Allan Poe, Stephane Mallarme, Paul Verlaine, Paul Valery, Juan Ramoz Jimenez, and Jorge Guillen offer examples of pure poetry.

Q

Quatrain: A four-line stanza of a poem or an entire poem consisting of four lines. The following quatrain is from Robert Herrick's ''To Live Merrily, and to Trust to Good Verses'': Round, round, the root do's run; And being ravisht thus, Come, I will drink a Tun To my *Propertius.*

R

Raisonneur: A character in a drama who functions as a spokesperson for the dramatist's views. The *raisonneur* typically observes the play without becoming central to its action. *Raisonneurs* were very common in plays of the nineteenth century.

Realism: A nineteenth-century European literary movement that sought to portray familiar characters, situations, and settings in a realistic manner. This was done primarily by using an objective narrative point of view and through the buildup of accurate detail. The standard for success of any realistic work depends on how faithfully it transfers common experience into fictional forms. The realistic method may be altered or extended, as in stream of consciousness writing, to record highly subjec-

tive experience. Seminal authors in the tradition of Realism include Honore de Balzac, Gustave Flaubert, and Henry James.

Refrain: A phrase repeated at intervals throughout a poem. A refrain may appear at the end of each stanza or at less regular intervals. It may be altered slightly at each appearance. Some refrains are nonsense expressions—as with ''Nevermore'' in Edgar Allan Poe's ''The Raven''—that seem to take on a different significance with each use.

Renaissance: The period in European history that marked the end of the Middle Ages. It began in Italy in the late fourteenth century. In broad terms, it is usually seen as spanning the fourteenth, fifteenth, and sixteenth centuries, although it did not reach Great Britain, for example, until the 1480s or so. The Renaissance saw an awakening in almost every sphere of human activity, especially science, philosophy, and the arts. The period is best defined by the emergence of a general philosophy that emphasized the importance of the intellect, the individual, and world affairs. It contrasts strongly with the medieval worldview, characterized by the dominant concerns of faith, the social collective, and spiritual salvation. Prominent writers during the Renaissance include Niccolo Machiavelli and Baldassare Castiglione in Italy, Miguel de Cervantes and Lope de Vega in Spain, Jean Froissart and Francois Rabelais in France, Sir Thomas More and Sir Philip Sidney in England, and Desiderius Erasmus in Holland.

Repartee: Conversation featuring snappy retorts and witticisms. Masters of *repartee* include Sydney Smith, Charles Lamb, and Oscar Wilde. An example is recorded in the meeting of ''Beau'' Nash and John Wesley: Nash said, ''I never make way for a fool,'' to which Wesley responded, ''Don't you? I always do,'' and stepped aside.

Resolution: The portion of a story following the climax, in which the conflict is resolved. The resolution of Jane Austen's *Northanger Abbey* is neatly summed up in the following sentence: ''Henry and Catherine were married, the bells rang and everybody smiled.''

Restoration: See *Restoration Age*

Restoration Age: A period in English literature beginning with the crowning of Charles II in 1660 and running to about 1700. The era, which was characterized by a reaction against Puritanism, was the first great age of the comedy of manners. The finest literature of the era is typically witty and urbane, and often lewd. Prominent Restoration Age writers include William Congreve, Samuel Pepys, John Dryden, and John Milton.

Revenge Tragedy: A dramatic form popular during the Elizabethan Age, in which the protagonist, directed by the ghost of his murdered father or son, inflicts retaliation upon a powerful villain. Notable features of the revenge tragedy include violence, bizarre criminal acts, intrigue, insanity, a hesitant protagonist, and the use of soliloquy. Thomas Kyd's *Spanish Tragedy* is the first example of revenge tragedy in English, and William Shakespeare's *Hamlet* is perhaps the best. Extreme examples of revenge tragedy, such as John Webster's *The Duchess of Malfi,* are labeled "tragedies of blood." Also known as Tragedy of Blood.

Revista: The Spanish term for a vaudeville musical revue. Examples of *revistas* include Antonio Guzman Aguilera's *Mexico para los mexicanos,* Daniel Vanegas's *Maldito jazz,* and Don Catarino's *Whiskey, morfina y marihuana* and *El desterrado.*

Rhetoric: In literary criticism, this term denotes the art of ethical persuasion. In its strictest sense, rhetoric adheres to various principles developed since classical times for arranging facts and ideas in a clear, persuasive, appealing manner. The term is also used to refer to effective prose in general and theories of or methods for composing effective prose. Classical examples of rhetorics include *The Rhetoric of Aristotle,* Quintillian's *Institutio Oratoria,* and Cicero's *Ad Herennium.*

Rhetorical Question: A question intended to provoke thought, but not an expressed answer, in the reader. It is most commonly used in oratory and other persuasive genres. The following lines from Thomas Gray's "Elegy Written in a Country Churchyard" ask rhetorical questions: Can storied urn or animated bust Back to its mansion call the fleeting breath? Can Honour's voice provoke the silent dust, Or Flattery soothe the dull cold ear of Death?

Rhyme: When used as a noun in literary criticism, this term generally refers to a poem in which words sound identical or very similar and appear in parallel positions in two or more lines. Rhymes are classified into different types according to where they fall in a line or stanza or according to the degree of similarity they exhibit in their spellings and sounds. Some major types of rhyme are "masculine" rhyme, "feminine" rhyme, and "triple" rhyme. In a masculine rhyme, the rhyming sound falls in a single accented syllable, as with "heat"

and "eat." Feminine rhyme is a rhyme of two syllables, one stressed and one unstressed, as with "merry" and "tarry." Triple rhyme matches the sound of the accented syllable and the two unaccented syllables that follow: "narrative" and "declarative." Robert Browning alternates feminine and masculine rhymes in his "Soliloquy of the Spanish Cloister": Gr-r-r—there go, my heart's abhorrence! Water your damned flower-pots, do! If hate killed men, Brother Lawrence, God's blood, would not mine kill you! What? Your myrtle-bush wants trimming? Oh, that rose has prior claims— Needs its leaden vase filled brimming? Hell dry you up with flames! Triple rhymes can be found in Thomas Hood's "Bridge of Sighs," George Gordon Byron's satirical verse, and Ogden Nash's comic poems.

Rhyme Royal: A stanza of seven lines composed in iambic pentameter and rhymed *ababbcc.* The name is said to be a tribute to King James I of Scotland, who made much use of the form in his poetry. Examples of rhyme royal include Geoffrey Chaucer's *The Parlement of Foules,* William Shakespeare's *The Rape of Lucrece,* William Morris's *The Early Paradise,* and John Masefield's *The Widow in the Bye Street.*

Rhyme Scheme: See *Rhyme*

Rhythm: A regular pattern of sound, time intervals, or events occurring in writing, most often and most discernably in poetry. Regular, reliable rhythm is known to be soothing to humans, while interrupted, unpredictable, or rapidly changing rhythm is disturbing. These effects are known to authors, who use them to produce a desired reaction in the reader. An example of a form of irregular rhythm is sprung rhythm poetry; quantitative verse, on the other hand, is very regular in its rhythm.

Rising Action: The part of a drama where the plot becomes increasingly complicated. Rising action leads up to the climax, or turning point, of a drama. The final "chase scene" of an action film is generally the rising action which culminates in the film's climax.

Rococo: A style of European architecture that flourished in the eighteenth century, especially in France. The most notable features of *rococo* are its extensive use of ornamentation and its themes of lightness, gaiety, and intimacy. In literary criticism, the term is often used disparagingly to refer to a decadent or over-ornamental style. Alexander Pope's "The Rape of the Lock" is an example of literary *rococo.*

Roman a clef: A French phrase meaning "novel with a key." It refers to a narrative in which real persons are portrayed under fictitious names. Jack Kerouac, for example, portrayed various real-life beat generation figures under fictitious names in his *On the Road.*

Romance: A broad term, usually denoting a narrative with exotic, exaggerated, often idealized characters, scenes, and themes. Nathaniel Hawthorne called his *The House of the Seven Gables* and *The Marble Faun* romances in order to distinguish them from clearly realistic works.

Romantic Age: See *Romanticism*

Romanticism: This term has two widely accepted meanings. In historical criticism, it refers to a European intellectual and artistic movement of the late eighteenth and early nineteenth centuries that sought greater freedom of personal expression than that allowed by the strict rules of literary form and logic of the eighteenth-century neoclassicists. The Romantics preferred emotional and imaginative expression to rational analysis. They considered the individual to be at the center of all experience and so placed him or her at the center of their art. The Romantics believed that the creative imagination reveals nobler truths—unique feelings and attitudes—than those that could be discovered by logic or by scientific examination. Both the natural world and the state of childhood were important sources for revelations of "eternal truths." "Romanticism" is also used as a general term to refer to a type of sensibility found in all periods of literary history and usually considered to be in opposition to the principles of classicism. In this sense, Romanticism signifies any work or philosophy in which the exotic or dreamlike figure strongly, or that is devoted to individualistic expression, self-analysis, or a pursuit of a higher realm of knowledge than can be discovered by human reason. Prominent Romantics include Jean-Jacques Rousseau, William Wordsworth, John Keats, Lord Byron, and Johann Wolfgang von Goethe.

Romantics: See *Romanticism*

Russian Symbolism: A Russian poetic movement, derived from French symbolism, that flourished between 1894 and 1910. While some Russian Symbolists continued in the French tradition, stressing aestheticism and the importance of suggestion above didactic intent, others saw their craft as a form of mystical worship, and themselves as mediators between the supernatural and the mundane. Russian symbolists include Aleksandr Blok, Vyacheslav Ivanovich Ivanov, Fyodor Sologub, Andrey Bely, Nikolay Gumilyov, and Vladimir Sergeyevich Solovyov.

S

Satire: A work that uses ridicule, humor, and wit to criticize and provoke change in human nature and institutions. There are two major types of satire: "formal" or "direct" satire speaks directly to the reader or to a character in the work; "indirect" satire relies upon the ridiculous behavior of its characters to make its point. Formal satire is further divided into two manners: the "Horatian," which ridicules gently, and the "Juvenalian," which derides its subjects harshly and bitterly. Voltaire's novella *Candide* is an indirect satire. Jonathan Swift's essay "A Modest Proposal" is a Juvenalian satire.

Scansion: The analysis or "scanning" of a poem to determine its meter and often its rhyme scheme. The most common system of scansion uses accents (slanted lines drawn above syllables) to show stressed syllables, breves (curved lines drawn above syllables) to show unstressed syllables, and vertical lines to separate each foot. In the first line of John Keats's *Endymion,* "A thing of beauty is a joy forever:" the word "thing," the first syllable of "beauty," the word "joy," and the second syllable of "forever" are stressed, while the words "A" and "of," the second syllable of "beauty," the word "a," and the first and third syllables of "forever" are unstressed. In the second line: "Its loveliness increases; it will never" a pair of vertical lines separate the foot ending with "increases" and the one beginning with "it."

Scene: A subdivision of an act of a drama, consisting of continuous action taking place at a single time and in a single location. The beginnings and endings of scenes may be indicated by clearing the stage of actors and props or by the entrances and exits of important characters. The first act of William Shakespeare's *Winter's Tale* is comprised of two scenes.

Science Fiction: A type of narrative about or based upon real or imagined scientific theories and technology. Science fiction is often peopled with alien creatures and set on other planets or in different dimensions. Karel Capek's *R.U.R.* is a major work of science fiction.

Second Person: See *Point of View*

Semiotics: The study of how literary forms and conventions affect the meaning of language. Semioticians include Ferdinand de Saussure, Charles Sanders Pierce, Claude Levi-Strauss, Jacques Lacan, Michel Foucault, Jacques Derrida, Roland Barthes, and Julia Kristeva.

Sestet: Any six-line poem or stanza. Examples of the sestet include the last six lines of the Petrarchan sonnet form, the stanza form of Robert Burns's ''A Poet's Welcome to his love-begotten Daughter,'' and the sestina form in W. H. Auden's ''Paysage Moralise.''

Setting: The time, place, and culture in which the action of a narrative takes place. The elements of setting may include geographic location, characters' physical and mental environments, prevailing cultural attitudes, or the historical time in which the action takes place. Examples of settings include the romanticized Scotland in Sir Walter Scott's ''Waverley'' novels, the French provincial setting in Gustave Flaubert's *Madame Bovary,* the fictional Wessex country of Thomas Hardy's novels, and the small towns of southern Ontario in Alice Munro's short stories.

Shakespearean Sonnet: See *Sonnet*

Signifying Monkey: A popular trickster figure in black folklore, with hundreds of tales about this character documented since the 19th century. Henry Louis Gates Jr. examines the history of the signifying monkey in *The Signifying Monkey: Towards a Theory of Afro-American Literary Criticism,* published in 1988.

Simile: A comparison, usually using ''like'' or ''as'', of two essentially dissimilar things, as in ''coffee as cold as ice'' or ''He sounded like a broken record.'' The title of Ernest Hemingway's ''Hills Like White Elephants'' contains a simile.

Slang: A type of informal verbal communication that is generally unacceptable for formal writing. Slang words and phrases are often colorful exaggerations used to emphasize the speaker's point; they may also be shortened versions of an often-used word or phrase. Examples of American slang from the 1990s include ''yuppie'' (an acronym for Young Urban Professional), ''awesome'' (for ''excellent''), wired (for ''nervous'' or ''excited''), and ''chill out'' (for relax).

Slant Rhyme: See *Consonance*

Slave Narrative: Autobiographical accounts of American slave life as told by escaped slaves. These works first appeared during the abolition movement of the 1830s through the 1850s. Olaudah Equiano's *The Interesting Narrative of Olaudah Equiano, or Gustavus Vassa, The African* and Harriet Ann Jacobs's *Incidents in the Life of a Slave Girl* are examples of the slave narrative.

Social Realism: See *Socialist Realism*

Socialist Realism: The Socialist Realism school of literary theory was proposed by Maxim Gorky and established as a dogma by the first Soviet Congress of Writers. It demanded adherence to a communist worldview in works of literature. Its doctrines required an objective viewpoint comprehensible to the working classes and themes of social struggle featuring strong proletarian heroes. A successful work of socialist realism is Nikolay Ostrovsky's *Kak zakalyalas stal* (*How the Steel Was Tempered*). Also known as Social Realism.

Soliloquy: A monologue in a drama used to give the audience information and to develop the speaker's character. It is typically a projection of the speaker's innermost thoughts. Usually delivered while the speaker is alone on stage, a soliloquy is intended to present an illusion of unspoken reflection. A celebrated soliloquy is Hamlet's ''To be or not to be'' speech in William Shakespeare's *Hamlet.*

Sonnet: A fourteen-line poem, usually composed in iambic pentameter, employing one of several rhyme schemes. There are three major types of sonnets, upon which all other variations of the form are based: the ''Petrarchan'' or ''Italian'' sonnet, the ''Shakespearean'' or ''English'' sonnet, and the ''Spenserian'' sonnet. A Petrarchan sonnet consists of an octave rhymed *abbaabba* and a ''sestet'' rhymed either *cdecde, cdccdc,* or *cdedce.* The octave poses a question or problem, relates a narrative, or puts forth a proposition; the sestet presents a solution to the problem, comments upon the narrative, or applies the proposition put forth in the octave. The Shakespearean sonnet is divided into three quatrains and a couplet rhymed *abab cdcd efef gg.* The couplet provides an epigrammatic comment on the narrative or problem put forth in the quatrains. The Spenserian sonnet uses three quatrains and a couplet like the Shakespearean, but links their three rhyme schemes in this way: *abab bcbc cdcd ee.* The Spenserian sonnet develops its theme in two parts like the Petrarchan, its final six lines resolving a problem, analyzing a narrative, or applying a proposition put forth in its first eight lines. Examples of sonnets can be found in Petrarch's *Canzoniere,* Edmund Spenser's *Amoretti,* Elizabeth Barrett

Browning's *Sonnets from the Portuguese,* Rainer Maria Rilke's *Sonnets to Orpheus,* and Adrienne Rich's poem "The Insusceptibles."

Spenserian Sonnet: See *Sonnet*

Spenserian Stanza: A nine-line stanza having eight verses in iambic pentameter, its ninth verse in iambic hexameter, and the rhyme scheme ababbcbcc. This stanza form was first used by Edmund Spenser in his allegorical poem *The Faerie Queene.*

Spondee: In poetry meter, a foot consisting of two long or stressed syllables occurring together. This form is quite rare in English verse, and is usually composed of two monosyllabic words. The first foot in the following line from Robert Burns's "Green Grow the Rashes" is an example of a spondee: Green grow the rashes, O

Sprung Rhythm: Versification using a specific number of accented syllables per line but disregarding the number of unaccented syllables that fall in each line, producing an irregular rhythm in the poem. Gerard Manley Hopkins, who coined the term "sprung rhythm," is the most notable practitioner of this technique.

Stanza: A subdivision of a poem consisting of lines grouped together, often in recurring patterns of rhyme, line length, and meter. Stanzas may also serve as units of thought in a poem much like paragraphs in prose. Examples of stanza forms include the quatrain, *terza rima, ottava rima,* Spenserian, and the so-called *In Memoriam* stanza from Alfred, Lord Tennyson's poem by that title. The following is an example of the latter form: Love is and was my lord and king, And in his presence I attend To hear the tidings of my friend, Which every hour his couriers bring.

Stereotype: A stereotype was originally the name for a duplication made during the printing process; this led to its modern definition as a person or thing that is (or is assumed to be) the same as all others of its type. Common stereotypical characters include the absent- minded professor, the nagging wife, the troublemaking teenager, and the kindhearted grandmother.

Stream of Consciousness: A narrative technique for rendering the inward experience of a character. This technique is designed to give the impression of an ever-changing series of thoughts, emotions, images, and memories in the spontaneous and seemingly illogical order that they occur in life. The

textbook example of stream of consciousness is the last section of James Joyce's *Ulysses.*

Structuralism: A twentieth-century movement in literary criticism that examines how literary texts arrive at their meanings, rather than the meanings themselves. There are two major types of structuralist analysis: one examines the way patterns of linguistic structures unify a specific text and emphasize certain elements of that text, and the other interprets the way literary forms and conventions affect the meaning of language itself. Prominent structuralists include Michel Foucault, Roman Jakobson, and Roland Barthes.

Structure: The form taken by a piece of literature. The structure may be made obvious for ease of understanding, as in nonfiction works, or may obscured for artistic purposes, as in some poetry or seemingly "unstructured" prose. Examples of common literary structures include the plot of a narrative, the acts and scenes of a drama, and such poetic forms as the Shakespearean sonnet and the Pindaric ode.

Sturm und Drang: A German term meaning "storm and stress." It refers to a German literary movement of the 1770s and 1780s that reacted against the order and rationalism of the enlightenment, focusing instead on the intense experience of extraordinary individuals. Highly romantic, works of this movement, such as Johann Wolfgang von Goethe's *Gotz von Berlichingen,* are typified by realism, rebelliousness, and intense emotionalism.

Style: A writer's distinctive manner of arranging words to suit his or her ideas and purpose in writing. The unique imprint of the author's personality upon his or her writing, style is the product of an author's way of arranging ideas and his or her use of diction, different sentence structures, rhythm, figures of speech, rhetorical principles, and other elements of composition. Styles may be classified according to period (Metaphysical, Augustan, Georgian), individual authors (Chaucerian, Miltonic, Jamesian), level (grand, middle, low, plain), or language (scientific, expository, poetic, journalistic).

Subject: The person, event, or theme at the center of a work of literature. A work may have one or more subjects of each type, with shorter works tending to have fewer and longer works tending to have more. The subjects of James Baldwin's novel *Go Tell It on the Mountain* include the themes of father-son relationships, religious conversion, black life, and sexuality. The subjects of Anne Frank's

Diary of a Young Girl include Anne and her family members as well as World War II, the Holocaust, and the themes of war, isolation, injustice, and racism.

Subjectivity: Writing that expresses the author's personal feelings about his subject, and which may or may not include factual information about the subject. Subjectivity is demonstrated in James Joyce's *Portrait of the Artist as a Young Man,* Samuel Butler's *The Way of All Flesh,* and Thomas Wolfe's *Look Homeward, Angel.*

Subplot: A secondary story in a narrative. A subplot may serve as a motivating or complicating force for the main plot of the work, or it may provide emphasis for, or relief from, the main plot. The conflict between the Capulets and the Montagues in William Shakespeare's *Romeo and Juliet* is an example of a subplot.

Surrealism: A term introduced to criticism by Guillaume Apollinaire and later adopted by Andre Breton. It refers to a French literary and artistic movement founded in the 1920s. The Surrealists sought to express unconscious thoughts and feelings in their works. The best-known technique used for achieving this aim was automatic writing—transcriptions of spontaneous outpourings from the unconscious. The Surrealists proposed to unify the contrary levels of conscious and unconscious, dream and reality, objectivity and subjectivity into a new level of "super-realism." Surrealism can be found in the poetry of Paul Eluard, Pierre Reverdy, and Louis Aragon, among others.

Suspense: A literary device in which the author maintains the audience's attention through the build-up of events, the outcome of which will soon be revealed. Suspense in William Shakespeare's *Hamlet* is sustained throughout by the question of whether or not the Prince will achieve what he has been instructed to do and of what he intends to do.

Syllogism: A method of presenting a logical argument. In its most basic form, the syllogism consists of a major premise, a minor premise, and a conclusion. An example of a syllogism is: Major premise: When it snows, the streets get wet. Minor premise: It is snowing. Conclusion: The streets are wet.

Symbol: Something that suggests or stands for something else without losing its original identity. In literature, symbols combine their literal meaning with the suggestion of an abstract concept. Literary symbols are of two types: those that carry complex associations of meaning no matter what their con-

texts, and those that derive their suggestive meaning from their functions in specific literary works. Examples of symbols are sunshine suggesting happiness, rain suggesting sorrow, and storm clouds suggesting despair.

Symbolism: This term has two widely accepted meanings. In historical criticism, it denotes an early modernist literary movement initiated in France during the nineteenth century that reacted against the prevailing standards of realism. Writers in this movement aimed to evoke, indirectly and symbolically, an order of being beyond the material world of the five senses. Poetic expression of personal emotion figured strongly in the movement, typically by means of a private set of symbols uniquely identifiable with the individual poet. The principal aim of the Symbolists was to express in words the highly complex feelings that grew out of everyday contact with the world. In a broader sense, the term "symbolism" refers to the use of one object to represent another. Early members of the Symbolist movement included the French authors Charles Baudelaire and Arthur Rimbaud; William Butler Yeats, James Joyce, and T. S. Eliot were influenced as the movement moved to Ireland, England, and the United States. Examples of the concept of symbolism include a flag that stands for a nation or movement, or an empty cupboard used to suggest hopelessness, poverty, and despair.

Symbolist: See *Symbolism*

Symbolist Movement: See *Symbolism*

Sympathetic Fallacy: See *Affective Fallacy*

T

Tale: A story told by a narrator with a simple plot and little character development. Tales are usually relatively short and often carry a simple message. Examples of tales can be found in the work of Rudyard Kipling, Somerset Maugham, Saki, Anton Chekhov, Guy de Maupassant, and Armistead Maupin.

Tall Tale: A humorous tale told in a straightforward, credible tone but relating absolutely impossible events or feats of the characters. Such tales were commonly told of frontier adventures during the settlement of the west in the United States. Tall tales have been spun around such legendary heroes as Mike Fink, Paul Bunyan, Davy Crockett, Johnny Appleseed, and Captain Stormalong as well as the real-life William F. Cody and Annie Oakley. Literary use of tall tales can be found in Washington Irving's *History of New York,* Mark Twain's *Life on the Mississippi,* and in the German R. F. Raspe's *Baron Munchausen's Narratives of His Marvellous Travels and Campaigns in Russia.*

Tanka: A form of Japanese poetry similar to *haiku.* A *tanka* is five lines long, with the lines containing five, seven, five, seven, and seven syllables respectively. Skilled *tanka* authors include Ishikawa Takuboku, Masaoka Shiki, Amy Lowell, and Adelaide Crapsey.

Teatro Grottesco: See *Theater of the Grotesque*

Terza Rima: A three-line stanza form in poetry in which the rhymes are made on the last word of each line in the following manner: the first and third lines of the first stanza, then the second line of the first stanza and the first and third lines of the second stanza, and so on with the middle line of any stanza rhyming with the first and third lines of the following stanza. An example of *terza rima* is Percy Bysshe Shelley's ''The Triumph of Love'': As in that trance of wondrous thought I lay This was the tenour of my waking dream. Methought I sate beside a public way Thick strewn with summer dust, and a great stream Of people there was hurrying to and fro Numerous as gnats upon the evening gleam,. . .

Tetrameter: See *Meter*

Textual Criticism: A branch of literary criticism that seeks to establish the authoritative text of a literary work. Textual critics typically compare all known manuscripts or printings of a single work in order to assess the meanings of differences and revisions. This procedure allows them to arrive at a definitive version that (supposedly) corresponds to the author's original intention. Textual criticism was applied during the Renaissance to salvage the classical texts of Greece and Rome, and modern works have been studied, for instance, to undo deliberate correction or censorship, as in the case of novels by Stephen Crane and Theodore Dreiser.

Theater of Cruelty: Term used to denote a group of theatrical techniques designed to eliminate the psychological and emotional distance between actors and audience. This concept, introduced in the 1930s in France, was intended to inspire a more intense theatrical experience than conventional theater allowed. The ''cruelty'' of this dramatic theory signified not sadism but heightened actor/audience involvement in the dramatic event. The theater of cruelty was theorized by Antonin Artaud in his *Le Theatre et son double* (*The Theatre and Its Double*), and also appears in the work of Jerzy Grotowski, Jean Genet, Jean Vilar, and Arthur Adamov, among others.

Theater of the Absurd: A post-World War II dramatic trend characterized by radical theatrical innovations. In works influenced by the Theater of the absurd, nontraditional, sometimes grotesque characterizations, plots, and stage sets reveal a meaningless universe in which human values are irrelevant. Existentialist themes of estrangement, absurdity, and futility link many of the works of this movement. The principal writers of the Theater of the Absurd are Samuel Beckett, Eugene Ionesco, Jean Genet, and Harold Pinter.

Theater of the Grotesque: An Italian theatrical movement characterized by plays written around the ironic and macabre aspects of daily life in the World War I era. Theater of the Grotesque was named after the play *The Mask and the Face* by Luigi Chiarelli, which was described as ''a grotesque in three acts.'' The movement influenced the work of Italian dramatist Luigi Pirandello, author of *Right You Are, If You Think You Are.* Also known as *Teatro Grottesco.*

Theme: The main point of a work of literature. The term is used interchangeably with thesis. The theme of William Shakespeare's *Othello*—jealousy—is a common one.

Thesis: A thesis is both an essay and the point argued in the essay. Thesis novels and thesis plays share the quality of containing a thesis which is supported through the action of the story. A master's thesis and a doctoral dissertation are two theses required of graduate students.

Thesis Play: See *Thesis*

Three Unities: See *Unities*

Tone: The author's attitude toward his or her audience may be deduced from the tone of the work. A formal tone may create distance or convey politeness, while an informal tone may encourage a friendly, intimate, or intrusive feeling in the reader. The author's attitude toward his or her subject matter may also be deduced from the tone of the words he or she uses in discussing it. The tone of John F. Kennedy's speech which included the appeal to ''ask not what your country can do for you'' was intended to instill feelings of camaraderie and national pride in listeners.

Tragedy: A drama in prose or poetry about a noble, courageous hero of excellent character who, because of some tragic character flaw or *hamartia*, brings ruin upon him- or herself. Tragedy treats its subjects in a dignified and serious manner, using poetic language to help evoke pity and fear and bring about catharsis, a purging of these emotions. The tragic form was practiced extensively by the ancient Greeks. In the Middle Ages, when classical works were virtually unknown, tragedy came to denote any works about the fall of persons from exalted to low conditions due to any reason: fate, vice, weakness, etc. According to the classical definition of tragedy, such works present the ''pathetic''—that which evokes pity—rather than the tragic. The classical form of tragedy was revived in the sixteenth century; it flourished especially on the Elizabethan stage. In modern times, dramatists have attempted to adapt the form to the needs of modern society by drawing their heroes from the ranks of ordinary men and women and defining the nobility of these heroes in terms of spirit rather than exalted social standing. The greatest classical example of tragedy is Sophocles' *Oedipus Rex.* The ''pathetic'' derivation is exemplified in ''The Monk's Tale'' in Geoffrey Chaucer's *Canterbury Tales.* Notable works produced during the sixteenth century revival include William Shakespeare's *Hamlet, Othello,* and *King Lear.* Modern dramatists working in the tragic tradition include Henrik Ibsen, Arthur Miller, and Eugene O'Neill.

Tragedy of Blood: See *Revenge Tragedy*

Tragic Flaw: In a tragedy, the quality within the hero or heroine which leads to his or her downfall. Examples of the tragic flaw include Othello's jealousy and Hamlet's indecisiveness, although most great tragedies defy such simple interpretation.

Transcendentalism: An American philosophical and religious movement, based in New England from around 1835 until the Civil War. Transcendentalism was a form of American romanticism that had its roots abroad in the works of Thomas Carlyle, Samuel Coleridge, and Johann Wolfgang von Goethe. The Transcendentalists stressed the importance of intuition and subjective experience in communication with God. They rejected religious dogma and texts in favor of mysticism and scientific naturalism. They pursued truths that lie beyond the ''colorless'' realms perceived by reason and the senses and were active social reformers in public education, women's rights, and the abolition of slavery. Prominent members of the group include Ralph Waldo Emerson and Henry David Thoreau.

Trickster: A character or figure common in Native American and African literature who uses his ingenuity to defeat enemies and escape difficult situations. Tricksters are most often animals, such as the spider, hare, or coyote, although they may take the form of humans as well. Examples of trickster tales include Thomas King's *A Coyote Columbus Story,* Ashley F. Bryan's *The Dancing Granny* and Ishmael Reed's *The Last Days of Louisiana Red.*

Trimeter: See *Meter*

Triple Rhyme: See *Rhyme*

Trochee: See *Foot*

U

Understatement: See *Irony*

Unities: Strict rules of dramatic structure, formulated by Italian and French critics of the Renaissance and based loosely on the principles of drama discussed by Aristotle in his *Poetics.* Foremost among these rules were the three unities of action, time, and place that compelled a dramatist to: (1) construct a single plot with a beginning, middle, and end that details the causal relationships of action and character; (2) restrict the action to the events of a single day; and (3) limit the scene to a single place or city. The unities were observed faithfully by continental European writers until the Romantic Age, but they were never regularly observed in English drama. Modern dramatists are typically more concerned with a unity of impression or emotional effect than with any of the classical unities. The unities are observed in Pierre Corneille's tragedy *Polyeuctes* and Jean-Baptiste Racine's *Phedre.* Also known as Three Unities.

Urban Realism: A branch of realist writing that attempts to accurately reflect the often harsh facts of modern urban existence. Some works by Stephen Crane, Theodore Dreiser, Charles Dickens, Fyodor Dostoyevsky, Emile Zola, Abraham Cahan, and Henry Fuller feature urban realism. Modern examples include Claude Brown's *Manchild in the Promised Land* and Ron Milner's *What the Wine Sellers Buy.*

Utopia: A fictional perfect place, such as ''paradise'' or ''heaven.'' Early literary utopias were included in Plato's *Republic* and Sir Thomas More's

Utopia, while more modern utopias can be found in Samuel Butler's *Erewhon,* Theodor Herzka's *A Visit to Freeland,* and H. G. Wells' *A Modern Utopia.*

Utopian: See *Utopia*

Utopianism: See *Utopia*

V

Verisimilitude: Literally, the appearance of truth. In literary criticism, the term refers to aspects of a work of literature that seem true to the reader. Verisimilitude is achieved in the work of Honore de Balzac, Gustave Flaubert, and Henry James, among other late nineteenth-century realist writers.

Vers de societe: See *Occasional Verse*

Vers libre: See *Free Verse*

Verse: A line of metered language, a line of a poem, or any work written in verse. The following line of verse is from the epic poem *Don Juan* by Lord Byron: ''My way is to begin with the beginning.''

Versification: The writing of verse. Versification may also refer to the meter, rhyme, and other mechanical components of a poem. Composition of a ''Roses are red, violets are blue'' poem to suit an occasion is a common form of versification practiced by students.

Victorian: Refers broadly to the reign of Queen Victoria of England (1837-1901) and to anything with qualities typical of that era. For example, the qualities of smug narrowmindedness, bourgeois materialism, faith in social progress, and priggish morality are often considered Victorian. This stereotype is contradicted by such dramatic intellectual developments as the theories of Charles Darwin, Karl Marx, and Sigmund Freud (which stirred strong debates in England) and the critical attitudes of serious Victorian writers like Charles Dickens and George Eliot. In literature, the Victorian Period was the great age of the English novel, and the latter part of the era saw the rise of movements such as decadence and symbolism. Works of Victorian lit-

erature include the poetry of Robert Browning and Alfred, Lord Tennyson, the criticism of Matthew Arnold and John Ruskin, and the novels of Emily Bronte, William Makepeace Thackeray, and Thomas Hardy. Also known as Victorian Age and Victorian Period.

Victorian Age: See *Victorian*

Victorian Period: See *Victorian*

W

Weltanschauung: A German term referring to a person's worldview or philosophy. Examples of *weltanschauung* include Thomas Hardy's view of the human being as the victim of fate, destiny, or impersonal forces and circumstances, and the disillusioned and laconic cynicism expressed by such poets of the 1930s as W. H. Auden, Sir Stephen Spender, and Sir William Empson.

Weltschmerz: A German term meaning ''world pain.'' It describes a sense of anguish about the nature of existence, usually associated with a melancholy, pessimistic attitude. *Weltschmerz* was expressed in England by George Gordon, Lord Byron in his *Manfred* and *Childe Harold's Pilgrimage,* in France by Viscount de Chateaubriand, Alfred de Vigny, and Alfred de Musset, in Russia by Aleksandr Pushkin and Mikhail Lermontov, in Poland by Juliusz Slowacki, and in America by Nathaniel Hawthorne.

Z

Zarzuela: A type of Spanish operetta. Writers of *zarzuelas* include Lope de Vega and Pedro Calderon.

Zeitgeist: A German term meaning ''spirit of the time.'' It refers to the moral and intellectual trends of a given era. Examples of *zeitgeist* include the preoccupation with the more morbid aspects of dying and death in some Jacobean literature, especially in the works of dramatists Cyril Tourneur and John Webster, and the decadence of the French Symbolists.

Cumulative Author/Title Index

Nationality/Ethnicity Index

Spanish

Garcia Lorca, Federico
The House of Bernarda Alba: V4

Swedish

Strindberg, August
Miss Julie: V4

Subject/Theme Index